Dictionary
German – English
English – German

Wörterbuch
Deutsch – Englisch
Englisch – Deutsch

Berlitz Publishing
Union, NJ · Munich · Singapore

Edited by the Berlitz Editorial Staff

Cover photo by ID Image Direkt CD-ROM GmbH, Germany

© 2004 Berlitz Publishing/APA Publications GmbH & Co. Verlag KG
Singapore Branch, Singapore

Trademark Reg. U.S. Patent Office and other countries.
Marca Registrada.
Used under license from Berlitz Investment Corporation.

Berlitz Publishing
95 Progress Street
Union, NJ 07083
USA

Printed in Austria
ISBN 981-246-373-9

Contents

Inhaltsverzeichnis

Preface

In selecting the vocabulary and phrases for this dictionary, the editors have had the traveller's needs foremost in mind. This book will prove a useful companion to casual tourists and business travellers alike who appreciate the reassurance a small and practical dictionary can provide. It offers them—as well as beginners and students—all the basic vocabulary they will encounter and have to use, giving the key words and expressions to allow them to cope in everyday situations.

Like our successful phrase books and travel guides, these dictionaries— created with the help of a computer data bank— are designed to slip into your pocket or purse, and thus have a role as handy companions at all times.

Besides just about everything you normally find in dictionaries, there are these Berlitz bonuses:

- simplified pronunciation after each foreign-word entry, making it easy to read and enunciate words whose spelling may look forbidding

- a unique, practical glossary to simplify reading a foreign restaurant menu and to take the mystery out of complicated dishes and indecipherable names on bills of fare

- useful information on how to tell the time and how to count, on conjugating irregular verbs, commonly seen abbreviations and converting to the metric system, in addition to basic phrases.

While no dictionary of this size can pretend to completeness, we are confident this dictionary will help you get most out of your trip abroad.

Berlitz Publishing

Vorwort

Bei der Auswahl der Wörter und Wendungen, die in diesem Wörterbuch enthalten sind, wurde besonderer Wert auf den Alltags- und Reisewortschatz gelegt. Dieses handliche und praktische, mithilfe einer Datenbank erstellte Wörterbuch wird sich deshalb für alle Reisenden, ob Touristen oder Geschäftsleute, aber auch für Anfänger und Sprachschüler als nützlicher Begleiter erweisen. Es enthält den Grundwortschatz und alle wichtigen Ausdrücke, die man benötigt, um sich in jeder alltäglichen Situation zurechtzufinden.

Dieses Wörterbuch passt in jede Jacken- oder Handtasche und ist so immer griffbereit. Neben all dem, was man von einem kompakten Wörterbuch erwartet, bietet es noch folgende besonderen Vorteile:

• Die internationale Lautschrift (IPA) nach jedem englischen Stichwort erleichtert Ihnen die richtige Aussprache.

• Ein sorgfältig zusammengestellter Menü-Sprachführer hilft Ihnen beim Lesen der Speise- und Getränkekarte und entschlüsselt all die unbekannten Gerichte und Zutaten.

• Ferner finden Sie nützliche Übersichten zu Zeitangaben, Grund- und Ordnungszahlen, unregelmäßigen Verben und gebräuchlichen Abkürzungen sowie die allerwichtigsten Redewendungen, um im Alltag und unterwegs zurechtzukommen.

Selbstverständlich kann kein Wörterbuch dieses Formats Anspruch auf Vollständigkeit erheben. Wir glauben jedoch, dass sich die Benutzer dieses kleinen Nachschlagewerks gut gerüstet auf die Reise machen können.

Berlitz Publishing

German-English

Deutsch-Englisch

Introduction

The dictionary has been designed to take account of your practical needs. Unnecessary linguistic information has been avoided. The entries are listed in alphabetical order, regardless of whether the entry word is printed in a single word or in two or more separate words.

When an entry is followed by sub-entries such as expressions and locutions, these, too, have been listed in alphabetical order.

Each main-entry word is followed by a phonetic transcription (see Guide to Pronunciation). Following the transcription is the part of speech of the entry word whenever applicable. When an entry word may be used as more than one part of speech, the translations are grouped together after the respective part of speech.

Considering the complexity of the rules for constructing the plural of German nouns, we have supplied the plural form whenever in current use.

German feminine headwords with regular endings are shown as follows:

Adressat ... *m* (pl ∼en), **-in** *f* addressee
Freund ... *m* (pl ∼e), **-in** *f* friend
Kassierer ... *m* (pl ∼), **-in** *f* cashier

The feminine forms of these headwords are: **Adressatin** (pl ∼nen), **Freundin** (pl ∼nen), **Kassiererin** (pl ∼nen).

Each time an entry word is repeated in plural or in sub-entries, a tilde (∼) is used to represent the full entry word. Two dots above the tilde (∼̈) means that, in the plural, the word takes an Umlaut.

In plurals of compounds only the part that changes is written out fully, whereas the unchanged part is represented by a hyphen.

Entry:	Abenteuer (pl ∼)	Plural:	Abenteuer
	Abend (pl ∼e)		Abende
	Satz (pl ∼̈e)		Sätze
	Geschäftsmann (pl -leute)		Geschäftsleute

An asterisk (*) in front of a verb indicates that the verb is irregular. For details, refer to the lists of irregular verbs.

Abbreviations

®	registered trademark	*ntpl*	neuter plural
adj	adjective	*num*	numeral
adv	adverb	*p*	past tense
Am	American	*pl*	plural
art	article	*plAm*	plural (American)
conj	conjunction	*pp*	past participle
f	feminine	*pr*	present tense
fpl	feminine plural	*pref*	prefix
m	masculine	*prep*	preposition
mpl	masculine plural	*pron*	pronoun
n	noun	*v*	verb
nAm	noun (American)	*vAm*	verb (American)
nt	neuter		

Guide to Pronunciation

Each main entry in this part of the dictionary is followed by a phonetic transcription which shows you how to pronounce the words. This transcription should be read as if it were English. It is based on Standard British pronunciation, though we have tried to take account of General American pronunciation also. Below, only those letters and symbols are explained which we consider likely to be ambiguous or not immediately understood.

The syllables are separated by hyphens, and stressed syllables are printed in *italics*.

Of course, the sounds of any two languages are never exactly the same, but if you follow carefully our indications, you should be able to pronounce the foreign words in such a way that you'll be understood. To make your task easier, our transcriptions occasionally simplify slightly the sound system of the language while still reflecting the essential sound differences.

Consonants

g	always hard, as in **g**o
kh	a **k**-sound where the tongue doesn't quite touch the roof of the mouth, so that the air continues to come out, with a sound of friction between the tongue and the roof of the mouth; after back vowels (e.g. **ah, o, oo**) like **ch** in Scottish lo**ch**, otherwise more like **h** in **h**uge
r	pronounced in the back of the mouth
s	always hard, as in **s**o
zh	a soft, voiced **sh**, like **s** in plea**s**ure

Vowels and Diphthongs

aa	long **a**, as in c**ar**
ah	a short version of **aa**; between **a** in c**a**t and **u** in c**u**t
ai	like **air**, without any **r**-sound
eh	like **e** in g**e**t
er	as in oth**er**, without any **r**-sound

ew a "rounded **ee**-sound"; say the vowel sound **ee** (as in s**ee**), and while saying it, round your lips as for **oo** (as in s**oo**n), without moving your tongue; when your lips are in the **oo** position, but your tongue is in the **ee** position, you should be pronouncing the correct sound

igh as in s**igh**

o always as in h**o**t (British pronunciation)

ou as in l**ou**d

ur as in f**ur**, but with rounded lips and no **r**-sound

1) A bar over a vowel symbol (e.g. **ēw**) shows that this sound is long.

2) Raised letters (e.g. **yaa**) should be pronounced only fleetingly.

3) German vowels (i.e. not diphthongs) are pure. Therefore, you should try to read a transcription like **oa** without moving tongue or lips while pronouncing the sound.

4) Some German words borrowed from French contain nasal vowels, which we transcribe with a vowel symbol plus **ng** (e.g. **ahng**). This **ng** should *not* be pronounced, and serves solely to indicate nasal quality of the preceding vowel. A nasal vowel is pronounced simultaneously through the mouth and the nose.

A

Aal (aal) *m* (pl ⁓e) eel

ab (ahp) *prep* as from; *adv* off; **⁓ und zu** occasionally

abändern (*ahp*-ehn-derrn) *v* change

Abbildung (*ahp*-bil-doong) *f* (pl ⁓en) picture

***abbrechen** (*ahp*-breh-khern) *v* *break off; pull down; call off; *give up

abbremsen (*ahp*-brehm-zern) *v* slow down

Abbruch (*ahp*-brookh) *m* demolition

abdrehen (*ahp*-dräy-ern) *v* turn off

Abend (aa-bernt) *m* (pl ⁓e) night, evening

Abenddämmerung (aa-bernt-deh-mer-roong) *f* dusk

Abendessen (aa-bernt-eh-sern) *nt* supper; dinner

abends (aa-bernts) *adv* at night

Abenteuer (aa-bern-toi-err) *nt* (pl ⁓) adventure

aber (aa-berr) *conj* but

Aberglaube (aa-berr-glou-ber) *m* superstition

***abfahren** (*ahp*-faa-rern) *v* pull out

Abfahrt (*ahp*-faart) *f* departure

Abfahrtszeit (*ahp*-faarts-tsight) *f* (pl ⁓en) time of departure

Abfall (*ahp*-fahl) *m* (pl ⁓e) garbage; litter, rubbish, refuse

Abfalleimer (*ahp*-fahl-igh-merr) *m* (pl ⁓) rubbish bin, dustbin; trash can *Am*

***abfallen** (*ahp*-fah-lern) *v* slope

abfassen (*ahp*-fah-sern) *v* *draw up

abfertigen (*ahp*-fehr-ti-gern) *v* dispatch

Abfluss (*ahp*-flooss) *m* drain

Abführmittel (*ahp*-fewr-mi-terl) *nt* (pl ⁓) laxative

abgelegen (*ahp*-ger-läy-gern) *adj* far-off, remote

abgeneigt (*ahp*-ger-nighkt) *adj* averse

abgenutzt (*ahp*-ger-nootst) *adj* worn-out

Abgeordnete (*ahp*-ger-or-dner-ter) *m/f* (pl ⁓n) deputy; Member of Parliament

abgerundet (*ahp*-ger-roon-dert) *adj* rounded

Abgesandte (*ahp*-ger-zahn-ter) *m/f* (pl ⁓n) delegate, envoy

abgeschieden (*ahp*-ger-shee-dern) *adj* isolated

abgesehen von (*ahp*-ger-zāy-ern) apart from

Abgrund (*ahp*-groont) *m* (pl ⁓e) abyss, precipice

Abhandlung (*ahp*-hahn-dloong) *f* (pl ⁓en) essay

Abhang (*ahp*-hahng) *m* (pl ⁓e) slope

***abhängen von** (*ahp*-hehng-ern) depend on

abhängig (*ahp*-hehng-ikh) *adj* dependant

***abheben** (*ahp*-hāy-bern) *v* *withdraw

abholen (*ahp*-hōa-lern) *v* pick up, collect, fetch

Abkommen (*ahp*-ko-mern) *nt* (pl ⁓) agreement

Abkürzung (*ahp*-kewr-tsoong) *f* (pl ⁓en) abbreviation

***abladen** (*ahp*-laa-dern) *v* unload

***ablaufen** (*ahp*-lou-fern) *v* expire

ablehnen (*ahp*-lāy-nern) *v* reject

ableiten (*ahp*-ligh-tern) *v* deduce, infer

Ablenkung (*ahp*-lehng-koong) *f* diversion

abliefern (*ahp*-lee-ferrn) *v* deliver

ablösen (*ahp*-lūr-zern) *v* relieve

abmachen (*ahp*-mah-khern) *v* agree on

abmelden (*ahp*-mehl-dern) report off duty; cancel the registration; **sich ⁓**

check out

abmühen (*ahp*-mew-ern): **sich ~** labo(u)r

Abnahme (*ahp*-naa-mer) *f* (pl ~n) decrease

*abnehmen (*ahp*-nay-mern) *v* *take away; decrease; slim

Abneigung (*ahp*-nigh-goong) *f* dislike, antipathy

Abonnement (ah-bo-ner-*mahng*) *nt* (pl ~s) subscription

Abonnent (ah-bo-*nehnt*) *m* (pl ~en), **-in** *f* subscriber

*abraten (*ahp*-raa-tern) *v* dissuade from

Abreise (*ahp*-righ-zer) *f* departure

abreisen (*ahp*-righ-zern) *v* depart, *set out

Absatz (*ahp*-zahts) *m* (pl ~e) heel; paragraph

abschaffen (*ahp*-shah-fern) *v* abolish

abschalten (*ahp*-shahl-tern) *v* switch off

abscheulich (ahp-*shoi*-likh) *adj* hideous, terrible

Abschied (*ahp*-sheet) *m* parting

*abschießen (*aab*-shee-sern) *v* launch

*abschließen (*ahp*-shlee-sern) *v* *shut off

Abschluss (*ahp*-shlooss) *m* issue

*abschneiden (*ahp*-shnigh-dern) *v* *cut off; chip

Abschnitt (*ahp*-shnit) *m* (pl ~e) section; extract

abschrauben (*ahp*-shrou-bern) *v* unscrew

Abschrift (*ahp*-shrift) *f* (pl ~en) copy

abschüssig (*ahp*-shew-sikh) *adj* sloping, slanting

*absenden (*ahp*-zehn-dern) *v* *send off

Absicht (*ahp*-zikht) *f* (pl ~en) purpose, intention

absichtlich (*ahp*-zikht-likh) *adj* deliberate, on purpose, intentional

absolut (ahp-zoa-*loot*) *adj* sheer

absplittern (*ahp*-shpli-terrn) *v* chip

Abstammung (*ahp*-shtah-moong) *f* origin

Abstand (*ahp*-shtahnt) *m* space

Abstieg (*ahp*-shteek) *m* descent

Abstimmung (*ahp*-shti-moong) *f* vote

abstoßend (*ahp*-shtoa-sernt) *adj* revolting, repellent

abstrakt (ahps-*trahkt*) *adj* abstract

abstürzen (*ahp*-shtewr-tsern) *v* crash

absurd (ahp-*zoort*) *adj* absurd

Abszess (ahps-tsehss) *m* (pl ~e) abscess

Abteil (ahp-*tighl*) *nt* (pl ~e) compartment

Abteilung (ahp-*tigh*-loong) *f* (pl ~en) division, department; section

*abtragen (*ahp*-traa-gern) *v* wear out

Abtreibung (*ahp*-trigh-boong) *f* abortion

abtrocknen (*ahp*-tro-knern) *v* dry

abwärts (*ahp*-vehrts) *adv* downwards

*abwaschen (*ahp*-vah-shern) *v* wash up

abwechselnd (*ahp*-veh-kserlnt) *adj* alternate

Abwechslung (*ahp*-veh-ksloong) *f* variation

Abwehr (*ahp*-vayr) *f* defence, defense *Am*

*abweichen (*ahp*-vigh-khern) *v* deviate

Abweichung (*ahp*-vigh-khoong) *f* (pl ~en) difference; deviation

abwenden (*ahp*-vehn-dern) *v* avert

Abwertung (*ahp*-vair-toong) *f* devaluation

abwesend (*ahp*-vay-zernt) *adj* absent

Abwesenheit (*ahp*-vay-zern-hight) *f* absence

abwischen (*ahp*-vi-shern) *v* wipe

abzahlen (*ahp*-tsaa-lern) *v* *pay on account

abzeichnen (*ahp*-tsighkh-nern) *v*
initial; endorse

*abziehen (*ahp*-tsee-ern) *v* deduct

Abzug (*ahp*-tsōōk) *m* (pl ≈e) print;
trigger

Achse (*ah*-kser) *f* (pl ∼n) axle

Acht (ahkht) *f* notice; **sich in ∼
*nehmen** beware; ∼ ***geben** look out;
∼ ***geben auf** watch; attend to; mind

acht (ahkht) *num* eight

achtbar (*ahkht*-baar) *adj* respectable

achte (*ahkh*-ter) *num* eighth

achten (*ahkh*-tern) *v* respect; ∼ **auf**
mind; *pay attention to

Achtung (*ahkh*-toong) *f* esteem;
respect; ∼! look out!

achtzehn (*ahkh*-tsāyn) *num* eighteen

achtzehnte (*ahkh*-tsāyn-ter) *num*
eighteenth

achtzig (*ahkh*-tsikh) *num* eighty

Acker (*ah*-kerr) *m* (pl ≈) field

Adapter (ah-*dahp*-terr) *m* (pl ∼s)
adapter

addieren (ah-*dee*-rern) *v* count; add

Addition (ah-di-ts^y*ōan*) *f* (pl ∼en)
addition

Adel (*aa*-derl) *m* nobility

Ader (*aa*-derr) *f* (pl ∼n) vein

Adler (*aa*-dlerr) *m* (pl ∼) eagle

administrativ (aht-mi-ni-strah-*teef*)
adj administrative

adoptieren (ah-dop-*tee*-rern) *v* adopt

Adressat (ah-dreh-*saat*) *m* (pl ∼en),
-in *f* addressee

Adresse (ah-*dreh*-ser) *f* (pl ∼n)
address

adressieren (ah-dreh-*see*-rern) *v*
address

Adverb (aht-*vehrp*) *nt* (pl ∼en) adverb

Affe (*ah*-fer) *m* (pl ∼n) monkey

Afrika (*ah*-fri-kaa) Africa

Afrikaner (ah-fri-*kaa*-nerr) *m* (pl ∼),
-in *f* African

afrikanisch (ah-fri-*kaa*-nish) *adj*
African

Agent (ah-*gehnt*) *m* (pl ∼en), **-in** *f*
agent

Agentur (ah-gehn-*tōōr*) *f* (pl ∼en)
agency

aggressiv (ah-greh-*seef*) *adj*
aggressive

Ägypten (eh-*gewp*-tern) Egypt

Ägypter (eh-*gewp*-terr) *m* (pl ∼), **-in** *f*
Egyptian

ägyptisch (eh-*gewp*-tish) *adj*
Egyptian

ähnlich (*ain*-likh) *adj* similar; alike

Ähnlichkeit (*ain*-likh-kight) *f* (pl ∼en)
similarity; resemblance

Ahnung (*aa*-noong) *f* notion

Ahorn (*aa*-horn) *m* (pl ∼e) maple

Aids (aidz) *nt* Aids

Airbag (*ehr*-berg) *m* (pl ∼s) airbag

Akademie (ah-kah-day-*mee*) *f* (pl ∼n)
academy

Akkord (ah-*kort*) *m* (pl ∼e) agreement

Akku (*ah*-koo) *m* (pl ∼s) battery

Akne (*ah*-kner) *f* acne

Akt (ahkt) *m* (pl ∼e) act; nude

Akte (*ahk*-ter) *f* (pl ∼n) record; **Akten**
file

Aktentasche (*ahk*-tern-tah-sher) *f* (pl
∼n) briefcase, attaché case

Aktie (*ahk*-ts^{y}er) *f* (pl ∼n) share;
Aktien stocks and shares

Aktion (ahk-ts^y*ōan*) *f* (pl ∼en) action

aktiv (ahk-*teef*) *adj* active

Aktivität (ahk-ti-vi-*tait*) *f* (pl ∼en)
activity

aktuell (ahk-too-*ehl*) *adj* current,
topical

akut (ah-*kōōt*) *adj* acute

Akzent (ahk-*tsehnt*) *m* (pl ∼e) accent

akzeptieren (ahk-tsehp-*tee*-rern) *v*
accept

Alarm (ah-*lahrm*) *m* alarm

alarmieren (ah-lahr-*mee*-rern) *v* alarm

albern (*ahl*-berrn) *adj* foolish, silly

Album (*ahl*-boom) *nt* (pl Alben) album

Algebra (*ahl*-gay-brah) *f* algebra

Algerien (ahl-*gāy*-rʸern) Algeria

Algerier (ahl-*gāy*-rʸerr) *m* (pl ∼), **-in** *f* Algerian

Alkohol (*ahl*-koa-hol) *m* alcohol

alkoholisch (ahl-koa-*hōa*-lish) *adj* alcoholic

all (ahl) *num* all; **alle** *num* all; *adv* finished

Allee (ah-*lāy*) *f* (pl ∼n) avenue

allein (ah-*lighn*) *adv* alone

allenfalls (*ah*-lern-fahls) *adv* at most

allerdings (ah-lerr-dings) *adv* indeed

Allergie (ah-lehr-*gee*) *f* (pl ∼n) allergy

allerlei (ah-lerr-ligh) *adj* various, all sorts of

alles (*ah*-lerss) *pron* everything; ∼ **inbegriffen** all included

allgemein (ahl-ger-*mighn*) *adj* general; public; common; universal; **im Allgemeinen** in general

Alliierte (ah-li-*eer*-ter) *m/f* ally

allmächtig (ahl-*mehkh*-tikh) *adj* omnipotent

allmählich (ahl-*mai*-likh) *adj* gradual

alltäglich (ahl-*tāyk*-likh) *adj* ordinary, everyday; daily

Alpen (*ahl*-pern) *pl* Alps *pl*

Alphabet (ahl-fah-*bāyt*) *nt* alphabet

als (ahls) *conj* when; than; ∼ **ob** as if

also (*ahl*-zōa) *conj* so

Alt (ahlt) *m* (pl ∼e) alto

alt (ahlt) *adj* old, ancient; aged

Altar (ahl-*taar*) *m* (pl ∼e) altar

altbacken (*ahlt*-bah-kern) *adj* stale

Alter (*ahl*-terr) *nt* age; old age

Alternative (ahl-tehr-nah-*tee*-ver) *f* (pl ∼n) alternative

Altertum (*ahl*-terr-tōōm) *nt* antiquity

altmodisch (ahlt-*mōa*-dish) *adj* old-fashioned, ancient; quaint

Ambulanz (ahm-boo-*lahnts*) *f* (pl ∼en) ambulance

Ameise (aa-migh-zer) *f* (pl ∼n) ant

Amerika (ah-*māy*-ri-kah) America

Amerikaner (ah-may-ri-*kaa*-nerr) *m* (pl ∼), **-in** *f* American

amerikanisch (ah-may-ri-*kaa*-nish) *adj* American

Amethyst (ah-may-*tewst*) *m* (pl ∼en) amethyst

Amnestie (ahm-nay-*stee*) *f* amnesty

Ampel (*ahm*-perl) *f* traffic lights *pl*

Amsel (*ahm*-zerl) *f* (pl ∼n) blackbird

Amt (ahmt) *nt* (pl ∼er) office

Amulett (ah-moo-*leht*) *nt* (pl ∼e) lucky charm, charm

amüsant (ah-mew-*zahnt*) *adj* entertaining

amüsieren (ah-mew-*zee*-rern) *v* amuse; entertain

an (ahn) *prep* on, to, at

Analphabet (ah-nahl-fah-*bāyt*) *m* (pl ∼en), **-in** *f* illiterate

Analyse (ah-nah-*lēw*-zer) *f* (pl ∼n) analysis

analysieren (ah-nah-lew-*zee*-rern) *v* analyse

Ananas (*ah*-nah-nahss) *f* pineapple

Anarchie (ah-nahr-*khee*) *f* anarchy

Anatomie (ah-nah-toa-*mee*) *f* anatomy

anbauen (*ahn*-bou-ern) *v* cultivate, raise

Anbetracht: in ∼ (in *ahn*-ber-trahkht) considering, regarding

*anbieten (*ahn*-bee-tern) *v* offer; present

Anblick (*ahn*-blik) *m* sight; look

*anbrennen (*ahn*-breh-nern) *v* *burn

Andenken (*ahn*-dehng-kern) *nt* (pl ∼) souvenir; remembrance; memory

ander (*ahn*-derr) *adj* other; different

ändern (*ehn*-derrn) *v* change; alter

anders (*ahn*-derrs) *adv* otherwise

andersherum (*ahn*-derrs-heh-room) *adv* the other way round

anderswo (*ahn*-derrs-vōa) *adv* elsewhere

Änderung (*ehn*-der-roong) *f* (pl ~en) change; alteration

andrehen (*ahn*-drāy-ern) *v* turn on

*anerkennen (*ahn*-ehr-keh-nern) *v* recognize

Anerkennung (*ahn*-ehr-keh-noong) *f* (pl ~en) recognition

Anfall (*ahn*-fahl) *m* (pl ~e) fit

Anfang (*ahn*-fahng) *m* start, beginning; **Anfangs-** initial; primary

*anfangen (*ahn*-fahng-ern) *v* start, commence, *begin

Anfänger (*ahn*-fehng-err) *m* (pl ~), **-in** *f* learner, beginner

anfangs (*ahn*-fahngs) *adv* at first

Anfangsbuchstabe (*ahn*-fahngs-bōōkh-shtaa-ber) *m* (pl ~n) initial

anfassen (*ahn*-fah-sern) touch, *take, grab; **mit anfassen** help, lend a hand

anfeuchten (*ahn*-foikh-tern) *v* moisten

Anführer (*ahn*-fēw-rerr) *m* (pl ~), **-in** *f* leader

Anführungszeichen (*ahn*-fēw-roongs-tsigh-khern) *ntpl* quotation marks

Angabe (*ahn*-gaa-ber) *f* (pl ~n) data *pl*

*angeben (*ahn*-gāy-bern) *v* indicate; declare; show off

angeboren (*ahn*-ger-bōa-rern) *adj* natural

Angebot (*ahn*-ger-bōāt) *nt* (pl ~e) offer; supply

angebracht (*ahn*-ger-brahkht) *adj* proper

angegliedert (*ahn*-ger-glee-derrt) *adj* affiliated

*angehen (*ahn*-gāy-ern) *v* concern

Angehörige (*ahn*-ger-hūr-ri-ger) *m/f* relative, relation

Angeklagte (*ahn*-ger-klaak-ter) *m/f* (pl ~n) accused

Angelegenheit (*ahn*-ger-lāy-gern-hight) *f* (pl ~en) affair, business, concern

Angelgeräte (*ahng*-erl-ger-rai-ter) *ntpl* fishing tackle, fishing gear

Angelhaken (*ahng*-erl-haa-kern) *m* (pl ~) fishing hook

angeln (*ahng*-erln) *v* fish, angle

Angelrute (*ahng*-erl-rōō-ter) *f* (pl ~n) fishing rod

Angelschein (*ahng*-erl-shighn) *m* (pl ~e) fishing licence

Angelschnur (*ahng*-erl-shnōōr) *f* (pl ~e) fishing line

angemessen (*ahn*-ger-meh-sern) *adj* appropriate; adequate, convenient, suitable

angenehm (*ahn*-ger-nāym) *adj* pleasant; enjoyable, pleasing, agreeable

Angestellte (*ahn*-ger-shtehl-ter) *m/f* (salaried) employee, *colloquial* white-collar worker

*angreifen (*ahn*-grigh-fern) *v* attack, assault

Angriff (*ahn*-grif) *m* (pl ~e) attack

Angst (ahngst) *f* (pl ~e) fright, fear; dread; ~ ***haben** *be afraid

ängstlich (*ehngst*-likh) *adj* afraid

*anhaben (*ahn*-haa-bern) *v* *wear

*anhalten (*ahn*-hahl-tern) *v* stop; pull up; prevent; **anhaltend** continuous

Anhalter (*ahn*-hahl-terr) *m* (pl ~), **-in** *f* hitchhiker; **per ~ *fahren** hitchhike

Anhang (*ahn*-hahng) *m* (pl ~e) annex

Anhänger (*ahn*-hehng-err) *m* (pl ~), **-in** *f* supporter; advocate; pendant; trailer

anhäufen (*ahn*-hoi-fern) *v* pile

anheften (*ahn*-hayf-tern) *v* attach

Anhöhe (*ahn*-hūr-er) *f* (pl ~n) rise

anhören (*ahn*-hūr-rern) *v* listen

Anker (*ahng*-kerr) *m* (pl ~) anchor

Anklage (*ahn*-klaa-ger) *f* (pl ~n)

charge

anklagen (*ahn-klaa-gern*) *v* accuse, charge

ankleben (*ahn-klāy-bern*) *v* *stick

ankleiden (*ahn-kligh-dern*) *v* dress

anklicken (*ahn-klee-kern*) *v* click (on)

anklopfen (*ahn-klo-pfern*) *v* knock

*ankommen (*ahn-ko-mern*) *v* arrive

ankreuzen (*ahn-kroi-tsern*) *v* mark

ankündigen (*ahn-kewn-di-gern*) *v* announce

Ankündigung (*ahn-kewn-di-goong*) *f* (pl ~en) announcement

Ankunft (*ahn-koonft*) *f* arrival; coming

Ankunftszeit (*ahn-koonfts-tsight*) *f* (pl ~en) time of arrival

Anlage (*ahn-laa-ger*) *f* (pl ~n) investment; public garden

Anlass (*ahn-lahss*) *m* (pl ~e) cause, occasion

anlegen (*ahn-lāy-gern*) *v* dock; invest

Anleihe (*ahn-ligh-er*) *f* (pl ~n) loan

anmelden (*ahn-mehl-dern*) *v* announce; register; *make an appointment; **sich anmelden** check in

Anmeldung (*ahn-mehl-doong*) *f* reception; announcement

anmerken (*ahn-mehr-kern*) *v* note

annähernd (*ahn-nai-errnt*) *adj* approximate

*annehmen (*ahn-nāy-mern*) *v* accept; assume, suppose; adopt; **angenommen dass** supposing that

annullieren (ah-noo-*lee*-rern) *v* cancel

Annullierung (ah-noo-*lee*-roong) *f* (pl ~en) cancellation

anonym (ah-noa-*nēwm*) *adj* anonymous

anpassen (*ahn-pah-sern*) *v* adapt; adjust

anprobieren (*ahn-proa-bee-rern*) *v* try on

*anraten (*ahn-raa-tern*) *v* recommend

anregen (*ahn-rāy-gern*) *v* incite

Anregung (*ahn-rāy-goong*) *f* impulse

anrichten (*ahn-rikh-tern*) *v* cause

Anruf (*ahn-rōōf*) *m* (pl ~e) telephone call, call

*anrufen (*ahn-rōō-fern*) *v* phone, ring up, call; call up *Am*

anrühren (*ahn-rēw-rern*) *v* touch

anschauen (*ahn-shou-ern*) *v* look at

Anschauung (*ahn-shou-oong*) *f* (pl ~en) idea, outlook

Anschein (*ahn-shighn*) *m* semblance

anscheinend (*ahn-shigh-nernt*) *adv* apparently

Anschlag (*ahn-shlaak*) *m* attack, attempt

*anschließen (*ahn-shlee-sern*) *v* connect; **sich ~** join

Anschluss (*ahn-shlooss*) *m* (pl ~e) connection

*anschreiben (*ahn-shrigh-bern*) *v* score

Anschrift (*ahn-shrift*) *f* (pl ~en) address

Ansehen (*ahn-zāy-ern*) *nt* reputation

*ansehen (*ahn-zāy-ern*) *v* look at; regard

Ansicht (*ahn-zikht*) *f* (pl ~en) view, opinion; **der ~ *sein** *take the view; **zur ~** on approval

Ansichtskarte (*ahn-zikhts-kahr-ter*) *f* (pl ~n) picture postcard, postcard

Anspannung (*ahn-shpah-noong*) *f* (pl ~en) strain

anspornen (*ahn-shpor-nern*) *v* stimulate

Ansprache (*ahn-shpraa-kher*) *f* (pl ~n) speech

*ansprechen (*ahn-shpreh-khern*) *v* address

Anspruch (*ahn-shprookh*) *m* (pl ~e) claim

Anstalt (*ahn-shtahlt*) *f* (pl ~en) institute; asylum

anständig (*ahn*-shtehn-dikh) *adj* decent

anstatt (ahn-*shtaht*) *prep* instead of

anstecken (*ahn*-shteh-kern) *v* infect

ansteckend (*ahn*-shteh-kernt) *adj* contagious, infectious

anstellen (*ahn*-shteh-lern) *v* appoint; engage

Anstoß (*ahn*-shtōass) *m* kickoff

*anstoßen (*ahn*-shtōa-sern) push, bump into; nudge; clink; ~ **auf** *drink to

anstößig (*ahn*-shtūr-sikh) *adj* offensive

*anstreichen (*ahn*-shtrigh-khern) *v* paint

Anstrengung (*ahn*-shtrehng-oong) *f* (pl ~en) effort, strain

Anteil (*ahn*-tighl) *m* share, part, portion

Antenne (ahn-*teh*-ner) *f* (pl ~n) aerial

Antibiotikum (ahn-ti-bi-*ōa*-ti-koom) *nt* (pl -ka) antibiotic

antik (ahn-*teek*) *adj* antique

Antipathie (ahn-ti-pah-*tee*) *f* dislike

Antiquität (ahn-ti-kvi-*tait*) *f* (pl ~en) antique

Antiquitätenhändler (ahn-ti-kvi-*tai*-tern-hehn-dlerr) *m* (pl ~), **-in** *f* antique dealer

Antrag (*ahn*-traak) *m* (pl ~e) motion

*antreiben (*ahn*-trigh-bern) *v* *drive (on)

Antwort (*ahnt*-vort) *f* (pl ~en) answer; reply; **als** ~ in reply

antworten (*ahnt*-vor-tern) *v* answer; reply

anvertrauen (*ahn*-fehr-trou-ern) *v* commit

*anwachsen (*ahn*-vah-ksern) *v* increase

Anwalt (*ahn*-vahlt) *m* (pl ~e) solicitor, attorney

Anwältin (*ahn*-vehlt-in) *f* (pl ~nen)

solicitor, attorney

*anweisen (*ahn*-vigh-zern) *v* designate

Anweisung (*ahn*-vigh-zoong) *f* (pl ~en) direction; money order

*anwenden (*ahn*-vehn-dern) *v* apply

Anwendung (*ahn*-vehn-doong) *f* (pl ~en) application

anwesend (*ahn*-vāy-zernt) *adj* present

Anwesenheit (*ahn*-vāy-zern-hight) *f* presence

Anzahl (*ahn*-tsaal) *f* (pl ~en) number; quantity

Anzahlung (*ahn*-tsaa-loong) *f* (pl ~en) down payment

Anzeichen (*ahn*-tsigh-khern) *nt* (pl ~) indication

Anzeige (*ahn*-tsigh-ger) *f* (pl ~n) notice; advertisement; ticket

*anziehen (*ahn*-tsee-ern) *v* attract; *put on

anziehend (*ahn*-tsee-ernt) *adj* attractive

Anziehung (*ahn*-tsee-oong) *f* attraction

Anzug (*ahn*-tsōōk) *m* (pl ~e) suit

anzünden (*ahn*-tsewn-dern) *v* *light

Anzünder (*ahn*-tsewn-derr) *m* (pl ~) lighter

apart (ah-*pahrt*) *adj* striking

Aperitif (ah-peh-ri-*teef*) *m* (pl ~s) aperitif; drink

Apfel (*ah*-pferl) *m* (pl ~) apple

Apfelsine (ah-pferl-*zee*-ner) *f* (pl ~n) orange

Apotheke (ah-poa-*tāy*-ker) *f* (pl ~n) pharmacy, chemist's; drugstore *Am*

Apotheker (ah-poa-*tāy*-kerr) *m* (pl ~), **-in** *f* chemist, pharmacist *Am*

Apparat (ah-pah-*raat*) *m* (pl ~e) machine, apparatus

Appartement (ah-pahr-ter-*mahng*) *nt* (pl ~e) apartment *Am*

Appell (ah-*pehl*) *m* (pl ~e) appeal

Appetit (ah-pay-*teet*) *m* appetite

Aprikose (ah-pri-*kōa*-zer) *f* (pl ∼n) apricot

April (ah-*pril*) April

Aquarell (ah-kvah-*rehl*) *nt* (pl ∼e) water-colo(u)r

Äquator (eh-*kvaa*-tor) *m* equator

Araber (*aa*-rah-berr) *m* (pl ∼), **-in** *f* Arab

arabisch (ah-*raa*-bish) *adj* Arab

Arbeit (*ahr*-bight) *f* (pl ∼en) labo(u)r, work; job

arbeiten (*ahr*-bigh-tern) *v* work; operate

Arbeiter (*ahr*-bigh-terr) *m* (pl ∼), **-in** *f* workman, workwoman, labo(u)rer, (female) worker, (female) employee

Arbeitgeber (*ahr*-bight-gāy-berr) *m* (pl ∼), **-in** *f* employer

Arbeitnehmer (*ahr*-bight-nāy-merr) *m* (pl ∼), **-in** *f* employee

Arbeitsamt (*ahr*-bights-ahmt) *nt* (pl ∼er) employment exchange

Arbeitsbewilligung (*ahr*-bights-ber-vi-li-goong) *f* (pl ∼en) work permit; labor permit *Am*, green card *Am*

arbeitslos (*ahr*-bights-lōáss) *adj* unemployed

Arbeitslosigkeit (*ahr*-bights-lōá-zikh-kight) *f* unemployment

Archäologe (ar-kheh-oa-*lōa*-ger) *m* (pl ∼n) archaeologist

Archäologie (ar-kheh-oa-loa-*gee*) *f* archaeology

Archäologin (ar-kheh-oa-*lōá*-gin) *f* (pl ∼nen) archaeologist

Architekt (ahr-khi-*tehkt*) *m* (pl ∼en), **-in** *f* architect

Architektur (ahr-khi-tehk-*tōōr*) *f* architecture

Archiv (ahr-*kheef*) *nt* (pl ∼e) archives *pl*

Argentinien (ahr-gehn-*tee*-nyern) Argentina

Argentinier (ahr-gehn-*tee*-nyerr) *m* (pl ∼), **-in** *f* Argentinian

argentinisch (ahr-gehn-*tee*-nish) *adj* Argentinian

Ärger (*ehr*-gerr) *m* anger

ärgerlich (*ehr*-gerr-likh) *adj* annoying

ärgern (*ehr*-gerrn) *v* annoy

Argument (ahr-goo-*mehnt*) *nt* (pl ∼e) argument

argumentieren (ahr-goo-mehn-*tee*-rern) *v* argue

Arkade (ahr-*kaa*-der) *f* (pl ∼n) arcade

Arm (ahrm) *m* (pl ∼e) arm; **∼ in Arm** arm-in-arm

arm (ahrm) *adj* poor

Armaturenbrett (ahr-mah-*tōō*-rern-breht) *nt* dashboard

Armband (*ahrm*-bahnt) *nt* (pl ∼er) bracelet

Armbanduhr (*ahrm*-bahnt-ōōr) *f* (pl ∼en) wristwatch

Armee (ahr-*māy*) *f* (pl ∼n) army

Ärmel (*ehr*-merl) *m* (pl ∼) sleeve

Ärmelkanal (*ehr*-merl-kah-naal) *m* English Channel

Armlehne (*ahrm*-lāy-ner) *f* (pl ∼n) arm

ärmlich (*ehrm*-likh) *adj* poor

Armreif (*ahrm*-righf) *m* (pl ∼en) bangle

Armut (*ahr*-mōōt) *f* poverty

Aroma (ah-*rōá*-mah) *nt* aroma

Arsch (ahrsh) *m* vulgar arse, bum

Art (ahrt) *f* (pl ∼en) species, sort; way, manner

Arterie (ahr-*tāy*-ryer) *f* (pl ∼n) artery

artig (*ahr*-tikh) *adj* good

Artikel (ahr-*tee*-kerl) *m* (pl ∼) article

Artischocke (ahr-ti-*sho*-ker) *f* (pl ∼n) artichoke

Arznei (ahrts-*nigh*) *f* (pl ∼en) drug

Arzt (ahrtst) *m* (pl ∼e), **Ärztin** *f* doctor, physician; **praktischer Arzt** general practitioner

ärztlich (*ehrtst*-likh) *adj* medical

Asbest (ahss-*behst*) *m* asbestos

Asche (*ah*-sher) *f* ash

Aschenbecher (*ah*-shern-beh-kherr) *m* (pl ~) ashtray

Asiate (ah-z^y*aa*-ter) *m* (pl ~n), **Asiatin** *f* Asian

asiatisch (ah-z^y*aa*-tish) *adj* Asian

Asien (*aa*-z^yern) Asia

Aspekt (ahss-*pehkt*) *m* (pl ~e) aspect

Asphalt (ahss-*fahlt*) *m* asphalt

Aspirin (ahss-pi-*reen*) *nt* aspirin

Assistent (ah-siss-*tehnt*) *m* (pl ~en), **-in** *f* assistant

assoziieren (ah-soa-tsi-*ee*-rern) *v* associate

Ast (ahst) *m* (pl ~e) branch

Asthma (*ahst*-mah) *nt* asthma

Astronomie (ah-stroa-noa-*mee*) *f* astronomy

Asyl (ah-z*ēwl*) *nt* (pl ~e) asylum

Atem (*aa*-term) *m* breath

Äther (*ai*-terr) *m* ether

Äthiopien (eh-ti-*ōa*-p^yern) Ethiopia

Äthiopier (eh-ti-*ōa*-p^yerr) *m* (pl ~), **-in** *f* Ethiopian

äthiopisch (eh-ti-*ōa*-pish) *adj* Ethiopian

Athlet (aht-*lāyt*) *m* (pl ~en), **-in** *f* athlete

Atlantik (aht-*lahn*-tik) *m* Atlantic

atmen (*aat*-mern) *v* breathe

Atmosphäre (aht-moa-*sfai*-rer) *f* atmosphere

Atmung (*aat*-moong) *f* respiration, breathing

Atom (ah-*tōam*) *nt* (pl ~e) atom; **Atom-** atomic

atomar (ah-toa-*maar*) *adj* atomic

Attest (ah-*tehst*) *nt* (pl ~e) certificate

Attraktion (ah-trahk-*ts^yōan*) *f* (pl ~en) attraction

Aubergine (oa-behr-*zhee*-ner) *f* eggplant

auch (oukh) *adv* too, also; as well

auf (ouf) *prep* on, upon; at

aufbauen (*ouf*-bou-ern) *v* construct; erect

aufblähen (*ouf*-blai-ern) *v* inflate

aufblasbar (*ouf*-blaass-baar) *adj* inflatable

aufdecken (*ouf*-deh-kern) *v* uncover

Aufenthalt (*ouf*-ehnt-hahlt) *m* (pl ~e) stay; delay

Aufenthaltsgenehmigung (*ouf*-ehnt-hahlts-ger-nāy-mi-goong) *f* (pl ~en) residence permit

*auffallen (*ouf*-fah-lern) *v* *strike

auffallend (*ouf*-fah-lernt) *adj* striking

auffassen (*ouf*-fah-sern) *v* conceive

auffordern (*ouf*-for-derrn) *v* ask

Aufführung (*ouf*-fēw-roong) *f* (pl ~en) show, performance

Aufgabe (*ouf*-gaa-ber) *f* (pl ~n) duty, task; exercise

*aufgeben (*ouf*-gāy-bern) *v* *give up, quit; post, mail

*aufgehen (*ouf*-gāy-ern) *v* *rise

aufgliedern (*ouf*-glee-derrn) *v* *break down

aufgrund (ouf-*groont*) *prep* owing to, because of

*aufhalten (*ouf*-hahl-tern) *v*: **sich ~** stay

aufhängen (*ouf*-hehng-ern) *v* *hang

Aufhänger (*ouf*-hehng-err) *m* (pl ~) hanger

Aufhängung (*ouf*-hehng-oong) *f* suspension

*aufheben (*ouf*-hāy-bern) *v* lift

aufheitern (*ouf*-high-terrn) *v* cheer up

aufhören (*ouf*-hūr-rern) *v* cease, expire, stop; **~ mit** discontinue, quit

Aufkleber (*ouf*-klāy-ber) *m* sticker

aufknöpfen (*ouf*-knur-pfern) *v* unbutton

aufknoten (*ouf*-knōa-tern) *v* untie

Auflage (*ouf*-laa-ger) *f* (pl ~n) edition

auflösen (*ouf*-lūr-zern) *v* dissolve;

sich ~ dissolve

aufmachen (*ouf*-mah-khern) *v* *undo; unfasten

aufmerksam (*ouf*-mehrk-zaam) *adj* attentive

Aufmerksamkeit (*ouf*-mehrk-zaam-kight) *f* attention; notice

Aufnahme (*ouf*-naa-mer) *f* (pl ~n) reception; shot; recording

***aufnehmen** (*ouf*-nāy-mern) *v* pick up

aufopfern (*ouf*-o-pferrn) *v* sacrifice

aufpassen (ouf-pah-sern) *v* *pay attention; watch out; **~ auf** look after

aufräumen (*ouf*-roi-mern) *v* tidy up

aufrecht (*ouf*-rehkht) *adj* upright, erect; *adv* upright

***aufrechterhalten** (*ouf*-rehkht-ehr-hahl-tern) *v* maintain

aufregen (*ouf*-rāy-gern) *v* excite; **aufregend** exciting

Aufregung (*ouf*-rāy-goong) *f* excitement

aufreihen (*ouf*-righ-ern) *v* thread

aufrichten (*ouf*-rikh-tern) *v* erect

aufrichtig (*ouf*-rikh-tikh) *adj* sincere, honest; true

Aufruhr (*ouf*-rōōr) *m* revolt, rebellion; riot

Aufsatz (*ouf*-zahts) *m* (pl ~e) essay

***aufschieben** (*ouf*-shee-bern) *v* delay; postpone

***aufschließen** (*ouf*-shlee-sern) *v* unlock

Aufschrei (*ouf*-shrigh) *m* (pl ~e) cry

***aufschreiben** (*ouf*-shrigh-bern) *v* *write down

Aufschub (*ouf*-shōōp) *m* delay; respite

aufsehenerregend (*ouf*-zāy-ern-ehr-rāy-gernt) *adj* sensational

Aufsicht (*ouf*-zikht) *f* supervision

Aufstand (*ouf*-shtahnt) *m* (pl ~e) rebellion; revolt, rising

***aufstehen** (*ouf*-shtāy-ern) *v* *rise,

*get up

***aufsteigen** (*ouf*-shtigh-gern) *v* ascend

Aufstieg (*ouf*-shteek) *m* climb; ascent; rise

auftauen (*ouf*-tou-ern) *v* thaw

Auftrag (*ouf*-traak) *m* (pl ~e) order

***auftreten** (*ouf*-trāy-tern) *v* appear

Auftritt (*ouf*-trit) *m* (pl ~e) appearance

aufwachen (*ouf*-vah-khern) *v* wake up

Aufwand (*ouf*-vahnt) *m* expenditure

aufwärts (*ouf*-vehrts) *adv* upwards

aufzeichnen (*ouf*-tsighkh-nern) *v* record

Aufzeichnung (*ouf*-tsighkh-noong) *f* (pl ~en) note

***aufziehen** (*ouf*-tsee-ern) *v* *wind; raise

Aufzug (*ouf*-tsōōk) *m* (pl ~e) lift; elevator *Am*

Auge (*ou*-ger) *nt* (pl ~n) eye

Augenarzt (*ou*-gern-ahrtst) *m* (pl ~e), **-ärztin** *f* oculist

Augenblick (*ou*-gern-blik) *m* (pl ~e) moment; second, instant

augenblicklich (*ou*-gern-blik-likh) *adv* instantly

Augenbraue (*ou*-gern-brou-er) *f* (pl ~n) eyebrow

Augenbrauenstift (*ou*-gern-brou-ern-shtift) *m* (pl ~e) eyebrow pencil

Augenlid (*ou*-gern-leet) *nt* (pl ~er) eyelid

Augenwimper (*ou*-gern-vim-perr) *f* (pl ~n) eyelash

Augenzeuge (*ou*-gern-tsoi-ger) *m* (pl ~n), **-zeugin** *f* eyewitness

August (ou-*goost*) August

aus (ouss) *prep* out of; from; for

ausarbeiten (*ouss*-ahr-bigh-tern) *v* elaborate

ausatmen (*ouss*-aat-mern) *v* expire, exhale

ausbessern (*ouss*-beh-serrn) *v* mend

ausbeuten (*ouss*-boi-tern) *v* exploit

ausbilden (*ouss*-bil-dern) *v* educate; train

Ausbildung (*ouss*-bil-doong) *f* training

ausbreiten (*ouss*-brigh-tern) *v* expand; *spread

Ausbruch (*ouss*-brookh) *m* (pl ⁓e) outbreak

ausdehnen (*ouss*-dāy-nern) *v* expand

Ausdehnung (*ouss*-dāy-noong) *f* extension

*ausdenken (*ouss*-dehng-kern) *v* imagine

Ausdruck (*ouss*-drook) *m* (pl ⁓e) term, expression; ⁓ ***geben** express

ausdrücken (*ouss*-drew-kern) *v* express

ausdrücklich (*ouss*-drewk-likh) *adj* express, explicit

Auseinandersetzung (ouss-igh-*nahn*-derr-zeh-tsoong) *f* (pl ⁓en) discussion, argument; dispute

Ausfahrt (*ouss*-faart) *f* (pl ⁓en) exit

*ausfallen (*ouss*-fah-lern) *v* *fall out, *come out; not to *take place, *be cancelled; turn out

Ausflug (*ouss*-flōok) *m* (pl ⁓e) excursion; trip

Ausfuhr (*ouss*-fōor) *f* exports *pl*, exportation

ausführen (*ouss*-fēw-rern) *v* perform; export; execute, implement

ausführlich (*ouss*-fēwr-likh) *adj* detailed

ausfüllen (*ouss*-few-lern) *v* fill in; fill out *Am*

Ausgabe (*ouss*-gaa-ber) *f* (pl ⁓n) issue, edition; expense

Ausgang (*ouss*-gahng) *m* (pl ⁓e) way out, exit

Ausgangspunkt (*ouss*-gahngs-poongkt) *m* (pl ⁓e) starting point

*ausgeben (*ouss*-gāy-bern) *v* *spend;

issue

ausgedehnt (*ouss*-ger-dāynt) *adj* extensive; broad

*ausgehen (*ouss*-gāy-ern) *v* *go out

ausgenommen (*ouss*-ger-no-mern) *prep* except

ausgesetzt (*ouss*-ger-zehtst) subject to

ausgezeichnet (*ouss*-ger-tsighkh-nert) *adj* fine, excellent

Ausgleich (*ouss*-glighkh) *m* (pl ⁓e) compensation

*ausgleichen (*ouss*-gligh-khern) *v* equalize; compensate

*ausgleiten (*ouss*-gligh-tern) *f* slip

Ausgrabung (*ouss*-graa-boong) *f* (pl ⁓en) excavation

Ausguss (*ouss*-gooss) *m* (pl ⁓e) sink

*aushalten (*ouss*-hahl-tern) *v* sustain

ausharren (*ouss*-hah-rern) *v* *keep up

Auskunft (*ouss*-koonft) *f* (pl ⁓e) information

*ausladen (*ouss*-laa-dern) *v* discharge, unload

Auslage (*ouss*-laa-ger) *f* (pl ⁓n) display

Ausland (*ouss*-lahnt) *nt* foreign countries *pl*; **im** ⁓ (im *ouss*-lahnt) abroad

Ausländer (*ouss*-lehn-derr) *m* (pl ⁓), **-in** *f* foreigner, alien

ausländisch (*ouss*-lehn-dish) *adj* foreign, alien

*auslassen (*ouss*-lah-sern) *v* *leave out, omit

auslegen (*ouss*-lāy-gern) *v* display

*auslesen (*ouss*-lāy-zayn) *v* select

ausliefern (*ouss*-lee-ferrn) *v* deliver; extradite

auslöschen (*ouss*-lur-shern) *v* extinguish, *put out

Ausmaß (*ouss*-maass) *nt* (pl ⁓e) extent; size

Ausnahme (*ouss*-naa-mer) *f* (pl ⁓n)

exception

ausnahmsweise (*ouss*-naams-vigh-zer) for once, for a change

*ausnehmen (*ouss*-nāy-mern) *v* exempt

ausnutzen (*ouss*-noo-tsern) *v* exploit

auspacken (*ouss*-pah-kern) *v* unpack, unwrap

Auspuff (*ouss*-poof) *m* (pl ⁓e) exhaust

Auspuffgase (*ouss*-poof-gaa-zer) *ntpl* exhaust gases

Auspufftopf (*ouss*-poof-topf) *m* silencer; muffler *Am*

ausrangieren (*ouss*-rahng-zhee-rern) *v* discard

ausrechnen (*ouss*-rehkh-nern) *v* calculate

*ausreißen (*ouss*-righ-sern) *v* extract

Ausreißer (*ouss*-righ-serr) *m* (pl ⁓), **-in** *f* runaway

Ausruf (*ouss*-rōof) *m* (pl ⁓e) exclamation

*ausrufen (*ouss*-rōo-fern) *v* exclaim

ausruhen (*ouss*-rōo-ern) *v* rest

ausrüsten (*ouss*-rewss-tern) *v* equip

Ausrüstung (*ouss*-rewss-toong) *f* outfit, equipment; gear, kit

ausrutschen (*ouss*-roo-chern) *v* slip

aussaugen (*ouss*-zou-gern) *v* *bleed

ausschalten (*ouss*-shahl-tern) *v* switch off; disconnect

ausschimpfen (*ouss*-shim-pfern) *v* call names

Ausschlag (*ouss*-shlaak) *m* rash

*ausschließen (*ouss*-shlee-sern) *v* exclude

ausschließlich (*ouss*-shleess-likh) *adv* exclusively; solely

Ausschnitt (*ouss*-shnit) *m* neck, décolleté; cutting; detail; extract, part

Ausschreitung (*ouss*-shrigh-toong) *f* (pl ⁓en) excess

Ausschuss (*ouss*-shooss) *m* (pl ⁓e) committee

Aussehen (*ouss*-zāy-ern) *nt* look

*aussehen (*ouss*-zāy-ern) *v* look

Außenbezirke (*ou*-sern-ber-tseer-ker) *mpl* outskirts *pl*

Außenseite (*ou*-sern-zigh-ter) *f* exterior, outside

außer (*ou*-serr) *prep* beyond, besides; but, except; out of; ⁓ **wenn** unless

außerdem (*ou*-serr-dāym) *adv* moreover

äußere (*oi*-serr-rer) *adj* outward, outside, external; **Äußere** (*oi*-ser-rer) *nt* outside

außergewöhnlich (*ou*-serr-ger-vūrn-likh) *adj* exceptional

außerhalb (*ou*-serr-hahlp) *prep* outside

äußerlich (*oi*-serr-likh) *adj* external, exterior

äußern (*oi*-serrn) *v* express; utter

außerordentlich (ou-serr-*or*-dernt-likh) *adj* extraordinary

äußerst *adj* extreme, utmost; very

Äußerung (*oi*-ser-roong) *f* (pl ⁓en) expression

Aussicht[1] (*ouss*-zikht) *f* view; sight

Aussicht[2] (*ouss*-zikht) *f* (pl ⁓en) prospect, outlook

Aussprache (*ouss*-shpraa-kher) *f* pronunciation

*aussprechen (*ouss*-shpreh-khern) *v* pronounce

ausstatten (*ouss*-shtah-tern) *v* equip

*aussteigen (*ouss*-shtigh-gern) *v* *get off

ausstellen (*ouss*-shteh-lern) *v* exhibit; *show

Ausstellung (*ouss*-shteh-loong) *f* (pl ⁓en) exhibition; display, show, exposition

Ausstellungsraum (*ouss*-shteh-loongs-room) *m* (pl ⁓e) showroom

Ausstoß (*ouss*-shtōäss) *m* output

austauschen (*ouss*-tou-shern) *v*

exchange

austeilen (*ouss*-tigh-lern) *v* *deal

Auster (*ouss*-terr) *f* (pl ⁀n) oyster

Australien (*ouss-traa*-l[y]ern) Australia

Australier (ouss-*traa*-l[y]err) *m* (pl ⁀), **-in** *f* Australian

australisch (ouss-*traa*-lish) *adj* Australian

ausüben (*ouss-ēw̄*-bern) *v* exercise; practise

Ausverkauf (*ouss*-fehr-kouf) *m* clearance sale

ausverkauft (*ouss*-fehr-kouft) *adj* sold out

Auswahl (*ouss*-vaal) *f* choice; selection; assortment; variety

auswählen (*ouss*-vai-lern) *v* select

Auswanderer (*ouss*-vahn-der-rerr) *m* (pl ⁀), **Auswanderin** *f* emigrant

auswandern (*ouss*-vahn-derrn) *v* emigrate

Auswanderung (*ouss*-vahn-der-roong) *f* emigration

auswechseln (*ouss*-veh-kserln) *v* exchange

Ausweg (*ouss*-vāyk) *m* (pl ⁀e) way out

Ausweis (*ouss*-vighss) *m* (pl ⁀e) identity card

*ausweisen (*ouss*-vigh-zern) *v* expel; **sich ⁀** prove one's identity

auswendig (*ouss*-vehn-dikh) *adv* by heart

auswischen (*ouss*-vi-shern) *v* wipe

auszeichnen (*ouss*-tsighkh-nern) *v*: **sich ⁀** excel

*ausziehen (*ouss*-tsee-ern) *v* extract; take off; **sich ⁀** undress

Auszug (*ouss*-tsōōk) *m* (pl ⁀e) excerpt

authentisch (ou-*tehn*-tish) *adj* authentic

Auto (*ou*-toa) *nt* (pl ⁀s) automobile; **⁀ *fahren** *drive (a car); **mit dem ⁀ *fahren** *go by car

Autobahn (*ou*-toa-baan) *f* (pl ⁀en) motorway; highway *Am*

Autofahrer (*ou*-toa-faa-rerr) *m* (pl ⁀), **-in** *f* motorist

Autokarte (*ou*-toa-kahr-ter) *f* (pl ⁀n) road map

Automat (ou-toa-*maat*) *m* (pl ⁀en) slot machine

automatisch (ou-toa-*maa*-tish) *adj* automatic

Automobilklub (ou-toa-moa-*beel*-kloop) *m* (pl ⁀s) automobile club

autonom (ou-toa-*nōām*) *adj* autonomous

Autopsie (ou-toa-*psee*) *f* autopsy

Autor (*ou*-tor) *m* (pl ⁀en), **-in** *f* author

autoritär (ou-toa-ri-*tair*) *adj* authoritarian

Autovermietung (*ou*-toa-fehr-mee-toong) *f* car hire; car rental *Am*

B

Baby (*bāy*-bi) *nt* (pl ⁀s) baby

Babysitter (*bāy*-bi-si-terr) *m* (pl ⁀) babysitter

Baby-Tragetasche (*bāy*-bi-traa-ger-tah-sher) *f* (pl ⁀n) carrycot

Bach (bahkh) *m* (pl ⁀e) brook, stream

Backbord (*bahk*-bord) *nt* port

backen (*bah*-kern) *v* bake

Backenknochen (*bah*-kern-kno-khern) *m* (pl ⁀) cheekbone

Backenzahn (*bah*-kern-tsaan) *m* (pl ⁀e) molar

Bäcker (*beh*-kerr) *m* (pl ~), **-in** *f* baker

Bäckerei (beh-ker-*righ*) *f* (pl ~en) bakery

Backofen (*bahk*-ōā-fern) *m* (pl ~) oven

Backpflaume (*bahk*-pflou-mer) *f* (pl ~n) prune

Bad (baat) *nt* (pl ~er) bath

Badeanzug (*baa*-der-ahn-tsōōk) *m* (pl ~e) swimsuit, bathing-suit

Badehose (*baa*-der-hōā-zer) *f* (pl ~n) swimmingtrunks, bathing trunks, bathing suit

Bademantel (*baa*-der-mahn-terl) *m* (pl ~) bathrobe

Bademütze (*baa*-der-mew-tser) *f* (pl ~n) bathing cap

baden (*baa*-dern) *v* bathe

Badesalz (*baa*-der-zahlts) *nt* (pl ~e) bath salts

Badetuch (*baa*-der-tōōkh) *nt* (pl ~er) bath towel

Badezimmer (*baa*-der-tsi-merr) *nt* (pl ~) bathroom

Bahn (baan) *f* (pl ~en) railway; track

Bahnhof (*baan*-hōāf) *m* (pl ~e) station; depot *Am*

Bahnsteig (*baan*-shtighk) *m* (pl ~e) platform

Bahnübergang (*baan*-ēw-berr-gahng) *m* (pl ~e) crossing, level crossing

Bakterie (bahk-*tāy*-r^y er) *f* (pl ~n) bacterium

bald (bahlt) *adv* soon; shortly

Balken (*bahl*-kern) *m* (pl ~) beam

Balkon (bahl-*kawng*) *m* (pl ~s) balcony; circle

Ball (bahl) *m* (pl ~e) ball

Ballett (bah-*leht*) *nt* (pl ~s) ballet

Ballon (bah-*lawng*) *m* (pl ~e) balloon

Bambus (*bahm*-booss) *m* bamboo

Banane (bah-*naa*-ner) *f* (pl ~n) banana

Band[1] (bahnt) *nt* (pl ~er) band; ribbon; tape

Band[2] (bahnt) *m* (pl ~e) volume

Bande (*bahn*-der) *f* (pl ~n) gang

Bandscheibe (*bahnt*-shigh-ber) *f* (pl ~n) disc; **Bandscheibenvorfall** *m* slipped disc

bange (*bahng*-er) *adj* afraid

Bank[1] (bahngk) *f* (pl ~en) bank

Bank[2] (bahngk) *f* (pl ~e) bench

Bankkonto (*bahngk*-kon-toa) *nt* (pl -konten) bank account

Banknote (*bahngk*-nōā-ter) *f* (pl ~n) banknote, *Am* bill

bankrott (bahng-*krot*) *adj* bankrupt

Bar (baar) *f* (pl ~s) bar; saloon

Bär (bair) *m* (pl ~en) bear

Bardame (*baar*-daa-mer) *f* (pl ~n) barmaid

Bargeld (*baar*-gehlt) *nt* cash

Bariton (*baa*-ri-ton) *m* (pl ~e) baritone

barock (bah-*rok*) *adj* baroque

Barometer (bah-roa-*māy*-terr) *nt* (pl ~) barometer

Barsch (bahrsh) *m* (pl ~e) perch, bass

Bart (bahrt) *m* (pl ~e) beard

Baseball (*bāyss*-bōal) *m* baseball

Basilika (bah-*zee*-li-kah) *f* (pl -ken) basilica

Basis (*baa*-ziss) *f* (pl Basen) basis; base

Baskenmütze (*bahss*-kern-mew-tser) *f* (pl ~n) beret

Bass (bahss) *m* (pl ~e) bass

basteln (*bahss*-terln) *v* *build, *make; work at a hobby

Batterie (bah-ter-*ree*) *f* (pl ~n) battery

Bau (bou) *m* construction

Bauch (boukh) *m* (pl ~e) belly

Bauchschmerzen (*boukh*-shmehr-tsern) *mpl* stomach ache

bauen (*bou*-ern) *v* construct, *build

Bauer (*bou*-err) *m* (pl ~n) farmer; peasant; pawn

Bäuerin (*boi*-er-rin) *f* (pl ∼nen) farmer's wife

Bauernhaus (*bou*-errn-houss) *nt* (pl ∼er) farmhouse

Bauernhof (*bou*-errn-h<u>oa</u>f) *m* (pl ∼e) farm

baufällig (*bou*-feh-likh) *adj* dilapidated

Bauholz (*bou*-holts) *nt* timber

Baukunst (*bou*-koonst) *f* architecture

Baum (boum) *m* (pl ∼e) tree

Baumschule (*boum*-sh<u>oo</u>-ler) *f* (pl ∼n) nursery

Baumwolle (*boum*-vo-ler) *f* cotton; **Baumwoll-** cotton

Bazille (bah-*tsi*-ler) *f* (pl ∼n) germ

beabsichtigen (ber-*ahp*-zikh-ti-gern) *v* intend; aim at

beachten (ber-*ahkh*-tern) *v* attend to; observe

beachtlich (ber-*ahkht*-likh) *adj* considerable

Beachtung (ber-*ahkh*-toong) *f* consideration

Beamte (ber-*ahm*-ter) *m* (pl ∼n), **Beamtin** *f* official; officer

beanspruchen (ber-*ahn*-shproo-khern) *v* claim

beantworten (ber-*ahnt*-vor-tern) *v* answer

beaufsichtigen (ber-*ouf*-zikh-ti-gern) *v* supervise

bebauen (ber-*bou*-ern) *v* cultivate

beben (*bay*-bern) *v* tremble

Becher (*beh*-kherr) *m* (pl ∼) mug, tumbler

Becken (*beh*-kern) *nt* (pl ∼) basin; pelvis

bedächtig (ber-*dehkh*-tikh) *adj* wary

Bedarf (ber-*dahrf*) *m* need

Bedauern (ber-*dou*-errn) *nt* regret

bedauern (ber-*dou*-errn) *v* regret

bedecken (ber-*deh*-kern) *v* cover

bedeckt (ber-*dehkt*) *adj* covered;

overcast, cloudy

bedenklich (ber-*dehngk*-likh) *adj* critical

bedeuten (ber-*doi*-tern) *v* *mean

bedeutend (ber-*doi*-ternt) *adj* considerable, big; important; capital, substantial

Bedeutung (ber-*doi*-toong) *f* (pl ∼en) meaning, sense; importance; **von ∼ *sein** matter

bedeutungsvoll (ber-*doi*-toongs-fol) *adj* significant

bedienen (ber-*dee*-nern) *v* serve; wait on, attend on

Bedienung (ber-*dee*-noong) *f* service

bedingt (ber-*dingkt*) *adj* conditional

Bedingung (ber-*ding*-oong) *f* (pl ∼en) condition; term

bedingungslos (ber-*ding*-oongs-l<u>oa</u>ss) *adj* unconditional

bedrohen (ber-*dr<u>oa</u>*-ern) *v* threaten

bedrohlich (ber-*dr<u>oa</u>*-likh) *adj* threatening

Bedrohung (ber-*dr<u>oa</u>*-oong) *f* (pl ∼en) threat

bedrücken (ber-*drew*-kern) *v* oppress

Bedürfnis (ber-*dewrf*-niss) *nt* (pl ∼se) need

beeilen (ber-*igh*-lern) *v*: **sich ∼** hurry

beeindrucken (ber-*ighn*-droo-kern) *v* impress

beeinflussen (ber-*ighn*-floo-sern) *v* influence; affect

beenden (ber-*ehn*-dern) *v* end, finish

beerdigen (ber-*air*-di-gern) *v* bury

Beere (*b<u>ay</u>*-rer) *f* (pl ∼n) berry; currant

Beet (b<u>ay</u>t) *nt* bed; patch

befahrbar (ber-*faar*-baar) *adj* passable; navigable

*befahren (ber-*faa*-rern) *v* *drive on, sail

befassen (ber-*fah*-sern) *v*: **sich ∼ mit** *deal with

Befehl (ber-*f<u>ay</u>l*) *m* (pl ∼e) order;

command

*befehlen (ber-*fay*-lern) *v* order; command

befestigen (ber-*fehss*-ti-gern) *v* fasten; attach

befeuchten (ber-*foikh*-tern) *v* damp

beflecken (ber-*fleh*-kern) *v* stain

befördern (ber-*furr*-derrn) *v* promote

Beförderung (ber-*furr*-der-roong) *f* (pl ~en) transport; promotion

befragen (ber-*fraa*-gern) *v* query

befreien (ber-*frigh*-ern) *v* free

befreit (ber-*fright*) *adj* exempt

Befreiung (beh-*frigh*-oong) *f* liberation; exemption

befriedigen (ber-*free*-di-gern) *v* satisfy

Befriedigung (ber-*free*-di-goong) *f* satisfaction

Befugnis (ber-*fook*-niss) *f* (pl ~se) authority

befugt (ber-*fookt*) *adj* qualified

befürchten (ber-*fewrkh*-tern) *v* fear

begabt (ber-*gaapt*) *adj* gifted, talented

Begabung (ber-*gaa*-boong) *f* faculty, talent

begegnen (ber-*gay*-gnern) *v* *meet; encounter, *come across; **zufällig ~** run into

Begegnung (ber-*gay*-gnoong) *f* (pl ~en) encounter

*begehen (ber-*gay*-ern) *v* commit

Begehren (ber-*gay*-rern) *nt* wish

begehren (ber-*gay*-rern) *v* wish; desire

begehrenswert (ber-*gay*-rerns-vayrt) *adj* desirable

begeistern (ber-*gighss*-terrn) *v* inspire; **begeistert** *adj* enthusiastic; keen

Begeisterung (ber-*gighss*-ter-roong) *f* enthusiasm

begierig (ber-*gee*-rikh) *adj* eager

Beginn (ber-*gin*) *m* beginning

*beginnen (ber-*gi*-nern) *v* *begin;

wieder ~ recommence

begleiten (ber-*gligh*-tern) *v* accompany; conduct

beglückwünschen (ber-*glewk*-vewnshern) *v* congratulate, compliment

*begraben (ber-*graa*-bern) *v* bury

Begräbnis (ber-*graip*-niss) *nt* (pl ~se) funeral, burial

*begreifen (ber-*grigh*-fern) *v* *understand; *see

Begriff (ber-*grif*) *m* (pl ~e) notion

begrüßen *v* greet, *say hello, welcome; approve

begünstigen (ber-*gewns*-ti-gern) *v* favo(u)r

behaglich (ber-*haak*-likh) *adj* cosy, cozy *Am*

Behaglichkeit (ber-*haak*-likh-kight) *f* (pl ~en) comfort

*behalten (ber-*hahl*-tern) *v* remember

Behälter (ber-*hehl*-terr) *m* (pl ~) container

behandeln (ber-*hahn*-derln) *v* treat; handle

Behandlung (ber-*hahn*-dloong) *f* (pl ~en) treatment; **kosmetische ~** beauty treatment

behaupten (ber-*houp*-tern) *v* claim

*behelfen (ber-*hehl*-fern) *v*: **sich ~ mit** *make do with

beherbergen (ber-*hehr*-behr-gern) *v* lodge

beherrschen (ber-*hehr*-shern) *v* master

Behörde (ber-*hurr*-der) *f* (pl ~n) authorities *pl*

behutsam (ber-*hoot*-zaam) *adj* gentle

bei (bigh) *prep* at, with; near, by

Beichte (*bighkh*-ter) *f* (pl ~n) confession

beichten (*bighkh*-tern) *v* confess

beide (*bigh*-der) *adj* both, either; **einer von beiden** either

Beifall (*bigh*-fahl) *m* applause; ~

klatschen clap

beifügen (*bigh*-few-gern) v attach

beige (bayzh) adj beige

Beil (bighl) nt (pl ⁓e) axe

Beilage (*bigh*-laa-ger) f (pl ⁓n) enclosure; supplement

beiläufig (*bigh*-loi-fikh) adj casual

beilegen (*bigh*-lay-gern) v enclose

Bein (bighn) nt (pl ⁓e) leg; bone

beinahe (*bigh*-naa-er) adv nearly, almost

beiseite (bigh-*zigh*-ter) adv aside

Beispiel (*bigh*-shpeel) nt (pl ⁓e) instance, example; **zum ⁓** for instance, for example

***beißen** (*bigh*-sern) v *bite

Beistand (*bigh*-shtahnt) m assistance

Beitrag (*bigh*-traak) m (pl ⁓e) contribution

bejahen (ber-*yaa*-ern) v approve; **bejahend** affirmative

bejahrt (ber-*yaart*) adj aged

bekämpfen (ber-*kehm*-pfern) v combat

bekannt (ber-*kahnt*) adj well-known; ⁓ **machen** (ber-*kahnt*-mah-khern) v announce; introduce

Bekannte (ber-*kahn*-ter) m/f (pl ⁓n) friend, acquaintance

Bekanntmachung (ber-*kahnt*-mah-khoong) f (pl ⁓en) announcement; communiqué

Bekanntschaft (ber-*kahnt*-shahft) f (pl ⁓en) acquaintance

bekehren (ber-*kay*-rern) v convert

***bekennen** (ber-*keh*-nern) v confess

***bekommen** (ber-*ko*-mern) v *get; receive

bekömmlich (ber-*kurm*-likh) adj easily digestible

bekümmert (ber-*kew*-merrt) adj worried

Belagerung (ber-*laa*-ger-roong) f (pl ⁓en) siege

belanglos (ber-*lahng*-loass) adj insignificant

belasten (ber-*lahss*-tern) v charge

belästigen (ber-*lehss*-ti-gern) v bother

Belästigung (ber-*lehss*-ti-goong) f (pl ⁓en) bother

Belastung (ber-*lahss*-toong) f (pl ⁓en) charge

Beleg (ber-*layk*) m (pl ⁓e) voucher

belegt adj taken, reserved, full; engaged, busy; **belegtes Brot** sandwich

beleibt (ber-*lighpt*) adj corpulent

beleidigen (ber-*ligh*-di-gern) v offend, insult; **beleidigend** adj offensive

Beleidigung (ber-*ligh*-di-goong) f (pl ⁓en) offence, offense Am; insult

beleuchten v light, illuminate

Beleuchtung (ber-*loikh*-toong) f lighting, illumination

Belgien (*behl*-gⁱern) Belgium

Belgier (*behl*-gⁱern) m (pl ⁓), **-in** f Belgian

belgisch (*behl*-gish) adj Belgian

Belichtung (ber-*likh*-toong) f exposure

Belichtungsmesser (ber-*likh*-toongs-meh-serr) m (pl ⁓) exposure meter

beliebig (ber-*lee*-bikh) adj any, optional

beliebt (ber-*leept*) adj popular

bellen (*beh*-lern) v bark, bay

belohnen (ber-*loa*-nern) v reward

Belohnung (ber-*loa*-noong) f (pl ⁓en) reward; prize

bemächtigen (ber-*mehk*-ti-gern) v: **sich ⁓** secure

bemerken (ber-*mehr*-kern) v notice; note; remark

bemerkenswert (ber-*mehr*-kerns-vayrt) adj noticeable

Bemerkung (ber-*mehr*-koong) f (pl ⁓en) remark

bemitleiden (ber-*mit*-ligh-dern) v pity

bemühen (ber-*mēw*-ern) v trouble; **sich ~** try

benachbart (ber-*nahkh*-baart) adj neighbo(u)ring

benachrichtigen (ber-*naakh*-rikh-ti-gern) v notify

*benehmen (ber-*nāy*-mern) v: **sich ~** act, behave

beneiden (ber-*nigh*-dern) v envy

Benennung (ber-*neh*-noong) f (pl ~en) denomination

benutzen (ber-*noo*-tsern) v use; utilize

Benutzer (ber-*noo*-tserr) m (pl ~), **-in** f user

Benzin (behn-*tseen*) nt petrol; fuel; gasoline Am, gas Am

Benzinpumpe (behn-*tseen*-poom-per) f (pl ~n) petrol pump; fuel pump Am; gas pump Am

Benzintank (behn-*tseen*-tahngk) m petrol tank, gas tank Am

beobachten (ber-*ōa*-bahkh-tern) v watch

Beobachtung (ber-*ōa*-bahkh-toong) f (pl ~en) observation

bequem (ber-*kvāym*) adj comfortable; convenient, easy

Bequemlichkeit (ber-*kvāym*-likh-kight) f (pl ~en) comfort

beraten v advise, *give s.o. advice; discuss, debate; *be in conference

beratschlagen (ber-*raat*-shlaa-gern) v discuss, advise

Beratung (ber-*raa*-toong) f (pl ~en) discussion, advice

Beratungsstelle (ber-*raa*-toongs-shteh-ler) f (pl ~n) health centre, health center Am

berauscht (ber-*rousht*) adj intoxicated

berechnen (ber-*rehkh*-nern) v calculate

berechtigt (ber-*rehkh*-tikht) adj authorized; justified

bereden (ber-*rāy*-dern) v discuss

Bereich (ber-*righkh*) m reach; range

bereit (ber-*right*) adj ready; prepared

bereits (ber-*rights*) adv already

bereitwillig (ber-*right*-vi-likh) adj cooperative

Berg (behrk) m (pl ~e) mountain; mount

Bergbau (*behrk*-bou) m mining

Bergkette (*behrk*-keh-ter) f (pl ~n) mountain range

Bergmann (*behrk*-mahn) m (pl -leute) miner

Bergsteigen (*behrk*-shtigh-gern) nt mountaineering

Bergwerk (*behrk*-vehrk) nt (pl ~e) mine

Bericht (ber-*rikht*) m (pl ~e) account; report; notice

berichten (ber-*rikh*-tern) v inform; report

Berichterstatter (ber-*rikht*-err-shtah-terr) m (pl ~), **-in** f reporter

Berichtigung (ber-*rikh*-ti-goong) f (pl ~en) correction

Bernstein (*behrn*-shtighn) m amber

*bersten (*behrs*-tern) v *burst; crack

berüchtigt (ber-*rewkh*-tikht) adj notorious

berücksichtigen v consider, *take into consideration, allow for, *take into account

Beruf (ber-*rōōf*) m (pl ~e) profession; trade

beruflich (ber-*rōōf*-likh) adj professional

beruhigen (ber-*rōō*-i-gern) v calm down; reassure

Beruhigungsmittel (ber-*rōō*-i-goongs-mi-terl) nt (pl ~) sedative; tranquillizer

berühmt (ber-*rēwmt*) adj famous, noted

berühren (ber-*rēw*-rern) v touch

Berührung (ber-*rew*-roong) *f* (pl ⁓en)
touch, contact

besagen (ber-*zaa*-gern) *v* *say, *mean

Besatzung (ber-*zah*-tsoong) *f* (pl ⁓en)
crew

beschädigen (ber-*shai*-di-gern) *v*
damage

beschaffen (ber-*shah*-fern) *v* provide

beschäftigen (ber-*shehf*-ti-gern) *v*
employ; **sich ⁓ mit** attend to;
beschäftigt *adj* engaged, busy

Beschäftigung (ber-*shehf*-ti-goong) *f*
(pl ⁓en) business, occupation;
employment; job

Bescheid (ber-*shight*) *m* notice,
information

bescheiden (ber-*shigh*-dern) *adj*
modest; humble

Bescheidenheit (ber-*shigh*-dern-
hight) *f* modesty

Bescheinigung (ber-*shigh*-ni-goong)
f (pl ⁓en) certificate

beschlagnahmen (ber-*shlaak*-naa-
mern) *v* confiscate

beschleunigen (ber-*shloi*-ni-gern) *v*
accelerate

*beschließen (ber-*shlee*-sern) *v*
decide

Beschluss (ber-*shlooss*) *m* (pl ⁓e)
decision

beschmutzt (ber-*shmootst*) *adj* soiled

beschränken (ber-*shrehng*-kern) *v*
limit

*beschreiben (ber-*shrigh*-bern) *v*
describe

Beschreibung (ber-*shrigh*-boong) *f*
(pl ⁓en) description

beschriften (ber-*shrif*-tern) *v* label

beschuldigen (ber-*shool*-di-gern) *v*
accuse; blame

Beschwerde (ber-*shvayr*-der) *f* (pl ⁓n)
complaint

beschweren (ber-*shvay*-rern) *v*: **sich
⁓** complain

beschwindeln (ber-*shvin*-derln) *v*
cheat

beseitigen (ber-*zigh*-ti-gern) *v*
eliminate; remove

Beseitigung (ber-*zigh*-ti-goong) *f*
removal

Besen (*bay*-zern) *m* (pl ⁓) broom

besessen (ber-*zeh*-sern) *adj*
possessed

Besessenheit (ber-*zeh*-sern-hight) *f*
obsession

besetzen (ber-*zeh*-tsern) *v* occupy;
besetzt *adj* engaged; occupied

Besetzung (ber-*zeh*-tsoong) *f* (pl ⁓en)
occupation

besichtigen (ber-*zikh*-ti-gern) *v* view

besiegen (ber-*zee*-gern) *v* *beat;
defeat; conquer

Besitz (ber-*zits*) *m* possession;
property

*besitzen (ber-*zi*-tsern) *v* possess, own

Besitzer (ber-*zi*-tserr) *m* (pl ⁓), **-in** *f*
owner

besondere (ber-*zon*-derr) *adj* special,
particular; separate

besonders (ber-*zon*-derrs) *adv* most
of all, especially

besonnen (ber-*zo*-nern) *adj* sensible,
calm

besorgen (ber-*zor*-gern) *v* procure;
look after, *do; **besorgt** *adj* anxious,
concerned

Besorgtheit (ber-*zorkt*-hight) *f* worry,
anxiety

Besprechung (ber-*shpreh*-khoong) *f*
(pl ⁓en) discussion; review

bespritzen (ber-*shpri*-tsern) *v* splash

besser (*beh*-serr) *adj* better; superior

beständig (ber-*shtehn*-dikh) *adj*
permanent; constant, steady

Bestandteil (ber-*shtahnt*-tighl) *m* (pl
⁓e) element; ingredient

bestätigen (ber-*shtai*-ti-gern) *v*
acknowledge, confirm

Bestätigung (ber-*shtai*-ti-goong) *f* (pl ~en) confirmation

Bestattung (ber-*shtah*-toong) *f* (pl ~en) burial

beste (beh-*sterr*) *adj* best

*****bestechen** (ber-*shteh*-khern) *v* bribe, corrupt

Bestechung (ber-*shteh*-khoong) *f* (pl ~en) bribery, corruption

Besteck (ber-*shtehk*) *nt* cutlery

*****bestehen** (ber-*shtāy*-ern) *v* exist; insist; pass; ~ **aus** consist of

*****besteigen** (ber-*shtigh*-gern) *v* mount, ascend

bestellen (ber-*shteh*-lern) *v* order

Bestellung (ber-*shteh*-loong) *f* (pl ~en) order; **auf ~ gemacht** made to order

Bestellzettel (ber-*shtehl*-tseh-terl) *m* (pl ~) order form

besteuern (ber-*shtoi*-errn) *v* tax

Besteuerung (ber-*shtoi*-er-roong) *f* taxation

bestimmen (ber-*shti*-mern) *v* define, determine; destine

bestimmt (ber-*shtimt*) *adj* certain; definite

Bestimmung (ber-*shti*-moong) *f* (pl ~en) definition

Bestimmungsort (ber-*shti*-moongs-ort) *m* (pl ~e) destination

bestrafen (ber-*shtraa*-fern) *v* punish

bestrebt (ber-*shträypt*) *adj* anxious

*****bestreiten** (ber-*shtrigh*-tern) *v* dispute

bestürzt (ber-*shtewrtst*) *adj* dismayed, shocked

Besuch (ber-*zōōkh*) *m* (pl ~e) visit; call

besuchen (ber-*zōō*-khern) *v* visit; call on

betasten (ber-*tahss*-tern) *v* *feel

Betäubung (ber-*toi*-boong) *f* (pl ~en) anaesthesia

Betäubungsmittel (ber-*toi*-boongs-mi-terl) *nt* (pl ~) anaesthetic

Bete (*bāy*-ter) *f* (pl ~n) beetroot

beteiligen (ber-*tigh*-li-gern) *v*: **sich ~ an** join

beteiligt (ber-*tigh*-likht) *adj* involved, concerned

beten (*bāy*-tern) *v* pray

Beton (bay-*tawng*) *m* concrete

betonen (ber-*tōa*-nern) *v* emphasize, stress

Betonung (ber-*tōa*-noong) *f* accent, stress

betrachten (ber-*trahkh*-tern) *v* consider; regard

beträchtlich (ber-*trehkht*-likh) *adj* considerable; *adv* pretty, quite

Betrag (ber-*traak*) *m* (pl ~e) amount

*****betragen** (ber-*traa*-gern) *v* amount to

*****betreffen** (ber-*treh*-fern) *v* concern; touch

betreffs (ber-*trehfs*) *prep* about, regarding, concerning

*****betreten** (ber-*trāy*-tern) *v* enter

Betrieb (bertreep) *m* enterprise; **in ~** working

Betriebsstörung (ber-*treeps*-shtūr-roong) *f* (pl ~en) breakdown

betrübt (ber-*trēwpt*) *adj* sad

Betrug (ber-*trōōk*) *m* deceit; fraud; swindle

*****betrügen** (ber-*trēw*-gern) *v* cheat; deceive; swindle

Betrüger (ber-*trēw*-gerr) *m* (pl ~), **-in** *f* swindler

betrunken (ber-*troong*-kern) *adj* drunk

Bett (beht) *nt* (pl ~en) bed

Bettdecke (*beht*-deh-ker) *f* (pl ~n) blanket; bedspread

betteln (*beh*-terln) *v* beg

Bettler (*beht*-lerr) *m* (pl ~), **-in** *f* beggar

Bettzeug (*beht*-tsoik) *nt* bedding

beugen (*boi*-gern) *v* bow

Beule (*boi*-ler) *f* (pl ~n) dent; lump

beunruhigen (ber-*oon*-rōō-i-gern) *v*: **sich ~** worry

beunruhigt (ber-*oon*-rōō-ikht) *adj* worried

beurteilen (ber-*oor*-tigh-lern) *v* judge

Beutel (*boi*-terl) *m* (pl ~) pouch

Bevölkerung (ber-*furl*-ker-roong) *f* population

bevor (ber-*foār*) *conj* before

bewachen (ber-*vah*-khern) *v* guard

bewaffnen (ber-*vahf*-nern) *v* arm

bewahren (ber-*vaa*-rern) *v* *keep; preserve

bewaldet (ber-*vahl*-dert) *adj* wooded

bewegen (ber-*vāy*-gern) *v* move, stir

beweglich (ber-*vāyk*-likh) *adj* mobile; movable

Bewegung (ber-*vāy*-goong) *f* (pl ~en) movement, motion

Beweis (ber-*vighss*) *m* (pl ~e) proof, evidence; token

***beweisen** (ber-*vigh*-zern) *v* prove; *show, demonstrate

***bewerben** (ber-*vehr*-bern) *v*: **sich ~** apply

Bewerber (ber-*vehr*-berr) *m* (pl ~), **-in** *f* candidate

Bewerbung (ber-*vehr*-boong) *f* (pl ~en) application

bewilligen (ber-*vi*-li-gern) *v* allow; grant

Bewilligung (ber-*vi*-li-goong) *f* permission

bewirten (ber-*veer*-tern) *v* entertain

bewohnbar (ber-*vōān*-baar) *adj* habitable, inhabitable

bewohnen (ber-*vōā*-nern) *v* inhabit

Bewohner (ber-*vōā*-nerr) *m* (pl ~), **-in** *f* inhabitant

bewölkt (ber-*vurlkt*) *adj* cloudy, overcast

Bewölkung (ber-*vurl*-koong) *f* clouds

bewundern (ber-*voon*-derrn) *v* admire

Bewunderung (ber-*voon*-der-roong) *f* admiration

bewusst (ber-*voost*) *adj* conscious; aware

bewusstlos (ber-*voost*-lōāss) *adj* unconscious

Bewusstsein (ber-*voost*-zighn) *nt* consciousness

bezahlen (ber-*tsaa*-lern) *v* *pay

Bezahlung (ber-*tsaa*-loong) *f* (pl ~en) payment

bezaubernd (ber-*tsou*-berrnt) *adj* enchanting; glamorous

bezeichnen (ber-*tsighkh*-nern) *v* mark; **bezeichnend** *adj* typical, characteristic

bezeugen (ber-*tsoi*-gern) *v* testify

***beziehen** (ber-*tsee*-ern) *v* move into; cover; **sich ~ auf** refer to

Beziehung (ber-*tsee*-oong) *f* (pl ~en) relation, connection; reference

Bezirk (ber-*tseerk*) *m* (pl ~e) district

Bezug: in ~ auf (in ber-*tsook* ouf) as regards

Bezugsschein (ber-*tsōōks*-shighn) *m* (pl ~e) coupon

bezwecken (ber-*tsveh*-kern) *v* aim at

bezweifeln (ber-*tsvigh*-ferln) *v* doubt, query

BH (bay-*haa*) *m colloquial* bra

Bibel (*bee*-berl) *f* (pl ~n) bible

Biber (*bee*-berr) *m* (pl ~) beaver

Bibliothek (bi-bli-oa-*tāyk*) *f* (pl ~en) library

***biegen** (*bee*-gern) *v* *bend

biegsam (*beek*-zaam) *adj* flexible; supple

Biegung (*bee*-goong) *f* (pl ~en) turn, bend; curve

Biene (*bee*-ner) *f* (pl ~n) bee

Bienenkorb (*bee*-nern-korp) *m* (pl ~e) beehive

Bier (beer) *nt* (pl ⁓e) beer; ale

Biergarten (*beer*-gahr-tern) *m* beer garden

*bieten (*bee*-tern) *v* offer

Bilanz (bi-*lahnts*) *f* (pl ⁓en) balance

Bild (bilt) *nt* (pl ⁓er) picture; image

bilden (*bil*-dern) *v* shape

Bildhauer (*bilt*-hou-err) *m* (pl ⁓), **-in** *f* sculptor

Bildschirm (*bilt*-sheerm) *m* (pl ⁓e) screen

Billard (bi-l^yahrt) *nt* billiards *pl*

billig (*bi*-likh) *adj* cheap, inexpensive; reasonable

billigen (*bi*-li-gern) *v* approve of

Billigung (*bi*-li-goong) *f* approval

*binden (*bin*-dern) *v* tie; *bind

Bindestrich (*bin*-der-shtrikh) *m* (pl ⁓e) hyphen

Binse (*bin*-zer) *f* (pl ⁓n) rush

Biologie (bi-oa-loa-*gee*) *f* biology

Birne (*beer*-ner) *f* (pl ⁓n) pear; light bulb

bis (biss) *prep* to, till, until; *conj* till; ⁓ **zu** till

Bischof (*bi*-shof) *m* (pl ⁓e) bishop

bisher (biss-*hāyr*) *adv* so far

Biss (biss) *m* (pl ⁓e) bite

bisschen bit

Bissen (*bi*-sern) *m* (pl ⁓) bite

Bitte (*bi*-ter) *f* (pl ⁓n) request

bitte (*bi*-ter) please; here you are

*bitten (*bi*-tern) *v* ask; request; beg

bitter (*bi*-terr) *adj* bitter

blank (blahngk) *adj* broke

Blase (*blaa*-zer) *f* (pl ⁓n) blister; bladder; bubble

*blasen (*blaa*-zern) *v* *blow

Blasenentzündung (*blaa*-zern-ehnt-tsewn-doong) *f* cystitis

Blaskapelle (*blaass*-kah-peh-ler) *f* (pl ⁓n) brass band

Blatt (blaht) *nt* (pl ⁓er) leaf; sheet; page

Blattgold (*blaht*-golt) *nt* gold leaf

blau (blou) *adj* blue

Blazer (*blāy*-zerr) *m* (pl ⁓) blazer

Blech (blehkh) *nt* sheet metal; baking tray; *colloquial* rubbish

Blei (bligh) *nt* lead

*bleiben (*bligh*-bern) *v* stay; remain; *keep; **bleibend** lasting

bleich (blighkh) *adj* pale

bleichen (*bligh*-khern) *v* bleach

bleifrei (*bligh*-frigh) *adj* unleaded

Bleistift (*bligh*-shtift) *m* (pl ⁓e) pencil

Bleistiftspitzer (*bligh*-shtift-shpi-tserr) *m* (pl ⁓) pencil sharpener

blenden (*blehn*-dern) *v* blind; **blendend** glaring

Blick (blik) *m* (pl ⁓e) look; glimpse; glance

blind (blint) *adj* blind

Blinddarm (*blint*-dahrm) *m* (pl ⁓e) appendix

Blinddarmentzündung (*blint*-dahrm-ehnt-tsewn-doong) *f* appendicitis

Blindenhund (*blin*-dern-hoont) *m* (pl ⁓e) guide dog

Blinker (*bling*-kerr) *m* (pl ⁓) indicator; blinker *Am*

Blitz (blits) *m* (pl ⁓e) lightning; flash

Blitzlicht (*blits*-likht) *nt* (pl ⁓er) flash bulb

blockieren (blo-*kee*-rern) *v* block

blöde (*blūr*-der) *adj* dumb

blond (blont) *adj* fair, blond

Blondine (blon-*dee*-ner) *f* (pl ⁓n) blonde

bloß (blōass) *adj* naked, bare; *adv* only

blühen (*blēw*-ern) *v* blossom

Blume (*blōo*-mer) *f* (pl ⁓n) flower

Blumenbeet (*blōo*-mern-bāyt) *nt* (pl ⁓e) flowerbed

Blumenblatt (*blōo*-mern-blaht) *nt* (pl ⁓er) petal

Blumenhändler (*blōo*-mern-hehn-dlerr) *m* (pl ⁓), **-in** *f* florist

Blumenhandlung (*bloo*-mern-hahn-dloong) *f* (pl ⌐en) flower shop

Blumenkohl (*bloo*-mern-koal) *m* cauliflower

Blumenzwiebel (*bloo*-mern-tsvee-berl) *f* (pl ⌐n) bulb

Bluse (*bloo*-zer) *f* (pl ⌐n) blouse

Blut (bloot) *nt* blood

Blutarmut (*bloot*-ahr-moot) *f* anaemia

Blutdruck (*bloot*-drook) *m* blood pressure

bluten (*bloo*-tern) *v* *bleed

Blutgefäß (*bloot*-ger-faiss) *nt* (pl ⌐e) blood vessel

Blutsturz (*bloot*-shtoorts) *m* (pl ⌐e) h(a)emorrhage

Blutvergiftung (*bloot*-fehr-gif-toong) *f* blood poisoning

Boden[1] (*boa*-dern) *m* soil, earth

Boden[2] (*boa*-dern) *m* (pl ⌐) bottom, ground; attic

Bogen (*boa*-gern) *m* (pl ⌐) arch; bow

bogenförmig (*boa*-gern-furr-mikh) *adj* arched

Bogengang (*boa*-gern-gahng) *m* (pl ⌐e) arcade

Bohne (*boa*-ner) *f* (pl ⌐n) bean

bohren (*boa*-rern) *v* bore, drill

Bohrer (*boa*-rerr) *m* (pl ⌐) drill

Boje (*boa*-^yer) *f* (pl ⌐n) buoy

Bolivianer (boa-li-*v*^y*aa*-nerr) *m* (pl ⌐), **-in** *f* Bolivian

bolivianisch (boa-li-*v*^y*aa*-nish) *adj* Bolivian

Bolivien (boa-*lee*-v^yern) Bolivia

Bolzen (*bol*-tsern) *m* (pl ⌐) bolt

bombardieren (bom-bahr-*dee*-rern) *v* bomb

Bombe (*bom*-ber) *f* (pl ⌐n) bomb

Bonbon (bawng-*bawng*) *m* (pl ⌐s) sweet; candy *Am*

Boot (boat) *nt* (pl ⌐e) boat

Bord: an ⌐ (ahn bort) aboard

Bordell (bor-*dehl*) *nt* (pl ⌐e) brothel

borgen (*bor*-gern) *v* borrow

Börse (*burr*-zer) *f* (pl ⌐n) stock exchange; stock market, exchange; purse

bösartig (*burss*-ahr-tikh) *adj* vicious, malignant

Böse (*bur*-zer) *nt* harm

böse (*bur*-zer) *adj* cross, angry; ill, wicked, evil

boshaft (*boass*-hahft) *adj* malicious

Botanik (boa-*taa*-nik) *f* botany

Bote (*boa*-ter) *m* (pl ⌐n), **Botin** *f* messenger

Botschaft (*boat*-shahft) *f* (pl ⌐en) embassy

Botschafter (*boat*-shahf-terr) *m* (pl ⌐), **-in** *f* ambassador

Boutique (boo-*tik*) *f* (pl ⌐n) boutique

Bowling (*boa*-ling) *nt* bowling

boxen (*bo*-ksern) *v* box

Boxkampf (*boks*-kahmpf) *m* (pl ⌐e) boxing match

brach (braakh) *adj* waste

Brand (brahnt) *m* (pl ⌐e) fire

Brandwunde (*brahnt*-voon-der) *f* (pl ⌐n) burn

Brasilianer (brah-zi-*l*^y*aa*-nerr) *m* (pl ⌐), **-in** *f* Brazilian

brasilianisch (brah-zi-*l*^y*aa*-nish) *adj* Brazilian

Brasilien (brah-*zee*-l^yern) Brazil

*braten (*braa*-tern) *v* fry; roast

Bratensoße (*braa*-tern-zoa-ser) *f* (pl ⌐n) gravy

Bratkartoffeln (*braat*- kahr-*to*-ferln) *fpl* fried potatoes *pl*

Bratpfanne (*braat*-pfah-ner) *f* (pl ⌐n) frying pan

Bratrost (*braat*-rost) *m* (pl ⌐e) grill

Bratspieß (*braat*-shpeess) *m* (pl ⌐e) spit

Brauch (broukh) *m* (pl ⌐e) usage

brauchbar (*broukh*-baar) *adj* useful; usable

brauchen (*brou*-khern) *v* need

brauen (*brou*-ern) *v* brew

Brauerei (brou-er-*righ*) *f* (pl ~en) brewery

braun (broun) *adj* brown; tanned

Brause (*brou*-zer) *f* fizz

Braut (brout) *f* (pl ~e) bride

Bräutigam (*broi*-ti-gahm) *m* (pl ~e) bridegroom

brav (braaf) *adj* good

Brecheisen (*brehkh*-igh-zern) *nt* (pl ~) crowbar

*brechen (*breh*-khern) *v* *break; crack; fracture

breit (bright) *adj* broad, wide

Breite (*brigh*-ter) *f* (pl ~n) breadth, width

Breitengrad (*brigh*-tern-graat) *m* (pl ~e) latitude

Bremse (*brehm*-zer) *f* (pl ~n) brake

Bremslichter (*brehms*-likh-terr) *ntpl* brake lights

Bremstrommel (*brehms*-tro-merl) *f* (pl ~n) brake drum

*brennen (*breh*-nern) *v* *burn

Brennpunkt (*brehn*-poongkt) *m* (pl ~e) focus

Brennstoff (*brehn*-shtof) *m* (pl ~e) fuel

Brett (breht) *nt* (pl ~er) plank, board

Bridge (brij) *nt* bridge

Brief (breef) *m* (pl ~e) letter; **eingeschriebener ~** registered letter

Briefkasten (*breef*-kahss-tern) *m* (pl ~) letterbox; pillarbox; mailbox *Am*

Briefmarke (*breef*-mahr-ker) *f* (pl ~n) postage stamp, stamp

Briefpapier (*breef*-pah-peer) *nt* stationery

Brieftasche (*breef*-tah-sher) *f* (pl ~n) wallet; billfold *Am*

Briefumschlag (*breef*-oom-shlaak) *m* (pl ~e) envelope

brillant (bri-*l'ahnt*) *adj* brilliant

Brille (*bri*-ler) *f* (pl ~n) spectacles, glasses

*bringen (*bring*-ern) *v* *bring; *take

Brise (*bree*-zer) *f* (pl ~n) breeze

Brite (*bri*-ter) *m* (pl ~n), **Britin** *f* Briton

britisch (*bri*-tish) *adj* British

Brocken (*bro*-kern) *m* (pl ~) lump

Brombeere (*brom*-bāy-rer) *f* (pl ~n) blackberry

Bronchitis (bron-*khee*-tiss) *f* bronchitis

Bronze (*brawng*-ser) *f* bronze

bronzen (*brawng*-sern) *adj* bronze

Brosche (*bro*-sher) *f* (pl ~n) brooch

Broschüre (bro-*shēw*-rer) *f* (pl ~n) brochure

Brot (brōat) *nt* (pl ~e) bread

Brötchen (*brūrt*-khern) *nt* (pl ~) roll, bun

Bruch (brookh) *m* (pl ~e) fracture, break; hernia

Bruchstück (*brookh*-shtewk) *nt* (pl ~e) fraction; fragment

Brücke (*brew*-ker) *f* (pl ~n) bridge

Bruder (*brōō*-derr) *m* (pl ~) brother

Brüllen (*brew*-lern) *nt* roar

brüllen (*brew*-lern) *v* roar

brummen (*broo*-mern) *v* growl

Brunnen (*broo*-nern) *m* (pl ~) well

Brunnenkresse (*broo*-nern-kreh-ser) *f* watercress

Brust (broost) *f* (pl ~e) chest; breast, bosom

Brustkasten (*broost*-kahss-tern) *m* chest

Brustschwimmen (*broost*-shvi-mern) *nt* breaststroke

Brüstung (*brewss*-toong) *f* (pl ~en) rail

brutal (broo-*taal*) *adj* brutal

brutto (*broo*-toa) *adj* gross

Bub (bōōp) *m* (pl ~en) boy

Bube (*bōō*-ber) *m* (pl ~n) knave

Buch (bo͞okh) *nt* (pl ⸚er) book
Buche (bo͞o-kher) *f* (pl ⸜n) beech
buchen (bo͞o-khern) *v* book
Bücherei (bew-kher-*righ*) *f* library
Bücherstand (bew-kherr-shtahnt) *m* (pl ⸚e) bookstand
Buchhändler (bo͞okh-hehn-dlerr) *m* (pl ⸜), **-in** *f* bookseller
Buchhandlung (bo͞okh-hahn-dloong) *f* (pl ⸜en) bookstore
Buchladen (bo͞okh-laa-dern) *m* (pl ⸚) bookstore
Büchse (bew-kser) *f* (pl ⸜n) tin, can
Büchsenöffner (bew-ksern-urf-nerr) *m* (pl ⸜) can opener
Buchstabe (bo͞okh-shtaa-ber) *m* (pl ⸜n) letter
buchstabieren (bo͞okh-shtah-*bee*-rern) *v* *spell
Bucht (bookht) *f* (pl ⸜en) creek, bay, inlet
Buchung (bo͞okh-oong) *f* booking; reservation
bücken (bew-kern) *v*: **sich ~** *bend down
Bude (bo͞o-der) *f* (pl ⸜n) booth
Budget (bew-*jay*) *nt* (pl ⸜s) budget
Büfett (bew-*feht*) *nt* (pl ⸜e) buffet
Bügeleisen (bēw-gerl-igh-zern) *nt* (pl ⸜) iron
bügelfrei (bēw-gerl-frigh) *adj* drip-dry, wash and wear
bügeln (bēw-gerln) *v* iron; press
Bühne (bēw-ner) *f* (pl ⸜n) stage
Bulgare (bool-*gaa*-rer) *m* (pl ⸜n), **Bulgarin** *f* Bulgarian
Bulgarien (bool-*gaa*-rʸern) Bulgaria
bulgarisch (bool-*gaa*-rish) *adj* Bulgarian
Bummel (boo-merl) *m* stroll
bummeln (boo-merln) *v* stroll
Bund¹ (boont) *m* (pl ⸚e) waistband

Bund² (boont) *m* (pl ⸚e) alliance, union; **Bundes-** federal
Bündel (bewn-derl) *nt* (pl ⸜) bundle
bündeln (bewn-derln) *v* bundle
bündig (bewn-dikh) *adj* brief
Bündnis (bewnt-niss) *nt* (pl ⸜se) alliance
bunt (boont) *adj* colo(u)rful; gay; **buntes Glas** stained glass
Burg (boork) *f* (pl ⸜en) castle, stronghold
Bürger (bewr-gerr) *m* (pl ⸜), **-in** *f* citizen; **Bürger-** civilian, civic
bürgerlich (bewr-gerr-likh) *adj* middle-class
Bürgermeister (bewr-gerr-mighss-terr) *m* (pl ⸜), **-in** *f* mayor
Bürgersteig (bewr-gerr-shtighk) *m* (pl ⸚e) pavement; sidewalk *Am*
Bürgschaft (bewr-gerr-shahft) *f* (pl ⸜en) guarantee
Büro (bew-*rōa*) *nt* (pl ⸜s) office
Büroangestellte (bew-*rōa*-ahn-ger-shtehl-ter) *m/f* (pl ⸜n) clerk
Bürokratie (bew-roa-krah-*tee*) *f* bureaucracy
Bürostunden (bew-*rōa*-shtoon-dern) *fpl* office hours
Bürste (bewrs-ter) *f* (pl ⸜n) brush
bürsten (bewrs-tern) *v* brush
Bus (booss) *m* (pl ⸜se) bus
Busch (boosh) *m* (pl ⸚e) bush
Busen (bo͞o-zern) *m* (pl ⸜) bosom
Bushaltestelle (booss-hahl-ter-shteh-ler) *f* bus stop
Buße (bo͞o-ser) *f* (pl ⸜n) penalty
Büste (bewss-ter) *f* (pl ⸜n) bust
Büstenhalter (bewss-tern-hahl-terr) *m* (pl ⸜) brassiere, bra
Butter (boo-terr) *f* butter
Butterbrot (boo-terr-brōat) *nt* (pl ⸜e) sandwich

C

Café (kah-*fay*) *nt* (pl ~s) café

Camper (*kehm*-perr) *m* (pl ~) camper

Camping (*kehm*-ping) *nt* (pl ~s) camping

Campingplatz (*kehm*-ping-plahts) *m* (pl ~e) camping site

CD-Spieler (*tsay*-day shpee-lerr) *m* (pl ~) CD-player

Celsius (*tsehl*-zi-ooss) centigrade

Cembalo (*chehm*-bah-loa) *nt* (pl ~s) harpsichord

Chalet (shah-*lay*) *nt* (pl ~s) chalet

Champignon (*shahm*-pi-n^yawng) *m* (pl ~s) mushroom

Chance (*shahng*-ser) *f* (pl ~n) chance

Chaos (*kaa*-oss) *nt* chaos

Charakter (kah-*rahk*-terr) *m* (pl ~e) character

charakterisieren (kah-rahk-ter-ri-*zee*-rern) *v* characterize

charakteristisch (kah-rahk-ter-*riss*-tish) *adj* characteristic

Charakterzug (kah-*rahk*-terr-tsook) *m* (pl ~e) characteristic

charmant (shahr-*mahnt*) *adj* charming

Charterflug (*chahr*-terr-flook) *m* (pl ~e) charter flight

Chauffeur (sho-*fürr*) *m* (pl ~e) chauffeur

Chef (shehf) *m* (pl ~s), **-in** *f* boss; manager

Chemie (khay-*mee*) *f* chemistry

chemisch (*khay*-mish) *adj* chemical

China (*khee*-nah) China

Chinese (khi-*nay*-zer) *m* (pl ~n), **Chinesin** *f* Chinese

chinesisch (khi-*nay*-zish) *adj* Chinese

Chirurg (khi-*roork*) *m* (pl ~en), **-in** *f* surgeon

Chlor (kloar) *nt* chlorine

Choke (choak) *m* choke

Chor (koar) *m* (pl ~e) choir

Christ (krist) *m* (pl ~en) Christian

christlich (*krist*-likh) *adj* Christian

Christus (*kriss*-tooss) Christ

Chrom (kroam) *nt* chromium

chronisch (*kroa*-nish) *adj* chronic

chronologisch (kroa-noa-*loa*-gish) *adj* chronological

Clown (kloun) *m* (pl ~s) clown

Cocktail (*kok*-tayl) *m* (pl ~s) cocktail

Compact Disc (*kom*-pakt disk) *f* (pl ~s) compact disc

Computer (kom-*p^yoo*-terr) *m* computer

Container (kon-*tay*-nerr) *m* (pl ~) container

Creme (kraym) *f* cream

Curry (*kur*-ri) *m* curry

D

da (daa) *conj* as, since, because

Dach (dahkh) *nt* (pl ∺er) roof

Dachziegel (dahkh-tsee-gerl) *m* (pl ∺) tile

dafür (daa-*fewr*) *pron, adv, conj* for it, for them; instead; in return

dagegen (daa-*gay*-gern) *pron, adv, conj* against it, against that; by comparison; on the other hand, whereas

damalig (daa-maa-likh) *adj* contemporary

damals (daa-maals) *adv* then

Dame (daa-mer) *f* (pl ∺n) lady

Damenbinde (daa-mern-bin-der) *f* (pl ∺n) sanitary towel

Damentoilette (daa-mern-twah-leh-ter) *f* (pl ∺n) powder room, ladies' room

Damenunterwäsche (daa-mern-oon-terr-veh-sher) *f* lingerie

Damespiel (daa-mer-shpeel) *nt* draughts; checkers *plAm*

damit (dah-*mit*) *conj* so that

Damm (dahm) *m* (pl ∺e) dam; dike; embankment

Dampf (dahmpf) *m* (pl ∺e) steam

Dampfer (dahm-pferr) *m* (pl ∺) steamer

Däne (dai-ner) *m* (pl ∺n)

Dänemark (dai-ner-mahrk) Denmark

Dänin (dai-nin) *f* (pl ∺nen) Dane

dänisch (dai-nish) *adj* Danish

dankbar (dahngk-baar) *adj* thankful, grateful

Dankbarkeit (dahngk-baar-kight) *f* gratitude

danke (dahng-ker) thank you, *colloquial* thanks; ∼ **schön** thank you

danken (dahng-kern) *v* thank

dann (dahn) *adv* then

darauf (dah-*rouf*) *adv* then

darlegen (*daar*-lay-gern) *v* state

Darm (dahrm) *m* (pl ∺e) gut, intestine

darstellen (*daar*-shteh-lern) *v* interpret

Darstellung (*daar*-shteh-loong) *f* (pl ∼en) presentation, diagram; version

darum (daa-room) *conj* therefore

das (dahss) *pron* that

Dasein (*daa*-zighn) *nt* existence

dass (dahss) *conj* that

Daten (*daa*-tern) *pl* data, facts

Dattel (*dah*-terl) *f* (pl ∼n) date

Datum (*daa*-toom) *nt* (pl Daten) date

Dauer (*dou*-err) *f* duration

dauerhaft (*dou*-err-hahft) *adj* lasting, permanent

Dauerkarte (*dou*-err-kahr-ter) *f* (pl ∼n) season ticket

dauern (*dou*-errn) *v* last; **dauernd** permanent

Dauerwelle (*dou*-err-veh-ler) *f* perm(anent wave)

Daumen (*dou*-mern) *m* (pl ∼) thumb

Daune (*dou*-ner) *f* (pl ∼n) down

Daunendecke (*dou*-nern-deh-ker) *f* (pl ∼n) eiderdown

Debatte (day-*bah*-ter) *f* (pl ∼n) debate

Deck (dehk) *nt* (pl ∼s) deck

Decke (*deh*-ker) *f* (pl ∼n) blanket; ceiling

Deckel (*deh*-kerl) *m* (pl ∼) lid; top, cover

decken (*deh*-kern) *v* roof; *lay; cover; protect, cover up for; mark

Defekt (day-*fehkt*) *m* (pl ∼e) fault

definieren (day-fi-*nee*-rern) *v* define

Definition (day-fi-ni-ts$^y\overline{oo}$an) *f* (pl ∼en) definition

Defizit (*day*-fi-tsit) *nt* (pl ∼e) deficit

dehnbar (*dayn*-baar) *adj* elastic

dehnen (*day*-nern) *v* stretch

Deich (dighkh) *m* (pl ∼e) dike; dam

dein (dighn) *pron* your

Dekoration (day-koa-rah-*ts^{y}ōan*) *f* (pl ~en) decoration

Delegation (day-lay-gah-*ts^{y}ōan*) *f* (pl ~en) delegation

demnächst *f* soon, shortly, in the near future

Demokratie (day-moa-krah-*tee*) *f* (pl ~n) democracy

demokratisch (day-moa-*kraa*-tish) *adj* democratic

Demonstration (day-mon-strah-*ts^{y}ōan*) *f* (pl ~en) demonstration

demonstrieren (day-mon-*stree*-rern) *v* demonstrate

*denken (*dehng*-kern) *v* *think; guess, reckon; ~ **an** *think of; **sich ~** imagine

Denker (*dehng*-kerr) *m* (pl ~), **-in** *f* thinker

Denkmal (*dehngk*-maal) *nt* (pl ≈er) monument; memorial

denkwürdig (*dehnk*-vewr-dikh) *adj* memorable

denn (dehn) *conj* for

dennoch (*deh*-nokh) *adv* still, however; *conj* yet

Deo(dorant) (day-oa-doa-*rahnt*) *nt* deodorant

deponieren (day-poa-*nee*-rern) *v* deposit, *leave

Depot (day-*pōa*) *nt* (pl ~s) warehouse

deprimieren (day-pri-*mee*-rern) *v* depress

der (dāyr) *art* (f die, nt das) the *art*; *pron* that; which

derartig (*dāyr*-ahr-tikh) *adj* similar

dermaßen (*dāyr*-maa-sern) *adv* so

desertieren (day-zehr-*tee*-rern) *v* desert

deshalb (*dehss*-hahlp) *adv* therefore

Desinfektionsmittel (dehss-in-fehk-*ts^{y}ōans*-mi-terl) *nt* (pl ~) disinfectant

desinfizieren (dehss-in-fi-*tsee*-rern) *v* disinfect

deswegen (*dehss*-vāy-gern) *adv* therefore

Detektiv (day-tehk-*teef*) *m* (pl ~e), **-in** *f* detective

deutlich (*doit*-likh) *adj* clear; distinct, plain

deutsch (doich) *adj* German

Deutsche (*doi*-cher) *m/f* (pl ~n) German

Deutschland (*doich*-lahnt) Germany

Devise (day-*vee*-zer) *f* (pl ~n) motto

Dezember (day-*tsehm*-berr) December

Dezimalsystem (day-tsi-*maal*-zewss-tāym) *nt* decimal system

Dia (*dee*-ah) *nt* (pl ~s) slide

Diabetes (di-ah-*bāy*-tehss) *m* diabetes

Diabetiker (di-ah-*bāy*-ti-kerr) *m* (pl ~), **-in** *f* diabetic

Diagnose (di-ah-*gnōa*-zer) *f* (pl ~n) diagnosis

diagnostizieren (di-ah-gnoss-ti-*tsee*-rern) *v* diagnose

diagonal (di-ah-goa-*naal*) *adj* diagonal

Diagonale (di-ah-goa-*naa*-ler) *f* (pl ~n) diagonal

Diagramm (di-ah-*grahm*) *nt* (pl ~e) chart

Diamant (di-ah-*mahnt*) *m* (pl ~en) diamond

Diät (di-*ait*) *f* diet

dich (dikh) *pron* you, yourself

dicht (dikht) *adj* thick; dense; ~ **bevölkert** populous

Dichter (*dikh*-terr) *m* (pl ~), **-in** *f* poet

Dichtung (*dikh*-toong) *f* poetry

dick (dik) *adj* thick, fat; corpulent, stout, big; bulky

Dicke (*di*-ker) *f* thickness

die (dee) *art*; *pron* the; this; that; who, which

Dieb (deep) *m* (pl ~e) thief

Diebstahl (*deep*-shtaal) *m* (pl ⁓e) robbery, theft

dienen (*dee*-nern) *v* serve

Diener (*dee*-nerr) *m* (pl ⁓), **-in** *f* servant; domestic, valet; boy, maid

Dienst (deenst) *m* (pl ⁓e) service

Dienstag (*deens*-taak) *m* Tuesday

Dienststelle (*deenst*-steh-ler) *f* (pl ⁓n) agency

dies (deess) *pron* this

diese (*dee*-zer) *pron* these

Diesel (*dee*-zerl) *m* diesel

dieser (*dee*-zer) *pron* this

diesig (*dee*-zikh) *adj* hazy

Digitaluhr (di-gi-*taal*-ōōr) *f* (pl ⁓en) digital clock, digital watch

Diktat (dik-*taat*) *nt* (pl ⁓e) dictation

Diktator (dik-*taa*-tor) *m* (pl ⁓en) dictator

diktieren (dik-*tee*-rern) *v* dictate

Ding (ding) *nt* (pl ⁓e) thing

Diphtherie (dif-tay-*ree*) *f* diphtheria

Diplom (di-*plōam*) *nt* (pl ⁓e) certificate; diploma; **ein ⁓ erlangen** graduate

Diplomat (di-ploa-*maat*) *m* (pl ⁓en), **-in** *f* diplomat

dir (deer) *pron* you, yourself

direkt (di-*rehkt*) *adj* direct

Direktor (di-*rehk*-tor) *m* (pl ⁓en), **-in** *f* manager, director; headmaster, headmistress; principal

Dirigent (di-ri-*gehnt*) *m* (pl ⁓en), **-in** *f* conductor

dirigieren (di-ri-*gee*-rern) *v* conduct

Diskussion (diss-koo-s^y*ōan*) *f* (pl ⁓en) discussion

diskutieren (diss-koo-*tee*-rern) *v* discuss; argue

Distel (*diss*-terl) *f* (pl ⁓n) thistle

Disziplin (diss-tsi-*pleen*) *f* discipline

doch (dokh) *conj* yet

Dock (dok) *nt* (pl ⁓s) dock

Doktor (*dok*-tor) *m* (pl ⁓en), **-in** *f* doctor

dolmetschen (*dol*-meh-chern) *v* interpret

Dolmetscher (*dol*-meh-cherr) *m* (pl ⁓), **-in** *f* interpreter

Dom (dōam) *m* (pl ⁓e) cathedral

Donner (*do*-nerr) *m* thunder

donnern (*do*-nerrn) *v* thunder

Donnerstag (*do*-nerrs-taak) *m* Thursday

Doppelbett (*do*-perl-beht) *nt* (pl ⁓en) twin beds

doppelt (*do*-perlt) *adj* double

Doppelzimmer (*do*-perl- tsi-merr) *nt* double room

Dorf (dorf) *nt* (pl ⁓er) village

Dorn (dorn) *m* (pl ⁓en) thorn

dort (dort) *adv* there

dorthin (*dort*-hin) *adv* there

Dose (*dōa*-zer) *f* (pl ⁓n) box; tin, can

Dosenöffner (*dōa*-zern-urf-nerr) *m* (pl ⁓) tin opener, *Am* can opener

Dosis (*dōa*-ziss) *f* (pl Dosen) dose

Dotter (*do*-terr) *nt* (pl ⁓) yolk

Drache (*drah*-kher) *m* (pl ⁓n) dragon

Draht (draat) *m* (pl ⁓e) wire

Drama (*draa*-mah) *nt* (pl Dramen) drama

dramatisch (drah-*maa*-tish) *adj* dramatic

drängen (*drehng*-ern) *v* push; urge

draußen (*drou*-sern) *adv* outside, outdoors; **nach ⁓** outwards

Dreck (drehk) *m* muck

dreckig (*dreh*-kikh) *adj* dirty, filthy

drehen (*drāy*-ern) *v* twist

Drehtür (*drāy*-tēwr) *f* (pl ⁓en) revolving door

Drehung (*drāy*-oong) *f* (pl ⁓en) turn, twist

drei (drigh) *num* three

Dreieck (*drigh*-ehk) *nt* (pl ⁓e) triangle

dreieckig (*drigh*-eh-kikh) *adj* triangular

dreißig (*drigh*-sikh) *num* thirty

dreißigste (*drigh*-sikhs-ter) *num* thirtieth

drei viertel (drigh-*feer*-terl) *adj* three-quarter

dreizehn (*drigh*-tsayn) *num* thirteen

dreizehnte (*drigh*-tsayn-ter) *num* thirteenth

dressieren (dreh-*see*-rern) *v* train

dringend (*dring*-ernt) *adj* pressing, urgent

Dringlichkeit (*dring*-likh-kight) *f* urgency

Drink (dringk) *m* (pl ~s) drink

drinnen (*dri*-nern) *adv* inside

dritte (*dri*-ter) *num* third

Droge (*droa*-ger) *f* (pl ~n) drug

Drogerie (droa-ger-*ree*) *f* (pl ~n) pharmacy, chemist's; drugstore *Am*

drohen (*droa*-ern) *v* threaten

Drohung (*droa*-oong) *f* (pl ~en) threat

Drossel (*dro*-serl) *f* (pl ~n) thrush

drüben (*drew*-bern) *adv* across; over there

Druck (drook) *m* pressure

drucken (*droo*-kern) *v* print

drücken (*drew*-kern) *v* press

Drucker (*droo*-kerr) *m* printer

Druckknopf (*drook*-knopf) *m* (pl ~e) push button

Drucksache (*drook*-zah-kher) *f* (pl ~n) printed matter

Drüse (*drew*-zer) *f* (pl ~n) gland

Dschungel (*joong*-erl) *m* jungle

du (doo) *pron* you

Duft *m* (dooft) (pleasant) smell, scent, fragrance

dulden (*dool*-dern) *v* *bear

dumm (doom) *adj* dumb, stupid

Düne (*dew*-ner) *f* (pl ~n) dune

Dünger (*dewng*-err) *m* dung, manure

dunkel (*doong*-kerl) *adj* dark, dim; obscure

Dunkelheit (*doong*-kerl-hight) *f* dark

dünn (dewn) *adj* thin; sheer; weak

Dunst (doonst) *m* (pl ~e) haze; vapo(u)r

durch (doorkh) *prep* through; by

durchaus (doorkh-*ouss*) *adv* quite

durchbohren (doorkh-*boa*-rern) *v* pierce

*****durchdringen** (doorkh-*dring*-ern) *v* penetrate

Durcheinander (doorkh-igh-*nahn*-derr) *m* (nt) muddle, mess

*****durcheinander bringen** (doorkh-igh-*nahn*-derr-bring-ern) *v* muddle

Durchfahrt (*doorkh*-faart) *f* passage

Durchfall (*doorkh*-fahl) *m* diarrh(o)ea

*****durchfallen** (*doorkh*-fah-lern) *v* fail

durchführbar (doorkh-*fewr*-baar) *adj* feasible

durchführen (*doorkh*-few-rern) *v* carry out

Durchgang (*doorkh*-gahng) *m* (pl ~e) passage

Durchgangsstraße (*doorkh*-gahngs-shtraa-ser) *f* (pl ~n) thoroughfare

durchmachen (*doorkh*-mah-khern) *v* *go through

durchnässen (doorkh-*neh*-sern) *v* soak

durchqueren (doorkh-*kvay*-rern) *v* pass through

Durchsage (*doorkh*-zaa-ger) *f* announcement, newsflash

durchscheinend (doorkh-*shigh*-nernt) *adj* sheer

Durchschlag (*doorkh*-shlaak) *m* (pl ~e) carbon copy; strainer

Durchschnitt (*doorkh*-shnit) *m* average

durchschnittlich (*doorkh*-shnit-likh) *adj* medium, average; *adv* on the average

durchsichtig (*doorkh*-zikh-tikh) *adj* transparent

durchsuchen (doorkh-*zoo*-khern) *v*

search

*dürfen (*dewr*-fern) *v* *be allowed to; *may

dürr (dewr) *adj* dry; skinny

Dürre (*dew*-rer) *f* drought

Durst (doorst) *m* thirst

durstig (*doors*-tikh) *adj* thirsty

Dusche (*doo*-sher) *f* (pl ∼n) shower

Düsenflugzeug (*dew*-zern-flóok-tsoik) *nt* (pl ∼e) jet

düster (*déwss*-terr) *adj* sombre, somber *Am*; gloomy

Düsterkeit (*déwss*-terr-kight) *f* gloom

Dutzend (*doo*-tsernt) *nt* (pl ∼e) dozen

Dynamo (dew-*naa*-moa) *m* (pl ∼s) dynamo

E

Ebbe (*eh*-ber) *f* low tide

eben (*āy*-bern) *adj* level, flat; smooth, even

Ebene (*āy*-ber-ner) *f* (pl ∼n) plain

ebenfalls (*āy*-bern-fahls) *adv* as well, likewise, also

Ebenholz (*āy*-bern-holts) *nt* ebony

ebenso (*āy*-bern-zōa) *adv* just as, equally; likewise; ∼ **sehr** as much; ∼ **viel** just as much, just as many; ∼ **wie** as well as

Echo (*eh*-khoa) *nt* (pl ∼s) echo

echt (ehkht) *adj* true; genuine, authentic

Ecke (*eh*-ker) *f* (pl ∼n) corner

edel (*āy*-derl) *adj* noble

Edelstein (*āy*-derl-shtighn) *m* (pl ∼e) gem, stone

Efeu (*āy*-foi) *m* ivy

egal (ay-*gaal*) *adj*: ∼ ***sein** not matter

egoistisch (ay-goa-*iss*-tish) *adj* egoi(t)stic

Ehe (*āy*-er) *f* (pl ∼n) marriage; matrimony

ehe (*āy*-er) *conj* before

ehemalig (*āy*-er-maa-likh) *adj* former

Ehepaar (*āy*-er-paar) *nt* (pl ∼e) married couple

eher (*āy*-err) *adv* before; rather

Ehering (*āy*-er-ring) *m* (pl ∼e) wedding ring

ehrbar (*āyr*-baar) *adj* respectable

Ehre (*āy*-rer) *f* (pl ∼n) hono(u)r; glory

ehren (*āy*-rern) *v* hono(u)r

ehrenwert (*āy*-rern-vāyrt) *adj* hono(u)rable

ehrerbietig (*āyr*-ehr-bee-tikh) *adj* respectful

Ehrerbietung (*āyr*-ehr-bee-toong) *f* respect

Ehrfurcht (*āyr*-foorkht) *f* respect

Ehrgefühl (*āyr*-ger-fēwl) *nt* sense of hono(u)r

ehrgeizig (*āyr*-gigh-tsikh) *adj* ambitious

ehrlich (*āyr*-likh) *adj* honest; straight

Ehrlichkeit (*āyr*-likh-kight) *f* honesty

ehrwürdig (*āyr*-vewr-dikh) *adj* venerable

Ei (igh) *nt* (pl ∼er) egg

Eiche (*igh*-kher) *f* (pl ∼n) oak

Eichel (*igh*-kherl) *f* (pl ∼n) acorn

Eichhörnchen (*ighkh*-hurrn-khern) *nt* (pl ∼) squirrel

Eid (ight) *m* (pl ∼e) vow, oath

Eidechse (*igh*-dehk-ser) *f* lizzard

Eidotter (*igh*-do-terr) *nt* (pl ∼) egg yolk

Eierbecher (*igh*-err-beh-kherr) *m* (pl ∼) eggcup

Eierkuchen (*igh*-err-koo-khern) *m* (pl ∼) omelette

Eifer (*igh*-ferr) *m* zeal; diligence

Eifersucht (*igh*-ferr-zookht) *f* jealousy

eifersüchtig (*igh*-ferr-zewkh-tikh) *adj* envious, jealous

eifrig (*igh*-frikh) *adj* zealous, diligent

Eigelb (*igh*- gehlp) *nt* yolk, yellow

eigen (*igh*-gern) *adj* own

Eigenschaft (*igh*-gern-shahft) *f* (pl ∼en) property, quality

Eigenschaftswort (*igh*-gern-shahfts-vort) *nt* (pl ∼er) adjective

eigentlich (*igh*-gernt-likh) *adv* really

Eigentum (*igh*-gern-toom) *nt* property

Eigentümer (*igh*-gern-tew-merr) *m* (pl ∼) proprietor, owner

eigentümlich (*igh*-gern-tewm-likh) *adj* peculiar

Eigentümlichkeit (*igh*-gern-tewm-likh-kight) *f* (pl ∼en) peculiarity

eignen (*igh*-gnern) *v*: **sich** ∼ qualify

Eile (*igh*-ler) *f* haste, hurry; speed; **Eil-** express

eilen (*igh*-lern) *v* hurry; hasten, rush

eilig (*igh*-likh) *adv* in a hurry

Eilzustellung (*ighl*-tsoo-shteh-loong) *f* special delivery

Eimer (*igh*-merr) *m* (pl ∼) bucket, pail

ein (ighn) *art* (f eine, nt ein) a *art*; ∼ **anderer** another

einander (igh-*nahn*-derr) *pron* each other

einatmen (*ighn*-aat-mern) *v* inhale

Einbahnstraße (*ighn*-baan shtraa-ser) *f* one-way street**Einband** (*ighn*-bahnt) *m* (pl ∼e) binding

einbilden (*ighn*-bil-dern) *v*: **sich** ∼ fancy, imagine

Einbildung (*ighn*-bil-doong) *f* fantasy, imagination

*einbrechen (*ighn*-breh-khern) *v* burgle

Einbrecher (*ighn*-breh-kherr) *m* (pl

∼), **-in** *f* burglar

einbüßen (*ighn*-bew-sern) *v* *lose

*eindringen (*ighn*-dring-ern) *v* invade; trespass

Eindringling (*ighn*-dring-ling) *m* (pl ∼e) trespasser

Eindruck (*ighn*-drook) *m* (pl ∼e) impression; sensation

eindrucksvoll (*ighn*-drooks-fol) *adj* impressive

einfach (*ighn*-fahkh) *adj* simple

Einfahrt (*ighn*-faart) *f* (pl ∼en) entry

Einfall (*ighn*-fahl) *m* (pl ∼e) idea; invasion, raid

Einfluss (*ighn*-flooss) *m* (pl ∼e) influence

einflussreich (*ighn*-flooss-righkh) *adj* influential

einfügen (*ighn*-few-gern) *v* insert

Einfuhr (*ighn*-foor) *f* import

einführen (*ighn*-few-rern) *v* import; introduce

Einführung (*ighn*-few-roong) *f* (pl ∼en) introduction

Einfuhrzoll (*ighn*-foor-tsol) *m* duty, import duty

Eingang (*ighn*-gahng) *m* (pl ∼e) entry; entrance, way in; **kein** ∼ no admittance

eingebildet (*ighn*-ger-bil-dert) *adj* conceited

Eingeborene (*ighn*-ger-boa-rer-ner) *m/f* (pl ∼n) native

eingehend (*ighn*-gay-ernt) *adj* detailed

eingeschlossen (*ighn*-ger-shlo-sern) included; locked in

Eingeweide (*ighn*-ger-vigh-der) *pl* bowels *pl*, intestines, insides

Eingreifen (*ighn*-grigh-fern) *nt* interference

einheimisch (*ighn*-high-mish) *adj* native

Einheit (*ighn*-hight) *f* (pl ∼en) unit;

unity

einholen (*ighn*-hōā-lern) *v* *catch up; *get

einige (*igh*-ni-ger) *pron* some

einkassieren (*ighn*-kah-see-rern) *v* cash

Einkauf (*ighn*-kouf) *m* purchase

einkaufen (*ighn*-kou-fern) *v* shop

Einkaufstasche (*ighn*-koufs-tah-sher) *f* (pl ∿n) shopping bag

Einkaufszentrum (*ighn*-koufs-tsehn-troom) *nt* (pl -zentren) shopping centre, mall

einkerben (*ighn*-kehr-bern) *v* carve

Einkommen (*ighn*-ko-mern) *nt* (pl ∿) revenue, income

Einkommenssteuer (*ighn*-ko-merns-shtoi-err) *f* income tax

einkreisen (*ighn*-krigh-zern) *v* encircle

Einkünfte (*ighn*-kewnf-ter) *fpl* revenue

*einladen (*ighn*-laa-dern) *v* invite; ask

Einladung (*ighn*-laa-doong) *f* (pl ∿en) invitation

*einlassen (*ighn*-lah-sern) *v* admit

einleitend (*ighn*-ligh-ternt) *adj* preliminary

einmachen (*ighn*-mah-khern) *v* preserve

einmal (*ighn*-maal) *adv* once; some time

einmischen (*ighn*-mi-shern) *v*: **sich ∿** intervene; interfere with

Einnahme (*ighn*-naa-mer) *f* capture; **Einnahmen** earnings *pl*

*einnehmen (*ighn*-nāy-mern) *v* cash; occupy, *take up; capture

einpacken (*ighn*-pah-kern) *v* pack up

einräumen (*ighn*-roi-mern) *v* admit; *put in

einrichten (*ighn*-rikh-tern) *v* furnish; institute

Einrichtung (*ighn*-rikh-toong) *f* (pl

∿en) furniture; installation; institution; facility

eins (ighns) *num* one

einsam (*ighn*-zaam) *adj* lonely

einsammeln (*ighn*-zah-merln) *v* collect

Einsatz (*ighn*-zahts) *m* (pl ∿e) bet

einschalten (*ighn*-shahl-tern) *v* turn on, switch on

einschenken (*ighn*-shehng-kern) *v* pour

einschiffen (*ighn*-shi-fern) *v*: **sich ∿** embark

Einschiffung (*ighn*-shi-foong) *f* embarkation

*einschließen (*ighn*-shlee-sern) *v* include, comprise; involve; encircle, *shut in, circle

einschließlich (*ighn*-shleess-likh) *adv* inclusive

Einschnitt (*ighn*-shnit) *m* (pl ∿e) cut

Einschränkung (*ighn*-shrehng-koong) *f* (pl ∿en) restriction, qualification

*einschreiben (*ighn*-shrigh-bern) *v* book; enter, register

Einschreibung (*ighn*-shrigh-boong) *f* (pl ∿en) booking

*einschreiten (*ighn*-shrigh-tern) *v* interfere

*einsehen (*ighn*-zāy-ern) *v* *see

einseitig (*ighn*-zigh-tikh) *adj* one-sided

Einsicht (*ighn*-zikht) *f* vision; insight

einsperren (*ighn*-shpeh-rern) *v* lock up

einspritzen (*ighn*-shpri-tsern) *v* inject

einst (ighnst) *adv* once

*einsteigen (*ighn*-shtigh-gern) *v* *get on; embark

einstellen (*ighn*-shteh-lern) *v* stop, discontinue; tune in; garage; employ

Einstellung (*ighn*-shteh-loong) *f* (pl ∿en) attitude

einstimmig (*ighn*-shti-mikh) *adj* unanimous

einstöpseln (*ighn*-shtur-pserln) *v* plug in

einstufen (*ighn*-shtoo-fern) *v* grade

einteilen (*ighn*-tigh-lern) *v* classify

*****eintragen** (*ighn*-traa-gern) *v* list, book

einträglich (*ighn*-traik-likh) *adj* profitable

Eintragung (*ighn*-traa-goong) *f* (pl ~en) entry; registration

Eintreffen (*ighn*-treh-fern) *nt* arrival

*****eintreffen** (*ighn*-treh-fern) *v* arrive

*****eintreten** (*ighn*-trāy-tern) *v* enter

Eintritt (*ighn*-trit) *m* entrance; entry; admission; ~ **verboten** no entry

Eintrittsgeld (*ighn*-trits-gehlt) *nt* entrance fee

einverleiben (*ighn*-fehr-ligh-bern) *v* annex

einverstanden! (*ighn*-fehr-shtahn-dern) all right!

Einverständnis (*ighn*-fehr-shtehnt-niss) *nt* approval

Einwand (*ighn*-vahnt) *m* (pl ~e) objection; ~ *****erheben gegen** object to

Einwanderer (*ighn*-vahn-der-rerr) *m* (pl ~), **Einwanderin** *f* immigrant

einwandern (*ighn*-vahn-derrn) *v* immigrate

Einwanderung (*ighn*-vahn-der-roong) *f* immigration

einwandfrei (*ighn*-vahnt-frigh) *adj* faultless

einweichen (*ighn*-vigh-khern) *v* soak

*****einwenden** (*ighn*-vehn-dern) *v* object; **etwas einzuwenden *****haben gegen** mind

einwickeln (*ighn*-vi-kerln) *v* wrap

einwilligen (*ighn*-vi-li-gern) *v* consent

Einwilligung (*ighn*-vi-li-goong) *f* consent

Einwohner (*ighn*-voā-nerr) *m* (pl ~), **-in** *f* inhabitant

Einzahl (*ighn*-tsaal) *f* singular

Einzelhandel (*ighn*-tserl-hahn-derl) *m* retail trade

Einzelhändler (*ighn*-tserl-hehn-dlerr) *m* (pl ~), **-in** *f* retailer

Einzelheit (*ighn*-tserl-hight) *f* (pl ~en) detail

einzeln (*ighn*-tserln) *adj* individual; **im Einzelnen** specially

Einzelne (*ighn*-tserl-ner) *m/f* (pl ~n) individual

Einzelzimmer (*ighn*-tserl-tsi-merr) *nt* single room; private room

*****einziehen** (*ighn*-tsee-ern) *v* move in; confiscate

einzig (*ighn*-tsikh) *adj* only; sole, single

einzigartig (*ighn*-tsikh-ahr-tikh) *adj* unique

Eis (ighss) *nt* ice; ice cream; ~ **laufen** *v* skate

Eisbahn (*ighss*-baan) *f* (pl ~en) skating rink

Eisbeutel (*ighss*-boi-terl) *m* (pl ~) ice bag

Eisen (*igh*-zern) *nt* iron

Eisenbahn (*igh*-zern-baan) *f* (pl ~en) railway; railroad *Am*

Eisenbahnfähre (*igh*-zern-baan-fai-rer) *f* (pl ~n) train ferry

Eisenwaren (*igh*-zern-vaa-rern) *fpl* hardware

Eisenwarenhandlung (*igh*-zern-vaa-rern-hahn-dloong) *f* (pl ~en) hardware store

eisern (*igh*-zerrn) *adj* iron

eisig (*igh*-zikh) *adj* freezing

Eislauf (*ighss*-louf) *n* ice-skating

Eisschrank (*ighss*-shrahngk) *m* (pl ~e) fridge, refrigerator

Eiswasser (*ighss*-vah-serr) *nt* iced water

eitel (*igh*-terl) *adj* vain

Eiter (*igh*-terr) *m* pus

Eiweiß (*igh*-vighss) *nt* (egg-)white, albumen; protein

ekelhaft (*āy*-kerl-hahft) *adj* disgusting

Ekuador (ay-kvah-*dōar*) Ecuador

Ekuadorianer (ay-kvah-doa-r'*aa*-nerr) *m* (pl ∼), **-in** *f* Ecuadorian

Ekzem (ehk-*tsāym*) *nt* eczema

elastisch (ay-*lahss*-tish) *adj* elastic

Elch (ehlkh) *m* (pl ∼e) moose

Elefant (ay-lay-*fahnt*) *m* (pl ∼en) elephant

elegant (ay-lay-*gahnt*) *adj* smart, elegant

Eleganz (ay-lay-*gahnts*) *f* elegance

Elektriker (ay-*lehk*-tri-kerr) *m* (pl ∼), **-in** *f* electrician

elektrisch (ay-*lehk*-trish) *adj* electric

Elektrizität (ay-lehk-tri-tsi-*tait*) *f* electricity

elektronisch (ay-lehk-*trōa*-nish) *adj* electronic

Element (ay-lay-*mehnt*) *nt* (pl ∼e) element

elementar (ay-lay-mern-*taar*) *adj* primary

Elend (*āy*-lehnt) *nt* misery

elend (*āy*-lehnt) *adj* miserable

Elendsviertel (*āy*-lehnts-feer-terl) *nt* slum

elf (ehlf) *num* eleven; **Elf** *f* soccer team

Elfe (*ehl*-fer) *f* (pl ∼n) elf

Elfenbein (*ehl*-fern-bighn) *nt* ivory

elfte (*ehlf*-ter) *num* eleventh

Ellbogen (*ehl*-bōa-gern) *m* (pl ∼) elbow

Elster (*ehls*-terr) *f* (pl ∼n) magpie

Eltern (*ehl*-terrn) *pl* parents *pl*

E-Mail (*i*-māyl) *f* (pl ∼s) e-mail

Email (ay-*migh*) *f* enamel

emailliert (ay-mah-*ʸeert*) *adj* enamelled

Emanzipation (ay-mahn-tsi-pah-

ts*ʸōan*) *f* emancipation

Embargo (ehm-*bahr*-goa) *nt* embargo

Emblem (ehm-*blāym*) *nt* (pl ∼e) emblem

eminent (ay-mi-*nehnt*) *adj* outstanding

Empfang (ehm-*pfahng*) *m* (pl ∼e) reception; receipt

***empfangen** (ehm-*pfahng*-ern) *v* receive

Empfänger (ehm-*pfehng*-err) *m* (pl ∼), **-in** *f* receiver, recipient

Empfängnis (ehm-*pfehng*-niss) *f* conception

Empfangsdame (ehm-*pfahngs*-daa-mer) *f* (pl ∼n) receptionist

***empfehlen** (ehm-*pfāy*-lern) *v* recommend; advise

Empfehlung (ehm-*pfāy*-loong) *f* (pl ∼en) recommendation; advice

empfindlich (ehm-*pfint*-likh) *adj* sensitive

Empfindung (ehm-*pfin*-doong) *f* (pl ∼en) perception; sensation

empörend (ehm-*pūr*-rernt) *adj* revolting, shocking

Ende (*ehn*-der) *nt* end; ending, issue

enden (*ehn*-dern) *v* end; finish

endgültig (*ehnt*-gewl-tikh) *adj* eventual

endlich (*ehnt*-likh) *adv* at last

Endstation (*ehnt*-shtah-ts*ʸōan*) *f* (pl ∼en) terminal

Energie (ay-nehr-*gee*) *f* energy; power

energisch (ay-*nehr*-gish) *adj* energetic

eng (ehng) *adj* narrow; tight; **enger machen** tighten; **enger *werden** tighten

Engel (*ehng*-erl) *m* (pl ∼) angel

England (*ehng*-lahnt) England; Britain

Engländer (*ehng*-lehn-derr) *m* (pl ∼) Englishman; Briton

Engländerin (*ehng*-lehn-der-rin) *f* (pl

~nen) Englishwoman; Briton

englisch (*ehng*-lish) *adj* English; British

Engpass (*ehng*-pahss) *m* (pl ~e) bottleneck

engstirnig (*ehng*-shteer-nikh) *adj* narrow-minded

Enkel (*ehng*-kerl) *m* (pl ~) grandson

Enkelin (*ehng*-ker-lin) *f* (pl ~nen) granddaughter

entbehren (ehnt-*bay*-rern) *v* spare

*entbinden von (ehnt-*bin*-dern) discharge of

Entbindung (ehnt-*bin*-doong) *f* (pl ~en) delivery, childbirth

entdecken (ehnt-*deh*-kern) *v* discover; detect

Entdeckung (ehnt-*deh*-koong) *f* (pl ~en) discovery

Ente (*ehn*-ter) *f* (pl ~n) duck

entfalten (ehnt-*fahl*-tern) *v* unfold; expand

entfernen (ehnt-*fehr*-nern) *v* *take away

entfernt (ehnt-*fehrnt*) *adj* distant; faraway, remote; **entferntest** furthest

Entfernung (ehnt-*fehr*-noong) *f* (pl ~en) distance; way

Entfernungsmesser (ehnt-*fehr*-noongs-meh-serr) *m* (pl ~) range finder

entgegengesetzt (ehnt-*gay*-gern-ger-zehtst) *adj* opposite; contrary

entgegenkommend (ehnt-*gay*-gern-ko-mernt) *adj* oncoming

*entgehen (ehnt-*gay*-ern) *v* escape

*enthalten (ehnt-*hahl*-tern) *v* contain, include; deny; **sich ~** abstain from

enthüllen (ehnt-*hew*-lern) *v* reveal

Enthüllung (ehnt-*hew*-loong) *f* (pl ~en) revelation

*entkommen (ehnt-*ko*-mern) *v* escape

entkorken (ehnt-*kor*-kern) *v* uncork

*entladen (ehnt-*laa*-dern) *v* discharge

entlang (ehnt-*lahng*) *prep* along, past

*entlassen (ehnt-*lah*-sern) *v* dismiss, fire

entlegen (ehnt-*lay*-gern) *adj* out of the way

*entleihen (ehnt-*ligh*-ern) *v* borrow

Entlohnung (ehnt-*loa*-noong) *f* (pl ~en) remuneration

*entnehmen (ehnt-*nay*-mern) *v* *take from; infer from**Entrüstung** (ehnt-*rewss*-toong) *f* indignation

entschädigen (ehnt-*shai*-di-gern) *v* remunerate

Entschädigung (ehnt-*shai*-di-goong) *f* (pl ~en) indemnity

*entscheiden (ehnt-*shigh*-dern) *v* decide

Entscheidung (ehnt-*shigh*-doong) *f* (pl ~en) decision

*entschließen: sich ~ (ehnt-*shlee*-sern) *v* decide

entschlossen (ehnt-*shlo*-sern) *adj* resolute, determined

Entschluss (ehnt-*shlooss*) *m* (pl ~e) decision

entschuldigen (ehnt-*shool*-di-gern) *v* excuse; *forgive; **sich ~** apologize

Entschuldigung (ehnt-*shool*-di-goong) *f* (pl ~en) apology, excuse; **Entschuldigung!** sorry!

Entsetzen (ehnt-*zeh*-tsern) *nt* horror

entsetzlich (ehnt-*zehts*-likh) *adj* horrible

*entsinnen (ehnt-*zi*-nern) *v*: **sich ~** recollect

entspannen (ehnt-*shpah*-nayn) *v*: **sich ~** relax

Entspannung (ehnt-*shpah*-noong) *f* (pl ~en) relaxation

entsprechend (ehnt-*shpreh*-khernt) *adj* adequate; equivalent

*entstehen (ehnt-*shtay*-ern) *v* *arise

entstellt (ehnt-*shtehlt*) *adj* deformed

enttäuschen (ehnt-*toi*-shern) *v*

disappoint; *let down; *be disappointing

Enttäuschung (ehnt-*toi*-shoong) f (pl ⁓en) disappointment

entwässern (ehnt-*veh*-serrn) v drain

entweder ... oder (ehnt-*vāy*-derr ... *ōā*-derr) conj either ... or

*****entwerfen** (ehnt-*vehr*-fern) v design

entwerten (ehnt-*vāy*r-tern) v devalue

entwickeln (ehnt-*vi*-kerln) v develop

Entwicklung (ehnt-*vi*-kloong) f (pl ⁓en) development

entwischen (ehnt-*vi*-shern) v slip

Entwurf (ehnt-*voorf*) m (pl ⁓e) design

entzücken (ehnt-*tsew*-kern) v delight; **entzückend** delightful; **entzückt** delighted

entzündbar (ehnt-*tsewnt*-baar) adj inflammable

entzünden (ehnt-*tsewn*-dern) v *become septic

Entzündung (ehnt-*tsewn*-doong) f (pl ⁓en) inflammation

entzwei (ehnt-*tsvigh*) adj broken

Enzyklopädie (ehn-tsew-kloa-peh-dee) f (pl ⁓n) encyclop(a)edia

Epidemie (ay-pi-day-*mee*) f (pl ⁓n) epidemic

Epilepsie (ay-pi-leh-*psee*) f epilepsy

episch (*āy*-pish) adj epic

Episode (ay-pi-z*ōā*-der) f (pl ⁓n) episode

Epos (*āy*-poss) nt (pl Epen) epic

er (āyr) pron he

erbärmlich (ehr-*behrm*-likh) adj miserable

Erbe (*ehr*-ber) m heir; successor; nt inheritance, heritage

erben (*ehr*-bern) v inherit

erblich (*ehrp*-likh) adj hereditary

erblicken (ehr-*bli*-kern) v glance; glimpse

*****erbrechen** (ehr-*breh*-khern) v vomit

Erbschaft (*ehrp*-shahft) f (pl ⁓en) inheritance; legacy

Erbse (*ehr*-pser) f (pl ⁓n) pea

Erdball (*āyrt*-bahl) m globe

Erdbeben (*āyrt*-*bāy*-bern) nt (pl ⁓) earthquake

Erdbeere (*āyrt*-*bāy*-rer) f (pl ⁓n) strawberry

Erdboden (*āyrt*-*bōā*-dern) m soil

Erde (*āyr*-der) f earth; soil

Erdgas (*āyrt*-gaass) nt natural gas

Erdgeschoss (*āyrt*-ger-shoss) nt ground floor

Erdkunde (*āyrt*-koon-der) f geography

Erdnuss (*āyrt*-nooss) f (pl ⁓e) peanut

Erdteil (*āyrt*-tighl) m (pl ⁓e) continent

ereignen (ehr-*igh*-gnern) v: **sich ⁓** happen; occur

Ereignis (ehr-*igh*-gniss) nt (pl ⁓se) event; happening, occurrence

erfahren (ehr-*faa*-rern) adj experienced; skilled

*****erfahren** (ehr-*faa*-rern) v experience

Erfahrung (ehr-*faa*-roong) f (pl ⁓en) experience

*****erfinden** (ehr-*fin*-dern) v invent

Erfinder (ehr-*fin*-derr) m (pl ⁓), **-in** f inventor

erfinderisch (ehr-*fin*-der-rish) adj inventive

Erfindung (ehr-*fin*-doong) f (pl ⁓en) invention

Erfolg (ehr-*folk*) m (pl ⁓e) success

erfolglos (ehr-*folk*-lōāss) adj unsuccessful

erfolgreich (ehr-*folk*-righkh) adj successful

erforderlich (ehr-*for*-derr-likh) adj requisite

erfordern (ehr-*for*-derrn) v require

Erfordernis (ehr-*for*-derr-niss) nt (pl ⁓se) requirement

erforschen (ehr-*for*-shern) v explore

erfreulich (ehr-*froi*-likh) *adj* enjoyable

erfreut (ehr-*froit*) *adj* pleased, glad

erfrischen (ehr-*fri*-shern) *v* refresh; **erfrischend** refreshing

Erfrischung (ehr-*fri*-shoong) *f* refreshment

ergänzen (ehr-*gehn*-tsern) *v* complete; **sich ~** complement one another

*****ergeben** (ehr-*gāy*-bern) *v*: **sich ~** result; surrender

Ergebnis (ehr-*gāyp*-niss) *nt* (pl ~se) result; issue, effect, outcome

*****ergreifen** (ehr-*grigh*-fern) *v* seize; *catch, grasp

*****erhalten** (ehr-*hahl*-tern) *v* obtain

erhältlich (ehr-*hehlt*-likh) *adj* obtainable

*****erheben** (ehr-*hāy*-bern) *v* raise; **sich ~** *arise

Erhebung (ehr-*hāy*-boong) *f* (pl ~en) mound, hillock

erhöhen (ehr-*hūr*-ern) *v* raise

Erhöhung (ehr-*hūr*-oong) *f* (pl ~en) increase; rise; raise *Am*

erholen: sich ~ (ehr-*hōa*-lern) *v* recover

Erholung (ehr-*hōa*-loong) *f* recreation; recovery

Erholungsheim (ehr-*hōa*-loongs-highm) *nt* (pl ~e) rest home

Erholungsort (ehr-*hōa*-loongs-ort) *m* (pl ~e) holiday resort

erinnern (ehr-*i*-nerrn) *v* remind; **sich ~** recall, remember

Erinnerung (ehr-*i*-ner-roong) *f* (pl ~en) memory; remembrance

erkälten (ehr-*kehl*-tern) *v*: **sich ~** catch a cold

Erkältung (ehr-*kehl*-toong) *f* (pl ~en) cold

*****erkennen** (ehr-*keh*-nern) *v* recognize; acknowledge

erkenntlich (ehr-*kehnt*-likh) *adj* grateful

erklärbar (ehr-*klair*-baar) *adj* accountable

erklären (ehr-*klai*-rern) *v* explain; declare

Erklärung (ehr-*klai*-roong) *f* (pl ~en) explanation; statement; declaration

Erkrankung (ehr-*krahng*-koong) *f* (pl ~en) illness; disease

erkundigen (ehr-*koon*-di-gern) *v*: **sich ~** enquire, inquire

Erkundigung (ehr-*koon*-di-goong) *f* (pl ~en) enquiry

erlangen (ehr-*lahng*-ern) *v* obtain

erlauben (ehr-*lou*-bern) *v* allow, permit; **erlaubt *sein** *be allowed

Erlaubnis (ehr-*loup*-niss) *f* permission

erläutern (ehr-*loi*-terrn) *v* explain; elucidate

Erläuterung (ehr-*loi*-ter-roong) *f* (pl ~en) explanation

erleben (ehr-*lāy*-bern) *v* experience

erledigen (ehr-*lāy*-di-gern) *v* settle

erleichtern (ehr-*lighkh*-terrn) *v* relieve

Erleichterung (ehr-*lighkh*-ter-roong) *f* (pl ~en) relief

*****erleiden** (ehr-*ligh*-dern) *v* suffer

erlesen (ehr-*lāy*-zern) *adj* select

erleuchten (ehr-*loikh*-tern) *v* illuminate

*****erliegen** (ehr-*lee*-gern) *v* succumb

Erlös (ehr-*lūrss*) *m* (pl ~e) produce

erlösen (ehr-*lūr*-zern) *v* deliver, redeem

Erlösung (ehr-*lūr*-zoong) *f* delivery

Ermächtigung (ehr-*mehkh*-ti-goong) *f* (pl ~en) authorization

Ermäßigung (ehr-*mai*-si-goong) *f* (pl ~en) reduction

ermitteln (ehr-*mi*-terln) *v* *find out

ermüden (ehr-*mēw*-dern) *v* tire

ermutigen (ehr-*mōo*-ti-gern) *v* encourage

ernähren (ehr-*nai*-rern) *v* *feed

*ernennen (ehr-*neh*-nern) v nominate, appoint

Ernennung (ehr-*neh*-noong) f (pl ⁓en) nomination, appointment

erneuern (ehr-*noi*-errn) v renew

Ernst (ehrnst) m gravity, seriousness

ernst (ehrnst) adj serious; grave; severe

ernsthaft (*ehrnst*-hahft) adj bad

Ernte (*ehrn*-ter) f (pl ⁓n) crop; harvest

Eroberer (ehr-*ōa*-ber-rerr) m (pl ⁓) conqueror

erobern (ehr-*ōa*-berrn) v conquer

Eroberung (ehr-*ōa*-ber-roong) f (pl ⁓en) conquest

eröffnen (ehr-*urf*-nern) v open

Eröffnung (ehr-*urf*-noong) f opening

erörtern (ehr-*urr*-terrn) v discuss; argue

Erörterung (ehr-*urr*-ter-roong) f (pl ⁓en) deliberation

erpressen (ehr-*preh*-sern) v blackmail; extort

Erpressung (ehr-*preh*-soong) f (pl ⁓en) blackmail; extortion

erregen (ehr-*rāy*-gern) v excite

Erregung (ehr-*rāy*-goong) f emotion; excitement

erreichbar (ehr-*righkh*-baar) adj attainable

erreichen (ehr-*righ*-khern) v reach, attain; achieve; *catch

errichten (ehr-*rikh*-tern) v construct; erect; found

erröten (ehr-*rūr*-tern) v blush

Ersatz (ehr-*zahts*) m substitute

Ersatzfüllung (ehr-*zahts*-few-loong) f (pl ⁓en) refill

Ersatzreifen (ehr-*zahts*-righ-fern) m (pl ⁓) spare tyre, spare tire Am

Ersatzteil (ehr-*zahts*-tighl) nt (pl ⁓e) spare part

erschaffen (ehr-*shah*-fern) v create

erschallen (ehr-*shah*-lern) v sound

Erscheinen (ehr-*shigh*-nern) nt appearance

*erscheinen (ehr-*shigh*-nern) v appear; seem

erschöpfen (ehr-*shur*-pfern) v exhaust; **erschöpft** tired

*erschrecken (ehr-*shreh*-kern) v *be frightened; frighten, terrify, scare

ersetzen (ehr-*zeh*-tsern) v replace, substitute

*ersinnen (ehr-*zi*-nern) v invent

Ersparnisse (ehr-*shpaar*-ni-ser) fpl savings pl

erstarrt (ehr-*shtahrt*) adj numb

Erstaunen (ehr-*shtou*-nern) nt amazement, astonishment

erstaunen (ehr-*shtou*-nern) v amaze; surprise

erstaunlich (ehr-*shtoun*-likh) adj astonishing, striking

erste (*āyrs*-ter) num first; adj initial; foremost

erstens (*āyrs*-terns) adv first(ly), in the first place

ersticken (ehr-*shti*-kern) v choke

erstklassig (*āyrst*-klah-sikh) adj first-class

erstrangig (*āyrst*-rahng-ikh) adj first-rate

Ertrag (ehr-*traak*) m (pl ⁓e) produce

*ertragen (ehr-*traa*-gern) v endure, *bear

erträglich (ehr-*trāyk*-likh) adj tolerable

*ertrinken (ehr-*tring*-kern) v drown; *be drowned

erwachsen (ehr-*vah*-ksern) adj adult, grown-up

Erwachsene (ehr-*vah*-kser-ner) m/f (pl ⁓n) adult, grown-up

*erwägen (ehr-*vai*-gern) v consider

Erwägung (ehr-*vai*-goong) f (pl ⁓en) consideration

erwähnen (ehr-*vai*-nern) v mention

Erwähnung (ehr-*vai*-noong) *f* (pl ⁓en) mention

erwarten (ehr-*vahr*-tern) *v* expect; anticipate; await

Erwartung (ehr-*vahr*-toong) *f* (pl ⁓en) expectation

erweitern (ehr-*vigh*-terrn) *v* extend; enlarge, widen

Erwerb (ehr-*vehrp*) *m* purchase

*erwerben (ehr-*vehr*-bern) *v* acquire; *buy

erwischen (ehr-*vi*-shern) *v* *catch

erwürgen (ehr-*vewr*-gern) *v* strangle, choke

Erz (āyrts) *nt* (pl ⁓e) ore

erzählen (ehr-*tsai*-lern) *v* *tell; relate

Erzählung (ehr-*tsai*-loong) *f* (pl ⁓en) tale

Erzbischof (*ehrts*-bi-shof) *m* (pl ⁓e) archbishop

erzeugen (ehr-*tsoi*-gern) *v* generate

*erziehen (ehr-*tsee*-ern) *v* *bring up

Erziehung (ehr-*tsee*-oong) *f* education

es (ehss) *pron* it

Esel (*āy*-zerl) *m* (pl ⁓) donkey

Essay (*eh*-say) *m* (pl ⁓s) essay

essbar (*ehss*-baar) *adj* edible

Essen (*eh*-sern) *nt* food

*essen (*eh*-sern) *v* *eat; **zu Abend ⁓** dine

Essenz (eh-*sehnts*) *f* essence

Essig (*eh*-sikh) *m* vinegar

Esslöffel (*ehss*-lur-ferl) *m* (pl ⁓) tablespoon

Esszimmer (*ehss*-tsi-merr) *nt* dining room

Etage (ay-*taa*-zher) *f* (pl ⁓n) stor(e)y; floor *Am*

Etappe (ay-*tah*-per) *f* (pl ⁓n) stage

Etikett (ay-ti-*keht*) *nt* (pl ⁓e) label, tag

etliche (*eht*-li-kher) *adj* several

Etui (eht-*vee*) *nt* (pl ⁓s) case

etwa (*eht*-vah) *adv* about, approximately

etwas (*eht*-vahss) *pron* something

EU (ay-*ōōr*) *f* EU

euch (oikh) *pron* you; yourselves

euer (*oi*-err) *pron* your

Eule (*oi*-ler) *f* (pl ⁓n) owl

Euro (*oi*-roh) *m* (pl ⁓, ⁓s), Euro

Europa (oi-*rōa*-pah) Europe

Europäer (oi-roa-*pai*-err) *m* (pl ⁓), **-in** *f* European

europäisch (oi-roa-*pai*-ish) *adj* European

evakuieren (ay-vah-koo-*ee*-rern) *v* evacuate

eventuell (ay-vehn-too-*ehl*) *adj* possible

Evolution (ay-voa-loo-*ts*ᵛ*ōan*) *f* (pl ⁓en) evolution

ewig (*āy*-vikh) *adj* eternal

Ewigkeit (*āy*-vikh-kight) *f* eternity

exakt (eh-*ksahkt*) *adj* precise, very

Examen (eh-*ksaa*-mern) *nt* (pl ⁓) examination

Exemplar (eh-ksehm-*plaar*) *nt* (pl ⁓e) specimen; copy

exklusiv (ehks-kloo-*zeef*) *adj* exclusive

exotisch (eh-*ksōa*-tish) *adj* exotic

Expedition (ehks-pay-di-*ts*ᵛ*ōan*) *f* (pl ⁓en) expedition

Experiment (ehks-pay-ri-*mehnt*) *nt* (pl ⁓e) experiment

experimentieren (ehks-pay-ri-mehn-*tee*-rern) *v* experiment

explodieren (ehks-ploa-*dee*-rern) *v* explode

Explosion (ehks-ploa-*z*ᵛ*ōan*) *f* (pl ⁓en) blast, explosion

explosiv (ehks-ploa-*zeef*) *adj* explosive

Export (ehks-*port*) *m* export

exportieren (ehks-por-*tee*-rern) *v* export

extravagant (*ehks*-trah-vah-gahnt) *adj* extravagant

Extrem (ehks-*trāym*) *nt* (pl ⁓e) extreme

extrem (ehks-*trāym*) *adj* extreme

F

Fabel (*faa*-berl) *f* (pl ⁓n) fable

Fabrik (fah-*breek*) *f* (pl ⁓en) factory; mill, works *pl*

Fabrikant (fah-bri-*kahnt*) *m* (pl ⁓en), **-in** *f* manufacturer

Fach (fahkh) *nt* (pl ⁓er) section; trade, profession

Fächer (*feh*-kherr) *m* (pl ⁓) fan

fachkundig (*fahkh*-koon-dikh) *adj* expert

Fachmann (*fahkh*-mahn) *m* (pl -leute) expert

Fackel (*fah*-kerl) *f* (pl ⁓n) torch

Faden (*faa*-dern) *m* (pl ⁓) thread

fähig (*fai*-ikh) *adj* able; capable

Fähigkeit (*fai*-ikh-kight) *f* (pl ⁓en) ability; faculty, capacity

Fahne (*faa*-ner) *f* (pl ⁓n) flag

Fahrbahn (*faar*-baan) *f* (pl ⁓en) carriageway; lane; roadway *Am*

Fährboot (*fair*-bōat) *nt* (pl ⁓e) ferry-boat

Fähre (*fai*-rer) *f* ferry(boat)

***fahren** (*faa*-rern) *v* *drive; *ride; sail

Fahrer (*faa*-rerr) *m* (pl ⁓), **-in** *f* driver

Fahrgast (*faar*-gahst) *m* passenger

Fahrgeld (*faar*-gehlt) *nt* fare

Fahrgestell (*faar*-ger-shtehl) *nt* (pl ⁓e) chassis

Fahrkarte (*faar*-kahr-ter) *f* (pl ⁓n) ticket

Fahrkartenautomat (*faar*-kahr-tern-ou-toa-maat) *m* (pl ⁓en) ticket machine

Fahrplan (*faar*-plaan) *m* (pl ⁓e) timetable, schedule

Fahrrad (*faar*-raat) *nt* (pl ⁓er) cycle, bicycle

Fahrschule (*faar*-shōo-ler) *f* driving school

Fahrt (faart) *f* (pl ⁓en) ride, drive

Fährte (*fair*-ter) *f* (pl ⁓n) trail

Fahrzeug (*faar*-tsoik) *nt* (pl ⁓e) vehicle

Faktor (*fahk*-tor) *m* (pl ⁓en) factor

Fakultät (fah-kool-*tait*) *f* (pl ⁓en) faculty

Falke (*fahl*-ker) *m* (pl ⁓n) hawk

Fall (fahl) *m* (pl ⁓e)case; instance; **auf jeden** ⁓ at any rate; **im** ⁓ in case of

Falle (*fah*-ler) *f* (pl ⁓n) trap

***fallen** (*fah*-lern) *v* *fall; ⁓ *lassen** drop

fällig (*feh*-likh) *adj* due

falls (fahls) *conj* in case, if

Fallschirm (*fahl*-sheerm) *m* parachute

falsch (fahlsh) *adj* wrong, mistaken; false

fälschen (*fehl*-shern) *v* forge, counterfeit

Fälschung (*fehl*-shoong) *f* (pl ⁓en) fake

Falte (*fahl*-ter) *f* (pl ⁓n) fold; crease; wrinkle

falten (*fahl*-tern) *v* fold

Familie (fah-*mee*-l*ʸ*er) *f* (pl ⁓n) family

Familienname (fah-*mee*-l*ʸ*ern-naa-mer) *m* surname

fanatisch (fah-*naa*-tish) *adj* fanatical

***fangen** (*fahng*-ern) *v* *catch; capture

Fantasie (fahn-tah-*see*) *f* fancy

fantastisch (fahn-*tahss*-tish) *adj*

fantastic

Farbe (*fahr*-ber) *f* (pl ⁓n) colo(u)r; paint; dye

farbecht (*fahrb*-ehkht) *adj* fast-dyed

färben (*fehr*-bern) *v* dye

farbenblind (*fahr*-bern-blint) *adj* colo(u)r-blind

farbenfroh (*fahr*-bern-froa) *adj* colo(u)rful

Farbfilm (*fahrp*-film) *m* (pl ⁓e) colo(u)r film

farbig (*fahr*-bikh) *adj* colo(u)red

Farbton (*fahrp*-toan) *m* (pl ⁓e) shade

Fasan (fah-*zaan*) *m* (pl ⁓e) pheasant

Faschismus (fah-*shiss*-mooss) *m* fascism

Faschist (fah-*shist*) *m* (pl ⁓en), **-in** *f* fascist

faschistisch (fah-*shiss*-tish) *adj* fascist

Faser (*faa*-zerr) *f* (pl ⁓n) fibre

Fass (fahss) *nt* (pl ⁓er) barrel; cask

Fassade (fah-*saa*-der) *f* (pl ⁓n) façade

Fässchen (*fehss*-khern) *nt* (pl ⁓) keg

fassen (*fah*-sern) *v* grip

Fassung (*fah*-soong) *f* (pl ⁓en) frame, socket; composure

fast (fahst) *adv* nearly, almost

faul (foul) *adj* lazy, idle

Faust (foust) *f* (pl ⁓e) fist

Fausthandschuhe (*foust*-hahnt-shoo-er) *mpl* mittens *pl*

Favorit (fah-voa-*reet*) *m* (pl ⁓en), **-in** *f* favo(u)rite

Fax (faaks) *nt* (pl ⁓) fax

faxen (faa-ksern) to send by fax

Februar (*fay*-broo-aar) February

***fechten** (*fehkh*-tern) *v* fence

Feder (*fay*-derr) *f* (pl ⁓n) feather; pen; spring

Federball (*fay*-derr-bahl) (**-spiel** *nt*) *m* badminton

Federung (*fay*-der-roong) *f* suspension

Fee (fay) *f* (pl ⁓n) fairy

fegen (*fay*-gern) *v* *sweep

Fehlen (*fay*-lern) *nt* want

fehlen (*fay*-lern) *v* fail; **fehlend** missing

Fehler (*fay*-lerr) *m* (pl ⁓) mistake; error, fault

fehlerhaft (*fay*-lerr-hahft) *adj* faulty

Fehlgeburt (*fayl*-ger-boort) *f* (pl ⁓en) miscarriage

Fehlschlag (*fayl*-shlaak) *m* (pl ⁓e) failure

Fehltritt (*fayl*-trit) *m* slip

Feier (*figh*-err) *f* (pl ⁓n) celebration

feierlich (*figh*-err-likh) *adj* solemn

Feierlichkeit (*figh*-err-likh-kight) *f* (pl ⁓en) ceremony

feiern (*figh*-errn) *v* celebrate

Feiertag (*figh*-err-taak) *m* (pl ⁓e) holiday

Feige (*figh*-ger) *f* (pl ⁓n) fig

feige (*figh*-ger) *adj* cowardly

Feigling (*fighk*-ling) *m* (pl ⁓e) coward

Feile (*figh*-ler) *f* (pl ⁓n) file

fein (fighn) *adj* fine; delicate

Feind (fighnt) *m* (pl ⁓e), **-in** *f* enemy

feindlich (*fighnt*-likh) *adj* hostile

Feinkost (*fighn*-kost) *f* delicatessen

Feinkostgeschäft (*fighn*-kost-ger-shehft) *nt* (pl ⁓e) deli(catessen)

Feinschmecker (*fighn*-shmeh-kerr) *m* (pl ⁓), **-in** *f* gourmet

Feld (fehlt) *nt* (pl ⁓er) field

Feldbett (*fehlt*-beht) *nt* (pl ⁓en) camp bed

Feldstecher (*fehlt*-shteh-kherr) *m* (pl ⁓) field glasses, binoculars *pl*

Felge (*fehl*-ger) *f* (pl ⁓n) rim

Fell (fehl) *nt* (pl ⁓e) skin

Felsblock (*fehls*-blok) *m* (pl ⁓e) boulder

Felsen (*fehl*-zern) *m* (pl ⁓) rock

felsig (*fehl*-zikh) *adj* rocky

Fenster (*fehns*-terr) *nt* (pl ⁓) window

Fensterbrett (*fehns*-terr-breht) *nt* (pl

~er) windowsill

Fensterladen (*fehns*-terr-laa-dern) *m* (pl ⁓) shutter

Ferien (*fāy*-r^yern) *pl* vacation, holidays *pl*

Ferienlager (*fāy*-r^yern-laa-gerr) *nt* (pl ⁓) holiday camp

Ferkel (*fehr*-kerl) *nt* (pl ⁓) piglet

fern (fehrn) *adj* far; **ferner** *adj* further; *adv* moreover

Ferngespräch (*fehrn*-ger-shpraikh) *nt* (pl ⁓e) long-distance call

Fernglas (*fehrn*-glaas) *nt* (pl ~er) binoculars *pl*

Fernsehen (*fehrn*-zāy-ern) *nt* television

Fernseher (*fehrn*-zāy-err) *m* television set

Fernsehgerät (*fehrn*-zāy-ger-rait) *nt* television set

Fernsprecher (*fehrn*-shprai-kherr) *m* phone

Ferse (*fehr*-zer) *f* (pl ⁓n) heel

fertig (*fehr*-tikh) *adj* ready; finished; ⁓ **machen** *v* prepare; finish

Fertigkeit (*fehr*-tikh-kight) *f* art, skill

fesseln (*feh*-serln) *v* fascinate

Fest (fehst) *nt* (pl ⁓e) feast

fest (fehst) *adj* firm; fixed, permanent; solid; *adv* tight

*festhalten (*fehst*-hahl-tern) *v* *hold; **sich** ⁓ *hold on

Festival (*fehss*-ti-vahl) *nt* (pl ⁓s) festival

Festkörper (*fehst*-kurr-perr) *m* (pl ⁓) solid

Festland (*fehst*-lahnt) *nt* mainland; continent

festlich (*fehst*-likh) *adj* festive

festmachen (*fehst*-mah-khern) *v* fasten

Festmahl (*fehst*-maal) *nt* (pl ~er) banquet

Festnahme (*fehst*-naa-mer) *f* (pl ⁓n)

arrest; capture

*festnehmen (*fehst*- nāy-mern) *v* arrest

festsetzen (*fehst*-zeh-tsern) *v* determine; stipulate

feststecken (*fehst*-shteh-kern) *v* pin

feststellen (*fehst*-shteh-lern) *v* notice; ascertain, establish; diagnose

Festung (*fehss*-toong) *f* (pl ⁓en) fortress

Fett (feht) *nt* (pl ⁓e) grease, fat

fett (feht) *adj* fat; greasy

fettig (*feh*-tikh) *adj* greasy, fatty

feucht (foikht) *adj* wet; damp, moist, humid

Feuchtigkeit (*foikh*-tikh-kight) *f* damp; moisture, humidity

Feuchtigkeitscreme (*foikh*-tikh-kights-krāym) *f* (pl ⁓s) moisturizing cream

feudal (foi-*daal*) *adj* feudal; sumptuous, classy

Feuer (*foi*-err) *nt* (pl ⁓) fire

Feueralarm (*foi*-err-ah-lahrm) *m* fire alarm

feuerfest (*foi*-err-fehst) *adj* fireproof

Feuerlöscher (*foi*-err-lur-sherr) *m* (pl ⁓) fire extinguisher

feuersicher (*foi*-err-zi-kherr) *adj* fireproof

Feuerwehr (*foi*-err-vāyr) *f* fire brigade

Feuerzeug (*foi*-err-tsoik) *nt* (pl ⁓e) cigarette lighter

Feuilleton (*fur^{ee}*-er-taw̄ng) *nt* (pl ⁓s) feature pages

Fieber (*fee*-berr) *nt* fever

fiebrig (*fee*-brikh) *adj* feverish

Figur (fi-*gōōr*) *f* (pl ⁓en) figure

Fiktion (fik-ts^y*ōan*) *f* (pl ⁓en) fiction

Filiale (fi-lee-*aa*-ler) *f* branch

Film (film) *m* (pl ⁓e) film; movie

filmen (*fil*-mern) *v* film

Filmleinwand (*film*-lighn-vahnt) *f* screen

Filter (*fil*-terr) *m* (pl ~) filter

Filz (filts) *m* felt

Finanzamt (fi-*nahnts*-ahmt) *nt* tax office, revenue office

Finanzen (fi-*nahn*-tsern) *pl* finances *pl*

finanziell (fi-nahn-*ts^{y}ehl*) *adj* financial

finanzieren (fi-nahn-*tsee*-rern) *v* finance

***finden** (*fin*-dern) *v* *find; *come across; consider

Finger (*fing*-err) *m* (pl ~) finger; **kleine ~** little finger

Fingerabdruck (*fing*-err-ahp-drook) *m* (pl ~e) fingerprint

Fingergelenk (*fing*-err-ger-lehngk) *nt* (pl ~e) knuckle

Fingerhut (*fing*-err-hōōt) *m* (pl ~e) thimble

Fink (fingk) *m* (pl ~en) finch

Finne (*fi*-ner) *m* (pl ~n), **-in** *f* Finn

finnisch (*fi*-nish) *adj* Finnish

Finnland (*fin*-lahnt) Finland

finster (*fins*-terr) *adj* dark

Finsternis (*fins*-terr-niss) *f* (pl ~se) dark; eclipse

Firma (*feer*-mah) *f* (pl -men) firm, company

Firnis (*feer*-niss) *m* varnish

Fisch (fish) *m* (pl ~e) fish

fischen (*fi*-shern) *v* fish

Fischer (*fi*-sherr) *m* (pl ~) fisherman

Fischerei (fi-sher-*righ*) *f* fishing industry

Fischerin (*fi*-sher-rin) *f* (pl ~) fisherwoman

Fischgräte (*fish*-grai-ter) *f* (pl ~n) fishbone

Fischhandlung (*fish*-hahn-dloong) *f* (pl ~en) fish shop

Fischnetz (*fish*-nehts) *nt* (pl ~e) fishing net

fit (fit) *adj colloquial* fit, in good shape

FKK-Strand (ehf-kaa-*kaa*-shtrahnt) *m* (pl ~e) nudist beach

flach (flahkh) *adj* smooth, plane, level, flat

Fläche (*fleh*-kher) *f* (pl ~n) area

Flamingo (flah-*ming*-goa) *m* (pl ~s) flamingo

Flamme (*flah*-mer) *f* (pl ~n) flame

Flanell (flah-*nehl*) *m* flannel

Flasche (*flah*-sher) *f* (pl ~n) bottle

Flaschenöffner (*flah*-shern-urf-nerr) *m* (pl ~) bottle opener

Fleck (flehk) *m* (pl ~e) stain; spot, speck; **blauer ~** bruise

fleckenlos (*fleh*-kern-lōass) *adj* spotless, stainless

Fleckenentferner (*fleh*-kern-ehnt-*fehr*-nerr)) *m* stain remover

Fleisch (flighsh) *nt* meat; flesh

Fleischer (*fligh*-sherr) *m* (pl ~), **-in** *f* butcher

Fleiß (flighss) *m* diligence

fleißig (*fligh*-sikh) *adj* diligent, industrious

flicken (*fli*-kern) *v* mend, patch

Fliege (*flee*-ger) *f* (pl ~n) fly; bow tie

***fliegen** (*flee*-gern) *v* *fly

***fliehen** (*flee*-ern) *v* escape

***fließen** (*flee*-sern) *v* flow; **fließend** fluent

Flitterwochen (*fli*-terr-vo-khern) *fpl* honeymoon

Floh (fl ōa) *m* flea

Floß (flōass) *nt* (pl ~e) raft

Flöte (*flūr*-ter) *f* (pl ~n) flute

flott (flot) *adj* quick, speedy, brisk; smart

Flotte (*flo*-ter) *f* (pl ~n) fleet

Fluch (flookh) *m* (pl ~e) curse

fluchen (*flōō*-khern) *v* curse, *swear

Flucht (flookht) *f* escape

flüchten (*flewkh*-tern) *v* escape

Flug (flōōk) *m* (pl ~e) flight

Flügel (*flēw*-gerl) *m* (pl ~) wing; grand piano

Flughafen (*flook*-haa-fern) *m* (pl ～) airport

Flugkapitän (*flook*-kah-pi-tain) *m* (pl ～e) captain

Fluglinie (*flook*-lee-n^yer) *f* (pl ～n) airline

Flugplatz (*flook*-plahts) *m* (pl ～e) airfield

Flugzeug (*flook*-tsoik) *nt* (pl ～e) aeroplane; plane, aircraft; airplane *Am*

Flugzeugabsturz (*flook*-tsoik-ahp-shtoorts) *m* (pl ～e) plane crash

Flur (*floor*) *m* (pl ～e) corridor

Fluss (*flooss*) *m* (pl ～e) river

flüssig (*flew*-sikh) *adj* liquid, fluid

Flüssigkeit (*flew*-sikh-kight) *f* (pl ～en) fluid

Flussufer (*flooss*-ōō-ferr) *nt* (pl ～) riverside, river bank

flüstern (*flewss*-terrn) *v* whisper

Flut (*floot*) *f* high tide, flood

Föderation (fur-day-rah-*ts^yōan*) *f* (pl ～en) federation

Folge (*fol*-ger) *f* (pl ～n) result, issue, consequence; sequel; series, sequence

folgen (*fol*-gern) *v* follow; **folgend** following, subsequent

folglich (*folk*-likh) *adv* consequently

Folklore (folk-*lōa*-rer) *f* folklore

Föhn (*fūrn*) *m* (pl ～s) foehn, föhn; hairdryer

Fonds (*fawng*) *m* (pl ～) fund

foppen (*fo*-pern) *v* kid

forcieren (for-*see*-rern) *v* strain; force

fordern (*for*-derrn) *v* demand, claim

fördern (*furr*-derrn) *v* promote

Forderung (*for*-der-roong) *f* (pl ～en) demand, claim

Forelle (foa-*reh*-ler) *f* trout

Form (form) *f* (pl ～en) form, shape

Format (for-*maat*) *nt* (pl ～e) size

Formel (*for*-merl) *f* (pl ～n) formula

formen (*for*-mern) *v* form; model

förmlich (*furrm*-likh) *adj* formal

Formular (for-moo-*laar*) *nt* (pl ～e) form

Forschung (*for*-shoong) *f* (pl ～en) research

Forst (forst) *m* (pl ～e) forest

Förster (*furrs*-terr) *m* (pl ～), **-in** *f* forester

Fort (*fōar*) *nt* (pl ～s) fort

fort (fort) *adv* gone

fortdauern (*fort*-dou-errn) *v* continue

*fortfahren (*fort*-faa-rern) *v* carry on, *go on, *go ahead, proceed; continue; ～ **mit** *keep on

fortgeschritten (*fort*-ger-shri-tern) *adj* advanced

fortlaufend (*fort*-lou-fernt) *adj* continuous

fortschicken (*fort*-shi-kern) *v* dismiss

*fortschreiten (*fort*-shrigh-tern) *v* advance

Fortschritt (*fort*-shrit) *m* (pl ～e) advance, progress

fortschrittlich (*fort*-shrit-likh) *adj* progressive

fortsetzen (*fort*-zeh-tsern) *v* continue

fortwährend (*fort*-vai-rernt) *adv* continually

Foto (*fōa*-toa) *nt* (pl ～s) photo

Fotogeschäft (*fōa*-toa-ger-shehft) *nt* (pl ～e) camera shop

Fotograf (foa-toa-*graaf*) *m* (pl ～en), **-in** *f* photographer

Fotografie (foa-toa-toa-grah-*fee*) *f* photography

fotografieren (foa-toa-grah-*fee*-rern) *v* photograph

Fotokopie (foa-toa-koa-*pee*) *f* (pl ～n) photocopy

Foyer (fwah-*^yay*) *nt* (pl ～s) foyer, lobby

Fracht (frahkht) *f* (pl ～en) freight, cargo

Frage (*fraa*-ger) *f* (pl ～n) inquiry,

question, query; issue, problem
fragen (*fraa*-gern) *v* ask; **sich ~**
wonder; **fragend** interrogative
Fragezeichen (*fraa*-ger-tsigh-khern)
nt (pl ~) question mark
Fragment (frah-*gmehnt*) *nt* (pl ~e)
fragment
frankieren (frahng-*kee*-rern) *v* stamp
franko (*frahng*-koa) *adj* post-paid
Frankreich (*frahngk*-righkh) France
Franse (*frahn*-zer) *f* (pl ~n) fringe
Franzose (frahn-*tsoa*-zer) *m* (pl ~n)
Frenchman
Französin (frahn-*tsur*-zin) *f* (pl ~nen)
Frenchwoman
französisch (frahn-*tsur*-zish) *adj*
French
Frau (frou) *f* (pl ~en) woman; wife;
gnädige ~ madam; **~ Miller** Mrs., Ms.
Miller
Frauenarzt (*frou*-ern-ahrtst) *m* (pl ~e)
gynaecologist
Frauenärztin (*frou*-ern-ehrts-tin) *f* (pl
~nen) gynaecologist
Fräulein (*froi*-lighn) *nt* (pl ~) miss
frech (frehkh) *adj* bold, impertinent
frei (frigh) *adj* free; vacant
freigebig (*frigh*-gay-bikh) *adj*
generous, liberal
*freihalten (*frigh*-hahl-tern) *v* *keep
clear, *keep open
Freiheit (*frigh*-hight) *f* (pl ~en)
freedom; liberty
Freikarte (*frigh*-kahr-ter) *f* (pl ~n) free
ticket
Freitag (*frigh*-taak) *m* Friday
freiwillig (*frigh*-vi-likh) *adj* voluntary
Freiwillige (*frigh*-vi-li-ger) *m/f* (pl ~n)
volunteer
Freizeit (*frigh*-tsight) *f* spare time
fremd (frehmt) *adj* strange; foreign
Fremde (*frehm*-der) *m/f* (pl ~n)
stranger; foreigner
Fremdenverkehr (*frehm*-dern-fehr-

kayr) *m* tourism
Frequenz (fray-*kvehnts*) *f* (pl ~en)
frequency
Freude (*froi*-der) *f* (pl ~n) joy;
pleasure, gladness
freudig (*froi*-dikh) *adj* joyful
freuen (*froi*-ern) *v*: **sich ~** *be
delighted
Freund (froint) *m* (pl ~e), **-in** *f* friend
freundlich (*froint*-likh) *adj* friendly,
kind
Freundschaft (*froint*-shahft) *f* (pl ~en)
friendship
freundschaftlich (*froint*-shahft-likh)
adj friendly
Frieden (*free*-dern) *m* peace
Friedhof (*freet*-hoaf) *m* (pl ~e)
cemetery
friedlich (*freet*-likh) *adj* peaceful
*frieren (*free*-rern) *v* *freeze
frisch (frish) *adj* fresh
Friseur (fri-*zurr*) *m* (pl ~e)
hairdresser, barber
Frist (frist) *f* (pl ~en) term
Frisur (fri-*zoor*) *f* (pl ~en) hairdo
froh (froa) *adj* glad, joyful
fröhlich (*frur*-likh) *adj* merry, jolly,
cheerful
fromm (from) *adj* pious
Frosch (frosh) *m* (pl ~e) frog
Frost (frost) *m* frost
Frösteln (*frurss*-terln) *nt* shiver, chill
frösteln (*frurss*-terln) *v* shiver
Frostschutzmittel (*frost*-shoots-mi-
terl) *nt* (pl ~) antifreeze
Frottierstoff (fro-*teer*-shtof) *m* (pl ~e)
towelling
Frucht (frookht) *f* (pl ~e) fruit
fruchtbar (*frookht*-baar) *adj* fertile
Fruchtsaft (*frookht*-zahft) *m* (pl ~e)
fruit juice
früh (frew) *adj* early
früher (*frew*-err) *adj* former, prior,
previous; *adv* formerly

Frühling (*frew*-ling) *m* spring; springtime

Frühstück (*frew*-shtewk) *nt* breakfast

Fuchs (fooks) *m* (pl ⁀e) fox

fühlbar (*fewl*-baar) *adj* noticeable

fühlen (*few*-lern) *v* *feel

führen (*few*-rern) *v* carry; *lead, guide, direct, conduct; **führend** *adj* leading

Führer (*few*-rerr) *m* (pl ∼), **-in** *f* guide; guidebook

Führerschein (*few*-rerr-shighn) *m* driving licence

Führung (*few*-roong) *f* leadership; management

Fülle (*few*-ler) *f* plenty

füllen (*few*-lern)*v* fill

Füller (*few*-lerr) *m* (pl ∼) fountain pen

Füllung (*few*-loong) *f* (pl ∼en) stuffing, filling

Fund (foont) *m* discovery, find

Fundbüro (*foont*-bew-rōā) *nt* (pl ∼s) lost property office

Fundsachen (*foont*-zah-khern) *fpl* lost and found

fünf (fewnf) *num* five

fünfte (*fewnf*-ter) *num* fifth

fünfzehn (*fewnf*-tsāyn) *num* fifteen

fünfzehnte (*fewnf*-tsāyn-ter) *num* fifteenth

fünfzig (*fewnf*-tsikh) *num* fifty

funkelnd (*foong*-kerlnt) *adj* sparkling

Funken (*foong*-kern) *m* (pl ∼) spark

Funktion (foongk-tsᵞ*ōan*) *f* (pl ∼en) function; operation

funktionieren (foongk-tsᵞoa-*nee*-rern) *v* work

funktionsunfähig (foongk-tsᵞ*ōans*-oon-fai-ikh) *adj* out of order

für (fewr) *prep* for

Furcht (foorkht) *f* terror, fear

furchtbar (*foorkht*-baar) *adj* terrible, dreadful, awful

fürchten (*fewrkh*-tern) *v* fear

fürchterlich (*fewrkh*-terr-likh) *adj* frightful

furchterregend (*foorkht*-ehr-rāy-gernt) *adj* terrifying

Furunkel (foo-*roong*-kerl) *m* (pl ∼) boil

Fürwort (*fewr*-vort) *nt* (pl ⁀er) pronoun

Fusion (foo-zᵞ*ōan*) *f* (pl ∼en) merger

Fuß (fōōss) *m* (pl ⁀e) foot; **zu ∼** walking, on foot

Fußball (*fōōss*-bahl) *m* (pl ⁀e) football; soccer

Fußballspiel (*fōōss*-bahl-shpeel) *nt* (pl ∼e) football match

Fußboden (*fōōss*-bōā-dern) *m* (pl ⁀) floor

Fußbremse (*fōōss*-brehm-zer) *f* (pl ∼n) foot brake

Fußgänger (*fōōss*-gehng-err) *m* (pl ∼), **-in** *f* pedestrian; **∼ verboten** no pedestrians

Fußgängerübergang (*fōōss*-gehng-err-ēw-berr-gahng) *m* (pl ⁀e) pedestrian crossing

Fußknöchel (*fōōss*-knur-kherl) *m* (pl ∼) ankle

Fußtritt (*fōōss*-trit) *m* (pl ∼e) kick

Fußweg (*fōōss*-vāyk) *m* (pl ∼e) footpath

Futter¹ (*foo*-terr) *nt* (pl ∼) feed; chow

Futter² (*foo*-terr) *nt* (pl ∼) lining

G

Gabe (*gaa*-ber) *f* (pl ∼n) gift; faculty

Gabel (*gaa*-berl) *f* (pl ∼n) fork

gabeln (*gaa*-berln) *v*: **sich ∼** fork

Gabelung (*gaa*-ber-loong) *f* (pl ∼en) fork

gähnen (*gai*-nern) *v* yawn

Galerie (gah-ler-*ree*) *f* (pl ∼n) gallery

Galle (*gah*-ler) *f* gall; bile

Gallenblase (*gah*-lern-blaa-zer) *f* (pl ∼n) gall bladder

Gallenstein (*gah*-lern-shtighn) *m* (pl ∼e) gallstone

Galopp (gah-*lop*) *m* gallop

Gang¹ (gahng) *m* (pl ∼e) aisle; course; gear

Gang² (gahng) *m* walk, pace; **in ∼ *bringen** launch

Gangschaltung (*gahng*-shahl-toong) *f* gearshift, gear lever

Gans (gahns) *f* (pl ∼e) goose

Gänsehaut (*gehn*-zer-hout) *f* goose flesh, goose bumps *Am*

ganz (gahnts) *adj* whole; total, entire, complete; *adv* entirely; quite

Ganze (*gahn*-tser) *nt* whole

gänzlich (*gehnts*-likh) *adj* total, utter; *adv* altogether, wholly, completely

Garage (gah-*raa*-zher) *f* (pl ∼n) garage

Garantie (gah-rahn-*tee*) *f* (pl ∼n) guarantee

garantieren (gah-rahn-*tee*-rern) *v* guarantee

Garderobe (gahr-der-*rōa*-ber) *f* (pl ∼n) cloakroom; wardrobe; checkroom *Am*

Garderobenschrank (gahr-der-*rōa*-bern-shrahngk) *m* (pl ∼e) closet *Am*

Garderobenständer (gahr-der-*rōa*-bern-shtehn-derr) *m* (pl ∼) hat rack

Gardine (gahr-*dee*-ner) *f* curtain

*gären (*gai*-rern) *v* ferment

Garn (gahrn) *nt* (pl ∼e) yarn

Garnele (gahr-*nāy*-ler) *f* (pl ∼n) shrimp

garstig (*gahrs*-tikh) *adj* nasty

Garten (*gahr*-tern) *m* (pl ∼) garden; **zoologischer ∼** zoological gardens

Gartenbau (*gahr*-tern-bou) *m* horticulture

Gärtner (*gehrt*-nerr) *m* (pl ∼) gardener

Gärtnerei (gehrt-ner-*righ*) *f* market garden; nursery

Gärtnerin (*gehrt*-ner-rin) *f* (pl ∼nen) gardener

Gas (gaass) *nt* (pl ∼e) gas

Gasherd (*gaass*-hāyrt) *m* (pl ∼e) gas cooker

Gasofen (*gaass*-ōā-fern) *m* (pl ∼) gas stove

Gaspedal (*gaass*-pay-daal) *nt* (pl ∼e) accelerator

Gasse (*gah*-ser) *f* alley, lane

Gast (gahst) *m* (pl ∼e) visitor, guest

Gästezimmer (*gehss*-ter-tsi-merr) *nt* (pl ∼) spare room, guest room

gastfreundlich (*gahst*-froint-likh) *adj* hospitable

Gastfreundschaft (*gahst*-froint-shahft) *f* hospitality

Gastgeber (*gahst*-gāy-berr) *m* (pl ∼), **-in** *f* host(ess)

Gasthof (*gahst*-hōaf) *m* (pl ∼e) inn

Gaststätte (*gahst*-shteh-ter) *f* (pl ∼n) restaurant; roadhouse *Am*

Gatte (*gah*-ter) *m* (pl ∼n) husband

Gatter (*gah*-terr) *nt* (pl ∼) fence

Gattin (*gah*-tin) *f* (pl ∼nen) wife

Gattung (*gah*-toong) *f* (pl ∼en) breed

Gebäck (ger-*behk*) *nt* cake, pastry

Gebärde (ger-*bair*-der) *f* (pl ∼n) sign

Gebärmutter (ger-*bair*-moo-terr) *f* womb

Gebäude (ger-*boi*-der) *nt* (pl ∼) building; construction, house, premises *pl*

*geben (*gay*-bern) *v* *give

Gebet (ger-*bayt*) *nt* (pl ~e) prayer

Gebiet (ger-*beet*) *nt* (pl ~e) zone, area, region; territory; field

Gebirge (ger-*beer*-ger) *nt* (pl ~) mountain range

gebirgig (ger-*beer*-gikh) *adj* mountainous

Gebirgspass (ger-*beerks*-pahss) *m* (pl ~e) mountain pass

Gebiss (ger-*biss*) *nt* (pl ~e) denture; **künstliches** ~ false teeth

geboren (ger-*bōa*-rern) *adj* born

Gebrauch (ger-*broukh*) *m* use

gebrauchen (ger-*brou*-khern) *v* apply, use; **gebraucht** *adj* second-hand

Gebrauchsanweisung (ger-*broukhs*-ahn-vigh-zoong) *f* (pl ~en) directions for use

Gebrauchsgegenstand (ger-*broukhs*-*gay*-gern-shtahnt) *m* (pl ~e) utensil

Gebühr (ger-*bēwr*) *f* (pl ~en) charge; **Gebühren** dues *pl*; **gebühren-pflichtige Verkehrsstraße** turnpike *Am*

gebührend (ger-*bēw*-rernt) *adj* proper

Geburt (ger-*bōort*) *f* (pl ~en) birth

Geburtsort (ger-*bōorts*-ort) *m* (pl ~e) place of birth

Geburtstag (ger-*boorts*-taak) *m* (pl ~e) birthday

Gedächtnis (ger-*dehkht*-niss) *nt* memory

Gedanke (ger-*dahng*-ker) *m* (pl ~n) thought; idea

gedankenlos (ger-*dahng*-kern-*lōass*) *adj* careless

Gedankenstrich (ger-*dahng*-kern-shtrikh) *m* (pl ~e) dash

Gedenkfeier (ger-*dehngk*-figh-err) *f* (pl ~n) commemoration

Gedicht (ger-*dikht*) *nt* (pl ~e) poem

Geduld (ger-*doolt*) *f* patience

geduldig (ger-*dool*-dikh) *adj* patient

geeignet (ger-*igh*-gnert) *adj* convenient, suitable, proper, appropriate

Gefahr (ger-*faar*) *f* (pl ~en) danger; risk, peril

gefährlich (ger-*fair*-likh) *adj* dangerous; perilous

Gefährte (ger-*fair*-ter) *m* (pl ~n) companion

Gefährtin (ger-*fair*-tin) *f* (pl ~nen) companion

Gefälle (ger-*feh*-ler) *nt* gradient

*gefallen (ger-*fah*-lern) *v* please

gefällig (ger-*feh*-likh) *adj* obliging; enjoyable

Gefälligkeit (ger-*feh*-likh-kight) *f* (pl ~en) favo(u)r

gefangen *adj* caught, captured; ~ ***nehmen** *v* capture

Gefangene (ger-*fahng*-er-ner) *m/f* (pl ~n) prisoner

Gefängnis (ger-*fehng*-niss) *nt* (pl ~se) jail, prison

Gefäß (ger-*faiss*) *nt* (pl ~e) vessel

Gefecht (ger-*fehkht*) *nt* (pl ~e) combat

Geflügel (ger-*flēw*-gerl) *nt* fowl, poultry

Geflügelhändler (ger-*flēw*-gerl-hehn-dlerr) *m* (pl ~), **-in** *f* poulterer

Geflüster (ger-*flewss*-terr) *nt* whisper

gefräßig (ger-*frai*-sikh) *adj* greedy

*gefrieren (ger-*free*-rern) *v* *freeze

Gefrierpunkt (ger-*freer*-poongkt) *m* freezing point

Gefrierkost (ger-*freer*-kost) *f* frozen food

Gefrierschutzmittel (ger-*freer*-shoots-mi-terl) *nt* (pl ~) antifreeze

Gefühl (ger-*fēwl*) *nt* (pl ~e) feeling

gefüllt (ger-*fewlt*) *adj* stuffed

gegen (*gay*-gern) *prep* against; versus

Gegend (*gay*-gernt) *f* (pl ~en) region,

area; district, country

Gegensatz (*gāy*-gern-zahts) *m* (pl *x*e) contrast

gegensätzlich (*gāy*-gern-zehts-likh) *adj* opposite

gegenseitig (*gāy*-gern-zigh-tikh) *adj* mutual

Gegenstand (*gāy*-gern-shtahnt) *m* (pl *x*e) article, object

Gegenteil (*gāy*-gern-tighl) *nt* reverse, contrary; **im** *~* on the contrary

gegenüber (*gāy*-gern-*ēw*-berr) *prep* opposite, facing

***gegenüberstehen** (*gāy*-gern-*ēw*-berr-shtāy-ern) *v* face

Gegenwart (*gāy*-gern-vahrt) *f* present; presence

gegenwärtig (*gāy*-gern-vehr-tikh) *adj* present; current

Gegenwind (*gāy*-gern-vint) *m* head wind

Gegner (*gāy*-gnerr) *m* (pl *~*), **-in** *f* opponent

Gehalt (ger-*hahlt*) *nt* (pl *x*er) salary, pay

Gehaltserhöhung (ger-*hahlts*-ehr-hūr-oong) *f* (pl *x*en) rise

gehässig (ger-*heh*-sikh) *adj* spiteful

geheim (ger-*highm*) *adj* secret

Geheimnis (ger-*highm*-niss) *nt* (pl *x*se) secret; mystery

geheimnisvoll (ger-*highm*-niss-fol) *adj* mysterious

***gehen** (*gāy*-ern)*v* *go; walk

Gehirn (ger-*heern*) *nt* (pl *x*e) brain

Gehirnerschütterung (ger-*heern*-ehr-shew-ter-roong) *f* concussion

Gehör (ger-*hūr*) *nt* hearing

gehorchen (ger-*hor*-khern) *v* obey

gehören (ger-*hūr*-rern) *v* belong

Gehorsam (ger-*hōar*-zaam) *m* obedience

gehorsam (ger-*hōar*-zaam) *adj* obedient

Gehsteig (*gāy*-shtigh) *m* pavement, *Am* sidewalk

Gehweg (*gāy*-vāyk) *m* (pl *x*e) sidewalk *Am*

Geier (*gigh*-err) *m* (pl *~*) vulture

Geige (*gigh*-ger) *f* (pl *x*n) violin

geil *adj colloquial* super, 'brilliant; *vulgar* randy

Geisel (*gigh*-zerl) *f* (pl *x*n) hostage

Geist (gighst) *m* (pl *x*er) ghost, soul, spirit, mind; spook

geistig (*gighss*-tikh) *adj* mental; spiritual

Geistliche (*gighst*-li-kher) *m/f* (pl *x*n) minister, clergyman, clergywoman

geistreich (*gighst*-righkh) *adj* witty

geizig (*gigh*-tsikh) *adj* miserly, stingy

gekrümmt (ger-*krewmt*) *adj* curved

Gelächter (ger-*lehkh*-terr) *nt* laughter

gelähmt (ger-*laimt*) *adj* lame

Gelände (ger-*lehn*-der) *nt* terrain; site

Geländer (ger-*lehn*-derr) *nt* (pl *~*) rail

gelassen (ger-*lah*-sern) *adj* quiet

gelb (gehlp) *adj* yellow

Gelbsucht (*gehlp*-zookht) *f* jaundice

Geld (gehlt) *nt* money

Geldanlage (*gehlt*-ahn-laa-ger) *f* (pl *x*n) investment

Geldautomat (*gehlt*-ou-toa-maat) *m* (pl *x*en) cash dispenser, automatic teller *Am*

Geldbeutel (*gehlt*-boi-terl) *m* (pl *~*) purse

Geldstrafe (*gehlt*-shtraa-fer) *f* (pl *x*n) fine

gelegen (ger-*lāy*-gern) *adj* situated

Gelegenheit (ger-*lāy*-gern-hight) *f* (pl *x*en) chance, opportunity, occasion

Gelegenheitskauf (ger-*lāy*-gern-hights-kouf) *m* (pl *x*e) bargain

gelegentlich (ger-*lāy*-gernt-likh) *adv* occasionally

Gelehrte (ger-*lāyr*-ter) *m/f* (pl *x*n) scholar

Gelenk (ger-*lehngk*) *nt* (pl ⁓e) joint

gelenkig (ger-*lehng*-kikh) *adj* supple

geliebt (ger-*leept*) *adj* beloved

***gelingen** (ger-*ling*-ern) *v* manage, succeed

***gelten** (*gehl*-tern) *v* *be valid, apply

Gemälde (ger-*mail*-der) *nt* (pl ⁓) picture, painting

gemäß (ger-*maiss*) *prep* according to; in accordance with

gemäßigt (ger-*mai*-sikht) *adj* moderate

gemein (ger-*mighn*) *adj* vulgar, coarse

Gemeinde (ger-*mighn*-der) *f* (pl ⁓n) community; congregation

gemeinsam (ger-*mighn*-zaam) *adj* common; *adv* jointly

Gemeinschaft (ger-*mighn*-shahft) *f* community

gemeinschaftlich (ger-*mighn*-shahft-likh) *adj* joint

gemischt (ger-*misht*) *adj* mixed

Gemüse (ger-*mēw*-zer) *nt* (pl ⁓) greens *pl*, vegetable

Gemüsegarten (ger-*mēw*-zer-gahr-tern) *m* (pl ⁓) kitchen garden

Gemüsehändler (ger-*mēw*-zer-hehn-dlerr) *m* (pl ⁓), **-in** *f* greengrocer; vegetable merchant

gemütlich (ger-*mēwt*-likh) *adj* cosy, cozy *Am*

genau (ger-*nou*) *adj* exact; precise, accurate, careful, punctual; correct; *adv* just, exactly

genehmigen (ger-*nāy*-mi-gern) *v* approve

Genehmigung (ger-*nāy*-mi-goong) *f* (pl ⁓en) permission, authorization; permit

geneigt (ger-*nighkt*) *adj* inclined

General (gay-nay-*raal*) *m* (pl ⁓e) general

Generation (gay-nay-rah-*tsᵞōan*) *f* (pl ⁓en) generation

Generator (gay-nay-*raa*-tor) *m* (pl ⁓en) generator

***genesen** (ger-*nāy*-zern) *v* recover

Genesung (ger-*nāy*-zoong) *f* cure, recovery

Genie (zhay-*nee*) *nt* (pl ⁓s) genius

***genießen** (ger-*nee*-sern) *v* enjoy

Genossenschaft (ger-*no*-sern-shahft) *f* (pl ⁓en) cooperative

genug (ger-*nōōk*) *adv* enough

genügend (ger-*nēw*-gernt) *adj* enough, sufficient

Genugtuung (ger-*nōōk*-tōō-oong) *f* satisfaction

Genuss (ger-*nooss*) *m* (pl ⁓e) enjoyment, delight

Geologie (gay-oa-loa-*gee*) *f* geology

Geometrie (gay-oa-may-*tree*) *f* geometry

Gepäck (ger-*pehk*) *nt* luggage, baggage

Gepäckaufbewahrung (ger-*pehk*-ouf-ber-vaa-roong) *f* left luggage office; baggage check *Am*

Gepäcknetz (ger-*pehk*-nehts) *nt* (pl ⁓e) luggage rack

Gepäckwagen (ger-*pehk*-vaa-gern) *m* (pl ⁓) luggage van

Geplauder (ger-*plou*-derr) *nt* chat

gerade (ger-*raa*-der) *adj* straight; even; *adv* just

geradeaus (ger-raa-der-*ouss*) *adv* straight on, straight ahead

geradewegs (ger-*raa*-der-*vāyks*) *adv* straight

Gerät (ger-*rait*) *nt* (pl ⁓e) appliance; tool, implement, utensil

geräumig (ger-*roi*-mikh) *adj* spacious, roomy, large

Geräusch (ger-*roish*) *nt* (pl ⁓e) noise

gerecht (ger-*rehkht*) *adj* fair; righteous, right, just

Gerechtigkeit (ger-*rehkh*-tikh-kight) *f* justice

Gericht (ger-*rikht*) *nt* (pl ⁓e) court; dish

Gerichtshof (ger-*rikhts*-hoāf) *m* (pl ⁓e) law court

Gerichtsverfahren (ger-*rikhts*-fehr-faa-rern) *nt* (pl ⁓) lawsuit, trial

gering (ger-*ring*) *adj* minor, small; **geringer** inferior; **geringst** least

geringfügig (ger-*ring*-fēw-gikh) *adj* petty, slight

Geringschätzung (ger-*ring*-shehtsoong) *f* contempt

*gerinnen (ger-*ri*-nern) *v* coagulate

Gerippe (ger-*ri*-per) *nt* (pl ⁓) skeleton

gern (gehrn) *adv* willingly; **⁓ *haben** like, care for, love; **⁓ *mögen** like, *be fond of

gerne (*gehr*-ner) *adv* gladly

Gerste (*gehrs*-ter) *f* barley

Geruch (ger-*rookh*) *m* (pl ⁓e) smell, odo(u)r

Gerücht (ger-*rewkht*) *nt* (pl ⁓e) rumo(u)r

Gerüst (ger-*rewst*) *nt* (pl ⁓e) scaffolding

gesamt (ger-*zahmt*) *adj* overall

Gesamtsumme (ger-*zahmt*-zoo-mer) *f* (pl ⁓n) total

Gesäß (ger-*zaiss*) *nt* (pl ⁓e) bottom

Geschäft (ger-*shehft*) *nt* (pl ⁓e) shop; business; deal; **Geschäfte machen mit** *deal with

geschäftlich (ger-*shehft*-likh) *adj* on business

Geschäftsfrau (ger-*shehfts*-frou) *f* (pl -en) tradeswoman, businesswoman

Geschäftsführer (ger-*shehfts*-fēw-rerr) *m* (pl ⁓), **-in** *f* manager, managing director

Geschäftsmann (ger-*shehfts*-mahn) *m* (pl -leute) tradesman, businessman

geschäftsmäßig (ger-*shehfts*-mai-sikh) *adj* business-like

Geschäftsreise (ger-*shehfts*-righ-zer) *f* (pl ⁓n) business trip

Geschäftszeit (ger-*shehfts*-tsight) *f* (pl ⁓en) business hours

*geschehen (ger-*shāy*-ern) *v* happen, occur

gescheit (ger-*shight*) *adj* smart, clever

Geschenk (ger-*shehngk*) *nt* (pl ⁓e) gift, present

Geschichte (ger-*shikh*-ter) *f* (pl ⁓n) history; story, tale

geschichtlich (ger-*shikht*-likh) *adj* historical

Geschick (ger-*shik*) *nt* fortune

geschickt (ger-*shikt*) *adj* skilful, skilled

Geschirr (ger-*sheer*) *nt* dishes *pl*, crockery, tableware

Geschirrtuch (ger-*sheer*-tōōkh) *nt* (pl ⁓er) tea cloth; kitchen towel *Am*

Geschlecht (ger-*shlehkht*) *nt* (pl ⁓er) sex; gender

Geschlechtskrankheit (ger-*shlehkhts*-krahngk-hight) *f* (pl ⁓en) venereal disease

geschlossen (ger-*shlo*-sern) *adj* shut, closed

Geschmack (ger-*shmahk*) *m* taste; flavo(u)r

geschmacklos (ger-*shmahk*-lōāss) *adj* tasteless

geschmeidig (ger-*shmigh*-dikh) *adj* supple, flexible; smooth

Geschöpf (ger-*shurpf*) *nt* (pl ⁓e) creature

Geschoss¹ (ger-*shoss*), **Geschoß** (ger-*shohs*) *nt* (pl ⁓e), floor

Geschoss² (ger-*shoss*), **Geschoß** (ger-*shohs*) *nt* (pl ⁓e), missile; bullet

Geschwätz (ger-*shvehts*) *nt* chat

geschwind (ger-*shvint*) *adj* swift

Geschwindigkeit (ger-*shvin*-dikh-kight) *f* (pl ⁓en) speed; rate

Geschwindigkeitsbegrenzung (ger-*shvin*-dikh-kights-ber-grehn-tsoong)

f (pl ~en) speed limit

Geschwindigkeitsmesser (ger-*shvin*-dikh-kights-meh-serr) *m* (pl ~) speedometer

Geschwindigkeitsübertretung (ger-*shvin*-dikh-kights-ēw-berr-trāy-toong) *f* (pl ~en) speeding

Geschwister (ger-*shvis*-terr) *pl* brothers and sisters

geschwollen (ger-*shvo*-lern) *adj* swollen

Geschwulst (ger-*shvoolst*) *f* (pl ~e) tumo(u)r, growth; swelling

Geschwür (ger-*shvēwr*) *nt* (pl ~e) sore, ulcer

Gesellschaft (ger-*zehl*-shahft) *f* (pl ~en) society, company; **Gesellschafts-** social

Gesellschaftsanzug (ger-*zehl*-shahfts-ahn-tsōōk) *m* (pl ~e) evening dress

Gesetz (ger-*zehts*) *nt* (pl ~e) law

gesetzlich (ger-*zehts*-likh) *adj* lawful; legal

gesetzmäßig (ger-*zehts*-mai-sikh) *adj* legal

Gesicht (ger-*zikht*) *nt* (pl ~er) face

Gesichtscreme (ger-*zikhts*-krāym) *f* (pl ~s) face cream

Gesichtsmassage (ger-*zikhts*-mah-saa-zher) *f* (pl ~n) face massage

Gesichtspackung (ger-*zikhts*-pah-koong) *f* (pl ~en) face pack

Gesichtszug (ger-*zikhts*-tsōōk) *m* (pl ~e) feature

gesondert (ger-*zon*-derrt) *adv* separately

gespannt (ger-*shpahnt*) *adj* curious; tense

Gespenst (ger-*shpehnst*) *nt* (pl ~er) spook, phantom

Gespräch (ger-*shpraikh*) *nt* (pl ~e) conversation, talk; discussion

gesprächig (ger-*shprai*-khikh) *adj* talkative

gesprenkelt (ger-*shprehng*-kerlt) *adj* spotted

Gestalt (ger-*shtahlt*) *f* (pl ~en) figure

Geständnis (ger-*shtehnt*-niss) *nt* (pl ~se) confession

gestatten (ger-*shtah*-tern) *v* allow, permit

***gestehen** (ger-*shtāy*-ern) *v* confess

Gestell (ger-*shtehl*) *nt* (pl ~e) frame

gestern (*gehss*-terrn) *adv* yesterday

gestikulieren (gehss-ti-koo-*lee*-rern) *v* gesticulate

gestreift (ger-*shtrighft*) *adj* striped

Gestrüpp (ger-*shtrewp*) *nt* (pl ~e) scrub

gesund (ger-*zoont*) *adj* healthy, well

Gesundheit (ger-*zoont*-hight) *f* health

Getränk (ger-*trehngk*) *nt* (pl ~e) beverage; **alkoholfreies ~** soft drink; **alkoholische Getränke** spirits

Getreide (ger-*trigh*-der) *nt* corn, grain

getrennt (ger-*trehnt*) *adj* separate; *adv* separately

Getriebe (ger-*tree*-ber) *nt* gearbox

Getue (ger-*tōō*-er) *nt* fuss

geübt (ger-*ēwpt*) *adj* skilled

Gewächshaus (ger-*vehks*-houss) *nt* (pl ~er) greenhouse

gewagt (ger-*vaakt*) *adj* risky

gewähren (ger-*vai*-rern) *v* grant, extend

Gewalt (ger-*vahlt*) *f* violence, force; **vollziehende ~** executive

Gewaltakt (ger-*vahlt*-ahkt) *m* (pl ~e) act of violence

gewaltig (ger-*vahl*-tikh) *adj* huge

gewaltsam (ger-*vahlt*-zaam) *adj* violent

Gewand (ger-*vahnt*) *nt* (pl ~er) robe

gewandt (ger-*vahnt*) *adj* smart, skilful

Gewebe (ger-*vāy*-ber) *nt* (pl ~) tissue

Gewehr (ger-*vāyr*) *nt* (pl ~e) rifle, gun

Gewerbe (ger-*vehr*-ber) *nt* (pl ~)

trade, business

Gewerkschaft (ger-*vehrk*-shahft) *f* (pl ~en) trade union

Gewicht (ger-*vikht*) *nt* (pl ~e) weight

gewillt (ger-*vilt*) *adj* inclined

Gewinn (ger-*vin*) *m* (pl ~e) benefit; gain, profit, winnings *pl*

***gewinnen** (ger-*vi*-nern) *v* gain, *win

gewiss (ger-*viss*) *adj* certain

Gewissen (ger-*vi*-sern) *nt* conscience

Gewitter (ger-*vi*-terr) *nt* (pl ~) thunderstorm

gewöhnen (ger-*vūr*-nern) *v* accustom

Gewohnheit (ger-*vōan*-hight) *f* (pl ~en) custom, habit

gewöhnlich (ger-*vūrn*-likh) *adj* customary, plain, ordinary, usual; common; *adv* as a rule, usually

gewohnt (ger-*vōant*) *adj* accustomed; habitual, regular, normal; ~ ***sein** *be used to

gewöhnt (ger-*vūrnt*) *adj* accustomed

Gewölbe (ger-*vurl*-ber) *nt* (pl ~) arch; vault

gewunden (ger-*voon*-dern) *adj* winding

gewürfelt (ger-*vewr*-ferlt) *adj* chequered

Gewürz (ger-*vewrts*) *nt* (pl ~e) spice

gewürzt (ger-*vewrtst*) *adj* spiced

Gezeiten (ger-*tsigh*-tern) *pl* tides *pl*

geziert (ger-*tseert*) *adj* affected

Gicht (gikht) *f* gout

Giebel (*gee*-berl) *m* (pl ~) gable

Gier (geer) *f* greed

gierig (*gee*-rikh) *adj* greedy

***gießen** (*gee*-sern) *v* pour

Gift (gift) *nt* (pl ~e) poison

giftig (*gif*-tikh) *adj* poisonous

Gipfel (*gi*-pferl) *m* (pl ~) height, top, summit, peak

Gips (gips) *m* plaster

Gitarre (gi-*tah*-rer) *f* (pl ~n) guitar

Gitter (*gi*-terr) *nt* (pl ~) railing

Glanz (glahnts) *m* glare, gloss

glänzen (*glehn*-tsern) *v* *shine

glänzend (*glehn*-tsernt) *adj* brilliant, magnificent; glossy

Glanzleistung (*glahnts*-lighss-toong) *f* (pl ~en) feat

glanzlos (*glahnts*-lōass) *adj* mat, dull

Glas (glaass) *nt* (pl ~er) glass

gläsern (*glai*-zerrn) *adj* glass

glasieren (glah-*zee*-rern) *v* glaze

glatt (glaht) *adj* even; smooth

Glatteis (*glaht*-ighss) *nt* black ice

Glatze (*glah*-tser) *f* bald head, bald patch

Glaube (*glou*-ber) *m* belief; faith

glauben (*glou*-bern) *v* believe

gläubig (*gloi*-big) *adj* believing, religious

Gläubiger (*gloi*-bi-gerr) *m* (pl ~) creditor

glaubwürdig (*gloub*-vewr-dikh) *adj* credible

gleich (glighkh) *adj* equal; alike; level; even; *adv* alike

***gleichen** (*gligh*-khern) *v* resemble

gleichfalls (*glighkh*-fahls) *adv* also

gleichförmig (*glighkh*-furr-mikh) *adj* uniform

gleichgesinnt (*glighkh*-ger-zint) *adj* like-minded

Gleichgewicht (*glighkh*-ger-vikht) *nt* balance

gleichgültig (*glighkh*-gewl-tikh) *adj* indifferent

Gleichheit (*glighkh*-hight) *f* equality

Gleichstrom (*glighkh*-shtrōam) *m* direct current

gleichwertig (*glighkh*-vāyr-tikh) *adj* equivalent

gleichzeitig (*glighkh*-tsigh-tikh) *adj* simultaneous

Gleis (glighss) *nt* (pl ~e) track

***gleiten** (*gligh*-tern) *v* glide, *slide

Gletscher (*gleh*-cherr) *m* (pl ~) glacier

Glied (gleet) *nt* (pl ⁓er) limb; link

glitschig (*gli*-chikh) *adj* slippery

global (gloa-*baal*) *adj* broad

Glocke (*glo*-ker) *f* (pl ⁓n) bell

Glockenspiel (*glo*-kern-shpeel) *nt* (pl ⁓e) chimes *pl*

Glück (glewk) *nt* luck; happiness; fortune

glücklich (*glewk*-likh) *adj* lucky; happy, fortunate

Glückwunsch (*glewk*-voonsh) *m* (pl ⁓e) congratulation

Glühbirne (*glēw*-beer-ner) *f* (pl ⁓n) light bulb

glühen (*glēw*-ern) *v* glow

Glut (gloot) *f* glow

Gnade (*gnaa*-der) *f* grace; mercy

Gold (golt) *nt* gold

golden (*gol*-dern) *adj* golden

Goldschmied (*golt*-shmeet) *m* (pl ⁓e) goldsmith

Golf (golf) *m* (pl ⁓e) gulf; *nt* golf

Golfklub (*golf*-kloop) *m* (pl ⁓s) golfclub

Golfplatz (*golf*-plahts) *m* (pl ⁓e) golf links, golf course

Gondel (*gon*-derl) *f* (pl ⁓n) gondola

Gott (got) *m* (pl ⁓er) god

Gottesdienst (*go*-terss-deenst) *m* (pl ⁓e) (church) service

Göttin (*gur*-tin) *f* (pl ⁓nen) goddess

göttlich (*gurt*-likh) *adj* divine

Gouverneur (goo-vehr-*nūr*) *m* (pl ⁓e) governor

Grab (graap) *nt* (pl ⁓er) grave, tomb

Graben (*graa*-bern) *m* (pl ⁓) ditch

*graben (*graa*-bern) *v* *dig

Grabstein (*graap*-shtighn) *m* (pl ⁓e) gravestone, tombstone

Grad (graat) *m* (pl ⁓e) degree

Graf (graaf) *m* (pl ⁓en) earl, count

Gräfin (*grai*-fin) *f* (pl ⁓nen) countess

grämen (*grai*-mern) *v*: **sich ⁓** grieve

Gramm (grahm) *nt* (pl ⁓e) gram

Grammatik (grah-*mah*-tik) *f* grammar

Granit (grah-*neet*) *m* granite

Grafik (*graa*-fik) *f* (pl ⁓en) graph

grafisch (*graa*-fish) *adj* graphic

Gras (graass) *nt* grass

Grashalm (*graass*-hahlm) *m* (pl ⁓e) blade of grass

Grat (graat) *m* (pl ⁓e) ridge

Gräte (*grai*-ter) *f* (pl ⁓n) bone, fishbone

gratis (*graa*-tiss) *adv* free

gratulieren (grah-too-*lee*-rern) *v* congratulate, compliment

grau (grou) *adj* grey

grauenhaft (*grou*-ern-hahft) *adj* horrible

grausam (*grou*-zaam) *adj* cruel, harsh

gravieren (grah-*vee*-rern) *v* engrave

greifbar (*grighf*-baar) *adj* handy, available, tangible

*greifen (*grigh*-fern) *v* *take

Grenze (*grehn*-tser) *f* (pl ⁓n) frontier, border; boundary, limit, bound

Grieche (*gree*-kher) *m* (pl ⁓n) Greek

Griechenland (*gree*-khern-lahnt) Greece

Griechin (*gree*-khin) *f* (pl ⁓nen) Greek

griechisch (*gree*-khish) *adj* Greek

Griff (grif) *m* (pl ⁓e) grip, grasp; clutch

Grill (gril) *m* grill

Grille (*gri*-ler) *f* (pl ⁓n) cricket; whim

grillen (*gri*-lern) *v* grill

Grinsen (*grin*-zern) *nt* grin

grinsen (*grin*-zern) *v* grin

Grippe (*gri*-per) *f* flu, influenza

grob (grawp) *adj* rude, coarse, gross

Gros (gross) *nt* gross

groß (*grōass*) *adj* big; great, large, tall; major

großartig (*grōass*-ahr-tikh) *adj* terrific, grand, superb, magnificent

Großbritannien (*grōass*-bri-*tah*-nⁱern) Great Britain

Großbuchstabe (*grōass*-bookhshtaa-ber) *m* (pl ~n) capital letter

Größe (*grūr*-ser) *f* (pl ~n) size

Großeltern (*grōass*-ehl-terrn) *pl* grandparents *pl*

Großhandel (*grōass*-hahn-derl) *m* wholesale

Großhändler (*grōass*-hehn-dlerr) *m* (pl ~), **-in** *f* wholesale dealer

Großmutter (*grōass*-moo-terr) *f* (pl ~) grandmother

Großvater (*grōass*-faa-terr) *m* (pl ~) grandfather

*großziehen (*grōass*-tsee-ern) *v* *bring up; rear

großzügig (*grōass*-tsew-gikh) *adj* generous, liberal

Grotte (*gro*-ter) *f* (pl ~n) grotto

Grube (*grōo*-ber) *f* (pl ~n) hole, pit

grün (grewn) *adj* green; **grüne Versicherungskarte** green card

Grund (groont) *m* (pl ~e) ground; cause, reason; **Grund-** primary

gründen (grewn-dern) *v* establish, found; base

Grundgesetz (groont-ger-zehts) *nt* (pl ~e) constitution

Grundlage (groont-laa-ger) *f* (pl ~n) basis, base

grundlegend (groont-lāy-gernt) *adj* fundamental, essential, basic

gründlich (grewnt-likh) *adj* thorough

Grundriss (groont-riss) *m* (pl ~e) plan

Grundsatz (groont-zahts) *m* (pl ~e) principle

Grundschule (groont-shōo-ler) *f* primary school, elementary school

Grundstück (groont-shtewk) *nt* (pl ~e) grounds; property; (building) site

Gruppe (*groo*-per) *f* (pl ~n) group; set, party

gruselig (*grōo*-zer-likh) *adj* creepy

Gruß (grōoss) *m* (pl ~e) greeting

grüßen (*grēw*-sern) *v* greet; salute

gucken (*goo*-kern) *v* look

Gulasch (*goo*-lash) *nt* goulash

gültig (*gewl*-tikh) *adj* valid

Gummi (*goo*-mi) *m* rubber; gum

Gummiband (*goo*-mi-bahnt) *nt* (pl ~er) rubber band, elastic

Gunst (goonst) *f* grace

günstig (*gewns*-tikh) *adj* favo(u)rable

gurgeln (*goor*-gerln) *v* gargle

Gurke (*goor*-ker) *f* (pl ~n) cucumber

Gürtel (*gewr*-terl) *m* (pl ~) belt

Gusseisen (*gooss*-igh-zern) *nt* cast iron

gut (gōot) *adj* good; right; *adv* well; **gut!** all right!; well!; **~ gelaunt** in a good mood

Güter (*gēw*-terr) *ntpl* goods *pl*

Güterzug (*gēw*-terr-tsōok) *m* (pl ~e) goods train; freight train *Am*

gutgläubig (*gōot*-gloi-bikh) *adj* credulous

gütig (*gēw*-tikh) *adj* kind

gutmütig (*gōot*-mēw-tikh) *adj* good-natured

Gutschein (*gōot*-shighn) *m* (pl ~e) voucher

Gymnasium (gewm-*naa*-s^{y}oom) *nt* high school, grammar school

Gynäkologe (gew-neh-koa-*lōā*-ger) *m* (pl ~n) gynaecologist

Gynäkologin (gew-neh-koa-*lōā*-gin) *f* (pl ~nen) gynaecologist

H

Haar (*haar*) *nt* (pl ~e) hair

Haarbürste (*haar*-bewrs-ter) *f* (pl ~n) hairbrush

haarig (*haa*-rikh) *adj* hairy

Haarklemme (*haar*-kleh-mer) *f* (pl ~n) hairgrip; bobby pin *Am*

Haarnadel (*haar*-naa-derl) *f* (pl ~n) hairpin

Haarschnitt (*haar*-shnit) *m* (pl ~e) haircut

Habe (*haa*-ber) *f* possessions, belongings *pl*

***haben** (*haa*-bern) *v* *have

Habicht (*haa*-bikht) *m* (pl ~e) hawk

hacken (*hah*-kern) *v* chop

Hackfleisch (*hak*- flighsh) *nt* minced meat, mince

Hafen (*haa*-fern) *m* (pl ~) harbo(u)r, port

Hafer (*haa*-ferr) *m* oats *pl*

Haft (hahft) *f* custody, imprisonment

haftbar (*hahft*-baar) *adj* responsible

haften (*hahf*-tern) *v* *stick; *be liable, *be (held) responsible

Häftling (*hehft*-ling) *m* (pl ~e) prisoner

Hagel (*haa*-gerl) *m* hail

Hahn (haan) *m* (pl ~e) cock; tap

Hähnchen (*hain*-khern) *nt* chicken

Hai (high) *m* (pl ~e) shark

häkeln (*hai*-kerln) *v* crochet

Haken (*haa*-kern) *m* (pl ~) hook

halb (hahlp) *adj* half; **Halb-** semi-

halbieren (hahl-*bee*-rern) *v* halve

Halbinsel (*hahlp*-in-zerl) *f* (pl ~n) peninsula

Halbkreis (*hahlp*-krighss) *m* (pl ~e) semicircle

halbwegs (*hahlp*-vāyks) *adv* halfway

Halbzeit (*hahlp*-tsight) *f* half time

Hälfte (*hehlf*-ter) *f* (pl ~n) half

Halle (*hah*-ler) *f* (pl ~n) hall

hallo! (hah-*lōa*) hello!

Hals (hahls) *m* (pl ~e) neck; throat

Halsband (*hahls*-bahnt) *nt* (pl ~er) collar; beads *pl*

Halsentzündung (*hahls*-ehnt-tsewn-doong) *f* (pl ~en) laryngitis

Halskette (*hahls*-keh-ter) *f* (pl ~n) necklace

Halsschmerzen (*hahls*-shmehr-tsern) *mpl* sore throat

Halt (hahlt) *m* grip

haltbar (*hahlt*-baar) *adj* durable, lasting; strong, solid; tolerable

***halten** (*hahl*-tern) *v* *hold, *keep; **halt!** stop!; ~ **für** reckon, count

Haltestelle (*hahl*-ter-shteh-ler) *f* (pl ~n) stop

Haltung (*hahl*-toong) *f* (pl ~en) position

Hammelfleisch (*hah*-merl-flighsh) *nt* mutton

Hammer (*hah*-merr) *m* (pl ~) hammer

Hämorrhoiden (heh-moa-roa-*ee*-dern) *fpl* piles *pl*, h(a)emorrhoids *pl*

Hand (hahnt) *f* (pl ~e) hand; **Hand-** manual; **eine ~ voll** a handful

Handarbeit (*hahnt*-ahr-bight) *f* (pl ~en) handwork, handicraft; needlework

Handbremse (*hahnt*-brehm-zer) *f* (pl ~n) handbrake

Handbuch (*hahnt*-bōokh) *nt* (pl ~er) handbook

Handcreme (*hahnt*-krāym) *f* (pl ~s) hand cream

Händedruck (*hehn*-der-drook) *m* hand-shake

Handel (*hahn*-derl) *m* trade, commerce; business; **Handels-** commercial

handeln (*hahn*-derln) *v* act; trade; bargain

Handelsware (*hahn*-derls-vaa-rer) *f*
merchandise

Handfläche (*hahnt*-fleh-kher) *f* (pl
~n) palm

handgearbeitet (*hahnt*-ger-ahr-bigh-
tert) *adj* hand-made

Handgelenk (*hahnt*-ger-lehngk) *nt* (pl
~e) wrist

Handgepäck (*hahnt*-ger-pehk) *nt*
hand luggage, hand baggage *Am*

Handgriff (*hahnt*-grif) *m* (pl ~e)
handle

handhaben (*hahnt*-haa-bern) *v*
handle

Handkoffer (*hahnt*-ko-ferr) *m* (pl ~)
suitcase

Händler (*hehn*-dlerr) *m* (pl ~), **-in** *f*
merchant; trader, dealer

handlich (*hahnt*-likh) *adj* handy;
manageable

Handlung (*hahn*-dloong) *f* (pl ~en)
deed, action; plot

Handschellen (*hahnh*-sheh-lern) *fpl*
handcuffs *pl*

Handschrift (*hahnt*-shrift) *f* (pl ~en)
handwriting

Handschuh (*hahnt*-sh$\overline{oo}$) *m* (pl ~e)
glove

Handtasche (*hahnt*-tah-sher) *f* (pl ~n)
handbag, bag

Handtuch (*hahnt*-t$\overline{oo}$kh) *nt* (pl ~er)
towel

Handwerk (*hahnt*-vehrk) *nt*
handicraft

Handy *nt* mobile phone

Hanf (hahnf) *m* hemp

Hang (hahng) *m* (pl ~e) hillside

Hängebrücke (*hehng*-er-brew-ker) *f*
(pl ~n) suspension bridge

Hängematte (*hehng*-er-mah-ter) *f* (pl
~n) hammock

*hängen (*hehng*-ern) *v* *hang

Harfe (*hahr*-fer) *f* (pl ~n) harp

Harke (*hahr*-ker) *f* (pl ~n) rake

harmlos (*hahrm*-l$\overline{oo}$ass) *adj* harmless

Harmonie (hahr-moa-*nee*) *f* harmony

hart (hahrt) *adj* hard

hartnäckig (*hahrt*-neh-kikh) *adj*
dogged, obstinate, stubborn

Harz (hahrts) *m* resin

Hase (*haa*-zer) *m* (pl ~n) hare

Haselnuss (*haa*-zerl-nooss) *f* (pl ~e)
hazelnut

Hass (hahss) *m* hatred, hate

hassen (*hah*-sern) *v* hate

hässlich (*hehss*-likh) *adj* ugly

Hast (hahst) *f* haste

hastig (*hahss*-tikh) *adj* hasty

Haufen (*hou*-fern) *m* (pl ~) heap, lot;
pile; bunch

häufig (*hoi*-fikh) *adj* frequent; *adv*
often

Häufigkeit (*hoi*-fikh-kight) *f*
frequency

Haupt (houpt) *nt* (pl ~er) head; chief;
Haupt- capital; leading, main, chief;
major

Hauptbahnhof (*houpt*-baan-h$\overline{oa}$f) *m*
(pl ~e) central station

Häuptling (*hoipt*-ling) *m* (pl ~e)
chieftain

Hauptmahlzeit (*houpt*-maal-tsight) *f*
(pl ~en) dinner

Hauptquartier (*houpt*-kvahr-teer) *nt*
(pl ~e) headquarters *pl*

hauptsächlich (*houpt*-zehkh-likh) *adj*
cardinal, primary; *adv* especially,
mainly

Hauptstadt (*houpt*-shtaht) *f* (pl ~e)
capital

Hauptstraße (*houpt*-shtraa-ser) *f* (pl
~n) main road; main street

Hauptstrecke (*houpt*-shtreh-ker) *f* (pl
~n) main line

Hauptverkehrsstraße (*houpt*-fehr-
k$\overline{a}$yrs-shtraa-ser) *f* (pl ~n)
thoroughfare

Hauptverkehrszeit (*houpt*-fehr-kāyrs-tsight) f (pl ~en) rush hour, peak hour

Hauptwort (*houpt*-vort) nt (pl ≈er) noun

Haus (houss) nt (pl ≈er) house; home; **im ~** indoors, indoor; **nach Hause** home; **zu Hause** home, at home

Hausangestellte (*houss*-ahn-ger-shtehl-ter) f (pl ~n) housemaid

Hausarbeit (*houss*-ahr-bight) f (pl ~en) housekeeping, housework; homework

Hausbesitzer (*houss*-ber-zi-tserr) m (pl ~) landlord

Häuserblock (*hoi*-zerr-blok) m (pl ~s) house block *Am*

Hausfrau (*houss*-frou) f (pl ~en) housewife

Haushalt (*houss*-hahlt) m (pl ~e) housekeeping, household

Haushälter (*houss*-hehl-ter-r) m (pl ~), **-in** f housekeeper

häuslich (*hoiss*-likh) adj domestic

Hausmeister (*houss*-mighss-terr) m (pl ~), **-in** f janitor, caretaker, concierge

Hausschlüssel (*houss*-shlew-serl) m (pl ~) latchkey

Hausschuh (*houss*-shōō) m (pl ~e) slipper

Haustier (*houss*-teer) nt (pl ~e) pet

Haut (hout) f skin; hide

Hautausschlag (*hout*-ouss-shlaak) m rash

Hautkrem (*hout*-krāym) f (pl ~s) skin cream

Hebamme (*hāyp*-ah-mer) f (pl ~n) midwife

Hebel (*hāy*-berl) m (pl ~) lever

*heben (*hāy*-bern) v lift; raise

Hebräisch (hay-*brai*-ish) nt Hebrew

Hecht (hehkht) m (pl ~e) pike

Hecke (*heh*-ker) f (pl ~n) hedge

Heckenschütze (*heh*-kern-shew-tser) m (pl ~n) sniper

Heer (hāyr) nt (pl ~e) army

Hefe (*hāy*-fer) f yeast

Heft (hehft) nt (pl ~e) note-book; issue

heftig (*hehf*-tikh) adj fierce; violent, severe, intense

Heftklammer (*hehft*-klah-merr) f (pl ~n) staple

Heftpflaster (*hehft*-pflahss-terr) nt (pl ~) adhesive tape, plaster

Heide (*high*-der) f (pl ~n) heath, moor; m heathen, pagan

Heidekraut (*high*-der-krout) nt heather

Heidin (*high*-din) f (pl ~nen) heathen, pagan

heidnisch (*hight*-nish) adj heathen, pagan

heikel (*high*-kerl) adj precarious, critical

Heilbad (*highl*-baat) nt (pl ≈er) spa

Heilbutt (*highl*-boot) m (pl ~e) halibut

heilen (*high*-lern) v cure, heal

heilig (*high*-likh) adj holy, sacred

Heilige (*high*-li-ger) m/f (pl ~n) saint

Heiligtum (*high*-likh-tōōm) nt (pl ≈er) shrine

Heilmittel (*highl*-mi-terl) nt (pl ~) remedy

Heim (highm) nt (pl ~e) home; asylum

Heimat (*high*-maat) f home, native country

Heimatland (*high*-maat-lahnt) nt (pl ≈er) native country

*heimgehen (*highm*-gāy-ern) v *go home

heimlich (*highm*-likh) adj secret

Heimweh (*highm*-vāy) nt homesickness

Heirat (*high*-raat) f (pl ~en) wedding

heiraten (*high*-raa-tern) v marry

heiser (*high*-zerr) adj hoarse

heiß (highss) adj warm, hot

*heißen (*high*-sern) v *be called

heiter (*high*-terr) *adj* cheerful

Heiterkeit (*high*-terr-kight) *f* gaiety

heizen (*high*-tsern) *v* heat

Heizkörper (*hights*-kurr-perr) *m* (pl ~) radiator

Heizofen (*hights*-ōa-fern) *m* (pl ~) heater

Heizöl (*hights*-ūrl) *nt* fuel oil

Heizung (*high*-tsoong) *f* (pl ~en) heating

Held (hehlt) *m* (pl ~en) hero

*****helfen** (*hehl*-fern) *v* help; assist, aid

Helfer (*hehl*-ferr) *m* (pl ~), **-in** *f* helper

hell (hehl) *adj* bright, light; pale

hellhörig (*hehl*-hūr-rikh) *adj* noisy

Helm (hehlm) *m* (pl ~e) helmet

Hemd (hehmt) *nt* (pl ~en) shirt; vest

Henne (*heh*-ner) *f* (pl ~n) hen

her (hāyr) *adv* ago

herab (heh-*rahp*) *adv* down

herabsetzen (heh-*rahp*-zeh-tsern) *v* reduce, lower

*****herabsteigen** (heh-*rahp*-shtigh-gern) *v* descend

herannahend (heh-*rahn*-naa-ernt) *adj* oncoming

heraus (heh-*rouss*) *adv* out

herausfordern (heh-*rouss*-for-derrn) *v* challenge, dare

Herausforderung (heh-*rouss*-for-der-roong) *f* (pl ~en) challenge

*****herausgeben** (heh-*rouss*-gāy-bern) *v* publish

*****herausnehmen** (heh-*rouss*-nāy-mern) *v* *take out

herausstellen (heh-*rouss*-shteh-lern) *v*: **sich ~** prove

Herberge (*hehr*-behr-ger) *f* (pl ~n) hostel

Herbst (hehrpst) *m* autumn; fall *Am*

Herd (hāyrt) *m* (pl ~e) hearth; stove

Herde (*hāyr*-der) *f* (pl ~n) herd, flock

herein (heh-*righn*) in (here); **herein!** come in!

Hering (*hāy*-ring) *m* (pl ~e) herring

Herkunft (*hāyr*-koonft) *f* origin

Herr (hehr) *m* (pl ~en) gentleman; mister; **mein ~** sir

Herrentoilette (heh-rern-twah-leh-ter) *f* (pl ~n) men's room

Herrin (*heh*-rin) *f* (pl ~nen) mistress

herrlich (*hehr*-likh) *adj* wonderful, lovely; splendid

Herrschaft (*hehr*-shahft) *f* domination; dominion, rule, reign

herrschen (*hehr*-shern) *v* rule

Herrscher (*hehr*-sherr) *m* (pl ~), **-in** *f* ruler; sovereign

herstellen (*hāy*-r-shteh-lern) *v* manufacture; produce

herum (heh-*room*) *adv* about

herunter (heh-*roon*-terr) *adv* down

*****herunterlassen** (heh-*roon*-terr-lah-sern) *v* lower

hervorragend (hehr-*fōar*-raa-gernt) *adj* outstanding, excellent

Herz (hehrts) *nt* (pl ~en) heart

Herzklopfen (*hehrts*-klo-pfern) *nt* palpitation

herzlich (*hehrts*-likh) *adj* hearty, cordial

herzlos (*hehrts*-lōass) *adj* heartless

Herzog (*hehr*-tsōāk) *m* (pl ~e) duke

Herzogin (*hehr*-tsōā-gin) *f* (pl ~nen) duchess

Herzschlag (*hehrts*-shlaak) *m* (pl ~e) heart attack

Herzschrittmacher (*hehrts*-shrit-mah-kherr) *m* (pl ~) (cardiac) pacemaker

heterosexuell (*hay*-tay-roa-zeh-ksoo-ehl) *adj* heterosexual

Heu (hoi) *nt* hay

Heuchelei (hoi-kher-*ligh*) *f* hypocrisy

heucheln (*hoi*-kherln) *v* simulate

Heuchler (*hoikh*-lerr) *m* (pl ~), **-in** *f* hypocrite

heuchlerisch (*hoikh*-ler-rish) *adj*

hypocritical

heulen (*hoi*-lern) *v* roar

Heuschnupfen (*hoi*-shnoo-pfern) *m* hay fever

Heuschrecke (*hoi*-shreh-ker) *f* (pl ~n) grasshopper

heute (*hoi*-ter) *adv* today; ~ **Abend** tonight; ~ **Morgen** this morning; ~ **Nachmittag** this afternoon; ~ **Nacht** tonight

heutzutage (*hoit*-tsoo-taa-ger) *adv* nowadays

Hexe (*heh*-kser) *f* (pl ~n) witch

Hexenschuss (*heh*-ksern-shooss) *m* lumbago

hier (heer) *adv* here

Hierarchie (hi-ay-rahr-*khee*) *f* (pl ~n) hierarchy

Hilfe (*hil*-fer) *f* help; assistance, aid; **erste** ~ first aid

hilfreich (*hilf*-righkh) *adj* helpful

Himbeere (*him*-bāy-rer) *f* (pl ~n) raspberry

Himmel (*hi*-merl) *m* sky; heaven

hinab (hi-*nahp*) *adv* down

hinauf (hi-*nouf*) *adv* up

***hinaufsteigen** (hi-*nouf*-shtigh-gern) *v* ascend

hinaus (hi-*nouss*) *adv* out

hindern (*hin*-derrn) *v* hinder, embarrass; impede

Hindernis (*hin*-derr-niss) *nt* (pl ~se) obstacle; impediment

hinein (hi-*nighn*) *adv* in

***hineingehen** (hi-*nighn*-gāy-ern) *v* *go in

hinken (*hing*-kern) *v* limp

hinreichend (*hin*-righ-khernt) *adj* sufficient

Hinrichtung (*hin*-rikh-toong) *f* (pl ~en) execution

hinsichtlich (*hin*-zikht-likh) *prep* as regards, regarding, about, with reference to, concerning

hinten (*hin*-tern) *adv* behind

hinter (*hin*-terr) *prep* behind; after

Hintergrund (*hin*-terr-groont) *m* (pl ~e) background

Hinterhalt (*hin*-terr-hahlt) *m* (pl ~e) ambush

hinterlegen (hin-terr-*lāy*-gern) *v* deposit

Hintern (*hin*-terrn) *m* bottom

Hinterrad (*hin*-terr-raat) *nt* rear wheel, back wheel

Hinterseite (*hin*-terr-zigh-ter) *f* (pl ~n) rear

***hinübergehen** (hi-*nēw*-berr-gāy-ern) *v* cross

hinunter (hi-*noon*-terr) *adv* downstairs

hinzufügen (hin-*tsoo*-fēw-gern) *v* add

Hinzufügung (hin-*tsoo*-fēw-goong) *f* (pl ~en) addition

Hirt (heert) *m* (pl ~en), **-in** *f* shepherd

Historiker (hiss-*tōa*-ri-kerr) *m* (pl ~), **-in** *f* historian

historisch (hiss-*tōa*-rish) *adj* historic

Hitze (*hi*-tser) *f* heat

hoch (hōakh) *adj* high; tall

Hochebene (*hōakh*-āy-ber-ner) *f* (pl ~n) plateau

Hochland (*hōakh*-lahnt) *nt* uplands *pl*

hochmütig (*hōakh*-mēw-tikh) *adj* haughty, proud

hochnäsig (*hōakh*-nai-zikh) *adj* snooty

Hochsaison (*hōakh*-zeh-zawng) *f* high season, peak season

Hochsommer (*hōakh*-zo-merr) *m* midsummer

höchst (hūrkhst) *adj* extreme

höchstens (*hūrkhst*-erns) *adv* at most

Höchstgeschwindigkeit (*hūrkhst*-ger-shvin-dikh-kight) *f* speed limit

Hochzeit (*hokh*-tsight) *f* (pl ~en) wedding

Hochzeitsreise (*hokh*-tsights-righ-zer) *f* (pl ~n) honeymoon

*hochziehen (*hōakh*-tsee-ern) *v* pull up, hoist

Hof (*hōaf*) *m* (pl ~e) yard; court

hoffen (*ho*-fern) *v* hope

Hoffnung (*hof*-noong) *f* (pl ~en) hope

hoffnungslos (*hof*-noongs-lōass) *adj* hopeless

hoffnungsvoll (*hof*-noongs-fol) *adj* hopeful

höflich (*hūrf*-likh) *adj* polite, courteous, civil

Höhe (*hūr*-er) *f* (pl ~n) height; altitude

Höhepunkt (*hūr*-er-poongkt) *m* (pl ~e) height; zenith

höher (*hūr*-err) *adj* upper

hohl (*hōal*) *adj* hollow

Höhle (*hūr*-ler) *f* (pl ~n) cavern, cave; den

Höhlung (*hūr*-loong) *f* (pl ~en) cavity

Hohn (*hōan*) *m* scorn

holen (*hōa*-lern) *v* fetch; *get, collect

Holland (*ho*-lahnt) Holland

Holländer (*ho*-lehn-derr) *m* (pl ~) Dutchman

Holländerin (*ho*-lehn-der-rin) *f* (pl ~nen) Dutchwoman

holländisch (*ho*-lehn-dish) *adj* Dutch

Hölle (*hur*-ler) *f* hell

holperig (*hol*-per-rikh) *adj* rough, bumpy

Holz (*holts*) *nt* wood

hölzern (*hurl*-tserrn) *adj* wooden

Holzkohle (*holts*-kōa-ler) *f* charcoal

Holzschnitzerei (*holts*-shni-tser-righ) *f* (pl ~en) wood-carving

Holzschuh (*holts*-shōō) *m* (pl ~e) wooden shoe

homosexuell (*hoa*-moa-zeh-ksoo-ehl) *adj* homosexual

Honig (*hōa*-nikh) *m* honey

Honorar (hoa-noa-*raar*) *nt* (pl ~e) fee

Hopfen (*ho*-pfern) *m* hop

hörbar (*hūr*-baar) *adj* audible

hören (*hūr*-rern) *v* *hear

Hörer (*hūr*-rerr) *m* (pl ~) receiver

Horizont (hoa-ri-*tsont*) *m* horizon

Horn (horn) *nt* (pl ~er) horn

Horsd'œuvre (or-*dūr*vr) *nt* (pl ~s) hors-d'œuvre

Hose (*hōa*-zer) *f* (pl ~n) trousers *pl*, slacks *pl*; pants *plAm*; **kurze ~** shorts *pl*

Hosenanzug (*hōa*-zern-ahn-tsōok) *m* (pl ~e) pant suit

Hosenträger (*hōa*-sern-trai-gerr) *mpl* braces *pl*; suspenders *plAm*

Hotel (hoa-*tehl*) *nt* (pl ~s) hotel

hübsch (hewpsh) *adj* good-looking, pretty; nice, fair, lovely

Hubschrauber (*hoop*-shrou-berr) *m* (pl ~) helicopter

Huf (*hōof*) *m* (pl ~e) hoof

Hufeisen (*hōof*-igh-zern) *nt* (pl ~) horseshoe

Hüfte (hewf-ter) *f* (pl ~n) hip

Hügel (*hēw*-gerl) *m* (pl ~) hill

hügelig (*hēw*-ger-likh) *adj* hilly

Huhn (*hōōn*) *nt* (pl ~er) hen; chicken

Hühnerauge (*hēw*-nerr-ou-ger) *nt* (pl ~n) corn

huldigen (*hool*-di-gern) *v* hono(u)r

Huldigung (*hool*-di-goong) *f* (pl ~en) tribute, homage

Hülle (hew-ler) *f* (pl ~n) sleeve

Hummer (*hoo*-merr) *m* (pl ~) lobster

Humor (hoo-*mōar*) *m* humo(u)r

humorvoll (hoo-*mōar*-fol) *adj* humorous

Hund (hoont) *m* (pl ~e) dog

Hundehütte (*hoon*-der-hew-ter) *f* (pl ~n) kennel

hundert (*hoon*-derrt) *num* hundred

Hündin (*hewn*-din) *f* (pl ~nen) bitch

Hunger (*hoong*-err) *m* hunger

hungrig (*hoong*-rikh) *adj* hungry

Hupe (*hōō*-per) *f* (pl ~n) hooter; horn

hupen (*hōō*-pern) *v* hoot; toot *Am*,

honk *Am*
hüpfen (*hew*-pfern) *v* hop, skip
Hure (*hōō*-rer) *f* (pl ⁓n) whore
Husten (*hōōss*-tern) *m* cough
husten (*hōōss*-tern) *v* cough
Hut (hōōt) *m* (pl ⁓e) hat
hüten (*hēw*-tern) *v*: **sich ⁓** beware
Hütte (*hew*-ter) *f* (pl ⁓n) cabin, hut

Hygiene (hew-gʸ*āy*-ner) *f* hygiene
hygienisch (hew-gʸ*āy*-nish) *adj*
hygienic
Hymne (*hewm*-ner) *f* (pl ⁓n) hymn
Hypothek (hew-poa-*tāyk*) *f* (pl ⁓en)
mortgage
hysterisch (hewss-*tāy*-rish) *adj*
hysterical

I

ich (ikh) *pron* I
Ideal (i-day-*aal*) *nt* (pl ⁓e) ideal
ideal (i-day-*aal*) *adj* ideal
Idee (i-*dāy*) *f* (pl ⁓n) idea
identifizieren (i-dehn-ti-fi-*tsee*-rern) *v*
identify
Identifizierung (i-dehn-ti-fi-*tsee*-
roong) *f* (pl ⁓en) identification
identisch (i-*dehn*-tish) *adj* identical
Identität (i-dehn-ti-*tait*) *f* identity
idiomatisch (i-dʸoa-*maa*-tish) *adj*
idiomatic
Idiot (i-dʸ*ōat*) *m* (pl ⁓en), **-in** *f* idiot
Idol (i-*dōal*) *nt* (pl ⁓e) idol
Igel (*ee*-gerl) *m* (pl ⁓) hedgehog
ignorieren (i-gnoa-*ree*-rern) *v* ignore
ihm (eem) *pron* him
ihn (een) *pron* him
Ihnen (*ee*-nern) *pron* you
ihnen (*ee*-nern) *pron* them
Ihr (eer) *pron* your
ihr (eer) *pron* you; their; her
Ikone (i-*kōa*-ner) *f* (pl ⁓n) icon
illegal (*i*-lay-gaal) *adj* illegal
Illusion (i-loo-zʸ*ōan*) *f* (pl ⁓en) illusion
Illustration (i-looss-trah-*ts*ʸ*ōan*) *f* (pl
⁓en) illustration
illustrieren (i-looss-*tree*-rern) *v*
illustrate
imaginär (i-mah-gi-*nair*) *adj*

imaginary
Imbiss (*im*-biss) *m* (pl ⁓e) lunch; snack
Imitation (i-mi-tah-*ts*ʸ*ōan*) *f* (pl ⁓en)
imitation
immer (*i*-merr) *adv* always; ever; **⁓
wieder** again and again
immerzu (i-merr-*tsōō*) *adv* all the time
immunisieren (i-mōō-ni-*zee*-rern) *v*
immunize
Immunität (i-mōō-ni-*tait*) *f* immunity
impfen (*im*-pfern) *v* vaccinate,
inoculate
Impfung (*im*-pfoong) *f* (pl ⁓en)
vaccination, inoculation
imponieren (im-poa-*nee*-rern) *v*
impress
Import (im-*port*) *m* import
Importeur (im-por-*tūrr*) *m* (pl ⁓e)
importer
importieren (im-por-*tee*-rern) *v*
import
imposant (im-poa-*zahnt*) *adj*
imposing
impotent (*im*-poa-tehnt) *adj* impotent
Impotenz (*im*-poa-tehnts) *f* impotence
improvisieren (im-proa-vi-*zee*-rern) *v*
improvise
Impuls (im-*pools*) *m* (pl ⁓e) impulse,
urge
impulsiv (im-pool-*zeef*) *adj* impulsive

imstande (im-*shtahn*-der) *adv* able; ~ ***sein zu** *be able to

in (in) *prep* in; at, into, inside

indem (in-*dāym*) *conj* by; while

Inder (*in*-derr) *m* (pl ~), **-in** *f* Indian

Index (*in*-dehks) *m* (pl ~e) index

Indianer (in-*d*ʸ*aa*-nerr) *m* (pl ~), **-in** *f* (Red, American) Indian, native American

indianisch (in-*d*ʸ*aa*-nish) *adj* Indian

Indien (*in*-dʸern) India

indirekt (*in*-di-rehkt) *adj* indirect

indisch (*in*-dish) *adj* Indian

individuell (in-di-vi-doo-*ehl*) *adj* individual

Individuum (in-di-*vee*-doo-oom) *nt* (pl -duen) individual

Indonesien (in-doa-*nāy*-zʸern) Indonesia

Indonesier (in-doa-*nāy*-zʸerr) *m* (pl ~), **-in** *f* Indonesian

indonesisch (in-doa-*nāy*-zish) *adj* Indonesian

indossieren (in-do-*see*-rern) *v* endorse

Industrie (in-dooss-*tree*) *f* (pl ~n) industry

Industriegebiet (in-dooss-*tree*-ger-beet) *nt* (pl ~e) industrial area

industriell (in-dooss-tri-*ehl*) *adj* industrial

Infanterie (in-fahn-ter-*ree*) *f* infantry

Infektion (in-fehk-tsʸ*ōan*) *f* (pl ~en) infection

Infinitiv (*in*-fi-ni-teef) *m* (pl ~e) infinitive

Inflation (in-flah-tsʸ*ōan*) *f* inflation

infolge (in-*fol*-ger) *prep* owing to

Information (in-for-maa-tsʸ*ōan*) *f* (pl ~en) information

informell (*in*-for-mehl) *adj* informal

informieren (in-for-*mee*-rern) *v* inform

infrarot (*in*-frah-rōat) *adj* infra-red

Ingenieur (in-zhay-*n*ʸ*ūrr*) *m* (pl ~e) engineer

Ingwer (*ing*-verr) *m* ginger

Inhaber (*in*-haa-berr) *m* (pl ~), **-in** *f* occupant; bearer

inhaftieren (in-hahf-*tee*-rern) *v* imprison

Inhalt (*in*-hahlt) *m* contents *pl*

Inhaltsverzeichnis (*in*-hahlts-fehr-tsighkh-niss) *nt* (pl ~se) table of contents

Initiative (i-ni-tsʸ*ah*-*tee*-ver) *f* initiative

Injektion (in-ʸehk-tsʸ*ōan*) *f* (pl ~en) injection

inländisch (*in*-lehn-dish) *adj* domestic

inmitten (in-*mi*-tern) *prep* among, amid

innen (*i*-nern) *adv* inside

Innenseite (*i*-nern-zigh-ter) *f* (pl ~n) inside

inner (*i*-nerr) *adj* inside; internal

Innere (*i*-ner-rer) *nt* interior; **im Innern** within, inside

innerhalb (*i*-nerr-hahlp) *prep* within, inside

Inschrift (*in*-shrift) *f* (pl ~en) inscription

Insekt (in-*zehkt*) *nt* (pl ~en) insect; bug *Am*

Insektengift (in-*zehk*-tern-gift) *nt* (pl ~e) insecticide

Insektenschutzmittel (in-*zehk*-tern-shoots-mi-terl) *nt* (pl ~) insect repellent

Insel (*in*-zerl) *f* (pl ~n) island

insgesamt (ins-ger-*zahmt*) *adv* altogether

Inspektion (in-spehk-tsʸ*ōan*) *f* (pl ~en) inspection

inspizieren (in-spi-*tsee*-rern) *v* inspect

Installateur (in-stah-lah-*tūrr*) *m* (pl ~e) plumber

installieren (in-stah-*lee*-rern) *v* install

Instandhaltung (in-*shtahnt*-hahl-toong) *f* maintenance

Instandsetzung (in-*shtahnt*-zeh-tsoong) *f* repair

Instinkt (in-*stingkt*) *m* (pl ⁓e) instinct

Institut (in-sti-*tōōt*) *nt* (pl ⁓e) institute

Institution (in-sti-too-*ts*ʸ*ōān*) *f* (pl ⁓en) institution

Instrument (in-stroo-*mehnt*) *nt* (pl ⁓e) instrument

Intellekt (in-teh-*lehkt*) *m* intellect

intellektuell (in-teh-lehk-too-*ehl*) *adj* intellectual

intelligent (in-teh-li-*gehnt*) *adj* clever, intelligent

Intelligenz (in-teh-li-*gehnts*) *f* intelligence

intensiv (in-tehn-*zeef*) *adj* intense

interessant (in-tay-reh-*sahnt*) *adj* interesting

Interesse (in-tay-*reh*-ser) *nt* (pl ⁓n) interest

interessieren (in-tay-reh-*see*-rern) *v* interest

interessiert (in-tay-reh-*seert*) *adj* interested

intern (in-*tehrn*) *adj* internal; resident

Internat (in-tehr-*naat*) *nt* (pl ⁓e) boarding school

international (in-tehr-nah-ts*ʸ*oa-*naal*) *adj* international

Internet (*in*-tehr-neht) *nt* Internet

Interview (in-tehr-*v*ʸ*ōō*) *nt* (pl ⁓s) interview

intim (in-*teem*) *adj* intimate

Invalide (in-vah-*lee*-der) *m/f* (pl ⁓n) invalid

invalide (in-vah-*lee*-der) *adj* disabled, handicapped *Am*; invalid

Invasion (in-vah-z*ʸ*ōān) *f* (pl ⁓en) invasion

Inventar (in-vehn-*taar*) *nt* (pl ⁓e) inventory

investieren (in-vehss-*tee*-rern) *v* invest

Investition (in-vehss-ti-ts*ʸ*ōān) *f* (pl ⁓en) investment

inwendig (*in*-vehn-dikh) *adj* inner

inzwischen (in-*tsvi*-shern) *adv* in the meantime, meanwhile

Irak (i-*raak*) Iraq

irakisch (i-*raa*-kish) *adj* Iraqi

Iran (i-*raan*) Iran

Iraner (i-*raa*-nʸerr) *m* (pl ⁓), **-in** *f* Iranian

iranisch (i-*raa*-nish) *adj* Iranian

Ire (*ee*-rer) *m* (pl ⁓n) Irishman

irgendein (*eer*-gernt-ighn) *adj* any

irgendetwas (*eer*-gernt-eht-vahss) *pron* anything

irgendjemand (*eer*-gernt-ʸ*āy*-mahnt) *pron* anybody

irgendwie (*eer*-gernt-vee) *adv* anyhow

irgendwo (*eer*-gernt-vōa) *adv* somewhere

Irin (*ee*-rin) *f* (pl ⁓nen) Irishwoman

irisch (*ee*-rish) *adj* Irish

Irland (*eer*-lahnt) Ireland

Ironie (i-roa-*nee*) *f* irony

ironisch (i-*rōā*-nish) *adj* ironical

Irre (*i*-rer) *m/f* (pl ⁓n) lunatic

irre (*i*-rer) *adj* mad

irreal (*i*-ray-aal) *adj* unreal

irren (*i*-rern) *v* err; **sich ⁓** *be mistaken

irreparabel (i-reh-pah-*raa*-berl) *adj* irreparable

irritieren (i-ri-*tee*-rern) *v* annoy, irritate

Irrsinn (*eer*-zin) *m* lunacy

irrsinnig (*eer*-zi-nikh) *adj* lunatic

Irrtum (*eer*-tōōm) *m* (pl ⁓er) error, mistake

Island (*eess*-lahnt) Iceland

Isländer (*eess*-lehn-derr) *m* (pl ⁓), **-in** *f* Icelander

isländisch (*eess*-lehn-dish) *adj* Icelandic

Isolation (i-zoa-lah-ts*ʸ*ōān) *f* (pl ⁓en) isolation

isolieren (i-zoa-*lee*-rern) *v* isolate; insulate

Isolierung (i-zoa-*lee*-roong) *f* (pl ~en) insulation

Israel (*iss*-rah-ehl) Israel

Israeli (iss-rah-$\overline{ay}$-li) *m/f* (pl ~s) Israeli

israelisch (iss-rah-$\overline{ay}$-lish) *adj* Israeli

Italien (i-*taa*-l^{y}ern) Italy

Italiener (i-tah-*l^{y}ay*-nerr) *m* (pl ~), **-in** *f* Italian

italienisch (i-tah-*l^{y}ay*-nish) *adj* Italian

J

ja (^{y}aa) yes

Jacht (^{y}ahkht) *f* (pl ~en) yacht

Jacke (^{y}*ah*-ker) *f* (pl ~n) jacket

Jackett (zhah-*keht*) *nt* (pl ~s) jacket

Jade (^{y}*aa*-der) *m* jade

Jagd (^{y}aakt) *f* hunt, chase

jagen (^{y}*aa*-gern) *v* hunt

Jäger (^{y}*ai*-gerr) *m* (pl ~), **-in** *f* hunter

Jahr (^{y}aar) *nt* (pl ~e) year

Jahrestag (^{y}*aa*-rerss-taak) *m* (pl ~e) anniversary

Jahreszeit (^{y}*aa*-rerss-tsight) *f* (pl ~en) season

Jahrhundert (^{y}aar-*hoon*-derrt) *nt* (pl ~e) century

jährlich (^{y}*air*-likh) *adj* yearly, annual; *adv* per annum

jähzornig (^{y}*ai*-tsor-nikh) *adj* hot-tempered

Jalousie (zhah-loo-*zee*) *f* (pl ~n) blind; shutter

Jammer (^{y}*ah*-merr) *m* misery

jämmerlich (^{y}*eh*-merr-likh) *adj* lamentable

Januar (^{y}*ah*-noo-aar) January

Japan (^{y}*aa*-pahn) Japan

Japaner (^{y}ah-*paa*-nerr) *m* (pl ~), **-in** *f* Japanese

japanisch (^{y}ah-*paa*-nish) *adj* Japanese

je ... je (^{y}$\overline{ay}$) the ... the

Jeans (*bloo*-jeens) *pl* jeans *pl*; **Jeansjacke** *f* denim jacket

jedenfalls (^{y}*$\overline{ay}$*-dern-fahls) *adv* at any rate

jeder (^{y}*$\overline{ay}$*-derr) *pron* each, every; everyone

jedermann (^{y}*$\overline{ay}$*-derr-mahn) *pron* everyone, everybody; anyone

jedoch (^{y}ay-*dokh*) *conj* yet, but, only, however; *adv* though

jemals (^{y}*$\overline{ay}$*-maals) *adv* ever

jemand (^{y}*$\overline{ay}$*-mahnt) *pron* someone, somebody

jene (^{y}*$\overline{ay}$*-ner) *pron* those; those

jener (^{y}*$\overline{ay}$*-nerr) *pron* that; that

jenseits (^{y}*$\overline{ay}$n*-zights) *prep* across, beyond; *adv* beyond

Jersey (*jurr*-si) *m* (pl ~s) jersey

jetzt (^{y}ehtst) *adv* now; **bis ~** so far

jeweilig (^{y}*$\overline{ay}$*-vigh-likh) *adj* respective

Joch (^{y}okh) *nt* (pl ~e) yoke

Jockei (*jo*-ki) *m* (pl ~s) jockey

Jod (^{y}*$\overline{oa}$t*) *nt* iodine

Johannisbeere (^{y}*oa*-hah-niss-b$\overline{ay}$-rer) *f* (pl ~n) blackcurrant

Jolle (^{y}*o*-ler) *f* (pl ~n) dinghy

Jordanien (^{y}or-*daa*-n^{y}ern) Jordan

Jordanier (^{y}or-*daa*-n^{y}err) *m* (pl ~), **-in** *f* Jordanian

jordanisch (^{y}or-*daa*-nish) *adj* Jordanian

Journalismus (zhoor-nah-*liss*-mooss) *m* journalism

Journalist (zhoor-nah-*list*) *m* (pl ~en),

-in *f* journalist
Jubiläum (ʸoo-bi-*lai*-oom) *nt* (pl
-läen) jubilee
Jucken (ʸ*oo*-kern) *nt* itch
jucken (ʸ*oo*-kern) *v* itch
Jude (ʸ*oo*-der) *m* (pl ‿n) Jew
Jüdin (ʸ*oo*-din) *f* (pl ‿nen) Jew
jüdisch (ʸ*ew*-dish) *adj* Jewish
Jugend (ʸ*oo*-gernt) *f* youth
Jugendherberge (ʸ*oo*-gernt-hehr-
behr-ger) *f* (pl ‿n) youth hostel
jugendlich (ʸ*oo*-gernt-likh) *adj*
juvenile
Jugendliche (ʸ*oo*-gernt-li-kher) *m/f*
(pl ‿n) youth, teenager
Juli (ʸ*oo*-li) July

jung (ʸoong) *adj* young
Junge (ʸ*oong*-er) *m* (pl ‿n) boy; lad
Jungfrau (ʸ*oongk*-frou) *f* (pl ‿en)
virgin
Junggeselle (ʸ*oong*-ger-zeh-ler) *m*
(pl ‿n) bachelor
Juni (ʸ*oo*-ni) June
Jurist (ʸoo-*rist*) *m* (pl ‿en), **-in** *f*
lawyer
Justitiar (ʸoo-*sti*-tsi-aar) *m* lawyer,
legal adviser
Justiz (ʸoos-*teets*) *f* justice
Juwel (ʸoo-*vāyl*) *nt* (pl ‿en) jewel; gem
Juwelier (ʸoo-vay-*leer*) *m* (pl ‿e)
jeweller

K

Kabarett (kah-bah-*reht*) *nt* (pl ‿e)
cabaret; revue, floor show
Kabel (*kaa*-berl) *nt* (pl ‿) cable; flex;
electric cord
Kabelfernsehen (*kaa*-berl-fehrn-zāy-
ern) *nt* cable television
Kabeljau (*kaa*-berl-ʸou) *m* (pl ‿e) cod
Kabine (kah-*bee*-ner) *f* (pl ‿n) cabin
Kabinett (kah-bi-*neht*) *nt* (pl ‿e)
cabinet
Kachel (*kah*-kherl) *f* (pl ‿n) tile
Käfer (*kai*-ferr) *m* (pl ‿) beetle; bug
Kaffee (*kah*-fay) *m* coffee
Kaffeelöffel (*kah*-fay-lur-ferl) *m* (pl ‿)
coffee-spoon
Kaffeemaschine (*kah*-fay-mah-shee-
ner) *f* (pl ‿n) coffee machine
Käfig (*kai*-fikh) *m* (pl ‿e) cage
kahl (kaal) *adj* bald; naked, bare
Kai (kigh) *m* (pl ‿s) dock, wharf, quay
Kaiser (*kigh*-zerr) *m* (pl ‿) emperor
Kaiserin (*kigh*-zer-rin) *f* (pl ‿nen)

empress
kaiserlich (*kigh*-zerr-likh) *adj*
imperial
Kaiserreich (*kigh*-zerr-righkh) *nt* (pl
‿e) empire
Kajüte (kah-ʸ*ew*-ter) *f* (pl ‿n) cabin
Kakao (kah-*kou*) *m* cocoa; Getränk
(hot) chocolate
Kalb (kahlp) *nt* (pl ‿er) calf
Kalbfleisch (*kahlp*-flighsh) *nt* veal
Kalbleder (*kahlp*-lāy-derr) *nt* calf skin
Kalender (kah-*lehn*-derr) *m* (pl ‿)
calendar
Kalk (kahlk) *m* lime
Kalkulation (kahl-koo-lah-ts*ʸōān*) *f*
(pl ‿en) calculation
Kalorie (kah-loa-*ree*) *f* (pl ‿n) calorie
kalt (kahlt) *adj* cold
Kälte (*kehl*-ter) *f* cold
Kalzium (*kahl*-ts*ʸ*oom) *nt* calcium
Kamel (kah-*māyl*) *nt* (pl ‿e) camel
Kamera (*kah*-may-rah) *f* (pl ‿s)

camera

Kamin (kah-*meen*) m (pl ⁀e) fireplace

Kamm (kahm) m (pl ⁀e) comb

kämmen (*keh*-mern) v comb

Kampagne (kahm-*pah*-n^yer) f (pl ⁀n) campaign

Kampf (kahmpf) m (pl ⁀e) battle; combat, struggle, fight

kämpfen (*kehm*-pfern) v *fight; combat, struggle, battle

Kanada (kah-nah-dah) Canada

Kanadier (kah-*naa*-d^yerr) m (pl ⁀), **-in** f Canadian

kanadisch (kah-*naa*-dish) adj Canadian

Kanal (kah-*naal*) m (pl ⁀e) canal; channel

Kanarienvogel (kah-*naa*-r^yern-fōa-gerl) m (pl ⁀) canary

Kandidat (kahn-di-*daat*) m (pl ⁀en), **-in** f candidate

Känguru (kehng-goo-roo) nt (pl ⁀s) kangaroo

Kaninchen (kah-*neen*-khern) nt (pl ⁀) rabbit

Kanne (*kah*-ner) f can; pot

Kanone (kah-*nōa*-ner) f (pl ⁀n) gun

Kante (*kahn*-ter) f (pl ⁀n) edge

Kantine (kahn-*tee*-ner) f (pl ⁀n) canteen

Kanu (*kah*-nōō) nt (pl ⁀s) canoe

Kanzel (*kahn*-tserl) f (pl ⁀n) pulpit

Kap (kahp) nt (pl ⁀s) cape

Kapelle (kah-*peh*-ler) f (pl ⁀n) band; chapel

Kaper (*kaa*-perr) f (pl ⁀n) caper

kapern (*kaa*-perrn) v hijack

Kapital (kah-pi-*taal*) nt capital

Kapitalismus (kah-pi-tah-*liss*-mooss) m capitalism

Kapitän (kah-pi-*tain*) m (pl ⁀e) captain

Kapitel (kah-*pi*-terl) nt chapter

Kapitulation (kah-pi-too-lah-ts^y*ōan*) f (pl ⁀en) capitulation

Kapsel (*kah*-pserl) f (pl ⁀n) capsule

kaputt (kah-*poot*) adj broken

Kapuze (kah-*pōō*-tser) f (pl ⁀n) hood

Karamelle (kah-rah-*meh*-ler) f (pl ⁀n) caramel

Karat (kah-*raat*) nt carat

Kardinal (kahr-di-*naal*) m (pl ⁀e) cardinal; **Kardinal-** cardinal

kariert (kah-*reert*) adj chequered

karmesinrot (kahr-may-*zeen*-rōat) adj crimson

Karneval (*kahr*-ner-vahl) m carnival

Karo (*kaa*-roa) nt (pl ⁀s) check

Karosserie (kah-ro-ser-*ree*) f (pl ⁀n) motor body Am

Karotte (kah-*ro*-ter) f (pl ⁀n) carrot

Karpfen (*kahr*-pfern) m (pl ⁀) carp

Karren (*kah*-rern) m (pl ⁀) cart

Karriere (kah-r^y*ay*-rer) f (pl ⁀n) career

Karte (*kahr*-ter) f (pl ⁀n) card; map; ticket

Kartenspiel (*kahr*-tern-shpeel) nt card game

Kartoffel (kahr-*to*-ferl) f (pl ⁀n) potato

Karton (kahr-*tawng*) m (pl ⁀s) carton

Karussell (kah-roo-*sehl*) nt (pl ⁀s) merry-go-round

Kaschmir (*kahsh*-meer) m cashmere

Käse (*kai*-zer) m cheese

Kaserne (kah-*zehr*-ner) f (pl ⁀n) barracks pl

Kasino (kah-*zee*-noa) nt (pl ⁀s) casino

Kasse (*kah*-ser) f (pl ⁀n) pay desk; cashier Am; box office

Kassierer (kah-*see*-rerr) m (pl ⁀), **-in** f cashier

Kastanie (kahss-*taa*-n^yer) f (pl ⁀n) chestnut

kastanienbraun (kahss-*taa*-n^yern-broun) adj chestnut

Kasten (*kahss*-tern) m case, crate; box

Katakombe (kah-tah-*kom*-ber) f (pl ⁀n) catacomb

Katalog (kah-tah-*lōak*) m (pl ⁀e)

catalogue

Katarrh (kah-*tahr*) *m* (pl ⁓e) catarrh

Katastrophe (kah-tahss-*trōa*-fer) *f* (pl ⁓n) catastrophe, disaster

Kategorie (kah-tay-goa-*ree*) *f* (pl ⁓n) category

Kater (*kaa*-terr) *m* hangover

Kathedrale (kah-tay-*draa*-ler) *f* (pl ⁓n) cathedral

katholisch (kah-*tōa*-lish) *adj* catholic

Katze (*kah*-tser) *f* (pl ⁓n) cat; pussy-cat

kauen (*kou*-ern) *v* chew

Kauf (kouf) *m* (pl ⁓e) purchase

Kauffrau (*kouf*-frou) *f* (pl ⁓en) dealer; merchant

kaufen (*kou*-fern) *v* *buy; purchase

Käufer (*koi*-ferr) *m* (pl ⁓), **-in** *f* buyer, purchaser

Kaufhaus (*kouf*-houss) *nt* (pl ⁓er) department store

Kaufmann (*kouf*-mahn) *m* (pl -leute) dealer; merchant

Kaufpreis (*kouf*-prighss) *m* (pl ⁓e) purchase price

Kaugummi (*kou*-goo-mi) *m* chewing gum

kaum (koum) *adv* hardly, scarcely, barely

Kaution (kou-*tsʸōan*) *f* (pl ⁓en) bail

Kaviar (*kaa*-vi-ahr) *m* caviar

Kegelbahn (*kāy*-gerl-baan) *f* (pl ⁓en) bowling alley

Kegeln (*kāy*-gerln) *nt* bowling

Kehle (*kāy*-ler) *f* (pl ⁓n) throat

kehren (*kāy*-rern) *v* turn; sweep

Kehrseite (*kāyr*-zigh-ter) *f* (pl ⁓n) reverse

Keil (kighl) *m* (pl ⁓e) wedge

Keim (kighm) *m* (pl ⁓e) germ

kein (kighn) *pron* no

keiner (*kigh*-nerr) *pron* none; ⁓ **von beiden** neither

keinesfalls (*kigh*-nerss-fahls) *adv* by

no means

keineswegs (*kigh*-nerss-*vāyks*) *adv* by no means

Keks (kāyks) *m* (pl ⁓e) biscuit; cookie *Am*; cracker *Am*

Keller (*keh*-lerr) *m* (pl ⁓) cellar

Kellner (*kehl*-nerr) *m* (pl ⁓) waiter; bartender, barman

Kellnerin (*kehl*-ner-rin) *f* (pl ⁓nen) waitress

Kenia (*kāy*-nʸah) Kenya

***kennen** (*keh*-nern) *v* *know

Kenner (*keh*-nerr) *m* (pl ⁓) connoisseur

Kenntnis (*kehnt*-niss) *f* (pl ⁓se) knowledge

Kennzeichen (*kehn*-tsigh-khern) *nt* (pl ⁓) characteristic, feature; registration number; licence number *Am*

kennzeichnen (*kehn*-tsighkh-nern) *v* mark

Keramik (kay-*raa*-mik) *f* (pl ⁓en) ceramics *pl*

Kerl (kehrl) *m* (pl ⁓e) chap, fellow

Kern (kehrn) *m* (pl ⁓e) essence; heart, core; pip, stone; nucleus; **Kern-** nuclear

Kernenergie (*kehrn*-ay-nehr-gee) *f* nuclear energy

Kerngehäuse (*kehrn*-ger-hoi-zer) *nt* (pl ⁓) core

Kerosin (kay-roa-*zeen*) *nt* kerosene

Kerze (*kehr*-tser) *f* (pl ⁓n) candle

Kessel (*keh*-serl) *m* (pl ⁓) kettle

Kette (*keh*-ter) *f* (pl ⁓n) chain

keuchen (*koi*-khern) *v* pant

Keule (*koi*-ler) *f* (pl ⁓n) club

Khaki (*kaa*-ki) *nt* khaki

kichern (*ki*-kherrn) *v* giggle, chuckle

Kiebitz (*kee*-bits) *m* (pl ⁓e) pewit

Kiefer (*kee*-ferr) *m* (pl ⁓) jaw

Kiel (keel) *m* (pl ⁓e) keel

Kieme (*kee*-mer) *f* (pl ⁓n) gill

Kies (keess) *m* gravel

Kieselstein (*kee*-zerl-shtighn) *m* (pl ~e) pebble

Kilo (*kee*-loa) *nt* (pl ~s) kilogram

Kilometer (ki-loa-*māy*-terr) *m* (pl ~) kilometre, kilometer *Am*

Kilometerzahl (ki-loa-*māy*-terr-tsaal) *f* distance in kilometres (kilometers *Am*)

Kind (kint) *nt* (pl ~er) child; kid; **kleines ~** tot

Kindergarten (*kin*-derr-gahr-tern) *m* (pl ~) kindergarten

Kinderkrippe (*kin*-derr-kri-per) *f* (pl ~n) nursery

Kinderlähmung (*kin*-derr-lai-moong) *f* polio

Kindermädchen (*kin*-derr-mait-khern) *nt* (pl ~) nurse

Kinderwagen (*kin*-derr-vaa-gern) *m* (pl ~) pram; baby carriage *Am*

Kinderzimmer (*kin*-derr-tsi-merr) *nt* (pl ~) children's room, nursery

Kinn (kin) *nt* chin

Kino (*kee*-noa) *nt* (pl ~s) cinema; pictures; movie theater *Am*, movies *Am*

Kiosk (ki-*osk*) *m* (pl ~e) kiosk

Kirche (*keer*-kher) *f* (pl ~n) chapel, church

Kirchhof (*keerkh*-hōaf) *m* (pl ~e) graveyard, churchyard

Kirchturm (*keerkh*-toorm) *m* (pl ~e) steeple

Kirmes (*keer*-mehss) *f* (pl ~sen) fair

Kirsche (*keer*-sher) *f* (pl ~n) cherry

Kissen (*ki*-sern) *nt* (pl ~) cushion; pillow

Kissenbezug (*ki*-sern-ber-tsōok) *m* (pl ~e) pillowcase

Kiste (*kiss*-ter) *f* (pl ~n) crate

kitzeln (*ki*-tserln) *v* tickle

Klage (*klaa*-ger) *f* (pl ~n) complaint

klagen (*klaa*-gern) *v* complain

Klammer (*klah*-merr) *f* (pl ~n) clamp

Klang (klahng) *m* (pl ~e) sound; tone

Klaps (klahps) *m* (pl ~e) smack

klar (klaar) *adj* clear; pure; serene

klären (*klai*-rern) *v* clarify

klarstellen (*klaar*-shteh-lern) *v* clarify

Klasse (*klah*-ser) *f* (pl ~n) class; form

Klassenkamerad (*klah*-sern-kah-mer-raat) *m* (pl ~en), **-in** *f* classmate

Klassenzimmer (*klah*-sern-tsi-merr) *nt* (pl ~) classroom

klassisch (*klah*-sish) *adj* classical

klatschen (*klah*-chern) *v* clap

Klatschmohn (*klahch*-mōan) *m* (pl ~e) poppy

Klaue (*klou*-er) *f* (pl ~n) claw

Klausel (*klou*-zerl) *f* (pl ~n) clause, stipulation

Klavier (klah-*veer*) *nt* (pl ~e) piano

kleben (*klāy*-bern) *v* *stick; paste

Klebestreifen (*klāy*-ber-shtrigh-fern) *m* (pl ~) adhesive tape

klebrig (*klāy*-brikh) *adj* sticky

Klebstoff (*klāyp*-shtof) *m* (pl ~e) gum

Klecks (klehks) *m* (pl ~e) stain, spot, blot

Klee (klāy) *m* clover

Kleeblatt (*klāy*-blaht) *nt* (pl ~er) shamrock

Kleid (klight) *nt* (pl ~er) dress; frock, robe, gown; **Kleider** clothes *pl*

kleiden (*kligh*-dern) *v* suit; **sich ~** dress

Kleiderbügel (*kligh*-derr-bēw-gerl) *m* (pl ~) coat hanger

Kleiderhaken (*kligh*-derr-haa-kern) *m* (pl ~) peg

Kleiderschrank (*kligh*-derr-shrahngk) *m* (pl ~e) wardrobe

Kleidung (*kligh*-doong) *f* clothes *pl*

klein (klighn) *adj* little, small; minor, petty, short

Kleingeld (*klighn*-gehlt) *nt* petty cash, change

Kleinhandel (*klighn*-hahn-derl) *m*
retail trade

Kleinhändler (*klighn*-hehn-dlerr) *m*
(pl ~), **-in** *f* retailer

Kleinkind (*klighn*-kint) *nt* (pl ~er)
toddler

kleinlich (*klighn*-likh) *adj* stingy

Kleinod (*klighn*-ōāt) *nt* (pl ~e) gem

Klemme (*kleh*-mer) *f* (pl ~n) clamp

klettern (*kleh*-terrn) *v* climb

Klient (kli-*ehnt*) *m* (pl ~en), **-in** *f*
customer, client

Klima (*klee*-mah) *nt* climate

Klimaanlage (*klee*-mah-ahn-laa-ger)
f (pl ~n) air conditioning

klimatisiert (kli-mah-ti-*zeert*) *adj* air-
conditioned

Klinge (*kling*-er) *f* (pl ~n) blade

Klingel (*kling*-erl) *f* (pl ~n) bell

klingeln (*kling*-erln) *v* *ring (the bell)

*klingen (*kling*-ern) *v* sound

Klinik (*klee*-nik) *f* (pl ~en) clinic;
hospital

Klinke (*kling*-ker) *f* (door)handle

Klippe (*kli*-per) *f* (pl ~n) cliff

Klo (kl ōā) *nt colloquial* loo

Klopfen (*klo*-pfern) *nt* knock, tap

klopfen (*klo*-pfern) *v* knock

Kloster (*klōāss*-terr) *nt* (pl ~) cloister;
convent; monastery

Klotz (klots) *m* (pl ~e) block; log

Klub (kloop) *m* (pl ~s) club

klug (klōōk) *adj* bright, clever

Klumpen (*kloom*-pern) *m* (pl ~)
chunk; lump

klumpig (*kloom*-pikh) *adj* lumpy

knabbern (*knahb*-errn) *v* nibble

Knall (knahl) *m* crack, bang

knapp (knahp) *adj* scarce; tight;
concise

Knappheit (*knahp*-hight) *f* shortage

*kneifen (*knigh*-fern) *v* pinch

Kneifzange (*knighf*-tsahng-er) *f* (pl
~n) pincers *pl*

Kneipe (*knigh*-per) *f* (pl ~n) pub

Knie (knee) *nt* (pl ~) knee

knien (*knee*-ern) *v* *kneel

Kniescheibe (*knee*-shigh-ber) *f* (pl
~n) kneecap

knirschen (*kneer*-shern) *v* creak

Knoblauch (*knōāp*-loukh) *m* garlic

Knöchel (*knur*-kherl) *m* knuckle;
ankle

Knochen (*kno*-khern) *m* (pl ~) bone

Knopf (knopf) *m* (pl ~e) button; knob

knöpfen (*knur*-pfern) *v* button

Knopfloch (*knopf*-lokh) *nt* (pl ~er)
buttonhole

Knorpel (*knor*-perl) *m* cartilage

Knospe (*knoss*-per) *f* (pl ~n) bud

Knoten (*knōā*-tern) *m* (pl ~) knot

knoten (*knōā*-tern) *v* knot, tie

Knotenpunkt (*knōā*-tern-poongkt) *m*
(pl ~e) junction

Knüppel (*knew*-perl) *m* (pl ~) club

knusprig (*knooss*-prikh) *adj* crisp

Koch (kokh) *m* (pl ~e) cook

Köchin (*kur*-khin) *f* (pl ~nen) cook

Kochbuch (*kokh*-bōōkh) *nt* (pl ~er)
cookery book; cookbook *Am*

kochen (*ko*-khern) *v* cook; boil

Kocher (*ko*-kherr) *m* (pl ~) cooker

Kode (kōāt) *m* (pl ~s) code

Köder (*kūr*-derr) *m* (pl ~) bait

Koffein (ko-fay-*een*) *nt* caffeine

koffeinfrei (ko-fay-*een*-frigh) *adj*
decaffeinated

Koffer (*ko*-ferr) *m* (pl ~) case, bag;
trunk

Kofferraum (*ko*-ferr-roum) *m* (pl ~e)
boot; trunk *Am*

Kognak (*ko*-nʸahk) *m* cognac

Kohl (kōāl) *m* cabbage

Kohle (*kōā*-ler) *f* (pl ~n) coal

Kokain (koa-kah-*een*) *nt* cocaine

Kokosnuss (*kōā*-koss-nooss) *f* (pl ~e)
coconut

Kolben (*kol*-bern) *m* (pl ~) piston

Kolbenring (*kol*-bern-ring) *m* (pl ～e)
piston ring

Kollege (ko-*lāy*-ger) *m* (pl ～n)
colleague

Kollegin (ko-*lāy*-gin) *f* (pl ～nen)
colleague

Kollektion (ko-lehk-ts^y*ōan*) *f* (pl ～en)
collection

kollektiv (ko-lehk-*teef*) *adj* collective

Kolonie (koa-loa-*nee*) *f* (pl ～n) colony

Kolonne (koa-*lo*-ner) *f* (pl ～n) column

Kolumbianer (koa-loom-b^y*aa*-nerr)
m (pl ～), **-in** *f* Colombian

kolumbianisch (koa-loom-b^y*aa*-nish)
adj Colombian

Kolumbien (koa-*loom*-b^{y}ern)
Colombia

Koma (*kōa*-mah) *nt* coma

Kombination (kom-bi-nah-ts^y*ōan*) *f*
(pl ～en) combination

kombinieren (kom-bi-*nee*-rern) *v*
combine

Komfort (kom-*fōar*) *m* comfort

komfortabel (kom-for- *taa*-berl) *adj*
luxurious

Komiker (*kōa*-mi-kerr) *m* (pl ～), **-in** *f*
comedian

komisch (*kōa*-mish) *adj* funny, comic;
strange, queer

Komma (*ko*-mah) *nt* (pl ～ta) comma

***kommen** (*ko*-mern) *v* *come; ～
lassen *send for

Kommentar (ko-mehn-*taar*) *m* (pl ～e)
comment

kommentieren (ko-mehn-*tee*-rern) *v*
comment

kommerziell (ko-mehr-ts^y*ehl*) *adj*
commercial

Kommission (ko-mi-s^y*ōan*) *f* (pl ～en)
commission; committee

Kommode (ko-*mōa*-der) *f* (pl ～n)
bureau *Am*; chest of drawers

Kommune (ko-*mōō*-ner) *f* (pl ～n)
commune

Kommunikation (ko-moo-ni-kah-
ts^y*ōan*) *f* communication

Kommunismus (ko-moo-*niss*-mooss)
m communism

Kommunist (ko-moo-*nist*) *m* (pl ～en),
-in *f* communist

Komödie (ko-*mūr*-d^{y}er) *f* (pl ～n)
comedy

kompakt (kom-*pahkt*) *adj* compact

Kompass (*kom*-pahss) *m* (pl ～e)
compass

Kompetenz (kom-pay-*tehnts*) *f* (pl
～en) capacity

Komplex (kom-*plehks*) *m* (pl ～e)
complex

Kompliment (kom-pli-*mehnt*) *nt* (pl
～e) compliment

kompliziert (kom-pli-*tseert*) *adj*
complicated

Komponist (kom-poa-*nist*) *m* (pl ～en),
-in *f* composer

Komposition (kom-poa-zi-ts^y*ōan*) *f*
(pl ～en) composition

Kompott (kom-*pot*) *nt* stewed fruit

Kondensmilch (kon-*dens*-milkh) *f*
evaporated milk; condensed milk

Konditor (kon-*dee*-tor) *m* (pl ～en), **-in**
f confectioner

Konditorei (kon-di-toa-*righ*) *f* (pl ～en)
pastry shop

Kondom (kon-*dom*) *m* (pl ～s) condom

Konferenz (kon-fay-*rehnts*) *f* (pl ～en)
conference

Konfitüre (kon-fi-*tēw*-rer) *f* jam

Konflikt (kon-*flikt*) *m* (pl ～e) conflict

Kongress (kon-*grehss*) *m* (pl ～e)
congress

König (*kūr*-nikh) *m* (pl ～e) king

Königin (*kūr*-ni-gin) *f* (pl ～nen) queen

königlich (*kūr*-nik-likh) *adj* royal

Königreich (*kūr*-nik-righkh) *nt* (pl ～e)
kingdom

konkret (kon-*krait*) *adj* concrete

Konkurrent (kon-koo-*rehnt*) *m* (pl

~en), **-in** *f* competitor; rival

Konkurrenz (kon-koo-*rehnts*) *f* competition; rivalry

*können (*kur*-nern) *v* *can; *be able to; *might

konservativ (kon-zehr-vah-*teef*) *adj* conservative

Konservatorium (kon-zehr-vah-*tōā*-rʸoom) *f* (pl -rien) music academy

Konserve (kon-*zehr*-vern) *f* tinned food, canned food

Konstruktion (kon-strook-*tsʸōān*) *f* (pl ~en) construction

Konsul (*kon*-zool) *m* (pl ~n) consul

Konsulat (kon-zoo-*laat*) *nt* (pl ~e) consulate

Konsultation (kon-zool-tah-*tsʸōān*) *f* (pl ~en) consultation

konsultieren (kon-zool-*tee*-rern) *v* consult

Konsument (kon-zoo-*mehnt*) *m* (pl ~en), **-in** *f* consumer

Kontakt (kon-*tahkt*) *m* (pl ~e) touch, contact

Kontaktlinsen (kon-*tahkt*-lin-zern) *fpl* contact lenses

Kontinent (kon-ti-*nehnt*) *m* (pl ~e) continent

kontinental (kon-ti-nehn-*taal*) *adj* continental

Konto (*kon*-toa) *nt* (pl -ten) account

Kontrast (kon-*trahst*) *m* (pl ~e) contrast

Kontrollabschnitt (kon-*trol*-ahp-shnit) *m* (pl ~e) counterfoil, stub

Kontrolle (kon-*tro*-ler) *f* (pl ~n) control, inspection; supervision

kontrollieren (kon-troa-*lee*-rern) *v* control, check

konvertieren (kon-vehr-*tee*-rern) *v* convert

Konzentration (kon-tsehn-trah-*tsʸōān*) *f* (pl ~en) concentration

konzentrieren (kon-tsehn-*tree*-rern) *v* concentrate

Konzern (kon-*tsehrn*) *m* (pl ~e) concern

Konzert (kon-*tsehrt*) *nt* (pl ~e) concert

Konzertsaal (kon-*tsehrt*-zaal) *m* (pl -säle) concert hall

Konzession (kon-tseh-sʸōān) *f* (pl ~en) concession; licence, permission

kooperativ (koa-oa-pay-rah-*teef*) *adj* co-operative

koordinieren (koa-or-di-*nee*-rern) *v* coordinate

Koordinierung (koa-or-di-*nee*-roong) *f* coordination

Kopf (kopf) *m* (pl ~e) head

Kopfhörer (*kopf*- hūr-rerr) *m* headphone

Kopfkissen (*kopf*-ki-sern) *nt* (pl ~) pillow

Kopfschmerzen (*kopf*-shmehr-tsern) *mpl* headache

Kopie (koa-*pee*) *f* (pl ~n) copy

kopieren (koa-*pee*-rern) *v* copy

Koralle (koa-*rah*-ler) *f* (pl ~n) coral

Korb (korp) *m* (pl ~e) basket

Kordel (*kor*-derl) *f* (pl ~n) tape

Korinthe (koa-*rin*-ter) *f* (pl ~n) currant

Korken (*kor*-kern) *m* (pl ~) cork

Korkenzieher (*kor*-kern-tsee-err) *m* (pl ~) corkscrew

Korn (korn) *nt* (pl ~er) corn, grain

Kornfeld (*korn*-fehlt) *nt* (pl ~er) cornfield

Körper (*kurr*-perr) *m* (pl ~) body

körperbehindert (*kurr*-perr-ber-hin-derrt) *adj* disabled

korpulent (kor-poo-*lehnt*) *adj* corpulent, stout

korrekt (ko-*rehkt*) *adj* correct

Korrespondent (ko-rehss-pon-*dehnt*) *m* (pl ~en), **-in** *f* correspondent

Korrespondenz (ko-rehss-pon-*dehnts*) *f* correspondence

korrespondieren (ko-rehss-pon-*dee*-

rern) v correspond

korrigieren (ko-ri-*gee*-rern) v correct

korrupt (ko-*roopt*) adj corrupt

Korsett (kor-*zeht*) nt (pl ~s) corset

Kosmetika (koss-*māy*-ti-kah) ntpl cosmetics pl

Kost (kost) f fare; food

kostbar (*kost*-baar) adj expensive, valuable

Kosten (*koss*-tern) pl cost

kosten (*koss*-tern) v *cost; taste

kostenlos (*koss*-tern-lōass) adj free of charge

köstlich (*kurst*-likh) adj delicious; delightful

kostspielig (*kost*-shpee-likh) adj expensive

Kostüm (koss-*tewm*) nt costume

Kotelett (kot-*leht*) nt (pl ~e) cutlet, chop; **Koteletten** sideburns pl

Krabbe (*krah*-ber) f (pl ~n) crab; prawn

Krach (krahkh) m (pl ~e) noise; row

krachen (*krah*-khern) v crack

Kraft (krahft) f (pl ~e) force, strength; power; energy

Kraftfahrer (*krahft*-faa-rerr) m (pl ~) motorist

kräftig (*krehf*-tikh) adj strong

Kraftwerk (*krahft*-vehrk) nt (pl ~e) power station

Kragen (*kraa*-gern) m (pl ~) collar

Krähe (*krai*-er) f (pl ~n) crow

Krampf (krahmpf) m (pl ~e) convulsion; cramp

Krampfader (*krahmpf*-aa-derr) f (pl ~n) varicose vein

Kran (kraan) m (pl ~e) crane

krank (krahngk) adj sick, ill

kränken (*krehng*-kern) v offend, *hurt, injure

Krankenhaus (*krahng*-kern-houss) nt (pl ~er) hospital

Krankenpfleger (*krahng*-kern-pflāy-ger) m (pl ~) nurse

Krankenschwester (*krahng*-kern-shvehss-terr) f (pl ~n) nurse

Krankenwagen (*krahng*-kern-vaa-gern) m (pl ~) ambulance

Krankheit (*krahngk*-hight) f (pl ~en) sickness, illness, disease; ailment

Krater (*kraa*-terr) m (pl ~) crater

kratzen (*krah*-tsern) v scratch

Kratzer (*krah*-tserr) m (pl ~) scratch

kraulen (*krou*-lern) v crawl

Kraut (krout) nt (pl ~er) herb

Krawatte (krah-*vah*-ter) f (pl ~n) necktie, tie

Krebs (krāyps) m cancer

Kredit (kray-*deet*) m (pl ~e) credit

kreditieren (kray-di-*tee*-rern) v credit

Kreditkarte (kray-*deet*-kahr-ter) f (pl ~n) credit card; charge plate Am

Kreide (*krigh*-der) f chalk

Kreis (krighss) m (pl ~e) circle; ring, sphere

kreischen (*krigh*-shern) v shriek, scream

Kreislauf (*krighss*-louf) m circulation; cycle

Krem (krāym) f (pl ~s) cream

kremfarben (*krāym*-fahr-bern) adj cream

Kreuz (kroits) nt (pl ~e) cross

kreuzen (*kroi*-tsern) v cross; **sich ~** intersect

Kreuzfahrt (*kroits*-faart) f (pl ~en) cruise

Kreuzigung (*kroi*-tsi-goong) f (pl ~en) crucifixion

Kreuzung (*kroi*-tsoong) f (pl ~en) crossing, crossroads, intersection

Kreuzzug (*kroits*-tsōōk) m (pl ~e) crusade

Kricket (*kri*-kert) nt cricket

*kriechen (*kree*-khern) v *creep, crawl

Krieg (kreek) m (pl ~e) war

kriegen (*kree*-gern) v *get

Kriegsgefangene (*kreeks*-ger-fahng-er-ner) *m* (pl ⁓n) prisoner of war

Kriegsschiff (*kreeks*-shif) *nt* (pl ⁓e) man-of-war

Krimi (*kri*-mee) *m colloquial* thriller, murder mystery

Kriminalität (kri-mi-nah-li-*tait*) *f* criminality

Kriminalroman (kri-mi-*naal*-roa-maan) *m* (pl ⁓e) detective story

kriminell (kri-mi-*nehl*) *adj* criminal

Krippe (*kri*-per) *f* (pl ⁓n) manger

Krise (*kree*-zer) *f* (pl ⁓n) crisis

Kristall (kriss-*tahl*) *nt* crystal

Kritik (kri-*teek*) *f* (pl ⁓en) criticism

Kritiker (*kree*-ti-kerr) *m* (pl ⁓), **-in** *f* critic

kritisch (*kree*-tish) *adj* critical

kritisieren (kri-ti-*zee*-rern) *v* criticize

Krokodil (kroa-koa-*deel*) *nt* (pl ⁓e) crocodile

Krone (*kroa*-ner) *f* (pl ⁓n) crown

krönen (*krūr*-nern) *v* crown

Kröte (*krūr*-ter) *f* (pl ⁓n) toad

Krücke (*krew*-ker) *f* (pl ⁓n) crutch

Krug (krōōk) *m* (pl ⁓e) pitcher, jug, jar

Krümel (*krēw*-merl) *m* (pl ⁓) crumb

krumm (kroom) *adj* curved, bent; crooked

Krümmung (*krew*-moong) *f* (pl ⁓en) bend

Kruste (*krooss*-ter) *f* (pl ⁓n) crust

Kruzifix (kroo-tsi-*fiks*) *nt* (pl ⁓e) crucifix

Kuba (*kōō*-bah) Cuba

Kubaner (koo-*baa*-nerr) *m* (pl ⁓), **-in** *f* Cuban

kubanisch (koo-*baa*-nish) *adj* Cuban

Küche (*kew*-kher) *f* (pl ⁓n) kitchen

Kuchen (*kōō*-khern) *m* (pl ⁓) cake

Küchenchef (*kew*-khern-shehf) *m* (pl ⁓s) chef

Kuckuck (*koo*-kook) *m* (pl ⁓e) cuckoo

Kugel (*kōō*-gerl) *f* (pl ⁓n) sphere; bullet

Kugelschreiber (*kōō*-gerl-shrigh-berr) *m* (pl ⁓) ballpoint pen, Biro

Kuh (kōō) *f* (pl ⁓e) cow

kühl (kēwl) *adj* cool; chilly

kühlen (*kēw*-lern) *v* cool, chill

Kühlschrank (*kēwl*-shrahngk) *m* (pl ⁓e) fridge, refrigerator

kühn (kēwn) *adj* bold

Kühnheit (*kēwn*-hight) *f* nerve

Küken (kew-kern) *nt* (pl ⁓) chicken

kultivieren (kool-ti-*vee*-rern) *v* cultivate

kultiviert (kool-ti-*veert*) *adj* cultured

Kultur (kool-*tōōr*) *f* (pl ⁓en) culture

Kümmel (*kew*-merl) *m* caraway

Kummer (*koo*-merr) *m* sorrow, grief

kümmern (*kew*-merrn) *v* mind; **sich ⁓ um** look after, *take care of

Kunde (*koon*-der) *m* (pl ⁓n) customer, client

kündigen (*kewn*-di-gern) *v* *give notice; *colloquial* fire, sack

Kündigung (*kewn*-di-goong) *f* notice

Kundin (*koon*-din) *f* (pl ⁓nen) customer, client

Kundgebung (*koont*-gāy-boong) *f* (pl ⁓en) demonstration

Kunst (koonst) *f* (pl ⁓e) art; **die schönen Künste** fine arts

Kunstakademie (*koonst*-ah-kah-day-mee) *f* (pl ⁓n) art school

Kunstausstellung (*koonst*-ooss-shteh-loong) *f* (pl ⁓en) art exhibition

Kunstgalerie (*koonst*-gah-ler-ree) *f* (pl ⁓n) art gallery

Kunstgeschichte (*koonst*-ger-shikh-ter) *f* art history

Kunstgewerbe (*koonst*-ger-vehr-ber) *nt* arts and crafts

Künstler (*kewnst*-lerr) *m* (pl ⁓), **-in** *f* artist

künstlerisch (*kewnst*-ler-rish) *adj* artistic

künstlich (*kewnst*-likh) *adj* artificial

Kunstsammlung (*koonst*-zahm-loong) *f* (pl ~en) art collection

Kunstseide (*koonst*-zigh-der) *f* rayon

Kunststoff (*koonst*-shtof) *m* (pl ~e) plastic; **Kunststoff-** plastic

Kunstwerk (*koonst*-vehrk) *nt* (pl ~e) work of art

Kupfer (*koo*-pferr) *nt* copper

Kupon (koo-*pawng*) *m* (pl ~s) coupon

Kuppel (*koo*-perl) *f* (pl ~n) dome

Kupplung (*koop*-loong) *f* (pl ~en) clutch

Kur (*koor*) *f* (pl ~en) cure

Kurs (koors) *m* (pl ~e) rate of exchange; course

Kursus (*koor*-zooss) *m* (pl Kurse) course

Kurve (*koor*-ver) *f* (pl ~n) curve, turning, bend

kurz (koorts) *adj* short; brief; **binnen kurzem** shortly

Kürze: in ~ (in *kewr*-tser) soon

kurzfristig (*koorts*-fris-tikh) *adj* short term

kurzgefasst (*koorts*-ger-fahst) *adj* concise

kürzlich (*kewrts*-likh) *adv* recently, lately

Kurzschluss (*koorts*-shlooss) *m* short circuit

kurzsichtig (*koorts*-zikh-tikh) *adj* short-sighted

Kusine (koo-*zee*-ner) *f* (pl ~n) cousin

Kuss (kooss) *m* (pl ~e) kiss

küssen (*kew*-sern) *v* kiss

Küste (*kewss*-ter) *f* (pl ~n) coast, shore; seaside

Kutsche (*koo*-cher) *f* (pl ~n) carriage, coach

L

labil (lah-*beel*) *adj* unstable

Laboratorium (lah-boa-rah-*toa*-rʸoom) *nt* (pl -rien) laboratory

Labyrinth (lah-bew-*rint*) *nt* (pl ~e) labyrinth

Lächeln (*leh*-kherln) *nt* smile

lächeln (*leh*-kherln) *v* smile

Lachen (*lah*-khern) *nt* laugh

lachen (*lah*-khern) *v* laugh

lächerlich (*leh*-kherr-likh) *adj* ridiculous; ludicrous

lachhaft (*lahkh*-hahft) *adj* ludicrous

Lachs (lahks) *m* (pl ~e) salmon

Lack (lahk) *m* (pl ~e) lacquer; varnish

lackieren (lah-*kee*-rern) *v* varnish

Laden (*laa*-dern) *m* (pl ~) store

***laden** (*laa*-dern) *v* load; charge

Ladeninhaber (*laa*-dern-in-haa-berr)

m (pl ~), **-in** *f* shopkeeper

Ladentisch (*laa*-dern-tish) *m* (pl ~e) counter

Laderaum (*laa*-der-roum) *m* (pl ~e) hold

Ladung (*laa*-doong) *f* (pl ~en) freight, charge, cargo

Lage (*laa*-ger) *f* (pl ~n) location; situation; position, site

Lager (*laa*-gerr) *nt* (pl ~) warehouse, depot; camp

Lagerhaus (*laa*-gerr-houss) *nt* (pl ~er) store house

lagern (*laa*-gerrn) *v* store

Lagerraum (*laa*-gerr-roum) *m* (pl ~e) depository

Lagerung (*laa*-ger-roong) *f* storage

Lagune (lah-*goo*-ner) *f* (pl ~n) lagoon

lahm (laam) *adj* lame

lähmen (*lai*-mern) *v* paralyse, paralyze *Am*

Laib (lighp) *m* (pl ⌐e) loaf

Laie (*ligh*-er) *m* (pl ⌐n) layman

Laken (*laa*-kern) *nt* (pl ⌐) sheet

Lakritze (lah-*kri*-tser) *f* liquorice

Lamm (lahm) *nt* (pl ⌐er) lamb

Lammfleisch (*lahm*-flighsh) *nt* lamb

Lampe (*lahm*-per) *f* (pl ⌐n) lamp

Lampenschirm (*lahm*-pern-sheerm) *m* (pl ⌐e) lampshade

Land (lahnt) *nt* (pl ⌐er) country, land; **an ~** ashore; **an ~ *gehen** land; disembark

Landebahn (*lahn*-der-baan) *f* runway

landen (*lahn*-dern) *v* land; disembark

Landesgrenze (*lahn*-derss-grehn-tser) *f* (pl ⌐n) boundary

Landhaus (*lahnt*-houss) *nt* (pl ⌐er) country house

Landkarte (*lahnt*-kahr-ter) *f* (pl ⌐n) map

ländlich (*lehnt*-likh) *adj* rustic, rural

Landschaft (*lahnt*-shahft) *f* (pl ⌐en) countryside; landscape, scenery

Landsitz (*lahnt*-zits) *m* (pl ⌐e) estate

Landstraße (*lahnt*-shtraa-ser) *f* (pl ⌐n) highway

Landung (*lahn*-doong) *f* landing

Landwirtschaft (*lahnt*-veert-shahft) *f* agriculture; **Landwirtschafts-** agricultural

Landzunge (*lahnt*-tsoong-er) *f* (pl ⌐n) headland

lang (lahng) *adj* long; tall; **lange** *adv* long

Länge (*lehng*-er) *f* length; **der ~ nach** lengthways

Längengrad (*lehng*-ern-graat) *m* (pl ⌐e) longitude

länglich (*lehng*-likh) *adj* oblong

langsam (*lahng*-zaam) *adj* slow

längst (lehngst) *adv* long ago

langweilen (*lahng*-vigh-lern) *v* bore; annoy

langweilig (*lahng*-vigh-likh) *adj* dull, boring; unpleasant

langwierig (*lahng*-vee-rikh) *adj* long

Lappen (*lah*-pern) *m* (pl ⌐) cloth

Lärm (lehrm) *m* noise

*lassen (*lah*-sern) *v* *let; *leave, allow to

lässig (*leh*-sikh) *adj* easy-going

Last (lahst) *f* (pl ⌐en) burden; charge, load; trouble

lästig (*lehss*-tikh) *adj* troublesome, inconvenient; annoying

Lastwagen (*lahst*-vaa-gern) *m* (pl ⌐) lorry; truck *Am*

Lateinamerika (lah-*tighn*-ah-māy-ri-kah) Latin America

lateinamerikanisch (lah-*tighn*-ah-may-ri-kaa-nish) *adj* Latin-American

Laterne (lah-*tehr*-ner) *f* (pl ⌐n) lantern

Lauf (louf) *m* (pl ⌐e) course

Laufbahn (*louf*-baan) *f* career

*laufen (*lou*-fern) *v* *run

Laune (*lou*-ner) *f* (pl ⌐n) spirit, mood; whim, fancy

Laus (louss) *f* (pl ⌐e) louse

laut (lout) *adj* loud; *adv* aloud

läuten (*loi*-tern) *v* *ring

Lautsprecher (*lout*-shpreh-kherr) *m* (pl ⌐) loudspeaker

lauwarm (*lou*-vahrm) *adj* tepid, lukewarm

Lawine (lah-*vee*-ner) *f* (pl ⌐n) avalanche

Leben (*lāy*-bern) *nt* (pl ⌐) life; lifetime; **am ~** alive

leben (*lāy*-bern) *v* live

lebend (*lāy*-bernt) *adj* live, alive

Lebensgefahr (*lāy*-berns- ger-faar) *f* (mortal) danger

Lebensmittel (*lāy*-berns-mi-terl) *pl* groceries *pl*

Lebensmittelgeschäft (*lāy*-berns-mi-terl-ger-shehft) *nt* (pl ⁓e) grocer's

Lebensmittelhändler (*lāy*-berns-mi-terl-hehn-dlerr) *m* (pl ⁓), **-in** *f* grocer

Lebensstandard (*lāy*-berns-shtahn-dahrt) *m* standard of living

Lebensversicherung (*lāy*-berns-fehr-zi-kher-roong) *f* (pl ⁓en) life insurance

Leber (*lāy*-berr) *f* (pl ⁓n) liver

lebhaft (*lāyp*-hahft) *adj* brisk, vivid, lively, active

Leck (lehk) *nt* (pl ⁓s) leak

leck (lehk) *adj* leaky

lecken (*leh*-kern) *v* leak; lick

lecker (*leh*-kerr) *adj* appetizing; delicious, good, tasty

Leckerbissen (*leh*-kerr-bi-sern) *m* (pl ⁓) delicacy

Leder (*lāy*-derr) *nt* leather; **Leder-** leather

ledern (*lāy*-derrn) *adj* leather

ledig (*lāy*-dikh) *adj* single

leer (lāyr) *adj* empty; blank

leeren (*lāy*-rern) *v* empty

Leerung (*lāy*-roong) *f* (pl ⁓en) collection

legal (lay-*gahl*) *adj* legal

legen (*lāy*-gern) *v* *lay, *put

Lehne (*lāy*-ner) *f* back

lehnen (*lāy*-nern) *v* *lean

Lehnstuhl (*lāyn*-shtōol) *m* (pl ⁓e) armchair, easy chair

Lehrbuch (*lāyr*-bōokh) *nt* (pl ⁓er) textbook

Lehre (*lāy*-rer) *f* (pl ⁓n) teachings *pl*

lehren (*lāy*-rern) *v* *teach

Lehrer (*lāy*-rerr) *m* (pl ⁓), **-in** *f* schoolteacher, schoolmaster, master; teacher; instructor

Lehrgang (*lāyr*-gahng) *m* (pl ⁓e) course

lehrreich (*lāyr*-righkh) *adj* instructive

Leib (lighp) *m* (pl ⁓er) body

Leiche (*ligh*-kher) *f* (pl ⁓n) corpse

leicht (lighkht) *adj* light; gentle, slight

Leichtigkeit (*lighkh*-tikh-kight) *f* ease

Leid (light) *nt* sorrow, grief; **(es) tut mir Leid** (I'm) sorry

Leiden (*ligh*-dern) *nt* (pl ⁓) disease; suffering

*leiden (*ligh*-dern) *v* suffer

Leidenschaft (*ligh*-dern-shahft) *f* (pl ⁓en) passion

leidenschaftlich (*ligh*-dern-shahft-likh) *adj* passionate

leider (*ligh*-derr) *adv* unfortunately

leidlich (*light*-likh) *adv* fairly, quite

*leihen (*ligh*-ern) *v* *lend, borrow

Leim (lighm) *m* glue

Leine (*ligh*-ner) *f* (pl ⁓n) cord; lead; leash

Leinen (*ligh*-nern) *nt* linen

leise (*ligh*-zer) *adj* quiet; low; gentle

Leiste (*lighss*-ter) *f* (pl ⁓n) groin

leisten (*lighss*-tern) *v* achieve; offer; **sich ⁓** afford

Leistung (*lighss*-toong) *f* (pl ⁓en) achievement

leistungsfähig (*lighss*-toongs-fai-ikh) *adj* efficient

Leistungsfähigkeit (*lighss*-toongs-fai-ikh-kight) *f* (pl ⁓en) capacity

leiten (*ligh*-tern) *v* head

Leiter[1] (*ligh*-terr) *m* (pl ⁓), **-in** *f* leader

Leiter[2] (*ligh*-terr) *f* (pl ⁓n) ladder

Leitplanke (*light*-plahng-ker) *f* (pl ⁓n) crash barrier

Leitung (*ligh*-toong) *f* (pl ⁓en) lead

Leitungswasser (*ligh*-toongs-vah-serr) *nt* tap water

Lektion (lehk-ts⁽ʸ⁾*ōan*) *f* (pl ⁓en) lesson

lenken (*lehng*-kern) *v* steer; guide, direct

Lektor (*lehk*-tor) *m* (pl ⁓en), **-in** *f* reader

Lepra (*lāy*-prah) *f* leprosy

Lerche (*lehr*-kher) *f* (pl ⁓n) lark

lernen (*lehr*-nern) *v* *learn;

auswendig ~ memorize

Leselampe (*lāy*-zer-lahm-per) *f* (pl ~n) reading lamp

*lesen (*lāy*-zern) *v* *read

Leser (*lāy*-zer) *m*, **-in** *f* reader

leserlich (*lāy*-zerr-likh) *adj* legible

Lesesaal (*lāy*-zer-zaal) *m* (pl -säle) reading room

letzt (lehtst) *adj* last; ultimate, final; past

leuchten (*loikh*-tern) *v* *shine; **leuchtend** bright; luminous

Leuchtturm (*loikht*-toorm) *m* (pl ẍe) lighthouse

leugnen (*loi*-gnern) *v* deny

Leute (*loi*-ter) *pl* people *pl*

Libanese (li-bah-*nāy*-zer) *m* (pl ~n) Lebanese

Libanesin (li-bah-*nāy*-zin) *f* (pl ~nen) Lebanese

libanesisch (li-bah-*nāy*-zish) *adj* Lebanese

Libanon (*lee*-bah-non) Lebanon

liberal (li-bay-*raal*) *adj* liberal

Liberia (li-*bāy*-rʸah) Liberia

Liberier (li-*bāy*-rʸerr) *m* (pl ~), **-in** *f* Liberian

liberisch (li-*bāy*-rish) *adj* Liberian

Licht (likht) *nt* (pl ~er) light

Lichtbild (*likht*-bilt) *nt* (pl ~er) photograph

Lichtung (*likh*-toong) *f* (pl ~en) clearing

Lid (leet) *nt* eyelid

lieb (leep) *adj* dear; affectionate, sweet

Liebe (*lee*-ber) *f* love

lieben (*lee*-bern) *v* love

liebenswürdig (*lee*-berns-vewr-dikh) *adj* lovable

lieber (*lee*-berr) *adv* sooner, rather

Liebesgeschichte (*lee*-berss-ger-shikh-ter) *f* (pl ~n) love story

Liebhaber (*leep*-haa-berr) *m* (pl ~),

-in *f* lover

Liebhaberei (leep-haa-ber-*righ*) *f* (pl ~en) hobby

liebkosen (*leep*-kōa-zern) *v* hug

Liebling (*leep*-ling) *m* (pl ~e) darling, sweetheart; favo(u)rite; pet; **Lieblings-** favo(u)rite; pet

Liebreiz (*leep*-rights) *m* charm

Lied (leet) *nt* (pl ~er) song; tune

lieferbar (*lee*-fer-baar) *adj* in stock

liefern (*lee*-ferrn) *v* furnish, supply, provide

Lieferung (*lee*-fer-roong) *f* (pl ~en) supply; delivery

Lieferwagen (*lee*-ferr-vaa-gern) *m* (pl ~) delivery van, pick-up van

Liege (*lee*-ger) *f* (pl ~n) camp-bed; cot *Am*

*liegen (*lee*-gern) *v* *lie

Liegestuhl (*lee*-ger-shtōōl) *m* (pl ẍe) deck chair

Likör (li-*kūrr*) *m* (pl ~e) liqueur

lila (*lee*-lah) *adj* lilac

Lilie (*lee*-lʸer) *f* (pl ~n) lily

Limonade (li-moa-*naa*-der) *f* (pl ~n) lemonade

Limone (li-*mōa*-ner) *f* (pl ~n) lime

Linde (*lin*-der) *f* (pl ~n) lime

Lindenbaum (*lin*-dern-boum) *m* (pl ẍe) limetree

Lineal (li-nay-*aal*) *nt* (pl ~e) ruler

Linie (*lee*-nʸer) *f* (pl ~n) line

linke (*ling*-ker) *adj* left-hand, left

links (lingks) *adv* (on, to the) left; **nach links**to the left

linkshändig (lingks-hehn-dikh) *adj* left-handed

Linse (*lin*-zer) *f* (pl ~n) lens

Lippe (*li*-per) *f* (pl ~n) lip

Lippenstift (*li*-pern-shtift) *m* (pl ~e) lipstick

List (list) *f* (pl ~en) trick, ruse

Liste (*liss*-ter) *f* (pl ~n) list

listig (*liss*-tikh) *adj* cunning, sly

Liter (*lee*-terr) *m* (pl ~) litre
literarisch (li-tay-*raa*-rish) *adj* literary
Literatur (li-tay-rah-*toor*) *f* literature
Lizenz (li-*tsehnts*) *f* (pl ~en) licence
Lob (*loap*) *nt* praise; glory
loben (*loa*-bern) *v* praise
Loch (lokh) *nt* (pl ~er) hole
Locke (*lo*-ker) *f* (pl ~n) curl
locken (*lo*-kern) *v* curl
Lockenwickler (*lo*-kern-vi-klerr) *m* (pl ~) curler
locker (*lo*-kerr) *adj* loose; lax
lockern (*lo*-kerrn) *v* loosen
lockig (*lo*-kikh) *adj* curly
Löffel (*lur*-ferl) *m* (pl ~) spoon
Logik (*loa*-gik) *f* logic
logisch (*loa*-gish) *adj* logical
Lohn (loan) *m* (pl ~e) wages *pl*, salary, pay
lohnen (*loa*-nern) *v*: **sich** ~ *be worthwhile; *pay
Lohnerhöhung (*loan*-ehr-hur-oong) *f* (pl ~en) raise *Am*
lokal (loa-*kaal*) *adj* local
Lokomotive (loa-koa-moa-*tee*-ver) *f* (pl ~n) engine, locomotive
Lorbeer (*loar*-bair) *m* laurel, bay
Los (loass) *nt* (pl ~e) lot
löschen (*lur*-shern) *v* extinguish
lose (*loa*-zer) *adj* loose
Lösegeld (*lur*-zer-gehlt) *nt* (pl ~er) ransom
lösen (*lur*-zern) *v* solve
löslich (*lurss*-likh) *adj* soluble
Lösung (*lur*-zoong) *f* (pl ~en) solution
Lotse (*loa*-tser) *m* (pl ~n) pilot, guide
Lötstelle (*lurt*-shteh-ler) *f* (pl ~n) joint
Lotterie (lo-ter-*ree*) *f* (pl ~n) lottery

Löwe (*lur*-ver) *m* (pl ~n) lion
Löwenzahn (*lur*-vern-tsaan) *m* dandelion
loyal (lwah-*ᵞaal*) *adj* loyal
Lücke (*lew*-ker) *f* (pl ~n) gap
Luft (looft) *f* (pl ~e) air; sky; breath
luftdicht (*looft*-dikht) *adj* airtight
Luftdruck (*looft*-drook) *m* atmospheric pressure
lüften (*lewf*-tern) *v* air, ventilate
Luftfilter (*looft*-fil-terr) *m* (pl ~) air-filter
luftig (*looft*-tikh) *adj* airy
Luftkrankheit (*looft*-krahngk-hight) *f* airsickness
Luftpost (*looft*-post) *f* airmail
Luftpumpe (*looft*-poom-per) *f* air pump
Lüftung (*lewf*-toong) *f* ventilation
Luftzug (*looft*-tsook) *m* draught, draft *Am*
Lüge (*lew*-ger) *f* (pl ~n) lie
*lügen (*lew*-gern) *v* lie
Luke (*loo*-ker) *f* (pl ~n) hatch; porthole
Lumpen (*loom*-pern) *m* (pl ~) rag
Lunge (*loong*-er) *f* (pl ~n) lung
Lungenentzündung (*loong*-ern-ehnt-tsewn-doong) *f* pneumonia
Lust (loost) *f* desire; zest; ~ ***haben zu** *feel like, fancy
lustig (*looss*-tikh) *adj* gay
Lustspiel (*loost*-shpeel) *nt* (pl ~e) comedy
lutschen (*loo*-chern) *v* suck
luxuriös (loo-ksoo-rᵞ*urss*) *adj* luxurious
Luxus (*loo*-ksooss) *m* luxury

M

machen (*mah*-khern) *v* *make; *have; cause to

Macht (mahkht) *f* (pl ⁀e) power; force, might

Machtbefugnis (*mahkht*-ber-fook-niss) *f* (pl ⁀se) authority

mächtig (*mehkh*-tikh) *adj* powerful, mighty

machtlos (*mahkht*-lōass) *adj* powerless

Mädchen (*mait*-khern) *nt* (pl ⁀) girl

Mädchenname (*mait*-khern-naa-mer) *m* (pl ⁀n) maiden name

Magen (*maa*-gern) *m* (pl ⁀) stomach

Magengeschwür (*maa*-gern-ger-shvēwr) *nt* (pl ⁀e) gastric ulcer

Magenschmerzen (*maa*-gern-shmehr-tsern) *mpl* stomach-ache

Magenverstimmung (*maa*-gern-fehr-shti-moong) *f* indigestion

mager (*maa*-gerr) *adj* thin; lean

Magie (mah-*gee*) *f* magic

Magnet (mah-*gnāyt*) *m* (pl ⁀en) magneto

magnetisch (mah-*gnāy*-tish) *adj* magnetic

Mahl (maal) *nt* (pl ⁀er) meal

mahlen (*maa*-lern) *v* *grind

Mahlzeit (*maal*-tsight) *f* (pl ⁀en) meal

Mai (migh) May

Mais (mighss) *m* maize; corn *Am*

Maiskolben (*mighss*-kol-bern) *m* (pl ⁀) corn on the cob

Major (mah-*yōar*) *m* (pl ⁀e) major

Majoran (*mah*-ʸo-raan) *m* marjoram

Makel (*maa*-kerl) *m* (pl ⁀) blot

Makler (*maa*-klerr) *m* (pl ⁀), **-in** *f* broker

Makrele (mah-*krāy*-ler) *f* (pl ⁀n) mackerel

Mal (maal) *nt* (pl ⁀e) time

mal (maal) times

malaiisch (mah-*ligh*-ish) *adj* Malay

Malaria (mah-*laa*-rʸah) *f* malaria

Malaysia (mah-*ligh*-zʸah) Malaysia

malen (*maa*-lern) *v* paint

Maler (*maa*-lerr) *m* (pl ⁀), **-in** *f* painter

malerisch (*maa*-ler-rish) *adj* picturesque, scenic

Malkasten (*maal*-kahss-tern) *m* (pl ⁀) paintbox

Mammut (*mah*-moot) *nt* (pl ⁀e) mammoth

man (mahn) *pron* one

manche (*mahn*-kher) *pron* some

manchmal (*mahnkh*-maal) *adv* sometimes

Mandarine (mahn-dah-*ree*-ner) *f* (pl ⁀n) mandarin, tangerine

Mandat (mahn-*daat*) *nt* (pl ⁀e) mandate

Mandel (*mahn*-derl) *f* (pl ⁀n) almond; **Mandeln** tonsils *pl*

Mandelentzündung (*mahn*-derl-ehnt-tsewn-doong) *f* tonsilitis

Mangel (*mahng*-erl) *m* (pl ⁀) want, lack, scarcity, shortage; deficiency, fault

mangelhaft (*mahng*-erl-hahft) *adj* defective; faulty

mangeln (*mahng*-erln) *v* fail; lack

Manieren (mah-*nee*-rern) *fpl* manners *pl*

Maniküre (mah-ni-*kēw*-rer) *f* (pl ⁀n) manicure

maniküren (mah-ni-*kēw*-rern) *v* manicure

Mann (mahn) *m* (pl ⁀er) man; husband

Mannequin (mah-ner-*kañg*) *nt* (pl ⁀s) model, mannequin

männlich (*mehn*-likh) *adj* male; masculine

Mannschaft (*mahn*-shahft) *f* (pl ⁀en)

team

Manschettenknöpfe (mahn-*sheh*-tern-knur-pfer) *mpl* cuff links *pl*

Mantel (*mahn*-terl) *m* (pl ∺) coat, overcoat

Manuskript (mah-noo-*skript*) *nt* (pl ∼e) manuscript

Mappe (*mah*-per) *f* portfolio, briefcase

Märchen (*mair*-khern) *nt* (pl ∼) fairytale

Margarine (mahr-gah-*ree*-ner) *f* margarine

Marine (mah-*ree*-ner) *f* navy; **Marine-** naval

Marionettentheater (mah-rio-*nehtern*-tay-*aa*-terr) *nt* (pl ∼) puppet show

maritim (mah-ri-*teem*) *adj* maritime

Mark (mahrk) *nt* marrow

Marke (*mahr*-ker) *f* (pl ∼n) brand

Markise (mahr-*kee*-zer) *f* (pl ∼n) sunblind

Markstein (*mahrk*-shtighn) *m* (pl ∼e) landmark

Markt (mahrkt) *m* (pl ∺e) market

Marktplatz (*mahrkt*-plahts) *m* (pl ∺e) marketplace

Marmelade (mahr-mer-*laa*-der) *f* (pl ∼n) marmalade; jam

Marmor (*mahr*-mor) *m* marble

Marokkaner (mah-ro-*kaa*-nerr) *m* (pl ∼), **-in** *f* Moroccan

marokkanisch (mah-ro-*kaa*-nish) *adj* Moroccan

Marokko (mah-*ro*-koa) Morocco

Marsch (mahrsh) *m* (pl ∺e) march

marschieren (mahr-*shee*-rern) *v* march

Märtyrer (*mehr*-tew-rerr) *m* (pl ∼), **-in** *f* martyr

März (mehrts) March

Marzipan (*mahr*-tsi-paan) *nt* marzipan

Masche (*mah*-sher) *f* (pl ∼n) mesh

Maschine (mah-*shee*-ner) *f* (pl ∼n) machine; engine; aircraft

Masern (*maa*-zerrn) *pl* measles

Maske (*mahss*-ker) *f* (pl ∼n) mask

Maß (maass) *nt* (pl ∼e) measure; **nach** ∼ tailor-made

Massage (mah-*saa*-zher) *f* (pl ∼n) massage

Masse (*mah*-ser) *f* (pl ∼n) bulk; crowd

Massenproduktion (*mah*-sern-proa-dook-ts^y*oān*) *f* mass production

Masseur (mah-*sūrr*) *m* (pl ∼e) masseur

massieren (mah-*see*-rern) *v* massage

mäßig (*mai*-sikh) *adj* moderate

massiv (mah-*seef*) *adj* solid, massive

Maßnahme (*maass*-naa-mer) *f* (pl ∼n) measure

Maßstab (*maass*-shtaap) *m* (pl ∺e) scale; standard

Mast (mahst) *m* (pl ∼e) mast

Mastdarm (*mahst*-dahrm) *m* (pl ∺e) rectum

Material (mah-tay-r^y*aal*) *nt* (pl ∼ien) material

Materie (mah-*tāy*-r^{y}er) *f* (pl ∼n) matter

materiell (mah-tay-r^y*ehl*) *adj* material

Mathematik (mah-tay-mah-*teek*) *f* mathematics

mathematisch (mah-tay-*maa*-tish) *adj* mathematical

Matratze (mah-*trah*-tser) *f* (pl ∼n) mattress

Matrose (mah-*trōā*-zer) *m* (pl ∼n) sailor, seaman

Matsch (mahch) *m* slush

matt (maht) *adj* mat; dull, dim

Matte (*mah*-ter) *f* (pl ∼n) mat

Mauer (*mou*-err) *f* (pl ∼n) wall

mauern (*mou*-errn) *v* *lay bricks

Maul (moul) *nt* (pl ∺er) mouth

Maulesel (*moul*-āy-zerl) *m* (pl ∼) mule

Maultier (*moul*-teer) *nt* (pl ∼e) mule

Maurer (*mou*-rerr) *m* (pl ∼), **-in** *f*

bricklayer

Maus (mouss) *f* (pl ⁓e) mouse

Mausoleum (mou-zoa-*lāy*-oom) *nt* (pl -leen) mausoleum

Mechaniker (may-*khaa*-ni-kerr) *m* (pl ⁓), **-in** *f* mechanic

mechanisch (may-*khaa*-nish) *adj* mechanical

Mechanismus (may-khah-*niss*-mooss) *m* (pl -men) mechanism; machinery

Medaille (may-*dah*-l^yer) *f* (pl ⁓n) medal

meditieren (may-di-*tee*-rern) *v* meditate

Medizin (may-di-*tseen*) *f* medicine

medizinisch (may-di-*tsee*-nish) *adj* medical

Meer (māyr) *nt* (pl ⁓e) sea

Meeresküste (*māy*-rerss-kewss-ter) *f* (pl ⁓n) seashore

Meerrettich (*māyr*-reh-tikh) *m* horseradish

Meerschweinchen (*māyr*-shvighn-khern) *nt* (pl ⁓) guinea pig

Meerwasser (*māyr*-vah-serr) *nt* sea water

Mehl (māyl) *nt* flour

mehr (māyr) *adv* more; **etwas ⁓** some more; **nicht ⁓** no longer

mehrere (*māy*-rer-rer) *pron* several

Mehrheit (*māyr*-hight) *f* (pl ⁓en) majority; bulk

Mehrzahl (*māyr*-tsaal) *f* plural

*meiden (*migh*-dern) *v* avoid

Meile (*migh*-ler) *f* (pl ⁓n) mile

Meilenstand (*migh*-lern-shtahnt) *m* mileage

Meilenstein (*migh*-lern-shtighn) *m* (pl ⁓e) milestone

mein (mighn) *pron* my, mine

Meineid (*mighn*-ight) *m* (pl ⁓e) perjury

meinen (*migh*-nern) *v* *mean

Meinung (*migh*-noong) *f* (pl ⁓en) view, opinion

Meißel (*migh*-serl) *m* (pl ⁓) chisel

meist (mighst) *adj* most

meistens (*migh*-sterns) *adv* mostly

Meister (*mighss*-terr) *m* (pl ⁓), **-in** *f* champion; master

Meisterschaft (*mighss*-terr-shahft) *f* championship

Meisterstück (*mighss*-terr-shtewk) *nt* (pl ⁓e) masterpiece

melden (*mehl*-dern) *v* report

Meldung (*mehl*-doong) *f* (pl ⁓en) report; mention

meliert (*may*-leert) *adj* mixed

Melodie (may-loa-*dee*) *f* (pl ⁓n) melody; tune

melodisch (may-*lōa*-dish) *adj* tuneful

Melone (may-*lōa*-ner) *f* (pl ⁓n) melon

Menge (*mehng*-er) *f* (pl ⁓n) amount; plenty, lot; crowd, mass

Mensch (mehnsh) *m* (pl ⁓en) man; human being

Menschheit (*mehnsh*-hight) *f* humanity, mankind

menschlich (*mehnsh*-likh) *adj* human

Menstruation (mehns-troo-ah-ts^y*ōan*) *f* menstruation

merken (*mehr*-kern) *v* notice

Merkmal (*mehrk*-maal) *nt* (pl ⁓e) indication

merkwürdig (*mehrk*-vewr-dikh) *adj* remarkable; singular

Messe (*meh*-ser) *f* (pl ⁓n) fair; Mass

*messen (*meh*-sern) *v* measure

Messer (*meh*-serr) *nt* (pl ⁓) knife; *m* gauge

Messing (*meh*-sing) *nt* brass

Metall (may-*tahl*) *nt* (pl ⁓e) metal

metallisch (may-*tah*-lish) *adj* metal

Meter (*māy*-terr) *nt* (pl ⁓) metre, meter *Am*

Methode (may-*tōa*-der) *f* (pl ⁓n) method

methodisch (may-*tōa*-dish) *adj*
methodical

metrisch (*māy*-trish) *adj* metric

Metzger (*mehts*-gerr) *m* (pl ~), **-in** *f*
butcher

Meuterei (moi-ter-*righ*) *f* (pl ~en)
mutiny

Mexikaner (meh-ksi-*kaa*-nerr) *m* (pl
~), **-in** *f* Mexican

mexikanisch (meh-ksi-*kaa*-nish) *adj*
Mexican

Mexiko (*meh*-ksi-koa) Mexico

mich (mikh) *pron* me; myself

Miete (*mee*-ter) *f* (pl ~n) rent

mieten (*mee*-tern) *v* hire, rent; lease;
engage

Mieter (*mee*-terr) *m* (pl ~), **-in** *f* tenant

Mietvertrag (*meet*-fehr-traak) *m* (pl
~e) lease

Migräne (mi-*grai*-ner) *f* migraine

Mikrofon (mi-kroa-*fōan*) *nt* (pl ~e)
microphone, *colloquial* mike

Mikrowellenherd (*mi*-kroa-veh-lern-
hāyrt) *m* (pl ~e) microwave oven

Milch (milkh) *f* milk

milchig (*mil*-khikh) *adj* milky

mild (milt) *adj* mild; mellow

mildern (*mil*-derrn) *v* soften

Milieu (mi-*l'ūr*) *nt* (pl ~s) milieu

Militär (mi-li-*tair*) *nt* army, armed
forces

militärisch (mi-li-*tai*-rish) *adj* military

Million (mi-*l'ōan*) *f* (pl ~en) million

Millionär (mi-l'oa-*nair*) *m* (pl ~e)
millionaire

Minderheit (*min*-derr-hight) *f* (pl ~en)
minority

minderjährig (*min*-derr-*y*ai-rikh) *adj*
under age

minderwertig (*min*-derr-vāyr-tikh)
adj inferior

mindest (*min*-derst) *adj* least

mindestens (*min*-ders-terns) *adv* at
least

Mineral (mi-ner-*raal*) *nt* (pl ~e)
mineral

Mineralwasser (mi-ner-*raal*-vah-serr)
nt mineral water

Miniatur (mi-n'ah-*tōōr*) *f* (pl ~en)
miniature

Minimum (*mi*-ni-moom) *nt* minimum

Minister (mi-*niss*-terr) *m* (pl ~), **-in** *f*
minister

Ministerium (mi-niss-*tāy*-r'oom) *nt*
(pl -rien) ministry

Ministerpräsident (mi-*niss*-terr-preh-
zi-dehnt) *m* (pl ~en), **-in** *f* Prime
Minister

Minute (mi-*nōō*-ter) *f* (pl ~n) minute

Minze (*min*-tser) *f* (pl ~n) mint

mir (meer) *pron* me

mischen (*mi*-shern) *v* mix; shuffle

Mischung (*mi*-shoong) *f* (pl ~en)
mixture

missbilligen (miss-*bi*-li-gern) *v*
disapprove

Missbrauch (*miss*-broukh) *m* (pl ~e)
misuse, abuse

Misserfolg (*miss*-ehr-folk) *m* (pl ~e)
failure

*missfallen (miss-*fah*-lern) *v*
displease

Missgeschick (*miss*-ger-shik) *nt* (pl
~e) misfortune; disaster

missgestaltet (*miss*-ger-shtahl-tert)
adj deformed

missgönnen (miss-*gur*-nern) *v* grudge

misslich (*miss*-likh) *adj* delicate

Misstrauen (*miss*-trou-ern) *nt*
suspicion

misstrauen (miss-*trou*-ern) *v* mistrust

misstrauisch (*miss*-trou-ish) *adj*
suspicious

Missverständnis (*miss*-fehr-shtehnt-
niss) *nt* (pl ~se) misunderstanding

*missverstehen (*miss*-fehr-shtāy-ern)
v *misunderstand

Misthaufen (*mist*-hou-fern) *m* (pl ~)

dunghill

mit (mit) *prep* with; by

Mitarbeit (*mit*-ahr-bight) *f* co-operation

*mitbringen (*mit*-bring-ern) *v* *bring

mitfühlend (*mit*-fēw-lernt) *adj* sympathetic

Mitgefühl (*mit*-ger-fēwl) *nt* sympathy

Mitglied (*mit*-gleet) *nt* (pl ∼er) associate, member

Mitgliedschaft (*mit*-gleet-shahft) *f* membership

Mitleid (*mit*-light) *nt* pity; ∼ ***haben mit** pity

*mitnehmen (*mit*-nāy-mern) *v* *take along; exhaust

Mittag (*mi*-taak) *m* noon, midday

Mittagessen (*mi*-taak-eh-sern) *nt* lunch; luncheon, dinner

mittags (*mi*-taaks) *adv* (at) noon, midday

Mitte (*mi*-ter) *f* midst, middle

mitteilen (*mit*-tigh-lern) *v* communicate, notify, inform

Mitteilung (*mit*-tigh-loong) *f* (pl ∼en) communication, information

Mittel (*mi*-terl) *nt* (pl ∼) means; remedy; **empfängnisverhütendes** ∼ contraceptive

Mittelalter (*mi*-terl-ahl-terr) *nt* Middle Ages

mittelalterlich (*mi*-terl-ahl-terr-likh) *adj* mediaeval

mittelmäßig (*mi*-terl-mai-sikh) *adj* medium; moderate

Mittelmeer (*mi*-terl-māyr) *nt* Mediterranean

Mittelpunkt (*mi*-terl-poongkt) *m* (pl ∼e) centre, center *Am*

Mittelstand (*mi*-terl-shtahnt) *m* middle class

mitten in (*mi*-tern in) in the middle of

Mitternacht (*mi*-terr-nahkht) *f* midnight

mittler (*mit*-ler-rer) *adj* middle, medium

mittlerweile (mit-lerr-*vigh*-ler) *adv* in the meantime, meanwhile

Mittwoch (*mit*-vokh) *m* Wednesday

mitzählen (*mit*-tsai-lern) *v* count

Mixer (*mi*-kserr) *m* (pl ∼) mixer

Möbel (*mūr*-berl) *ntpl* furniture

mobil (moa-*beel*) *adj* mobile

möblieren (mur-*blee*-rern) *v* furnish

Mode (*mōa*-der) *f* (pl ∼n) fashion

Modell (moa-*dehl*) *nt* (pl ∼e) model

modellieren (moa-deh-*lee*-rern) *v* model

Modem (*mōa*-derm) *nt* (pl ∼s) modem

modern (moa-*dehrn*) *adj* modern; fashionable

modifizieren (moa-di-fi-*tsee*-rern) *v* modify

*mögen (*mūr*-gern) *v* like, fancy; *may

möglich (*mūrk*-likh) *adj* possible; eventual

Möglichkeit (*mūrk*-likh-kight) *f* (pl ∼en) possibility

Mohair (moa-*hair*) *m* mohair

Mohn (mōan) *m* (pl ∼e) poppy

Mohrrübe (*mōar*-rēw-ber) *f* (pl ∼n) carrot

Molkerei (mol-ker-*righ*) *f* (pl ∼en) dairy

mollig (*mo*-likh) *adj* plump

Moment (moa-*mehnt*) *m* (pl ∼e) moment

Monarch (moa-*nahrkh*) *m* (pl ∼en), **-in** *f* ruler, monarch

Monarchie (moa-nahr-*khee*) *f* (pl ∼n) monarchy

Monat (*mōa*-naht) *m* (pl ∼e) month

monatlich (*mōa*-naht-likh) *adj* monthly

Mönch (murnkh) *m* (pl ∼e) monk

Mond (mōant) *m* (pl ∼e) moon

Mondlicht (*mōant*-likht) *nt* moonlight

Monolog (moa-noa-*lōag*) m (pl ~e)
monologue

Monopol (moa-noa-*pōal*) nt (pl ~e)
monopoly

monoton (moa-noa-*tōan*) adj
monotonous

Montag (*mōan*-taak) m Monday

Monteur (mon-*tūrr*) m (pl ~e)
mechanic

montieren (mon-*tee*-rern) v assemble

Monument (moa-noo-*mehnt*) nt (pl
~e) monument

Moor (*mōar*) nt (pl ~e) moor

Moorhuhn (*mōar*-hōon) nt (pl ~er)
grouse

Moos (*mōass*) nt (pl ~e) moss

Moped (*mōa*-peht) nt (pl ~s) moped;
motorbike Am

Moral (moa-*raal*) f moral; morality

moralisch (moa-*raa*-lish) adj moral

Morast (moa-*rahst*) m swamp

Mord (mort) m (pl ~e) murder,
assassination

morden (*mor*-dern) v murder

Mörder (*murr*-derr) m (pl ~), **-in** f
murderer

Morgen (*mor*-gern) m (pl ~) morning

morgen (*mor*-gern) adv tomorrow

Morgendämmerung (*mor*-gern-deh-
mer-roong) f dawn

Morgenrock (*mor*-gern-rok) m (pl ~e)
dressing gown

morgens (*mor*-gerns) adv in the
morning

Morgenzeitung (*mor*-gern-tsigh-
toong) f (pl ~en) morning paper

Morphium (*mor*-f'oom) nt morphine,
morphia

Mosaik (moa-zah-*eek*) nt (pl ~en)
mosaic

Moschee (mo-*shāy*) f (pl ~n) mosque

Moskito (moss-*kee*-toa) m (pl ~s)
mosquito

Moskitonetz (moss-*kee*-toa-nehts) nt

(pl ~e) mosquito net

Motel (moa-*tehl*) nt (pl ~s) motel

Motiv (moa-*teef*) nt (pl ~e) motive;
pattern

Motor (*mōa*-tor) m (pl ~en) engine,
motor

Motorboot (*mōa*-tor-bōat) nt (pl ~e)
motorboat

Motorhaube (*mōa*-tor-hou-ber) f (pl
~n) bonnet; hood Am

Motorrad (*mōa*-tor-raat) nt (pl ~er)
motorcycle

Motorroller (*mōa*-tor-ro-lerr) m (pl ~)
scooter

Motorschiff (*mōa*-tor-shif) nt (pl ~e)
motor ship

Motte (*mo*-ter) f (pl ~n) moth

Möwe (*mūr*-ver) f (pl ~n) gull

Mücke (*mew*-ker) f (pl ~n) mosquito

müde (*mew*-der) adj tired; weary

Mühe (*mew*-er) f (pl ~n) trouble;
difficulty, pains; **sich ~ *geben**
bother

Mühle (*mew*-ler) f (pl ~n) mill

Müll (mewl) m garbage, trash

Müller (*mew*-lerr) m (pl ~), **-in** f miller

Multiplikation (mool-ti-pli-kah-
ts'*ōan*) f (pl ~en) multiplication

multiplizieren (mool-ti-pli-*tsee*-rern)
v multiply

Mumm (moom) m guts

Mumps (moomps) m mumps

Mund (moont) m (pl ~er) mouth

Mundart (*moont*-ahrt) f (pl ~en)
dialect

münden (*mewn*-dern) adj *flow into;
*lead into

mündig (*mewn*-dikh) adj of age

mündlich (*mewnt*-likh) adj oral,
verbal

Mündung (*mewn*-doong) f (pl ~en)
mouth

Mundwasser (*moont*-vah-serr) nt
mouthwash

Münze (*mewn*-tser) *f* (pl ∾n) coin; token

Münzwäscherei (*mewnts*-veh-sher-righ) *f* (pl ∾en) launderette

Murmel (*moor*-merl) *f* (pl ∾n) marble

Muschel (*moo*-sherl) *f* (pl ∾n) seashell, shell; mussel

Museum (moo-*zāy*-oom) *nt* (pl Museen) museum

Musical (*m*y*ōō*-zi-kerl) *nt* (pl ∾s) musical comedy

Musik (moo-*zeek*) *f* music

musikalisch (moo-zi-*kaa*-lish) *adj* musical

Musiker (*mōō*-zi-kerr) *m* (pl ∾), **-in** *f* musician

Musikinstrument (moo-*zeek*-in-stroo-mehnt) *nt* (pl ∾e) musical instrument

Muskatnuss (mooss-*kaat*-nooss) *f* (pl ∾e) nutmeg

Muskel (*mooss*-kerl) *m* (pl ∾n) muscle

muskulös (mooss-koo-*lūrss*) *adj* muscular

Muße (*mōō*-ser) *f* leisure

***müssen** (*mew*-sern) *v* *must; need to, *have to, *be obliged to, *should; *be bound to

müßig (*mēw*-sikh) *adj* idle

Muster (*mooss*-terr) *nt* (pl ∾) pattern; sample

Mut (*mōōt*) *m* courage

mutig (*mōō*-tikh) *adj* brave, courageous; plucky

Mutter (*moo*-terr) *f* (pl ∾) mother

Muttersprache (*moo*-terr-shpraa-kher) *f* native language, mother tongue

Mütze (*mew*-tser) *f* (pl ∾n) cap

Mythos (*mēw*-toss) *m* (pl Mythen) myth

N

Nabel (*naa*-berl) *m* (pl ∾) navel

nach (naakh) *prep* to; towards, for; at; after; **unterwegs ∾** bound for

nachahmen (*naakh*-aa-mern) *v* copy; imitate

Nachahmung (*naakh*-aa-moong) *f* imitation

Nachbar (*nahkh*-baar) *m* (pl ∾n) neighbo(u)r

Nachbarschaft (*nahkh*-baar-shahft) *f* (pl ∾en) neighbo(u)rhood; vicinity

nachdem (naakh-*dāym*) *conj* after

***nachdenken** (*naakh*-dehng-kern) *v* *think

nachdenklich (*naakh*-dehngk-likh) *adj* thoughtful

nachfolgen (*naakh*-fol-gern) *v*

succeed

Nachfrage (*naakh*-fraa-ger) *f* (pl ∾n) demand; inquiry

nachfragen (*naakh*-fraa-gern) *v* inquire

***nachgeben** (*naakh*-gāy-bern) *v* *give in, indulge

nachher (naakh-*hāyr*) *adv* afterwards

Nachkomme (*naakh*-ko-mer) *m* (pl ∾n) descendant

nachlässig (*naakh*-leh-sikh) *adj* neglectful, careless

nachmachen (*naakh*-mah-khern) *v* imitate

Nachmittag (*naakh*-mi-taak) *m* (pl ∾e) afternoon

Nachname (*naakh*-naa-mer) *m* family

name

nachprüfen (*naakh*-prēw-fern) *v* verify

Nachricht (*naakh*-rikht) *f* (pl ~en) news *pl*; message; information; **Nachrichten** news

Nachsaison (*naakh*-zeh-zawng) *f* low season

*nachsenden (*naakh*-zehn-dern) *v* forward

nächst (naikhst) *adj* next, following

nachstreben (*naakh*-shtray-bern) *v* pursue

Nacht (nahkht) *f* (pl ~e) night; **bei ~** by night; **über ~** overnight

Nachteil (*naakh*-tighl) *m* (pl ~e) disadvantage

nachteilig (*naakh*-tigh-likh) *adj* harmful

Nachtflug (*nahkht*-flook) *m* (pl ~e) night flight

Nachthemd (*nahkht*-hehmt) *nt* (pl ~en) nightdress

Nachtigall (*nahkh*-ti-gahl) *f* (pl ~en) nightingale

Nachtisch (*naakh*-tish) *m* (pl ~e) dessert, sweet

Nachtklub (*nahkht*-kloop) *m* (pl ~s) cabaret

Nachtkrem (*nahkht*-kraym) *f* (pl ~s) night cream

nächtlich (*nehkht*-likh) *adj* nightly

Nachtlokal (*nahkht*-loa-kaal) *nt* (pl ~e) nightclub

Nachttarif (*nahkht*-tah-reef) *m* (pl ~e) night rate

Nachtzug (*nahkht*-tsook) *m* (pl ~e) night train

Nacken (*nah*-kern) *m* (pl ~) nape of the neck

nackt (nahkt) *adj* naked; nude, bare

Nadel (*naa*-derl) *f* (pl ~n) needle

Nagel (*naa*-gerl) *m* (pl ~) nail

Nagelbürste (*naa*-gerl-bewrs-ter) *f* (pl ~n) nailbrush

Nagelfeile (*naa*-gerl-figh-ler) *f* (pl ~n) nail file

Nagellack (*naa*-gerl-lahk) *m* nail polish

nagelneu (*naa*-gerl-noi) *adj* brand-new

Nagelschere (*naa*-gerl-shāy-rer) *f* (pl ~n) nail scissors *pl*

Nähe (*nāy*-er) *f* vicinity

nahe (*naa*-er) *adj* nearby, near; close

nähen (*nai*-ern) *v* sew; sew up

nähern (*nai*-errn) *v*; **sich ~** approach

nahezu (*naa*-er-tsōō) *adv* practically

Nähmaschine (*nai*-mah-shee-ner) *f* (pl ~n) sewing machine

nahrhaft (*naar*-hahft) *adj* nutritious, nourishing

Nahrung (*naa*-roong) *f* food

Nahrungsmittel (*naa*-roongs-mi-terl) *ntpl* foodstuffs *pl*

Nahrungsmittelvergiftung (*naa*-roongs-mi-terl-fehr-gif-toong) *f* food poisoning

Naht (naat) *f* (pl ~e) seam

nahtlos (*naat*-lōāss) *adj* seamless

Nahverkehrszug (*naa*-fehr-kāyrs-tsōōk) *m* (pl ~e) local train

Nähzeug (*nai*-tsoik) *nt* sewing-kit

naiv (nah-*eef*) *adj* naïve

Name (*naa*-mer) *m* (pl ~n) name; fame; denomination; **im Namen von** on behalf of, in the name of

nämlich (*naim*-likh) *adv* namely

Narbe (*nahr*-ber) *f* (pl ~n) scar

Narkose (nahr-*kōā*-zer) *f* narcosis

Narr (nahr) *m* (pl ~en) fool

Narzisse (nahr-*tsi*-ser) *f* (pl ~n) daffodil

naschen (*nah*-shern) *v* nibble; **gern ~** have a sweet tooth

Nase (*naa*-zer) *f* (pl ~n) nose

Nasenbluten (*naa*-zern-blōō-tern) *nt* nosebleed

Nasenloch (*naa*-zern-lokh) *nt* (pl ⸚er) nostril

Nashorn (*naass*-horn) *nt* (pl ⸚er) rhinoceros

nass (nahss) *adj* wet; damp, moist

Nässe (*neh*-ser) *f* wetness

Nation (nah-ts^y*oan*) *f* (pl ⁓en) nation

national (nah-ts^yoa-*naal*) *adj* national

Nationalhymne (nah-ts^yoa-*naal*-hewm-ner) *f* (pl ⁓n) national anthem

Natur (nah-*toor*) *f* nature

natürlich (nah-*tewr*-likh) *adj* natural; *adv* naturally

Naturschutzgebiet (nah-*toor*-shoots-ger-beet) *nt* nature reserve, wildlife reserve; national park

Naturschutzpark (nah-*toor*-shoots-pahrk) *m* (pl ⁓s) national park

Naturwissenschaft (nah-*toor*-vi-sern-shahft) *f* physics

Navigation (nah-vi-gah-ts^y*oan*) *f* navigation

Nebel (*nay*-berl) *m* (pl ⁓) fog, mist; haze

nebelig (*nay*-ber-likh) *adj* foggy, misty

Nebellampe (*nay*-berl-lahm-per) *f* (pl ⁓n) foglamp

neben (*nay*-bern) *prep* next to, beside

nebenan (*nay*-bern-*ahn*) *adv* next-door

Nebenanschluss (*nay*-bern-ahn-shlooss) *m* (pl ⸚e) extension

Nebenbedeutung (*nay*-bern-ber-doi-toong) *f* (pl ⁓en) connotation

nebeneinander (*nay*-bern- igh-nahn-derr) *adv* side by side; next to one another

Nebenfluss (*nay*-bern-flooss) *m* (pl ⸚e) tributary

Nebengebäude (*nay*-bern-ger-boi-der) *nt* (pl ⁓) annex

nebensächlich (*nay*-bern-zehkh-likh) *adj* minor, irrelevant

neblig (*nay*-blik) *adj* foggy, misty

necken (*neh*-kern) *v* tease

Neffe (*neh*-fer) *m* (pl ⁓n) nephew

Negativ (nay-gah-*teef*) *nt* (pl ⁓e) negative

negativ (nay-gah-*teef*) *adj* negative

Neid (night) *m* envy

neidisch (*nigh*-dish) *adj* envious

neigen (*nigh*-gern) *v* *be inclined to; tend; **sich** ⁓ slant

Neigung (*nigh*-goong) *f* (pl ⁓en) incline; inclination, tendency

nein (nighn) no

Nelke (*nel*-ker) *f* carnation; clove

*nennen (*neh*-nern) *v* call; name; mention

Nerv (nehrf) *m* (pl ⁓en) nerve

nervös (nehr-*vürss*) *adj* nervous

Nerz (nehrts) *m* (pl ⁓e) mink

Nest (nehst) *nt* (pl ⁓er) nest

nett (neht) *adj* nice, pleasant, kind; neat

netto (*neh*-toa) *adj* net

Netz (nehts) *nt* (pl ⁓e) net; network

Netzhaut (*nehts*-hout) *f* retina

neu (noi) *adj* new

Neuerwerbung (*noi*-ehr-vehr-boong) *f* (pl ⁓en) acquisition

Neugier (*noi*-geer) *f* curiosity

neugierig (*noi*-gee-rikh) *adj* curious, inquisitive

Neuigkeit (*noi*-ikh-kight) *f* (pl ⁓en) news

Neujahr (*noi*-^yaar) New Year

neulich (*noi*-likh) *adv* recently

neun (noin) *num* nine

neunte (*noin*-ter) *num* ninth

neunzehn (*noin*-tsayn) *num* nineteen

neunzehnte (*noin*-tsayn-ter) *num* nineteenth

neunzig (*noin*-tsikh) *num* ninety

Neuralgie (noi-rahl-*gee*) *f* neuralgia

Neurose (noi-*roa*-zer) *f* (pl ⁓n) neurosis

Neuseeland (noi-z$\overline{ay}$-lahnt) New Zealand

neutral (noi-*traal*) *adj* neutral

nicht (nikht) *adv* not

Nichte (*nikh*-ter) *f* (pl ⁓n) niece

nichtig (*nikh*-tikh) *adj* void

nichts (nikhts) *pron* nothing; nil

nichtsdestoweniger (nikhts-dehss-toa-*vay*-ni-gerr) *adv* nevertheless

nichts sagend (*nikhts*-zaa-gernt) *adj* insignificant

Nickel (*ni*-kerl) *m* nickel

Nicken (*ni*-kern) *nt* nod

nicken (*ni*-kern) *v* nod

nie (nee) *adv* never

nieder (*nee*-derr) *adv* down; over

niedergeschlagen (*nee*-derr-ger-shlaa-gern) *adj* depressed; down, low, sad, blue

Niedergeschlagenheit (*nee*-derr-ger-shlaa-gern-hight) *f* depression

Niederlage (*nee*-derr-laa-ger) *f* (pl ⁓n) defeat

Niederlande (*nee*-derr-lahn-der) *fpl* the Netherlands

Niederländer (*nee*-derr-lehn-derr) *m* (pl ⁓) Dutchman

Niederländerin (*nee*-derr-lehn-der-rin) *f* (pl ⁓nen) Dutchwoman

niederländisch (*nee*-derr-lehn-dish) *adj* Dutch

niederlassen (*nee*-derr-lah-sern) *v*: **sich** ⁓ settle down

niederlegen (*nee*-derr-l$\overline{ay}$-gern) *v*: **sich** ⁓ *lie down

***niederreißen** (*nee*-derr-righ-sern) *v* demolish

Niederschläge (*nee*-derr-shlai-ger) *mpl* precipitation

***niederschlagen** (*nee*-derr-shlaa-gern) *v* knock down

niederträchtig (*nee*-derr-trehkh-tikh) *adj* foul, mean

niedrig (*nee*-drikh) *adj* low

niemals (*nee*-maals) *adv* never

niemand (*nee*-mahnt) *pron* nobody, no one

Niere (*nee*-rer) *f* (pl ⁓n) kidney

niesen (*nee*-zern) *v* sneeze

Nigeria (ni-g$\overline{ay}$-r^{y}ah) Nigeria

Nigerianer (ni-gay-r^{y}aa-nerr) *m* (pl ⁓), **-in** *f* Nigerian

nigerianisch (ni-gay-r^{y}aa-nish) *adj* Nigerian

Nikotin (ni-koa-*teen*) *nt* nicotine

nirgends (*neer*-gernts) *adv* nowhere

Niveau (ni-*v$\overline{oa}$*) *nt* (pl ⁓s) level

noch (nokh) *adv* still; yet; ⁓ **ein** another; ⁓ **einmal** once more; **weder ... ⁓** neither ... nor

nochmals (*nokh*-maals) *adv* again

nominell (noa-mi-*nehl*) *adj* nominal

Nonne (*no*-ner) *f* (pl ⁓n) nun

Norden (*nor*-dern) *m* north

nördlich (*nurrt*-likh) *adj* northern, northerly, north

Nordosten (nort-*oss*-tern) *m* northeast

Nordpol (*nort*-p$\overline{oa}$l) *m* North Pole

Nordsee (*nort*-z$\overline{ay}$) *f* North Sea

Nordwesten (nort-*vehss*-tern) *m* north-west

Norm (norm) *f* (pl ⁓en) standard

normal (nor-*maal*) *adj* normal; regular

normalerweise (nor-*maa*-lerr-vigh-zer) *adv* normally, usually

Norwegen (*nor*-v$\overline{ay}$-gern) Norway

Norweger (*nor*-v$\overline{ay}$-gerr) *m* (pl ⁓), **-in** *f* Norwegian

norwegisch (*nor*-v$\overline{ay}$-gish) *adj* Norwegian

Not (n$\overline{oa}$t) *f* (pl ⁓e) distress, misery; need

Notar (noa-*taar*) *m* (pl ⁓e) notary

Notarzt (*n$\overline{oa}$t*-ahrtst) *m* doctor on emergency call

Notausgang (*n$\overline{oa}$t*-ouss-gahng) *m* (pl ⁓e) emergency exit

Note (*noa*-ter) *f* note; banknote; mark

Notfall (*nōat*-fahl) *m* (pl ≈e) emergency

notieren (*noa*-teer-ern) *v* note down, *make a note

nötig (*nūr*-tikh) *adj* necessary; ~ *haben need

Notiz (noa-*teets*) *f* (pl ~en) note

Notizblock (noa-*teets*-blok) *m* (pl ≈e) writing pad

Notizbuch (noa-*teets*-bōokh) *nt* (pl ≈er) notebook

Notlage (*nōat*-laa-ger) *f* emergency

Notsignal (*nōat*-zi-gnaal) *nt* (pl ≈e) distress signal

Nottreppe (*nōat*-treh-per) *f* (pl ~n) fire escape

notwendig (*nōat*-vehn-dikh) *adj* necessary

Notwendigkeit (*nōat*-vehn-dikh-kight) *f* (pl ~en) need, necessity

Nougat (*nōo*-gaht) *m* nougat

November (noa-*vehm*-berr) November

Nuance (new-*ahng*-ser) *f* (pl ~n) nuance

nüchtern (*newkh*-terrn) *adj* matter-of-fact; sober

nuklear (noo-klay-*aar*) *adj* nuclear

Null (nool) *f* (pl ~en) nought; zero

Nummer (*noo*-merr) *f* (pl ~n) number; size; act

Nummernschild (*noo*-merrn-shilt) *nt* (pl ≈er) registration plate; licence plate *Am*

nun (nōon) *adv* now

nur (nōor) *adv* merely; only, exclusively

Nuss (nooss) *f* (pl ≈e) nut

Nussknacker (*nooss*-knah-kerr) *m* (pl ~) nutcrackers *pl*

Nussschale (*nooss*-shaa-ler) *f* (pl ~n) nutshell

Nutzen (*noo*-tsern) *m* profit; benefit; interest; utility, use

nützen (*new*-tsern) *v* *be of use

nützlich (*newts*-likh) *adj* useful

nutzlos (*noots*-lōass) *adj* useless; idle

Nylon (*nigh*-lon) *nt* nylon

O

Oase (oa-*aa*-zer) *f* (pl ~n) oasis

ob (op) *conj* whether; ~ ... oder whether ... or

Obdach (*op*-dahkh) *nt* cover

oben (*ōa*-bern) *adv* above; upstairs; overhead; nach ~ up; upstairs; ~ auf on top of

Ober (*ōa*-berr) *m* (pl ~) waiter

ober (*ōa*-berr) *adj* superior, upper; Ober- chief

Oberdeck (*ōa*-berr-dehk) *nt* main deck

Oberfläche (*ōa*-berr-fleh-kher) *f* (pl ~n) surface

oberflächlich (*ōa*-berr-flehkh-likh) *adj* superficial

oberhalb (*ōa*-berr-hahlp) *prep* over

Oberkellner (*ōa*-berr-kehl-nerr) *m* (pl ~) head waiter

Oberschenkel (*ōa*-berr-shehng-kerl) *m* (pl ~) thigh

Oberseite (*ōa*-berr-zigh-ter) *f* (pl ~n) top side

Oberst (*ōa*-berrst) *m* (pl ~en) colonel

oberst (*ōa*-berrst) *adj* top

obgleich (op-*glighkh*) *conj* although,

though
Obhut (*op*-hoot) *f* custody
Objekt (op-*ʸehkt*) *nt* (pl ~e) object
objektiv (op-*ʸehk-teef*) *adj* objective
obligatorisch (oa-bli-gah-*tōa*-rish) *adj* compulsory, obligatory
Observatorium (op-zehr-vah-*tōa*-rʸoom) *nt* (pl -rien) observatory
Obst (*ōapst*) *nt* fruit
Obstgarten (*ōapst*-gahr-tern) *m* (pl ⸚) orchard
obszön (ops-*tsȳrn*) *adj* obscene
obwohl (op-*vōal*) *conj* although, though
Ochse (*o*-kser) *m* (pl ~n) ox
oder (*ōa*-derr) *conj* or
Ofen (*ōa*-fern) *m* (pl ⸚) stove; furnace
offen (*o*-fern) *adj* open
offenbaren (o-fern-*baa*-rern) *v* reveal
offenherzig (o-fern-hehr-tsikh) *adj* open
offensichtlich (o-fern-zikht-likh) *adj* obvious, apparent, evident
offensiv (o-fehn-*zeef*) *adj* offensive
Offensive (o-fehn-*zee*-ver) *f* (pl ~n) offensive
öffentlich (*ur*-fernt-likh) *adj* public
offiziell (o-fi-*tsʸehl*) *adj* official
Offizier (o-fi-*tseer*) *m* (pl ~e) officer
öffnen (*urf*-nern) *v* open
Öffnung (*urf*-noong) *f* (pl ~en) opening
Öffnungszeiten (*urf*-noongs-tsigh-tern) *fpl* business hours
oft (oft) *adv* often; frequently
ohne (*ōa*-ner) *prep* without
ohnehin (ōa-ner-*hin*) *adv* anyway
ohnmächtig (*ōan*-mehkh-tikh) *adj* unconscious; ~ **werden** faint
Ohr (ōar) *nt* (pl ~en) ear
Ohrenschmerzen (*ōa*-rern-shmehr-tsern) *mpl* earache
Ohrring (*ōar*-ring) *m* (pl ~e) earring
Oktober (ok-*tōa*-berr) October

Öl (ūrl) *nt* (pl ~e) oil
ölen (*ūr*-lern) *v* lubricate
Ölfilter (*ūrl*-fil-terr) *nt* (pl ~) oil filter
Ölgemälde (*ūrl*-ger-mail-der) *nt* (pl ~) oil painting
ölig (*ūr*-likh) *adj* oily
Olive (oa-*lee*-ver) *f* (pl ~n) olive
Olivenöl (oa-*lee*-vern-ūrl) *nt* olive oil
Ölquelle (*ūrl*-kveh-ler) *f* (pl ~n) oil well
Ölraffinerie (*ūrl*-rah-fi-ner-ree) *f* (pl ~n) oil refinery
Oma (*ōa*-mah) *f* (pl ~s) grandmother, grandma
Onkel (*ong*-kerl) *m* (pl ~) uncle
Onyx (*ōa*-newks) *m* (pl ~e) onyx
Opa (*ōa*-pah) *m* (pl ~s) grandfather, granddad
Opal (oa-*paal*) *m* (pl ~e) opal
Oper (*ōa*-perr) *f* (pl ~n) opera
Operation (oa-pay-rah-*tsʸōan*) *f* (pl ~en) operation; surgery
Operette (oa-pay-*reh*-ter) *f* (pl ~n) operetta
operieren (oa-pay-*ree*-rern) *v* operate
Opernhaus (*ōa*-perrn-houss) *nt* (pl ⸚er) opera house
Opfer (*o*-pferr) *nt* (pl ~) sacrifice; casualty, victim
Opposition (o-poa-zi-*tsʸōan*) *f* opposition
Optiker (*op*-ti-kerr) *m* (pl ~), **-in** *f* optician
Optimismus (op-ti-*miss*-mooss) *m* optimism
Optimist (op-ti-*mist*) *m* (pl ~en), **-in** *f* optimist
optimistisch (op-ti-*miss*-tish) *adj* optimistic
orange (oa-*rahng*-zher) *adj* orange
Orchester (or-*kehss*-terr) *nt* (pl ~) orchestra
Orden (*or*-dern) *m* (pl ~) congregation
ordentlich (*or*-dernt-likh) *adj* tidy

ordinär (or-di-*nair*) *adj* vulgar
ordnen (*or*-dnern) *v* arrange; sort
Ordnung (*or*-dnoong) *f* order;
method, system; **in ~** in order; **in
Ordnung!** okay!
Organ (or-*gaan*) *nt* (pl ~e) organ
Organisation (or-gah-ni-zah-*ts'ōan*) *f*
(pl ~en) organization
organisch (or-*gaa*-nish) *adj* organic
organisieren (or-gah-ni-*zee*-rern) *v*
organize
Orgel (*or*-gerl) *f* (pl ~n) organ
Orient (*ōa*-ri-ehnt) *m* Orient
orientalisch (oa-ri-ehn-*taa*-lish) *adj*
oriental
orientieren (oa-ri-ehn-*tee*-rern) *v*:
sich ~ orientate o.s.
original (oa-ri-gi-*naal*) original, real,
genuine
originell (oa-ri-gi-*nehl*) *adj* original
ornamental (or-nah-mehn-*taal*) *adj*
ornamental
Ort (ort) *m* (pl ~e) place

orthodox (or-toa-*doks*) *adj* orthodox
örtlich (*urrt*-likh) *adj* local; regional
Ortsansässige (*orts*-ahn-zeh-si-ger)
m/f (pl ~n) resident
Ortsgespräch (*orts*-ger-shpraikh) *nt*
(pl ~e) local call
Ortsnetzkennzahl (*orts*-nehts-kehn-
tsaal) *f* area code
Osten (*oss*-tern) *m* east
Ostern (*ōass*-terrn) Easter
Österreich (*ūrss*-ter-righkh) Austria
Österreicher (*ūrss*-ter-righ-kherr) *m*
(pl ~), **-in** *f* Austrian
österreichisch (*ūr*-ster-righ-khish)
adj Austrian
östlich (*urst*-likh) *adj* eastern, easterly
Ostsee (*osst*- zāy) *f*: **die Ostsee** the
Baltic (Sea)
Ouvertüre (oo-vehr-*tēw*-rer) *f* (pl ~n)
overture
oval (oa-*vaal*) *adj* oval
Ozean (*ōa*-tsay-aan) *m* (pl ~e) ocean

P

Paar (paar) *nt* (pl ~e) pair; couple
Pacht (pahkht) *f* lease
Päckchen (*pehk*-khern) *nt* (pl ~)
packet
packen (*pah*-kern) *v* pack
Packpapier (*pahk*-pah-peer) *nt*
wrapping paper
Paddel (*pah*-derl) *nt* (pl ~) paddle
Paket (pah-*kāyt*) *nt* (pl ~e) parcel,
package
Pakistan (*paa*-kiss-taan) Pakistan
Pakistaner (paa-kiss-*taa*-nerr) *m* (pl
~), **-in** *f* Pakistani
pakistanisch (paa-kiss-*taa*-nish) *adj*
Pakistani

Palast (pah-*lahst*) *m* (pl ~e) palace
Palme (*pahl*-mer) *f* (pl ~n) palm (tree)
Pampelmuse (pahm-perl-*mōō*-zer) *f*
(pl ~n) grapefruit
Paneel (pah-*nāyl*) *nt* (pl ~e) panel
Panik (*paa*-nik) *f* panic
Panne (*pah*-ner) *f* (pl ~n) breakdown;
eine ~ *haben *break down
Pantoffel (pahn-*to*-ferl) *m* (pl ~n)
slipper
Papagei (pah-pah-*gigh*) *m* (pl ~e)
parrot
Papier (pah-*peer*) *nt* paper
Papiere (pah-*pee*-rer) *pl* documents,
papers; identification

Papierkorb (pah-*peer*-korp) *m* (pl ⁓e) wastepaper basket

Papierserviette (pah-*peer*-zehr-vʸeh-ter) *f* (pl ⁓n) paper napkin

Papiertaschentuch (pah-*peer*-tah-shern-tōōkh) *nt* (pl ⁓er) tissue

Pappe (*pah*-per) *f* cardboard; **Papp-** cardboard

Papst (paapst) *m* (pl ⁓e) pope

Parade (pah-*raa*-der) *f* (pl ⁓n) parade; review

parallel (pah-rah-*lāyl*) *adj* parallel

Parallele (pah-rah-*lāy*-ler) *f* (pl ⁓n) parallel

Parfüm (pahr-*fewm*) *nt* (pl ⁓s) scent; perfume

Park (pahrk) *m* (pl ⁓s) park

parken (*pahr*-kern) *v* park; **Parken verboten** no parking

Parkett (pahr-keht) *nt* parquet; stalls *pl*

Parkgebühr (*pahrk*-ger-bēwr) *f* (pl ⁓en) parking fee

Parkhaus (*pahrk*-houss) *nt* multistor(e)y car park

Parkleuchte (*pahrk*-loikh-ter) *f* (pl ⁓n) parking light

Parkplatz (*pahrk*-plahts) *m* (pl ⁓e) car park, parking lot *Am*

Parkuhr (*pahrk*-ōōr) *f* (pl ⁓en) parking meter

Parkzone (*pahrk*-tsōa-ner) *f* (pl ⁓n) parking zone

Parlament (pahr-lah-*mehnt*) *nt* (pl ⁓e) parliament

parlamentarisch (pahr-lah-mehn-*taa*-rish) *adj* parliamentary

Partei (pahr-*tigh*) *f* (pl ⁓en) party; side

parteiisch (pahr-*tigh*-ish) *adj* partial

Partie (pahr-*tee*) *f* (pl ⁓n) batch

Partner (*pahrt*-nerr) *m* (pl ⁓), **-in** *f* associate; partner

Party (*paar*-ti) *f* (pl -ties) party

Parzelle (pahr-*tseh*-ler) *f* (pl ⁓n) plot

Pass (pahss) *m* (pl ⁓e) passport

Passagier (pah-sah-*zheer*) *m* (pl ⁓e) passenger

Passant (pah-*sahnt*) *m* (pl ⁓en), **-in** *f* passer-by

passen (*pah*-sern) *v* fit; suit; ⁓ **zu** match

passend (*pah*-sernt) *adj* adequate, proper; convenient

passieren (pah-*see*-rern) *v* pass; happen

Passion (pah-sʸōan) *f* passion

passiv (*pah*-seef) *adj* passive

Passfoto (*pahss*-fōa-toa) *nt* (pl ⁓s) passport photograph

Passkontrolle (*pahss*-kon-tro-ler) *f* (pl ⁓n) passport control

Paste (*pahss*-ter) *f* (pl ⁓n) paste

Pastete (pahss-*teh*-ter) *f* pie, pastry

Pastor (*pahss*-tor) *m* (pl ⁓en), **-in** *f* rector, clergyman, clergywoman

Pate (*paa*-ter) *m* (pl ⁓n) godfather

Patent (pah-*tehnt*) *nt* (pl ⁓e) patent

Pater (*paa*-terr) *m* (pl ⁓) father

Patient (pah-tsʸehnt) *m* (pl ⁓en), **-in** *f* patient

Patin (*paa*-tin) f (pl ⁓nen) godmother

Patriot (pah-tri-*ōat*) *m* (pl ⁓en), **-in** *f* patriot

Patrone (pah-*trōa*-ner) *f* (pl ⁓n) cartridge

patrouillieren (pah-trool-ʸ*ee*-rern) *v* patrol

Pauschalsumme (pou-*shaal*-zoo-mer) *f* (pl ⁓n) lump sum

Pause (*pou*-zer) *f* (pl ⁓n) pause; break, interval, intermission

pausieren (pou-*zee*-rern) *v* pause

Pavillon (*pah*-vi-lʸawnḡ) *m* (pl ⁓s) pavilion

Pazifismus (pah-tsi-*fiss*-mooss) *m* pacifism

Pazifist (pah-tsi-*fist*) *m* (pl ⁓en), **-in** *f* pacifist

pazifistisch (pah-tsi-*fiss*-tish) *adj* pacifist

Pech (pehkh) *nt* bad luck

Pedal (pay-*daal*) *nt* (pl ~en) pedal

peinlich (*pighn*-likh) *adj* embarrassing, awkward

Peitsche (*pigh*-cher) *f* (pl ~n) whip

Pelikan (*pāy*-li-kaan) *m* (pl ~e) pelican

Pelz (pehlts) *m* (pl ~e) fur

Pelzmantel (*pehlts*-mahn-terl) *m* (pl ~) fur coat

Pendler (*pehn*-dlerr) *m* (pl ~), **-in** *f* commuter

Penicillin (peh-ni-tsi-*leen*) *nt* penicillin

Pension (pahng-s^y*ōan*) *f* (pl ~en) board; boardinghouse; pension

pensioniert (pahng-s^yoa-*neert*) *adj* retired

perfekt (pehr-*fehkt*) *adj* perfect

Perfektion (pehr-fehk-*ts*^y*ōan*) *f* perfection

periodisch (pay-r^y*ōā*-dish) *adj* periodical

Perle (*pehr*-ler) *f* (pl ~n) pearl; bead

perlend (*pehr*-lernt) *adj* sparkling

Perlmutt (*pehrl*-moot) *nt* mother of pearl

Perser (*pehr*-zerr) *m* (pl ~), **-in** *f* Persian

Persien (*pehr*-z^yern) Persia

persisch (*pehr*-zish) *adj* Persian

Person (pehr-*zōan*) *f* (pl ~en) person; **pro ~** per person

Personal (pehr-zoa-*naal*) *nt* staff, personnel

Personenzug (pehr-z*ōā*-nern-ts*ōō*k) *m* (pl ~e) passenger train

persönlich (pehr-z*ǖ*rn-likh) *adj* personal, private

Persönlichkeit (pehr-z*ǖ*rn-likh-kight) *f* (pl ~en) personality

Perspektive (pehr-spehk-*tee*-ver) *f* (pl ~n) perspective

Perücke (peh-*rew*-ker) *f* (pl ~n) wig

Pessimismus (peh-si-*miss*-mooss) *m* pessimism

Pessimist (peh-si-*mist*) *m* (pl ~en), **-in** *f* pessimist

pessimistisch (peh-si-*miss*-tish) *adj* pessimistic

Petersilie (pay-terr-*zee*-l^yer) *f* parsley

Petroleum (pay-*trōā*-lay-oom) *nt* petroleum, oil; paraffin

Pfad (pfaat) *m* (pl ~e) trail, lane, path

Pfadfinder (*pfaat*-fin-derr) *m* (pl ~) boy scout, scout

Pfadfinderin (*pfaat*-fin-der-rin) *f* (pl ~nen) girl guide

Pfand (pfahnt) *nt* (pl ~er) security; deposit

Pfandflasche (*pfahnt*-flah-sher) *f* returnable bottle

Pfanne (*pfah*-ner) *f* (pl ~n) saucepan, pan

Pfarrer (*pfah*-rerr) *m* (pl ~), **-in** *f* clergyman, clergywoman; rector, parson

Pfarrhaus (*pfahr*-houss) *nt* (pl ~er) vicarage, parsonage

Pfau (pfou) *m* (pl ~en) peacock

Pfeffer (*pfeh*-ferr) *m* pepper

Pfefferminze (*pfeh*-ferr-min-tser) *f* peppermint

Pfeife (*pfigh*-fer) *f* (pl ~n) pipe; whistle

*pfeifen (*pfigh*-fern) *v* whistle

Pfeifenreiniger (*pfigh*-fern-righ-ni-gerr) *m* (pl ~) pipe cleaner

Pfeil (pfighl) *m* (pl ~e) arrow

Pfeiler (*pfigh*-lerr) *m* (pl ~) column, pillar

Pferd (pfāyrt) *nt* (pl ~e) horse

Pferderennen (*pfāyr*-der-reh-nern) *nt* (pl ~) horserace

Pferdestärke (*pfāyr*-der-shtehr-ker) *f* (pl ~n) horsepower

Pfiff (pfif) *m* whistle

Pfingsten (*pfings*-tern) Whitsun; Pentecost *Am*

Pfirsich (*pfeer*-zikh) *m* (pl ⁓e) peach
Pflanze (*pflahn*-tser) *f* (pl ⁓n) plant
pflanzen (*pflahn*-tsern) *v* plant
Pflaster (*pflahss*-terr) *nt* (pl ⁓) plaster; pavement
pflastern (*pflahss*-terrn) *v* pave
Pflaume (*pflou*-mer) *f* (pl ⁓n) plum
Pflege (*pflāy*-ger) *f* care
Pflegeeltern (*pflāy*-ger-ehl-terrn) *pl* foster parents *pl*
pflegen (*pflāy*-gern) *v* nurse; tend; would
Pfleger (*pflāy*-gerr) *m* male nurse
Pflegespülung (*pflāy*-ger-shpēw-loong) *f* (pl ⁓en) conditioner
Pflicht (pflikht) *f* (pl ⁓en) duty
pflücken (*pflew*-kern) *v* pick
Pflug (pflook) *m* (pl ⁓e) plough
pflügen (*pflēw*-gern) *v* plough
Pforte (*pforr*-ter) *f* gate, door
Pförtner (*pfurrt*-nerr) *m* (pl ⁓), **-in** *f* porter
Pfosten (*pfoss*-tern) *m* (pl ⁓) pole, post
Pfote (*pfoa*-ter) *f* (pl ⁓n) paw
pfui! (pfoo⁰⁰) shame!
Pfund (pfoont) *nt* (pl ⁓e) pound
pfuschen (*pfoo*-shern) *v* bungle
Pfütze (*pfew*-tser) *f* (pl ⁓n) puddle
Phase (*faa*-zer) *f* (pl ⁓n) stage; phase
Philippinen (fi-li-*pee*-nern) *pl* Philippines *pl*
Philosoph (fi-loa-*zōaf*) *m* (pl ⁓en), **-in** *f* philosopher
Philosophie (fi-loa-soa-*fee*) *f* (pl ⁓n) philosophy
phonetisch (foa-*nāy*-tish) *adj* phonetic
Physik (few-*zeek*) *f* physics
Physiker (*fēw*-zi-kerr) *m* (pl ⁓), **-in** *f* physicist
Physiologie (few-zʸoa-loa-*gee*) *f* physiology
physisch (*fēw*-zish) *adj* physical

Pianist (pʸah-*nist*) *m* (pl ⁓en), **-in** *f* pianist
Pickel (*pi*-kerl) *m* (pl ⁓) pimple
Pickles (*pi*-kerls) *pl* pickles *pl*
Picknick (*pik*-nik) *nt* picnic
picknicken (*pik*-ni-kern) *v* picnic
Pier (peer) *m* (pl ⁓s) pier, jetty
pikant (pi-*kahnt*) *adj* spicy, savo(u)ry
Pilger (*pil*-gerr) *m* (pl ⁓), **-in** *f* pilgrim
Pilgerfahrt (*pil*-gerr-faart) *f* (pl ⁓en) pilgrimage
Pille (*pi*-ler) *f* (pl ⁓n) pill
Pilot (pi-*lōat*) *m* (pl ⁓en), **-in** *f* pilot
Pilz (pilts) *m* (pl ⁓e) mushroom; toadstool
Pinguin (ping-goo-*een*) *m* (pl ⁓e) penguin
Pinsel (*pin*-zerl) *m* (pl ⁓) brush, paintbrush
Pinzette (pin-*tseh*-ter) *f* (pl ⁓n) tweezers *pl*
Pionier (pi-oa-*neer*) *m* (pl ⁓e) pioneer
Piste (*piss*-ter) *f* course; piste; runway
Pistole (piss-*tōa*-ler) *f* (pl ⁓n) pistol
pittoresk (pi-toa-*rehsk*) *adj* picturesque
plädieren (pleh-*dee*-rern) *v* plead
Plage (*plaa*-ger) *f* (pl ⁓n) plague
Plakat (plah-*kaat*) *nt* (pl ⁓e) poster, placard
Plan (plaan) *m* (pl ⁓e) plan; scheme; project; map; schedule
planen (*plaa*-nern) *v* plan
Planet (plah-*nāyt*) *m* (pl ⁓en) planet
Planetarium (plah-nay-*taa*-rʸoom) *nt* (pl -rien) planetarium
planmäßig (*plaan*-mai-sikh) *adj* scheduled; according to plan, as planned
Plantage (plahn-*taa*-zher) *f* (pl ⁓n) plantation
Plastik *f* sculpture *nt* plastic
Platin (plah-*teen*) *nt* platinum
platt (plaht) *adj* flat

Platte (*plah*-ter) *f* (pl ⁓n) plate, sheet; dish

Plattenspieler (*plah*-tern-shpee-lerr) *m* (pl ⁓) record player

Platz (plahts) *m* (pl ⁓e) spot; seat; room; square

Platzanweiser (*plahts*-ahn-vigh-zerr) *m* (pl ⁓) usher

Platzanweiserin (*plahts*-ahn-vigh-zer-rin) *f* (pl ⁓nen) usherette

platzen (*plaht*-sern) *v* *burst, explode, *blow up

plaudern (*plou*-derrn) *v* chat

pleite (*pligh*-ter) *adj colloquial* broke, bankrupt

Plombe (*plom*-ber) *f* (pl ⁓n) filling

plötzlich (*plurts*-likh) *adj* sudden; *adv* suddenly

Plunder (*ploon*-derr) *m* junk

plündern (*plewn*-derrn) *v* plunder, rob

plus (plooss) *adv* plus

pneumatisch (pnoi-*maa*-tish) *adj* pneumatic

pochen (*po*-khern) *v* tap

Pocken (*po*-kern) *fpl* smallpox

Pokal (poa-*kaal*) *m* (pl ⁓e) cup

Pole (*p$\overline{oa}$*-ler) *m* (pl ⁓n) Pole

Polen (*p$\overline{oa}$*-lern) Poland

Police (poa-*lee*-ser) *f* (pl ⁓n) policy

polieren (poa-*lee*-rern) *v* polish

Polin (*p$\overline{oa}$*-lin) *f* (pl ⁓nen) Pole

Polio (*p$\overline{oa}$*-l^{y}oa) *f* polio

Politik (poa-li-*teek*) *f* politics; policy

Politiker (poa-*lee*-ti-kerr) *m* (pl ⁓), **-in** *f* politician

politisch (poa-*lee*-tish) *adj* political

Polizei (poa-li-*tsigh*) *f* police *pl*

Polizeiwache (poa-li-*tsigh*-vah-kher) *f* (pl ⁓n) police station

Polizist (poa-li-*tsist*) *m* (pl ⁓en) policeman

Polizistin (poa-li-*tsis*-tin) *f* (pl ⁓nen) policewoman

polnisch (*pol*-nish) *adj* Polish

Polster (*pols*-terr) *nt* (pl ⁓) pad

polstern (*pols*-terrn) *v* upholster

Polyp (poa-*l$\overline{ew}$p*) *m* (pl ⁓en) octopus

Pommes frites (pom-*frit*) chips, French fries *Am*

Pony (*po*-ni) *nt* (pl ⁓s) pony

Popmusik (*pop*-moo-zeek) *f* pop music

Portier (por-*t^y$\overline{ay}$*) *m* (pl ⁓s) doorman, doorkeeper

Portion (por-*ts^y$\overline{oa}$n*) *f* (pl ⁓en) helping, portion

Porto (*por*-toa) *nt* postage

portofrei (*por*-toa-frigh) *adj* postage paid

Porträt (por-*trai*) *nt* (pl ⁓s) portrait

Portugal (*por*-too-gahl) Portugal

Portugiese (por-too-*gee*-zer) *m* (pl ⁓n) Portuguese

Portugiesin (por-too-*gee*-zin) *f* (pl ⁓nen) Portuguese

portugiesisch (por-too-*gee*-zish) *adj* Portuguese

Porzellan (por-tser-*laan*) *nt* porcelain, china

Position (poa-zi-*ts^y$\overline{oa}$n*) *f* (pl ⁓en) position

Positiv (*p$\overline{oa}$*-zi-teef) *nt* (pl ⁓e) positive

positiv (*p$\overline{oa}$*-zi-teef) *adj* positive

Post (post) *f* post, mail

Postamt (*post*-ahmt) *nt* (pl ⁓er) post-office

Postanweisung (*post*-ahn-vigh-zoong) *f* (pl ⁓en) postal order; mail order *Am*

Postbote (*post*-b$\overline{oa}$-ter) *m* (pl ⁓n) postman

Postdienst (*post*-deenst) *m* postal service

Posten (*poss*-tern) *m* (pl ⁓) item; post

Postfach (*post*-fahkh) *nt* P.O. Box

Postkarte (*post*-kahr-ter) *f* (pl ⁓n) postcard, card

postlagernd (*post*-laa-gerrnt) *adj*

poste restante
Postleitzahl (*post*-light-tsaal) *f* (pl
~en) zip code *Am*
Pracht (prahkht) *f* splendo(u)r
prächtig (*prehkh*-tikh) *adj*
magnificent; glorious, splendid,
gorgeous, superb, wonderful, fine
Präfix (*preh*-fiks) *nt* (pl ~e) prefix
prahlen (*praa*-lern) *v* boast
praktisch (*prahk*-tish) *adj* practical
Praline (prah-*lee*-ner) *f* (pl ~n)
chocolate
Prämie (*prai*-m^{y}er) *f* (pl ~n) premium
Präposition (preh-poa-zi-ts^y$\overline{oa}$n) *f* (pl
~en) preposition
Präsent (preh-*zehnt*) *nt* (pl ~e) present
Präservativ (preh-zehr-vah-*teef*) *nt*
condom, contraceptive
Präsident (preh-zi-*dehnt*) *m* (pl ~en),
-in *f* president
Praxis (*prah*-ksiss) *f* practice
präzis (preh-*tseess*) *adj* precise, exact
predigen (*pray̅*-di-gern) *v* preach
Predigt (*pray̅*-dikht) *f* (pl ~en) sermon
Preis (prighss) *m* (pl ~e) cost, price;
award, prize; **den ~ festsetzen** price
Preisgericht (*prighss*-ger-rikht) *nt* (pl
~e) jury
Preisliste (*prighss*-liss-ter) *f* (pl ~n)
price list
Preisnachlass (*prighss*-naakh-lahss)
m (pl ~e) reduction
Prellung (*preh*-loong) *f* bruise
Premierminister (prer-*m^{y}ay̅*-mi-niss-
terr) *m* (pl ~), **-in** *f* premier
Presse (*preh*-ser) *f* press
Pressekonferenz (*preh*-ser-kon-fay-
rehnts) *f* (pl ~en) press conference
pressen (*preh*-sern) *v* press; squeeze
Prestige (prehss-*tee*-zher) *nt* prestige
Priester (*preess*-terr) *m* (pl ~), **-in** *f*
priest
prima (*pree*-mah) *adj* first-rate
Prinz (prints) *m* (pl ~en) prince

Prinzessin (prin-*tseh*-sin) *f* (pl ~nen)
princess
Prinzip (prin-*tseep*) *nt* (pl ~ien)
principle
Priorität (pri-oa-ri-*tait*) *f* (pl ~en)
priority
privat (pri-*vaat*) *adj* private
Privatleben (pri-*vaat*-lay̅-bern) *nt*
privacy
Probe (*pr$\overline{oa}$*-ber) *f* (pl ~n) test;
rehearsal
proben (*pr$\overline{oa}$*-bern) *v* rehearse
probieren (proa-*bee*-rern) *v* try,
attempt
Problem (proa-*blay̅m*) *nt* (pl ~e)
problem; question
Produkt (proa-*dookt*) *nt* (pl ~e)
product
Produktion (proa-dook-ts^y$\overline{oa}$n) *f*
production
Produzent (proa-doo-*tsehnt*) *m* (pl
~en), **-in** *f* producer
produzieren (proa-doo-*tsee*-rern) *v*
produce, *make
Professor (proa-*feh*-sor) *m* (pl ~en),
-in *f* professor
profitieren (proa-fi-*tee*-rern) *v* profit,
benefit
Programm (proa-*grahm*) *nt* (pl ~e)
programme
progressiv (proa-greh-*seef*) *adj*
progressive
Projekt (proa-^{y}*ehkt*) *nt* (pl ~e) project
proklamieren (proa-klah-*mee*-rern) *v*
proclaim
Promenade (proa-mer-*naa*-der) *f* (pl
~n) esplanade, promenade
Propaganda (proa-pah-*gahn*-dah) *f*
propaganda
Propeller (proa-*peh*-lerr) *m* (pl ~)
propeller
Prophet (proa-*fay̅t*) *m* (pl ~en), **-in** *f*
prophet
proportional (proa-por-ts^{y}oa-*naal*)

adj proportional

Prospekt (proa-*spehkt*) *m* (pl ~e) prospectus

Prostituierte (proa-sti-too-*eer*-ter) *f* (pl ~n) prostitute

Protein (proa-tay-*een*) *nt* (pl ~e) protein

Protest (proa-*tehst*) *m* (pl ~e) protest

protestantisch (proa-tehss-*tahn*-tish) *adj* Protestant

protestieren (proa-tehss-*tee*-rern) *v* protest

Protokoll (proa-toa-*kol*) *nt* (pl ~e) minutes

Provinz (proa-*vints*) *f* (pl ~en) province

provinziell (proa-vin-*ts*^y*ehl*) *adj* provincial

Prozent (proa-*tsehnt*) *nt* (pl ~e) percent

Prozentsatz (proa-*tsehnt*-zahts) *m* (pl ~e) percentage

Prozess (proa-*tsehss*) *m* (pl ~e) lawsuit, process

Prozession (proa-tseh-*s*^y*oan*) *f* (pl ~en) procession

prüfen (*prew*-fern) *v* check, examine; test

Prügel (*prew*-gerl) *pl* spanking

prügeln (*prew*-gerln) *pl* *beat, thrash; **sich ~** (*have a) fight

Psychiater (psew-khi-*aa*-terr) *m* (pl ~), **-in** *f* psychiatrist

psychisch (*psew*-khish) *adj* psychic

Psychoanalytiker (psew-khoa-ah-nah-*lew*-ti-kerr) *m* (pl ~), **-in** *f* analyst, psychoanalyst

Psychologe (psew-khoa-*loa*-ger) *m*

(pl ~n) psychologist

Psychologie (psew-khoa-loa-*gee*) *f* psychology

Psychologin (psew-khoa-*loa*-gin) *f* (pl ~nen) psychologist

psychologisch (psew-khoa-*loa*-gish) *adj* psychological

Publikum (*poo*-bli-koom) *nt* audience, public

Pudding (*poo*-ding) *m* pudding

Pudel (*poo*-derl) *m* poodle

Puder (*poo*-derr) *m* powder

Puderdose (*poo*-derr-*doa*-zer) *f* (pl ~n) powder compact

Pullover (poo-*loa*-verr) *m* (pl ~) pullover, sweater

Puls (pools) *m* (pl ~e) pulse

Pulsschlag (*pools*-shlaak) *m* pulse

Pult (poolt) *nt* (pl ~e) desk

Pulver (*pool*-verr) *nt* powder

Pumpe (*poom*-per) *f* (pl ~n) pump

pumpen (*poom*-pern) *v* pump

Punkt (poongkt) *m* (pl ~e) point; full stop, period; item, issue

pünktlich (*pewngkt*-likh) *adj* punctual

Puppe (*poo*-per) *f* (pl ~n) doll

Puppentheater (*poo*-pern-tay-*aa*-terr) *nt* (pl ~) puppet show

pur (poor) *adj* pure; neat

purpur (*poor*-poor) *adj* purple

Pute (*poo*-ter) *f* turkey

Putz (poots) *m* plaster

putzen (*poo*-tsern) *v* brush

Puzzlespiel (*pah*-zerl-shpeel) *nt* (pl ~e) jigsaw puzzle

Pyjama (pi-*zhaa*-mah) *m* (pl ~s) pyjamas *pl*

Q

Quadrat (kvah-*draat*) *nt* (pl ⁓e) square

quadratisch (kvah-*draa*-tish) *adj* square

Qual (kvaal) *f* (pl ⁓en) torment

quälen (*kvai*-lern) *v* torment

qualifiziert (kvah-li-fi-*tseert*) *adj* qualified

Qualität (kvah-li-*tait*) *f* (pl ⁓en) quality

Qualle (*kvah*-ler) *f* (pl ⁓n) jellyfish

Qualm (kvahlm) *m* (dense) smoke

Quantität (kvahn-ti-*tait*) *f* (pl ⁓en) quantity

Quarantäne (kah-rahn-*tai*-ner) *f* quarantine

Quark (kvahrk) *m* quark, curd cheese

Quartal (kvahr-*taal*) *nt* (pl ⁓e) quarter

Quartier (kvar-teer) *nt* accommodation

Quatsch (kvahch) *m* rubbish

quatschen (*kvah*-chern) *v* talk rubbish

Quecksilber (*kvehk*-zil-berr) *nt* mercury

Quelle (*kveh*-ler) *f* (pl ⁓n) source, spring, well; fountain

quer (kvāyr) *adv* athwart

quetschen (*kveh*-chern) *v* bruise

Quetschung (*kveh*-choong) *f* (pl ⁓en) bruise

Quittung (*kvi*-toong) *f* (pl ⁓en) receipt

Quote (*kvōa*-ter) *f* (pl ⁓n) quota

R

Rabatt (rah-*baht*) *m* (pl ⁓e) reduction, rebate, discount

Rabe (*raa*-ber) *m* (pl ⁓n) raven

Rache (*rah*-kher) *f* revenge

Rachen (*rah*-khern) *m* throat

Rad (raat) *nt* (pl ⁓er) wheel; cycle, bicycle

Radfahrer (*raat*-faa-rerr) *m* (pl ⁓), **-in** *f* cyclist

Radieschen (rah-*dees*-khern) *nt* radish

Radiergummi (rah-*deer*-goo-mi) *m* (pl ⁓s) eraser, rubber

Radierung (rah-*dee*-roong) *f* (pl ⁓en) etching

radikal (rah-di-*kaal*) *adj* radical

Radio (*raa*-dᶻoa) *nt* (pl ⁓s) radio

Raffinerie (rah-fi-ner-*ree*) *f* (pl ⁓n) refinery

Rahm (raam) *m* cream

Rahmen (*raa*-mern) *m* (pl ⁓) frame

Rakete (rah-*kāy*-ter) *f* (pl ⁓n) rocket

Rampe (*rahm*-per) *f* (pl ⁓n) ramp

Rand (rahnt) *m* (pl ⁓er) brim, edge, border; margin; verge; rim

Randstein (*rahnt*-shtighn) *m* curb

Rang (rahng) *m* (pl ⁓e) grade, rank

ranzig (*rahn*-tsikh) *adj* rancid

rasch (rahsh) *adj* fast

Rasen (*raa*-zern) *m* (pl ⁓) lawn

rasen (*raa*-zern) *v* rage; *speed

rasend (*raa*-zernt) *adj* furious

Rasierapparat (rah-*zeer*-ah-pah-raat) *m* (pl ⁓e) electric razor; shaver

rasieren (rah-*zee*-rern) *v* shave; **sich ⁓** shave

Rasierklinge (rah-*zeer*-kling-er) *f* (pl ⁓n) razor blade

Rasierkrem (rah-*zeer*-krāym) *f* (pl ⁓s) shaving cream

Rasierpinsel (rah-*zeer*-pin-zerl) *m* (pl ∼) shaving brush

Rasierseife (rah-*zeer*-zigh-fer) *f* (pl ∼n) shaving soap

Rasierwasser (rah-*zeer*-vah-serr) *nt* aftershave lotion

raspeln (*rahss*-perln) *v* grate

Rasse (*rah*-ser) *f* (pl ∼n) race; breed; **Rassen-** racial

Rast (rahst) *f* rest

Rat (raat) *m* (pl ∼e) advice, counsel; council, board

***raten** (*raa*-tern) *v* guess; advise

Ratenzahlung (*raa*-tern-tsaa-loong) *f* (pl ∼en) instal(l)ment

Ratgeber (*raat*-gāy-berr) *m* (pl ∼), **-in** *f* counsellor

Rathaus (*raat*-houss) *nt* (pl ∼er) town hall

Ration (rah-*ts*ᵞ*ōān*) *f* (pl ∼en) ration

Rätsel (*rai*-tserl) *nt* (pl ∼) riddle, puzzle; mystery, enigma

rätselhaft (*rai*-tserl-hahft) *adj* mysterious

Ratsmitglied (*raats*-mit-gleet) *nt* (pl ∼er) councillor

Ratte (*rah*-ter) *f* (pl ∼n) rat

Raub (roup) *m* robbery

rauben (*rou*-bern) *v* rob

Räuber (*roi*-berr) *m* (pl ∼), **-in** *f* robber

Raubtier (*roup*-teer) *nt* (pl ∼e) beast of prey

Rauch (roukh) *m* smoke

rauchen (*rou*-khern) *v* smoke; **Rauchen verboten** no smoking

Raucher (*rou*-kherr) *m* (pl ∼), **-in** *f* smoker

Raucherabteil (*rou*-kherr-ahp-tighl) *nt* (pl ∼e) smoking compartment, smoker

rau (rou) *adj* bleak; harsh; hoarse

Raum (roum) *m* (pl ∼e) space, room

räumen (*roi*-mern) *v* vacate

Raupe (*rou*-per) *f* caterpillar

Rausch (roush) *m* drunkenness

Rauschgift (*roush*-gift) *nt* (pl ∼e) narcotic

Reaktion (ray-ahk-*ts*ᵞ*ōān*) *f* (pl ∼en) reaction

realisieren (ray-ah-li-*zee*-rern) *v* realize

rebellieren (ray-beh-*lee*-rern) *v* revolt

Rebhuhn (*rehp*-hōōn) *nt* (pl ∼er) partridge

Rechnen (*rehkh*-nern) *nt* arithmetic

rechnen (*rehkh*-nern) *v* reckon

Rechner (*rehkh*-nerr) *m* (pl ∼s) calculator

Rechnung (*rehkh*-noong) *f* (pl ∼en) bill; check *Am*

Recht (rehkht) *nt* (pl ∼e) right; law, justice; **mit ∼** rightly; **∼ *haben** *be right

recht (rehkht) *adj* right; right-hand; *adv* fairly, rather

Rechteck (*rehkht*-ehk) *nt* (pl ∼e) rectangle, oblong

rechteckig (*rehkht*-eh-kikh) *adj* rectangular

rechtlich (*rehkht*-likh) *adj* legal

rechtmäßig (*rehkht*-mai-sikh) *adj* legitimate

rechts (rehkhts) *adv* on the right; **nach ∼** to the right

Rechtsanwalt (*rehkhts*-ahn-vahlt) *m* (pl ∼e) lawyer; barrister

Rechtsanwältin (*rehkhts*-ahn-vehlt-in) *f* (pl ∼nen) lawyer; barrister

rechtschaffen (*rehkht*-shah-fern) *adj* hono(u)rable

Rechtschreibung (*rehkht*-shrigh-boong) *f* spelling

rechtswidrig (*rehkhts*-vee-drikh) *adj* unlawful

rechtzeitig (*rehkht*-tsigh-tikh) *adv* in time

Recycling (ray-*sighk*-ling) *nt* recycling

Redakteur (ray-dahk-*tūrr*) *m* (pl ∼e)
editor

Rede (*rāy*-der) *f* (pl ∼n) speech

reden (*rāy*-dern) *v* talk

Redewendung (*rāy*-der-vehn-doong)
f (pl ∼en) phrase

redlich (*rāyt*-likh) *adj* right, fair

reduzieren (ray-doo-*tsee*-rern) *v*
reduce

Reeder (*rāy*-derr) *m* (pl ∼), **-in** *f*
shipowner

Referenz (ray-fay-*rehnts*) *f* (pl ∼en)
reference

Reflektor (ray-*flehk*-tor) *m* (pl ∼en)
reflector

Reformation (ray-for-mah-*ts*ʸ*ōan*) *f*
reformation

Regal (ray-*gaal*) *nt* (pl ∼e) shelf

Regatta (ray-*gah*-tah) *f* (pl Regatten)
regatta

Regel (*rāy*-gerl) *f* (pl ∼n) rule; **in der ∼**
as a rule

regelmäßig (*rāy*-gerl-mai-sikh) *adj*
regular

regeln (*rāy*-gerln) *v* regulate; settle

Regelung (*rāy*-ger-loong) *f* (pl ∼en)
regulation; arrangement, settlement

Regen (*rāy*-gern) *m* rain

Regenbogen (*rāy*-gern-bōa-gern) *m*
(pl ∼̈) rainbow

Regenguss (*rāy*-gern-gooss) *m* (pl
∼̈e) downpour

Regenmantel (*rāy*-gern-mahn-terl) *m*
(pl ∼̈) mackintosh, raincoat

Regenschauer (*rāy*-gern-shou-err) *m*
(pl ∼) shower

Regenschirm (*rāy*-gern-sheerm) *m*
(pl ∼e) umbrella

Regie (ray-*zhee*) *f* direction

regieren (ray-*gee*-rern) *v* govern; rule,
reign

Regierung (ray-*gee*-roong) *f* (pl ∼en)
government; rule

Regime (ray-*zheem*) *nt* (pl ∼s) régime

Regisseur (ray-zhi-*sūrr*) *m* (pl ∼e)
director

regnen (*rāy*-gnern) *v* rain

regnerisch (*rāy*-gner-rish) *adj* rainy

regulieren (ray-goo-*lee*-rern) *v* adjust

Reh (rāy) *nt* roe

Rehabilitation (ray-hah-bi-li-tah-
*ts*ʸ*ōan*) *f* rehabilitation

Reibe (*righ*-ber) *f* (pl ∼n) grater

*reiben (*righ*-bern) *v* rub, grate

Reibung (*righ*-boong) *f* (pl ∼en)
friction

Reich (righkh) *nt* (pl ∼e) empire;
kingdom; **Reichs-** imperial

reich (righkh) *adj* rich; wealthy

reichen (*righ*-khern) *v* suffice; pass

reichlich (*righkh*-likh) *adj* plentiful,
abundant

Reichtum (*righkh*-tēw-merr) *m* (pl
∼̈er) riches *pl*, wealth

reif (righf) *adj* ripe, mature

Reife (*righ*-fer) *f* maturity

Reifen (*righ*-fern) *m* (pl ∼) tyre, tire

Reifendruck (*righ*-fern-drook) *m* tyre
pressure, tire pressure *Am*

Reifenpanne (*righ*-fern-pah-ner) *f* (pl
∼n) blowout; puncture; flat tyre, flat
tire *Am*

Reihe (*righ*-er) *f* (pl ∼n) line, row; file,
rank; turn

Reihenfolge (*righ*-ern-fol-ger) *f* order,
sequence

Reiher (*righ*-err) *m* (pl ∼) heron

Reim (righm) *m* (pl ∼e) rhyme

rein (righn) *adj* clean; pure; sheer

reinigen (*righ*-ni-gern) *v* clean;
chemisch ∼ dry-clean

Reinigung (*righ*-ni-goong) *f* (pl ∼en)
cleaning; **chemische ∼** dry cleaner's

Reinigungsmittel (*righ*-ni-goongs-
mi-terl) *nt* (pl ∼) cleaning fluid;
detergent

Reis (righss) *m* rice

Reise (*righ*-zer) *f* (pl ∼n) voyage,

journey; trip

Reisebüro (*righ*-zer-bew-*rōā*) *nt* (pl ~s) travel agency

Reisebus (*righ*-zer-booss) *m* (pl ~se) coach

Reisegeschwindigkeit (*righ*-zer-ger-shvin-dikh-kight) *f* cruising speed

reisen (*righ*-zern) *v* travel

Reisende (*righ*-zern-der) *m/f* (pl ~n) travel(l)er

Reisepass (*righ*-zer-pahs) *m* passport

Reiseplan (*righ*-zer-plaan) *m* (pl ~e) itinerary

Reisescheck (*righ*-zer-shehk) *m* (pl ~s) traveller's cheque; traveler's check *Am*

Reisespesen (*righ*-zer-shpāy-zern) *pl* travelling expenses

Reiseversicherung (*righ*-zer-fehr-zi-kher-roong) *f* travel insurance

*reißen (*righ*-sern) *v* *tear

Reißnagel (*righss*-naa-gerl) *m* (pl ~) thumbtack *Am*

Reißverschluss (*righss*-fehr-shlooss) *m* (pl ~e) zipper, zip

Reißzwecke (*righss*-tsveh-ker) *f* (pl ~n) drawing pin; thumbtack *Am*

*reiten (*righ*-tern) *v* *ride

Reiter (*righ*-terr) *m* (pl ~), **-in** *f* rider, horseman

Reitschule (*right*-shōō-ler) *f* (pl ~n) riding school

Reitsport (*right*-shport) *m* riding

Reiz (rights) *m* (pl ~e) attraction; glamo(u)r

reizbar (*rights*-baar) *adj* quick-tempered, irritable

reizen (*righ*-tsern) *v* irritate

reizend (*righ*-tsernt) *adj* adorable, graceful

Reizmittel (*rights*-mi-terl) *nt* (pl ~) stimulant

Reklame (ray-*klaa*-mer) *f* (pl ~n) publicity

Rekord (ray-*kort*) *m* (pl ~e) record

Rekrut (ray-*krōōt*) *m* (pl ~en), **-in** *f* recruit

relativ (ray-lah-*teef*) *adj* comparative, relative

Relief (ray-*l^yehf*) *nt* (pl ~s) relief

Religion (ray-li-g^y*ōān*) *f* (pl ~en) religion

religiös (ray-li-g^y*ūrss*) *adj* religious

Reliquie (ray-*lee*-kvi-er) *f* (pl ~n) relic

Rennbahn (*rehn*-baan) *f* (pl ~en) racecourse, racetrack

Rennen (*reh*-nern) *nt* (pl ~) race

*rennen (*reh*-nern) *v* *run

Rennpferd (*rehn*-pfāyrt) *nt* (pl ~e) racehorse

Rennstrecke (*rehn*-shtreh-ker) *f* (pl ~n) racetrack

renovieren (ray-noa-*vee*-rern) *v* renovate

rentabel (rehn-*taa*-berl) *adj* paying

Rente (*rehn*-ter) *f* (pl ~n) pension

Reparatur (ray-pah-rah-*tōōr*) *f* (pl ~en) reparation

reparieren (ray-pah-*ree*-rern) *v* repair

Repertoire (ray-pehr-*twaar*) *nt* (pl ~s) repertory

repräsentativ (ray-preh-zehn-tah-*teef*) *adj* representative

Reproduktion (ray-proa-dook-ts^y*ōān*) *f* (pl ~en) reproduction

reproduzieren (ray-proa-doo-*tsee*-rern) *v* reproduce

Reptil (rehp-*teel*) *nt* (pl ~e) reptile

Republik (ray-poo-*bleek*) *f* (pl ~en) republic

republikanisch (ray-poo-bli-*kaa*-nish) *adj* republican

Reserve (ray-*zehr*-ver) *f* (pl ~n) reserve

Reserverad (ray-*zehr*-ver-raat) *nt* (pl ~er) spare wheel

reservieren (ray-zehr-*vee*-rern) *v* reserve; book

reserviert (ray-zehr-*veert*) *adj* reserved

Reservierung (ray-zehr-*vee*-roong) *f* (pl ~en) reservation; booking

Reservoir (ray-zehr-*vwaar*) *nt* (pl ~s) reservoir

resolut (ray-zoa-*lo͞ot*) *adj* resolute

Respekt (ray-*spehkt*) *m* esteem, regard, respect

Rest (rehst) *m* (pl ~e) rest; remainder, remnant

Restaurant (rehss-toa-*rah͞ng*) *nt* (pl ~s) restaurant

Restbestand (*rehst*-ber-shtahnt) *m* (pl ~e) remainder

Resultat (ray-zool-*taat*) *nt* (pl ~e) issue

retten (*reh*-tern) *v* rescue, save

Retter (*reh*-terr) *m* (pl ~), **-in** *f* savio(u)r

Rettich (*reh*-tikh) *m* (pl ~e) radish

Rettung (*reh*-toong) *f* (pl ~en) rescue

Rettungsboot (*reh*-toongs-bōat) *nt* lifeboat

Rettungsgürtel (*reh*-toongs-gewr-terl) *m* (pl ~) lifebelt

Reue (*roi*-er) *f* repentance

Revolution (ray-voa-loo-*ts*ʸ*ōan*) *f* (pl ~en) revolution

revolutionär (ray-voa-loo-tsʸoa-*nair*) *adj* revolutionary

Revolver (ray-*vol*-verr) *m* (pl ~) revolver, gun

Rezept (ray-*tsehpt*) *nt* (pl ~e) recipe; prescription

Rezeption (ray-tsehp-*ts*ʸ*ōan*) *f* reception office

Rhabarber (rah-*bahr*-berr) *m* rhubarb

Rheumatismus (roi-mah-*tiss*-mooss) *m* rheumatism

Rhythmus (*rewt*-mooss) *m* (pl -men) rhythm

richten (*rikh*-tern) *v* direct; fix; ~ **auf** aim at

Richter (*rikh*-terr) *m* (pl ~), **-in** *f* judge; magistrate

richtig (*rikh*-tikh) *adj* right, correct, just; proper, appropriate

Richtigkeit (*rikh*-tikh-kīght) *f* correctness

Richtlinie (*rikht*-lee-nʸer) *f* (pl ~n) directive

Richtung (*rikh*-toong) *f* (pl ~en) direction; way

*riechen (*ree*-khern) *v* *smell

Riegel (*ree*-gerl) *m* (pl ~) bolt

Riemen (*ree*-mern) *m* (pl ~) strap

Riese (*ree*-zer) *m* (pl ~n) giant

riesenhaft (*ree*-zern-hahft) *adj* gigantic

riesig (*ree*-zikh) *adj* enormous, huge

Riff (rif) *nt* (pl ~e) reef

Rille (*ri*-ler) *f* (pl ~n) groove

Rind (rint) *nt* cow, beef

Rinde (*rin*-der) *f* (pl ~n) bark

Rinderbraten (*rin*-derr-braa-tern) *m* roast beef

Rindfleisch (*rint*-flighsh) *nt* beef

Ring (ring) *m* (pl ~e) ring

Ringen (*ring*-ern) *nt* struggle

*ringen (*ring*-ern) *v* struggle

Rippe (*ri*-per) *f* (pl ~n) rib

Risiko (*ree*-zi-koa) *nt* (pl ~s) risk; chance, hazard

riskant (riss-*kahnt*) *adj* risky

Riss (riss) *m* (pl ~e) crack; tear; cave

Ritter (*ri*-terr) *m* (pl ~) knight

Rivale (ri-*vaa*-ler) *m* (pl ~n) rival

Rivalin (ri-*vaa*-lin) *f* (pl ~nen) rival

rivalisieren (ri-vah-li-*zee*-rern) *v* rival

Rivalität (ri-vah-li-*tait*) *f* rivalry

Robbe (*ro*-ber) *f* (pl ~n) seal

robust (roa-*boost*) *adj* robust

Rock (rok) *m* (pl ~e) skirt

rodeln (*rōa*-derln) *v* sledge, go sledging

Rogen (*rōa*-gern) *m* roe

Roggen (*ro*-gern) *m* rye

roh (rōa) *adj* raw

Rohmaterial (*rōā*-mah-tay-r^yaal) *nt* (pl ~ien) raw material

Rohr (*rōār*) *nt* (pl ~e) tube, pipe; cane

Röhre (*rūr*-rer) *f* (pl ~n) tube

Rohstoff (*rōā*-shtof) *m* raw material

Rolle (*ro*-ler) *f* (pl ~n) roll; pulley

rollen (*ro*-lern) *v* roll

Roller (*ro*-lerr) *m* (pl ~) scooter

Rollstuhl (*rol*-shtōōl) *m* (pl ~̈e) wheelchair

Rolltreppe (*roal*-treh-per) *f* (pl ~n) escalator

Roman (roa-*maan*) *m* (pl ~e) novel

Romanschriftsteller (roa-*maan*-shrift-shteh-lerr) *m* (pl ~), **-in** *f* novelist

romantisch (roa-*mahn*-tish) *adj* romantic

Romanze (roa-*mahn*-tser) *f* (pl ~n) romance

römisch-katholisch (*rūr*-mish-kah-tōā-lish) *adj* Roman Catholic

röntgen (*rurnt*-gern) *v* X-ray

Röntgenaufnahme (*rurnt*-gern-ouf-naa-mer) *f*, **Röntgenbild** (*rurnt*-gern-bilt) *nt* X-ray

rosa (*rōā*-zah-rōāt) *adj* rose, pink

Rose (*rōā*-zer) *f* (pl ~n) rose

Rosenkohl (*rōā*-zern-kōāl) *m* sprouts *pl*

Rosenkranz (*rōā*-zern-krahnts) *m* (pl ~̈e) rosary, beads *pl*

Rosine (roa-*zee*-ner) *f* (pl ~n) raisin

Rost[1] (rost) *m* rust

Rost[2] (rost) *m* (pl ~e) grate

rösten (*rūrss*-tern) *v* roast

rostig (*ross*-tikh) *adj* rusty

rot (rōat) *adj* red

Rotkehlchen (*rōāt*-kāyl-khern) *nt* (pl ~) robin

Rotwild (*rōāt*-vilt) *nt* deer

Rouge (rōōzh) *nt* rouge

Roulett (roo-*leht*) *nt* roulette

Route (*rōō*-ter) *f* (pl ~n) route

Routine (roo-*tee*-ner) *f* routine

Rübe (*rēw*-ber) *f* (pl ~n) beet

Rubin (roo-*been*) *m* (pl ~e) ruby

Rubrik (roo-*breek*) *f* (pl ~en) column

Ruck (rook) *m* (pl ~e) tug, wrench

Rücken (*rew*-kern) *m* (pl ~) back

Rückenschmerzen (*rew*-kern-shmehr-tsern) *mpl* backache

Rückfahrkarte (*rewk*-faar-kahr-ter) *f* return (ticket)

Rückfahrt (*rewk*-faart) *f* return journey; **Hin- und ~** round trip *Am*

Rückflug (*rewk*-flōōk) *m* (pl ~̈e) return flight

Rückgang (*rewk*-gahng) *m* recession, depression

Rückgrat (*rewk*-graat) *nt* (pl ~e) spine, backbone

Rückkehr (*rewk*-kāyr) *f* return

Rücklicht (*rewk*-likht) *nt* (pl ~er) taillight

Rückreise (*rewk*-righ-zer) *f* return journey

Rucksack (*rook*-zahk) *m* (pl ~̈e) rucksack; knapsack

Rückschlag (*rewk*-shlaak) *m* (pl ~̈e) reverse

Rückseite (*rewk*-zigh-ter) *f* back

Rücksicht (*rewk*-zikht) *f* consideration

rücksichtsvoll (*rewk*-zikhts-fol) *adj* considerate

Rücksitz (*rewk*-zits) *m* back seat

rückständig (*rewk*-shtehn-dikh) *adj* overdue; out-of-date

Rücktritt (*rewk*-trit) *m* resignation

rückvergüten (*rewk*-fehr-gēw-tern) *v* refund

Rückvergütung (*rewk*-fehr-gēw-toong) *f* (pl ~en) refund

rückwärts (*rewk*-vehrts) *adv* backwards; ~ *fahren *v* reverse

Rückwärtsgang (*rewk*-vehrts-gahng) *m* reverse

Rückweg (*rewk*-vāyk) *m* way back

Rückzahlung (*rewk*-tsaa-loong) *f* (pl ~en) repayment

Ruder (*rōō*-derr) *nt* (pl ~) helm; oar

Ruderboot (*rōō*-derr-bōat) *nt* (pl ~e) rowing boat

rudern (*rōō*-derrn) *v* row

Ruf (rōōf) *m* (pl ~e) call; cry, scream; fame, reputation

***rufen** (*rōō*-fern) *v* call; cry, shout

Ruhe (*rōō*-er) *f* quiet

ruhelos (*rōō*-er-lōass) *adj* restless

Ruhelosigkeit (*rōō*-er-lōā-zikh-kight) *f* unrest

ruhen (*rōō*-ern) *v* rest

ruhig (*rōō*-ikh) *adj* calm; tranquil, quiet, serene; restful

Ruhm (rōōm) *m* celebrity, fame; glory

rühren (*rēw*-rern) *v* stir; move

rührend (*rēw*-rernt) *adj* touching

Rührung (*rēw*-roong) *f* emotion

Ruine (roo-*ee*-ner) *f* (pl ~n) ruins

ruinieren (roo-i-*nee*-rern) *v* ruin

Rumäne (roo-*mai*-ner) *m* (pl ~n) Rumanian

Rumänien (roo-*mai*-nʸern) Rumania

Rumänin (roo-*mai*-nin) *f* (pl ~nen) Rumanian

rumänisch (roo-*mai*-nish) *adj* Rumanian

rund (roont) *adj* round

Runde (*roon*-der) *f* (pl ~n) round

Rundfunk (*roont*-foongk) *m* wireless

rundherum (*roont*-heh-room) *adv* around

Rundreise (*roont*-righ-zer) *f* (pl ~n) tour

Russe (*roo*-ser) *m* (pl ~n) Russian

Russin (*roo*-sin) *f* (pl ~nen) Russian

russisch (*roo*-sish) *adj* Russian

Russland (*rooss*-lahnt) Russia

Rüstung (*rewss*-toong) *f* (pl ~en) armo(u)r

Rutschbahn (*rooch*-baan) *f* (pl ~en) slide

rutschen (*rooch*-ern) *v* slip; *slide

S

Saal (zaal) *m* (pl Säle) hall

Sache (*zah*-kher) *f* (pl ~en) matter; cause

sachlich (*zahkh*-likh) *adj* down-to-earth; substantial

sächlich (*zehkh*-likh) *adj* neuter

Sachverständige (*zahkh*-fehr-shtehn-di-ger) *m/f* (pl ~n) expert

Sack (zahk) *m* (pl ~e) sack; bag

Sackgasse (*zahk*-gah-ser) *f* (pl ~n) cul-de-sac

säen (*zai*-ern) *v* *sow

Safe (sāyf) *m* (pl ~s) safe

Saft (zahft) *m* (pl ~e) juice

saftig (*zahf*-tikh) *adj* juicy

Säge (*zai*-ger) *f* (pl ~n) saw

Sägemehl (*zai*-ger-māyl) *nt* sawdust

sagen (*zaa*-gern) *v* *say; *tell

Sahne (*zaa*-ner) *f* cream

Sahnebonbon (*zaa*-ner-bawng̅-bawng̅) *m* (pl ~s) toffee

sahnig (*zaa*-nikh) *adj* creamy

Saison (zeh-*zawng̅*) *f* (pl ~s) season; **außer** ~ off season

Saite (*zigh*-ter) *f* (pl ~n) string

Sakko (zah-*kōa*) *m*, *nt* jacket

Salat (zah-*laat*) *m* (pl ~e) salad; lettuce

Salatöl (zah-*laat*-ūrl) *nt* (pl ~e) salad oil

Salatsoße (zah-*laat*-zoa-ser) *nt* (pl

~en) salad dressing

Salbe (*zahl*-ber) *f* (pl ~n) salve, ointment

Saldo (*zahl*-doa) *m* (pl Salden) balance

Salmiakgeist (zahl-*m*ʸ*ahk*-gighst) *m* ammonia

Salon (zah-*lawng*) *m* (pl ~s) salon

Salz (zahlts) *nt* salt

Salzstreuer (zahlts-*shtroi*-err) *m* (pl ~) salt-cellar; salt shaker *Am*

salzen (*zahl*-tsern) *v* salt

salzig (*zahl*-tsikh) *adj* salty

Samen (*zaa*-mern) *m* (pl ~) seed

sammeln (*zah*-merln) *v* collect; gather

Sammler (*zahm*-lerr) *m* (pl ~), **-in** *f* collector

Sammlung (*zahm*-loong) *f* (pl ~en) collection

Samstag (*zahms*-taak) *m* Saturday

Samt (zahmt) *m* velvet

Sanatorium (zah-nah-*tōā*-rʸoom) *nt* (pl -rien) sanatorium

Sand (zahnt) *m* sand

Sandale (zahn-*daa*-ler) *f* (pl ~n) sandal

Sandbank (*zahnd*-bahngk) *f* sandbank

sandig (*zahn*-dikh) *adj* sandy

sanft (zahnft) *adj* gentle

Sänger (*zehng*-err) *m* (pl ~), **-in** *f* vocalist, singer

sanitär (zah-ni-*tair*) *adj* sanitary

Saphir (*zaa*-feer) *m* (pl ~e) sapphire

Sardelle (zahr-*deh*-ler) *f* (pl ~n) anchovy

Sardine (zahr-*dee*-ner) *f* (pl ~n) sardine

Sarg (zahrk) *m* coffin

Satellit (zah-teh-*leet*) *m* (pl ~en) satellite; **Satellitenfernsehen** *nt* satellite tv

Satin (sah-*tang*) *m* satin

satt (zaht) *adj* satisfied

Sattel (*zah*-terl) *m* (pl ~) saddle

Satz (zahts) *m* (pl ~e) sentence; set; rate

Sau (zou) *f* sow

sauber (*zou*-berr) *adj* clean

Sauberkeit (*zou*-berr-kight) *f* cleanness, cleanliness

säubern (*zoi*-berrn) *v* clean

Saudi-Arabien (zou-di-ah-*raa*-bʸern) Saudi Arabia

saudiarabisch (zou-di-ah-*raa*-bish) *adj* Saudi Arabian

sauer (*zou*-err) *adj* sour

Sauerstoff (*zou*-err-shtof) *m* oxygen

***saufen** (*zou*-fern) *v* *drink, *colloquial* booze

***saugen** (*zou*-gern) *v* suck

Säugetier (*zoi*-ger-teer) *nt* (pl ~e) mammal

Säugling (*zoik*-ling) *m* (pl ~e) infant

Säule (*zoi*-ler) *f* (pl ~n) pillar, column

Saum (zoum) *m* (pl ~e) hem

Sauna (*zou*-nah) *f* (pl ~s) sauna

Säure (*zoi*-rer) *f* (pl ~n) acid

schaben (*shaa*-bern) *v* scrape

Schach (shahkh) *nt* chess; **Schach!** check!

Schachbrett (*shahkh*-breht) *nt* (pl ~er) checkerboard *Am*

Schachtel (*shahkh*-terl) *f* (pl ~n) box

schade! (*shaa*-der) what a pity! **es ist** ~ it's a pity

Schädel (*shai*-derl) *m* (pl ~) skull

Schaden (*shaa*-dern) *m* (pl ~) damage; harm, mischief

schaden (*shaa*-dern) *v* harm

Schadenersatz (*shaa*-dern-ehr-zahts) *m* compensation, indemnity

schadhaft (*shaat*-hahft) *adj* defective

schädlich (*shait*-likh) *adj* harmful, hurtful

Schadstoff (*shaat*-shtof) *m* harmful substance, pollutant

Schaf (shaaf) *nt* (pl ~e) sheep

*schaffen (*shah*-fern) *v* create; *make

Schaffner (*shahf*-nerr) *m* (pl ~), **-in** *f* conductor; ticket collector

Schal (shaal) *m* (pl ~s) scarf, shawl

Schale (*shaa*-ler) *f* (pl ~n) bowl; skin, peel; shell

schälen (*shai*-lern) *v* peel

Schalentier (*shaa*-lern-teer) *nt* (pl ~e) shellfish

Schall (shahl) *m* sound

schalldicht (*shahl*-dikht) *adj* soundproof

Schallplatte (*shahl*-plah-ter) *f* (pl ~n) record, disc

schalten (*shahl*-tern) *v* change gear

Schalter (*shahl*-terr) *m* (pl ~) switch; counter

Schaltjahr (*shahlt*-ᵞaar) *nt* leap year

schämen (*shai*-mern) *v*: **sich ~** *be ashamed

Schande (*shahn*-der) *f* disgrace, shame

Schänke (*shehng*-ker) *f* (pl ~n) tavern

scharf (shahrf) *adj* sharp; keen

schärfen (*shehr*-fern) *v* sharpen

scharlachrot (*shahr*-lahkh-rōat) *adj* scarlet

Scharnier (shahr-*neer*) *nt* (pl ~e) hinge

Schatten (*shah*-tern) *m* (pl ~) shade; shadow

schattig (*shah*-tikh) *adj* shady

Schatz (shahts) *m* (pl ~e) treasure; darling, sweetheart

schätzen (*sheh*-tsern) *v* appreciate; estimate, value; esteem

Schätzung (*sheh*-tsoong) *f* appreciation

Schauder (*shou*-derr) *m* horror; shudder

schauen (*shou*-ern) *v* look

Schauer (*shou*-err) *m* (pl ~) shower

Schaufel (*shou*-ferl) *f* (pl ~n) spade, shovel

Schaufenster (*shou*-fehns-terr) *nt* (pl ~) shopwindow

Schaukel (*shou*-kerl) *f* (pl ~n) swing

schaukeln (*shou*-kerln) *v* *swing; rock

Schaum (shoum) *m* froth, lather; foam

schäumen (*shoi*-mern) *v* foam

Schaumgummi (*shoum*-goo-mi) *m* foam rubber

Schauspiel (*shou*-shpeel) *nt* (pl ~e) spectacle; play

Schauspieler (*shou*-shpee-lerr) *m* (pl ~) actor; comedian

Schauspielerin (*shou*-shpee-ler-rin) *f* (pl ~nen) actress; comedian

Schauspielhaus (*shou*-shpeel-houss) *nt* (pl ~er) theatre, theater *Am*

Scheck (shehk) *m* (pl ~s) cheque; check *Am*

Scheckbuch (*shehk*-bōokh) *nt* (pl ~er) chequebook; checkbook *Am*

Scheibe (*shigh*-ber) *f* (pl ~n) disc; pane

Scheibenwischer (*shigh*-bern-vi-sherr) *m* (pl ~) windscreen wiper; windshield wiper *Am*

Scheide (*shigh*-der) *f anat* vagina; sheath

*scheiden (*shigh*-dern) *v* divorce; **sich ~ lassen** get divorced

Scheidewand (*shigh*-der-vahnt) *f* (pl ~e) partition

Scheidung (*shigh*-doong) *f* (pl ~en) divorce

Schein (shighn) *m* (pl ~e) shine; appearance; certificate; note

scheinbar (*shighn*-baar) *adj* apparent

*scheinen (*shigh*-nern) *v* look, appear, seem

scheinheilig (*shighn*-high-likh) *adj* hypocritical

Scheinwerfer (*shighn*-vehr-ferr) *m* (pl ~) headlight, headlamp; spotlight, searchlight

Scheitel (*shigh*-terl) *m* (pl ~) parting

Schellfisch (*shehl*-fish) *m* (pl ⁓e) haddock

Schelm (shehlm) *m* (pl ⁓e) rascal

schelmisch (*shehl*-mish) *adj* mischievous

Schema (*shāy*-mah) *nt* (pl ⁓ta) scheme; diagram

Schenkel (*shehng*-kerl) *m* thigh; shank; calf

schenken (*shehng*-kern) *v* pour

Schenkung (*shehng*-koong) *f* (pl ⁓en) donation

Schere (*shāy*-rer) *f* (pl ⁓n) scissors *pl*

Scherz (shehrts) *m* joke

scheu (shoi) *adj* shy

scheuern (*shoi*-errn) *v* scrub

Scheune (*shoi*-ner) *f* (pl ⁓n) barn

scheußlich (*shoiss*-likh) *adj* horrible

Schi (shee) *m* (pl ⁓er) ski; ⁓ **laufen* ski

Schicht (shikht) *f* (pl ⁓en) layer; shift; gang

schicken (*shi*-kern) *v* **send*

Schicksal (*shik*-zaal) *nt* destiny, fate

*schieben (*shee*-bern) *v* push

Schiebetür (*shee*-ber-tēwr) *f* (pl ⁓en) sliding door

Schiedsrichter (*sheets*-rikh-terr) *m* (pl ⁓), -**in** *f* umpire

schief (sheef) *adj* slanting

Schiefer (*shee*-ferr) *m* slate

schielen (*shee*-lern) *v* squint

schielend (*shee*-lernt) *adj* cross-eyed

Schienbein (*sheen*-bighn) *nt* shin(bone)

Schiene (*shee*-ner) *f* (pl ⁓n) splint

*schießen (*shee*-sern) *v* **shoot, fire*

Schießpulver (*sheess*-pool-ferr) *nt* gunpowder

Schiff (shif) *nt* (pl ⁓e) boat, ship; vessel

Schifffahrt (*shif*-faart) *f* navigation

Schifffahrtslinie (*shif*-faarts-lee-nʸer) *f* (pl ⁓n) shipping line

Schiffswerft (*shifs*-vehrft) *f* (pl ⁓en) shipyard

Schihose (*shee*-hōa-zer) *f* (pl ⁓n) ski pants

Schilauf (*shee*-louf) *m* skiing

Schiläufer (*shee*-loi-ferr) *m* (pl ⁓), -**in** *f* skier

Schild (shilt) *m* shield; *nt* sign; nameplate

schildern (*shil*-derrn) *nt* describe

Schilderung (*shil*-der-roong) *f* description

Schildkröte (*shilt*-krūr-ter) *f* (pl ⁓n) turtle

Schilfrohr (*shilf*-rōar) *nt* (pl ⁓e) reed

Schilift (*shee*-lift) *m* (pl ⁓e) ski lift

Schimmel (*shi*-merl) *m* mildew

schimmelig (*shi*-mer-likh) *adj* mouldy

schimpfen (*shim*-pfern) *v* scold

Schinken (*shing*-kern) *m* (pl ⁓) ham

Schirm (sheerm) *m* (pl ⁓e) screen

Schischuhe (*shee*-shōo-er) *mpl* ski boots

Schisprung (*shee*-shproong) *m* (pl ⁓e) ski jump

Schistöcke (*shee*-shtur-ker) *mpl* ski sticks; ski poles *Am*

Schlacht (shlahkht) *f* (pl ⁓en) battle

Schlaf (shlaaf) *m* sleep; **im** ⁓ asleep

Schläfe (*shlai*-fer) *f* (pl ⁓n) temple

*schlafen (*shlaa*-fern) *v* **sleep*

schlaff (shlahf) *adj* limp

schlaflos (*shlaaf*-lōass) *adj* sleepless

Schlaflosigkeit (*shlaaf*-lōa-zikh-kight) *f* insomnia

Schlafmittel (*shlaaf*-mi-terl) *nt* (pl ⁓) sleeping pill

schläfrig (*shlaif*-rikh) *adj* sleepy

Schlafsaal (*shlaaf*-zaal) *m* (pl -säle) dormitory

Schlafsack (*shlaaf*-zahk) *m* (pl ⁓e) sleeping bag

Schlafwagen (*shlaaf*-vaa-gern) *m* (pl ⁓) sleeping car

Schlafzimmer (*shlaaf*-tsi-merr) *nt* (pl

~) bedroom

Schlag (shlaak) *m* (pl ⁓e) blow, slap; bump

Schlaganfall (shlaak-ahn-fahl) *m* (pl ⁓e) stroke

*schlagen (shlaa-gern) *v* *hit, slap, *strike, *beat; thump, bump; smack; whip; **sich ~** *fight

Schlager (shlaa-gerr) *m* (pl ~) hit

Schläger (shlai-gerr) *m* (pl ~) racket; bat; thug

Schlagwort (shlaak-vort) *nt* (pl ⁓er) slogan

Schlagzeile (shlaak-tsigh-ler) *f* (pl ~n) headline

Schlamm (shlahm) *m* mud

schlammig (shlah-mikh) *adj* muddy

schlampig (shlahm-pikh) *adj* sloppy

Schlange (shlahng-er) *f* (pl ~n) snake; queue; **~ *stehen** queue; stand in line *Am*

schlank (shlahngk) *adj* slim, slender

schlapp (shlahp) *adj* washed-out; listless; weak

schlau (shlou) *adj* bright, clever

Schlauch (shloukh) *m* (pl ⁓e) inner tube

schlecht (shlehkht) *adj* bad; ill, evil; **schlechter** *adj* worse; **schlechtest** *adj* worst; **~ gelaunt** in a bad mood

Schleier (shligh-err) *m* (pl ~) veil

Schleife (shligh-fer) *f* bow; ribbon; loop

*schleifen (shligh-fern) *v* sharpen

schleppen (shleh-pern) *v* drag; haul, tug, tow

Schlepper (shleh-perr) *m* (pl ~) tug

schleudern (shloi-derrn) *v* *throw; skid

Schleuse (shloi-zer) *f* (pl ~n) lock, sluice

schlicht (shlikht) *adj* simple, plain

*schließen (shlee-sern) *v* close, *shut; fasten; **in sich ~** imply

schließlich (shleess-likh) *adv* at last

schlimm (shlim) *adj* bad

Schlinge (shling-er) *f* (pl ~n) loop

Schlitten (shli-tern) *m* (pl ~) sledge, sled *Am*; sleigh

Schlittschuh (shlit-shoo) *m* (pl ⁓e) skate

Schlitz (shlits) *m* (pl ⁓e) slot; fly

Schloss (shloss) *nt* (pl Schlösser) lock; castle

Schlucht (shlookht) *f* (pl ~en) gorge

Schluck (shlook) *m* drink; sip

Schluckauf (shlook-ouf) *m* hiccup

Schlückchen (shlewk-khern) *nt* (pl ~) sip

schlucken (shloo-kern) *v* swallow

Schlüpfer (shlew-pferr) *m* (pl ~) panties *pl*

schlüpfrig (shlewpf-rikh) *adj* slippery

Schluss (shlooss) *m* (pl ⁓e) end, finish; conclusion

Schlüssel (shlew-serl) *m* (pl ~) key

Schlüsselbein (shlew-serl-bighn) *nt* (pl ⁓e) collarbone

Schlüsselloch (shlew-serl-lokh) *nt* (pl ⁓er) keyhole

Schlussfolgerung (shlooss-fol-ger-roong) *f* (pl ~en) conclusion

Schlusslicht (shlooss-likht) *nt* (pl ~er) rear light

Schlussverkauf (shlooss-fehr-kouf) *m* sales

schmackhaft (shmahk-hahft) *adj* enjoyable, savo(u)ry, tasty

schmal (shmaal) *adj* narrow

Schmalz (shmahlts) *n* lard; schmaltz

schmecken (shmeh-kern) *v* taste

*schmelzen (shmehl-tsern) *v* melt

Schmerz (shmehrts) *m* (pl ~en) ache, pain

schmerzen (shmehr-tsern) *v* ache

schmerzhaft (shmehrts-hahft) *adj* sore, painful

schmerzlos (shmehrts-lōass) *adj*

painless

Schmetterling (*shmeh*-terr-ling) *m* (pl ⁓e) butterfly

Schmetterlingsstil (*shmeh*-terr-lings-shteel) *m* butterfly stroke

Schmied (shmeet) *m* (pl ⁓e) smith, blacksmith

schmieren (*shmee*-rern) *v* grease; lubricate

schmierig (*shmee*-rikh) *adj* greasy

Schmieröl (*shmeer*-ūrl) *nt* (pl ⁓e) lubrication oil

Schmiersystem (*shmeer*-zewss-tāym) *nt* lubrication system

Schmierung (*shmee*-roong) *f* (pl ⁓en) lubrication

Schminke (*shming*-ker) *f* (pl ⁓n) make-up

Schmirgelpapier (*shmeer*-gerl-pah-peer) *nt* sandpaper

Schmuck (shmook) *m* jewellery

schmuggeln (*shmoo*-gerln) *v* smuggle

Schmutz (shmoots) *m* dirt

schmutzig (*shmoo*-tsikh) *adj* dirty; foul, filthy

Schnabel (*shnaa*-berl) *m* (pl ⁓) beak; nozzle

Schnalle (*shnah*-ler) *f* (pl ⁓n) buckle

Schnappschuss (*shnahp*-shooss) *m* (pl ⁓e) snapshot

Schnaps (shnahps) *m* spirits *pl*

schnarchen (*shnahr*-khern) *v* snore

Schnauze (*shnou*-tser) *f* (pl ⁓n) snout

Schnecke (*shneh*-ker) *f* (pl ⁓n) snail

Schnee (shnāy) *m* snow

schneebedeckt (*shnāy*-ber-dehkt) *adj* snowy

Schneesturm (*shnāy*-shtoorm) *m* (pl ⁓e) blizzard, snowstorm

*schneiden (*shnigh*-dern) *v* *cut

Schneider (*shnigh*-derr) *m* (pl ⁓) tailor

Schneiderin (*shnigh*-der-rin) *f* (pl ⁓nen) dressmaker

schneien (*shnigh*-ern) *v* snow

schnell (shnehl) *adj* fast; quick, rapid; **zu ⁓ *fahren** *speed

Schnelligkeit (*shneh*-likh-kight) *f* speed

Schnellimbiss (*shnehl*-im-biss) *m* snack bar, *colloquial* fastfood joint

Schnellkochtopf (*shnehl*-kokh-topf) *m* (pl ⁓e) pressure cooker

Schnellzug (*shnehl*-tsōōk) *m* (pl ⁓e) express train

Schnitt (shnit) *m* (pl ⁓e) cut

Schnitte (*shni*-ter) *f* (pl ⁓n) slice

Schnittlauch (*shnit*-loukh) *m* chives *pl*

Schnittwunde (*shnit*-voon-der) *f* cut

Schnitzel (*shni*-tserl) *nt* cutlet, schnitzel

schnitzen (*shni*-tsern) *v* carve

Schnitzerei (shni-tser-*righ*) *f* (pl ⁓en) carving

Schnorchel (*shnor*-kherl) *m* (pl ⁓) snorkel

Schnulze (*shnool*-tser) *f* (pl ⁓n) tearjerker

Schnupfen (*shnoo*-pfern) *m* cold

Schnur (shnōōr) *f* (pl ⁓e) string; line, twine

Schnurrbart (*shnoor*-baart) *m* (pl ⁓e) moustache

Schnürsenkel (*shnēwr*-zehng-kerl) *m* (pl ⁓) lace, shoelace

Schock (shok) *m* (pl ⁓s) shock

schockieren (sho-*kee*-rern) *v* shock

Schokolade (shoa-koa-*laa*-der) *f* chocolate

Scholle (*sho*-ler) *f* (pl ⁓n) plaice

schon (shōan) *adv* already

schön (shūrn) *adj* beautiful; pretty, fine

schonen (*shōa*-nern) *v* spare; *take care of; **sich ⁓** take it easy

Schönheit (*shūrn*-hight) *f* beauty

Schönheitssalon (*shūrn*-hights-zah-lawng) *m* (pl ∾s) beauty salon, beauty parlo(u)r

schöpfen (*shur*-pfern) *v* scoop, ladle; bale (out); *draw from

Schornstein (*shorn*-shtighn) *m* (pl ∾e) chimney

Schoß (shōas) *m* lap

Schotte (*sho*-ter) *m* (pl ∾n) Scot, Scotsman

Schottin (*sho*-tin) *f* (pl ∾nen) Scot, Scotswoman

schottisch (*sho*-tish) *adj* Scottish, Scotch

Schottland (*shot*-lahnt) Scotland

schräg (shraik) *adj* slanting

Schramme (*shrah*-mer) *f* (pl ∾n) graze, scratch

Schrank (shrahngk) *m* (pl ∾e) cupboard

Schranke (*shrahng*-ker) *f* (pl ∾n) barrier; **in Schranken *halten** restrain

Schraube (*shrou*-ber) *f* (pl ∾n) screw; propeller

schrauben (*shrou*-bern) *v* screw

Schraubenmutter (*shrou*-bern-moo-terr) *f* (pl ∾n) nut

Schraubenschlüssel (*shrou*-bern-shlew-serl) *m* (pl ∾) spanner, wrench

Schraubenzieher (*shrou*-bern-tsee-err) *m* (pl ∾) screwdriver

Schreck (shrehk) *m* fright, scare

*****schrecken** (*shreh*-kern) *v* frighten, scare, terrify

schrecklich (*shrehk*-likh) *adj* frightful, horrible, dreadful, awful, terrible

Schrei (shrigh) *m* (pl ∾e) cry, scream, yell, shout

Schreibblock (*shrighp*-blok) *m* (pl ∾e) writing-pad, pad

*****schreiben** (*shrigh*-bern) *v* *write

Schreibmaschine (*shrighp*-mah-shee-ner) *f* (pl ∾n) typewriter

Schreibpapier (*shrighp*-pah-peer) *nt* notepaper, writing paper

Schreibtisch (shrighp-tish) *m* (pl ∾e) bureau, desk

Schreibwaren (*shrighp*-vaa-rern) *fpl* stationery

Schreibwarenhandlung (*shrighp*-vaa-rern-hahn-dloong) *f* (pl ∾en) stationer's

*****schreien** (*shrigh*-ern) *v* cry, scream, yell, shout

Schrein (shrighn) *m* (pl ∾e) shrine

Schrift (shrift) *f* (hand)writing; type; typeface

schriftlich (*shrift*-likh) *adj* written; *adv* in writing

Schriftsteller (*shrift*-shteh-lerr) *m* (pl ∾), **-in** *f* writer

Schritt (shrit) *m* (pl ∾e) pace; step; move; ∾ *halten mit *keep up with

schroff (shrof) *adj* steep

Schrott (shrot) *m* tech scrap metal; *colloquial* junk

schrumpfen (*shroom*-pfern) *v* *shrink

Schub (shoōp) *m* (pl ∾e) push

Schubkarren (*shoōp*-kah-rern) *m* (pl ∾) wheelbarrow

Schublade (*shoōp*-laa-der) *f* (pl ∾n) drawer

schüchtern (*shewkh*-terrn) *adj* timid, shy

Schüchternheit (*shewkh*-terrn-hight) *f* timidity, shyness

Schuh (shoō) *m* (pl ∾e) shoe

Schuhgeschäft (*shoō*-ger-shehft) *nt* (pl ∾e) shoe shop

Schuhkrem (*shoō*-krāym) *f* (pl ∾s) shoe polish

Schuhmacher (*shoō*-mah-kherr) *m* (pl ∾), **-in** *f* shoemaker

Schuhwerk (*shoō*-vehrk) *nt* footwear

Schulbank (*shoōl*-bahngk) *f* (pl ∾e) desk

Schuld (shoolt) *f* (pl ⁓en) guilt, blame; debt

schulden (*shool*-dern) *v* owe

schuldig (*shool*-dikh) *adj* guilty; due; ⁓ ***sein** owe

Schuldirektor (*shool*-di-rehk-tor) *m* (pl ⁓en), **-in** *f* headmaster, headmistress, head teacher

Schule (*shoo*-ler) *f* (pl ⁓n) school; college; **höhere** ⁓ secondary school

Schüler (*shew*-lerr) *m* (pl ⁓) scholar, pupil; schoolboy

Schülerin (*shew*-ler-rin) *f* (pl ⁓nen) schoolgirl

Schulferien (*shool*-fāy-r ᵞern) *pl* holidays *pl*, *Am* vacation sg

Schullehrer (*shool*-lāy-rerr) *m* (pl ⁓), **-in** *f* teacher

Schulleiter (*shool*-ligh-terr) *m* (pl ⁓), **-in** *f* headmaster, headmistress, head teacher, principal

Schultasche (*shool*-tah-sher) *f* (pl ⁓n) satchel

Schulter (*shool*-terr) *f* (pl ⁓n) shoulder

Schuppe (*shoo*-per) *f* (pl ⁓n) scale; **Schuppen** *fpl* dandruff; *m* shed

Schürze (*shewr*-tser) *f* (pl ⁓n) apron

Schuss (shooss) *m* (pl ⁓e) shot

Schüssel (*shew*-serl) *f* (pl ⁓n) dish; basin

Schuster (*shoos*- terr) *m* shoemaker

Schutt (shoot) *m* litter

Schüttelfrost (*shew*-terl-frost) *m* shivering fit

schütteln (*shew*-terln) *v* *shake

schütten (*shew*-tern) *v* pour; **es schüttet** it's pouring (down), *Brit colloquial* it's bucketing (down)

Schutz (shoots) *m* protection; cover, shelter

Schutzbrille (*shoots*-bri-ler) *f* (pl ⁓n) goggles *pl*

schützen (*shew*-tsern) *v* protect; shelter

Schutzmann (*shoots*-mahn) *m* (pl ⁓er) policeman

schwach (shvahkh) *adj* weak, feeble, faint; poor; dim

Schwäche (*shveh*-kher) *f* (pl ⁓n) weakness

Schwager (*shvaa*-gerr) *m* (pl ⁓) brother-in-law

Schwägerin (*shvai*-ger-rin) *f* (pl ⁓nen) sister-in-law

Schwalbe (*shvahl*-ber) *f* (pl ⁓n) swallow

Schwamm (shvahm) *m* (pl ⁓e) sponge

Schwan (shvaan) *m* (pl ⁓e) swan

schwanger (*shvahng*-err) *adj* pregnant

Schwanz (shvahnts) *m* (pl ⁓e) tail

schwänzen (*shvehn*-tsern) *v* play truant

schwarz (shvahrts) *adj* black

Schwarzmarkt (*shvahrts*-mahrkt) *m* black market

schwatzen (*shvah*-tsern) *v* chat

Schwede (*shvāy*-der) *m* (pl ⁓n) Swede

Schweden (*shvāy*-dern) Sweden

Schwedin (*shvāy*-din) *f* (pl ⁓nen) Swede

schwedisch (*shvāy*-dish) *adj* Swedish

*schweigen (*shvigh*-gern) *v* *keep quiet, *be silent; **schweigend** silent; **zum Schweigen *bringen** silence

Schwein (shvighn) *nt* (pl ⁓e) pig

Schweinefleisch (*shvigh*-ner-flighsh) *nt* pork

Schweinsleder (*shvighns*-lāy-derr) *nt* pigskin

Schweiß (shvighss) *m* perspiration; sweat

schweißen (*shvigh*-sern) *v* weld

Schweiz (shvights) *f* Switzerland

Schweizer (*shvigh*-tserr) *m* (pl ⁓), **-in** *f* Swiss

schweizerisch (*shvigh*-tser-rish) *adj*

Swiss

Schwelle (*shveh*-ler) *f* (pl ~n)
threshold

***schwellen** (*shveh*-lern) *v* *swell

schwer (shvāyr) *adj* heavy; difficult

schwerfällig (*shvāyr*-feh-likh) *adj*
slow

schwerhörig (*shvāyr*-hūr-rikh) *adj*
hard of hearing

Schwerkraft (*shvāyr*-krahft) *f* gravity

Schwermut (*shvāyr*-mōōt) *f*
melancholy

Schwert (shvāyrt) *nt* (pl ~er) sword

Schwester (*shvehss*-terr) *f* (pl ~n)
sister; nurse

Schwiegereltern (*shvee*-gerr-ehl-
terrn) *pl* parents-in-law *pl*

Schwiegermutter (*shvee*-gerr-moo-
terr) *f* (pl ~) mother-in-law

Schwiegersohn (*shvee*-gerr-zōan) *m*
(pl ~e) son-in-law

Schwiegertochter (*shvee*-gerr-tokh-
terr) *f* (pl ~) daughter-in-law

Schwiegervater (*shvee*-gerr-faa-terr)
m (pl ~) father-in-law

schwierig (*shvee*-rikh) *adj* hard,
difficult

Schwierigkeit (*shvee*-rikh-kight) *f* (pl
~en) difficulty

Schwimmbad (*shvim*-baat) *nt* (pl ~er)
swimming pool

***schwimmen** (*shvi*-mern) *v* *swim;
float

Schwimmer (*shvi*-merr) *m* (pl ~), **-in** *f*
swimmer; float

Schwimmsport (*shvim*-shport) *m*
swimming

Schwindel (*shvin*-derl) *m* dizziness;
fraud

Schwindelgefühl (*shvin*-derl-ger-
fēwl) *nt* giddiness

schwindlig (*shvin*-dlikh) *adj* giddy,
dizzy

Schwingung (*shving*-oong) *f* (pl ~en)

vibration

Schwitzbad (*shvits*-baat) *nt* (pl ~er)
Turkish bath

schwitzen (*shvi*-tsern) *v* perspire,
sweat

***schwören** (*shvūr*-rern) *v* *swear; vow

schwul (shwōōl) *adj colloquial* gay

sechs (zehks) *num* six

sechste (*zehks*-ter) *num* sixth

sechzehn (*zehkh*-tsāyn) *num* sixteen

sechzehnte (*zehkh*-tsāyn-ter) *num*
sixteenth

sechzig (*zehkh*-tsikh) *num* sixty

Sediment (zay-di-*mehnt*) *nt* (pl ~e)
deposit

See (zāy) *m* (pl ~n) lake; *f* sea

Seebad (*zāy*-baat) *nt* (pl ~er) seaside
resort

Seehafen (*zāy*-haa-fern) *m* (pl ~)
seaport

Seehund (*zāy*-hoont) *m* (pl ~e) seal

Seeigel (*zāy*-ee-gerl) *m* (pl ~) sea
urchin

Seekarte (*zāy*-kahr-ter) *f* (pl ~n) chart

seekrank (*zāy*-krahngk) *adj* seasick

Seekrankheit (*zāy*-krahngk-hight) *f*
seasickness

Seele (*zāy*-ler) *f* (pl ~n) soul

Seemöwe (*zāy*-mūr-ver) *f* (pl ~n)
seagull

Seeräuber (*zāy*-roi-berr) *m* (pl ~)
pirate

Seereise (*zāy*-righ-zer) *f* (pl ~n) cruise

Seevogel (*zāy*-fōa-gerl) *m* (pl ~)
seabird

Seezunge (*zāy*-tsoong-er) *f* (pl ~n)
sole

Segel (*zāy*-gerl) *nt* (pl ~) sail

Segelboot (*zāy*-gerl-bōat) *nt* (pl ~e)
sailing boat

Segelflugzeug (*zāy*-gerl-flōōk-tsoik)
nt (pl ~e) glider

Segelklub (*zāy*-gerl-kloop) *m* (pl ~s)
yacht club

Segelsport (*zay*-gerl-shport) *m* yachting

Segeltuch (*zay*-gerl-tookh) *nt* canvas

Segen (*zay*-gern) *m* blessing

segnen (*zay*-gnern) *v* bless

***sehen** (*zay*-ern) *v* *see; notice; ~ *lassen *show

Sehenswürdigkeit (*zay*-erns-vewr-dikh-kight) *f* (pl ~en) sight

Sehne (*zay*-ner) *f* (pl ~n) sinew, tendon

sehnen (*zay*-nern) *v*: **sich ~ nach** long for

Sehnsucht (*zayn*-zookht) *f* (pl ~e) longing

sehr (*zayr*) *adv* quite, very

seicht (*zighkht*) *adj* shallow

Seide (*zigh*-der) *f* silk

seiden (*zigh*-dern) *adj* silken

Seife (*zigh*-fer) *f* (pl ~n) soap

Seifenpulver (*zigh*-fern-pool-ferr) *nt* soap powder

Seil (*zighl*) *nt* (pl ~e) rope, cord

sein (*zighn*) *pron* his

***sein** (*zighn*) *v* *be

seit (*zight*) *prep* since

seitdem (*zight*-*daym*) *conj* since

Seite (*zigh*-ter) *f* (pl ~n) way, side; page; **zur ~** aside

Seitenlicht (*zigh*-tern-likht) *nt* (pl ~er) sidelight

Seitenschiff (*zigh*-tern-shif) *nt* (pl ~e) aisle

Seitenstraße (*zigh*-tern-shtraa-ser) *f* (pl ~n) side street

seither (*zight*-*hayr*) *adv* since

seitwärts (*zight*-vehrts) *adv* sideways

Sekretär (zay-kray-*tair*) *m* (pl ~e), **-in** *f* secretary; assistant

Sekt (zehkt) *m* champagne

Sekunde (zay-*koon*-der) *f* (pl ~n) second

selb (zehlb) *pron* same

selbst (zehlpst) *pron* myself; yourself;

himself; herself; oneself; ourselves; yourselves; themselves

Selbstbedienung (*zehlpst*-ber-dee-noong) *f* self-service

Selbstbedienungsrestaurant (*zehlpst*-ber-dee-noongs-rehss-toa-rah*n̄g*) *nt* (pl ~s) cafeteria, self-service restaurant

selbstgemacht (*zehlpst*-ger-mahkht) *adj* home-made

Selbstklebeband (*zehlpst*-klay-ber-bahnt) *nt* scotch tape

Selbstlaut (*zehlpst*-lout) *m* (pl ~e) vowel

selbstlos (*zehlpst*-loass) *adj* unselfish

Selbstmord (*zehlpst*-mort) *m* (pl ~e) suicide

selbstständig (*zehlp*-shtehn-dikh) *adj* independent; self-employed

Selbstsucht (*zehlpst*-zookht) *f* selfishness

selbstsüchtig (*zehlpst*-zewkh-tikh) *adj* selfish

selbstverständlich (*zehlpst*-fehr-shtehnt-likh) *adj* self-evident; *adv* naturally, of course

Selbstverwaltung (*zehlpst*-fehr-vahl-toong) *f* self-government

Sellerie (*zeh*-ler-ree) *m* celery

selten (*zehl*-tern) *adj* rare; uncommon,; *adv* seldom, rarely

Selterswasser (*zehl*-terrs-vah-serr) *nt* soda-water

seltsam (*zehlt*-zaam) *adj* curious, odd, quaint

Senat (zay-*naat*) *m* senate

Senator (zay-naa-tor) *m* (pl ~en), **-in** *f* senator

***senden** (*zehn*-dern) *v* *send; transmit, *broadcast

Sender (*zehn*-derr) *m* (pl ~) transmitter; radio station

Sendung (*zehn*-doong) *f* (pl ~en) consignment; transmission, broadcast

Senf (zehnf) *m* mustard

senil (zay-*neel*) *adj* senile

senken (*zehng*-kern) *v* *cut

senkrecht (*zehngk*-rehkht) *adj* vertical, perpendicular

Sensation (zehn-zah-ts^y*oan*) *f* (pl ∼en) sensation

sensationell (zehn-zah-ts^{y}oa-*nehl*) *adj* sensational

sentimental (zehn-ti-mehn-*taal*) *adj* sentimental

September (zehp-*tehm*-berr) September

Serie (*zay*-r^{y}er) *f* (pl ∼n) series

seriös (zay-r^y*ürss*) *adj* serious

Serum (*zay*-room) *nt* (pl Seren) serum

Serviette (zehr-v^y*eh*-ter) *f* (pl ∼n) napkin, serviette

Sessel (*zeh*-serl) *m* (pl ∼) chair, armchair

setzen (*zeh*-tsern) *v* place; *lay, *put; **sich ∼** *sit down

Seuche (*soi*-kher) *f* epidemic

Sex (zehks) *m* sex

Sexualität (zeh-ksoo-ah-li-*tait*) *f* sexuality

sexuell (zeh-ksoo-*ehl*) *adj* sexual

Shampoo (shehm-*poo*) *nt* shampoo

sich (zikh) *pron* himself; herself; themselves

sicher (*zi*-kherr) *adj* safe, secure; sure

Sicherheit (*zi*-kherr-hight) *f* safety, security

Sicherheitsgurt (*zi*-kherr-hights-goort) *m* (pl ∼e) seat belt; safety belt

Sicherheitsnadel (*zi*-kherr-hights-naa-derl) *f* (pl ∼n) safety pin

sicherlich (*zi*-kherr-likh) *adv* surely

Sicherung (*zi*-kher-roong) *f* (pl ∼en) fuse

Sicht (zikht) *f* sight

sichtbar (*zikht*-baar) *adj* visible

Sichtweite (*zikht*-vigh-ter) *f* visibility

Sie (zee) *pron* you

sie (zee) *pron* she; her; they; them

Sieb (zeep) *nt* (pl ∼e) sieve

sieben[1] (*zee*-bern) *v* sift, sieve; strain

sieben[2] (*zee*-bern) *num* seven

sieb(en)te (*zee*-bern-ter) *num* seventh

siebzehn (*zeep*-tsayn) *num* seventeen

siebzehnte (*zeep*-tsayn-ter) *num* seventeenth

siebzig (*zeep*-tsikh) *num* seventy

Siedlung (*zeed*-loong) *f* settlement; housing estate

Sieg (zeek) *m* (pl ∼e) victory

Siegel (*zee*-gerl) *nt* (pl ∼) seal

siegen (*zee*-gern) *v* *win

Sieger (*zee*-gerr) *m* (pl ∼), **-in** *f* winner

Signal (zi-*gnaal*) *nt* (pl ∼e) signal

signalisieren (zi-gnah-li-*zee*-rern) *v* signal

Silbe (*zil*-ber) *f* (pl ∼n) syllable

Silber (*zil*-berr) *nt* silver; silverware

silbern (*zil*-berrn) *adj* silver

*singen (*zing*-ern) *v* *sing

*sinken (*zing*-kern) *v* *sink

Sinn (zin) *m* (pl ∼e) sense

sinnlos (*zin*-loáss) *adj* meaningless, useless

Sirene (zi-*ray*-ner) *f* (pl ∼n) siren

Sirup (*zee*-roop) *m* syrup

Sitte (*zi*-ter) *f* (pl ∼n) custom; **Sitten** morals

sittlich (*zit*-likh) *adj* moral

Sitz (zits) *m* (pl ∼e) seat

*sitzen (*zi*-tsern) *v* *sit

Sitzung (*zi*-tsoong) *f* (pl ∼en) session

Skandal (skahn-*daal*) *m* (pl ∼e) scandal

Skandinavien (skahn-di-*naa*-v^{y}ern) Scandinavia

Skandinavier (skahn-di-*naa*-v^{y}err) *m* (pl ∼), **-in** *f* Scandinavian

skandinavisch (skahn-di-*naa*-vish) *adj* Scandinavian

Skelett (skay-*leht*) *nt* (pl ~e) skeleton

Ski (shee) *m* ski; ~ **laufen** ski

Skizze (*ski*-tser) *f* (pl ~n) sketch

skizzieren (ski-*tsee*-rern) *v* sketch

Sklave (*sklaa*-ver) *m* (pl ~n) slave

Sklavin (*sklaa*-vin) *f* (pl ~nen) slave

Skulptur (skoolp-*toor*) *f* (pl ~en) sculpture

Slip (slip) *m* (pl ~s) briefs *pl*

Smaragd (smah-*rahkt*) *m* (pl ~e) emerald

Smoking (*smoa*-king) *m* (pl ~s) dinner jacket; tuxedo *Am*

Snackbar (*snehk*-baar) *f* (pl ~s) snack bar

so (zoa) *adv* so; such; thus; ~ **dass** so that

sobald als (zoa-*bahlt* ahls) as soon as

Socke (*zo*-ker) *f* (pl ~n) sock

Sodawasser (*zoa*-dah-vah-serr) *nt* soda water

Sodbrennen (*zoat*-breh-nern) *nt* heartburn

soeben (zoa-*ay*-bern) *adv* just now

Sofa (*zoa*-fah) *nt* (pl ~s) sofa

sofort (zoa-*fort*) *adv* at once; presently; straight away, immediately, instantly

sofortig (zoa-*for*-tikh) *adj* prompt

Software (*zoft*-vayr) *f* software

sogar (zoa-*gaar*) *adv* even

sogenannt (*zoa*-ger-nahnt) *adj* so-called

sogleich (zoa-*glighkh*) *adv* presently, immediately

Sohle (*zoa*-ler) *f* (pl ~n) sole

Sohn (zoan) *m* (pl ~e) son

solch (zolkh) *pron* such

Soldat (zol-*daat*) *m* (pl ~en), **-in** *f* soldier

solide (zoa-*lee*-der) *adj* firm

Soll (zol) *nt* debit

sollen (*zo*-lern) *v* *ought to, *shall

Sommer (*zo*-merr) *m* (pl ~) summer

Sommerzeit (zo-merr-*tsight*) *f* summer time

Sonderangebot (zon-derr-ahn-ger-boat) *nt* special offer

sonderbar (*zon*-derr-baar) *adj* funny, odd, peculiar; queer

sondern (*zon*-derrn) *conj* but

Sonnabend (*zon*-aa-bernt) *m* Saturday

Sonne (*zo*-ner) *f* (pl ~n) sun

sonnen (*zo*-nern) *v*: **sich ~** sunbathe, sun o.s.

Sonnenaufgang (*zo*-nern-ouf-gahng) *m* (pl ~e) sunrise

Sonnenbrand (*zo*-nern-brahnt) *m* sunburn

Sonnenbrille (*zo*-nern-bri-ler) *f* (pl ~n) sunglasses *pl*

Sonnenlicht (*zo*-nern-likht) *nt* sunlight

Sonnenöl (*zo*-nern-url) *nt* suntan oil

Sonnenschein (*zo*-nern-shighn) *m* sunshine

Sonnenschirm (*zo*-nern-sheerm) *m* (pl ~e) sunshade

Sonnenstich (*zo*-nern-shtikh) *m* sunstroke

Sonnenuntergang (*zo*-nern-oon-terr-gahng) *m* (pl ~e) sunset

sonnig (*zo*-nikh) *adj* sunny

Sonntag (*zon*-taak) *m* Sunday

sonst (zonst) *adv* otherwise; else

Sorge (*zor*-ger) *f* (pl ~n) care; trouble, concern, worry

sorgen für (*zor*-gern) see to, attend to, *take care of

sorgfältig (*zork*-fehl-tikh) *adj* neat; careful; thorough

Sorte (*zor*-ter) *f* (pl ~n) sort, kind

sortieren (zor-*tee*-rern) *v* sort, assort

Sortiment (zor-ti-*mehnt*) *nt* (pl ~e) assortment

Soße (*zoa*-ser) *f* (pl ~n) sauce

Souvenir (zoo-veh-*nir*) *nt* (pl ~s)

souvenir

sowie (zo-*vee*) *conj* as soon as, as well as

sowohl ... als auch (zoa-*vōal* ... ahls oukh) both ... and; ... as well as ...

sozial (zoa-ts*ʸaal*) *adj* social

Sozialismus (zoa-ts*ʸah-liss*-mooss) *m* socialism

Sozialist (zoa-t*ʸsah-list*) *m* (pl ⁓en), **-in** *f* socialist

sozialistisch (zoa-ts*ʸah-liss*-tish) *adj* socialist

spähen (*shpai*-ern) *v* peep

Spalt (shpahlt) *m* (pl ⁓e) crack, gap, slit

Spalte (*shpahl*-ter) *f* (pl ⁓n) cleft; column

spalten (*shpahl*-tern) *v* *split

Spanferkel (*shpaan*-fehr-kerl) *nt* sucking pig

Spange (*shpahng*-er) *f* clasp; (hair) slide;brace

Spanien (*shpaa*-n*ʸern*) Spain

Spanier (*shpaa*-n*ʸerr*) *m* (pl ⁓), **-in** *f* Spaniard

spanisch (*shpaa*-nish) *adj* Spanish

spannen (*shpah*-nern) *v* tighten

spannend (*shpah*-nernt) *adj* exciting, thrilling

Spannkraft (*shpahn*-krahft) *f* elasticity

Spannung (*shpah*-noong) *f* (pl ⁓en) pressure; stress, tension; voltage

sparen (*shpaa*-rern) *v* save, economize

Spargel (*shpahr*-gerl) *m* asparagus

Sparkasse (*shpaar*-kah-ser) *f* (pl ⁓n) savings bank

sparsam (*shpaar*-zaam) *adj* economical; thrifty

Spaß (shpaass) *m* fun, pleasure

spaßig (*shpaa*-sikh) *adj* funny, humorous

spät (shpait) *adj* late; **später**

afterwards

Spaten (*shpaa*-tern) *m* (pl ⁓) spade

spätestens (shpai-tehss-terns) *adv* at the latest

Spatz (shpahts) *m* sparrow

spazieren (shpah-*tsee*-rern) *v* walk

Spaziergang (shpah-*tseer*-gahng) *m* (pl ⁓e) walk

Spaziergänger (shpah-*tseer*-gehng-err) *m* (pl ⁓), **-in** *f* walker

Spazierstock (shpah-*tseer*-shtok) *m* (pl ⁓e) walking stick

Speck (shpehk) *m* bacon

Speer (shp*āyr*) *m* (pl ⁓e) spear

Speiche (*shpigh*-kher) *f* (pl ⁓n) spoke

Speichel (*shpigh*-kherl) *m* spit

Speise (*shpigh*-zer) *f* (pl ⁓n) fare

Speisekammer (*shpigh*-zer-kah-merr) *f* (pl ⁓n) larder

Speisekarte (*shpigh*-zer-kahr-ter) *f* (pl ⁓en) menu

speisen (*shpigh*-zern) *v* *eat

Speisesaal (*shpigh*-zer-zaal) *m* (pl -säle) dining-room

Speisewagen (*shpigh*-zer-vaa-gern) *m* (pl ⁓) dining car

Speisezimmer (*shpigh*-zer-tsi-merr) *nt* (pl ⁓) dining room

spekulieren (shpay-koo-*lee*-rern) *v* speculate

Spende (*shpehn*-der) *f* (pl ⁓n) donation

spenden (*shpehn*-dern) *v* donate

Sperling (*shpehr*-ling) *m* (pl ⁓e) sparrow

Sperre (*shpeh*-rerr) *f* barrier; road block

sperren (*shpeh*-rern) *v* block

Spesen (*shpay*-sern) *pl* expenses *pl*

spezialisieren (shpay-ts*ʸah*-li-*zee*-rern) *v*: **sich** ⁓ specialize

Spezialist (shpay-ts*ʸah-list*) *m* (pl ⁓en), **-in** *f* specialist

Spezialität (shpay-ts*ʸah*-li-*tait*) *f* (pl

speziell (shpay-ts^{y}ehl) adj special; peculiar; adv in particular

spezifisch (shpay-tsee-fish) adj specific

Spiegel (shpee-gerl) m (pl ~) looking-glass, mirror

Spiegelbild (shpee-gerl-bilt) nt (pl ~er) reflection

Spiegelei (shpee-gerl-igh) nt fried egg

Spiegelung (shpee-ger-loong) f (pl ~en) reflection

Spiel (shpeel) nt (pl ~e) game; play; match

spielen (shpee-lern) v play; act

Spieler (shpee-lerr) m (pl ~), **-in** f player

Spielkarte (shpeel-kahr-ter) f (pl ~n) playing card

Spielmarke (shpeel-mahr-ker) f (pl ~n) chip

Spielplatz (shpeel-plahts) m (pl ~e) playground, recreation ground

Spielstand (shpeel-shtahnt) m score

Spielwarenladen (shpeel-vaa-rern-laa-dern) m (pl ~) toyshop

Spielzeug (shpeel-tsoik) nt (pl ~e) toy

Spinat (shpi-naat) m spinach

Spinne (shpi-ner) f (pl ~n) spider

*spinnen (shpi-nern) v *spin

Spinnwebe (shpin-vāy-ber) f (pl ~n) spider's web

Spion (shpi-ōan) m (pl ~e) spy

Spirituosen (shpi-ri-too-ōa-zern) pl spirits, liquor

Spirituskocher (shpee-ri-tooss-ko-kherr) m (pl ~) spirit stove

spitz (shpits) adj pointed

Spitze (shpi-tser) f (pl ~n) point; peak; top; tip; spire; lace

Spitzname (shpits-naa-mer) m (pl ~n) nickname

Splitter (shpli-terr) m (pl ~) splinter; chip

spontan (shpon-taan) adj spontaneous

Sport (shport) m (pl ~e) sport

Sportjacke (shport-^{y}ah-ker) f (pl ~n) sports jacket, blazer

Sportkleidung (shport-kligh-doong) f sportswear

Sportler (shport-lerr) m (pl ~) sportsman

Sportlerin (shport-ler-rin) f (pl ~nen) sportswoman

sportlich (shport-likh) adj sporty; sporting

Sportwagen (shport-vaa-gern) m (pl ~) sports car

Spott (shpot) m mockery

Sprache (shpraa-kher) f (pl ~n) speech; language

Sprachführer (shpraakh-fēw-rerr) m (pl ~) phrase book

Sprachlabor (shpraakh-lah-bōar) nt (pl ~e) language laboratory

sprachlos (shpraakh-lōass) adj speechless

Spray (sprāy) nt (pl ~s) atomizer

*sprechen (shpreh-khern) v *speak, talk

Sprechstunde (shprehkh-shtoon-der) f (pl ~n) consultation hours

Sprechzimmer (shprehkh-tsi-merr) nt (pl ~) surgery

sprengen (shprehng-ern) v *blow up

Sprengstoff (shprehng-shtof) m (pl ~e) explosive

Sprichwort (shprikh-vort) nt (pl ~er) proverb

Springbrunnen (shpring-broo-nern) m (pl ~) fountain

*springen (shpring-ern) v jump; *leap

Spritze (shpri-tser) f (pl ~n) shot; syringe

spritzen (shpri-tsern) v splash; sprinkle, water; inject

Sprühregen (shprēw-rāy-gern) m

drizzle

Sprung (shproong) *m* (pl ⁓e) leap, jump

Spucke (shpoo-ker) *f* spit

spucken (shpoo-kern) *v* *spit

Spule (shpoo-ler) *f* (pl ⁓n) spool

spülen (shpew-lern) *v* rinse

Spülung (shpew-loong) *f* (pl ⁓en) rinse

Spur (shpoor) *f* (pl ⁓en) trace

spüren (shpew-rern) *v* sense

Staat (shtaat) *m* (pl ⁓en) state; **Staats-** national

Staatsangehörige (shtaats-ahn-ger-hür-ri-ger) *m* (pl ⁓n) subject

Staatsangehörigkeit (shtaats-ahn-ger-hür-rikh-kight) *f* nationality; citizenship

Staatsbeamte (shtaats-ber-ahm-ter) *m* (pl ⁓n) civil servant

Staatsmann (shtaats-mahn) *m* (pl ⁓er) statesman

Staatsoberhaupt (shtaats-oa-berr-houpt) *nt* (pl ⁓er) head of state

Stab (shtaap) *m* (pl ⁓e) stick; rod; bar

stabil (shtah-beel) *adj* stable

Stachel (shtah-kherl) *m* thorn; sting

Stachelbeere (shtah-kherl-bay-rer) *f* (pl ⁓n) gooseberry

Stachelschwein (shtah-kherl-shvighn) *m* (pl ⁓e) porcupine

Stadion (shtaa-dʸon) *nt* (pl -dien) stadium

Stadium (shtaa-dʸoom) *nt* (pl -dien) stage

Stadt (shtaht) *f* (pl ⁓e) town; city

Städter (shtai-terr) *mpl* townspeople *pl*

städtisch (shteh-tish) *adj* urban; municipal

Stadtverwaltung (shtaht-fehr-vahl-toong) *f* (pl ⁓en) municipality

Stadtviertel (shtaht-feer-terl) *nt* (pl ⁓) quarter

Stadtzentrum (shtaht-tsehn-troom) *nt* (pl -zentren) town centre, town center *Am*

Stahl (shtaal) *m* steel; **nichtrostender** ⁓ stainless steel

Stall (shtahl) *m* (pl ⁓e) stable

Stamm (shtahm) *m* (pl ⁓e) trunk; tribe

stammeln (shtah-merln) *v* stammer

stammen aus (shtah-mern) *v* *come from; date from; *be from

Stammgast (shtahm-gahst) *m* regular customer

stämmig (shteh-mikh) *adj* stout

stampfen (shtahm-pfern) *v* stamp

Stand (shtahnt) *m* (pl ⁓e) stand, stall; level

Standbild (shtahnt-bilt) *nt* (pl ⁓er) statue

Ständer (shtehn-derr) *m* stand

standhaft (shtahnt-hahft) *adj* steadfast

ständig (shtehn-dikh) *adj* permanent; constant

Standpunkt (shtahnt-poongkt) *m* (pl ⁓e) point of view

Stange (shtahng-er) *f* (pl ⁓n) rod; bar; carton

Stapel (shtaa-perl) *m* (pl ⁓) stack; heap

Stapellauf (shtaa-perl-louf) *m* launching

stapeln (shtaa-perln) *v* pile up

Star (shtaar) *m* (pl ⁓e) starling

stark (shtahrk) *adj* powerful, strong; solid

Stärke (shtehr-ker) *f* strength; starch

stärken (shtehr-kern) *v* strengthen; starch

starr (shtahr) *adj* numb

starren (shtah-rern) *v* gaze, stare

starrköpfig (shtahr-kur-pfikh) *adj* head-strong, obstinate; pig-headed

Start (shtahrt) *m* take-off

Startbahn (shtahrt-baan) *f* (pl ⁓en)

runway

starten (*shtahr*-tern) v *take off

Station (shtah-*ts'on*) f station

Statistik (shtah-*tiss*-tik) f (pl ∼en) statistics pl

statt (shtaht) prep instead of

***stattfinden** (*shtaht*-fin-dern) v *take place

stattlich (*shtaht*-likh) adj handsome, impressive

Stau (shtou) m traffic jam; tailback

Staub (shtoup) m dust

staubig (*shtou*-bikh) adj dusty

staubsaugen (*shtoup*-zou-gern) v hoover; vacuum Am

Staubsauger (*shtoup*-zou-gerr) m (pl ∼) vacuum cleaner

staunen (*shtou*-nern) v* be astonished, *be amazed

Steak (stāyk) nt (pl ∼s) steak

Stechen (*shteh*-khern) nt stitch

***stechen** (*shteh*-khern) v prick; *sting

Steckdose (*shtehk*-dōā-zer) f socket, outlet

stecken (*shteh*-kern) v *put

Steckenpferd (*shteh*-kern-pfāyrt) nt (pl ∼e) hobbyhorse; hobby

Stecker (*shteh*-kerr) m (pl ∼) plug

Stecknadel (*shtehk*-naa-derl) f (pl ∼n) pin

Steg (shtāyg) m footbridge

***stehen** (*shtāy*-ern) v *stand; **gut** ∼ *become

***stehlen** (*shtāy*-lern) v *steal

Stehplatz (*shtāy*-plahts) m standing room

steif (shtighf) adj stiff

***steigen** (*shtigh*-gern) v rise; climb

Steigung (*shtigh*-goong) f (pl ∼en) rise; ascent

steil (shtighl) adj steep

Stein (shtighn) m (pl ∼e) stone

Steinbruch (*shtighn*-brookh) m (pl ∼e) quarry

steinern (*shtigh*-nerrn) adj stone

Steingut (*shtighn*-gōot) nt crockery

Stelle (*shteh*-ler) f (pl ∼n) spot; station; passage; **wunde** ∼ sore

stellen (*shteh*-lern) v *put; place, *lay, *set

Stellung (*shteh*-loong) f (pl ∼en) position; job

Stellvertreter (*shtehl*-fehr-trāy-terr) m (pl ∼), **-in** f substitute; deputy

Stempel (*shtehm*-perl) m (pl ∼) stamp

Stenographie (shtay-noa-grah-*fee*) f shorthand

Steppdecke (*shtehp*-deh-ker) f (pl ∼n) quilt

***sterben** (*shtehr*-bern) v die; depart

sterblich (*shtehrp*-likh) adj mortal

steril (shtay-*reel*) adj sterile

sterilisieren (shtay-ri-li-*zee*-rern) v sterilize

Stern (shtehrn) m (pl ∼e) star

stetig (*shtāy*-tikh) adj even

Steuer (*shtoi*-err) f (pl ∼n) tax

Steuerbord (*shtoi*-err-bort) nt starboard

steuerfrei (*shtoi*-err-frigh) adj tax-free

Steuermann (*shtoi*-err-mahn) m (pl ∼er) helmsman, steersman

steuern (*shtoi*-errn) v navigate

Steuerrad (*shtoi*-err-raat) nt steering wheel

Steuerruder (*shtoi*-err-rōō-derr) nt (pl ∼) rudder

Stich (shtikh) m (pl ∼e) sting; bite; stitch; engraving, picture, print

Stichwort (*shtikh*-vort) nt cue; headword; key word

sticken (*shti*-kern) v embroider

Stickerei (shti-ker-*righ*) f (pl ∼en) embroidery

stickig (*shti*-kikh) adj stuffy

Stickstoff (*shti*-kshtof) m nitrogen

Stiefel (*shtee*-ferl) m (pl ∼) boot

Stiefkind (*shteef*-kint) nt (pl ∼er)

stepchild

Stiefmutter (*shteef*-moo-terr) *f* (pl ⁓) stepmother

Stiefvater (*shteef*-faa-terr) *m* (pl ⁓) stepfather

Stiel (shteel) *m* (pl ⁓e) handle; stem

Stier (shteer) *m* (pl ⁓e) bull

Stierkampf (*shteer*-kahmpf) *m* (pl ⁓e) bullfight

Stierkampfarena (*shteer*-kahmpf-ah-rāy-nah) *f* (pl -arenen) bullring

Stift (shtift) *m* pin; peg; pencil

stiften (*shtif*-tern) *v* found

Stiftung (*shtif*-toong) *f* (pl ⁓en) foundation

Stil (shteel) *m* (pl ⁓e) style

still (shtil) *adj* silent; still, calm, quiet

Stille (*shti*-ler) *f* silence; quiet

stillen (*shti*-lern) *v* nurse

Stille Ozean (*shti*-ler ōa-tsay-aan) Pacific Ocean

stillstehend (*shtil*-shtāy-ernt) *adj* stationary

Stimme (*shti*-mer) *f* (pl ⁓n) voice; vote

stimmen (*shti*-mern) *v* vote

Stimmung (*shti*-moong) *f* (pl ⁓en) spirits, mood; atmosphere

***stinken** (*shting*-kern) *v* *smell; *stink

Stipendium (shti-*pehn*-dʸoom) *nt* (pl -dien) grant, scholarship

Stirn (shteern) *f* forehead

Stock (shtok) *m* (pl ⁓e) stick; cane

Stockwerk (*shtok*-vehrk) *nt* (pl ⁓e) stor(e)y, floor

Stoff (shtof) *m* (pl ⁓e) matter; fabric; theme

stofflich (*shtof*-likh) *adj* material

stöhnen (*shtūr*-nern) *v* moan, groan

Stola (*shtōa*-lah) *f* (pl ⁓s) stole

stolpern (*shtol*-perrn) *v* stumble

Stolz (shtolts) *m* pride

stolz (shtolts) *adj* proud

stopfen (*shto*-pfern) *v* darn

Stopfgarn (*shtopf*-gahrn) *nt* darning

wool

stoppen (*shto*-pern) *v* stop; time

Stöpsel (*shtur*-pserl) *m* (pl ⁓) cork, stopper

Storch (shtorkh) *m* (pl ⁓e) stork

stören (*shtūr*-rern) *v* disturb; upset

stornieren (shtor-*nee*-rern) *v* cancel

Störung (*shtūr*-roong) *f* (pl ⁓en) disturbance

Stoß (shtōass) *m* (pl ⁓e) bump; push

Stoßdämpfer (*shtōass*-dehm-pferr) *m* (pl ⁓) shock absorber

***stoßen** (*shtōa*-sern) *v* bump; push; kick

Stoßstange (*shtōass*-shtahng-er) *f* (pl ⁓n) bumper

stottern (*shto*-terrn) *v* stutter

Strafe (*shtraa*-fer) *f* (pl ⁓n) punishment, penalty

strafen (*shtraa*-fern) *v* punish

straffen (*shtrah*-fern) *v* tighten

Strafrecht (*shtraaf*-rehkht) *nt* criminal law

Strafstoß (*shtraaf*-shtōass) *m* (pl ⁓e) penalty kick

Strahl (shtraal) *m* (pl ⁓en) beam, ray; squirt, spout, jet

strahlen (*shtraa*-lern) *v* *shine

Strähne (*shtrai*-ner) *f* strand; streak

stramm (shtrahm) *adj* tight

Strand (shtrahnt) *m* (pl ⁓e) beach

Straße (*shtraa*-ser) *f* (pl ⁓n) road, street

Straßenarbeiten (*shtraa*-sern-ahr-bigh-tern) *fpl* roadworks

Straßenbahn (*shtraa*-sern-baan) *f* (pl ⁓en) tram; streetcar *Am*

Straßenkreuzung (*shtraa*-sern-kroi-tsoong) *f* (pl ⁓en) junction

Straßennetz (*shtraa*-sern-nehts) *nt* (pl ⁓e) road system

Straßenseite (*shtraa*-sern-zigh-ter) *f* (pl ⁓n) roadside

Strauch (shtroukh) *m* (pl ⁓er) shrub

Strauß¹ (shtrouss) *m* (pl ⁀e) bunch, bouquet

Strauß² (shtrouss) *m* (pl ⁀e) ostrich

streben (shtrāy-bern) *v* aspire

strebsam (shtrāyp-zaam) *adj* ambitious

Strecke (shtreh-ker) *f* (pl ⁀n) stretch

Streich (shtrighkh) *m* trick, prank

***streichen** (shtrigh-khern) *v* paint; spread, apply; *strike

Streichholz (shtrighkh-holts) *nt* (pl ⁀er) match

Streichholzschachtel (shtrighkh-holts-shahkh-terl) *f* (pl ⁀n) matchbox

Streife (shtrigh-fer) *f* (pl ⁀n) patrol

Streifen (shtrigh-fern) *m* (pl ⁀) strip; stripe

Streik (shtrighk) *m* (pl ⁀s) strike

streiken (shtrigh-kern) *v* *strike

Streit (shtright) *m* quarrel; contest; fight, battle; **Streit-** controversial

***streiten** (shtrigh-tern) *v* quarrel; dispute, argue

Streitigkeit (shtrigh-tikh-kight) *f* (pl ⁀en) dispute

Streitkräfte (shtright-krehf-ter) *pl* armed forces

streitsüchtig (shtright-zewkh-tikh) *adj* rowdy

streng (shtrehng) *adj* strict; harsh, severe

Strich (shtrikh) *m* (pl ⁀e) line; dash

Strichpunkt (shtrikh-poongkt) *m* (pl ⁀e) semicolon

Strick (shtrik) *m* cord; rope

stricken (shtri-kern) *v* *knit

Stroh (shtrōa) *nt* straw

Strohdach (shtrōa-dahkh) *nt* (pl ⁀er) thatched roof

Strom (shtrōam) *m* (pl ⁀e) current

stromabwärts (shtrōam-ahp-vehrts) *adv* downstream

stromaufwärts (shtrōam-ouf-vehrts) *adv* upstream

strömen (shtrūr-mern) *v* flow; stream

Stromschnelle (shtrōam-shneh-ler) *f* (pl ⁀n) rapids *pl*

Strömung (shtrūr-moong) *f* (pl ⁀en) current

Stromverteiler (shtrōam-fehr-tigh-lerr) *m* distributor

Strophe (shtrōa-fer) *f* (pl ⁀n) stanza

Struktur (shtrook-tōor) *f* (pl ⁀en) structure; texture, fabric

Strumpf (shtroompf) *m* (pl ⁀e) stocking

Strumpfhose (shtroompf-hōa-zer) *f* (pl ⁀n) panty hose

Stück (shtewk) *nt* (pl ⁀e) piece; part; lump, morsel

Stückchen (shtewk-khern) *nt* (pl ⁀) scrap, bit

Student (shtoo-*dehnt*) *m* (pl ⁀en), **-in** *f* student

Studienrat (shtōō-d^yern-raat) *m* (pl ⁀e) master

studieren (shtoo-*dee*-rern) *v* study

Studium (shtōō-d^yoom) *nt* (pl -dien) study

Stufe (shtōō-fer) *f* (pl ⁀n) step

Stuhl (shtōol) *m* (pl ⁀e) chair

stumm (shtoom) *adj* mute; dumb

stumpf (shtoompf) *adj* blunt; dull

Stunde (shtoon-der) *f* (pl ⁀n) hour

stündlich (shtewnt-likh) *adj* hourly

Sturm (shtoorm) *m* (pl ⁀e) gale, storm

stürmen (shtewr-mern) *v* dash

stürmisch (shtewr-mish) *adj* stormy

Sturz (shtoorts) *m* (pl ⁀e) fall

stürzen (shtewr-tsern) *v* *fall; crash; rush

Stute (shtōō-ter) *f* (pl ⁀n) mare

Stütze (shtew-tser) *f* support; prop

stutzen (shtoo-tsern) *v* trim

stützen (shtew-tsern) *v* support; *hold up

Suaheli (swah-*hāy*-li) *nt* Swahili

Subjekt (zoop-^yehkt) *nt* (pl ⁀e) subject

Substantiv (*zoop*-stahn-teef) *nt* (pl ~e) noun

Substanz (zoop-*stahnts*) *f* (pl ~en) substance

subtil (zoop-*teel*) *adj* subtle

subtrahieren (zoop-trah-*hee*-rern) *v* subtract

Subvention (zoop-vehn-*ts'ōan*) *f* (pl ~en) subsidy

Suche (*zōō*-kher) *f* search

suchen (*zōō*-khern) *v* look for; *seek, search; hunt for

Sucher (*zōō*-kherr) *m* viewfinder

Sucht (zookht) *f* addiction; mania

süchtig (*zewkh*-tikh) *adj* addicted

Südafrika (*zēwt*-aa-fri-kah) South Africa

Süden (*zēw*-dern) *m* south

südlich (*zēwt*-likh) *adj* southern, southerly

Südosten (zēwt-*oss*-tern) *m* southeast

Südpol (*zēwt*-pōal) *m* South Pole

Südwesten (zēwt-*vehss*-tern) *m* southwest

Summe (*zoo*-mer) *f* (pl ~n) sum; amount

summen (*zoo*-mern) *v* hum

Sumpf (zoompf) *m* (pl ~e) bog, marsh

Sünde (*zewn*-der) *f* (pl ~n) sin

Sündenbock (*zewn*-dern-bok) *m* (pl ~e) scapegoat

Superlativ (*zōō*-pehr-lah-teef) *m* superlative

Supermarkt (*zōō*-pehr-mahrkt) *m* (pl ~e) supermarket

Suppe (*zoo*-per) *f* (pl ~n) soup

suspendieren (zooss-pehn-*dee*-rern) *v* suspend

süß (zēwss) *adj* sweet

süßen (*zēw*-sern) *v* sweeten

Süßigkeiten (*zēw*-sikh-kigh-tern) *fpl* sweets; candy *Am*

Süßwarengeschäft (*zēwss*-vaa-rern-ger-shehft) *nt* (pl ~e) sweetshop; candy store *Am*

Süßwasser (*zēwss*-vah-serr) *nt* fresh water

Sweatshirt (*svāy*-shurt) *nt* (pl ~s) sweater

Symbol (zewm-*bōal*) *nt* (pl ~e) symbol

Sympathie (zewm-pah-*tee*) *f* sympathy

sympathisch (zewm-*paa*-tish) *adj* nice, sympathetic

Symphonie (zewm-foa-*nee*) *f* (pl ~n) symphony

Symptom (zewmp-*tōam*) *nt* (pl ~e) symptom

Synagoge (zew-nah-*gōa*-ger) *f* (pl ~n) synagogue

Synonym (zew-noa-*nēwm*) *nt* (pl ~e) synonym

synthetisch (zewn-*tāy*-tish) *adj* synthetic

Syrer (*zēw*-rerr) *m* (pl ~), **-in** *f* Syrian

Syrien (*zēw*-r'ern) Syria

syrisch (*zēw*-rish) *adj* Syrian

System (zewss-*tāym*) *nt* (pl ~e) system

systematisch (zewss-tay-*maa*-tish) *adj* systematic

Szene (*stsāy*-ner) *f* (pl ~n) scene

T

Tabak (*taa*-bahk) *m* tobacco; pipe tobacco

Tabakhändler (*taa*-bahk-hehn-dlerr) *m* (pl ~) tobacconist

Tabakladen (*taa*-bahk-laa-dern) *m* (pl ∼) tobacconist's

Tabaksbeutel (*taa*-bahks-boi-terl) *m* (pl ∼) tobacco pouch

Tabelle (tah-*beh*-ler) *f* (pl ∼n) chart, table

Tablett (tah-*bleht*) *nt* (pl ∼s) tray

Tablette (tah-*bleh*-ter) *f* (pl ∼n) tablet

Tabu (tah-*bōō*) *nt* (pl ∼s) taboo

Tacho (*taa*-khoa) *m colloquial*, **Tachometer** *m*, *nt* speedometer

tadellos (*taa*-derl-lōāss) *adj* faultless

tadeln (*taa*-derln) *v* reprimand

Tafel (*taa*-ferl) (pl ∼n) board

Täfelung (*tai*-fer-loong) *f* panelling

Tag (taak) *m* (pl ∼e) day; **bei Tage** by day; **eines Tages** some day; **guten Tag!** hello!; **pro ∼** per day; **vierzehn Tage** fortnight

Tagebuch (*taa*-ger-bōōkh) *nt* (pl ∼er) diary

Tagesanbruch (*taa*-gerss-ahn-brookh) *m* daybreak, dawn

Tagesausflug (*taa*-gerss-ouss-flōōk) *m* (pl ∼e) day trip

Tageslicht (*taa*-gerss-likht) *nt* daylight

Tagesordnung (*taa*-gerss-or-dnoong) *f* (pl ∼en) agenda

Tageszeitung (*taa*-gerss-tsigh-toong) *f* (pl ∼en) daily

täglich (*taik*-likh) *adj* daily

tagsüber (*taaks*-ēw-berr) *adv* during the day

Tagung (*taa*-goong) *f* (pl ∼en) congress

Taille (*tah*-lʸer) *f* (pl ∼n) waist

Taktik (*tahk*-tik) *f* (pl ∼en) tactics *pl*

Tal (taal) *nt* (pl ∼er) valley

Talent (tah-*lehnt*) *nt* (pl ∼e) faculty, talent

Tampon (tahng-*pawng*) *m* (pl ∼s) tampon

Tank (tahngk) *m* (pl ∼s) tank

tanken (*tahng*-kern) *v* tank

Tankschiff (*tahngk*-shif) *nt* (pl ∼e) tanker

Tankstelle (*tahngk*-shteh-ler) *f* (pl ∼n) petrol station, service station, filling station; gas station *Am*

Tanne (*tah*-ner) *f* (pl ∼n) fir tree

Tante (*tahn*-ter) *f* (pl ∼n) aunt

Tanz (tahnts) *m* (pl ∼e) dance

tanzen (*tahn*-tsern) *v* dance

Tapete (tah-*pāy*-ter) *f* (pl ∼n) wallpaper

tapfer (*tah*-pferr) *adj* courageous, brave

Tapferkeit (*tah*-pferr-kight) *f* courage

Tarif (tah-*reef*) *m* (pl ∼e) tariff, rate

Tasche (*tah*-sher) *f* (pl ∼n) bag; pocket

Taschenbuch (*tah*-shern-bōōkh) *nt* (pl -bücher) paperback

Taschenlampe (*tah*-shern-lahm-per) *f* (pl ∼n) torch, flashlight

Taschenmesser (*tah*-shern-meh-serr) *nt* (pl ∼) pocketknife, penknife

Taschenrechner (*tah*-shern-rehkh-nerr) *m* pocket calculator

Taschentuch (*tah*-shern-tōōkh) *nt* (pl ∼er) handkerchief

Tasse (*tah*-ser) *f* (pl ∼n) cup

Tastatur (tahs-tah-*tōōr*) *f* keyboard

Taste (*tahs*-ter) *f* key

Tastsinn (*tahst*-zin) *m* touch

Tat (taat) *f* (pl ∼en) deed, act

Täter (*tai*-terr) *m* (pl ∼), **-in** *f* culprit; offender

Tätigkeit (*tai*-tikh-kight) *f* (pl ∼en) work; employment

Tatsache (*taat*-zah-kher) *f* (pl ∼n) fact

tatsächlich (taat-*zehkh*-likh) *adj* actual, factual; *adv* as a matter of fact, actually, in fact, in effect; really

Tau (tou) *m* dew; rope

taub (toup) *adj* deaf

Taube (*tou*-ber) *f* (pl ∼n) pigeon

tauchen (*tou*-khern) *v* dive

Tauchsieder (*toukh*-zee-derr) *m* (pl ∼) immersion heater

tauen (*tou*-ern) *v* thaw

Taufe (*tou*-fer) *f* (pl ⁓n) baptism, christening

taufen (*tou*-fern) *v* baptize, christen

tauglich (*touk*-likh) *adj* suitable; fit

Tausch (toush) *m* exchange

tauschen (*tou*-shern) *v* swap

täuschen (*toi*-shern) deceive; **sich ⁓** deceive o.s.; *be wrong, *be mistaken

Täuschung (*toi*-shoong) *f* (pl ⁓en) illusion

tausend (*tou*-zernt) *num* thousand

Tauwetter (*tou*-veh-terr) *nt* thaw

Taxameter (tah-ksah-*māy*-terr) *m* (pl ⁓) taximeter

Taxi (*tah*-ksi) *nt* (pl ⁓s) cab, taxi

Taxichauffeur (*tah*-ksi-sho-fūrr) *m* (pl ⁓e), **-in** *f* taxi driver

Taxifahrer (*tah*-ksi-faa-rerr) *m* (pl ⁓), **-in** *f* cab driver

Taxistand (*tah*-ksi-shtahnt) *m* (pl ⁓e) taxi rank; taxi stand *Am*

Team (teem) *nt* (pl ⁓s) team

Technik (*taykh*-nik) *f* (pl ⁓en) technique

Techniker (*tehkh*-ni-kerr) *m* (pl ⁓), **-in** *f* technician

technisch (*tehkh*-nish) *adj* technical

Technologie (tehkh-noa-loa-*gee*) *f* technology

Tee (tāy) *m* tea

Teekanne (*tāy*-kah-ner) *f* (pl ⁓n) teapot

Teelöffel (*tāy*-lur-ferl) *m* (pl ⁓) teaspoon

Teenager (*teen*-ay-jerr) *m* (pl ⁓) teenager

Teer (tāyr) *m* tar

Teeservice (*tāy*-zehr-veess) *nt* tea set

Teestube (*tāy*-shtoo-ber) *f* (pl ⁓n) tea-shop

Teestunde (*tāy*-shtoon-der) *f* tea

Teetasse (*tāy*-tah-ser) *f* (pl ⁓n) teacup

Teich (tighkh) *m* (pl ⁓e) pond

Teig (tighk) *m* dough; batter

Teil (tighl) *m* (pl ⁓e) part; share; volume

teilen (*tigh*-lern) *v* divide; share

Teilhaber (*tighl*-haa-berr) *m* (pl ⁓), **-in** *f* associate, partner

Teilnahme (*tighl*-naa-mer) *f* attendance

***teilnehmen** (*tighl*-nāy-mern) *v* participate

Teilnehmer (*tighl*-nāy-merr) *m* (pl ⁓), **-in** *f* participant

teils (tighls) *adv* partly

Teilung (*tigh*-loong) *f* (pl ⁓en) division

teilweise (*tighl*-vigh-zer) *adj* partial; *adv* partly

Teint (tang) *m* complexion

Telefon (tay-lay-*fōan*) *nt* (pl ⁓e) telephone, *colloquial* phone

Telefonbuch (tay-lay-*fōan*-bookh) *nt* (pl ⁓er) telephone directory; telephone book *Am*

telefonieren (tay-lay-foa-*nee*-rern) *v* telephone, *colloquial* phone

Telefonzentrale (tay-lay-*fōan*-tsehn-traa-ler) *f* (pl ⁓n) telephone exchange

Telegramm (tay-lay-*grahm*) *nt* (pl ⁓e) cable, telegram

Teleobjektiv (*tāy*-lay-op-ʸehk-teef) *nt* (pl ⁓e) telephoto lens

Telex (*tāy*-lehks) *nt* (pl ⁓e) telex

Teller (*teh*-lerr) *m* (pl ⁓) plate, dish

Tempel (*tehm*-perl) *m* (pl ⁓) temple

Temperatur (tehm-pay-rah-*tōor*) *f* (pl ⁓en) temperature

Tempo (*tehm*-poa) *nt* pace

Tendenz (tehn-*dehnts*) *f* (pl ⁓en) tendency

Tennis (*teh*-niss) *nt* tennis

Tennisplatz (*teh*-niss-plahts) *m* (pl ⁓e) tennis court

Tennisschuhe (*teh*-niss-shoo-er) *mpl* tennis shoes

Teppich (*teh*-pikh) *m* (pl ⁓e) carpet

Termin (tehr-*meen*) *m* (pl ⁓e) date; appointment; deadline

Terpentin (tehr-pehn-*teen*) *nt* turpentine

Terrasse (teh-*rah*-ser) *f* (pl ⁓n) terrace

Terror (*teh*-ror) *m* terrorism

Terrorismus (teh-ro-*riss*-mooss) *m* terrorism

Terrorist (teh-ro-*rist*) *m* (pl ⁓en), **-in** *f* terrorist

Test (tehst) *m* (pl ⁓s) test

Testament (tehss-tah-*mehnt*) *nt* (pl ⁓e) (last) will

testen (*tehss*-tern) *v* test

teuer (*toi*-err) *adj* expensive; dear, precious

Teufel (*toi*-ferl) *m* (pl ⁓) devil

Text (tehkst) *m* (pl ⁓e) text

Textilien (tehks-*tee*-lʸern) *pl* textiles

Thailand (*tigh*-lahnt) Thailand

Thailänder (*tigh*-lehn-derr) *m* (pl ⁓), **-in** *f* Thai

thailändisch (*tigh*-lehn-dish) *adj* Thai

Theater (tay-*aa*-terr) *nt* (pl ⁓) theatre, theater *Am*; drama

Thema (*tāy*-mah) *nt* (pl Themen) topic; theme

Theologie (tay-oa-loa-*gee*) *f* theology

theoretisch (tay-oa-*rāy*-tish) *adj* theoretical

Theorie (tay-oa-*ree*) *f* (pl ⁓n) theory

Therapie (tay-rah-*pee*) *f* (pl ⁓n) therapy

Thermometer (tehr-moa-*māy*-terr) *nt* (pl ⁓) thermometer

Thermosflasche (*tehr*-moss-flah-sher) *f* (pl ⁓n) thermos flask, vacuum flask

Thermostat (tehr-moa-*staat*) *m* (pl ⁓en) thermostat

These (*tāy*-zer) *f* (pl ⁓n) thesis

Thron (trōan) *m* (pl ⁓e) throne

Thunfisch (*tōōn*-fish) *m* (pl ⁓e) tuna

Thymian (*tēw*-mʸaan) *m* thyme

Tief (teef) *nt* low, depression

tief (teef) *adj* deep; low

Tiefe (*tee*-fer) *f* (pl ⁓n) depth

Tiefkühltruhe (*teef*-kēwl-trōō-er) *f* (pl ⁓n) deep-freeze

Tiefland (*teef*-lahnt) *nt* lowlands *pl*

Tier (teer) *nt* (pl ⁓e) beast, animal

Tierarzt (*teer*-ahrtst) *m* (pl ⁓e) veterinary surgeon

Tierärztin (*teer*-ehrts-tin) *f* (pl ⁓nen) veterinary surgeon

Tiger (*tee*-gerr) *m* (pl ⁓) tiger

tilgen (*til*-gern) *v* *pay off

Tinte (*tin*-ter) *f* (pl ⁓n) ink

Tintenfisch (*tin*-tern-fish) *m* octopus; squid

tippen (*ti*-pern) *v* type

Tisch (tish) *m* (pl ⁓e) table

Tischler (*tish*-lerr) *m* (pl ⁓), **-in** *f* carpenter

Tischtennis (*tish*-teh-niss) *nt* ping-pong, table tennis

Tischtuch (*tish*-tōōkh) *nt* (pl ⁓er) tablecloth

Titel (*tee*-terl) *m* (pl ⁓) title; degree

Toast (tōast) *m* (pl ⁓e) toast

Tochter (*tokh*-terr) *f* (pl ⁓) daughter

Tod (tōat) *m* death

Todesstrafe (*tōa*-derss-shtraa-fer) *f* death penalty

tödlich (*tūrt*-likh) *adj* mortal, fatal

Toilette (twah-*leh*-ter) *f* (pl ⁓n) lavatory, toilet; washroom *Am*

Toilettenartikel (twah-*leh*-tern-ahr-tee-kerl) *mpl* toiletry

Toilettenpapier (twah-*leh*-tern-pah-peer) *nt* toilet paper

toll (tol) *adj* terrific; crazy, mad

Tollwut (*tol*-vōōt) *f* rabies

Tomate (toa-*maa*-ter) *f* (pl ⁓n) tomato

Ton[1] (tōan) *m* (pl ⁓e) tone; note

Ton[2] (tōan) *m* clay

Tonleiter (*tōan*-ligh-terr) *f* (pl ⁓n) scale

Tonne (*to*-ner) *f* (pl ⁓n) barrel; ton,

cask

Topf (topf) *m* (pl ≈e) pot

Töpferware (*tur*-pferr-vaa-rer) *f* (pl ~n) ceramics *pl*, pottery, crockery

Tor¹ (tōar) *nt* (pl ~e) gate; goal

Tor² (tōar) *m* (pl ~en) fool

Torte (*tor*-ter) *f* (pl ~n) cake

Torwart (*tōar*-vahrt) *m* (pl ~e) goalkeeper

tot (tōat) *adj* dead

total (toa-*taal*) *adj* total

totalitär (toa-tah-li-*tair*) *adj* totalitarian

töten (*ūr*-tern) *v* kill

Toupet (too-*pāy*) *nt* (pl ~s) hair piece

Tourist (too-*rist*) *m* (pl ~en), **-in** *f* tourist

Touristenklasse (too-*riss*-tern-klah-ser) *f* tourist class

toxisch (*to*-ksish) *adj* toxic

Tracht (trahkht) *f* (pl ~en) national dress

Tradition (trah-di-tsᵞ*ōan*) *f* (pl ~en) tradition

traditionell (trah-di-tsᵞoa-*nehl*) *adj* traditional

tragbar (*traak*-baar) *adj* portable

träge (*trai*-ger) *adj* slack

*tragen (*traa*-gern) *v* carry; *bear; *wear

Träger (*trai*-gerr) *m* (pl ~) porter

tragisch (*traa*-gish) *adj* tragic

Tragödie (trah-*gūr*-dᵞer) *f* (pl ~n) tragedy

Trainer (*trai*-nerr) *m* (pl ~), **-in** *f* coach

trainieren (treh-*nee*-rern) *v* drill

Traktor (*trahk*-tor) *m* (pl ~en) tractor

Träne (*trai*-ner) *f* (pl ~n) tear

Transaktion (trans-ahk-tsᵞ*ōan*) *f* (pl ~en) deal, transaction

transatlantisch (trahns-aht-*lahn*-tish) *adj* transatlantic

Transformator (trahns-for-*maa*-tor) *m* (pl ~en) transformer

transpirieren (trahns-pi-*ree*-rern) *v* perspire

Transport (trahns-*port*) *m* (pl ~e) transportation

transportieren (trahns-por-*tee*-rern) *v* transport

Tratsch (traach) *m* gossip

tratschen (*traa*-chern) *v* gossip

Trauben (*trou*-bern) *fpl* grapes *pl*

trauen (*trou*-ern) *f*: **sich ~** dare

Trauer (*trou*-err) *f* mourning

Trauerspiel (*trou*-err-shpeel) *nt* (pl ~e) drama

Traum (troum) *m* (pl ≈e) dream

träumen (*troi*-mern) *v* *dream

traurig (*trou*-rikh) *adj* sad

Traurigkeit (*trou*-rikh-kight) *f* sadness

Treffen (*treh*-fern) *nt* (pl ~) meeting

*treffen (*treh*-fern) *v* *hit; *meet

treffend (*treh*-fernt) *adj* striking

Treffpunkt (*trehf*-poongkt) *m* (pl ~e) meeting place

*treiben (*trigh*-bern) *v* press, *drive; *do; float

Treibhaus (*trighp*-houss) *nt* (pl ~er) greenhouse

Treibkraft (*trighp*-krahft) *f* driving force

Treibstoff (*trighp*-shtof) *m* fuel

trennen (*treh*-nern) *v* separate, part; divide; disconnect

Trennung (*treh*-noong) *f* (pl ~en) division

Treppe (*treh*-per) *f* (pl ~n) stairs *pl*, staircase

*treten (*trāy*-tern) *v* step; kick

treu (troi) *adj* true, faithful

Tribüne (tri-*bēw*-ner) *f* (pl ~n) stand

Trichter (*trikh*-terr) *m* (pl ~) funnel

Trick (trik) *m* (pl ~s) trick

Trikot (tri-*kōa*) *nt* (pl ~s) shirt

trinkbar (*tringk*-baar) *adj* for drinking

*trinken (*tring*-kern) *v* *drink

Trinkgeld (*tringk*-gehlt) *nt* (pl ~er) tip,

gratuity

Trinkspruch (*tringk*-shprookh) *m* (pl ⁓e) toast

Trinkwasser (*tringk*-vah-serr) *nt* drinking water

Tritt (trit) *m* (pl ⁓e) step; kick

Triumph (tri-*oomf*) *m* triumph

triumphieren (tri-oom-*fee*-rern) *v* triumph; **triumphierend** triumphant

trocken (*tro*-kern) *adj* dry

trockenlegen (*tro*-kern-lā́y-gern) *v* drain

trocknen (*tro*-knern) *v* dry

Trockner (*tro*-knerr) *m* (pl ⁓) dryer

Trommel (*tro*-merl) *f* (pl ⁓n) drum

Trommelfell (*tro*-merl-fehl) *nt* eardrum

Trompete (trom-*pā́y*-ter) *f* (pl ⁓n) trumpet

Tropen (*trṓa*-pern) *pl* tropics *pl*

Tropfen (*tro*-pfern) *m* (pl ⁓) drop

tropisch (*trṓa*-pish) *adj* tropical

Trost (trōast) *m* comfort

trösten (*trǖ́rss*-tern) *v* comfort

Trostpreis (*trṓast*-prighss) *m* (pl ⁓e) consolation prize

trotz (trots) *prep* despite, in spite of

trotzdem (*trots*-dāym) *conj* nevertheless

trübe (*trǖ́w*-ber) *adj* dim

trübsinnig (*trǖ́wp*-zi-nikh) *adj* sad

Truhe (*trṓo*-er) *f* (pl ⁓n) chest

Truppen (*troo*-pern) *fpl* troops *pl*

Truthahn (*trṓot*-haan) *m* (pl ⁓e) turkey

Tscheche (*cheh*-kher) *m* (pl ⁓n) Czech

Tschechien (chek-*kheen*) *m* Czech Republic

Tschechin (*cheh*-khin) *f* (pl ⁓nen) Czech

tschechisch (*cheh*-khish) *adj* Czech

Tube (*tṓo*-ber) *f* (pl ⁓n) tube

Tuberkulose (too-behr-koo-*lṓa*-zer) *f* tuberculosis

Tuch (tōokh) *nt* (pl ⁓e) cloth; scarf

tüchtig (*tewkh*-tikh) *adj* capable

Tugend (*tṓo*-gernt) *f* (pl ⁓en) virtue

Tulpe (*tool*-per) *f* (pl ⁓n) tulip

Tumor (*tṓo*-mor) *m* (pl ⁓en) tumo(u)r

Tumult (too-*moolt*) *m* racket

*tun (tōon) *v* *do

Tunesien (too-*nā́y*-z^yern) Tunisia

Tunesier (too-*nā́y*-z^yerr) *m* (pl ⁓), **-in** *f* Tunisian

tunesisch (too-*nā́y*-zish) *adj* Tunisian

Tunika (*tṓo*-ni-kah) *f* (pl -ken) tunic

Tunnel (*too*-nerl) *m* (pl ⁓) tunnel

Tür (tēwr) *f* (pl ⁓en) door

Turbine (toor-*bee*-ner) *f* (pl ⁓n) turbine

Türke (*tewr*-ker) *m* (pl ⁓n) Turk

Türkei (tewr-*kigh*) Turkey

Türkin (*tewr*-kin) *f* (pl ⁓nen) Turk

türkisch (*tewr*-kish) *adj* Turkish

Türklingel (*tḗwr*-kling-erl) *f* (pl ⁓n) doorbell

Turm (toorm) *m* (pl ⁓e) tower

Turnen (*toor*-nern) *nt* gymnastics *pl*

Turner (*toor*-nerr) *m* (pl ⁓), **-in** *f* gymnast

Turnhalle (*toorn*-hah-ler) *f* (pl ⁓n) gymnasium

Turnhose (*toorn*-hōa-zer) *f* (pl ⁓n) trunks *pl*

Turnier (toor-*neer*) *nt* (pl ⁓e) tournament

Turnschuhe (*toorn*-shōo-er) *mpl* plimsolls *pl*, gym shoes; sneakers *plAm*

Tüte (*tḗw*-ter) *f* (pl ⁓n) paper bag, plastic bag

Tweed (tweet) *m* tweed

Typ (tēwp) *m* (pl ⁓en) type

Typhus (*tēw*-fooss) *m* typhoid

typisch (*tēw*-pish) *adj* typical

Tyrann (tew-*rahn*) *m* (pl ⁓en), **-in** *f* tyrant

U

U-Bahn ($\overline{oo}$-baan) f (pl ~en)
underground

Übel ($\overline{ew}$-berl) nt (pl ~n) harm, evil

übel ($\overline{ew}$-berl) adj sick; ~ *nehmen v
take offence (Am offense) at; ~
riechend adj smelly

Übelkeit ($\overline{ew}$-berl-kight) f (pl ~en)
nausea, sickness

üben ($\overline{ew}$-bern) v exercise; **sich ~**
practise

über ($\overline{ew}$-berr) prep over; above;
across; about; via; ~ ... **hinaus**
beyond

überall ($\overline{ew}$-berr-ahl) adv everywhere;
throughout, anywhere

überarbeiten ($\overline{ew}$-berr-ahr-bigh-tern)
v revise; **sich ~** overwork

Überarbeitung ($\overline{ew}$-berr-ahr-bigh-
toong) f (pl ~en) revision

Überbleibsel ($\overline{ew}$-berr-blighp-serl) nt
(pl ~) remainder, remnant

überdies ($\overline{ew}$-berr-deess) adv
furthermore, besides

überdrüssig ($\overline{ew}$-berr-drew-sikh) adj
weary; fed up with, tired of

übereilt ($\overline{ew}$-berr-ighlt) adj rash

Übereinkunft ($\overline{ew}$-berr-ighn-koonft) f
(pl ~e) settlement

übereinstimmen ($\overline{ew}$-berr-ighn-shti-
mern) v agree; correspond; **nicht ~**
disagree

Übereinstimmung ($\overline{ew}$-berr-ighn-
shti-moong) f agreement; **in ~ mit**
according to

Überfahrt ($\overline{ew}$-berr-faart) f crossing,
passage

Überfall ($\overline{ew}$-berr-fahl) m (pl ~e)
hold-up

überfällig ($\overline{ew}$-berr-feh-likh) adj
overdue

Überfluss ($\overline{ew}$-berr-flooss) m
abundance

überflüssig ($\overline{ew}$-berr-flew-sikh) adj
redundant, superfluous

überführen ($\overline{ew}$-berr-few-rern) v
convict

Überführung ($\overline{ew}$-berr-few-roong) f
(pl ~en) conviction

überfüllt ($\overline{ew}$-berr-fewlt) adj crowded

Übergabe ($\overline{ew}$-berr-gaa-ber) f
delivery; surrender

Übergang ($\overline{ew}$-berr-gahng) m (pl ~e)
transition; crossing

*übergeben ($\overline{ew}$-berr-gay-bern) v
hand over; commit; **sich ~** vomit

*übergehen ($\overline{ew}$-berr-gay-ern) v skip

Übergewicht ($\overline{ew}$-berr-ger-vikht) nt
overweight

Übergröße ($\overline{ew}$-berr-grur-ser) f (pl ~n)
outsize

überhaupt ($\overline{ew}$-berr-houpt) adv at all

überheblich ($\overline{ew}$-berr-hayp-likh) adj
presumptuous

überholen ($\overline{ew}$-berr-hoa-lern) v
*overtake; pass; overhaul;
Überholen verboten no overtaking;
no passing Am

Überleben ($\overline{ew}$-berr-lay-bern) nt
survival

überleben ($\overline{ew}$-berr-lay-bern) v
survive

überlegen ($\overline{ew}$-berr-lay-gern) v *think
over; deliberate; adj superior

übermorgen ($\overline{ew}$-berr-mor-gern) adv
the day after tomorrow

übermüdet ($\overline{ew}$-berr-mew-dert) adj
over-tired

übermütig ($\overline{ew}$-berr-mew-tikh) adj
presumptuous

übernachten ($\overline{ew}$-berr-nakh-tern) v
stay overnight

Übernachtung ($\overline{ew}$-berr-nakh-toong)
f overnight stay

*übernehmen ($\overline{ew}$-berr-nay-mern) v

*take over; *take charge of

überqueren (ew-berr- *kvāy*-rern) *v* cross

überragend (ew-berr-*raa*-gernt) *adj* superior; superlative

überraschen (ew-berr-*rah*-shern) *v* surprise

Überraschung (ew-berr-*rah*-shoong) *f* (pl ⁓en) surprise

überreden (ew-berr-*rāy*-dern) *v* persuade

überreichen (ew-berr-*righ*-khern) *v* *give

Überrest (*ew*-berr-rehst) *m* (pl ⁓e) remnant

***überschreiten** (ew-berr-*shrigh*-tern) *v* exceed

Überschrift (*ew*-berr-shrift) *f* (pl ⁓en) heading

Überschuss (*ew*-berr-shooss) *m* (pl ⁓e) surplus

überschüssig (*ew*-berr-shew-sikh) *adj* spare

Überschwemmung (ew-berr-*shveh*-moong) *f* (pl ⁓en) flood

überschwänglich (ew-berr-*shvehng*-likh) *adj* exuberant

überseeisch (ew-berr-*zāy*-ish) *adj* overseas

***übersehen** (ew-berr-*zāy*-ern) *v* overlook

übersetzen (ew-berr-*zeh*-tsern) *v* translate

Übersetzer (ew-berr-*zeh*-tserr) *m* (pl ⁓), **-in** *f* translator

Übersetzung (ew-berr-*zeh*-tsoong) *f* (pl ⁓en) translation; version

Übersicht (*ew*-berr-zikht) *f* (pl ⁓en) survey

überspannt (ew-berr-*shpahnt*) *adj* overstrung; eccentric

***übertragen** (ew-berr-*traa*-gern) *v* transfer

***übertreffen** (ew-berr-*treh*-fern) *v* *outdo, exceed

***übertreiben** (ew-berr-*trigh*-bern) *v* exaggerate

übertrieben (ew-berr-*tree*-bern) *adj* extravagant; excessive

übervoll (*ew*-berr-fol) *adj* chock-full

überwachen (ew-berr-*vah*-khern) *v* watch; patrol

überwachsen (ew-berr-*vah*-ksern) *adj* overgrown

überwältigen (ew-berr-*vehl*-ti-gern) *v* overwhelm

***überweisen** (ew-berr-*vigh*-zern) *v* remit

Überweisung (ew-berr-*vigh*-zoong) *f* (pl ⁓en) remittance

***überwinden** (ew-berr-*vin*-dern) *v* *overcome

überzeugen (ew-berr-*tsoi*-gern) *v* convince, persuade

Überzeugung (ew-berr-*tsoi*-goong) *f* (pl ⁓en) conviction; persuasion

***überziehen** (ew-berr-*tsee*-ern) *v* upholster

üblich (*ewp*-likh) *adj* customary, common; simple; frequent

übrig (*ew*-brikh) *adj* remaining

***übrig bleiben** (*ew*-brikh-bligh-bern) *v* remain

übrigens (*ew*-bri-gerns) *adv* by the way, besides

Übung (*ew*-boong) *f* (pl ⁓en) exercise

Ufer (*oo*-ferr) *nt* (pl ⁓) bank, shore

Uhr (oor) *f* (pl ⁓en) clock; watch; **um ... ~** at ... o'clock

Uhrmacher (*oor*-mah-kherr) *m* (pl ⁓), **-in** *f* watchmaker

Ulme (*ool*-mer) *f* (pl ⁓n) elm

ultraviolett (*ool*-trah-vi-oa-leht) *adj* ultraviolet

um (oom) *prep* round, about, around; **~ ... herum** round, around; **~ zu** to, in order to

umarmen (oom-*ahr*-mern) *v* embrace;

hug

Umarmung (oom-*ahr*-moong) f (pl ∼en) embrace; hug

*umbringen (oom-*bring*-ern) v kill

umdrehen (oom-*dray*-ern) v turn; invert; **sich ∼** turn round

Umdrehung (oom-*dray*-oong) f (pl ∼en) revolution

*umfallen (oom-*fah*-lern) v *fall (down, over); collapse

Umfang (oom-*fahng*) m bulk

umfangreich (oom-*fahng*-righkh) adj bulky, big; extensive

umfassen (oom-*fah*-sern) v comprise, contain

umfassend (oom-*fah*-sernt) adj comprehensive, extensive

Umfrage (oom-*fraa*-ger) f (pl ∼n) enquiry

Umgang (oom-*gahng*) m intercourse

*umgehen (oom-*gay*-bern) v surround

Umgebung (oom-*gay*-boong) f environment, surroundings pl; setting

*umgehen (oom-*gay*-ern) v by-pass; **∼ mit** associate with

Umgehungsstraße (oom-*gay*-oongs-shtraa-ser) f (pl ∼n) by-pass

umgekehrt (oom-*ger*-kayrt) adj reverse; adv upside-down

Umhang (oom-*hahng*) m (pl ∼e) cloak; cape

umher (oom-*hayr*) adv about, around

umherschweifen (oom-*hayr*-shvigh-fern) v roam, wander

umherwandern (oom-*hayr*-vahn-derrn) v wander

umkehren (oom-*kay*-rer) v turn round; turn back

Umkleidekabine (oom-*kligh*-der-kah-bee-ner) f (pl ∼n) cabin

Umkleideraum (oom-*kligh*-der-roum) m changing room, locker room

*umkommen (oom-*ko*-mern) v perish

Umkreis (oom-*krighss*) m radius

umkreisen (oom-*krigh*-zern) v circle

Umlauf (oom-*louf*) m circulation

Umleitung (oom-*ligh*-toong) f (pl ∼en) detour; diversion

umliegend (oom-*lee*-gernt) adj surrounding

umrechnen (oom-*rehkh*-nern) v convert

Umrechnungstabelle (oom-*rehkh*-noongs-tah-beh-ler) f (pl ∼n) conversion chart

umringen (oom-*ring*-ern) v surround

Umriss (oom-*riss*) m (pl ∼e) outline, contour

umrühren (oom-*rew*-rern) v stir

Umsatz (oom-*zahts*) m (pl ∼e) turnover

Umsatzsteuer (oom-*zahts*-shtoi-err) f turnover tax

Umschlag (oom-*shlaak*) m (pl ∼e) cover, jacket

Umschlagtuch (oom-*shlaak*-tookh) nt (pl ∼er) shawl

*umschließen (oom-*shlee*-sern) v encircle

Umschwung (oom-*shvoong*) m reverse

umsonst (oom-*zonst*) adv gratis; in vain

Umstand (oom-*shtahnt*) m (pl ∼e) circumstance; condition

*umsteigen (oom-*shtigh*-gern) v change

umstritten (oom-*shtri*-tern) adj controversial

Umtausch (oom-*toush*) m exchange

umtauschen (oom-*toush*-ern) v exchange

Umweg (oom-*vayk*) m (pl ∼e) detour

Umwelt (oom-*vehlt*) f environment

Umweltverschmutzung (oom-*vehlt*-fehr-shmoo-tsoong) f environmental pollution

*umwenden (*oom*-vehn-dern) *v* turn over

*umziehen (*oom*-tsee-ern) *v* move; sich ~ change

Umzug (*oom*-ts○○k) *m* (pl ⁀e) parade; move

unabhängig (*oon*-ahp-hehng-ikh) *adj* independent

Unabhängigkeit (*oon*-ahp-hehng-ikh-kight) *f* independence

unabsichtlich (*oon*-ahp-zikht-likh) *adj* unintentional

unähnlich (*oon*-ain-likh) *adj* unlike

unangebracht (*oon*-ahn-ger-brahkht) *adj* misplaced

unangenehm (*oon*-ahn-ger-nāym) *adj* unpleasant, disagreeable; nasty

unannehmbar (oon-ahn-*nāym*-baar) *adj* unacceptable

Unannehmlichkeit (*oon*-ahn-nāym-likh-kight) *f* (pl ⁀en) inconvenience

unanständig (*oon*-ahn-shtehn-dikh) *adj* indecent

unartig (*oon*-ahr-tikh) *adj* naughty

unauffällig (*oon*-ouf-feh-likh) *adj* inconspicuous

unaufhörlich (*oon*-ouf-hūrr-likh) *adj* continual

unbeantwortet (*oon*-ber-ahnt-vor-tert) *adj* unanswered

unbedeutend (*oon*-ber-doi-ternt) *adj* insignificant; petty

unbedingt (*oon*-ber-dingt) *adv* absolutely, without fail

unbefriedigend (*oon*-ber-free-di-gernt) *adj* unsatisfactory

unbefugt (*oon*-ber-f○○kt) *adj* unauthorized

unbegreiflich (*oon*-ber-grighf-likh) *adj* puzzling

unbegrenzt (*oon*-ber-grehntst) *adj* unlimited

unbekannt (*oon*-ber-kahnt) *adj* unknown; unfamiliar

Unbekannte (*oon*-ber-kahn-ter) *m/f* (pl ⁀n) stranger

unbekümmert (*oon*-ber-kew-merrt) *adj* carefree

unbeliebt (*oon*-ber-leept) *adj* unpopular

unbequem (*oon*-ber-kvāym) *adj* uncomfortable; inconvenient

Unbequemlichkeit (*oon*-ber-kvāym-likh-kight) *f* (pl ⁀en) inconvenience

unbeschädigt (*oon*-ber-shai-dikht) *adj* whole

unbescheiden (*oon*-ber-shigh-dern) *adj* immodest

unbeschränkt (*oon*-ber-shrehngkt) *adj* unlimited

unbesetzt (*oon*-ber-zehtst) *adj* unoccupied

unbesonnen (*oon*-ber-zo-nern) *adj* rash

unbestimmt (*oon*-ber-shtimt) *adj* indefinite

unbewohnbar (*oon*-ber-vōan-baar) *adj* uninhabitable

unbewohnt (*oon*-ber-vōant) *adj* uninhabited

unbewusst (*oon*-ber-voost) *adj* unaware

und (oont) *conj* and; ~ so weiter etcetera

undankbar (*oon*-dahngk-baar) *adj* ungrateful

undeutlich (*oon*-doit-likh) *adj* vague

undicht (*oon*-dikht) *adj* leaky; not tight

uneben (*oon*-āy-bern) *adj* uneven

unecht (*oon*-ehkht) *adj* false

unehrlich (*oon*-āyr-likh) *adj* crooked, dishonest

unempfindlich (*oon*-ehm-pfint-likh) *adj* insensitive

unendlich (oon-*ehnt*-likh) *adj* infinite, endless; immense

unentbehrlich (oon-ehnt-*bāyr*-likh)

adj essential

unentgeltlich (oon-ehnt-*gehlt*-likh) *adj* free of charge

unerfahren (*oon*-ehr-faa-rern) *adj* inexperienced

unerfreulich (*oon*-ehr-froi-likh) *adj* unpleasant

unerheblich (*oon*-ehr-h̄ayp-likh) *adj* insignificant

unerklärlich (oon-ehr-*klair*-likh) *adj* unaccountable

unermesslich (*oon*-ehr-*mehss*-likh) *adj* immense, vast

unerschwinglich (oon-ehr-*shving*-likh) *adj* prohibitive

unerträglich (oon-ehr-*traik*-likh) *adj* unbearable, intolerable

unerwartet (*oon*-ehr-vahr-tert) *adj* unexpected

unerwünscht (*oon*-ehr-vewnsht) *adj* undesirable

unfähig (*oon*-fai-ikh) *adj* unable, incompetent, incapable

Unfall (*oon*-fahl) *m* (pl ⁀e) accident

Unfallstation (*oon*-fahl-shtah-tsʸo͞an) *f* (pl ⁀en) first aid post

unfassbar (*oon*-fahss-baar) *adj* inconceivable

unfreundlich (*oon*-froint-likh) *adj* unkind, unfriendly

Unfug (*oon*-fōͦk) *m* nuisance; mischief

Ungar (*oong*-gahr) *m* (pl ⁀n) Hungarian

ungarisch (*oong*-gah-rish) *adj* Hungarian

Ungarn (*oong*-gahrn) Hungary

ungeachtet (*oon*-ger-ahkh-tert) *prep* regardless of, in spite of

ungebildet (*oon*-ger-bil-dert) *adj* uneducated

ungebräuchlich (*oon*-ger-broikh-likh) *adj* unusual

ungeduldig (*oon*-ger-dool-dikh) *adj* impatient

ungeeignet (*oon*-ger-igh-gnert) *adj* unsuitable

ungefähr (*oon*-ger-fair) *adv* approximately

ungehalten (*oon*-ger-hahl-tern) *adj* cross

ungeheuer (*oon*-ger-hoi-err) *adj* tremendous, enormous, huge, immense

ungelegen (*oon*-ger-lāy-gern) *adj* inconvenient

ungelernt (*oon*-ger-lehrnt) *adj* unskilled

ungemütlich (*oon*-ger-mēwt-likh) *adj* uncomfortable

ungenau (*oon*-ger-nou) *adj* incorrect, inaccurate

ungenießbar (*oon*-ger-neess-baar) *adj* inedible

ungenügend (*oon*-ger-nēw-gernt) *adj* insufficient

ungerade (*oon*-ger-raa-der) *adj* odd

ungerecht (*oon*-ger-rehkht) *adj* unjust, unfair

ungeschickt (*oon*-ger-shikt) *adj* clumsy, awkward

ungeschützt (*oon*-ger-shewtst) *adj* unprotected

ungesetzlich (*oon*-ger-zehts-likh) *adj* illegal

ungesund (*oon*-ger-zoont) *adj* unsound, unhealthy

ungewiss (*oon*-ger-viss) *adj* doubtful

ungewöhnlich (*oon*-ger-vūrn-likh) *adj* uncommon, unusual; exceptional

ungewohnt (*oon*-ger-vōant) *adj* unaccustomed

ungezogen (*oon*-ger-tsōa-gern) *adj* naughty, bad

Ungezwungenheit (*oon*-ger-tsvoong-ern-hight) *f* ease

unglaublich (oon-*gloup*-likh) *adj* incredible

ungleich (*oon*-glighkh) *adj* unequal; uneven

Unglück (*oon*-glewk) *nt* (pl ~e) misfortune; accident; calamity

unglücklich (*oon*-glewk-likh) *adj* unlucky; unhappy, unfortunate

unglücklicherweise (*oon*-glewk-li-kherr-vigh-zer) *adv* unfortunately

ungültig (*oon*-gewl-tikh) *adj* invalid

ungünstig (*oon*-gewns-tikh) *adj* unfavo(u)rable

Unheil (*oon*-highl) *nt* disaster; mischief

unheilbar (*oon*-highl-baar) *adj* incurable

unheilvoll (*oon*-highl-fol) *adj* sinister; fatal

unheimlich (*oon*-highm-likh) *adj* scary, creepy

unhöflich (*oon*-hūrf-likh) *adj* impolite

Uniform (oo-ni-*form*) *f* (pl ~en) uniform

Union (oo-n^y*ōan*) *f* (pl ~en) union

universal (oo-ni-vehr-*zaal*) *adj* universal

Universität (oo-ni-vehr-zi-*tait*) *f* (pl ~en) university

unklar (*oon*-klaar) *adj* obscure

Unkosten (*oon*-koss-tern) *pl* expenses *pl*

Unkraut (*oon*-krout) *nt* (pl ~er) weed

unkultiviert (*oon*-kool-ti-veert) *adj* uncultivated

unleserlich (*oon*-lāy-zerr-likh) *adj* illegible

unmittelbar (*oon*-mi-terl-baar) *adj* direct; immediate

unmöglich (*oon*-mūrk-likh) *adj* impossible

unnötig (*oon*-nūr-tikh) *adj* unnecessary

unnütz (*oon*-newts) *adj* vain

unordentlich (*oon*-or-dehnt-likh) *adj* slovenly, untidy

Unordnung (*oon*-or-dnoong) *f* disorder; mess; **in ~ *bringen** mess up

unparteiisch (*oon*-pahr-tigh-ish) *adj* impartial

unpassend (*oon*-pah-sernt) *adj* improper

unpersönlich (*oon*-pehr-zūrn-likh) *adj* impersonal

unpopulär (*oon*-poa-poo-lair) *adj* unpopular

unqualifiziert (*oon*-kvah-li-fi-tseert) *adj* unqualified

Unrecht (*oon*-rehkht) *nt* injustice; wrong; ~ *tun** wrong; ~ *haben** *be wrong

unrecht (*oon*-rehkht) *adj* wrong;

unregelmäßig (*oon*-rāy-gerl-mai-sikh) *adj* irregular

unrichtig (*oon*-rikh-tikh) *adj* incorrect

Unruhe (*oon*-rōō-er) *f* unrest

unruhig (*oon*-rōō-ikh) *adj* uneasy, restless

uns (oons) *pron* us; ourselves

unschätzbar (*oon*-shehts-baar) *adj* priceless

Unschuld (*oon*-shoolt) *f* innocence

unschuldig (*oon*-shool-dikh) *adj* innocent

unser (*oon*-zerr) *pron* our

unsicher (*oon*-zi-kherr) *adj* unsafe; uncertain

unsichtbar (*oon*-zikht-baar) *adj* invisible

Unsinn (*oon*-zin) *m* nonsense, rubbish

unsinnig (*oon*-zi-nikh) *adj* senseless

unsympathisch (*oon*-zewm-paa-tish) *adj* unpleasant

untauglich (*oon*-touk-likh) *adj* unfit

unten (*oon*-tern) *adv* beneath, below; underneath; downstairs; **nach ~** downwards

unter (*oon*-terr) *prep* under; beneath, below; among, amid; *adj* inferior;

Unter- subordinate; **~ anderem** among other things

***unterbrechen** (oon-terr-*breh*-khern) v interrupt

Unterbrechung (oon-terr-*breh*-khoong) f (pl ~en) interruption

***unterbringen** (oon-terr-bring-ern) v *undertake

unterdrücken (oon-terr-*drew*-kern) v oppress; suppress

Unterernährung (oon-terr-ehr-nai-roong) f malnutrition

Unterführung (oon-terr-*few*-roong) f Brit subway; Am pedestrian underpass; underpass

Untergang (oon-terr-gahng) m ruin, destruction

untergeordnet (oon-terr-ger-or-dnert) adj subordinate; minor, secondary

Untergeschoss (oon-terr-ger-shoss) nt basement

Untergrundbahn (oon-terr-groont-baan) f (pl ~en) subway Am

unterhalb (oon-terr-hahlp) prep under, below

Unterhalt (oon-terr-hahlt) m livelihood; upkeep

***unterhalten** (oon-terr-*hahl*-tern) v entertain, amuse

unterhaltsam (oon-terr-*hahlt*-zaam) adj entertaining, amusing

Unterhaltung (oon-terr-*hahl*-toong) f (pl ~en) conversation; entertainment, amusement

Unterhemd (oon-terr-hehmt) nt (pl ~en) undershirt

Unterhose (oon-terr-hōa-zer) f (pl ~n) pants pl; briefs pl, drawers, pl; shorts plAm; underpants plAm

unterirdisch (oon-terr-eer-dish) adj underground

Unterkunft (oon-terr-koonft) f (pl ~e) accommodation; lodgings pl

Untermieter (oon-terr-mee-terr) m (pl ~), **-in** f lodger

Unternehmen (oon-terr-*nāy*-mern) nt (pl ~) enterprise, business; concern, company

***unternehmen** (oon-terr-*nāy*-mern) v *undertake

Unternehmer (oon-terr-*nāy*-merr) m (pl ~), **-in** f businessman, businesswoman; contractor

Unternehmung (oon-terr-*nāy*-moong) f (pl ~en) undertaking

Unterredung (oon-terr-*rāy*-doong) f (pl ~en) interview

Unterricht (oon-terr-rikht) m instruction; lessons; tuition

unterrichten (oon-terr-*rikh*-tern) v *teach

Unterrock (oon-terr-rok) m (pl ~e) slip

unterschätzen (oon-terr-*sheh*-tsern) v underestimate

***unterscheiden** (oon-terr-*shigh*-dern) v distinguish; **sich ~** differ

Unterscheidung (oon-terr-*shigh*-doong) f distinction

Unterschied (oon-terr-sheet) m (pl ~e) difference, distinction; contrast

***unterschreiben** (oon-terr-*shrigh*-bern) v sign

Unterschrift (oon-terr-shrift) f (pl ~en) signature

unterst (oon-terrst) adj bottom

***unterstreichen** (oon-terr-*shtrigh*-khern) v underline

Unterströmung (oon-terr-shtrūr-moong) f undercurrent

unterstützen (oon-terr-*shtew*-tsern) v support; assist, aid

Unterstützung (oon-terr-*shtew*-tsoong) f (pl ~en) support; assistance, relief

untersuchen (oon-terr-z**ōō**-khern) v enquire, investigate

Untersuchung (oon-terr-*zōō-*khoong) *f* (pl ~en) enquiry, investigation, inquiry; checkup, examination

Untertasse (*oon*-terr-tah-ser) *f* (pl ~n) saucer

Untertitel (*oon*-terr-tee-terl) *m* (pl ~) subtitle

Unterwäsche (*oon*-terr-veh-sher) *fpl* underwear

unterwegs (oon-terr-*vāyks*) *adv* on the way

***unterweisen** (oon-terr-*vigh*-zern) *v* instruct

Unterweisung (oon-terr-*vigh*-zoong) *f* instruction

***unterwerfen** (oon-terr-*vehr*-fern) *v* subject; **sich ~** submit; **unterworfen** liable to

unterzeichnen (oon-terr-*tsighkh*-nern) *v* sign

untreu (*oon*-troi) *adj* unfaithful

unüberlegt (*oon*-ēw-berr-lāykt) *adj* unwise

unübertroffen (*oon*-ēw-berr-tro-fern) *adj* unsurpassed

ununterbrochen (*oon*-oon-terr-bro-khern) *adj* continuous

unverbleit (*oon*-fehr-blight) *adj* unleaded

unverdient (*oon*-fehr-deent) *adj* unearned

unverletzt (*oon*-fehr-lehtst) *adj* unhurt

unvermeidlich (oon-fehr-*might*-likh) *adj* unavoidable, inevitable

unvernünftig (*oon*-fehr-newnf-tikh) *adj* unreasonable

unverschämt (*oon*-fehr-shaimt) *adj* impudent, impertinent, insolent

Unverschämtheit (*oon*-fehr-shaimt-hight) *f* impertinence, insolence

unversehrt (*oon*-fehr-zāyrt) *adj* unbroken; intact

unverzüglich (oon-fehr-*tsēwk*-likh) *adj* prompt; *adv* immediately, instantly

unvollkommen (*oon*-fol-ko-mern) *adj* imperfect

unvollständig (*oon*-fol-shtehn-dikh) *adj* incomplete

unvorhergesehen (*oon*-fōar-hāyr-ger-zāy-ern) *adj* unexpected

unwahr (*oon*-vaar) *adj* untrue, false

unwahrscheinlich (*oon*-vaar-shighn-likh) *adj* unlikely, improbable

Unwetter (*oon*-veh-terr) *nt* (pl ~) tempest

unwichtig (*oon*-vikh-tikh) *adj* unimportant

unwiderruflich (*oon*-vee-derr-*rōōf*-likh) *adj* irrevocable

unwillig (*oon*-vi-likh) *adj* unwilling

unwissend (*oon*-vi-sernt) *adj* ignorant

unwohl (*oon*-vōal) *adj* unwell

unzerbrechlich (*oon*-tsehr-brehkh-likh) *adj* unbreakable

unzufrieden (*oon*-tsoo-free-dern) *adj* dissatisfied, discontented

unzugänglich (*oon*-tsōō-gerng-likh) *adj* inaccessible

unzulänglich (*oon*-tsōō-lehng-likh) *adj* inadequate

unzuverlässig (*oon*-tsōō-vehr-leh-sikh) *adj* untrustworthy, unreliable

unzweckmäßig (*oon*-tsvehk-mai-sikh) *adj* inefficient

uralt (*ōōr*-ahlt) *adj* ancient

Urin (oo-*reen*) *m* urine

Urkunde (*ōōr*-koon-der) *f* (pl ~n) certificate, document

Urlaub (*ōōr*-loup) *m* (pl ~e) holiday; leave; **auf ~** on holiday

Ursache (*ōōr*-zah-kher) *f* (pl ~n) cause; reason

Ursprung (*ōōr*-shproong) *m* (pl ~e) origin

ursprünglich ($\overline{oo}r$-shprewng-likh) *adj* original

Urteil (*oor*-tighl) *nt* (pl ≈e) judgment; sentence, verdict

urteilen (*oor*-tigh-lern) *v* judge

Urteilsspruch (*oor*-tighls-shprookh) *m* (pl ≈e) verdict

Uruguay (oo-roo-*gvigh*) Uruguay

uruguayisch (oo-roo-*gvigh*-ish) *adj* Uruguayan

Urwald ($\overline{oo}r$-vahlt) *m* (pl ≈er) jungle

V

vage (*vaa*-ger) *adj* faint

Vakuum (*vaa*-koo-oom) *nt* (pl Vakua) vacuum

Vanille (vah-*ni*-l^{y}er) *f* vanilla

Varieté (vah-ri-ay-*tay*) *nt* (pl ≈s) music hall, variety theatre (theater *Am*)

variieren (vah-ri-*ee*-rern) *v* vary

Vase (*vaa*-zer) *f* (pl ≈n) vase

Vaseline (vah-say-*lee*-ner) *f* vaseline

Vater (*faa*-terr) *m* (pl ≈) father; dad

Vaterland (*faa*-terr-lahnt) *nt* native country

Vati (*faa*-ti) *m* daddy

Vegetarier (vay-gay-*taa*-r^{y}err) *m* (pl ≈), **-in** *f* vegetarian

Vegetation (vay-gay-tah-ts$^y\overline{oa}n$) *f* (pl ≈en) vegetation

Veilchen (*fighl*-khern) *nt* (pl ≈) violet

Vene (*vay*-nay) *f* vein

Venezolaner (vay-nay-tsoa-*laa*-nerr) *m* (pl ≈), **-in** *f* Venezuelan

venezolanisch (vay-nay-tsoa-*laa*-nish) *adj* Venezuelan

Venezuela (vay-nay-tsoo-$\overline{ay}$-lah) Venezuela

Ventil (vehn-*teel*) *nt* (pl ≈e) valve

Ventilation (vehn-ti-lah-ts$^y\overline{oa}n$) *f* (pl ≈en) ventilation

Ventilator (vehn-ti-*laa*-tor) *m* (pl ≈en) fan, ventilator

ventilieren (vehn-ti-*lee*-rern) *v* ventilate

verabreden (fehr-*ahp*-ray-dern) *v* agree on, arrange; **sich ~** *make an appointment with, arrange to meet

Verabredung (fehr-*ahp*-ray-doong) *f* (pl ≈en) appointment; date, engagement

verabreichen (fehr-*ahp*-righ-khern) *v* administer

verabschieden (fehr-*ahp*-shee-dern) *v* dismiss; **sich ~** *say goodbye to

verachten (fehr-*ahkh*-tern) *v* despise, scorn

Verachtung (fehr-*ahkh*-toong) *f* scorn, contempt

veraltet (fehr-*ahl*-tert) *adj* ancient; out of date

Veranda (vay-*rahn*-dah) *f* (pl -den) veranda

veränderlich (fehr-*ehn*-derr-likh) *adj* variable

verändern (fehr-*ehn*-derrn) *v* alter; vary

Veränderung (fehr-*ehn*-der-roong) *f* (pl ≈en) alteration; variation

verängstigt (fehr-*ehngs*-tikht) *adj* frightened

veranschlagen (fehr-*ahn*-shlaa-gern) *v* evaluate, estimate

veranstalten (fehr-*ahn*-shtahl-tern) *v* organize, arrange

Veranstaltung (fehr-*ahn*-shtahl-toong) *f* event, meeting

verantwortlich (fehr-*ahnt*-vort-likh) *adj* responsible; liable

Verantwortlichkeit (fehr-*ahnt*-vort-likh-kight) *f* responsibility; liability

verausgaben (fehr-*ouss*-gaa-bern) *v* *spend

Verband (fehr-*bahnt*) *m* (pl ✕e) bandage; federation

Verbandskasten (fehr-*bahnts*-kahss-tern) *m* (pl ✕) first aid kit

Verbannung (fehr-*bah*-noong) *f* exile

***verbergen** (fehr-*behr*-gern) *v* *hide; conceal

verbessern (fehr-*beh*-serrn) *v* improve; correct

Verbesserung (fehr-*beh*-ser-roong) *f* (pl ✕en) improvement; correction

***verbieten** (fehr-*bee*-tern) *v* *forbid, prohibit

***verbinden** (fehr-*bin*-dern) *v* link, join, connect; combine; dress

Verbindung (fehr-*bin*-doong) *f* (pl ✕en) link; connection; relation; **sich in ~ setzen mit** contact

verblassen (fehr-*blah*-sern) *v* fade

verblüffen (fehr-*blew*-fern) *v* astonish; overwhelm

Verbot (fehr-*bōat*) *nt* (pl ✕e) prohibition

verboten (fehr-*bōa*-tern) *adj* prohibited

Verbrauch (fehr-*broukh*) *m* consumption

verbrauchen (fehr-*brou*-khern) *v* use up

Verbraucher (fehr-*brou*-kherr) *m* (pl ✕), **-in** *f* consumer

Verbrechen (fehr-*breh*-khern) *nt* (pl ✕) crime

Verbrecher (fehr-*breh*-kherr) *m* (pl ✕), **-in** *f* criminal

verbrecherisch (fehr-*breh*-kher-rish) *adj* criminal

verbreiten (fehr-*brigh*-tern) *v* *shed

***verbrennen** (fehr-*breh*-nern) *v* *burn; cremate

***verbringen** (fehr-*bring*-ern) *v* *spend

verbunden (fehr-*boon*-dern) *adj* joint

Verbündete (fehr-*bewn*-der-ter) *m/f* (pl ✕n) associate

Verdacht (fehr-*dahkht*) *m* suspicion

verdächtig (fehr-*dehkh*-tikh) *adj* suspicious

Verdächtige (fehr-*dehkh*-ti-ger) *m/f* (pl ✕n) suspect

verdächtigen (fehr-*dehkh*-ti-gern) *v* suspect

verdampfen (fehr-*dahm*-pfern) *v* evaporate

verdanken (fehr-*dahng*-kern) *v* owe

verdauen (fehr-*dou*-ern) *v* digest

verdaulich (fehr-*dou*-likh) *adj* digestible

Verdauung (fehr-*dou*-oong) *f* digestion

verdecken (fehr-*deh*-kern) *v* cover

***verderben** (fehr-*dehr*-bern) *v* *spoil; **leicht verderblich** perishable

verdicken (fehr-*di*-kern) *v* thicken

verdienen (fehr-*dee*-nern) *v* earn, *make; deserve, merit

Verdienst (fehr-*deenst*) *nt* (pl ✕e) merit; *m* earnings *pl*

verdorben (fehr-*dor*-bern) *adj* rotten

verdrehen (fehr-*drāy*-ern) *v* wrench

Verdruss (fehr-*drooss*) *m* annoyance

verdünnen (fehr-*dew*-nern) *v* dilute

verehren (fehr-*āy*-rern) *v* worship

Verein (fehr-*ighn*) *m* (pl ✕e) society, club

vereinigen (fehr-*igh*-ni-gern) *v* unite; join

Vereinigte Staaten United States, the States

Vereinigung (fehr-*igh*-ni-goong) *f* (pl ✕en) association; union

Verfahren (fehr-*faa*-rern) *nt* (pl ✕) procedure; process

*verfahren (fehr-*faa*-rern) v proceed

verfallen (fehr-*fah*-lern) adj expired

*verfallen (fehr-*fah*-lern) v expire

Verfallsdatum (fehr-*fahls*-daa-toom) nt expiry date; best-before date, best-by date, Am pull date; sell-by date

verfärben (fehr-*fehr*-bern) v: **sich ~** discolo(u)r

verfärbt (fehr-*fehrpt*) adj discolo(u)red

Verfasser (fehr-*fah*-serr) m (pl ~), **-in** f author

Verfassung (fehr-*fah*-soong) f condition; constitution

Verfechter (fehr-*fehkh*-terr) m (pl ~) champion

verfluchen (fehr-*floo*-khern) v curse

verfolgen (fehr-*fol*-gern) v carry on; chase, pursue

verfügbar (fehr-*fewk*-baar) adj available

verfügen über (fehr-*few*-gern) dispose of

Verfügung (fehr-*few*-goong) f disposal

verführen (fehr-*few*-rern) v seduce

vergangen (fehr-*gahng*-ern) adj past

Vergangenheit (fehr-*gahng*-ern-hight) f past

Vergaser (fehr-*gaa*-zerr) m (pl ~) carburettor

vergebens (fehr-*gāy*-berns) adv in vain

vergegenwärtigen (fehr-*gāy*-gern-*vehr*-ti-gern) v: **sich ~** realize

Vergehen (fehr-*gāy*-ern) nt (pl ~) offence, offense Am

*vergehen (fehr-*gāy*-ern) v pass; **sich ~** offend

*vergessen (fehr-*geh*-sern) v *forget

vergesslich (fehr-*gehss*-likh) adj forgetful

vergeuden (fehr-*goi*-dern) v waste

vergewaltigen (fehr-ger-*vahl*-ti-gern) v assault, rape

vergewissern (fehr-ger-*vi*-serrn) v: **sich ~** ascertain

*vergießen (fehr-*gee*-sern) v *shed

vergiften (fehr-*gif*-tern) v poison

Vergiftung (fehr-*gif*-toong) f poisoning

Vergleich (fehr-*glighkh*) m (pl ~e) comparison; compromise, settlement

*vergleichen (fehr-*gligh*-khern) v compare

Vergnügen (fehr-*gnēw*-gern) nt (pl ~) fun, pleasure; amusement; **mit ~** gladly

vergoldet (fehr-*gol*-dert) adj gilt

vergrößern (fehr-*grūr*-serrn) v enlarge; increase

Vergrößerung (fehr-*grūr*-ser-roong) f (pl ~en) enlargement

vergüten (fehr-*gēw*-tern) v remunerate

verhaften (fehr-*hahf*-tern) v arrest

Verhaftung (fehr-*hahf*-toong) f (pl ~en) arrest

verhalten (fehr-*hahl*-tern) v: **sich ~** behave; conduct o.s.

Verhalten (fehr-*hahl*-tern) nt behavio(u)r, conduct

Verhältnis (fehr-*hehlt*-niss) nt (pl ~se) proportion; affair

verhältnismäßig (fehr-*hehlt*-niss-mai-sikh) adj relative

verhandeln (fehr-*hahn*-derln) v negotiate

Verhandlung (fehr-*hahn*-dloong) f (pl ~en) negotiation

Verhängnis (fehr-*hehng*-niss) nt destiny

verhängnisvoll (fehr-*hehng*-niss-fol) adj ominous; fatal

verhätscheln (fehr-*heh*-cherln) v cuddle

verheerend (fehr-*hāy*-rernt) adj disastrous

verhindern (fehr-*hin*-derrn) *v* prevent

Verhör (fehr-*hūrr*) *nt* (pl ~e) interrogation, examination

verhören (fehr-*hūr*-rern) *v* interrogate

verhüten (fehr-*hēw*-tern) *v* prevent

verirrt (fehr-*eert*) *adj* lost

verjagen (fehr-*ʸaa*-gern) *v* chase

Verkauf (fehr-*kouf*) *m* (pl ~e) sale

verkaufen (fehr-*kou*-fern) *v* *sell; **zu ~** for sale

Verkäufer (fehr-*koi*-ferr) *m* (pl ~) salesman; shop assistant

Verkäuferin (fehr-*koi*-fer-rin) *f* (pl ~nen) salesgirl

verkäuflich (fehr-*koif*-likh) *adj* saleable

Verkehr (fehr-*kāyr*) *m* traffic

verkehren mit (fehr-*kāy*-rern) mix with

Verkehrsampel (fehr-*kāyrs*-ahm-perl) *f* (pl ~n) traffic light

Verkehrsmittel (fehr-*kāyrs*-mi-terl) *nt* (means of) transport

verkehrsreich (fehr-*kāyrs*-righkh) *adj* busy

Verkehrsstauung (fehr-*kāyrs*-shtou-oong) *f* (pl ~en) traffic jam, jam

verkehrt (fehr-*kāyrt*) *adj* false; *adv* inside out; **~ herum** (fehr-*kāyrt*-heh-room) *adj* reverse; *adv* upside down; inside out

verkleiden (fehr-*kl^ee-klighkh*-dern) *v*: **sich ~** disguise

Verkleidung (fehr-*kligh*-doong) *f* (pl ~en) disguise

verkrüppelt (fehr-*krew*-perlt) *adj* crippled

verkürzen (fehr-*kewr*-tsern) *v* shorten

Verlangen (fehr-*lahng*-ern) *nt* desire

verlangen (fehr-*lahng*-ern) *v* desire; demand; charge

verlängern (fehr-*lehng*-errn) *v* lengthen, extend; renew

Verlängerung (fehr-*lehng*-er-roong) *f*

(pl ~en) extension

Verlängerungsschnur (fehr-*lehng*-er-roongs-shnōōr) *f* (pl ~e) extension cord

verlangsamen (fehr-*lahng*-zaa-mern) *v* slow down

verlassen (fehr-*lah*-sern) *adj* desert

*****verlassen** (fehr-*lah*-sern) *v* *leave; desert; **sich ~ auf** rely on

*****verlaufen** (fehr-*lou*-fern) *v* *go, *take a ... course; **sich ~** *get lost, *lose one's way

verlegen (fehr-*lāy*-gern) *v* *mislay; *adj* embarrassed

Verlegenheit (fehr-*lāy*-gern-hight) *f* (pl ~) embarrassment; **in ~*bringen** embarrass

Verleger (fehr-*lāy*-gerr) *m* (pl ~), **-in** *f* publisher

Verleih (fehr-*ligh*) *m* hire, rental

*****verleihen** (fehr-*ligh*-ern) *v* grant

verlernen (fehr-*lehr*-nern) *v* unlearn

verletzbar (fehr-*lehts*-baar) *adj* vulnerable

verletzen (fehr-*leh*-tsern) *v* *hurt, injure; wound

Verletzung (fehr-*leh*-tsoong) *f* (pl ~en) injury; violation

Verleumdung (fehr-*loim*-doong) *f* (pl ~en) slander

verlieben (fehr-*lee*-bern) *v*: **sich ~ in** *fall in love with

verliebt (fehr-*leept*) *adj* in love

*****verlieren** (fehr-*lee*-rern) *v* *lose

verlobt (fehr-*lōapt*) *adj* engaged

Verlobte (fehr-*lōap*-ter) *m* (pl ~n) fiancé; *f* fiancée

Verlobung (fehr-*lōa*-boong) *f* (pl ~en) engagement

Verlobungsring (fehr-*lōa*-boongs-ring) *m* (pl ~e) engagement ring

Verlust (fehr-*loost*) *m* (pl ~e) loss

*****vermeiden** (fehr-*migh*-dern) *v* avoid

Vermerk (fehr-*mehrk*) *m* (pl ~e) note

vermieten (fehr-*mee*-tern) *v* *let;
lease; **zu ~** for hire

Vermieter (fehr-*mee*-terr) *m*, **-in** *f*
landlord, landlady

vermindern (fehr-*min*-derrn) *v* lessen,
decrease, reduce

vermischt (fehr-*misht*) *adj*
miscellaneous

vermissen (fehr-*miss*-ern) *v* miss

Vermisste (fehr-*miss*-ter) *m/f* (pl ~n)
missing person

vermitteln (fehr-*mi*-terln) *v* mediate

Vermittler (fehr-*mit*-lerr) *m* (pl ~), **-in** *f*
mediator; intermediary

Vermittlung (fehr-*mit*-loong) *f*
(telephone) exchange, *Am* central
office; operator

Vermögen (fehr-*mūr*-gern) *nt* (pl ~)
ability; fortune

vermuten (fehr-*mōō*-tern) *v* suspect;
guess, suppose

vermutlich (fehr-*mōōt*-likh) *adj*
presumable, probable

Vermutung (fehr-*mōō*-toong) *f* (pl
~en) guess

vernachlässigen (fehr-*naakh*-leh-si-
gern) *v* neglect

Vernachlässigung (fehr-*naakh*-leh-
si-goong) *f* (pl ~en) neglect

verneinend (fehr-*nigh*-nernt) *adj*
negative

vernichten (fehr-*nikh*-tern) *v* destroy;
wreck

Vernunft (fehr-*noonft*) *f* sense, reason

vernünftig (fehr-*newnf*-tikh) *adj*
reasonable

veröffentlichen (fehr-*ur*-fernt-li-
khern) *v* publish

Veröffentlichung (fehr-*ur*-fernt-li-
khoong) *f* (pl ~en) publication

verpachten (fehr-*pahkh*-tern) *v* lease

verpacken (fehr-*pahk*-ern) *v* pack
(up), wrap up

Verpackung (fehr-*pah*-koong) *f* (pl
~en) packing

verpassen (fehr-*pah*-sern) *v* miss

verpfänden (fehr-*pfehn*-dern) *v* pawn

verpflichten (fehr-*pflikh*-tern) *v*
oblige; **sich ~** engage; **verpflichtet
*sein zu** *be obliged to

Verpflichtung (fehr-*pflikh*-toong) *f*
(pl ~en) engagement

Verrat (fehr-*raat*) *m* treason

*verraten (fehr-*raa*-tern) *v* betray;
*give away

Verräter (fehr-*rai*-terr) *m* (pl ~), **-in** *f*
traitor

verrenkt (fehr-*rehngkt*) *adj* dislocated

verrichten (fehr-*rikh*-tern) *v* perform

verrückt (fehr-*rewkt*) *adj* mad, crazy;
idiotic

Vers (fehrs) *m* (pl ~e) verse

versagen (fehr-*zaa*-gern) *v* fail; deny

versammeln (fehr-*zah*-merln) *v*
assemble; **sich ~** gather

Versammlung (fehr-*zahm*-loong) *f* (pl
~en) assembly, meeting; rally

Versand (fehr-*zahnt*) *m* shipment,
transport

verschicken (fehr-*shi*-kern) *v*
dispatch

*verschieben (fehr-*shee*-bern) *v*
adjourn, *put off

verschieden (fehr-*shee*-dern) *adj*
different, distinct; varied;
verschiedene various; **~ *sein** vary

*verschießen (fehr-*shee*-sern) *v* fade

*verschlafen (fehr-*shlaa*-fern) *v*
*oversleep

*verschließen (fehr-*shlee*-sern) *v* lock

*verschlingen (fehr-*shling*-ern) *v*
swallow

verschlissen (fehr-*shli*-sern) *adj*
threadbare

verschlucken (fehr-*shlook*-ern) *v*
swallow; **sich ~** choke (on)

Verschluss (fehr-*shlooss*) *m* (pl ~e)
fastener

Verschmutzung (fehr-*shmoo*-tsoong) f pollution

*****verschreiben** (fehr-*shrigh*-bern) v prescribe

verschreibungspflichtig adj (fehr-*shrigh*-boongs-pflikh-tikh) (available on) prescription only

verschütten (fehr-*shew*-tern) v *spill

verschwenden (fehr-*shvehn*-dern) v waste

verschwenderisch (fehr-*shvehn*-der-rish) adj wasteful, lavish

Verschwendung (fehr-*shvehn*-doong) f waste

*****verschwinden** (fehr-*shvin*-dern) v disappear, vanish

*****verschwören** (fehr-*shvūr*-rern) v: **sich ~** conspire

Verschwörung (fehr-*shvūr*-roong) f (pl ~en) plot

Versehen (fehr-*zay*-ern) nt (pl ~) oversight; mistake

*****versehen mit** (fehr-*zay*-ern) v furnish with

*****versenden** (fehr-*zehn*-dern) v despatch; ship

versetzen (fehr-*zeh*-tsern) v move; transfer

versichern (fehr-*zi*-kherrn) v assure; insure

Versicherung (fehr-*zi*-kher-roong) f (pl ~en) insurance

Versicherungspolice (fehr-*zi*-kher-roongs-poa-lee-ser) f (pl ~n) insurance policy

Versöhnung (fehr-*zūr*-noong) f (pl ~en) reconciliation

versorgen (fehr-*zor*-gern) v look after

verspätet (fehr-*shpai*-tert) adj late

Verspätung (fehr-*shpai*-toong) f delay

versperren (fehr-*shpeh*-rern) v block

verspotten (fehr-*shpo*-tern) v mock

Versprechen (fehr-*shpreh*-khern) nt (pl ~) promise

*****versprechen** (fehr-*shpreh*-khern) v promise

Verstand (fehr-*shtahnt*) m brain; wits pl, sense, intellect, reason

verständig (fehr-*shtehn*-dikh) adj sensible

Verständigung (fehr-*shtehn*-di-goong) f understanding

verstauchen (fehr-*shtou*-khern) v sprain

Verstauchung (fehr-*shtou*-khoong) f (pl ~en) sprain

verstecken (fehr-*shteh*-kern) v *hide

*****verstehen** (fehr-*shtay*-ern) v *understand; *take; conceive

Versteigerung (fehr-*shtigh*-ger-roong) f (pl ~en) auction

verstellen (fehr-*shteh*-lern) v: **sich ~** pretend

verstimmen (fehr-*shti*-mern) v displease

verstopft (fehr-*shtopft*) adj blocked; congested; constipated

Verstopfung (fehr-*shto*-pfoong) f constipation

verstorben (fehr-*shtor*-bern) adj dead

Verstoß (fehr-*shtōass*) m offence, offense Am

verstreuen (fehr-*shtroi*-ern) v scatter

Versuch (fehr-*zōōkh*) m (pl ~e) try, attempt; trial, experiment

versuchen (fehr-*zōō*-khern) v try, attempt; tempt

Versuchung (fehr-*zōō*-khoong) f (pl ~en) temptation

verteidigen (fehr-*tigh*-di-gern) v defend

Verteidigung (fehr-*tigh*-di-goong) f defence, defense Am

Verteidigungsrede (fehr-*tigh*-di-goongs-*ray*-der) f (pl ~n) plea

verteilen (fehr-*tigh*-lern) v divide; distribute

Vertrag (fehr-*traak*) m (pl ~e)

agreement; contract; treaty

Vertrauen (fehr-*trou*-ern) *nt*
confidence; trust, faith

vertrauen (fehr-*trou*-ern) *v* trust

vertraulich (fehr-*trou*-likh) *adj*
confidential; familiar

vertraut (fehr-*trout*) *adj* familiar

*vertreiben (fehr-*trigh*-bern) *v* chase

*vertreten (fehr-*trāy*-tern) *v* represent

Vertreter (fehr-*trāy*-terr) *m* (pl ~), **-in** *f*
representative, agent

Vertretung (fehr-*trāy*-toong) *f* (pl ~en)
representation; agency

verüben (fehr-*ēw*-bern) *v* commit

Verunreinigung (fehr-*oon*-righ-ni-
goong) *f* pollution

verursachen (fehr-*ōōr*-zah-khern) *v*
cause

verurteilen (fehr-*oor*-tigh-lern) *v*
sentence

Verurteilte (fehr-*oor*-tighl-ter) *m/f* (pl
~n) convict

verwalten (fehr-*vahl*-tern) *v* manage

Verwaltung (fehr-*vahl*-toong) *f* (pl
~en) administration; management,
direction; rule, government;
Verwaltungs- administrative

Verwaltungsrecht (fehr-*vahl*-toongs-
rehkht) *nt* administrative law

verwandeln (fehr-*vahn*-derln) *v*
transform; **sich ~ in** turn into

verwandt (fehr-*vahnt*) *adj* related

Verwandte (fehr-*vahn*-ter) *m/f* (pl ~n)
relative, relation

Verwandtschaft (fehr-*vahnt*-shahft) *f*
family

verwechseln (fehr-*veh*-kserln) *v*
*mistake

verweigern (fehr-*vigh*-gerrn) *v* deny,
refuse

Verweigerung (fehr-*vigh*-ger-roong) *f*
(pl ~en) refusal

verweilen (fehr-*vigh*-lern) *v* stay

Verweis (fehr-*vighss*) *m* (pl ~e)

reference

*verweisen auf (fehr-*vigh*-zern) refer
to

*verwenden (fehr-*vehn*-dern) *v*
employ; apply

*verwerfen (fehr-*vehr*-fern) *v* turn
down, reject

verwickelt (fehr-*vi*-kerlt) *adj*
complicated, complex

verwirklichen (fehr-*veerk*-li-khern) *v*
realize

verwirren (fehr-*vi*-rern) *v* confuse;
embarrass

Verwirrung (fehr-*vi*-roong) *f*
confusion; disturbance

verwöhnen (fehr-*vūr*-nern) *v* *spoil

verwunden (fehr-*voon*-dern) *v* wound

verwundern (fehr-*voon*-derrn) *v*
amaze

Verwunderung (fehr-*voon*-der-roong)
f wonder

Verwundung (fehr-*voon*-doong) *f* (pl
~en) injury

Verzeichnis (fehr-*tsighkh*-niss) *nt* (pl
~se) index

*verzeihen (fehr-*tsigh*-ern) *v* *forgive;
excuse

Verzeihung (fehr-*tsigh*-oong) *f*
pardon; **Verzeihung!** sorry!

verzögern (fehr-*tsūr*-gerrn) *v* delay;
slow down

Verzögerung (fehr-*tsūr*-ger-roong) *f*
(pl ~en) delay

verzollen (fehr-*tso*-lern) *v* declare

verzweifeln (fehr-*tsvigh*-ferln) *v*
despair

verzweifelt (fehr-*tsvigh*-ferlt) *adj*
desperate

Verzweiflung (fehr-*tsvigh*-floong) *f*
despair

Vetter (*feh*-terr) *m* (pl ~n) cousin

Viadukt (vi-ah-*dookt*) *m* (pl ~e)
viaduct

vibrieren (vi-*bree*-rern) *v* vibrate

Videokamera (*vi*-deh-o-kah-may-rah) *f* (pl ~s) video camera

Videokassette (*vi*-deh-o-kah-seht-ter) *f* (pl ~n) video cassette

Videorekorder (*vi*-deh-o-ray-kor-derr) *m* (pl ~) video recorder, VCR

Vieh (fee) *nt* cattle *pl*

viel (feel) *adj* much, many; *adv* much, far; **zu ~** too much

vielleicht (fi-*lighkht*) *adv* maybe, perhaps

vielmehr (feel-*māyr*) *adv* rather

vielseitig (*feel*-zigh-tikh) *adj* all-round

vier (feer) *num* four

vierte (*feer*-ter) *num* fourth

Viertel (*feer*-terl) *nt* (pl ~) quarter

Vierteljahr (feer-terl-*y*aar) *nt* quarter of a year

vierteljährlich (*feer*-terl-*y*air-likh) *adj* quarterly

Viertelstunde (feer-terl-*shtoon*-der) *f* (pl ~n) quarter of an hour

vierzehn (*feer*-tsāyn) *num* fourteen

vierzehnte (*feer*-tsāyn-ter) *num* fourteenth

vierzig (*feer*-tsikh) *num* forty

Vikar (vi-*kaar*) *m* (pl ~e) vicar

Villa (*vi*-lah) *f* (pl Villen) villa

violett (vi-oa-*leht*) *adj* violet

Visitenkarte (vi-*zee*-tern-kahr-ter) *f* (pl ~n) visiting-card

Visum (*vee*-zoom) *nt* (pl Visa) visa

Vitamin (vi-tah-*meen*) *nt* (pl ~e) vitamin

Vitrine (vi-*tree*-ner) *f* (pl ~n) showcase

Vizepräsident (*fee*-tser-preh-zi-dehnt) *m* (pl ~en), **-in** *f* vice president

Vogel (*fōa*-gerl) *m* (pl ~) bird

Vokabular (voa-kah-boo-*laar*) *nt* vocabulary

vokal (voa-*kaal*) *adj* vocal

Volk (folk) *nt* (pl ~er) people; nation, folk; **Volks-** national; popular; vulgar

Volksfest (*folks*-fehst) *nt* funfair, carnival

Volkslied (*folks*-leet) *nt* (pl ~er) folk song

Volksschullehrer (*folks*-shōol-*lāy*-rerr) *m* (pl ~), **-in** *f* schoolmaster, teacher

Volkstanz (*folks*-tahnts) *m* (pl ~e) folk-dance

Volkswirt (*folks*-veert) *m* (pl ~e) economist

voll (fol) *adj* full; crowded; **brechend ~** chock-full

vollbesetzt (*fol*-ber-zehtst) *adj* full up

vollenden (fol-*ehn*-dern) *v* accomplish; complete

völlig (*fur*-likh) *adj* utter; *adv* completely, absolutely, quite

vollkommen (fol-*ko*-mern) *adj* perfect; *adv* completely

Vollkommenheit (fol-*ko*-mern-hight) *f* perfection

Vollkornbrot (*fol*-korn-brōat) *nt* wholemeal bread

Vollpension (*fol*-pahng-s*y*ōan) *f* full board, board and lodging, bed and board

vollständig (*fol*-shtehn-dikh) *adj* complete, whole

***vollziehen** (fol-*tsee*-ern) *v* execute

Volt (volt) *nt* volt

Volumen (voa-*lōo*-mern) *nt* (pl ~) volume

von (fon) *prep* of; from, off; by; with; **~ ... an** from, as from

vor (fōar) *prep* before; ahead of, in front of; to; **~ allem** essentially

***vorangehen** (foa-*rahn*-gāy-ern) *v* precede

Voranschlag (*fōar*-ahn-shlaak) *m* (pl ~e) estimate; budget

voraus (foa-*rouss*) *adv* forward; **im ~** in advance

vorausbezahlt (foa-*rouss*-ber-tsaalt) *adj* prepaid

voraussagen (foa-*rouss*-zaa-gern) *v* forecast

voraussetzen (foa-*rouss*-zeh-tsern) *v* assume; **vorausgesetzt dass** provided that

voraussichtlich (foa-*rouss*-zikht-likh) *adv* probably

Vorbehalt (*fōar*-ber-hahlt) *m* (pl ∼e) qualification

vorbei (foar-*bigh*) *adv* over; **an ... ∼** past

*vorbeifahren (foar-*bigh*-faa-rern) *v* pass *Am*

*vorbeigehen (foar-*bigh*-gāy-ern) *v* pass by

vorbereiten (*fōar*-ber-righ-tern) *v* prepare; arrange

Vorbereitung (*fōar*-ber-righ-toong) *f* (pl ∼en) preparation

vorbestellen (*fōar*-ber-shteh-lern) *v* reserve

vorbeugend (*fōar*-boi-gernt) *adj* preventive

Vorbildung (*fōar*-bil-doong) *f* background

*vorbringen (*fōar*-bring-ern) *v* *bring up

Vordergrund (for-derr-groont) *m* foreground

Vorderseite (for-derr-zigh-ter) *f* front

Vorfahr (*fōar*-faar) *m* (pl ∼en), **-in** *f* ancestor

Vorfahrt (*fōar*-faart) *f* right of way, priority

Vorfahrtsrecht (*fōar*-faarts-rehkht) *nt* right of way

Vorfall (*fōar*-fahl) *m* (pl ∼e) event

vorführen (*fōar*-fēw-rern) *v* exhibit

Vorgang (*fōar*-gahng) *m* (pl ∼e) process

Vorgänger (*fōar*-gehng-err) *m* (pl ∼), **-in** *f* predecessor

*vorgeben (*fōar*-gāy-bern) *v* pretend

Vorgehen (*fōar*-gāy-ern) *nt* policy

*vorgehen (*fōar*-gāy-ern) *v* act

vorgestern (*fōar*-gehss-terrn) *adv* the day before yesterday

vorhanden (fōar-*hahn*-dern) *adj* available

Vorhang (*fōar*-hahng) *m* (pl ∼e) curtain

Vorhängeschloss (*fōar*-hehng-er-shloss) *nt* (pl -schlösser) padlock

vorher (*fōar*-hāyr) *adv* in advance, before

vorhergehend (fōar-*hāyr*-gāy-ernt) *adj* previous, preceding, last

Vorhersage (fōar-*hāyr*-zaa-ger) *f* (pl ∼n) forecast

vorhersagen (fōar-*hāyr*-zaa-gern) *v* predict

*vorhersehen (fōar-*hāyr*-zāy-ern) *v* anticipate

vorig (*fōa*-rikh) *adj* previous, past

*vorkommen (*fōar*-ko-mern) *v* occur

vorläufig (*fōar*-loi-fikh) *adj* provisional, temporary; preliminary

Vorleger (*fōar*-lāy-gerr) *m* (pl ∼) rug

*vorlesen (*fōar*-lāy-zern) *v* *read (aloud); *read out to

Vorlesung (*fōar*-lāy-zoong) *f* (pl ∼en) lecture

Vormittag (*fōar*-mi-taak) *m* (pl ∼e) morning

Vorname (*fōar*-naa-mer) *m* (pl ∼n) first name, Christian name

vornehm (*fōar*-nāym) *adj* distinguished

Vorort (*fōar*-ort) *m* (pl ∼e) suburb

Vorrang (*fōar*-rahng) *m* priority

Vorrat (*fōar*-raat) *m* (pl ∼e) stock, store; provisions *pl*, supply

vorrätig (*fōar*-rai-tikh) *adj* available; ∼ ***haben** stock

Vorrecht (*fōar*-rehkht) *nt* (pl ∼e) privilege

Vorrichtung (*fōar*-rikh-toong) *f* (pl ∼en) appliance, apparatus

*vorschießen (*fōar*-shee-sern) *v* advance

Vorschlag (*fōar*-shlaak) *m* (pl ⁓e) proposition, proposal, suggestion

*vorschlagen (*fōar*-shlaa-gern) *v* suggest, propose

Vorschrift (*fōar*-shrift) *f* (pl ⁓en) regulation

Vorschuss (*fōar*-shooss) *m* (pl ⁓e) advance

*vorsehen (*fōar*-zāy-ern) *v*: **sich ⁓** look out

Vorsicht (*fōar*-zikht) *f* caution; precaution; **⁓!** look out! careful!

vorsichtig (*fōar*-zikh-tikh) *adj* careful; cautious

Vorsichtsmaßnahme (*fōar*-zikhts-maass-naa-mer) *f* (pl ⁓n) precaution

Vorsitzende (*fōar*-zi-tsern-der) *m/f* (pl ⁓n) chairman, chairwoman; president

Vorspeise (*fōar*-shpigh-zer) *f* (pl ⁓n) hors d'œuvre

Vorsprung (*fōar*-shproong) *m* lead

Vorstadt (*fōar*-shtaht) *f* (pl ⁓e) suburb

vorstädtisch (*fōar*-shteh-tish) *adj* suburban

Vorstand (*fōar*-shtahnt) *m* (pl ⁓e) direction

vorstellen (*fōar*-shteh-lern) *v* present, introduce; represent; **sich ⁓** fancy, imagine; conceive

Vorstellung (*fōar*-shteh-loong) *f* introduction; conception, idea; show

Vorteil (*foar*-tighl) *m* (pl ⁓e) advantage; profit, benefit

vorteilhaft (*foar*-tighl-hahft) *adj* advantageous; cheap

Vortrag (*fōar*-traak) *m* (pl ⁓e) lecture

Vorurteil (*fōar*-oor-tighl) *nt* (pl ⁓e) prejudice

Vorverkauf (*fōar*-fehr-kouf) *m* advance sale of tickets; advance booking

Vorverkaufskasse (*fōar*-fehr-koufs-kah-ser) *f* (pl ⁓n) box-office

Vorwand (*fōar*-vahnt) *m* (pl ⁓e) pretext, pretence

vorwärts (*fōar*-vehrts) *adv* ahead, forward, onwards; **⁓ *kommen** (*fōar*-vehrts-ko-mern) *v* *get on, get ahead

*vorwerfen (*fōar*-vehr-fern) *v* reproach; blame

Vorwurf (*fōar*-voorf) *m* (pl ⁓e) reproach; blame

vorzeitig (*fōar*-tsigh-tikh) *adj* premature

*vorziehen (*fōar*-tsee-ern) *v* prefer

Vorzug (*fōar*-tsōōk) *m* (pl ⁓e) preference

vorzüglich (fōar-*tsēwk*-likh) *adj* first-rate

Vulkan (vool-*kaan*) *m* (pl ⁓e) volcano

W

Waage (*vaa*-ger) *f* (pl ⁓n) scales *pl*, weighing machine

waagerecht (*vaa*-ger-rehkht) *adj* horizontal

wach (vahkh) *adj* awake; **⁓ *werden** wake up

Wache (*vah*-kher) *f* (pl ⁓n) guard

Wachs (vahks) *nt* wax

wachsam (*vahkh*-zaam) *adj* vigilant

*wachsen (*vah*-ksern) *v* *grow

Wachsfigurenkabinett (*vahks*-fi-gōō-rern-kah-bi-neht) *nt* (pl ⁓e) waxworks *pl*

Wachtel (*vahkh*-terl) *f* (pl ⁓n) quail

Wächter (*vehkh*-terr) *m* (pl ∿), **-in** *f* warden

wackeln (*vah-kerln*) *v* *shake, wobble; *be loose

wacklig (*vahk*-likh) *adj* unsteady, shaky, ramshackle

Wade (*vaa*-der) *f* (pl ∿n) calf

Waffe (*vah*-fer) *f* (pl ∿n) weapon, arm

Waffel (*vah*-ferl) *f* (pl ∿n) waffle, wafer

Wagen (*vaa*-gern) *m* (pl ∿) car; carriage, coach; cart; passenger car *Am*

wagen (*vaa*-gern) *v* dare; risk, venture

Wagenheber (*vaa*-gern-hāy-berr) *m* (pl ∿) jack

Waggon (vah-*gawng*) *m* (pl ∿s) wag(g)on

Wahl (vaal) *f* (pl ∿en) choice; pick, selection; election

wählen (*vai*-lern) *v* pick, *choose; elect

wählerisch (*vai*-ler-rish) *adj* particular

Wahlkreis (*vaal*-krighss) *m* (pl ∿e) constituency

Wahlrecht (*vaal*-rehkht) *nt* franchise; suffrage

Wahlspruch (*vaal*-shprookh) *m* (pl ∿e) slogan

Wahnsinn (*vaan*-zin) *m* madness

wahnsinnig (*vaan*-zi-nikh) *adj* crazy, insane

wahr (vaar) *adj* true; very

während (*vai*-rernt) *prep* for, during; *conj* while

wahrhaft (*vaar*-hahft) *adj* truthful

Wahrheit (*vaar*-hight) *f* (pl ∿en) truth

wahrnehmbar (*vaar*-nāym-baar) *adj* noticeable, perceptible

*wahrnehmen (*vaar*-nāy-mern) *v* perceive; note

wahrscheinlich (vaar-*shighn*-likh) *adj* likely, probable; *adv* probably

Währung (*vai*-roong) *f* (pl ∿en) currency; **fremde** ∿ foreign currency

Währungseinheit (*vai*-roongs-ighn-hight) *f* (pl ∿en) monetary unit

Waise (*vigh*-zer) *m/f* (pl ∿n) orphan

Wal (vaal) *m* (pl ∿e) whale

Wald (vahlt) *m* (pl ∿er) forest, wood

Walnuss (*vahl*-nooss) *f* (pl ∿e) walnut

Walzer (*vahl*-tserr) *m* (pl ∿) waltz

Wand (vahnt) *f* (pl ∿e) wall

wandern (*vahn*-derrn) *v* tramp, hike

Wandschrank (*vahnt*-shrahngk) *m* (pl ∿e) closet

Wandtafel (*vahnt*-taa-ferl) *f* (pl ∿n) blackboard

Wandteppich (*vahnt*-teh-pikh) *m* (pl ∿e) tapestry

Wange (*vahng*-er) *f* (pl ∿n) cheek

wanken (*vahng*-kern) *v* falter

wann (vahn) *adv* when; ∿ **immer** whenever

Wanne (*vahn*-er) *f* tub; bath(tub)

Wanze (*vahn*-tser) *f* (pl ∿n) bug

Ware (*vaa*-rer) *f* (pl ∿n) merchandise; **Waren** wares *pl*, goods *pl*

Warenhaus (*vaa*-rern-houss) *nt* (pl ∿er) drugstore *Am*

warm (vahrm) *adj* hot, warm

Wärme (*vehr*-mer) *f* warmth; heat

wärmen (*vehr*-mern) *v* warm

Wärmflasche (*vehrm*-flah-sher) *f* (pl ∿n) hot-water bottle

Warnblinkanlage (*vahrn*-blingk-ahn-laa-ger) *f* hazard warning lights *pl*

warnen (*vahr*-nern) *v* warn; caution

Warnung (*vahr*-noong) *f* (pl ∿en) warning

Warteliste (*vahr*-ter-liss-ter) *f* (pl ∿n) waiting list

warten (*vahr*-tern) *v* wait; ∿ **auf** await

Wärter (*vehr*-terr) *m* (pl ∿), **-in** *f* attendant

Wartesaal (*vahr*-ter-zaal) *m*, **Wartezimmer** (*vahr*-ter-tsi-merr) *nt* (pl ∿) waiting room

warum (vah-*room*) *adv* why

was (vahss) *pron* what; some; ~ ...
betrifft as regards; ~ **auch immer**
whatever

Waschanlage (*vahsh*-ahn-laa-ger) *f*
car wash; windscreen (*Am*
windshield) washer

waschbar (*vahsh*-baar) *adj* washable

Waschbecken (*vahsh*-beh-kern) *nt*
(pl ~) washbasin

Wäsche (*veh*-sher) *f* washing, laundry;
linen

Waschen (*vah*-shern) *nt* washing

*waschen (*vah*-shern) *v* wash

Wäscherei (veh-sher-*righ*) *f* (pl ~en)
laundry

Waschmaschine (*vahsh*-mah-shee-
ner) *f* (pl ~n) washing machine

Waschpulver (*vahsh*-pool-ferr) *nt* (pl
~) washing powder

Wasser (*vah*-serr) *nt* water;
fließendes ~ running water

wasserdicht (*vah*-serr-dikht) *adj*
waterproof, rainproof

Wasserfall (*vah*-serr-fahl) *m* (pl ~e)
waterfall

Wasserfarbe (*vah*-serr-fahr-ber) *f* (pl
~n) watercolo(u)r

Wasserhahn (*vah*-serr-haan) *m* (pl
~e) faucet *Am*

Wassermelone (*vah*-serr-may-*loa*-
ner) *f* (pl ~n) water-melon

Wasserpumpe (*vah*-serr-poom-per) *f*
(pl ~n) water pump

Wasserschi (*vah*-serr-shee) *m* (pl ~er)
water ski

Wasserstoff (*vah*-serr-shtof) *m*
hydrogen

Wasserstoffperoxid (vah-serr-shtof-
pehr-o-ksēwt) *nt* peroxide

Wasserstraße (*vah*-serr-shtraa-ser) *f*
(pl ~n) waterway

Wasserwaage (*vah*-serr-vaa-ger) *f* (pl
~n) level

waten (*vaa*-tern) *v* wade

Watt (vaht) *nt* tech watt

Watte (*vah*-ter) *f* cotton wool

*weben (*vāy*-bern) *v* *weave

Weber (*vāy*-berr) *m* (pl ~), **-in** *f*
weaver

Wechsel (*vehk*-serl) *m* (pl ~)
transition, change; exchange

Wechselgeld (*veh*-kserl-gehlt) *nt*
change

Wechselkurs (*veh*-kserl-koors) *m* (pl
~e) exchange rate

wechseln (*veh*-kserln) *v* change,
exchange; switch; vary

wechselseitig (*veh*-kserl-zigh-tikh)
adj mutual

Wechselstrom (*veh*-kserl-shtrōam) *m*
alternating current

Wechselstube (*veh*-kserl-shtōō-ber) *f*
(pl ~n) money exchange, exchange
office

wecken (*veh*-kern) *v* *wake, *awake

Wecker (*veh*-kerr) *m* (pl ~) alarm
clock

weder ... noch (*vāy*-derr ... *nokh*)
conj neither ... nor

Weg (vāyk) *m* (pl ~e) way; drive

weg (vehk) *adv* away; lost; off

wegen (*vāy*-gern) *prep* because of; for,
on account of

*wegfahren (*vehk*-faa-rern) *v* *drive
away

*weggehen (*vehk*-gāy-ern) *v* depart,
*leave; *go away

weglegen (*vehk*-lāy-gern) *v* *put away

*wegnehmen (*vehk*-nāy-mern) *v*
*take away

Wegrand (*vāyk*-rahnt) *m* (pl ~er)
wayside

Wegweiser (*vāyk*-vigh-zerr) *m* (pl ~)
milepost, signpost

wegwerfbar (*vehk*-vehrf-baar) *adj*
disposable

*wegwerfen (*vehk*-vehr-fern) *v*

*throw away

Wehen (*vāy*-ern) *fpl* labo(u)r

wehen (*vāy*-ern) *v* *blow

wehren (*vāy*-rern) *v*: **sich ~** defend o.s., *stand up for o.s.

*wehtun (vāy tōōn) *hurt

weiblich (*vighp*-likh) *adj* female; feminine

weich (vighkh) *adj* soft

weichen (*vigh*-khern) *v* yield

Weide (*vigh*-der) *f* (pl ~n) pasture

weiden (*vāy*-dern) *v* graze

Weihnachten (*vigh*-nahkh-tern) Xmas, Christmas

Weihrauch (*vigh*-roukh) *m* incense

weil (vighl) *conj* because; as

Weile (*vigh*-ler) *f* while

Wein (vighn) *m* (pl ~e) wine

Weinberg (*vighn*-behrk) *m* (pl ~e) vineyard

weinen (*vigh*-nern) *v* *weep, cry

Weinhändler (*vighn*-hehn-dlerr) *m* (pl ~), **-in** *f* wine merchant

Weinkarte (*vighn*-kahr-ter) *f* (pl ~n) wine list

Weinkeller (*vighn*-keh-lerr) *m* (pl ~) wine cellar

Weinlese (*vighn*-lāy-zer) *f* vintage

Weinrebe (*vighn*-rāy-ber) *f* (pl ~n) vine

Weise (*vigh*-zer) *f* (pl ~n) way, fashion, manner

weise (*vigh*-zer) *adj* wise

*weisen (*vigh*-zern) *v* direct

Weisheit (*vighss*-hight) *f* (pl ~en) wisdom

weiß (vighss) *adj* white

Weißfisch (*vighss*-fish) *m* (pl ~e) whiting

weit (vight) *adj* broad; wide, vast; **bei weitem** by far

weiter (*vigh*-terr) *adj* further; **und so ~** and so on

*weitergehen (*vigh*-terr-gāy-ern) *v*

*go on

Weizen (*vigh*-tsern) *m* wheat

welche (*vehl*-kher) *pron* what, which; who, which, that

welcher (*vehl*-kherr) *pron* who; which; **~ auch immer** whichever

Welle (*veh*-ler) *f* (pl ~n) wave

Wellenlänge (*veh*-lern-lehng-er) *f* (pl ~n) wavelength

wellig (*veh*-likh) *adj* wavy

Welt (vehlt) *f* world

Weltall (*vehlt*-ahl) *nt* universe

weltberühmt (*vehlt*-ber-rēwmt) *adj* world-famous

Weltkrieg (*vehlt*-kreek) *m* (pl ~e) world war

weltumfassend (*vehlt*-oom-fah-sernt) *adj* global

weltweit (*vehlt*-vight) *adj* world-wide

wem (vāym) *pron* whom

wen (vāyn) *pron* who(m), *colloquial* somebody

*wenden (*vehn*-dern) *v* turn

Wendepunkt (*vehn*-der-poongkt) *m* (pl ~e) turning point

Wendung (*vehn*-doong) *f* (pl ~en) turn

wenig (*vāy*-nikh) *adj* little; few; **zu ~** not enough

weniger (*vāy*-ni-gerr) *adj* minus; *adv* less

wenigstens (*vāy*-nikhs-terns) *adv* at least

wenn (vehn) *conj* if; when; **~ auch** though

wer (vāyr) *pron* who; **~ auch immer** whoever

Werbesendung (*vehr*-ber-zehn-doong) *f* (pl ~en) commercial

Werbung (*vehr*-boong) *f* (pl ~en) advertising

*werden (*vāyr*-dern) *v* *will, *shall; *become; *go, *get, *grow

*werfen (*vehr*-fern) *v* *throw; toss,

*cast

Werk (vehrk) nt (pl ~e) deed; work; works pl

Werkmeister (*vehrk*-mighss-terr) m (pl ~) foreman

Werkstatt (*vehrk*-shtaht) f (pl ~en) workshop

Werktag (*vehrk*-taak) m (pl ~e) working day

Werkzeug (*vehrk*-tsoik) nt (pl ~e) tool; utensil, implement

Werkzeugtasche (*vehrk*-tsoik-tah-sher) f (pl ~n) tool kit

Wert (vāyrt) m (pl ~e) worth, value

wert (vāyrt) adj dear; ~ ***sein** *be worth

wertlos (*vāyrt*-lōass) adj worthless

Wertsachen (*vāyrt*-zah-khern) fpl valuables pl

wertvoll (*vāyrt*-fol) adj valuable

Wesen (*vāy*-zern) nt (pl ~) being; essence

Wesensart (*vāy*-zerns-aart) f nature

wesentlich (*vāy*-zernt-likh) adj essential; vital

weshalb (vehss-hahlp) adv why

Wespe (*vehss*-per) f (pl ~n) wasp

Weste (*vehss*-ter) f (pl ~n) waistcoat, vest Am

Westen (*vehss*-tern) m west

westlich (*vehst*-likh) adj westerly; western

Wettbewerb (*veht*-ber-vehrp) m (pl ~e) competition, contest

Wette (*veh*-ter) f (pl ~n) bet

wetteifern (*veht*-igh-ferrn) v compete

wetten (*veh*-tern) v *bet

Wetter (*veh*-terr) nt weather

Wetterbericht (*veh*-terr-ber-rikht) m (pl ~e) weather forecast

Wettlauf (*veht*-louf) m (pl ~e) race

wichtig (*vikh*-tikh) adj important; **wichtigste** principal, main

Wichtigkeit (*vikh*-tikh-kight) f importance

Wichtigtuerei (vikh-tikh-tōō-er-*righ*) f fuss

wickeln (*vi*-kerln) v change the baby('s nappy, Am diaper); *wind; wrap up

Widerhall (*vee*-derr-hahl) m echo

widerlich (*vee*-derr-likh) adj disgusting

*widerrufen (vee-derr-*rōō*-fern) v recall; cancel

widersetzen (vee-derr-*zeh*-tsern) v: **sich ~** oppose

widersinnig (*vee*-derr-zi-nikh) adj absurd

widerspiegeln (*vee*-derr-shpee-gerln) v reflect

*widersprechen (vee-derr-*shpreh*-khern) v contradict; **widersprechend** contradictory

Widerspruch (*vee*-derr-shprookh) m (pl ~e) objection

Widerstand (*vee*-derr-shtahnt) m resistance

widerwärtig (*vee*-derr-vehr-tikh) adj revolting, repulsive, repellent

Widerwille (*vee*-derr-vi-ler) m aversion, dislike

widmen (*vit*-mern) v dedicate; devote

widrig (*vee*-drikh) adj nasty

wie (vee) adv how; conj like, like, such as; as; ~ **auch immer** any way; ~ **viel** how much; ~ **viele** how many

wieder (*vee*-derr) adv again; **hin und ~** now and then

*wieder aufnehmen (vee-derr-*ouf*-nāy-mern) v resume

wiedererlangen (*vee*-derr-ehr-lahng-ern) v recover

wiedererstatten (*vee*-derr-ehr-shtah-tern) v reimburse

Wiederherstellung (vee-derr-*hāyr*-shteh-loong) f reparation; revival

wiederholen (vee-derr-*hōa*-lern) v

repeat

Wiederholung (vee-derr-*hoa*-loong) f (pl ~en) repetition

Wiedersehen (vee-derr-*zay*-ern) nt reunion; **auf ~!** goodbye!, colloquial bye!

wiedervereinigen (vee-derr-fehr-igh-ni-gern) v reunite

Wiederverkäufer (vee-derr-fehr-koi-ferr) m (pl ~), **-in** f retailer

wieder verwerten (vee-derr-fehr-verr-tern) v recycle

Wiege (vee-ger) f (pl ~n) cradle

*wiegen** (vee-gern) v weigh

Wiese (vee-zer) f (pl ~n) meadow

wie viel (vi-feel) adv how much; how many

Wild (vilt) nt game

wild (vilt) adj wild; savage, fierce

wildern (vil-derrn) v poach

Wildleder (vilt-lay-derr) nt suede

Wildpark (vilt-pahrk) m (pl ~s) game reserve

Wille (vi-ler) m will

willig (vi-likh) adj willing, co-operative

Willkommen (vil-ko-mern) nt welcome

willkommen (vil-ko-mern) adj welcome

willkürlich (vil-kewr-likh) adj arbitrary

Wimperntusche (vim-perrn-too-sher) f (pl ~n) mascara

Wind (vint) m (pl ~e) wind

Windel (vin-derl) f (pl ~n) nappy, diaper Am

*winden** (vin-dern) v *wind; twist

Windhund (vint-hoont) m (pl ~e) greyhound

windig (vin-dikh) adj windy, gusty

Windmühle (vint-mew-ler) f (pl ~n) windmill

Windpocken (vint-po-kern) fpl chickenpox

Windschutzscheibe (vint-shoots-shigh-ber) f (pl ~n) windscreen; windshield Am

Windstoß (vint-shtoass) m (pl ~e) gust, blow

Wink (vingk) m (pl ~e) sign

Winkel (ving-kerl) m (pl ~) angle

winken (ving-kern) v wave

Winter (vin-terr) m (pl ~) winter

Wintersport (vin-terr-shport) m winter sports

winzig (vin-tsikh) adj tiny, minute

Wippe (vi-per) f (pl ~n) seesaw

wir (veer) pron we

wirbeln (veer-berln) v *spin

Wirbelsturm (veer-berl-shtoorm) m (pl ~e) hurricane

wirken (veer-kern) v operate

wirklich (veerk-likh) adj actual, real; true, substantial, very; adv indeed, really

Wirklichkeit (veerk-likh-kight) f reality

wirksam (veerk-zaam) adj effective

Wirkung (veer-koong) f (pl ~en) effect; consequence

wirkungsvoll (veer-koongs-fol) adj effective

Wirrwarr (veer-vahr) m muddle

Wirt (veert) m (pl ~e) landlord

Wirtin (veer-tin) f (pl ~nen) landlady

Wirtschaft (veert-shahft) f economy

wirtschaftlich (veert-shahft-likh) adj economic

Wirtshaus (veerts-houss) nt (pl ~er) public house; pub

*wissen** (vi-sern) v *know

Wissenschaft (vi-sern-shahft) f (pl ~en) science

Wissenschaftler (vi-sern-shahft-lerr) m (pl ~), **-in** f scientist

wissenschaftlich (vi-sern-shahft-likh) adj scientific

Witwe (*vit*-ver) *f* (pl ~n) widow

Witwer (*vit*-verr) *m* (pl ~) widower

Witz (vits) *m* (pl ~e) joke

witzig (*vi*-tsikh) *adj* humorous

wo (vōa) *adv* where; *conj* where; ~ **auch immer** anywhere; ~ **immer** wherever

Woche (*vo*-kher) *f* (pl ~n) week

Wochenende (*vo*-khern-ehn-der) *nt* (pl ~n) weekend

Wochenschau (*vo*-khern-shou) *f* (pl ~en) newsreel

Wochentag (*vo*-khern-taak) *m* (pl ~e) weekday

wöchentlich (*vur*-khernt-likh) *adj* weekly

wohl (vōal) *adj* well

Wohl (vōal) *nt* well-being, welfare; **zum** ~ cheers!, your health!

Wohlbefinden (*vōal*-ber-fin-dern) *nt* welfare; ease

wohl begründet (*vōal*-ber-grewn-dert) *adj* well-founded

wohlfühlen (*vōal*- few-lern) *v*: **sich** ~ *feel well, *feel good

wohlhabend (*vōal*-haa-bernt) *adj* prosperous; well-to-do

wohlschmeckend (*vōal*-shmeh-kernt) *adj* tasty

Wohlstand (*vōal*-shtahnt) *m* prosperity

Wohltätigkeit (*vōal*-tai-tikh-kight) *f* charity

Wohlwollen (*vōal*-vo-lern) *nt* goodwill

Wohnblock (*vōan*-blok) *m* (pl ~e) block of flats

Wohnboot (*vōan*-bōat) *nt* (pl ~e) houseboat

wohnen (*vōa*-nern) *v* live, reside

Wohngebäude (*vōan*-ger-boi-der) *nt* (pl ~) apartment house *Am*

wohnhaft (*vōan*-hahft) *adj* resident

Wohnmobil (*vōan*-moa-beel) *nt* camper (van); mobile home, *Am*

motorhome

Wohnsitz (*vōan*-zits) *m* (pl ~e) domicile, residence

Wohnung (*vōa*-noong) *f* (pl ~en) house; flat; apartment *Am*

Wohnwagen (*vōan*-vaa-gern) *m* (pl ~) trailer *Am*, caravan

Wohnzimmer (*vōan*-tsi-merr) *nt* (pl ~) living room, sitting room

Wolf (volf) *m* (pl ~e) wolf

Wolke (*vol*-ker) *f* (pl ~n) cloud

Wolkenbruch (*vol*-kern-brookh) *m* (pl ~e) cloud-burst

Wolkenkratzer (*vol*-kern-krah-tserr) *m* (pl ~) skyscraper

wolkig (*vol*-kikh) *adj* cloudy

Wolle (*vo*-ler) *f* wool

wollen (*vo*-lern) *adj* wool(l)en

***wollen** (*vo*-lern) *v* want, *will

Wolljacke (*vol*-ʸah-ker) *f* (pl ~n) cardigan

Wollpullover (*vol*-poo-lōa-verr) *m* (pl ~) jersey

Wort (vort) *nt* (pl ~er) word

Wörterbuch (*vurr*-terr-bōokh) *nt* (pl ~er) dictionary

Wortschatz (*vort*-shahts) *m* vocabulary

Wortwechsel (*vort*-veh-kserl) *m* (pl ~) argument

wovon (vōa-fon) *adv* about what?; what from, what of?; of, from, about which

wozu (vōa-tsōō) *adv* what for

Wrack (vrahk) *nt* (pl ~s) wreck

Wuchs (vōoks) *m* growth

wund (voont) *adj* sore

Wunde (*voon*-der) *f* (pl ~n) wound

Wunder (*voon*-derr) *nt* (pl ~) miracle; wonder, marvel

wunderbar (*voon*-derr-baar) *adj* marvel(l)ous; lovely, wonderful; swell; miraculous

wundern (*voon*-derrn) *v*: **sich** ~

marvel, *be surprised at

Wunsch (voonsh) *m* (pl ⁓e) wish; desire

wünschen (*vewn*-shern) *v* wish; want, desire

wünschenswert (*vewn*-sherns-*vay*rt) *adj* desirable

würdevoll (*vewr*-der-fol) *adj* dignified

würdig (*vewr*-dikh) *adj* worthy of

Wurf (voorf) *m* (pl ⁓e) throw; cast; litter

Würfel (*vewr*-ferl) *m* (pl ⁓) cube

würfeln (*vewr*-ferln) *v* *throw dice

Würfelzucker (*vewr*-ferl-tsoo-kerr) *m* lump sugar

Wurm (voorm) *m* (pl ⁓er) worm

Wurst (voorst) *f* (pl ⁓e) sausage

Würstchen (*vewrsst*-khern) *nt* small sausage; frankfurter; wiener; hot dog

Wurzel (*voor*-tserl) *f* (pl ⁓n) root

würzen (*vewr*-tsern) *v* flavo(u)r

wüst (vewst) *adj* desert; wild, fierce

Wüste (*vewss*-ter) *f* (pl ⁓n) desert

Wut (voot) *f* anger, rage, temper; passion

wüten (*vew*-tern) *v* rage

wütend (*vew*-ternt) *adj* furious, mad

Z

zäh (tsai) *adj* tough

Zahl (tsaal) *f* (pl ⁓en) number; figure

zahlen (*tsaa*-lern) *v* *pay

zählen (*tsai*-lern) *v* count

Zähler (*tsai*-lerr) *m* (pl ⁓) meter

zahlreich (*tsaal*-righkh) *adj* numerous

Zahlungsempfänger (*tsaa*-loongs-ehm-pfehng-err) *m* (pl ⁓), **-in** *f* payee

zahlungsunfähig (*tsaa*-loongs-oon-fai-ikh) *adj* bankrupt

Zahlwort (*tsaal*-vort) *nt* (pl ⁓er) numeral

zahm (tsaam) *adj* tame

zähmen (*tsai*-mern) *v* tame

Zahn (tsaan) *m* (pl ⁓e) tooth

Zahnarzt (*tsaan*-ahrtst) *m* (pl ⁓e) dentist

Zahnärztin (*tsaan*-ehrtstin) *f* (pl ⁓nen) dentist

Zahnbürste (*tsaan*-bewrs-ter) *f* (pl ⁓n) toothbrush

Zahnfleisch (*tsaan*-flighsh) *nt* gum

Zahnpasta (*tsaan*-pahss-taar) *f* (pl ⁓en) toothpaste

Zahnschmerzen (*tsaan*- shmehr-tsern) *ntpl* toothache *sg*

Zahnstocher (*tsaan*-shto-kherr) *m* (pl ⁓) toothpick

Zange (*tsahng*-er) *f* (pl ⁓n) pliers *pl*; tongs *pl*

Zank (tsahngk) *m* quarrel, dispute

zanken (*tsahng*-kern) *v* quarrel

Zäpfchen (*tsehpf*-khern) *nt* (pl ⁓) suppository

Zapfen (*tsahp*-fern) *m* peg; cone; icicle

zapfen (*tsahp*-fern) *v* tap, draw

zart (tsaart) *adj* gentle, delicate, tender

zärtlich (*tsairt*-likh) *adj* tender; affectionate

Zauber (*tsou*-berr) *m* spell; **Zauber-** magic

Zauberei (tsou-ber-*righ*) *f* magic

Zauberer (*tsou*-ber-rerr) *m* (pl ⁓) magician

zauberhaft (*tsou*-berr-hahft) *adj* enchanting

Zaun (tsoun) *m* (pl ⁓e) fence

Zebra (*tsay*-brah) *nt* (pl ~s) zebra

Zebrastreifen (*tsay*-brah-shtrigh-fern) *m* (pl ~) crosswalk *Am*

Zehe (*tsay*-er) *f* (pl ~n) toe

zehn (tsayn) *num* ten

zehnte (*tsayn*-ter) *num* tenth

Zeichen (*tsigh*-khern) *nt* (pl ~) sign; signal; mark; token

Zeichentrickfilm (*tsigh*-khern-trik-film) *m* (pl ~e) cartoon

zeichnen (*tsighkh*-nern) *v* *draw, sketch; mark

Zeichnung (*tsighkh*-noong) *f* (pl ~en) drawing, sketch

Zeigefinger (*tsigh*-ger-fing-err) *m* (pl ~) index finger

zeigen (*tsigh*-gern) *v* *show; display; point, point out, indicate; prove; **sich ~** appear

Zeile (*tsigh*-ler) *f* (pl ~n) line

Zeit (tsight) *f* (pl ~en) time; **in letzter ~** lately

Zeitabschnitt (*tsight*-ahp-shnit) *m* (pl ~e) period

Zeitgenosse (*tsight*-ger-no-ser) *m* (pl ~n) contemporary

zeitgenössisch (*tsight*-ger-nur-sish) *adj* contemporary

Zeitraum (*tsight*-roum) *m* (pl ~e) period

Zeitschrift (*tsight*-shrift) *f* (pl ~en) periodical; magazine, journal, review

zeitsparend (*tsight*-shpaa-rernt) *adj* time-saving

Zeitung (*tsigh*-toong) *f* (pl ~en) newspaper, paper

Zeitungshändler (*tsigh*-toongs-hehn-dlerr) *m* (pl ~) newsagent

Zeitungsstand (*tsigh*-toongs-shtahnt) *m* (pl ~e) newsstand

Zeitunterschied (*tsight*-oon-terr-sheet) *m* time difference

zeitweilig (*tsight*-vigh-likh) *adj* temporary

Zeitwort (*tsight*-vort) *nt* (pl ~er) verb

Zelle (*tseh*-ler) *f* (pl ~n) cell; booth

Zelt (tsehlt) *nt* (pl ~e) tent

zelten (*tsehl*-tern) *v* camp

Zeltplatz (*tsehlt*-plahts) *m* (pl ~e) camping site

Zement (tsay-*mehnt*) *m* cement

Zenit (tsay-*neet*) *m* zenith

Zensur (tsehn-*zoor*) *f* (pl ~en) mark; censorship

Zentimeter (tsehn-ti-*may*-terr) *m* (pl ~) centimetre, centimeter *Am*

zentral (tsehn-*traal*) *adj* central

Zentralheizung (tsehn-*traal*-high-tsoong) *f* (pl ~en) central heating

Zentrum (*tsehn*-troom) *nt* (pl -tren) centre, center *Am*

*zerbrechen (tsehr-*brehkh*-ern) *adj* *break

zerbrechlich (tsehr-*brehkh*-likh) *adj* fragile

zerfasern (tsehr-*faa*-zerrn) *v* fray

zerhacken (tsehr-*hah*-kern) *v* mince

zerknittern (tsehr-*kni*-terrn) *v* crease

zerlegen (tsehr-*lay*-gern) *v* carve; analyse

*zerreiben (tsehr-*righ*-bern) *v* *grind

*zerreißen (tsehr-*righ*-sern) *v* rip

zerren (*tseh*-rern) *v* pull, drag; *med* strain

zerstampfen (tsehr-*shtahm*-pfern) *v* mash

Zerstäuber (tsehr-*shtoi*-berr) *m* (pl ~) atomizer

zerstören (tsehr-*shtür*-rern) *v* destroy

Zerstörung (tsehr-*shtür*-roong) *f* destruction

Zettel (*tseh*-terl) *m* (pl ~) piece of paper; ticket, note; form

Zeug (tsoik) *nt* stuff; things *pl*

Zeuge (*tsoi*-ger) *m* (pl ~n) witness

Zeugin (*tsoi*-gin) *f* (pl ~nen) witness

Zeugnis (*tsoik*-niss) *nt* (pl ~se) certificate

Ziege (*tsee*-ger) f (pl ~n) goat

Ziegel (*tsee*-gerl) m (pl ~) brick

Ziegelstein (*tsee*-gerl-shtighn) m (pl ~e) brick

Ziegenbock (*tsee*-gern-bok) m (pl ~e) goat

Ziegenkäse (*tsee*-gern-kai-zer) m goat's milk cheese

Ziegenleder (*tsee*-gern-lāy-derr) nt kid

*ziehen (*tsee*-ern) v pull; *draw

Ziehung (*tsee*-oong) f (pl ~en) draw

Ziel (tseel) nt (pl ~e) aim; goal, object, target

zielen auf (*tsee*-lern) v aim at

Ziellinie (*tseel*-lee-nʸer) f (pl ~n) finish

Zielscheibe (*tseel*-shigh-ber) f (pl ~n) mark; target

ziemlich (*tseem*-likh) adv pretty, fairly, rather; somewhat, quite

Ziffer (*tsi*-ferr) f (pl ~n) digit; number

Zigarette (tsi-gah-*reh*-ter) f (pl ~n) cigarette

Zigarettenautomat (tsi-gah-*reh*-tern-ou-toa-maat) m cigarette machine

Zigarettenetui (tsi-gah-*reh*-tern-eht-vi) nt (pl ~s) cigarette case

Zigarettentabak (tsi-gah-*reh*-tern-taa-bahk) m cigarette tobacco

Zigarre (tsi-*gah*-rer) f (pl ~n) cigar

Zigarrenladen (tsi-*gah*-rern-laa-dern) m (pl ~) cigar shop

Zimmer (*tsi*-merr) nt (pl ~) room; chamber; ~ mit Frühstück bed and breakfast; ~ mit Vollpension room and board

Zimmerservice (*tsi*-merr-surr-viss) m room service

Zimmertemperatur (*tsi*-merr-tehm-pay-rah-tōōr) f room temperature

Zimt (tsimt) m cinnamon

Zink (tsingk) nt zinc

Zinn (tsin) nt tin, pewter

Zins (tsins) m (pl ~en) interest

Zirkus (*tseer*-kooss) m (pl ~se) circus

Zirkusarena (*tseer*-kooss-ah-rāy-nah) f (pl -arenen) ring

Zitat (tsi-*taat*) nt (pl ~e) quotation

zitieren (tsi-*tee*-rern) v quote

Zitrone (tsi-*trōa*-ner) f (pl ~n) lemon

zittern (*tsi*-terrn) v tremble, shiver

zivil (tsi-*veel*) adj civil

Zivilisation (tsi-vi-li-zah-tsʸ*ōan*) f (pl ~en) civilization

zivilisiert (tsi-vi-li-*zeert*) adj civilized

Zivilist (tsi-vi-*list*) m (pl ~en), **-in** f civilian

Zivilrecht (tsi-*veel*-rehkht) nt civil law

zögern (*tsūr*-gerrn) v hesitate

Zoll[1] (tsol) m (pl ~e) customs duty

Zoll[2] (tsol) m (pl ~) inch

Zollbehörde (*tsol*-ber-hūrr-der) f (pl ~n) customs pl

zollfrei (*tsol*-frigh) adj duty-free

Zöllner (*tsurl*-nerr) m (pl ~), **-in** f customs officer

Zone (*tsōa*-ner) f (pl ~n) zone

Zoo (tsōa) m (pl ~s) zoo

Zoologie (tsoa-oa-loa-*gee*) f zoology

Zorn (tsorn) m anger

zornig (*tsor*-nikh) adj angry

zu (tsōō) prep to; towards; adv too; closed, shut

Zubehör (*tsōō*-ber-hūrr) nt (pl ~e) accessories pl

zubereiten (*tsōō*-ber-righ-tern) v cook

*zubinden (*tsōō*-bin-dern) v tie (up)

zudecken (*tsōō*-deh-kern) v cover (up); conceal

züchten (*tsewkh*-tern) v *breed, raise; *grow

Zucker (*tsoo*-kerr) m sugar; **Stück ~** lump of sugar

Zuckerkrankheit (*tsoo*-kerr-krahngk-hight) f diabetes

*zuerkennen (*tsōō*-ehr-keh-nern) v award

zuerst (tsoo-*āyrst*) adv at first

Zufall (*tsoo*-fahl) *m* (pl ⁓e) chance; luck

zufällig (*tsoo*-feh-likh) *adj* accidental, casual, incidental; *adv* by chance

zufrieden (tsoo-*free*-dern) *adj* satisfied; happy, content

zufriedenstellen (tsoo-*free*-dern-shteh-lern) *v* satisfy

Zufuhr (*tsoo*-foor) *f* supply

Zug (tsook) *m* (pl ⁓e) train; procession; move; trait; **durchgehender ⁓** through train

Zugang (*tsoo*-gahng) *m* entry; approach

zugänglich (*tsoo*-gehng-likh) *adj* accessible

Zugbrücke (*tsook*-brew-ker) *f* (pl ⁓n) drawbridge

***zugeben** (*tsoo*-gāy-bern) *v* admit, acknowledge

zügeln (*tsew*-gerln) *v* curb

Zugeständnis (*tsoo*-ger-shtehnt-niss) *nt* (pl ⁓se) concession

zugetan (*tsoo*-ger-taan) *adj* attached to

zugleich (tsoo-*glighkh*) *adv* at the same time

zugunsten (tsoo-*goons*-tern) *prep* on behalf of

zuhören (*tsoo*-hūr-rern) *v* listen

Zuhörer (*tsoo*-hūr-rerr) *m* (pl ⁓), **-in** *f* listener, auditor

Zuhörerraum (*tsoo*-hūr-rerr-roum) *m* (pl ⁓e) auditorium

zujubeln (*tsoo*-ʸoo-berln) *v* cheer

Zukunft (*tsoo*-koonft) *f* future

zukünftig (*tsoo*-kewnf-tikh) *adj* future

Zulage (*tsoo*-laa-ger) *f* (pl ⁓n) allowance

Zulassung (*tsoo*-lah-soong) *f* (pl ⁓en) admission

zuletzt (tsoo-*lehtst*) *adv* at last

zumachen (*tsoo*-mah-khern) *v* close

zumindest (tsoo-*min*-derst) *adv* at least

Zunahme (*tsoo*-naa-mer) *f* increase

Zündkerze (*tsewnt*-kehr-tser) *f* (pl ⁓n) sparking plug

Zündung (*tsewn*-doong) *f* (pl ⁓en) ignition; ignition coil

***zunehmen** (*tsoo*-nāy-mern) *v* increase; gain weight; **zunehmend** progressive; increasing

Zuneigung (*tsoo*-nigh-goong) *f* affection

Zunge (*tsoong*-er) *f* (pl ⁓n) tongue

zurichten (*tsoo*-rikh-tern) *v* cook

zurück (tsoo-*rewk*) *adv* back

***zurückbringen** (tsoo-*rewk*-bring-ern) *v* *bring back

***zurückgeben** (tsoo-*rewk*- gāy-bern) *v* *give back, return

***zurückgehen** (tsoo-*rewk*-gāy-ern) *v* *go back; *get back

***zurückhalten** (tsoo-*rewk*-hahl-tern) *v* restrain

zurückkehren (tsoo-*rewk*-kāy-rern) *v* return

***zurückkommen** (tsoo-*rewk*-ko-mern) *v* return

***zurücklassen** (tsoo-*rewk*-lah-sern) *v* *leave behind

***zurückrufen** (tsoo-*rewk*-rōo-fern) *v* recall

zurückschicken (tsoo-*rewk*-shi-kern) *v* *send back

***zurücksenden** (tsoo-*rewk*-zehn-dern) *v* *send back

***zurücktreten** (tsoo-*rewk*-trāy-tern) *v* resign

***zurückweisen** (tsoo-*rewk*-vigh-zern) *v* reject

zurückzahlen (tsoo-*rewk*-tsaa-lern) *v* *repay, reimburse

***zurückziehen** (tsoo-*rewk*-tsee-ern) *v* *withdraw

zusammen (tsoo-*zah*-mern) *adv* together

Zusammenarbeit (tsoo-*zah*-mern-ahr-bight) *f* cooperation

*zusammenbinden (tsoo-*zah*-mern-bin-dern) *v* bundle

*zusammenbrechen (tsoo-*zah*-mern-breh-khern) *v* collapse

*zusammenfallen (tsoo-*zah*-mern-fah-lern) *v* coincide

zusammenfalten (tsoo-*zah*-mern-fahl-tern) *v* fold

Zusammenfassung (tsoo-*zah*-mern-fah-soong) *f* (pl ~en) résumé, summary

zusammenfügen (tsoo-*zah*-mern-fēw-gern) *v* join

Zusammenhang (tsoo-*zah*-mern-hahng) *m* (pl ~e) connection; coherence

Zusammenkunft (tsoo-*zah*-mern-koonft) *f* (pl ~e) assembly

zusammensetzen (tsoo-*zah*-mern-zeh-tsern) *v* assemble

Zusammensetzung (tsoo-*zah*-mern-zeh-tsoong) *f* (pl ~en) composition

zusammenstellen (tsoo-*zah*-mern-shteh-lern) *v* compile; compose, *make up

Zusammenstoß (tsoo-*zah*-mern-shtōass) *m* (pl ~e) collision; crash

*zusammenstoßen (tsoo-*zah*-mern-shtōa-sern) *v* bump; crash, collide

Zusammentreffen (tsoo-*zah*-mern-treh-fern) *nt* concurrence

*zusammenziehen (tsoo-*zah*-mern-tsee-ern) *v* tighten

zusätzlich (tsōō-zehts-likh) *adj* additional, extra

zuschauen (tsōō-shou-ern) *v* watch

Zuschauer (tsōō-shou-err) *m* (pl ~), -in *f* spectator

Zuschlag (tsōō-shlaak) *m* (pl ~e) surcharge

*zuschlagen (tsōō-shlaa-gern) *v* slam; *strike

zuschreiben (tsōō-shrigh-bern) *v* assign to

Zuschuss (tsōō-shooss) *m* (pl ~e) grant

Zustand (tsōō-shtahnt) *m* (pl ~e) state, condition

zustande *bringen (tsoo-*shtahn*-der *bring*-ern) effect; accomplish

Zustellung (tsōō-shteh-loong) *f* delivery

zustimmen (tsōō-shti-mern) *v* agree; consent

Zustimmung (tsōō-shti-moong) *f* consent; approval

Zutat (tsōō-taat) *f* (pl ~en) ingredient

Zutritt (tsōō-trit) *m* entrance, admittance, access

zuverlässig (tsōō-fehr-leh-sikh) *adj* trustworthy, reliable; sound

zuversichtlich (tsōō-fehr-zikht-likh) *adj* confident

zu viel (tsoo-*feel*) *pron* too much

zuvor (tsoo-*fōar*) *adv* before

*zuvorkommen (tsoo-*fōar*-ko-mern) *v* anticipate

zuvorkommend (tsoo-*fōar*-ko-mernt) *adj* thoughtful

*zuweisen (tsōō-vigh-zern) *v* assign to

Zuweisung (tsōō-vigh-zoong) *f* (pl ~en) assignment

zu wenig (tsoo-*vāy*-nikh) *pron* not enough

*zuziehen (tsōō-tsee-ern) *v*: sich ~ pull tight; contract

zwanglos (tsvahng-lōass) *adj* casual

zwangsweise (tsvahngs-vigh-zer) *adv* by force

zwanzig (tsvahn-tsikh) *num* twenty

zwanzigste (tsvahn-tsikhs-ter) *num* twentieth

Zweck (tsvehk) *m* (pl ~e) purpose; objective, design

zweckmäßig (tsvehk-mai-sikh) *adj* appropriate; efficient

zwei (tsvigh) *num* two

zweideutig (*tsvigh*-doi-tikh) *adj* ambiguous

Zweifel (*tsvigh*-ferl) *m* (pl ~) doubt; **ohne ~** without doubt

zweifelhaft (*tsvigh*-ferl-hahft) *adj* doubtful

zweifellos (*tsvigh*-ferl-lōass) *adv* undoubtedly

zweifeln (*tsvigh*-ferln) *v* doubt

Zweig (tsvighk) *m* (pl ~e) twig

Zweigstelle (*tsvighk*-shteh-ler) *f* (pl ~n) branch

zweimal (*tsvigh*-maal) *adv* twice

zweisprachig (*tsvigh*-shpraa-khikh) *adj* bilingual

zweite (*tsvigh*-ter) *num* second

zweiteilig (*tsvigh*-tigh-likh) *adj* two-piece

Zwerg (tsvehrk) *m* (pl ~e) dwarf

Zwieback (*tsvee*-bahk) *m* rusk, *Am* Zwieback

Zwiebel (*tsvee*-berl) *f* (pl ~n) onion; bulb

Zwielicht (*tsvee*-likht) *nt* twilight

Zwillinge (*tsvi*-li-nger) *mpl* twins *pl*

*zwingen (*tsving*-ern) *v* force; compel

Zwirn (tsveern) *m* thread

zwischen (*tsvi*-shern) *prep* between; among, amid

Zwischenfall (*tsvi*-shern-fahl) *m* (pl ~e) incident

Zwischenlandung (*tsvi*-shern-lahn-doong) *f* stopover

Zwischenraum (*tsvi*-shern-roum) *m* (pl ~e) space

Zwischenspiel (*tsvi*-shern-shpeel) *nt* (pl ~e) interlude

Zwischenzeit (*tsvi*-shern-tsight) *f* interim

zwölf (tsvurlf) *num* twelve

zwölfte (*tsvurlf*-ter) *num* twelfth

Zyklus (*tsēw*-klooss) *m* (pl Zyklen) cycle

Zylinder (tsi-*lin*-derr) *m* (pl ~) cylinder

Zylinderkopf (tsi-*lin*-derr-kopf) *m* (pl ~e) cylinder head

Aus der Speisekarte

Speisen

Aal eel

Abendbrot, Abendessen evening meal, supper

Allgäuer Bergkäse hard cheese from Bavaria resembling *Emmentaler*

Allgäuer Rahmkäse a mild and creamy Bavarian cheese

Altenburger a mild, soft goat's milk cheese

Ananas pineapple

Anis aniseed

~brot aniseed-flavoured cake or biscuit

Apfel apple

Apfelsine orange

Appenzeller (Käse) slightly bitter, fully flavoured cheese

Appetithäppchen,
Appetitschnittchen appetizer, canapé

Aprikose apricot

Artischocke artichoke

Artischockenherz artichoke heart

Aubergine aubergine (US eggplant)

Auflauf 1) soufflé 2) a meat, fish, fowl, fruit or vegetable dish which is oven-browned

Aufschnitt cold meat (US cold cuts)

Auster oyster

Backforelle baked trout

Backhähnchen, Backhendl,
Backhuhn fried chicken

Backobst dried fruit

Backpflaume prune

Backsteinkäse strong cheese from Bavaria resembling *Limburger*

Banane banana

Barsch perch

Bauernbrot rye or wholemeal bread

Bauernfrühstück breakfast usually consisting of eggs, bacon and potatoes

Bauernomelett diced bacon and onion omelet

Bauernschmaus sauerkraut garnished with bacon, smoked pork, sausages and dumplings or potatoes

Bauernsuppe a thick soup of sliced frankfurters and cabbage

Baumnuss walnut

Bayerische Leberknödel veal-liver dumplings, served with sauerkraut

Bedienung (nicht) (e)inbegriffen service (not) included

Beere berry

Beilage side dish, sometimes a garnish

belegtes Brot/Brötchen roll with any of a variety of garnishes

Berliner (Pfannkuchen) jam-filled doughnut (US jelly donut)

Berliner Luft dessert made of eggs and lemon, served with raspberry juice

Berner Platte a mound of sauerkraut or French beans liberally garnished with smoked pork chops, boiled bacon and beef, sausages, tongue, ham and boiled potatoes

Beuschel heart, kidney and liver of calf or lamb in a slightly sour sauce

Bienenstich cake with honey and almonds

Bierrettich black radish, generally cut, salted and served with beer

Biersuppe a sweet, spicy soup made on beer

Birchermus, Birchermüsli uncooked oats with raw, shredded fruit, chopped nuts in milk or yoghurt

Birne pear

Bischofsbrot fruit-nut cake

Biskuitrolle Swiss roll; jelly and butter-cream roll

Bismarckhering pickled herring, seasoned with onions

blau word to designate fish freshly poached

Blaubeere bilberry (US blueberry)

Blaukraut red cabbage

Blumenkohl cauliflower

Blutwurst black pudding (US blood sausage)

Bockwurst boiled sausage

Bohne bean

Bouillon broth, consommé

Brachse, Brasse bream

Bratapfel baked apple

Braten roast, joint

   ~soße gravy

Bratfisch fried fish

Brathähnchen, Brathendl, Brathuhn roast chicken

Bratkartoffel fried potato

Bratwurst fried sausage

Braunschweiger Kuchen rich cake with fruit and almonds

Brei porridge, mash, purée

Brezel salted, knot-shaped roll (US pretzel)

Bries, Brieschen, Briesel sweetbread

Brombeere blackberry

Brot bread

   ~suppe broth with stale bread

Brötchen roll

Brühe broth, consommé

Brunnenkresse watercress

Brüsseler Endivie chicory (US endive)

Brust breast

   ~stück brisket

Bückling bloater

Bulette meat- or fishball

Bündnerfleisch cured, dried beef served in very thin slices

Butt(e) brill

Champignon button mushroom

Chicorée chicory (US endive)

Cornichon small gherkin (US pickle)

Dampfnudel steamed sweet dumpling, served warm with vanilla sauce

Dattel date

deutsches Beefsteak hamburger, sometimes topped with a fried egg

doppeltes Lendenstück a thick fillet of beef (US tenderloin)

Dörrobst dried fruit

Dorsch cod

Dotterkäse cheese made from skimmed milk and egg-yolk

durchgebraten well-done

Egli perch

Ei egg

   ~dotter, ~gelb egg-yolk

   ~schnee beaten egg-white

   ~weiß egg-white

Eierauflauf egg soufflé

Eierkuchen pancake

Eierschwamm(erl) chanterelle mushroom

eingemacht preserved (of fruit or vegetables)

Eintopf stew, usually of meat and vegetables

Eis ice, ice-cream

   ~bombe ice-cream dessert

   ~krem ice-cream

Eisbein mit Sauerkraut pickled pig's knuckle with sauerkraut

Emmentaler (Käse) a semi-hard, robust Swiss cheese with holes

Endivie endive (US chicory)

Ente duck

Erbse pea

Erdbeere strawberry

Erdnuss peanut

errötende Jungfrau raspberries with cream

Essig vinegar

~gurke gherkin (US pickle)

Esskastanie chestnut

Extraaufschlag extra charge, supplementary charge

Fadennudel thin noodle, vermicelli

falscher Hase a meat loaf of beef and pork

Fasan pheasant

Faschiertes minced meat

faschiertes Laibchen meatball

Feige fig

Felchen variety of lake trout

Fenchel fennel

fester Preis, zu festem Preis fixed price

Filet fillet

~ Stroganoff thin slices of beef cooked in a sauce of sour cream, mustard and onions

Fisch fish

~klößchen fishball

~schüssel casserole of fish and diced bacon

Fladen pancake

Flädle, Flädli thin strips of pancake added to soup

flambiert flambé (food set aflame with brandy)

Flammeri a pudding made of rice or semolina and served with stewed fruit or vanilla custard

Fleisch meat

~käse seasoned meat loaf made of beef and other minced meats

~kloß meat dumpling

~roulade, ~vogel slice of meat rolled around a stuffing and braised; veal bird

Flunder flounder

Forelle trout

Frankfurter (Würstchen) frankfurter (sausage)

Frikadelle a meat, fowl or fish

dumpling

Frikassee fricassée, stew

frisch fresh

Frischling young wild boar

Froschschenkel frogs' legs

Frucht fruit

Frühlingssuppe soup with diced spring vegetables

Frühstück breakfast

Frühstückskäse a strong cheese with a smooth texture

Frühstücksspeck smoked bacon

Füllung stuffing, filling, forcemeat

Fürst-Pückler-Eis(bombe) chocolate, vanilla and strawberry ice-cream dessert

Gabelfrühstück brunch

Gans goose

Gänseklein goose giblets

Garnele shrimp

Garnitur garnish

Gebäck pastry

gebacken baked

gebraten roasted, fried

gedämpft steamed

Gedeck meal at a set price

gedünstet braised, steamed

Geflügel fowl

~klein giblets

Gefrorenes ice-cream

gefüllt stuffed

gegrillt grilled

gehackt minced or chopped

Gehacktes minced meat

gekocht cooked, boiled

Gelee 1) aspic 2) jelly 3) jam

gemischt mixed

Gemüse vegetable

gepökelt pickled

geräuchert smoked

Gericht dish

geröstet roasted

Gerste barley

gesalzen salted

geschmort stewed, braised

Geschnetzeltes meat cut into thin, small slices

Geselchtes cured and smoked pork

gesotten simmered, boiled

gespickt larded

gesülzt jellied, in aspic

Gewürz spice

~**gurke** gherkin (US pickle)

~**kuchen** spice cake

~**nelke** clove

gewürzt spiced, hot

Gipfel crescent-shaped roll

Gittertorte almond cake or tart with a raspberry topping

Gitzi kid

Glace ice-cream

Glattbutt brill

Gnagi cured pig's knuckle

Götterspeise fruit jelly dessert (US Jell-O)

Granat prawn

~**apfel** pomegranate

gratiniert oven-browned, gratinéed

Graubrot brown bread (US black bread)

Graupensuppe barley soup

Greyerzer (Käse) Gruyère, a cheese rich in flavour, smooth in texture

Griebenwurst a larded frying sausage

Grieß semolina

grilliert grilled

Gröstl grated, fried potatoes with pieces of meat

Gründling gudgeon

grüne Bohne French bean (US green bean)

Grünkohl kale

Gugelhopf, Gugelhupf a moulded cake with a hole in the centre; usually with almonds and raisins

Güggeli spring chicken

Gurke cucumber, gherkin

Hachse knuckle, shank

Hackbraten meat loaf of beef and pork

Hackfleisch minced meat

Haferbrei oatmeal, porridge

Haferflocken rolled oats

Hähnchen spring chicken

halb half

~**gar** rare (US underdone)

Hamme ham

Hammel(fleisch) mutton

Handkäse cheese made from sour milk, with a pungent aroma

Haschee hash

Hase hare

Hasenpfeffer jugged hare

Haselnuss hazelnut

Hauptgericht main course

hausgemacht, nach Art des Hauses home-made

Hausmannskost plain food

Haxe knuckle, shank

Hecht pike

Hefekranz ring-shaped cake

Heidelbeere bilberry (US blueberry)

Heilbutt halibut

heiß very warm (hot)

Hering herring

~ **Hausfrauenart** herring fillets with onions in sour cream

Heringskartoffeln a casserole of layers of herring and potatoes

Heringskönig John Dory (fish)

Herz heart

Himbeere raspberry

Himmel und Erde slices of black pudding served with mashed potatoes and apple sauce

Hirn brains

Hirsch stag (venison)

Hirse millet

hohe Rippe roast ribs of beef

Holsteiner Schnitzel breaded veal cutlet served with vegetables and

topped with a fried egg
Honig honey
Hörnchen crescent-shaped roll
Huhn chicken
Hühnchen chicken
Hühnerklein chicken giblets
Hummer lobster
Husarenfleisch braised beef, veal and pork fillets, with sweet peppers, onions and sour cream
Hutzelbrot bread made of prunes and other dried fruit
Imbiss snack
Ingwer ginger
italienischer Salat finely sliced veal, salami, tomatoes, anchovies, cucumber and celery in mayonnaise
(nach) Jägerart sautéed with mushrooms and sometimes onions
Jakobsmuschel scallop
Johannisbeere redcurrant
jung young, spring
Jungfernbraten roast pork with bacon
Kabeljau cod
Kaisergranat Norway lobster, Dublin Bay prawn
Kaiserschmarren delicious, fluffy pancakes with raisins served with a compote or chocolate sauce
Kalb(fleisch) veal
Kalbsbries veal sweetbread
Kalbskopf calf's head
Kalbsmilch veal sweetbread
Kalbsnierenbraten roast veal stuffed with kidneys
Kaldaunen tripe
kalt cold
Kaltschale chilled fruit soup
Kammmuschel scallop
kandierte Frucht crystallized fruit (US candied fruit)
Kaninchen rabbit
Kapaun capon

Kaper caper
Karamelkrem caramel custard
Karfiol cauliflower
Karotte carrot
Karpfen carp
Kartoffel potato
~**puffer** potato fritter
Käse cheese
~**platte** cheese board
~**stange** cheese straw, cheese stick
Kasseler Rippenspeer smoked pork chops, often served with sauerkraut
Kastanie chestnut
Katenrauchschinken country-style smoked ham
Katenwurst country-style smoked sausage
Katzenjammer cold slices of beef in mayonnaise with cucumbers or gherkins
Kaviar caviar
Keks biscuit (US cookie)
Kerbel chervil
Kesselfleisch boiled pork served with vegetables
Keule leg, haunch
Kieler Sprotte smoked sprat
Kipfel crescent-shaped roll
Kirsche cherry
Kitz kid
Kliesche dab
Klops meatball
Kloß dumpling
Klößchen small dumpling
Kluftsteak rumpsteak
Knackwurst a lightly garlic-flavoured sausage, generally boiled
Knoblauch garlic
Knochen bone ~**schinken** cured ham
Knödel dumpling
Knöpfli thick noodle
Kohl cabbage ~**rabi**, ~**rübe** turnip
~**roulade** cabbage leaves stuffed with minced meat

Kompott stewed fruit, compote

Konfitüre jam

Königinpastetchen vol-au-vent; puff-pastry shell filled with diced chicken and mushrooms

Königinsuppe creamy chicken soup with pieces of chicken breast

Königsberger Klops cooked meatball in white caper sauce

Kopfsalat green salad, lettuce

Korinthe currant

Kotelett chop, cutlet

Krabbe crab

Kraftbrühe broth, consommé

Krainer spiced pork sausage

Kranzkuchen ring-shaped cake

Krapfen 1) fritter 2) jam-filled doughnut (US jelly donut)

Krauskohl kale

Kraut cabbage

Kräutersoße herb dressing

Krautsalat coleslaw

Krautstiel white beet, Swiss chard

Krautwickel stuffed cabbage

Krebs freshwater crayfish

Krem cream, custard

~**schnitte** custard slice (US napoleon)

Kren horse-radish

~**fleisch** pork stew with vegetables and horse-radish

Kresse cress

Krustentier shellfish

Kuchen cake

Kukuruz maize (US corn)

Kümmel caraway

Kürbis pumpkin

Kuttelfleck, Kutteln tripe

Labskaus thick stew of minced, marinated meat with mashed potatoes

Lachs salmon

~**forelle** salmon trout

Lamm(fleisch) lamb

Languste spiny lobster, crawfish

Lattich lettuce

Lauch leek

Leber liver

~**käse** seasoned meat loaf made of minced liver, pork and bacon

Lebkuchen gingerbread

Leckerli honey-flavoured ginger biscuit

legiert thickened, usually with egg-yolk (refers to sauces or soups)

Leipziger Allerlei spring carrots, peas and asparagus (sometimes with mushrooms)

Lende loin

Lendenbraten roast tenderloin

Lendenstück fillet of beef (US tenderloin)

Limburger (Käse) a semi-soft, strong-smelling whole-milk cheese

Linse lentil

Linzer Torte almond cake or tart with a raspberry-jam topping

Löwenzahn young dandelion green, usually prepared as salad

Lunge light (lung of an animal)

Mahlzeit meal

Mainauer (Käse) semi-hard, full-cream round cheese with a red rind and yellow interior

Mainzer Rippchen pork chop

Mais maize (US corn)

Makrele mackerel

Makrone macaroon

Mandarine mandarin

Mandel almond

Mangold white beet, Swiss chard

Marille apricot

mariniert marinated, pickled

Mark (bone) marrow

Marmelade jam

Marone chestnut

Mastente fattened duckling

Masthühnchen broiler, spring

chicken

Matjeshering slightly salted young herring

Matrosenbrot a sandwich with chopped, hard-boiled eggs, anchovies and seasoning

Maulbeere mulberry

Maultasche a kind of ravioli filled with meat, vegetables and seasoning

Meerrettich horse-radish

Mehlnockerl small dumpling

Mehlsuppe brown-flour soup

Melone melon

Menü meal at a set price

Meringe(l) meringue

Mettwurst spiced and smoked pork sausage, usually for spreading on bread

Miesmuschel mussel

Milke sweetbread

Mirabelle small yellow plum

Mittagessen midday meal, lunch

Mohn poppy

Möhre, Mohrrübe carrot

Mondseer (Käse) whole-milk yellow cheese with a moist texture

Morchel morel mushroom

Morgenessen breakfast

Morgenrötesuppe thick soup of meat, tapioca, tomatoes and chicken stock

Mostrich mustard

Mus stewed fruit, purée, mash

Muschel mussel

Muskat(nuss) nutmeg

Nachspeise, Nachtisch dessert, sweet

naturell plain

Nelke clove

Nidel, Nidle cream

Niere kidney

Nierenstück loin

Nockerl small dumpling

Nudel noodle

Nürnberger Bratwurst frying sausage made of veal and pork

Nuss 1) nut 2) approx. rumpsteak

Obst fruit
~salat fruit salad

Ochs(enfleisch) beef

Ochsenauge fried egg (US sunny side up)

Ochsenmaulsalat ox muzzle salad

Ochsenschwanz oxtail

Ohr ear

Öl oil

Omelett(e) omelet

Palatschinken pancake usually filled with jam or cheese, sometimes served with a hot chocolate and nut topping

Pampelmuse grapefruit

paniert breaded

Paprikaschote sweet pepper

Paradeis(er), Paradiesapfel tomato

Pastetchen filled puff-pastry case

Pastete pastry, pie

Patisserie pastry

Pellkartoffel potato boiled in its jacket

Perlgraupe pearl barley

Petersilie parsley

Pfahlmuschel mussel

Pfannkuchen pancake

Pfeffer pepper
~kuchen very spicy gingerbread
~nuss ginger(bread)-nut
~schote hot pepper

Pfifferling chanterelle mushroom

Pfirsich peach
~ Melba peach-halves poached in syrup, served over vanilla ice-cream, topped with raspberry sauce and whipped cream

Pflaume plum

Pichelsteiner (Fleisch) meat and vegetable stew

pikant spiced, highly seasoned

Pilz mushroom

Platte platter

Plätzchen biscuit (US cookie)

Plätzli scallop, cutlet

pochiert poached

Pökelfleisch marinated meat

Pomeranzensoße sauce of bitter oranges, wine and brandy, usually served with duck

Pommes frites chips (US french fries)

Porree leek

Poulet chicken

Praline praline; chocolate with a sweet filling

Preiselbeere cranberry

Presskopf brawn (US headcheese)

Printe honey-flavoured biscuit (US cookie)

Pudding custard, pudding

Püree mash, purée

Puter turkey

Quargel a small, round cheese, slightly acid and salty

Quark(käse) fresh white cheese

Quitte quince

Radieschen radish

Ragout stew

Rahm cream

Rande beetroot

Räucheraal smoked eel

Räucherhering smoked herring

Räucherlachs smoked salmon

Räucherspeck smoked bacon

Rebhuhn partridge

Rechnung bill (US check)

Regensburger a highly spiced and smoked sausage

Reh deer, venison

~**pfeffer** jugged venison, fried and braised in its marinade, served with sour cream

Reibekuchen potato pancake

Reibkäse grated cheese

Reis rice

~**fleisch** veal braised with rice, tomatoes and other vegetables

Rettich black radish

Rhabarber rhubarb

Ribisel redcurrant

Rinderbrust brisket of beef

Rind(fleisch) beef

Rippe rib

Rippchen, Rippenspeer, Rippenstück, Rippli chop (usually smoked pork)

Rochen skate, ray

Rogen roe (generally cod's roe)

Roggenbrot rye bread

roh raw

Rohkost uncooked vegetables, vegetarian food

Rohschinken cured ham

Rollmops soused herring fillet rolled around chopped onions or gherkins

Rosenkohl brussels sprout

Rosine raisin

Rosmarin rosemary

Rostbraten rumpsteak

Rösti grated, fried (US hashed-brown) potatoes

Röstkartoffel roast potato

rote Beete/Rübe beetroot

rote Grütze fruit jelly served with cream

Rotkohl, Rotkraut red cabbage

Rotzunge lemon sole

Roulade beef olives; usually thin slices of beef, stuffed, rolled and braised

Rücken chine, saddle

Rüebli carrot

Rührei scrambled egg

russische Eier Russian eggs; egg-halves topped with caviar, served with remoulade sauce

Sachertorte rich chocolate layer cake with jam filling

Safran saffron

Saft juice

Sahne cream

Saibling char

Saitenwurst a variety of frankfurter or wiener sausage

Salat salad

Salbei sage

Salm salmon

Salz salt

  ~fleisch salted meat

  ~gurke pickled cucumber

  ~kartoffel boiled potato

Salzburger Nockerl dumpling made of beaten egg-yolks, egg-whites, sugar and flour, fried in butter

Sandmuschel clam

Sardelle anchovy

Sardellenring rolled anchovy

Sardine sardine, pilchard

Sattel chine, saddle

Saubohne broad bean

sauer sour

Sauerampfer sorrel

Sauerbraten pot roast marinated with herbs

Schalentier shellfish

Schalotte shallot

Schaschlik chunks of meat, slices of kidneys and bacon, grilled then braised in a spicy sauce of tomatoes, onions and bacon

Schaumrolle puff-pastry rolls filled with whipped cream or custard

Scheibe slice

Schellfisch haddock

Schildkrötensuppe turtle soup

Schillerlocke 1) smoked conger eel 2) pastry cornet with vanilla cream filling

Schinken ham

  ~brot ham sandwich, usually open (-faced)

Schlachtplatte cold meat, liver sausage and sauerkraut

Schlagobers, Schlagrahm,

Schlagsahne whipped cream

Schlegel leg, haunch

Schleie tench

Schmelzkäse a soft and pungent cheese, usually for spreading on bread

Schmorbraten pot roast

Schmorfleisch meat stew

Schnecke 1) cinnamon roll 2) snail

Schnepfe snipe

Schnittbohne sliced French bean

Schnitte slice, cut

Schnittlauch chive

Schnitzel cutlet

Schokolade chocolate

Scholle plaice

Schulter shoulder

Schwamm(erl) mushroom

schwarze Johannisbeere blackcurrant

Schwarzwälder Kirschtorte a chocolate layer cake filled with cream and cherries, flavoured with *Kirsch*

Schwarzwälder Schinken a variety of smoked ham from the Black Forest

Schwarzwurzel salsify

Schwein(efleisch) pork

Seezunge sole

Selchfleisch smoked pork

Sellerie celery

Semmel roll

  ~brösel breadcrumbs

  ~knödel dumpling made of diced white bread

Senf mustard

Siedfleisch boiled meat

Soße sauce, gravy

Spanferkel suck(l)ing pig

spanische Soße a brown sauce with herbs

Spargel asparagus

Spätzle, Spätzli thick noodle

Speck bacon
  ~knödel dumpling made with bacon, eggs and white bread
Speise food
  ~eis ice-cream
  ~karte menu, bill of fare
Spekulatius spiced biscuit (US cookie)
Spezialität speciality
  ~ des Hauses chef's speciality
  ~ des Tages day's speciality
Spiegelei fried egg (US sunny side up)
(am) Spieß (on the) spit
Spinat spinach
Sprossenkohl brussels sprout
Sprotte sprat
Stachelbeere gooseberry
Steckrübe turnip
Steinbuscher (Käse) semi-hard creamy cheese; strong and slightly bitter
Steinbutt turbot
Steingarnele prawn
Steinpilz boletus mushroom
Stelze knuckle of pork
Stierenauge fried egg (US sunny side up)
Stock mashed potatoes
  ~fisch stockfish, dried cod
Stollen loaf cake with raisins, almonds, nuts and candied lemon peel
Stoßsuppe caraway soup
Stotzen leg, haunch
Strammer Max slice of bread or sandwich with spiced minced pork (sometimes sausage or ham) served with fried eggs and onions
Streichkäse any soft cheese spread, with different flavours
Streuselkuchen coffee cake with a topping made of butter, sugar, flour and cinnamon

Strudel paper-thin layers of pastry filled with apple slices, nuts, raisins and jam or honey
Stück piece, slice
Sülze 1) jellied, in aspic 2) brawn (US headcheese)
Suppe soup
süß sweet
  ~sauer sweet-and-sour (of sauces)
Süßigkeit sweet (US candy)
Süßspeise dessert, pudding
Tagesgericht day's special
Tagessuppe day's soup
Tascherl pastry turnover with meat, cheese or jam filling
Tatar raw, spiced minced beef
Tatarenbrot open(-faced) sandwich with *Tatar*
Taube pigeon (US squab)
Teigwaren macaroni, noodles, spaghetti
Teller plate, dish
  ~gericht one-course meal
Thunfisch tunny (US tuna)
Thymian thyme
Tilsiter (Käse) semi-hard cheese, mildly pungent
Tomate tomato
Topfen fresh white cheese
  ~strudel flaky pastry filled with creamed, vanilla-flavoured white cheese, rolled and baked
Topfkuchen moulded cake with raisins
Törtchen small tart or cake
Torte layer cake, usually rich
Traube grape
Trüffel truffle
Truthahn turkey
Tunke sauce, gravy
Türkenkorn maize (US corn)
Vanille vanilla
verlorenes Ei poached egg
Voressen meat stew

Vorspeise starter, first course
Wacholderbeere juniper berry
Wachtel quail
Waffel waffle
Walnuss walnut
Wassermelone watermelon
Weinbeere, Weintraube grape
Weinkarte wine list
Weinkraut white cabbage, often braised with apples and simmered in wine
weiße Bohne haricot bean (US navy bean)
Weißbrot white bread
Weißkäse fresh white cheese
Weißkohl, Weißkraut white cabbage
Weißwurst sausage made of veal, flavoured with parsley, onion and lemon peel
Weizen wheat
Welschkorn maize (US corn)
Westfälischer Schinken a well-known variety of cured and smoked ham
Wiener Schnitzel breaded veal cutlet
Wiener Würstchen, Wienerli wiener, frankfurter (sausage)
Wild(bret) game, venison

Wildente wild duck
Wildschwein wild boar
Wilstermarschkäse semi-hard cheese, similar to *Tilsiter*
Windbeutel cream puff
Wirsing(kohl) savoy cabbage
Wittling whiting
Wurst sausage
Würstchen small sausage
würzig spiced
Zander pike-perch
Zervelat(wurst) a seasoned and smoked sausage made of pork, beef and bacon
Zichorie chicory (US endive)
Ziege goat
Zimt cinnamon
Zitrone lemon
Zucker sugar
Zunge tongue
Zutat (added) ingredient
Zwetsch(g)e plum
Zwiebel onion
   ~**fleisch** beef sautéed with onions
   ~**wurst** liver and onion sausage
Zwischenrippenstück approx. ribeye steak, entrecôte

Getränke

Abfüllung bottled, from wine brought directly from the grower
Abzug wine bottled on the estate or at the vineyard where the grapes were grown, e.g., *Schlossabzug, Kellerabzug*
Ahr the region, named after its tributary of the Rhine, has the continent's northernmost vineyards; the red wine—pale, delicious with a

fine aroma—is the best in Germany, which produces little red wine; try it around the towns of Ahrweiler, Neuenahr and Walporzheim
Apfelmost apple cider
Apfelsaft apple juice
Apfelwein apple cider with a highalcoholic content
Aprikosenlikör apricot liqueur
Auslese wine produced from choice

grapes

Baden this wine-producing region is situated in the southwestern part of Germany with Switzerland to the south and Alsace, France, to the west; vineyards are especially found on the outskirts of the Black Forest facing the valley of the Rhine; some examples of the wine are *Kaiserstuhl*, produced at the foot of a one-time volcano to the west of Freiburg, *Markgräfler, Mauerwein* and *Seewein* from the Lake of Constance

Beerenauslese wine produced from choice, very mature grapes resulting in a dessert wine

Bier beer
dunkles ~ dark
helles ~ light, lager

Bock(bier) a beer with a high malt content

Branntwein brandy, spirits

Brauner coffee with milk
kleiner ~ small cup of coffee with milk

Danziger Goldwasser a caraway seed-flavoured liqueur flecked with tiny golden leaves

Doppelkorn spirit distilled from grain

Dornkaat a grain-distilled spirit, slightly flavoured with juniper berries

Eierlikör egg liqueur

Eiskaffee iced coffee

Enzian spirit distilled from gentian root

Exportbier a beer with a higher hops content than lager beer

Flasche bottle

Flaschenbier bottled beer

Franken Franconia; the best vineyards of this wine-producing region around the River Main are situated in the vicinity of Iphofen, Escherndorf,

Randersacker, Rödelsee and Würzburg; Franconian white wine is dry, strong and full-bodied; Würzburg produces one of the area's best wines under the name *Steinwein*

Fruchtsaft fruit juice

Gewächs used together with the year on the label of quality wines

gezuckert sugar added, sweetened

Glühwein mulled wine

Himbeergeist spirit distilled from raspberries

Kabinett a term indicating that a wine is of high quality

Kaffee coffee
~ Hag caffeine-free
~ mit Sahne (und Zucker) with cream (and sugar)
~ mit Schlag(obers) served with whipped cream
schwarzer ~ black

Kakao cocoa

Kapuziner coffee with whipped cream and grated chocolate

Kirsch(wasser) spirit distilled from cherries

Klosterlikör herb liqueur

Kognak cognac

Korn(branntwein) spirit distilled from grain

Kümmel(branntwein) caraway-flavoured spirit

Likör liqueur, cordial

Limonade 1) soft drink 2) lemon drink

Lindenblütentee lime-blossom tea

Malzbier malt beer, with a low alcoholic content

Märzenbier beer with a high alcoholic content, brewed in March

Maß(krug) a large beer mug holding 1 litre (about 1 quart)

Milch milk
~kaffee half coffee and half hot milk

~mix milk shake

Mineralwasser mineral water

Mosel(–Saar–Ruwer) the official name of the Moselle region; the best Moselle wine is produced in only a part of the region, the mid-Moselle Valley which runs from Trittenheim to Traben-Trarbach; the best vineyards are those of Bernkastel, Brauneberg, Graach, Piesport, Wehlen and Zeltingen

Most must, young wine

Nahe a wine-producing region, named after its tributary of the River Rhine, in the vicinity of Bad Kreuznach; its white wine is full-bodied and may be compared to the best wine of Rhenish Hesse; the most celebrated vineyard is Schloss Böckelheim, owned by the state; other excellent wine is produced in the vicinity of Bad Kreuznach, Bretzenheim, Münster, Niederhausen, Norheim, Roxheim, Winzerheim

Naturwein unblended, unsweetened wine

Österreich Austria; very little of its wine is exported; the red—mainly from Burgenland—is not especially notable and is usually drunk only locally; probably the best-known Austrian wine is *Gumpoldskirchner*, produced to the south of Vienna, a good white wine which generations of Viennese have enjoyed; along the banks of the River Danube to the west of Vienna, good white wine is produced in the Wachau area (e.g., *Dürnsteiner, Loibner, Kremser*); in the immediate vicinity of the Austrian capital, table wine is produced (e.g., *Nussberger, Grinzinger, Badener*) of which the best is sometimes exported

Perlwein white, semi-sparkling wine

Pfalz Palatinate; in good years this region is often first among West Germany's wine-producing regions in terms of production, predominantly of white wine; in medieval times, the Palatinate gained a reputation for being "the wine cellar of the Holy Roman Empire" today's Palatinate is bounded on the north by Rhenish Hesse, to the east by the River Rhine, to the south and west by Alsace, and Saarland; some examples *Dürkheimer, Forster, Deidesheimer, Ruppertsberger* for white, *Dürkheimer* also for red

Pils(e)ner beer with a particularly strong aroma of hops

Pfefferminztee peppermint tea

Pflümli(wasser) spirit distilled from plums

Portwein port (wine)

Rhein Rhine vine is produced in five regions in the Rhine valley offering the country's best white wines

Rheingau region situated at the foot of the Taunus Mountains facing the River Rhine; its best wines are dessert wines which can be compared to fine Sauternes; a good red wine is produced in Assmannshausen

Rheinhessen Rhenish Hesse, of which Mainz is the capital; no less than 155 villages are dedicated to wine production; some produce wines of exceptional quality (Alsheim, Bingen, Bodenheim, Dienheim, Guntersblum, Ingelheim, Nackenheim, Nierstein, Oppenheim and Worms); wine of lesser quality is sold under the name of *Liebfrau(en)milch*

Schillerwein rosé wine

Schloss castle, denotes a wine estate

Schnaps brandy, spirits
Schokolade chocolate
Schweiz Switzerland; the most notable wines (both red and white) are produced in French- and Italian-speaking cantons; German-speaking cantons produce mostly light red wines
Sekt sparkling wine similar to Champagne
Sirup syrup
Sodawasser soda water
Spätlese wine produced from grapes picked late in the season, often resulting in full-bodied wine
Spezialbier more strongly brewed beer than *Vollbier*
Sprudel(wasser) soda water
Starkbier strong beer with a high malt content
Steinhäger juniper-flavoured spirit
Tee tea
~ **mit Milch** with milk
~ **mit Zitrone** with lemon
trocken dry
Trockenbeerenauslese wine produced from specially selected overripe grapes; usually results in a rich, full-bodied dessert wine
ungezuckert unsweetened

verbessert in reference to wine, "improved" or sweetened
Viertel ¼ litre (about ½ pint) of wine
Vollbier the typical German beer with an alcoholic content of 3-4%
Wachstum used on a wine label with the name of the grower, guarantees natural wine
Wasser water
Wein wine
Rotwein red wine
Schaumwein sparkling wine
Süßwein dessert wine
Weißwein white wine
Weinbrand brandy distilled from wine
Weißbier light beer brewed from wheat
Wermut vermouth
Württemberg wine from this region, rarely exported, must be drunk very young; the term *Schillerwein* is employed in the region to denote rosé wine; best wine is produced at Cannstatt, Feuerbach, Untertürckheim; *Stettener Brotwasser* is a noted wine
Zitronensaft lemon squash (US lemon soda)
Zwetschgenwasser spirit distilled from plums

Mini-Grammar

Here is a brief outline of some essential features of German grammar.

Articles

All nouns in German are either masculine, feminine or neuter, and they are classified by the article which precedes them.

1. **Definite article** (the):

			Plural:
masc.	*der* **Mann**	the man	*die* **Männer**
fem.	*die* **Frau**	the woman	*die* **Frauen**
neut.	*das* **Kind**	the child	*die* **Kinder**

2. **Indefinite article** (a/an):

masc.	*ein* **Zug**	a train
fem.	*eine* **Reise**	a trip
neut.	*ein* **Flugzeug**	a plane

Nouns and adjectives

1. All nouns are written with a capital letter. The rules for constructing the plural are very complex.

2. **Declension:** According to their use in the sentence, German articles, nouns and modifying adjectives undergo related changes. The tables below show the declension of all three parts of speech.

	masc. sing.	masc. plur.
subject	**der reiche Mann**	**die reichen Männer**
direct object	**den reichen Mann**	**die reichen Männer**
possessive	**des reichen Mannes**	**der reichen Männer**
indirect object	**dem reichen Mann**	**den reichen Männern**

	fem. sing.	fem. plur.
subject	**die schöne Frau**	**die schönen Frauen**
direct object	**die schöne Frau**	**die schönen Frauen**
possessive	**der schönen Frau**	**der schönen Frauen**
indirect object	**der schönen Frau**	**den schönen Frauen**

	neuter sing.	neuter plur.
subject	**das kleine Kind**	**die kleinen Kinder**
direct object	**das kleine Kind**	**die kleinen Kinder**

possessive	**des kleinen Kindes**	**der kleinen Kinder**
indirect object	**dem kleinen Kind**	**den kleinen Kindern**

The indefinite article is declined in a slightly different way, as is the modifying adjective.

	masc.	fem.
subject	**ein reicher Mann**	**eine schöne Frau**
direct object	**einen reichen Mann**	**eine schöne Frau**
possessive	**eines reichen Mannes**	**einer schönen Frau**
indirect object	**einem reichen Mann**	**einer schönen Frau**

	neuter	plur.
subject	**ein kleines Kind**	**keine* großen Leute**
direct object	**einen kleines Kind**	**keine großen Leute**
possessive	**eines kleinen Kindes**	**keiner großen Leute**
indirect object	**einem kleinen Kind**	**keinen großen Leuten**

If declined without an article the adjectives take the endings of the definite article, except in the possessive, which you'll hardly use: **guter Wein** (good wine), **kalte Milch** (cold milk), **warmes Wasser** (hot water).

3. **Demonstrative adjectives:** In spoken German "that" is usually expressed by the definite article, but contrary to the article, it is stressed. "This" **dieser, diese, dieses** and plural **diese** is declined like the definite article.

das Buch (that book)   **dieser Platz** (this seat)

4. **Possessive adjectives:** These agree in number and gender with the noun they modify, i.e., with the thing possessed and not the possessor. In singular they are declined like the indefinite article, and in plural like the definite. Note that **Ihr** meaning "your" in the polite form is capitalized.

	masc. or neut.	fem. or plur.
my	**mein**	**meine**
your	**dein**	**deine**
his/its	**sein**	**seine**
her	**ihr**	**ihre**
our	**unser**	**unsere**

---

* ein has no plural, but the negative **kein** (declined in singular like **ein**) does.

your	**euer**	**eure**
their	**ihr**	**ihre**
your (pol.)	**Ihr**	**Ihre**

5. **Comparatives and superlatives:** These are formed by adding **-er (-r)** and **-est** (**-st**) respectively, very often together with an umlaut.

alt (old)	**kurz** (short)
älter (older)	**kürzer** (shorter)
ältest (oldest)	**kürzest** (shortest)

Adverbs

Many adjectives are used in their undeclined form as adverbs.

| **schnell** | quick, quickly |
| **gut** | good, well |

There are a few irregularities:

glücklich — glücklicherweise	happy — happily
anders	differently
besonders	especially
gleichfalls	as well, (the) same

Viel indicates quantity and **sehr** intensity:

| **Er arbeitet viel.** | He works a lot. |
| **Er ist sehr müde.** | He's very tired. |

Personal pronouns

	subject	direct object	indirect object
I	**ich**	**mich**	**mir**
you	**du**	**dich**	**dir**
he	**er**	**ihn**	**ihm**
she	**sie**	**sie**	**ihr**
it	**es**	**es**	**ihm**
we	**wir**	**uns**	**uns**
you	**ihr**	**euch**	**euch**
they	**sie**	**sie**	**ihnen**
you	**Sie**	**Sie**	**Ihnen**

Note: There are two forms for "you" in German: **du** and **Sie; du** (plur.: **ihr**) is used when talking to relatives, close friends and children (and between young people); **Sie** (both sing. and plur.) in all other cases. **Sie** is written with a capital **S.** The verb has the same form as that of the 3rd person plural.

Verbs

These are two important **auxiliary verbs:**

sein (to be)	**haben** (to have)
ich bin (I am)	**ich habe** (I have)
du bist (you are)	**du hast** (you have)
er, sie, es ist (he, she, it is)	**er, sie, es hat** (he, she, it has)
wir sind (we are)	**wir haben** (we have)
ihr seid (you are)	**ihr habt** (you have)
sie sind (they are)	**sie haben** (they have)
Sie sind (you are)	**Sie haben** (you have)

The infinitive of practically all verbs ends in **-en.** Here are the endings for the present tense and past tense of a regular weak verb:

ich lieb*e*	I love	**ich lieb***te*	I loved
du lieb*st*	you love	**du lieb***test*	you loved
er, sie, es lieb*t*	he, she, it loves	**er, sie, es lieb***te*	he, she, it loved
wir lieb*en*	we love	**wir lieb***ten*	we loved
ihr lieb*t*	you love	**ihr lieb***tet*	you loved
sie, Sie lieb*en*	they, you love	**sie, Sie lieb***ten*	they, you loved

Irregular Verbs

The following list contains the most common strong and irregular verbs. In parentheses, we have given the irregular forms of the present tense, generally the second and the third persons singular (when they change their stem). If a compound verb or a verb with a prefix (*ab-, an-, auf-, aus-, be-, bei-, ein-, emp-, ent-, er-, mit-, nach-, um-, ver-, vor-, zer-, zu-,* etc.) is not listed, its forms may be found by looking up the simple verb.

Infinitive	Past	Past Participle	
backen (bäckst, bäckt)	backte/buk	gebacken	*bake*
befehlen (befiehlst, befiehlt)	befahl	befohlen	*(give an) order*
beginnen	begann	begonnen	*begin*
bekommen	bekam	bekommen	*get*
beißen	biss	gebissen	*bite*
bergen (birgst, birgt)	barg	geborgen	*salvage*
bersten (birst, birst)	barst	geborsten	*burst*
bewegen	bewog	bewogen	*induce*
beweisen	bewies	bewiesen	*prove*
bewerben	bewarb	beworben	*apply*
biegen	bog	gebogen	*bend*
bieten	bot	geboten	*offer*

binden	band	gebunden	*bind*
bitten	bat	gebeten	*request*
blasen (bläst, bläst)	blies	geblasen	*blow*
bleiben	blieb	geblieben	*remain*
braten (brätst, brät)	briet	gebraten	*roast*
brechen (brichst, bricht)	brach	gebrochen	*break*
brennen	brannte	gebrannt	*burn*
bringen	brachte	gebracht	*bring*
denken	dachte	gedacht	*think*
dringen	drang	gedrungen	*penetrate*
dürfen (darf, darfst, darf)	durfte	gedurft	*be allowed*
empfehlen (empfiehlst, empfiehlt)	empfahl	empfohlen	*recommend*
erschrecken (erschrickst, erschrickt)	erschrak	erschrocken	*frighten, be frightened*
erwägen	erwog	erwogen	*consider*
erweisen	erwies	erwiesen	*prove*
essen (isst, isst)	aß	gegessen	*eat*
fahren (fährst, fährt)	fuhr	gefahren	*go, drive*
fallen (fällst, fällt)	fiel	gefallen	*fall*
fangen (fängst, fängt)	fing	gefangen	*catch*
fechten (fichst, ficht)	focht	gefochten	*fence*
finden	fand	gefunden	*find*
flechten (flichtst, flicht)	flocht	geflochten	*plait*
fliegen	flog	geflogen	*fly*
fliehen	floh	geflohen	*flee*
fließen	floss	geflossen	*flow*
fressen (frisst, frisst)	fraß	gefressen	*eat (animals)*
frieren	fror	gefroren	*freeze*
gären	gor/gärte	gegoren/gegärt	*ferment*
geben (gibst, gibt)	gab	gegeben	*give*
gedeihen	gedieh	gediehen	*prosper*
gehen	ging	gegangen	*go*
gelingen*	gelang	gelungen	*succeed*
gelten (giltst, gilt)	galt	gegolten	*be valid*
genesen	genas	genesen	*convalesce*
genießen	genoss	genossen	*enjoy*
geschehen* (geschieht)	geschah	geschehen	*happen*
gewinnen	gewann	gewonnen	*win*
gießen	goss	gegossen	*pour*
gleichen	glich	geglichen	*resemble*
gleiten	glitt	geglitten	*glide*

---

* impersonal

graben (gräbst, gräbt)	grub	gegraben	*dig*
greifen	griff	gegriffen	*seize*
haben (hast, hat)	hatte	gehabt	*have*
halten (hältst, hält)	hielt	gehalten	*hold*
hängen	hing	gehangen	*be suspended*
hauen	hieb	gehauen	*hit, cut*
heben	hob	gehoben	*lift*
heißen	hieß	geheißen	*be called*
helfen (hilfst, hilft)	half	geholfen	*help*
kennen	kannte	gekannt	*know*
klingen	klang	geklungen	*sound*
kneifen	kniff	gekniffen	*pinch*
kommen	kam	gekommen	*come*
können (kann, kannst, kann)	konnte	gekonnt	*can*
kriechen	kroch	gekrochen	*crawl*
laden (lädst, lädt)	lud	geladen	*load*
lassen (lässt, lässt)	ließ	gelassen	*let, leave*
laufen (läufst, läuft)	lief	gelaufen	*run*
leiden	litt	gelitten	*suffer*
leihen	lieh	geliehen	*lend*
lesen (liest, liest)	las	gelesen	*read*
liegen	lag	gelegen	*lie, rest*
lügen	log	gelogen	*tell a lie*
mahlen	mahlte	gemahlen	*grind*
meiden	mied	gemieden	*avoid*
messen (misst, misst)	maß	gemessen	*measure*
misslingen	misslang	misslungen	*fail*
mögen (mag, magst, mag)	mochte	gemocht	*want, like*
müssen (muss, musst, muss)	musste	gemusst	*must*
nehmen (nimmst, nimmt)	nahm	genommen	*take*
nennen	nannte	genannt	*name*
pfeifen	pfiff	gepfiffen	*whistle*
raten (rätst, rät)	riet	geraten	*counsel*
reiben	rieb	gerieben	*rub*
reißen	riss	gerissen	*tear*
reiten	ritt	geritten	*ride*
rennen	rannte	gerannt	*run*
riechen	roch	gerochen	*smell*
ringen	rang	gerungen	*struggle*
rinnen	rann	geronnen	*flow, run*
rufen	rief	gerufen	*call*
saufen (säufst, säuft)	soff	gesoffen	*drink, booze*
schaffen	schuf	geschaffen	*create*
schallen	schallte/scholl	geschallt	*resound*

scheiden	schied	geschieden	*divorce*
scheinen	schien	geschienen	*shine, seem*
schieben	schob	geschoben	*push*
schießen	schoss	geschossen	*shoot*
schlafen (schläfst, schläft)	schlief	geschlafen	*sleep*
schlagen (schlägst, schlägt)	schlug	geschlagen	*beat*
schleichen	schlich	geschlichen	*creep*
schleifen	schliff	geschliffen	*sharpen*
schließen	schloss	geschlossen	*close*
schlingen	schlang	geschlungen	*twine*
schmeißen	schmiss	geschmissen	*hurl*
schmelzen (schmilzt, schmilzt)	schmolz	geschmolzen	*melt*
schneiden	schnitt	geschnitten	*cut*
schreiben	schrieb	geschrieben	*write*
schreien	schrie	geschrie(e)n	*scream*
schreiten	schritt	geschritten	*stride*
schweigen	schwieg	geschwiegen	*be silent*
schwellen (schwillst, schwillt)	schwoll	geschwollen	*swell*
schwimmen	schwamm	geschwommen	*swim*
schwinden	schwand	geschwunden	*diminish*
schwingen	schwang	geschwungen	*swing*
schwören	schwor	geschworen	*swear*
sehen	sah	gesehen	*see*
sein (bin, bist, ist, sind, seid, sind)	war	gewesen	*be*
senden	sandte	gesandt	*send*
singen	sang	gesungen	*sing*
sinken	sank	gesunken	*sink*
sinnen	sann	gesonnen	*meditate*
sitzen	saß	gesessen	*sit*
sollen (soll, sollst, soll)	sollte	gesollt	*must, shall*
spinnen	spann	gesponnen	*spin*
sprechen (sprichst, spricht)	sprach	gesprochen	*speak*
springen	sprang	gesprungen	*jump*
stechen (stichst, sticht)	stach	gestochen	*prick*
stehen	stand	gestanden	*stand*
stehlen (stiehlst, stiehlt)	stahl	gestohlen	*steal*
steigen	stieg	gestiegen	*mount*
sterben (stirbst, stirbt)	starb	gestorben	*die*
stinken	stank	gestunken	*stink*
stoßen (stößt, stößt)	stieß	gestoßen	*push*
streichen	strich	gestrichen	*stroke*
streiten	stritt	gestritten	*quarrel*
tragen (trägst, trägt)	trug	getragen	*carry*

treffen (triffst, trifft)	traf	getroffen	*het, meet*
treiben	trieb	getrieben	*drive, push*
treten (trittst, tritt)	trat	getreten	*tread*
trinken	trank	getrunken	*drink*
trügen	trog	getrogen	*deceive*
tun (tue, tust, tut)	tat	getan	*do*
verbergen	verbag	verborgen	*hide*
verderben (verdirbst, verdirbt)	verdarb	verdorben	*spoil*
verdrießen	verdross	verdrossen	*annoy*
vergessen (vergisst, vergisst)	vergaß	vergessen	*forget*
verlieren	verlor	verloren	*lose*
verzeihen	verzieh	verziehen	*forgive*
wachsen (wächst, wächst)	wuchs	gewachsen	*grow*
wägen	wog	gewogen	*consider*
waschen (wäschst, wäscht)	wusch	gewaschen	*wash*
weben	wob/webte	gewoben/gewebt	*weave*
weichen	wich	gewichen	*yield*
weisen	wies	gewiesen	*indicate*
wenden	wandte/ wendete	gewandt/ gewendet	*turn*
werben (wirbst, wirbt)	warb	geworben	*recruit*
werden (wirst, wird)	wurde	geworden	*become*
werfen (wirfst, wirft)	warf	geworfen	*throw*
wiegen	wog	gewogen	*weigh*
winden	wand	gewunden	*wind, twist*
wissen (weiß, weißt, weiß)	wusste	gewusst	*know*
wollen (will, willst, will)	wollte	gewollt	*want*
ziehen	zog	gezogen	*pull*
zwingen	zwang	gezwungen	*force*

German Abbreviations

Abf.	*Abfahrt*	departure
Abs.	*Absender*	sender
ACS	*Automobil-Club der Schweiz*	Automobile Association of Switzerland
ADAC	*Allgemeiner Deutscher Automobil-Club*	German Automobile Association
AG	*Aktiengesellschaft*	Ltd., Inc.
a. M.	*am Main*	on the river Main
Ank.	*Ankunft*	arrival
Anm.	*Anmerkung*	remark
a. Rh.	*am Rhein*	on the river Rhine
AvD	*Automobilclub von Deutschland*	Automobile Association of Germany
Bhf.	*Bahnhof*	train station
Bez.	*Bezirk*	district
BRD	*Bundesrepublik Deutschland*	Federal Republic of Germany
b. w.	*bitte wenden*	please turn over
bzw.	*beziehungsweise*	respectively
d. h.	*das heißt*	i.e.
DIN	*Deutsche Industrie-Norm*	German Industrial Standards
d. M.	*dieses Monats*	inst., of this month
EU	*Europäische Union*	EU, European Union
Ffm.	*Frankfurt am Main*	Frankfurt, West Germany
fl. W.	*fließendes Wasser*	running water
Fr.	*Franken; Frau*	franc; Mrs.
G	*Gasse*	lane
Gebr.	*Gebrüder*	brothers
gefl.	*gefälligst*	please, kindly
GmbH	*Gesellschaft mit beschränkter Haftung*	limited liability company
Hbf.	*Hauptbahnhof*	main railway station
Hr.	*Herr*	Mr.
Ing.	*Ingenieur*	engineer
Inh.	*Inhaber; Inhalt*	proprietor; contents
Kfm.	*Kaufmann*	merchant
Kfz.	*Kraftfahrzeug*	motor vehicle
KG	*Kommanditgesellschaft*	limited partnership
Lkw	*Lastkraftwagen*	lorry, truck
MEZ	*Mitteleuropäische Zeit*	Central European Time
MwSt	*Mehrwertsteuer*	VAT, value added tax
n. Chr.	*nach Christus*	A.D.

ÖAMTC	*Österreichischer Automobil-, Motorrad- und Touringclub*	Austrian Automobile, Motorcycle and Touring Association
OB	*Oberbürgermeister*	mayor (of a large city)
ÖBB	*Österreichische Bundesbahnen*	Austrian Federal Railways
OHG	*Offene Handelsgesellschaft*	ordinary partnership
Pfd.	*Pfund*	pound (weight)
Pkw	*Personenkraftwagen*	automobile
PS	*Pferdestärke*	hp, horsepower
PTT	*Post, Telefon, Telegraf*	Post and Telecommunications
Rp.	*Rappen*	1/100 of a franc
SBB	*Schweizerische Bundesbahnen*	Swiss Federal Railways
Str.	*Straße*	street
TCS	*Touring-Club der Schweiz*	Swiss Touring Association
u. a.	*unter anderem*	among other things
U-Bahn	*Untergrundbahn*	underground (GB), subway (US)
ü. d. M.	*über dem Meeresspiegel*	above sea level
UKW	*Ultrakurzwelle*	FM (radio)
ung./ugf.	*ungefähr*	approximately
UN, UNO	*Vereinte Nationen*	United Nations
usw.	*und so weiter*	etc., and so on
u. U.	*unter Umständen*	in certain cases
v. Chr.	*vor Christus*	B.C.
vgl.	*vergleiche*	compare
v. H.	*vom Hundert*	per cent
Wwe.	*Witwe*	widow
z. B.	*zum Beispiel*	e.g.
z. H.	*zu Händen*	to the attention of
z. Z.	*zur Zeit*	at present

Numerals

Cardinal numbers

0	null
1	eins
2	zwei
3	drei
4	vier
5	fünf
6	sechs
7	sieben
8	acht
9	neun
10	zehn
11	elf
12	zwölf
13	dreizehn
14	vierzehn
15	fünfzehn
16	sechzehn
17	siebzehn
18	achtzehn
19	neunzehn
20	zwanzig
21	einundzwanzig
22	zweiundzwanzig
23	dreiundzwanzig
30	dreißig
40	vierzig
50	fünfzig
60	sechzig
70	siebzig
80	achtzig
90	neunzig
100	(ein)hundert
101	hundert(und)eins
230	zweihundert(und)dreißig
538	fünfhundert(und)achtunddreißig
1 000	(ein)tausend
10 000	zehntausend
100 000	(ein)hunderttausend
1 000 000	eine Million

Ordinal numbers

1.	erste
2.	zweite
3.	dritte
4.	vierte
5.	fünfte
6.	sechste
7.	sieb(en)te
8.	achte
9.	neunte
10.	zehnte
11.	elfte
12.	zwölfte
13.	dreizehnte
14.	vierzehnte
15.	fünfzehnte
16.	sechzehnte
17.	siebzehnte
18.	achtzehnte
19.	neunzehnte
20.	zwanzigste
21.	einundzwanzigste
22.	zweiundzwanzigste
23.	dreiundzwanzigste
24.	vierundzwanzigste
25.	fünfundzwanzigste
26.	sechsundzwanzigste
27.	siebenundzwanzigste
28.	achtundzwanzigste
29.	neunundzwanzigste
30.	dreißigste
40.	vierzigste
50.	fünfzigste
60.	sechzigste
70.	siebzigste
80.	achtzigste
90.	neunzigste
100.	(ein)hundertste
230.	zweihundert(und)dreißigste
1 000.	(ein)tausendste

Time

Although official time in Germany, Austria and Switzerland is based on the 24-hour clock, the 12-hour system is used in conversation.

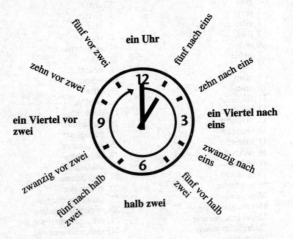

If you want to indicate a.m. or p.m., add *morgens*, *nachmittags* or *abends*. Thus:

acht Uhr morgens	8 a.m.
zwei Uhr nachmittags	2 p.m.
acht Uhr abends	8 p.m.

Days of the Week

Sonntag	Sunday	*Donnerstag*	Thursday
Montag	Monday	*Freitag*	Friday
Dienstag	Tuesday	*Samstag, Sonnabend*	Saturday
Mittwoch	Wednesday		

Some Basic Phrases

Nützliche Redewendungen

Please.	Bitte.
Thank you very much.	Vielen Dank.
Don't mention it.	Gern geschehen.
Good morning.	Guten Morgen.
Good afternoon.	Guten Tag (*nachmittags*).
Good evening.	Guten Abend.
Good night.	Gute Nacht.
Good-bye.	Auf Wiedersehen.
See you later.	Bis bald.
Where is/Where are…?	Wo ist/Wo sind…?
What do you call this?	Wie heißt dies?
What does that mean?	Was bedeutet das?
Do you speak English?	Sprechen Sie Englisch?
Do you speak German?	Sprechen Sie Deutsch?
Do you speak French?	Sprechen Sie Französisch?
Do you speak Spanish?	Sprechen Sie Spanisch?
Do you speak Italian?	Sprechen Sie Italienisch?
Could you speak more slowly, please?	Könnten Sie bitte etwas langsamer sprechen?
I don't understand.	Ich verstehe nicht.
Can I have…?	Kann ich … haben?
Can you show me…?	Können Sie mir … zeigen?
Can you tell me…?	Können Sie mir sagen …?
Can you help me, please?	Können Sie mir bitte helfen?
I'd like…	Ich hätte gern…
We'd like…	Wir hätten gern …
Please give me…	Geben Sie mir bitte …
Please bring me…	Bringen Sie mir bitte …
I'm hungry.	Ich habe Hunger.
I'm thirsty.	Ich habe Durst.
I'm lost.	Ich habe mich verirrt.
Hurry up!	Beeilen Sie sich!
There is/There are…	Es gibt …
There isn't/There aren't…	Es gibt keinen, keine, kein/Es gibt keine …

Arrival

Ankunft

Your passport, please.	Ihren Pass, bitte.
Do you have anything to declare?	Haben Sie etwas zu verzollen?
No, nothing at all.	Nein, gar nichts.
Can you help me with my luggage, please?	Können Sie mir mit meinem Gepäck helfen, bitte?

Where's the bus to the centre of town, please?	Wo ist der Bus zum Stadtzentrum, bitte?
This way, please.	Hier durch, bitte.
Where can I get a taxi?	Wo finde ich ein Taxi?
What's the fare to...?	Was kostet es bis ...?
Take me to this address, please.	Fahren Sie mich bitte zu dieser Adresse.
I'm in a hurry.	Ich habe es eilig.

Hotel — Hotel

My name is...	Mein Name ist ...
Do you have a reservation?	Haben Sie vorbestellt?
I'd like a room with a bath.	Ich hätte gern ein Zimmer mit Bad.
What's the price per night?	Wieviel kostet es pro Nacht?
May I see the room?	Kann ich das Zimmer sehen?
What's my room number, please?	Welche Zimmernummer habe ich, bitte?
There's no hot water.	Es kommt kein warmes Wasser.
May I see the manager, please?	Kann ich bitte den Direktor sprechen?
Did anyone telephone me?	Hat mich jemand angerufen?
Is there any mail for me?	Ist Post für mich da?
May I have my bill (check), please?	Kann ich bitte meine Rechnung haben?

Eating out — Gaststätten

Do you have a fixed-price menu?	Haben Sie ein Menü?
May I see the menu?	Kann ich die Speisekarte sehen?
May we have an ashtray, please?	Können wir bitte einen Aschenbecher haben?
Where's the toilet, please?	Wo ist die Toilette, bitte?
I'd like an hors d'uvre (starter).	Ich hätte gern eine Vorspeise.
Do you have any soup?	Haben Sie Suppe?
I'd like some fish.	Ich hätte gern Fisch.
What kind of fish do you have?	Was für Fisch haben Sie?
I'd like a steak.	Ich hätte gern ein Beefsteak.
What vegetables have you got?	Was für Gemüse haben Sie?
Nothing more, thanks.	Nein danke, nichts mehr.
What would you like to drink?	Was möchten Sie gern trinken?
I'll have a beer, please.	Ich nehme ein Bier, bitte.
I'd like a bottle of wine.	Ich möchte eine Flasche Wein.
May I have the bill (check), please?	Die Rechnung, bitte.
Is service included?	Ist Bedienung inbegriffen?
Thank you, that was a very good meal.	Danke, das Essen war sehr gut.

Travelling — Reisen

| Where's the railway station, please? | Wo ist der Bahnhof, bitte? |

Where's the ticket office, please?	Wo ist der Fahrkartenschalter, bitte?
I'd like a ticket to...	Ich möchte eine Fahrkarte nach ...
First or second class?	Erste oder zweite Klasse?
First class, please.	Erste Klasse, bitte.
Single or return (one way or roundtrip)?	Einfach oder hin und zurück?
Do I have to change trains?	Muss ich umsteigen?
What platform does the train for... leave from?	Auf welchem Bahnsteig fährt der Zug nach ... ab?
Where's the nearest underground (subway) station?	Wo ist die nächste U-Bahn-Station?
Where's the bus station, please?	Wo ist der Busbahnhof, bitte?
When's the first bus to...?	Wann fährt der erste Bus nach ...?
Please let me off at the next stop.	Bitte lassen Sie mich an der nächsten Haltestelle aussteigen.

Relaxing **Unterhaltung**

What's on at the cinema (movies)?	Was gibt es im Kino zu sehen?
What time does the film begin?	Wann beginnt der Film?
Are there any tickets for tonight?	Gibt es noch Karten für heute Abend?
Where can we go dancing?	Wohin können wir tanzen gehen?

Meeting people **Bekanntschaft schließen**

How do you do.	Guten Tag.
How are you?	Wie geht es Ihnen?
Very well, thank you. And you?	Sehr gut, danke. Und Ihnen?
May I introduce ...?	Darf ich Ihnen ... vorstellen?
My name is ...	Ich heiße ...
I'm very pleased to meet you.	Sehr erfreut.
How long have you been here?	Wie lange sind Sie schon hier?
It was nice meeting you.	Es war mir ein Vergnügen.
Do you mind if I smoke?	Stört es Sie, wenn ich rauche?
Do you have a light, please?	Haben Sie Feuer, bitte?
May I get you a drink?	Darf ich Ihnen etwas zum Trinken bestellen?
May I invite you for dinner tonight?	Darf ich Sie heute Abend zum Essen einladen?
Where shall we meet?	Wo treffen wir uns?

Shops, stores and services **Läden, Geschäfte usw.**

Where's the nearest bank, please?	Wo ist die nächste Bank, bitte?
Where can I cash some travellers' cheques?	Wo kann ich Reiseschecks einlösen?

Can you give me some small change, please?	Können Sie mir bitte Kleingeld geben?
Where's the nearest chemist's (pharmacy)?	Wo ist die nächste Apotheke?
How do I get there?	Wie komme ich dorthin?
Is it within walking distance?	Kann man zu Fuß gehen?
Can you help me, please?	Können Sie mir helfen, bitte?
How much is this? And that?	Wie viel kostet dies? Und das?
It's not quite what I want.	Es ist nicht ganz das, was ich möchte.
I like it.	Es gefällt mir.
Can you recommend something for sunburn?	Können Sie mir etwas gegen Sonnenbrand empfehlen?
I'd like a haircut, please.	Ich möchte mir die Haare schneiden lassen, bitte.
I'd like a manicure, please.	Ich möchte eine Maniküre, bitte.

Street directions

Wo? Wohin?

Can you show me on the map where I am?	Können Sie mir auf der Karte zeigen, wo ich bin?
You are on the wrong road.	Sie sind auf der falschen Straße.
Go/Walk straight ahead.	Fahren/Gehen Sie geradeaus.
It's on the left/on the right.	Es ist linker Hand/rechter Hand.

Emergencies

Im Notfall

Call a doctor quickly.	Rufen Sie schnell einen Arzt.
Call an ambulance.	Rufen Sie einen Krankenwagen.
Please call the police.	Rufen Sie bitte die Polizei.

Englisch-Deutsch

English-German

Erläuterungen

Die Gestaltung des Wörterverzeichnisses wird allen praktischen Anforderungen gerecht. Unnötige sprachwissenschaftliche Angaben wurden weggelassen. Alle Eintragungen sind alphabetisch geordnet, egal ob das Stichwort in einem Wort, mit Bindestrich oder als zwei oder mehr Wörter geschrieben wird. Untergeordnete Eintragungen wie übliche Redewendungen oder feste Ausdrücke sind ebenfalls alphabetisch geordnet.

Jedem Stichwort folgt eine Aussprachebezeichnung (siehe Erklärung der Lautschrift). Der Umschrift folgt gegebenenfalls die Angabe der Wortart. Kann eine Vokabel mehreren Wortarten angehören, so stehen die Wortbedeutungen nach der Angabe der entsprechenden Wortart. Die unregelmäßige Pluralform der Substantive wird im gegebenen Falle angeführt. Der Plural steht außerdem nach einigen Wörtern, deren Mehrzahlbildung nicht offensichtlich ist.

Soll eine Eintragung wiederholt werden (auch in unregelmäßigen Pluralformen), so vertritt die Tilde (~) die ganze vorangegangene Eintragung.

Ein waagrechter Strich vertritt den Teil einer Eintragung vor der abweichenden, ausgeschriebenen Wortendung.

Ein Sternchen (*) vor einem Verb bedeutet, dass es unregelmäßig konjugiert wird (siehe Tabelle der unregelmäßigen Verben).

Dieses Wörterbuch folgt der britischen Rechtschreibung. Alle Wörter und Wortbedeutungen, die in erster Linie dem amerikanischen Sprachkreis zugerechnet werden, sind entsprechend gekennzeichnet (siehe Tabelle der im Wörterverzeichnis verwendeten Abkürzungen).

Abkürzungen

®	eingetragenes Warenzeichen, Marke		
adj	Adjektiv	*ntpl*	Neutrum Plural
adv	Adverb	*num*	Numerale
Am	Amerikanisch	*p*	Präteritum
art	Artikel	*pl*	Plural
conj	Konjuktion	*plAm*	Plural (amerikanisch)
f	Femininum	*pp*	Partizip Perfekt
fpl	Femininum Plural	*pr*	Präsens
m	Maskulinum	*pref*	Präfix
mpl	Maskulinum Plural	*prep*	Präposition
n	Substantiv	*pron*	Pronomen
nAm	Substantiv (amerikanisch)	*v*	Verb
nt	Neutrum	*vAm*	Verb (amerikanisch)

Aussprache

In diesem Teil des Wörterbuchs ist zu jedem Stichwort die Aussprache in Internationaler Lautschrift (IPA) angegeben. Jedes einzelne Zeichen dieser Umschrift steht für einen ganz bestimmten Laut. Zeichen, die hier nicht erklärt sind, werden ungefähr wie die entsprechenden Buchstaben im Deutschen ausgesprochen.

Konsonanten

ð	wie s in Rose, aber gelispelt
ŋ	wie ng in Ring
r	schwer zu beschreiben! Die Zunge ist ungefähr in der gleichen Stellung wie bei ʒ (siehe unten), aber viel tiefer, und die Lippen sind eher in einer neutralen Stellung
s	immer wie in es
ʃ	wie sch in rasch
θ	wie s in es, aber gelispelt
v	wie w in wo
z	ein flüchtiger u-Laut, ungefähr wie in Ritual
z	wie s in Rose
ʒ	wie g in Etage

Vokale

aː	wie aa in Saal
æ	zwischen a in hat und ä in nächste
ʌ	ähnlich wie a in hat
e	wie e in fest
ɛ	wie e in best, aber mit der Zunge etwas tiefer
ə	wie e in haben, aber mit gedehnten Lippen (ungerundet)
əː	eher wie ö in lösen, aber mit gedehnten Lippen (ungerundet)
ɔ	wie o in Post

1) Ein Doppelpunkt (ː) bezeichnet die Länge des vorhergehenden Vokals.
2) Einige aus dem Französischen entlehnte Wörter enthalten nasale Vokale, die durch eine Tilde über dem Vokal bezeichnet werden (z.B. ã). Sie werden gleichzeitig durch Mund und Nase ausgesprochen.

Diphthonge

Ein Diphthong besteht aus zwei Vokalen, von denen der eine stärker (betont) und der andere schwächer (unbetont) ist und die zusammen als »gleitender« Laut ausgesprochen werden, wie z.B. **ai** in **Mai**. Im Englischen ist der zweite Vokal immer der schwächere. Manchmal folgt auf einen Diphthong noch ein [ə], wodurch der zweite Vokal etwas weiter abgeschwächt wird. Folgende Diphthonge sind zu beachten:

ei   nicht wie in **eins**! Der erste Laut ist **e** wie in **fest**
ou   ungerundetes **ö** mit folgendem flüchtigem **u**-Laut.

Betonung

Das Zeichen (') steht vor der Silbe mit Hauptton, (‚) vor einer Silbe mit Nebenton.

Amerikanische Aussprache

Unsere Umschrift gibt die übliche britische Aussprache an. Die amerikanische weicht davon in einigen Punkten ab (wobei es noch bedeutende regionale Unterschiede gibt). Hier einige der auffallendsten Abweichungen:
1) Im Gegensatz zum britischen Englisch wird **r** auch vor einem Konsonanten und am Wortende ausgesprochen.
2) In vielen Wörtern (z.B. *ask, castle, laugh* usw.) wird [ɑ:] zu [æ:].
3) Den [ɔ]-Laut spricht der Amerikaner [ē:], vielfach auch [ɔ:].
4) In Wörtern wie *duty, tune, new* usw. entfällt oft der [j]-Laut vor [u:].
5) Schließlich werden eine Anzahl von Wörtern anders betont.

A

a [ei, ə] *art* (an) ein *art*

abbey ['æbi] *n* Abtei *f*

abbreviation [ə,bri:vi'eiʃən] *n* Abkürzung *f*

aberration [,æbə'reiʃən] *n* Abweichung *f*

ability [ə'biləti] *n* Fähigkeit *f*; Vermögen *nt*

able ['eibəl] *adj* imstande; fähig; ***be ~ to** imstande *sein zu; *können

aboard [ə'bɔ:d] *adv* an Bord

abolish [ə'bɔliʃ] *v* abschaffen

abortion [ə'bɔ:ʃən] *n* Abtreibung *f*, Abgang *m*

about [ə'baut] *prep* über; betreffs, hinsichtlich; um; *adv* etwa; umher, herum

above [ə'bʌv] *prep* über; *adv* oben

abroad [ə'brɔ:d] *adv* ins Ausland, im Ausland

abscess ['æbses] *n* Abszess *m*

absence ['æbsəns] *n* Abwesenheit *f*

absent ['æbsənt] *adj* abwesend

absolutely ['æbsəlu:tli] *adv* völlig

abstain from [əb'stein] sich *enthalten

abstract ['æbstrækt] *adj* abstrakt

absurd [əb'sə:d] *adj* absurd, widersinnig

abundance [ə'bʌndəns] *n* Überfluss *m*

abundant [ə'bʌndənt] *adj* reichlich

abuse [ə'bju:s] *n* Missbrauch *m*

abyss [ə'bis] *n* Abgrund *m*

academy [ə'kædəmi] *n* Akademie *f*

accelerate [ək'seləreit] *v* beschleunigen

accelerator [ək'seləreitə] *n* Gaspedal *nt*

accent ['æksənt] *n* Akzent *m*; Betonung *f*

accept [ək'sept] *v* *annehmen; akzeptieren

access ['ækses] *n* Zutritt *m*

accessible [ək'sesəbəl] *adj* zugänglich

accessories [ək'sesəriz] *pl* Zubehör *nt*

accident ['æksidənt] *n* Unglück *nt*, Unfall *m*

accidental [,æksi'dentəl] *adj* zufällig

accommodate [ə'kɔmədeit] *v* *unterbringen

accommodation [ə,kɔmə'deiʃən] *n* Unterkunft *f*

accompany [ə'kʌmpəni] *v* begleiten

accomplish [ə'kʌmpliʃ] *v* vollenden; zustande *bringen

accordance: in ~ with [in ə'kɔ:dəns wið] gemäß

according to [ə'kɔ:diŋ tu:] gemäß; in Übereinstimmung mit

account [ə'kaunt] *n* Konto *nt*; Bericht *m*; **~ for** Rechenschaft ablegen über; **on ~ of** wegen

accountable [ə'kauntəbəl] *adj* erklärbar

accurate ['ækjurət] *adj* genau

accuse [ə'kju:z] *v* beschuldigen; anklagen

accused [ə'kju:zd] *n* Angeklagte *m/f*

accustom [ə'kʌstəm] *v* gewöhnen; **accustomed** gewöhnt, gewohnt

ache [eik] *v* schmerzen; *n* Schmerz *m*

achieve [ə'tʃi:v] *v* erreichen; leisten

achievement [ə'tʃi:vmənt] *n* Leistung *f*

acid ['æsid] *n* Säure *f*

acknowledge [ək'nɔlidʒ] *v* *erkennen; *zugeben; bestätigen

acne ['ækni] *n* Akne *f*

acorn ['eikɔ:n] *n* Eichel *f*

acquaintance [ə'kweintəns] *n* Bekanntschaft *f*, Bekannte *m/f*

acquire [əˈkwaiə] v *erwerben
acquisition [ˌækwiˈziʃən] n Neuerwerbung f
acquittal [əˈkwitəl] n Freispruch m
across [əˈkrɔs] prep über; jenseits; adv drüben
act [ækt] n Tat f; Akt m; Nummer f; v *vorgehen, handeln; sich *benehmen; spielen
action [ˈækʃən] n Aktion f, Handlung f
active [ˈæktiv] adj aktiv; lebhaft
activity [ækˈtivəti] n Aktivität f
actor [ˈæktə] n Schauspieler m
actress [ˈæktris] n Schauspielerin f
actual [ˈæktʃuəl] adj tatsächlich, wirklich
actually [ˈæktʃuəli] adv tatsächlich
acute [əˈkjuːt] adj akut
adapt [əˈdæpt] v anpassen
adapter [əˈdæptə] n Adapter m; Mehrfachstecker m
add [æd] v addieren; hinzufügen
addition [əˈdiʃən] n Addition f; Hinzufügung f
additional [əˈdiʃənəl] adj zusätzlich; nebensächlich
address [əˈdres] n Anschrift f; v adressieren; *ansprechen
addressee [ˌædreˈsiː] n Adressat m, -in f
adequate [ˈædikwət] adj angemessen; entsprechend, passend
adjective [ˈædʒiktiv] n Eigenschaftswort nt
adjourn [əˈdʒəːn] v *verschieben
adjust [əˈdʒʌst] v regulieren; anpassen
administer [ədˈministə] v verabreichen
administration [ədˌminiˈstreiʃən] n Verwaltung f
administrative [ədˈministrətiv] adj administrativ; Verwaltungs-; ~ law

Verwaltungsrecht nt
admiral [ˈædmərəl] n Admiral m
admiration [ˌædməˈreiʃən] n Bewunderung f
admire [ədˈmaiə] v bewundern
admission [ədˈmiʃən] n Eintritt m; Zulassung f
admit [ədˈmit] v *einlassen; einräumen, *zugeben
admittance [ədˈmitəns] n Zutritt m; no ~ kein Eingang
adopt [əˈdɔpt] v adoptieren; *annehmen
adorable [əˈdɔːrəbəl] adj reizend
adult [ˈædʌlt] n Erwachsene m/f; adj erwachsen
advance [ədˈvaːns] n Fortschritt m; Vorschuss m; v *fortschreiten; *vorschießen; in ~ im voraus, vorher
advanced [ədˈvaːnst] adj fortgeschritten
advantage [ədˈvaːntidʒ] n Vorteil m
advantageous [ˌædvənˈteidʒəs] adj vorteilhaft
adventure [ədˈventʃə] n Abenteuer nt
adverb [ˈædvəːb] n Adverb nt
advertisement [ədˈvəːtismənt] n Anzeige f
advertising [ˈædvətaiziŋ] n Werbung f
advice [ədˈvais] n Empfehlung f, Rat m
advise [ədˈvaiz] v *empfehlen, *raten
advocate [ˈædvəkət] n Befürworter m, -in f
aerial [ˈeəriəl] n Antenne f
aeroplane [ˈeərəplein] n Flugzeug nt
affair [əˈfɛə] n Angelegenheit f; Verhältnis nt
affect [əˈfekt] v beeinflussen; sich *beziehen auf
affected [əˈfektid] adj geziert
affection [əˈfekʃən] n Erkrankung f;

Zuneigung f

affectionate [ə'fekʃənit] adj lieb, zärtlich

affiliated [ə'filieitid] adj angegliedert

affirm [ə'fɔːm] v beteuern, bekräftigen

affirmative [ə'fɔːmətiv] adj bejahend

afford [ə'fɔːd] v sich leisten

afraid [ə'freid] adj ängstlich, bange; *be ~ Angst *haben

Africa ['æfrikə] Afrika

African ['æfrikən] adj afrikanisch; n Afrikaner m, -in f

after ['ɑːftə] prep nach; hinter; conj nachdem

afternoon [,ɑːftə'nuːn] n Nachmittag m; **this ~** heute Nachmittag

afterwards ['ɑːftəwədz] adv später; nachher

again [ə'gen] adv wieder; nochmals; **~ and again** immer wieder

against [ə'genst] prep gegen

age [eidʒ] n Alter nt; **of ~** mündig; **under ~** minderjährig

aged ['eidʒid] adj bejahrt; alt

agency ['eidʒənsi] n Agentur f; Dienststelle f; Vertretung f

agenda [ə'dʒendə] n Tagesordnung f

agent ['eidʒənt] n Agent m, -in f, Vertreter m, -in f

aggressive [ə'gresiv] adj aggressiv

ago [ə'gou] adv her

agree [ə'griː] v übereinstimmen; zustimmen

agreeable [ə'griːəbəl] adj angenehm

agreement [ə'griːmənt] n Vertrag m; Akkord m, Abkommen nt

agriculture ['ægrikʌltʃə] n Landwirtschaft f

ahead [ə'hed] adv vorwärts; **~ of** vor; *go ~ *fortfahren; **straight ~** geradeaus

aid [eid] n Hilfe f; v unterstützen, *helfen

Aids [eidz] n Aids nt

ailment ['eilmənt] n Leiden nt; Krankheit f

aim [eim] n Ziel nt; **~ at** v richten auf, zielen auf; beabsichtigen, bezwecken

air [ɛə] n Luft f; v lüften

airbag ['ɛəbæg] n Airbag m

air conditioning ['ɛəkən,diʃəniŋ] n Klimaanlage f; **air-conditioned** adj klimatisiert

aircraft ['ɛəkrɑːft] n (pl ~) Flugzeug nt; Maschine f

airfield ['ɛəfiːld] n Flugplatz m

air-filter ['ɛə,filtə] n Luftfilter m

airline ['ɛəlain] n Fluglinie f

airmail ['ɛəmeil] n Luftpost f

airplane ['ɛəplein] nAm Flugzeug nt

airport ['ɛəpɔːt] n Flughafen m

airsickness ['ɛə,siknəs] n Luftkrankheit f

airtight ['ɛətait] adj luftdicht

airy ['ɛəri] adj luftig

aisle [ail] n Seitenschiff nt; Gang m

alarm [ə'lɑːm] n Alarm m; v alarmieren; **~ clock** Wecker m

album ['ælbəm] n Album nt

alcohol ['ælkəhɔl] n Alkohol m

alcoholic [,ælkə'hɔlik] adj alkoholisch

ale [eil] n Bier nt

algebra ['ældʒibrə] n Algebra f

Algeria [æl'dʒiəriə] Algerien

Algerian [æl'dʒiəriən] adj algerisch; n Algerier m, -in f

alien ['eiliən] n Ausländer m, -in f; adj ausländisch

alike [ə'laik] adj gleich, ähnlich

alive [ə'laiv] adj am Leben, lebend

all [ɔːl] adj all, alle; **~ in** alles inbegriffen; **~ right!** gut!; **at ~** überhaupt

allergy ['ælədʒi] n Allergie f

alley ['æli] n Gasse f

alliance [ə'laiəns] n Bündnis nt

ally ['ælai] n Alliierte m/f

allot [ə'lɔt] v zuteilen

allow [ə'lau] v gestatten, bewilligen, erlauben; **~ to** *lassen; ***be allowed** erlaubt *sein; ***be allowed to** *dürfen

allowance [ə'lauəns] n Zulage f

all-round [ˌɔːl'raund] adj vielseitig

almond ['ɑːmənd] n Mandel f

almost ['ɔːlmoust] adv beinahe; fast

alone [ə'loun] adv allein

along [ə'lɔŋ] prep entlang

aloud [ə'laud] adv laut

alphabet ['ælfəbet] n Alphabet nt

already [ɔːl'redi] adv bereits, schon

also ['ɔːlsou] adv auch; gleichfalls, ebenfalls

altar ['ɔːltə] n Altar m

alter ['ɔːltə] v ändern, verändern

alteration [ˌɔːltə'reiʃən] n Veränderung f, Änderung f

alternate [ɔːl'təːnət] adj abwechselnd

alternative [ɔːl'təːnətiv] n Alternative f

although [ɔːl'ðou] conj obgleich, obwohl

altitude ['æltitjuːd] n Höhe f

alto ['æltou] n (pl ~s) Alt m

altogether [ˌɔːltə'geðə] adv gänzlich; insgesamt

always ['ɔːlweiz] adv immer

am [æm] v (pr be)

amaze [ə'meiz] v verwundern, erstaunen

amazement [ə'meizmənt] n Erstaunen nt

amazing [ə'meiziŋ] adj erstaunlich, unglaublich

ambassador [æm'bæsədə] n Botschafter m, -in f

amber ['æmbə] n Bernstein m

ambiguous [æm'bigjuəs] adj zweideutig

ambition [æm'biʃən] n Ehrgeiz m

ambitious [æm'biʃəs] adj strebsam; ehrgeizig

ambulance ['æmbjuləns] n Krankenwagen m, Ambulanz f

ambush ['æmbuʃ] n Hinterhalt m

America [ə'merikə] Amerika

American [ə'merikən] adj amerikanisch; n Amerikaner m, -in f

amethyst ['æmiθist] n Amethyst m

amid [ə'mid] prep unter; zwischen, inmitten

ammonia [ə'mouniə] n Salmiakgeist m

amnesty ['æmnisti] n Amnestie f

among [ə'mʌŋ] prep unter; zwischen, inmitten; **~ other things** unter anderem

amount [ə'maunt] n Menge f; Summe f, Betrag m; **~ to** v *betragen

amuse [ə'mjuːz] v *unterhalten, amüsieren

amusement [ə'mjuːzmənt] n Vergnügen nt, Unterhaltung f

amusing [ə'mjuːziŋ] adj unterhaltsam

anaemia [ə'niːmiə] n Blutarmut f

anaesthesia [ˌænis'θiːziə] n Betäubung f

anaesthetic [ˌænis'θetik] n Betäubungsmittel nt

analyse ['ænəlaiz] v zerlegen, analysieren

analysis [ə'næləsis] n (pl -ses) Analyse f

analyst ['ænəlist] n Psychoanalytiker m, -in f

anarchy ['ænəki] n Anarchie f

anatomy [ə'nætəmi] n Anatomie f

ancestor ['ænsestə] n Vorfahr m, -in f

anchor ['æŋkə] n Anker m

anchovy ['æntʃəvi] n Sardelle f

ancient ['einʃənt] adj alt; altmodisch, veraltet; uralt

and [ænd, ənd] conj und

applause

angel ['eindʒəl] n Engel m

anger ['æŋɡə] n Ärger m, Zorn m; Wut f

angle ['æŋɡəl] v angeln; n Winkel m

angry ['æŋɡri] adj zornig, böse

animal ['æniməl] n Tier nt

ankle ['æŋkəl] n Fußknöchel m

annex[1] ['æneks] n Nebengebäude nt; Anhang m

annex[2] [ə'neks] v einverleiben

anniversary [,æni'vɔːsəri] n Jahrestag m

announce [ə'nauns] v bekanntmachen, ankündigen

announcement [ə'naunsmənt] n Bekanntmachung f, Ankündigung f

annoy [ə'nɔi] v irritieren, ärgern; langweilen

annoyance [ə'nɔiəns] n Verdruss m

annoying [ə'nɔiiŋ] adj lästig, ärgerlich

annual ['ænjuəl] adj jährlich

annum: per ~ [pər 'ænəm] jährlich

anonymous [ə'nɔniməs] adj anonym

another [ə'nʌðə] adj noch ein; ein anderer

answer ['ɑːnsə] v antworten; beantworten; n Antwort f

ant [ænt] n Ameise f

antibiotic [,æntibai'ɔtik] n Antibiotikum nt

anticipate [æn'tisipeit] v erwarten, *vorhersehen; *zuvorkommen

antifreeze ['æntifriːz] n Gefrierschutzmittel nt

antipathy [æn'tipəθi] n Abneigung f

antique [æn'tiːk] adj antik; n Antiquität f; **~ dealer** Antiquitätenhändler m, -in f

antiquity [æn'tikwəti] n Altertum nt; **antiquities** pl Altertümer

antiseptic [,ænti'septik] n antiseptisches Mittel

antlers ['æntləz] pl Geweih nt

anxiety [æŋ'zaiəti] n Angst f, Sorge f

anxious ['æŋkʃəs] adj bestrebt; besorgt

any ['eni] adj irgendein

anybody ['enibɔdi] pron irgendjemand

anyhow ['enihau] adv irgendwie

anyone ['eniwʌn] pron jedermann

anything ['eniθiŋ] pron irgendetwas

anyway ['eniwei] adv ohnehin

anywhere ['eniweə] adv wo auch immer; überall

apart [ə'pɑːt] adv gesondert, getrennt; **~ from** abgesehen von

apartment [ə'pɑːtmənt] nAm Appartement nt, Wohnung f; **~ house** Am Wohngebäude nt; Mietshaus m

aperitif [ə'perətiv] n Aperitif m

apologize [ə'pɔlədʒaiz] v sich entschuldigen

apology [ə'pɔlədʒi] n Entschuldigung f

apparatus [,æpə'reitəs] n Vorrichtung f, Apparat m

apparent [ə'pærənt] adj scheinbar; offensichtlich

apparently [ə'pærəntli] adv anscheinend; offensichtlich

appeal [ə'piːl] n Appell m

appear [ə'piə] v *scheinen; sich zeigen; *erscheinen; *auftreten

appearance [ə'piərəns] n Erscheinung f, Erscheinen nt; Auftritt m

appendicitis [ə,pendi'saitis] n Blinddarmentzündung f

appendix [ə'pendiks] n (pl -dices, -dixes) Blinddarm m

appetite ['æpətait] n Appetit m

appetizer ['æpətaizə] n Appetithappen m

appetizing ['æpətaiziŋ] adj lecker

applaud [ə'plɔːd] v applaudieren

applause [ə'plɔːz] n Beifall m

apple ['æpəl] n Apfel m

appliance [ə'plaiəns] n Vorrichtung f, Gerät nt

application [,æpli'keiʃən] n Anwendung f; Gesuch nt; Bewerbung f

apply [ə'plai] v *verwenden; gebrauchen; sich *bewerben; *gelten

appoint [ə'pɔint] v anstellen, *ernennen

appointment [ə'pɔintmənt] n Verabredung f; Ernennung f

appreciate [ə'pri:ʃieit] v schätzen

appreciation [ə,pri:ʃi'eiʃən] n Würdigung f

apprentice [ə'prentis] n Auszubildende m(f), Lehrling m

approach [ə'proutʃ] v sich nähern; n Zugang m, Herangehensweise f

appropriate [ə'proupriət] adj richtig, zweckmäßig, geeignet, angemessen

approval [ə'pru:vəl] n Billigung f; Zustimmung f, Einverständnis nt; on ~ zur Ansicht

approve [ə'pru:v] v genehmigen, bejahen; ~ of billigen

approximate [ə'prɔksimət] adj annähernd

approximately [ə'prɔksimətli] adv etwa, ungefähr

apricot ['eiprikɔt] n Aprikose f

April ['eiprəl] April

apron ['eiprən] n Schürze f

Arab ['ærəb] adj arabisch; n Araber m, -in f

arbitrary ['a:bitrəri] adj willkürlich

arcade [a:'keid] n Bogengang m, Arkade f

arch [a:tʃ] n Bogen m; Gewölbe nt

archaeologist [,a:ki'ɔlədʒist] n Archäologe m; Archäologin f

archaeology [,a:ki'ɔlədʒi] n Archäologie f

archbishop [,a:tʃ'biʃəp] n Erzbischof m

arched [a:tʃt] adj bogenförmig

architect ['a:kitekt] n Architekt m, -in f

architecture ['a:kitektʃə] n Baukunst f, Architektur f

archives ['a:kaivz] pl Archiv nt

are [a:] v (pr be)

area ['ɛəriə] n Gegend f; Gebiet nt; Fläche f; ~ code Ortsnetzkennzahl f

Argentina [,a:dʒən'ti:nə] Argentinien

Argentinian [,a:dʒən'tiniən] adj argentinisch; n Argentinier m, -in f

argue ['a:gju:] v argumentieren, erörtern, diskutieren; *streiten

argument ['a:gjumənt] n Argument nt; Auseinandersetzung f; Wortwechsel m

arid ['ærid] adj trocken, dürr

*arise [ə'raiz] v sich *erheben, *entstehen

arithmetic [ə'riθmətik] n Rechnen nt

arm [a:m] n Arm m; Waffe f; Armlehne f; v bewaffnen

armchair ['a:mtʃɛə] n Sessel m, Lehnstuhl m

armed [a:md] adj bewaffnet; ~ forces Streitkräfte pl

armour ['a:mə] n Rüstung f

army ['a:mi] n Armee f

aroma [ə'roumə] n Aroma nt

around [ə'raund] prep um, um ... herum; adv rundherum

arrange [ə'reindʒ] v ordnen; vorbereiten

arrangement [ə'reindʒmənt] n Regelung f

arrest [ə'rest] v verhaften; n Festnahme f, Verhaftung f

arrival [ə'raivəl] n Ankunft f; Eintreffen nt

arrive [ə'raiv] v *ankommen, *eintreffen

arrow ['ærou] *n* Pfeil *m*

art [ɑːt] *n* Kunst *f*; Fertigkeit *f*; ~
collection Kunstsammlung *f*; ~
exhibition Kunstausstellung *f*; ~
gallery Kunstgalerie *f*; ~ **history**
Kunstgeschichte *f*; **arts and crafts**
Kunstgewerbe *nt*; ~ **school**
Kunstakademie *f*

artery ['ɑːtəri] *n* Arterie *f*

artichoke ['ɑːtitʃouk] *n* Artischocke *f*

article ['ɑːtikəl] *n* Gegenstand *m*;
Artikel *m*

artificial [,ɑːti'fiʃəl] *adj* künstlich

artist ['ɑːtist] *n* Künstler *m*, -in *f*

artistic [ɑː'tistik] *adj* künstlerisch

as [æz] *conj* wie; ebenso; da, weil; ~
from von … an; ab; ~ **if** als ob

asbestos [æz'bestɔs] *n* Asbest *m*

ascend [ə'send] *v* *aufsteigen;
*hinaufsteigen; *besteigen

ascent [ə'sent] *n* Steigung *f*; Aufstieg
m

ascertain [,æsə'tein] *v* feststellen;
sich vergewissern, ermitteln

ash [æʃ] *n* Asche *f*

ashamed [ə'ʃeimd] *adj* beschämt; *be
~ *v* sich schämen

ashore [ə'ʃɔː] *adv* ans Land, an Land

ashtray ['æʃtrei] *n* Aschenbecher *m*

Asia ['eiʃə] Asien

Asian ['eiʃən] *adj* asiatisch; *n* Asiate
m; Asiatin *f*

aside [ə'said] *adv* zur Seite, beiseite

ask [ɑːsk] *v* fragen; *bitten; *einladen

asleep [ə'sliːp] *adj* im Schlaf

asparagus [ə'spærəgəs] *n* Spargel *m*

aspect ['æspekt] *n* Aspekt *m*

asphalt ['æsfælt] *n* Asphalt *m*

aspire [ə'spaiə] *v* streben

aspirin ['æspərin] *n* Aspirin *nt*

assassination [ə,sæsi'neiʃən] *n*
Mord *m*

assault [ə'sɔːlt] *v* *angreifen;
vergewaltigen

assemble [ə'sembəl] *v* versammeln;
zusammensetzen, montieren

assembly [ə'sembli] *n* Versammlung
f, Zusammenkunft *f*, Montage *f*

assignment [ə'sainmənt] *n*
Zuweisung *f*

assign to [ə'sain] *v* *zuweisen;
zuschreiben

assist [ə'sist] *v* unterstützen, *helfen

assistance [ə'sistəns] *n* Hilfe *f*;
Unterstützung *f*, Beistand *m*

assistant [ə'sistənt] *n* Assistent *m*,
-in *f*

associate [ə'souʃiət] *n* Partner *m*, -in
f, Teilhaber *m*, -in *f*; Verbündete *m/f*;
Mitglied *nt*; *v* assoziieren; ~ **with** *v*
*umgehen mit

association [ə,sousi'eiʃən] *n*
Vereinigung *f*

assort [ə'sɔːt] *v* sortieren

assortment [ə'sɔːtmənt] *n* Auswahl *f*,
Sortiment *nt*

assume [ə'sjuːm] *v* *annehmen,
voraussetzen

assure [ə'ʃuə] *v* versichern

asthma ['æsmə] *n* Asthma *nt*

astonish [ə'stɔniʃ] *v* verblüffen

astonishing [ə'stɔniʃiŋ] *adj*
erstaunlich

astonishment [ə'stɔniʃmənt] *n*
Erstaunen *nt*

astronomy [ə'strɔnəmi] *n*
Astronomie *f*

astronaut ['æstrənɔːt] *n* Astronaut
m, -in *f*

asylum [ə'sailəm] *n* Asyl *nt*; Anstalt *f*,
Heim *nt*

at [æt] *prep* in, bei, auf; nach; ~ **all** *adv*
überhaupt

ate [et] *v* (p eat)

athlete ['æθliːt] *n* Athlet *m*, -in *f*

Atlantic [ət'læntik] Atlantik *m*

atmosphere ['ætməsfiə] *n*
Atmosphäre *f*; Stimmung *f*

atom ['ætəm] n Atom nt

atomic [ə'tɔmik] adj atomar; Atom-

atomizer ['ætəmaizə] n Zerstäuber m; Spray nt

attach [ə'tætʃ] v befestigen; anheften; beifügen; **attached to** zugetan

attack [ə'tæk] v *angreifen; n Angriff m

attain [ə'tein] v erreichen

attainable [ə'teinəbəl] adj erreichbar

attempt [ə'tempt] v probieren, versuchen; n Versuch m

attend [ə'tend] v beiwohnen; ~ **on** bedienen; ~ **to** sorgen für, sich beschäftigen mit; beachten, *Acht geben auf

attendance [ə'tendəns] n Teilnahme f

attendant [ə'tendənt] n Wärter m, -in f

attention [ə'tenʃən] n Aufmerksamkeit f; *pay ~ aufpassen

attentive [ə'tentiv] adj aufmerksam

attest [ə'test] v bescheinigen, beglaubigen

attic ['ætik] n (Dach)Boden m

attitude ['ætitjuːd] n Einstellung f

attorney [ə'təːni] n Anwalt m, Anwältin f

attract [ə'trækt] v *anziehen

attraction [ə'trækʃən] n Attraktion f; Anziehung f, Reiz m

attractive [ə'træktiv] adj anziehend

auburn ['ɔːbən] adj kastanienbraun

auction ['ɔːkʃən] n Versteigerung f

audible ['ɔːdibəl] adj hörbar

audience ['ɔːdiəns] n Publikum nt

auditor ['ɔːditə] n Zuhörer m, -in f

auditorium [,ɔːdi'tɔːriəm] n Zuhörerraum m

August ['ɔːgəst] August

aunt [ɑːnt] n Tante f

Australia [ɔ'streiliə] Australien

Australian [ɔ'streiliən] adj australisch; n Australier m, -in f

Austria ['ɔstriə] Österreich

Austrian ['ɔstriən] adj österreichisch; n Österreicher m, -in f

authentic [ɔ'θentik] adj authentisch; echt

author ['ɔːθə] n Verfasser m, -in f, Autor m, -in f

authoritarian [ɔ,θɔri'tɛəriən] adj autoritär

authority [ɔ'θɔrəti] n Befugnis f; Machtbefugnis f; Vollmacht f; authorities pl Behörde f

authorization [,ɔːθərai'zeiʃən] n Ermächtigung f; Genehmigung f

automatic [,ɔːtə'mætik] adj automatisch; ~ **teller** n Geldautomat m

automobile ['ɔːtəməbiːl] n Auto nt; ~ **club** Automobilklub m

autonomous [ɔ'tɔnəməs] adj autonom

autopsy ['ɔːtɔpsi] n Autopsie f

autumn ['ɔːtəm] n Herbst m

available [ə'veiləbəl] adj vorrätig, vorhanden, verfügbar

avalanche ['ævəlɑːnʃ] n Lawine f

avenue ['ævənjuː] n Allee f

average ['ævəridʒ] adj durchschnittlich; n Durchschnitt m; on the ~ durchschnittlich

averse [ə'vəːs] adj abgeneigt

aversion [ə'vəːʃən] n Widerwille m

avert [ə'vəːt] v abwenden

avoid [ə'vɔid] v *vermeiden; *meiden

await [ə'weit] v warten auf, erwarten

awake [ə'weik] adj wach

*awake [ə'weik] v wecken

award [ə'wɔːd] n Preis m; v *zuerkennen

aware [ə'wɛə] adj bewusst

away [ə'wei] adv weg; *go ~ *weggehen

awful ['ɔːfəl] adj furchtbar, schrecklich

awkward ['ɔ:kwəd] *adj* peinlich;
ungeschickt
awning ['ɔ:niŋ] *n* Markise *f*

axe [æks] *n* Beil *nt*
axle ['æksəl] *n* Achse *f*

B

baby ['beibi] *n* Baby *nt*; ~ **carriage**
Am Kinderwagen *m*
babysitter ['beibi,sitə] *n* Babysitter *m*
bachelor ['bætʃələ] *n* Junggeselle *m*
back [bæk] *n* Rücken *m*; *adv* zurück;
***go** ~ *zurückgehen
backache ['bækeik] *n*
Rückenschmerzen *mpl*
backbone ['bækboun] *n* Rückgrat *nt*
background ['bækgraund] *n*
Hintergrund *m*; Vorbildung *f*
backwards ['bækwədz] *adv*
rückwärts
bacon ['beikən] *n* Speck *m*
bacterium [bæk'ti:riəm] *n* (pl -ria)
Bakterie *f*
bad [bæd] *adj* schlecht; ernsthaft,
schlimm; ungezogen
bag [bæg] *n* Sack *m*; Tasche *f*,
Handtasche *f*; Koffer *m*
baggage ['bægidʒ] *n* Gepäck *nt*; ~
check *Am* Gepäckaufbewahrung *f*;
hand ~ *Am* Handgepäck *nt*
bail [beil] *n* Kaution *f*
bait [beit] *n* Köder *m*
bake [beik] *v* backen
baker ['beikə] *n* Bäcker *m*, -in *f*
bakery ['beikəri] *n* Bäckerei *f*
balance ['bæləns] *n* Gleichgewicht *nt*;
Bilanz *f*; Saldo *m*
balcony ['bælkəni] *n* Balkon *m*
bald [bɔ:ld] *adj* kahl
ball [bɔ:l] *n* Ball *m*
ballet ['bælei] *n* Ballett *nt*
balloon [bə'lu:n] *n* Ballon *m*

ballpoint pen ['bɔ:lpɔintpen] *n*
Kugelschreiber *m*
bamboo [bæm'bu:] *n* (pl ~s) Bambus *m*
banana [bə'nɑ:nə] *n* Banane *f*
band [bænd] *n* Kapelle *f*; Band *nt*
bandage ['bændidʒ] *n* Verband *m*
band-aid ['bændeid] *nAm*
Heftpflaster *nt*
bandit ['bændit] *n* Bandit *m*
bangle ['bæŋgəl] *n* Armreif *m*
banisters ['bænistəz] *pl*
Treppengeländer *nt*
bank [bæŋk] *n* Ufer *nt*; Bank *f*; *v*
deponieren; ~ **account** Bankkonto *nt*
bank note ['bæŋknout] *n* Banknote *f*,
Geldschein *m*
bankrupt ['bæŋkrʌpt] *adj*
zahlungsunfähig, bankrott
banquet ['bæŋkwit] *n* Festmahl *nt*
baptism ['bæptizəm] *n* Taufe *f*
baptize [bæp'taiz] *v* taufen
bar [bɑ:] *n* Bar *f*; Stange *f*
barbecue ['bɑ:bikju:] *n* Grillfest *nt*; *v*
grillen
barbed wire ['bɑ:bd waiə] *n*
Stacheldraht *m*
barber ['bɑ:bə] *n* Friseur *m*, -in *f*
bare [beə] *adj* nackt, bloß; kahl
barely ['beəli] *adv* kaum
bargain ['bɑ:gin] *n* Gelegenheitskauf
m; *v* handeln
baritone ['bæritoun] *n* Bariton *m*
bark [bɑ:k] *n* Rinde *f*; *v* bellen
barley ['bɑ:li] *n* Gerste *f*

barmaid ['bɑ:meid] n Bardame f

barman ['bɑ:mən] n (pl -men) Kellner m

barn [bɑ:n] n Scheune f

barometer [bə'rɔmitə] n Barometer nt

baroque [bə'rɔk] adj barock

barracks ['bærəks] pl Kaserne f

barrel ['bærəl] n Tonne f, Fass nt

barrier ['bæriə] n Schranke f

barrister ['bæristə] n Rechtsanwalt m, Rechtsanwältin f

bartender ['bɑ:,tendə] n Kellner m

base [beis] n Basis f; Grundlage f; v gründen auf

baseball ['beisbɔ:l] n Baseball m

basement ['beismənt] n Untergeschoss nt

basic ['beisik] adj grundlegend; basics npl Grundlagen pl

basilica [bə'zilikə] n Basilika f

basin ['beisən] n Schüssel f, Becken nt

basis ['beisis] n (pl bases) Grundlage f, Basis f

basket ['bɑ:skit] n Korb m

bass¹ [beis] n Bass m

bass² [bæs] n (pl ~) Barsch m

batch [bætʃ] n Partie f

bath [bɑ:θ] n Bad nt; ~ salts Badesalz nt; ~ towel Badetuch nt

bathe [beið] v baden

bathing cap ['beiðiŋkæp] n Bademütze f

bathing suit ['beiðiŋsu:t] n Badeanzug m; Badehose f

bathing trunks ['beiðiŋtrʌŋks] n Badehose f

bathrobe ['bɑ:θroub] n Bademantel m

bathroom ['bɑ:θru:m] n Badezimmer nt; Toiletten fpl

batter ['bætə] n Teig m

battery ['bætəri] n Batterie f; Akku m

battle ['bætəl] n Schlacht f; Streit m,

Kampf m; v kämpfen

bay [bei] n Bucht f; v bellen

*be [bi:] v *sein

beach [bi:tʃ] n Strand m; nudist ~ FKK-Strand m

bead [bi:d] n Perle f; beads pl Halsband nt; Rosenkranz m

beak [bi:k] n Schnabel m

beam [bi:m] n Strahl m; Balken m

bean [bi:n] n Bohne f

bear [bɛə] n Bär m

*bear [bɛə] v *tragen; dulden; *ertragen

beard [biəd] n Bart m

bearer ['bɛərə] n Inhaber m, -in f

beast [bi:st] n Tier nt; ~ of prey Raubtier nt

*beat [bi:t] v *schlagen; besiegen

beautiful ['bju:tifəl] adj schön

beauty ['bju:ti] n Schönheit f; ~ parlour Schönheitssalon m; ~ salon Schönheitssalon m; ~ treatment kosmetische Behandlung f

beaver ['bi:və] n Biber m

because [bi'kɔz] conj weil; da; ~ of aufgrund, wegen

*become [bi'kʌm] v *werden; gut *stehen

bed [bed] n Bett nt; ~ and board Vollpension f; ~ and breakfast Zimmer mit Frühstück

bedding ['bediŋ] n Bettzeug nt

bedroom ['bedru:m] n Schlafzimmer nt

bee [bi:] n Biene f

beech [bi:tʃ] n Buche f

beef [bi:f] n Rindfleisch nt

beefburger ['bi:fbɜ:gə] n Hamburger m

beehive ['bi:haiv] n Bienenkorb m

been [bi:n] v (pp be)

beer [biə] n Bier nt

beet [bi:t] n Rübe f

beetle ['bi:təl] n Käfer m

beetroot ['biːtruːt] n (rote) Bete f

before [bi'fɔː] prep vor; conj bevor; adv vorher; eher, zuvor

beg [beg] v betteln; *bitten

beggar ['begə] n Bettler m, -in f

***begin** [bi'gin] v *beginnen; *anfangen

beginner [bi'ginə] n Anfänger m, -in f

beginning [bi'giniŋ] n Beginn m; Anfang m

behalf: on ~ of [ɔn bi'hɑːf ɔv] im Namen von; zugunsten

behave [bi'heiv] v sich *benehmen

behavio(u)r [bi'heivjə] n Verhalten nt

behind [bi'haind] prep hinter; adv hinten

beige [beiʒ] adj beige

being ['biːiŋ] n Wesen nt

Belgian ['beldʒən] adj belgisch; n Belgier m, -in f

Belgium ['beldʒəm] Belgien

belief [bi'liːf] n Glaube m

believe [bi'liːv] v glauben

bell [bel] n Glocke f; Klingel f

bellboy ['belbɔi] n Hotelpage m

belly ['beli] n Bauch m

belong [bi'lɔŋ] v gehören

belongings [bi'lɔŋiŋz] pl Habe f

beloved [bi'lʌvd] adj geliebt

below [bi'lou] prep unterhalb; unter; adv unten

belt [belt] n Gürtel m

bench [bentʃ] n Bank f

bend [bend] n Kurve f, Biegung f; Krümmung f

***bend** [bend] v *biegen; **~ down** sich bücken

beneath [bi'niːθ] prep unter; adv unten

benefit ['benifit] n Gewinn m, Nutzen m; Vorteil m; v profitieren

bent [bent] adj (pp bend) krumm

beret ['berei] n Baskenmütze f

berry ['beri] n Beere f

berth [bəːθ] n Schlafwagenbett nt; Koje f

beside [bi'said] prep neben

besides [bi'saidz] adv überdies; übrigens; prep außer

best [best] adj best

bet [bet] n Wette f; Einsatz m

***bet** [bet] v wetten

betray [bi'trei] v *verraten

better ['betə] adj besser

between [bi'twiːn] prep zwischen

beverage ['bevəridʒ] n Getränk nt

beware [bi'wɛə] v sich in Acht *nehmen, sich hüten

bewitch [bi'witʃ] v verzaubern

beyond [bi'jɔnd] prep über ... hinaus; jenseits; außer; adv jenseits

bible ['baibəl] n Bibel f

bicycle ['baisikəl] n Fahrrad nt; Rad nt

bid [bid] n Gebot nt, Angebot nt; bieten

big [big] adj groß; umfangreich; dick; bedeutend

bike [baik] n colloquial Fahrrad nt; v radeln

bile [bail] n Galle f

bilingual [bai'liŋwəl] adj zweisprachig

bill [bil] n Rechnung f

billiards ['biljədz] pl Billard nt

billion ['biljən] n Milliarde f

***bind** [baind] v *binden

binding ['baindiŋ] n Einband m

binoculars [bi'nɔkjələz] pl Feldstecher m; Fernglas nt

biology [bai'ɔlədʒi] n Biologie f

birch [bəːtʃ] n Birke f

bird [bəːd] n Vogel m

biro® [bai'rou] n Kugelschreiber m

birth [bəːθ] n Geburt f

birthday ['bəːθdei] n Geburtstag m

biscuit ['biskit] n Keks m

bishop ['biʃəp] n Bischof m

bit [bit] *n* Stückchen *nt*; bisschen

bitch [bitʃ] *n* Hündin *f*

bite [bait] *n* Bissen *m*; Biss *m*; Stich *m*

*bite [bait] *v* *beißen

bitter [ˈbitə] *adj* bitter

black [blæk] *adj* schwarz; ~ **market** Schwarzmarkt *m*

blackberry [ˈblækbəri] *n* Brombeere *f*

blackbird [ˈblækbəːd] *n* Amsel *f*

blackboard [ˈblækbɔːd] *n* Wandtafel *f*

blackcurrant [ˌblækˈkʌrənt] *n* Johannisbeere *f*

blackmail [ˈblækmeil] *n* Erpressung *f*; *v* erpressen

blacksmith [ˈblæksmiθ] *n* Schmied *m*, -in *f*

bladder [ˈblædə] *n* Blase *f*

blade [bleid] *n* Klinge *f*; ~ **of grass** Grashalm *m*

blame [bleim] *n* Schuld *f*; Vorwurf *m*; *v* *vorwerfen, beschuldigen

blank [blæŋk] *adj* leer

blanket [ˈblæŋkit] *n* Decke *f*

blast [blɑːst] *n* Explosion *f*

blazer [ˈbleizə] *n* Sportjacke *f*, Blazer *m*

bleach [bliːtʃ] *v* bleichen

bleak [bliːk] *adj* rau

*bleed [bliːd] *v* bluten; aussaugen

bless [bles] *v* segnen

blessing [ˈblesiŋ] *n* Segen *m*

blind [blaind] *n* Jalousie *f*; *adj* blind; *v* blenden

blinker [ˈbliŋkə] *n* Blinklicht *nt*; Blinker *m*

blister [ˈblistə] *n* Blase *f*

blizzard [ˈblizəd] *n* Schneesturm *m*

block [blɔk] *v* versperren, blockieren, sperren; *n* Klotz *m*; ~ **of flats** Wohnblock *m*

blond [blɔnd] *n* Blonde *m*,*f*; *adj* blond

blonde [blɔnd] *n* Blondine *f*

blood [blʌd] *n* Blut *nt*; ~ **pressure** Blutdruck *m*; ~ **poisoning**

Blutvergiftung *f*; ~ **vessel** Blutgefäß *nt*

bloody [ˈblʌdi] *adj* blutig; *colloquial* verdammt

blossom [ˈblɔsəm] *n* Blüte *f*; blühen

blot [blɔt] *n* Klecks *m*; Makel *m*

blouse [blauz] *n* Bluse *f*

blow [blou] *n* Schlag *m*; Windstoß *m*

*blow [blou] *v* *blasen; wehen; ~ **up** sprengen; explodieren

blowout [ˈblouaut] *n* Reifenpanne *f*

blue [bluː] *adj* blau; niedergeschlagen

blunt [blʌnt] *adj* stumpf

blush [blʌʃ] *v* erröten

board [bɔːd] *n* Brett *nt*; Tafel; Pension *f*; Rat *m*; ~ **and lodging** Vollpension *f*

boardinghouse [ˈbɔːdiŋhaus] *n* Pension *f*

boarding school [ˈbɔːdiŋskuːl] *n* Internat *nt*

boast [boust] *v* prahlen

boat [bout] *n* Schiff *nt*, Boot *nt*

body [ˈbɔdi] *n* Körper *m*; Leib *m*

bodyguard [ˈbɔdigɑːd] *n* Leibwächter *m*

bog [bɔg] *n* Sumpf *m*

boil [bɔil] *v* kochen; *n* Furunkel *m*

bold [bould] *adj* kühn; frech

Bolivia [bəˈliviə] Bolivien

Bolivian [bəˈliviən] *adj* bolivianisch; *n* Bolivianer *m*, -in *f*

bolt [boult] *n* Riegel *m*; Bolzen *m*

bomb [bɔm] *n* Bombe *f*; *v* bombardieren

bond [bɔnd] *n* Obligation *f*

bone [boun] *n* Bein *nt*, Knochen *m*; Gräte *f*

bonnet [ˈbɔnit] *n* Motorhaube *f*

book [buk] *n* Buch *nt*; *v* reservieren, buchen; *einschreiben, *eintragen

booking [ˈbukiŋ] *n* Einschreibung *f*, Reservierung *f*

bookseller [ˈbukˌselə] *n* Buchhändler *m*, -in *f*

bookstand ['bukstænd] n
Bücherständer m

bookstore ['bukstɔ:] n Buchladen m,
Buchhandlung f

boot [bu:t] n Stiefel m; Kofferraum m

booth [bu:ð] n Bude f; Zelle f

booze [bu:z] n colloquial Alkohol m;
v saufen

border ['bɔ:də] n Grenze f, Rand m

bore¹ [bɔ:] v langweilen; bohren

bore² [bɔ:] v (p bear)

boring ['bɔ:riŋ] adj langweilig

born [bɔ:n] adj geboren

borrow ['bɔrou] v borgen; *entleihen

bosom ['buzəm] n Brust f, Busen m

boss [bɔs] n Chef m, -in f

botany ['bɔtəni] n Botanik f

both [bouθ] adj beide; **both ... and**
sowohl ... als auch

bother ['bɔðə] v belästigen; sich Mühe
*geben; n Belästigung f

bottle ['bɔtəl] n Flasche f; ~ **opener**
Flaschenöffner m; **hot-water ~**
Wärmflasche f

bottleneck ['bɔtəlnek] n Engpass m

bottom ['bɔtəm] n Boden m; Hintern
m, Gesäß nt; adj unterst

bought [bɔ:t] v (p, pp buy)

boulder ['bouldə] n Felsblock m

bound [baund] n Grenze f; *be ~ to
*müssen; ~ for unterwegs nach

boundary ['baundəri] n Grenze f;
Landesgrenze f

bouquet [bu'kei] n Strauß m

boutique [bu'ti:k] n Boutique f

bow¹ [bau] v beugen

bow² [bou] n Bogen m; ~ tie Fliege f

bowels ['bauəlz] pl Eingeweide pl

bowl [boul] n Schale f

bowling ['bouliŋ] n Bowling nt,
Kegeln nt; ~ **alley** Kegelbahn f

box¹ [bɔks] v boxen; **boxing match**
Boxkampf m

box² [bɔks] n Schachtel f

box office ['bɔks,ɔfis] n
Vorverkaufskasse f, Kasse f

boy [bɔi] n Junge m; Bursche m, Bub
m; Diener m; ~ **scout** Pfadfinder m

boyfriend ['bɔifrend] n Freund m
(eines Mädchens)

bra [brɑ:] n BH m, Büstenhalter m

bracelet ['breislit] n Armband nt

braces ['breisiz] pl Hosenträger mpl

brain [brein] n Gehirn nt; Verstand m;
~ **wave** Geistesblitz m

brake [breik] n Bremse f; ~ **drum**
Bremstrommel f; ~ **lights**
Bremslichter ntpl

branch [brɑ:ntʃ] n Ast m; Zweigstelle
f

brand [brænd] n Marke f;
Brandmarke f

brand-new [,brænd'nju:] adj
nagelneu

brass [brɑ:s] n Messing nt; ~ **band** n
Blaskapelle f

brassière ['bræziə] n Büstenhalter m

brave [breiv] adj mutig, tapfer

Brazil [brə'zil] Brasilien

Brazilian [brə'ziljən] adj
brasilianisch; n Brasilianer m, -in f

breach [bri:tʃ] n Bruch m

bread [bred] n Brot nt; **wholemeal ~**
Vollkornbrot nt

breadth [bredθ] n Breite f

break [breik] n Bruch m; Pause f

***break** [breik] v *brechen; ~ **down**
eine Panne *haben; aufgliedern;
zusammenbrechen

breakdown ['breikdaun] n
Betriebsstörung f, Panne f

breakfast ['brekfəst] n Frühstück nt

breast [brest] n Brust f

breaststroke ['breststrouk] n
Brustschwimmen nt

breath [breθ] n Atem m; Luft f

breathe [bri:ð] v atmen

breathing ['bri:ðiŋ] n Atmung f

breed [bri:d] *n* Rasse *f*; Gattung *f*

*breed [bri:d] *v* züchten

breeze [bri:z] *n* Brise *f*

brew [bru:] *v* brauen

brewery ['bru:əri] *n* Brauerei *f*

bribe [braib] *v* *bestechen

bribery ['braibəri] *n* Bestechung *f*

brick [brik] *n* Ziegelstein *m*, Ziegel *m*

bricklayer ['brikleiə] *n* Maurer *m*, -in *f*

bride [braid] *n* Braut *f*

bridegroom ['braidgru:m] *n* Bräutigam *m*

bridge [bridʒ] *n* Brücke *f*; Bridge *nt*

brief [bri:f] *adj* kurz; bündig

briefcase ['bri:fkeis] *n* Aktentasche *f*

briefs [bri:fs] *pl* Slip *m*, Unterhose *f*

bright [brait] *adj* hell; leuchtend; schlau, klug

brighten ['braitən] *v* aufhellen, erhellen

brilliant ['briljənt] *adj* glänzend; brillant

brim [brim] *n* Rand *m*

*bring [briŋ] *v* *bringen; *mitbringen; ~ **back** *zurückbringen; ~ **up** *erziehen; *großziehen; *vorbringen

brisk [brisk] *adj* lebhaft

Britain ['britən] England

British ['britiʃ] *adj* britisch; englisch

Briton ['britən] Brite *m*, -in *f*

broad [bro:d] *adj* breit; ausgedehnt, weit; global

broadcast ['bro:dka:st] *n* Sendung *f*

*broadcast ['bro:dka:st] *v* *senden

brochure ['brouʃuə] *n* Broschüre *f*

broke¹ [brouk] *v* (p break)

broke² [brouk] *adj* blank

broken ['broukən] *adj* (pp break) kaputt, entzwei

broker ['broukə] *n* Makler *m*, -in *f*

bronchitis [broŋ'kaitis] *n* Bronchitis *f*

bronze [bronz] *n* Bronze *f*; *adj* bronzen

brooch [broutʃ] *n* Brosche *f*

brook [bruk] *n* Bach *m*

broom [bru:m] *n* Besen *m*

brothel ['broθəl] *n* Bordell *nt*

brother ['brʌðə] *n* Bruder *m*

brother-in-law ['brʌðərinlɔ:] *n* (pl brothers-) Schwager *m*

brought [bro:t] *v* (p, pp bring)

brown [braun] *adj* braun

bruise [bru:z] *n* blauer Fleck, Quetschung *f*; *v* quetschen

brush [brʌʃ] *n* Bürste *f*; Pinsel *m*; *v* putzen, bürsten

brutal ['bru:təl] *adj* brutal

bubble ['bʌbəl] *n* Blase *f*

buck [bʌk] *n* Bock *m*; *colloquial* Dollar *m*

bucket ['bʌkit] *n* Eimer *m*

buckle ['bʌkəl] *n* Schnalle *f*

bud [bʌd] *n* Knospe *f*

buddy ['bʌdi] *n* *colloquial* Kumpel *m*

budget ['bʌdʒit] *n* Voranschlag *m*, Budget *nt*

buffet ['bufei] *n* Büfett *nt*

bug [bʌg] *n* Wanze *f*; Käfer *m*; *nAm* Insekt *nt*

*build [bild] *v* bauen

building ['bildiŋ] *n* Gebäude *nt*

bulb [bʌlb] *n* Zwiebel *f*; Blumenzwiebel *f*; **light** ~ Glühbirne *f*

Bulgaria [bʌl'geəriə] Bulgarien

Bulgarian [bʌl'geəriən] *adj* bulgarisch; *n* Bulgare *m*, Bulgarin *f*

bulk [bʌlk] *n* Umfang *m*; Masse *f*; Mehrheit *f*

bulky ['bʌlki] *adj* dick, umfangreich

bull [bul] *n* Stier *m*

bullet ['bulit] *n* Kugel *f*

bullfight ['bulfait] *n* Stierkampf *m*

bulletin ['bulitin] *n* Bekanntmachung *f*; ~ **board** schwarzes Brett

bullring ['bulriŋ] *n* Stierkampfarena *f*

bump [bʌmp] *v* *stoßen; *zusammenstoßen; *schlagen; *n*

Schlag *m*, Stoß *m*

bumper ['bʌmpə] *n* Stoßstange *f*

bumpy ['bʌmpi] *adj* holperig

bun [bʌn] *n* Brötchen *nt*

bunch [bʌntʃ] *n* Strauß *m*; Haufen *m*

bundle ['bʌndəl] *n* Bündel *nt*; *v* *zusammenbinden, bündeln

bunk [bʌŋk] *n* Koje *f*

buoy [bɔi] *n* Boje *f*

burden ['bə:dən] *n* Last *f*

bureau ['bjuərou] *n* (pl ~x, ~s) Schreibtisch *m*; *nAm* Kommode *f*

bureaucracy [bjuə'rɔkrəsi] *n* Bürokratie *f*

burglar ['bə:glə] *n* Einbrecher *m*, -in *f*

burgle ['bə:gəl] *v* *einbrechen

burial ['beriəl] *n* Bestattung *f*, Begräbnis *nt*

burn [bə:n] *n* Brandwunde *f*

***burn** [bə:n] *v* *brennen; *verbrennen; *anbrennen

***burst** [bə:st] *v* *bersten

bury ['beri] *v* beerdigen; *begraben

bus [bʌs] *n* Bus *m*

bush [buʃ] *n* Busch *m*

business ['biznəs] *n* Handel *m*, Gewerbe *nt*; Unternehmen *nt*, Geschäft *nt*; Beschäftigung *f*; Angelegenheit *f*; ~ hours

Öffnungszeiten *fpl*, Geschäftszeit *f*; ~ trip Geschäftsreise *f*; on ~ geschäftlich

business-like ['biznislaik] *adj* geschäftsmäßig

businessman ['biznəsmən] *n* (pl -men) Geschäftsmann *m*

businesswoman ['biznəswumən] *n* (pl -women) Geschäftsfrau *f*

bust [bʌst] *n* Büste *f*

busy ['bizi] *adj* beschäftigt; verkehrsreich

but [bʌt] *conj* aber; jedoch; *prep* außer

butcher ['butʃə] *n* Fleischer *m*, -in *f*

butter ['bʌtə] *n* Butter *f*

butterfly ['bʌtəflai] *n* Schmetterling *m*; ~ stroke Schmetterlingsstil *m*

buttocks ['bʌtəks] *pl* Gesäß *n*

button ['bʌtən] *n* Knopf *m*; *v* knöpfen

buttonhole ['bʌtənhoul] *n* Knopfloch *nt*

***buy** [bai] *v* kaufen; *erwerben

buyer ['baiə] *n* Käufer *m*, -in *f*

buzz [bʌz] *n* summen, brummen

by [bai] *prep* von, durch; mit; bei

bye-bye [bai'bai] *colloquial* Wiedersehen!, tschüs(s)!

bypass ['baipɑːs] *n* Umgehungsstraße *f*; *v* *umgehen

C

cab [kæb] *n* Taxi *nt*

cabaret ['kæbərei] *n* Kabarett *nt*; Nachtklub *m*

cabbage ['kæbidʒ] *n* Kohl *m*

cab driver ['kæb,draivə] *n* Taxifahrer *m*, -in *f*

cabin ['kæbin] *n* Kabine *f*; Hütte *f*; Umkleidekabine *f*; Kajüte *f*

cabinet ['kæbinət] *n* Kabinett *nt*

cable ['keibəl] *n* Kabel *nt*; ~ television Kabelfernsehen *nt*

café ['kæfei] *n* Café *nt*

cafeteria [,kæfə'tiəriə] *n* Selbstbedienungsrestaurant *nt*

caffeine ['kæfiːn] *n* Koffein *nt*

cage [keidʒ] *n* Käfig *m*

cake [keik] *n* Kuchen *m*; Torte *f*, Gebäck *nt*

calamity [kə'læməti] n Unglück nt
calcium ['kælsiəm] n Kalzium nt
calculate ['kælkjuleit] v berechnen, ausrechnen
calculation [ˌkælkju'leiʃən] n Kalkulation f
calculator ['kælkju'leitə] n Rechner m
calendar ['kæləndə] n Kalender m
calf [kɑːf] n (pl calves) Kalb nt; Wade f; ~ skin Kalbleder nt
call [kɔːl] v *rufen; *nennen; *anrufen; n Ruf m; Besuch m; Anruf m; long-distance ~ n Ferngespräch nt; *be called *heißen; ~ names ausschimpfen; ~ on besuchen; ~ up Am *anrufen
calm [kɑːm] adj ruhig, still; ~ down v beruhigen
calorie ['kæləri] n Kalorie f
came [keim] v (p come)
camel ['kæməl] n Kamel nt
camera ['kæmərə] n Kamera f; ~ shop Fotogeschäft nt
camp [kæmp] n Lager nt; v zelten
campaign [kæm'pein] n Kampagne f
camp bed [ˌkæmp'bed] n Liege f, Feldbett nt
camper ['kæmpə] n Camper m
camping ['kæmpiŋ] n Camping nt; ~ site Zeltplatz m, Campingplatz m
can [kæn] n Dose f; ~ opener Dosenöffner m; canned food Konserven fpl
*can [kæn] v *können
Canada ['kænədə] Kanada
Canadian [kə'neidiən] adj kanadisch; n Kanadier m, -in f
canal [kə'næl] n Kanal m
canary [kə'neəri] n Kanarienvogel m
cancel ['kænsəl] v annullieren; *widerrufen
cancellation [ˌkænsə'leiʃən] n Annullierung f

cancer ['kænsə] n Krebs m
candidate ['kændidət] n Kandidat m, -in f, Bewerber m, -in f
candle ['kændəl] n Kerze f
candy ['kændi] nAm Bonbon m; Süßigkeiten fpl ~ store Am Süßwarengeschäft nt
cane [kein] n Rohr nt; Stock m
canister ['kænistə] n Dose f
canoe [kə'nuː] n Kanu nt
canteen [kæn'tiːn] n Kantine f
canvas ['kænvəs] n Segeltuch nt
cap [kæp] n Mütze f
capable ['keipəbəl] adj tüchtig, fähig
capacity [kə'pæsəti] n Fähigkeit f; Leistungsfähigkeit f; Kompetenz f
cape [keip] n Umhang m; Kap nt
capital ['kæpitəl] n Hauptstadt f; Kapital nt; adj bedeutend, Haupt-; ~ letter Großbuchstabe m
capitalism ['kæpitəlizəm] n Kapitalismus m
capitulation [kə,pitju'leiʃən] n Kapitulation f
capsule ['kæpsjuːl] n Kapsel f
captain ['kæptin] n Kapitän m; Flugkapitän m
capture ['kæptʃə] v *gefangen nehmen, *fangen; *einnehmen; n Festnahme f; Einnahme f
car [kɑː] n Wagen m; ~ hire Autovermietung f, ~ park Parkplatz m; Parkhaus nt; ~ rental Am Autovermietung f
caramel ['kærəməl] n Karamelle f
carat ['kærət] n Karat nt
caravan ['kærəvæn] n Wohnwagen m
carburettor [ˌkɑːbju'retə] n Vergaser m
card [kɑːd] n Karte f; Postkarte f
cardboard ['kɑːdbɔːd] n Pappe f; adj Papp-
cardigan ['kɑːdigən] n Wolljacke f
cardinal ['kɑːdinəl] n Kardinal m; adj

Kardinal-, hauptsächlich

care [keə] n Pflege f; Sorge f; **~ about** v sich sorgen um; **~ for** v gern *haben; *take ~ of** sorgen für, sich kümmern um

career [kə'riə] n Laufbahn f, Karriere f

carefree ['keəfri:] adj unbekümmert

careful ['keəfəl] adj vorsichtig; sorgfältig, genau

careless ['keələs] adj gedankenlos, nachlässig

caretaker ['keə,teikə] n Hausmeister m, -in f

cargo ['ka:gou] n (pl ~es) Ladung f, Fracht f

carnival ['ka:nivəl] n Karneval m

carp [ka:p] n (pl ~) Karpfen m

carpenter ['ka:pintə] n Tischler m, -in f

carpet ['ka:pit] n Teppich m

carriage ['kærid3] n Wagen m; Kutsche f; **baby ~** Am Kinderwagen m

carrot ['kærət] n Mohrrübe f, Karotte f

carry ['kæri] v *tragen; führen; **~ on** verfolgen; *fortfahren; **~ out** durchführen

carrycot ['kærikɔt] n Baby-Tragetasche f

cart [ka:t] n Karren m, Wagen m

cartilage ['ka:tilid3] n Knorpel m

carton ['ka:tən] n Karton m; Stange f

cartoon [ka:'tu:n] n Zeichentrickfilm m

cartridge ['ka:trid3] n Patrone f

carve [ka:v] v zerlegen; einkerben; schnitzen

carving ['ka:viŋ] n Schnitzerei f

case [keis] n Fall m; Koffer m; Etui nt; **attaché ~** Aktentasche f; **in ~** falls; **in ~ of** im Fall

cash [kæʃ] n Bargeld nt; v

*einnehmen, einkassieren

cash dispenser [kæʃ di'spɔnsə] n Geldautomat m

cashier [kæ'ʃiə] n Kassierer m, -in f

cashmere ['kæʃmiə] n Kaschmir m

casino [kə'si:nou] n (pl ~s) Kasino nt

cask [ka:sk] n Tonne f, Fass nt

cassette [kə'set] n (Video- etc) Kassette f

cast [ka:st] n Wurf m

*cast** [ka:st] v *werfen; **cast iron** Gusseisen nt

castle ['ka:səl] n Schloß nt, Burg f

casual ['kæʒuəl] adj zwanglos; beiläufig, zufällig

casualty ['kæʒuəlti] n Opfer nt

cat [kæt] n Katze f

catacomb ['kætəkoum] n Katakombe f

catalogue ['kætəlɔg] n Katalog m

catarrh [kə'ta:] n Katarrh m

catastrophe [kə'tæstrəfi] n Katastrophe f

*catch** [kætʃ] v *fangen; *ergreifen; erwischen; *nehmen, erreichen

catchword ['kætʃwɔ:d] n Schlag-, Stichwort nt

category ['kætigəri] n Kategorie f

cathedral [kə'θi:drəl] n Dom m, Kathedrale f

catholic ['kæθəlik] adj katholisch

cattle ['kætəl] pl Vieh nt

caught [kɔ:t] v (p, pp catch)

cauliflower ['kɔliflauə] n Blumenkohl m

cause [kɔ:z] v verursachen; anrichten; n Ursache f, Grund m, Anlass m; Sache f; **~ to** machen

caution ['kɔ:ʃən] n Vorsicht f; v warnen

cautious ['kɔ:ʃəs] adj vorsichtig

cave [keiv] n Höhle f; Riss m

cavern ['kævən] n Höhle f

caviar ['kævia:] n Kaviar m

cavity ['kævəti] n Höhlung f

CD(-ROM) [si:'di:(-)] n CD(-ROM) f

cease [si:s] v aufhören

ceasefire ['si:sfaiə] n Waffenruhe f

ceiling ['si:liŋ] n Decke f

celebrate ['selibreit] v feiern

celebration [,seli'breiʃən] n Feier f

celebrity [si'lebrəti] n Ruhm m; Berühmtheit f

celery ['seləri] n Sellerie m

cell [sel] n Zelle f

cellar ['selə] n Keller m

cellphone ['selfoun] n Handy nt

cement [si'ment] n Zement m

cemetery ['semitri] n Friedhof m

censorship ['sensəʃip] n Zensur f

center ['sentə] nAm Zentrum nt; Mittelpunkt m

centigrade ['sentigreid] adj Celsius

centimetre ['sentimi:tə] n, Am centimeter Zentimeter m

central ['sentrəl] adj zentral; ~ heating Zentralheizung f; ~ station Hauptbahnhof m

centre ['sentə] n Zentrum nt; Mittelpunkt m

century ['sentʃəri] n Jahrhundert nt

ceramics [si'ræmiks] pl Töpferware f, Keramik f

ceremony ['serəməni] n Feierlichkeit f

certain ['sə:tən] adj bestimmt; gewiss

certainly ['sə:tənli] adv sicherlich, aber sicher

certificate [sə'tifikət] n Bescheinigung f; Attest nt, Urkunde f, Diplom nt, Zeugnis nt

chain [tʃein] n Kette f

chair [tʃeə] n Stuhl m; Sessel m

chairman ['tʃeəmən] n (pl -men) Vorsitzende m

chairwoman ['tʃeəwumən] n (pl -women) Vorsitzende f

chalet ['ʃælei] n Chalet nt

chalk [tʃɔ:k] n Kreide f

challenge ['tʃæləndʒ] v herausfordern; n Herausforderung f

chamber ['tʃeimbə] n Zimmer nt

champagne [ʃæm'pein] n Sekt m

champion ['tʃæmpjən] n Meister m, -in f; Verfechter m, -in f

chance [tʃɑ:ns] n Zufall m; Chance f, Gelegenheit f; Risiko nt; by ~ zufällig

change [tʃeindʒ] v abändern, ändern; wechseln; sich *umziehen; *umsteigen; n Änderung f; Kleingeld nt, Wechselgeld nt; for a ~ zur Abwechslung; ausnahmsweise

channel ['tʃænəl] n Kanal m; English Channel Ärmelkanal m

chaos ['keiɔs] n Chaos nt

chaotic [kei'ɔtik] adj chaotisch

chap [tʃæp] n Kerl m

chapel ['tʃæpəl] n Kirche f, Kapelle f

character ['kærəktə] n Charakter m; Buchstabe m

characteristic [,kærəktə'ristik] adj bezeichnend, charakteristisch; n Kennzeichen nt; Charakterzug m

characterize ['kærəktəraiz] v charakterisieren

charcoal ['tʃɑ:koul] n Holzkohle f

charge [tʃɑ:dʒ] v verlangen; belasten; anklagen; *laden; n Gebühr f, Belastung f, Ladung f, Last f; Anklage f; ~ plate Am Kreditkarte f; free of ~ unentgeltlich; in ~ of beauftragt mit; *take ~ of *übernehmen

charity ['tʃærəti] n Wohltätigkeit f

charm [tʃɑ:m] n Liebreiz m; Amulett nt

charming ['tʃɑ:miŋ] adj charmant

chart [tʃɑ:t] n Tabelle f, Diagramm nt; Seekarte f; conversion ~ Umrechnungstabelle f

chase [tʃeis] v verfolgen; *vertreiben; verjagen; n Jagd f

chasm ['kæzəm] n Spalt m

chassis ['ʃæsi] n (pl ~) Fahrgestell nt

chat [tʃæt] v plaudern, schwatzen; n Geschwätz nt, Geplauder nt

chauffeur ['ʃoufə] n Chauffeur m, -in f

cheap [tʃi:p] adj billig; vorteilhaft

cheat [tʃi:t] v *betrügen; beschwindeln

check [tʃek] v kontrollieren, prüfen; n Karo nt; nAm Rechnung f; Scheck m; **check!** Schach!; ~ **in** sich anmelden; ~ **out** sich abmelden

checkbook ['tʃekbuk] nAm Scheckbuch nt

checkerboard ['tʃekəbɔːd] nAm Schachbrett nt

checkers ['tʃekəz] plAm Damespiel nt

checkroom ['tʃekruːm] nAm Garderobe f

checkup ['tʃekʌp] n Untersuchung f

cheek [tʃi:k] n Wange f

cheekbone ['tʃi:kboun] n Backenknochen m

cheeky ['tʃi:ki] adj colloquial frech, unverschämt

cheer [tʃiə] v zujubeln; ~ **up** aufheitern

cheerful ['tʃiəfəl] adj fröhlich, heiter

cheese [tʃi:z] n Käse m

chef [ʃef] n Küchenchef m, -in f

chemical ['kemikəl] adj chemisch

chemist ['kemist] n Apotheker m, -in f; **chemist's** Apotheke f; Drogerie f

chemistry ['kemistri] n Chemie f

cheque [tʃek] n Scheck m

chequebook ['tʃekbuk] n Scheckbuch nt

chequered ['tʃekəd] adj kariert, gewürfelt

cherry ['tʃeri] n Kirsche f

chess [tʃes] n Schach nt

chest [tʃest] n Brust f; Brustkasten m;

Truhe f; ~ **of drawers** Kommode f

chestnut ['tʃesnʌt] n Kastanie f

chew [tʃu:] v kauen

chewing gum ['tʃu:iŋgʌm] n Kaugummi m

chicken ['tʃikin] n Huhn nt; Küken nt

chickenpox ['tʃikinpɔks] n Windpocken fpl

chief [tʃi:f] n Haupt nt; adj Ober-, Haupt-

chieftain ['tʃi:ftən] n Häuptling m

child [tʃaild] n (pl children) Kind nt

childbirth ['tʃaildbəːθ] n Entbindung f

childhood ['tʃaildhud] n Jugend f

Chile ['tʃili] Chile

Chilean ['tʃiliən] adj chilenisch; n Chilene m, Chilenin f

chill [tʃil] n Frösteln nt; v abkühlen

chilly ['tʃili] adj kühl

chimes [tʃaimz] pl Glockenspiel nt

chimney ['tʃimni] n Schornstein m

chin [tʃin] n Kinn nt

China ['tʃainə] China

china ['tʃainə] n Porzellan nt

Chinese [tʃai'ni:z] adj chinesisch; n Chinese m, Chinesin f

chink [tʃiŋk] n Spalt m

chip [tʃip] n Splitter m; Spielmarke f; v *abschneiden, absplittern; **chips** Pommes frites

chisel ['tʃizəl] n Meißel m

chives [tʃaivz] pl Schnittlauch m

chlorine ['klɔ:ri:n] n Chlor nt

chock-full [tʃɔk'ful] adj übervoll, brechend voll

chocolate ['tʃɔklət] n Schokolade f; Praline f

choice [tʃɔis] n Wahl f; Auswahl f

choir [kwaiə] n Chor m

choke [tʃouk] v ersticken; erwürgen; n Choke m

***choose** [tʃu:z] v wählen

chop [tʃɔp] n Kotelett nt; v hacken

Christ [kraist] Christus
christen ['krisən] v taufen
christening ['krisəniŋ] n Taufe f
Christian ['kristʃən] adj christlich; n
Christ m; ~ name Vorname m
Christmas ['krisməs] Weihnachten
chromium ['kroumiəm] n Chrom nt
chronic ['krɔnik] adj chronisch
chronological [,krɔnə'lɔdʒikəl] adj
chronologisch
chuckle ['tʃʌkəl] v glucksen
chunk [tʃʌŋk] n Klumpen m
church [tʃəːtʃ] n Kirche f
churchyard ['tʃəːtʃjaːd] n Kirchhof
m, Friedhof m
cigar [si'gaː] n Zigarre f; ~ shop
Zigarrenladen m
cigarette [,sigə'ret] n Zigarette f; ~
case Zigarettenetui nt; ~ lighter
Feuerzeug nt
cinema ['sinəmə] n Kino nt
cinnamon ['sinəmən] n Zimt m
circle ['səːkəl] n Kreis m; Balkon m; v
*einschließen, umkreisen
circulation [,səːkju'leiʃən] n
Kreislauf m; Umlauf m
circumstance ['səːkəmstæns] n
Umstand m
circus ['səːkəs] n Zirkus m
citizen ['sitizən] n Bürger m, -in f
citizenship ['sitizənʃip] n
Staatsangehörigkeit f
city ['siti] n Stadt f
civic ['sivik] adj Bürger-
civil ['sivəl] adj zivil; höflich; ~ law
Zivilrecht nt; ~ servant
Staatsbeamte m, Staatsbeamtin f
civilian [si'viljən] adj Bürger-; n
Zivilist m, -in f
civilization [,sivəlai'zeiʃən] n
Zivilisation f
civilized ['sivəlaizd] adj zivilisiert
claim [kleim] v fordern,
beanspruchen; behaupten; n

Forderung f, Anspruch m
clamp [klæmp] n Klemme f;
Klammer f
clap [klæp] v klatschen
clarify ['klærifai] v klarstellen, klären
class [klaːs] n Klasse f
classical ['klæsikəl] adj klassisch
classify ['klæsifai] v einteilen
classmate ['klaːsmeit] n
Klassenkamerad m, -in f
classroom ['klaːsruːm] n
Klassenzimmer nt
clause [klɔːz] n Klausel f
claw [klɔː] n Klaue f
clay [klei] n Ton m
clean [kliːn] adj rein, sauber; v
säubern, reinigen
cleaning ['kliːniŋ] n Reinigung f; ~
fluid Reinigungsmittel nt
clear [kliə] adj klar; deutlich; v
aufräumen
clearing ['kliəriŋ] n Lichtung f
cleft [kleft] n Spalte f
clergyman ['kləːdʒimən] n (pl -men)
Pastor m, Pfarrer m; Geistliche m
clerk [klaːk] n Büroangestellte m/f;
Beamte m, Beamtin f; Sekretär m, -in
f
clever ['klevə] adj intelligent; schlau,
gescheit, klug
click [klik] v klicken; ~ into place
einrasten
client ['klaiənt] n Kunde m, Kundin f;
Klient m, -in f
cliff [klif] n Klippe f
climate ['klaimit] n Klima nt
climb [klaim] v klettern; *steigen; n
Aufstieg m
clinic ['klinik] n Klinik f
cling [kliŋ] v: ~ to haften, kleben; sich
klammern an
cloak [klouk] n Umhang m
cloakroom ['kloukruːm] n Garderobe
f

clock [klɔk] n Uhr f; **at ... o'clock** um
... Uhr

cloister ['klɔistə] n Kloster nt

close¹ [klouz] v zumachen,
*schließen; **closed** adj zu,
geschlossen

close² [klous] adj nahe

closet ['klɔzit] n Wandschrank m;
nAm Garderobenschrank m

cloth [klɔθ] n Tuch nt; Lappen m

clothes [klouðz] pl Kleidung f,
Kleider

clothing ['klouðiŋ] n Kleidung f

cloud [klaud] n Wolke f; **clouds**
Bewölkung f

cloudy ['klaudi] adj bewölkt

clover ['klouvə] n Klee m

clown [klaun] n Clown m

club [klʌb] n Klub m; Verein m; Keule
f, Knüppel m

clumsy ['klʌmzi] adj ungeschickt

clutch [klʌtʃ] n Kupplung f; Griff m

coach [koutʃ] n Reisebus m; Wagen
m; Kutsche f; Trainer m, -in f

coal [koul] n Kohle f

coarse [kɔːs] adj grob; gemein

coast [koust] n Küste f

coat [kout] n Mantel m

coat hanger ['kout,hæŋə] n
Kleiderbügel m

cobweb ['kɔbweb] n Spinnwebe f,
Spinnennetz nt

cocaine [kou'kein] n Kokain nt

cock [kɔk] n Hahn m

cocktail ['kɔkteil] n Cocktail m

coconut ['koukənʌt] n Kokosnuss f

cod [kɔd] n (pl ~) Kabeljau m

code [koud] n Kode m

coffee ['kɔfi] n Kaffee m

cognac ['kɔnjæk] n Kognak m

coherence [kou'hiərəns] n
Zusammenhang m

coin [kɔin] n Münze f

coincide [,kouin'said] v
*zusammenfallen

cold [kould] adj kalt; n Kälte f;
Erkältung f; **catch a ~** sich erkälten

collaborate [kə'læbərait] v
zusammenarbeiten

collapse [kə'læps] v
*zusammenbrechen

collar ['kɔlə] n Halsband nt; Kragen m

collarbone ['kɔləboun] n
Schlüsselbein nt

colleague ['kɔliːg] n Kollege m,
Kollegin f

collect [kə'lekt] v sammeln; holen,
abholen; einsammeln

collection [kə'lekʃən] n Kollektion f,
Sammlung f; Leerung f

collective [kə'lektiv] adj kollektiv

collector [kə'lektə] n Sammler m, -in
f

college ['kɔlidʒ] n höhere
Lehranstalt; Schule f

collide [kə'laid] v *zusammenstoßen

collision [kə'liʒən] n Zusammenstoß
m

colloquial [kə'loukwiəl] adj
umgangssprachlich

Colombia [kə'lɔmbiə] Kolumbien

Colombian [kə'lɔmbiən] adj
kolumbianisch; n Kolumbianer m, -in
f

colonel ['kəːnəl] n Oberst m

colony ['kɔləni] n Kolonie f

colo(u)r ['kʌlə] n Farbe f; v färben; ~
film Farbfilm m

colo(u)r-blind ['kʌləblaind] adj
farbenblind

colo(u)red ['kʌləd] adj farbig

colo(u)rful ['kʌləfəl] adj bunt,
farbenfroh

column ['kɔləm] n Pfeiler m, Säule f;
Spalte f; Rubrik f; Kolonne f

coma ['koumə] n Koma nt

comb [koum] v kämmen; n Kamm m

combat ['kɔmbæt] n Kampf m,

Gefecht *nt*; *v* bekämpfen, kämpfen

combination [,kɔmbi'neiʃən] *n* Kombination *f*

combine [kəm'bain] *v* kombinieren; *verbinden

***come** [kʌm] *v* *kommen; ~ **across** begegnen; *finden

comedian [kə'mi:diən] *n* Schauspieler *m*, -in *f*; Komiker *m*, -in *f*

comedy ['kɔmədi] *n* Lustspiel *nt*, Komödie *f*; **musical ~** Musical *nt*

comfort ['kʌmfət] *n* Bequemlichkeit *f*, Behaglichkeit *f*, Komfort *m*; Trost *m*; *v* trösten

comfortable ['kʌmfətəbəl] *adj* bequem

comic ['kɔmik] *adj* komisch

comics ['kɔmiks] *pl* Comics *pl*

coming ['kʌmiŋ] *n* Ankunft *f*

comma ['kɔmə] *n* Komma *nt*

command [kə'ma:nd] *v* *befehlen; *n* Befehl *m*

commander [kə'ma:ndə] *n* Befehlshaber *m*

commemoration [kə,memə'reiʃən] *n* Gedenkfeier *f*

commence [kə'mens] *v* *anfangen

comment ['kɔment] *n* Kommentar *m*; *v* kommentieren

commerce ['kɔmə:s] *n* Handel *m*

commercial [kə'mə:ʃəl] *adj* kommerziell, Handels-; *n* Werbesendung *f*

commission [kə'miʃən] *n* Kommission *f*

commit [kə'mit] *v* *übergeben, anvertrauen; verüben, *begehen

committee [kə'miti] *n* Kommission *f*, Ausschuss *m*

common ['kɔmən] *adj* gemeinsam; üblich, allgemein; gewöhnlich

commune ['kɔmju:n] *n* Kommune *f*

communicate [kə'mju:nikeit] *v*

mitteilen

communication [kə,mju:ni'keiʃən] *n* Kommunikation *f*; Mitteilung *f*

communiqué [kə'mju:nikei] *n* Bekanntmachung *f*

communism ['kɔmjunizəm] *n* Kommunismus *m*

community [kə'mju:nəti] *n* Gemeinschaft *f*, Gemeinde *f*

commuter [kə'mju:tə] *n* Pendler *m*, -in *f*

compact ['kɔmpækt] *adj* kompakt

compact disc ['kɔmpækt disk] *n* Compact Disk *f*; **~ player** CD-Spieler *m*

companion [kəm'pænjən] *n* Gefährte *m*, Gefährtin *f*

company ['kʌmpəni] *n* Gesellschaft *f*; Firma *f*, Unternehmen *nt*

comparative [kəm'pærətiv] *adj* relativ

compare [kəm'peə] *v* *vergleichen

comparison [kəm'pærisən] *n* Vergleich *m*

compartment [kəm'pa:tmənt] *n* Abteil *nt*

compass ['kʌmpəs] *n* Kompass *m*

compel [kəm'pel] *v* *zwingen

compensate ['kɔmpənseit] *v* *ausgleichen

compensation [,kɔmpən'seiʃən] *n* Ausgleich *m*; Schadenersatz *m*

compete [kəm'pi:t] *v* wetteifern

competition [,kɔmpə'tiʃən] *n* Wettbewerb *m*; Konkurrenz *f*

competitor [kəm'petitər] *n* Konkurrent *m*, -in *f*

compile [kəm'pail] *v* zusammenstellen

complain [kəm'plein] *v* sich beschweren

complaint [kəm'pleint] *n* Beschwerde *f*

complete [kəm'pli:t] *adj* ganz,

vollständig; v vollenden

completely [kəm'pli:tli] adv
vollkommen, gänzlich, völlig

complex ['kɔmpleks] n Komplex m;
adj verwickelt

complexion [kəm'plekʃən] n Teint m

complicated ['kɔmplikeitid] adj
kompliziert, verwickelt

compliment ['kɔmplimənt] n
Kompliment nt; v gratulieren,
beglückwünschen

compose [kəm'pouz] v
zusammenstellen

composer [kəm'pouzə] n Komponist
m, -in f

composition [,kɔmpə'ziʃən] n
Komposition f; Zusammensetzung f

comprehensive [,kɔmpri'hensiv] adj
umfassend

comprise [kəm'praiz] v umfassen,
*einschließen

compromise ['kɔmprəmaiz] n
Kompromiss m

compulsory [kəm'pʌlsəri] adj
obligatorisch

computer [kəm'pju:tə] n Computer m

conceal [kən'si:l] v *verbergen

conceited [kən'si:tid] adj eingebildet

conceive [kən'si:v] v auffassen,
*verstehen; sich vorstellen

concentrate ['kɔnsəntreit] v
konzentrieren

concentration [,kɔnsən'treiʃən] n
Konzentration f

conception [kən'sepʃən] n
Vorstellung f; Empfängnis f

concern [kən'sə:n] v *angehen,
*betreffen; n Sorge f; Angelegenheit
f; Unternehmen nt, Konzern m

concerned [kən'sə:nd] adj besorgt;
beteiligt

concerning [kən'sə:niŋ] prep
hinsichtlich, betreffs

concert ['kɔnsət] n Konzert nt; ~ hall

Konzertsaal m

concession [kən'seʃən] n
Konzession f; Zugeständnis nt

concise [kən'sais] adj kurz, knapp,
prägnant

conclusion [kəŋ'klu:ʒən] n
Schlussfolgerung f, Schluss m

concrete ['kɔŋkri:t] adj konkret; n
Beton m

concussion [kəŋ'kʌʃən] n
Gehirnerschütterung f

condition [kən'diʃən] n Bedingung f;
Zustand m, Verfassung f

conditional [kən'diʃənəl] adj bedingt

conditioner [kən'diʃənə] n
Pflegespülung f; Weichspüler m

condom ['kɔndəm] n Kondom m,
Präservativ nt

conduct¹ ['kɔndʌkt] n Betragen nt

conduct² [kən'dʌkt] v führen;
begleiten; dirigieren

conductor [kən'dʌktə] n Schaffner
m, -in f; Dirigent m, -in f

confectioner [kən'fekʃənə] n
Konditor m, -in f

conference ['kɔnfərəns] n Konferenz
f

confess [kən'fes] v *gestehen;
beichten; *bekennen

confession [kən'feʃən] n Geständnis
nt; Beichte f

confidence ['kɔnfidəns] n Vertrauen
nt

confident ['kɔnfidənt] adj
zuversichtlich

confidential [,kɔnfi'denʃəl] adj
vertraulich

confirm [kən'fə:m] v bestätigen

confirmation [,kɔnfə'meiʃən] n
Bestätigung f

confiscate ['kɔnfiskeit] v *einziehen,
beschlagnahmen

conflict ['kɔnflikt] n Konflikt m

confuse [kən'fju:z] v verwirren

confusion [kən'fjuːʒən] *n*
Verwirrung *f*

congratulate [kəŋ'grætʃuleit] *v*
gratulieren, beglückwünschen

congratulation [kən‚grætʃu'leiʃən] *n*
Glückwunsch *m*

congregation [‚kɔŋgri'geiʃən] *n*
Gemeinde *f*; Orden *m*

congress [kɔŋgres] *n* Kongress *m*;
Tagung *f*

connect [kə'nekt] *v* *verbinden;
*anschließen

connection [kə'nekʃən] *n* Beziehung
f; Zusammenhang *m*; Verbindung *f*,
Anschluss *m*

connoisseur [‚kɔnə'səː] *n* Kenner *m*,
-in *f*

connotation [‚kɔnə'teiʃən] *n*
Nebenbedeutung *f*

conquer ['kɔŋkə] *v* erobern; besiegen

conqueror ['kɔŋkərə] *n* Eroberer *m*

conquest ['kɔŋkwest] *n* Eroberung *f*

conscience ['kɔnʃəns] *n* Gewissen *nt*

conscious ['kɔnʃəs] *adj* bewusst

consciousness ['kɔnʃəsnəs] *n*
Bewusstsein *nt*

consent [kən'sent] *v* einwilligen;
zustimmen; *n* Einwilligung *f*,
Zustimmung *f*

consequence ['kɔnsikwəns] *n*
Wirkung *f*, Folge *f*

consequently ['kɔnsikwəntli] *adv*
folglich

conservative [kən'səːvətiv] *adj*
konservativ

consider [kən'sidə] *v* betrachten;
*erwägen; der Ansicht *sein, *finden

considerable [kən'sidərəbəl] *adj*
beträchtlich; beachtlich, bedeutend

considerate [kən'sidərət] *adj*
rücksichtsvoll

consideration [kən‚sidə'reiʃən] *n*
Erwägung *f*; Rücksicht *f*, Beachtung *f*

considering [kən'sidəriŋ] *prep* in

Anbetracht

consignment [kən'sainmənt] *n*
Sendung *f*

consist of [kən'sist] *bestehen aus

conspire [kən'spaiə] *v* sich
*verschwören

constant ['kɔnstənt] *adj* beständig

constipation [‚kɔnsti'peiʃən] *n*
Verstopfung *f*

constituency [kən'stitʃuənsi] *n*
Wahlkreis *m*

constitution [‚kɔnsti'tjuːʃən] *n*
Aufbau *m*; Grundgesetz *nt*

construct [kən'strʌkt] *v* bauen;
aufbauen, errichten

construction [kən'strʌkʃən] *n*
Konstruktion *f*; Bau *m*; Gebäude *nt*

consul ['kɔnsəl] *n* Konsul *m*, -in *f*

consulate ['kɔnsjulət] *n* Konsulat *nt*

consult [kən'sʌlt] *v* konsultieren

consultation [‚kɔnsəl'teiʃən] *n*
Konsultation *f*; ~ **hours** *n*
Sprechstunde *f*

consume [kən'sjuːm] *v* konsumieren,
verzehren, verbrauchen; zerstören

consumer [kən'sjuːmə] *n*
Verbraucher *m*, -in *f*, Konsument *m*,
-in *f*

contact ['kɔntækt] *n* Kontakt *m*;
Berührung *f*; *v* sich in Verbindung
setzen mit; ~ **lenses** Kontaktlinsen
fpl

contagious [kən'teidʒəs] *adj*
ansteckend

contain [kən'tein] *v* *enthalten;
umfassen

container [kən'teinə] *n* Behälter *m*;
Container *m*

contemporary [kən'tempərəri] *adj*
zeitgenössisch; damalig; *n*
Zeitgenosse *m*; Zeitgenossin *f*

contempt [kən'tempt] *n* Verachtung
f, Geringschätzung *f*

content [kən'tent] *adj* zufrieden

contents ['kɔntents] pl Inhalt m

contest ['kɔntest] n Streit m; Wettbewerb m

continent ['kɔntinənt] n Kontinent m, Erdteil m; Festland nt

continental [,kɔnti'nentəl] adj kontinental

continual [kən'tinjuəl] adj unaufhörlich; **continually** adv fortwährend

continue [kən'tinju:] v fortsetzen; *fortfahren, fortdauern

continuous [kən'tinjuəs] adj fortlaufend, anhaltend, ununterbrochen

contour ['kɔntuə] n Umriss m

contraceptive [,kɔntrə'septiv] n empfängnisverhütendes Mittel

contract¹ ['kɔntrækt] n Vertrag m

contract² [kən'trækt] v sich *zusammenziehen

contractor [kən'træktə] n Unternehmer m, -in f

contradict [,kɔntrə'dikt] v *widersprechen

contradictory [,kɔntrə'diktəri] adj widersprechend, widersprüchlich

contrary ['kɔntrəri] n Gegenteil nt; adj entgegengesetzt; **on the ~** im Gegenteil

contrast ['kɔntrɑːst] n Kontrast m; Unterschied m, Gegensatz m

contribution [,kɔntri'bju:ʃən] n Beitrag m

control [kən'troul] n Kontrolle f; v kontrollieren

controversial [,kɔntrə'vəːʃəl] adj Streit-, umstritten

convenience [kən'vi:njəns] n Bequemlichkeit f

convenient [kən'vi:njənt] adj bequem; angemessen, geeignet, passend

convent ['kɔnvənt] n Kloster nt

conversation [,kɔnvə'seiʃən] n Unterhaltung f, Gespräch nt

convert [kən'vəːt] v bekehren; umrechnen, konvertieren

convict¹ [kən'vikt] v überführen

convict² ['kɔnvikt] n Verurteilte m/f

conviction [kən'vikʃən] n Überzeugung f; Überführung f

convince [kən'vins] v überzeugen

convulsion [kən'vʌlʃən] n Krampf m

cook [kuk] n Koch m, Köchin f; v kochen; zubereiten, zurichten

cookbook ['kukbuk] nAm Kochbuch nt

cooker ['kukə] n Kocher m; **gas ~** Gasherd m

cookery book ['kukəribuk] n Kochbuch nt

cookie ['kuki] nAm Keks m

cool [ku:l] adj kühl

cooperation [kou,ɔpə'reiʃən] n Zusammenarbeit f; Mitarbeit f

cooperative [kou'ɔpərətiv] adj kooperativ; willig, bereitwillig; n Genossenschaft f

coordinate [kou'ɔːdineit] v koordinieren

coordination [kou,ɔːdi'neiʃən] n Koordinierung f

cope [koup] v fertig werden, bewältigen

copper ['kɔpə] n Kupfer nt

copy ['kɔpi] n Kopie f; Abschrift f; Exemplar nt; v kopieren; nachahmen; **carbon ~** Durchschlag m

coral ['kɔrəl] n Koralle f

cord [kɔːd] n Seil nt; Leine f

cordial ['kɔːdiəl] adj herzlich

core [kɔː] n Kern m; Kerngehäuse nt

cork [kɔːk] n Korken m; Stöpsel m

corkscrew ['kɔːkskru:] n Korkenzieher m

corn [kɔːn] n Korn nt; Getreide nt;

Am Mais *m*; Hühnerauge *nt*; **~ on the cob** Maiskolben *m*

corner ['kɔːnə] *n* Ecke *f*

cornfield ['kɔːnfiːld] *n* Kornfeld *nt*

corpse [kɔːps] *n* Leiche *f*

corpulent ['kɔːpjulənt] *adj* korpulent; beleibt, dick

correct [kə'rekt] *adj* genau, korrekt, richtig; *v* korrigieren, verbessern

correction [kə'rekʃən] *n* Berichtigung *f*; Verbesserung *f*

correctness [kə'rektnəs] *n* Richtigkeit *f*

correspond [ˌkɔri'spɔnd] *v* korrespondieren; übereinstimmen

correspondence [ˌkɔri'spɔndəns] *n* Korrespondenz *f*

correspondent [ˌkɔri'spɔndənt] *n* Korrespondent *m*, -in *f*

corridor ['kɔridɔː] *n* Flur *m*

corrupt [kə'rʌpt] *adj* korrupt; *v* *bestechen

corruption [kə'rʌpʃən] *n* Bestechung *f*

corset ['kɔːsit] *n* Korsett *nt*

cosmetics [kɔz'metiks] *pl* Kosmetika *ntpl*

cost [kɔst] *n* Kosten *pl*; Preis *m*

***cost** [kɔst] *v* kosten

cosy ['kouzi] *adj* gemütlich, behaglich

cot [kɔt] *nAm* Liege *f*

cottage ['kɔtidʒ] *n* (kleines) Landhaus *nt*, *Am* Ferienhäuschen *nt*; **~ cheese** Hüttenkäse *m*

cotton ['kɔtən] *n* Baumwolle *f*; Baumwoll-

cotton wool ['kɔtənwul] *n* Watte *f*

couch [kauʃ] *n* Couch *f*

cough [kɔf] *n* Husten *m*; *v* husten

could [kud] *v* (p can)

council ['kaunsəl] *n* Rat *m*

councillor ['kaunsələ] *n* Ratsmitglied *nt*

counsel ['kaunsəl] *n* Rat *m*

counsellor ['kaunsələ] *n* Ratgeber *m*, -in *f*

count [kaunt] *v* zählen; addieren; mitzählen; *halten für; *n* Graf *m*

counter ['kauntə] *n* Ladentisch *m*; Schalter *m*

counterfeit ['kauntəfiːt] *v* fälschen

counterfoil ['kauntəfɔil] *n* Kontrollabschnitt *m*

countess ['kauntis] *n* Gräfin *f*

country ['kʌntri] *n* Land *nt*; Gegend *f*; **~ house** Landhaus *nt*

countryside ['kʌntrisaid] *n* Landschaft *f*

county ['kaunti] *n* Grafschaft *f*, *Am* (Land)Kreis *m*

couple ['kʌpəl] *n* Paar *nt*

coupon ['kuːpɔn] *n* Kupon *m*, Bezugs-schein *m*

courage ['kʌridʒ] *n* Tapferkeit *f*, Mut *m*

courageous [kə'reidʒəs] *adj* tapfer, mutig

course [kɔːs] *n* Kurs *m*; Gang *m*; Lauf *m*; Lehrgang *m*, Kursus *m*; **of ~** allerdings, selbstverständlich

court [kɔːt] *n* Gericht *nt*; Hof *m*

courteous ['kəːtiəs] *adj* höflich

cousin ['kʌzən] *n* Vetter *m*, Kusine *f*

cover ['kʌvə] *v* bedecken, verdecken; *n* Obdach *nt*, Schutz *m*; Deckel *m*; Umschlag *m*

cow [kau] *n* Kuh *f*

coward ['kauəd] *n* Feigling *m*

cowardly ['kauədli] *adj* feige

cozy ['kouzi] *adjAm* gemütlich, behaglich

crab [kræb] *n* Krabbe *f*

crack [kræk] *n* Riss *m*; *v* krachen; *brechen, *bersten

cracker ['krækə] *nAm* Keks *m*

cradle ['kreidəl] *n* Wiege *f*

cramp [kræmp] *n* Krampf *m*

crane [krein] *n* Kran *m*

crap [kræp] n vulgar Scheiße f

crash [kræʃ] n Zusammenstoß m; v *zusammenstoßen; abstürzen; ~ barrier Leitplanke f

crate [kreit] n Kiste f

crater ['kreitə] n Krater m

crawl [krɔːl] v *kriechen; kraulen; n Kraulstil m

crazy ['kreizi] adj verrückt; wahnsinnig

creak [kriːk] v knirschen

cream [kriːm] n Krem f; Sahne f; adj kremfarben

creamy ['kriːmi] adj sahnig

crease [kriːs] v zerknittern; n Falte f

create [kri'eit] v *schaffen; erschaffen

creative [kri'eitiv] adj kreativ, schöpferisch

creature ['kriːtʃə] n Geschöpf nt

credible ['kredibəl] adj glaubwürdig

credit ['kredit] n Kredit m; v kreditieren; ~ card Kreditkarte f

creditor ['kreditə] n Gläubiger m

credulous ['kredjuləs] adj gutgläubig

creek [kriːk] n Bucht f

*creep [kriːp] v *kriechen

creepy ['kriːpi] adj unheimlich, gruselig

cremate [kri'meit] v *verbrennen

crew [kruː] n Besatzung f

cricket ['krikit] n Kricket nt; Grille f

crime [kraim] n Verbrechen nt

criminal ['kriminəl] n Verbrecher m, -in f; adj verbrecherisch, kriminell; ~ law Strafrecht nt

criminality [ˌkrimi'næləti] n Kriminalität f

crimson ['krimzən] adj karmesinrot

crippled ['kripəld] adj verkrüppelt

crisis ['kraisis] n (pl crises) Krise f

crisp [krisp] adj knusprig

critic ['kritik] n Kritiker m, -in f

critical ['kritikəl] adj kritisch; entscheidend, heikel, bedenklich

criticism ['kritisizəm] n Kritik f

criticize ['kritisaiz] v kritisieren

crochet ['krouʃei] v häkeln

crockery ['krɔkəri] n Steingut nt, Töpferware f

crocodile ['krɔkədail] n Krokodil nt

crooked ['krukid] adj verdreht, krumm; unehrlich

crop [krɔp] n Ernte f

cross [krɔs] v *hinübergehen; adj ungehalten, böse; n Kreuz nt

cross-eyed ['krɔsaid] adj schielend

crossing ['krɔsiŋ] n Überfahrt f; Kreuzung f; Übergang m; Bahnübergang m

crossroads ['krɔsroudz] n Kreuzung f

crosswalk ['krɔswɔːk] nAm Zebrastreifen m

crow [krou] n Krähe f

crowbar ['kroubaː] n Brecheisen nt

crowd [kraud] n Masse f, Menge f

crowded ['kraudid] adj voll; überfüllt

crown [kraun] n Krone f; v krönen

crucifix ['kruːsifiks] n Kruzifix nt

crucifixion [ˌkruːsi'fikʃən] n Kreuzigung f

cruel [kruəl] adj grausam

cruise [kruːz] n Kreuzfahrt f, Seereise f

crumb [krʌm] n Krümel m

crusade [kruː'seid] n Kreuzzug m

crust [krʌst] n Kruste f

crutch [krʌtʃ] n Krücke f

cry [krai] v weinen; *schreien; *rufen; n Aufschrei m, Schrei m; Ruf m

crystal ['kristəl] n Kristall nt

Cuba ['kjuːbə] Kuba

Cuban ['kjuːbən] adj kubanisch; n Kubaner m, -in f

cube [kjuːb] n Würfel m

cuckoo ['kukuː] n Kuckuck m

cucumber ['kjuːkəmbə] n Gurke f

cuddle ['kʌdəl] v kuscheln

cuff links ['kʌfliŋks] *pl* Manschettenknöpfe *mpl*

cul-de-sac ['kʌldəsæk] *n* Sackgasse *f*

cultivate ['kʌltiveit] *v* bebauen; anbauen, kultivieren

culture ['kʌltʃə] *n* Kultur *f*

cultured ['kʌltʃəd] *adj* kultiviert

cunning ['kʌniŋ] *adj* listig

cup [kʌp] *n* Tasse *f*; Pokal *m*

cupboard ['kʌbəd] *n* Schrank *m*

curb [kə:b] *n* Randstein *m*; *v* zügeln

cure [kjuə] *v* heilen; *n* Kur *f*; Genesung *f*

curiosity [ˌkjuəri'ɔsəti] *n* Neugier *f*

curious ['kjuəriəs] *adj* gespannt, neugierig; seltsam

curl [kə:l] *v* locken; *n* Locke *f*

curler ['kə:lə] *n* Lockenwickler *m*

curly ['kə:li] *adj* lockig

currant ['kʌrənt] *n* Korinthe *f*; Beere *f*

currency ['kʌrənsi] *n* Währung *f*; **foreign ~** fremde Währung

current ['kʌrənt] *n* Strömung *f*; Strom *m*; *adj* laufend, aktuell, gegenwärtig; **alternating ~** Wechselstrom *m*; **direct ~** Gleichstrom *m*

curry ['kʌri] *n* Curry *m*

curse [kə:s] *v* fluchen; verfluchen; *n* Fluch *m*

curtain ['kə:tən] *n* Vorhang *m*

curve [kə:v] *n* Kurve *f*; Biegung *f*

curved [kə:vd] *adj* krumm, gekrümmt

cushion ['kuʃən] *n* Kissen *nt*

custody ['kʌstədi] *n* Haft *f*; Obhut *f*

custom ['kʌstəm] *n* Gewohnheit *f*; Sitte *f*

customary ['kʌstəməri] *adj* üblich, gewöhnlich

customer ['kʌstəmə] *n* Kunde *m*, Kundin *f*; Klient *m*, -in *f*

customs ['kʌstəmz] *pl* Zollbehörde *f*, **~ duty** Zoll *m*; **~ officer** Zollbeamte *m*, -beamtin *f*

cut [kʌt] *n* Einschnitt *m*; Schnitt *m*

***cut** [kʌt] *v* *schneiden; senken; **~ off** *abschneiden; abschalten

cutlery ['kʌtləri] *n* Besteck *nt*

cutlet ['kʌtlət] *n* Kotelett *nt*

cycle ['saikəl] *n* Rad *nt*; Fahrrad *nt*; Kreislauf *m*, Zyklus *m*

cyclist ['saiklist] *n* Radfahrer *m*, -in *f*

cylinder ['silində] *n* Zylinder *m*; **~ head** Zylinderkopf *m*

cystitis [si'staitis] *n* Blasenentzündung *f*

Czech [tʃek] *adj* tschechisch; *n* Tscheche *m*, Tschechin *f*

Czech Republic [tʃek ri'pʌblik] *n* Tschechien

D

dad [dæd] *n* Vater *m*

daddy ['dædi] *n* Vati *m*

daffodil ['dæfədil] *n* Narzisse *f*

daily ['deili] *adj* alltäglich, täglich; *n* Tageszeitung *f*

dairy ['dɛəri] *n* Molkerei *f*

dam [dæm] *n* Damm *m*; Deich *m*

damage ['dæmidʒ] *n* Schaden *m*; *v* beschädigen

damn [dæm] *v* verdammen; **~!** verdammt!

damp [dæmp] *adj* feucht; nass; *n* Feuchtigkeit *f*; *v* befeuchten

dance [dɑ:ns] *v* tanzen; *n* Tanz *m*

dandelion ['dændilaiən] *n* Löwenzahn *m*

dandruff ['dændrəf] n Schuppen

Dane [dein] n Däne m, Dänin f

danger ['deindʒə] n Gefahr f

dangerous ['deindʒərəs] adj gefährlich

Danish ['deiniʃ] adj dänisch

dare [deə] v sich trauen, wagen; herausfordern

dark [dɑːk] adj finster, dunkel; n Dunkelheit f, Finsternis f

darling ['dɑːliŋ] n Schatz m, Liebling m

darn [dɑːn] v stopfen

dash [dæʃ] v stürmen; n Gedankenstrich m

dashboard ['dæʃbɔːd] n Armaturenbrett nt

data ['deitə] pl Angabe f

date[1] [deit] n Datum nt; Verabredung f; v datieren; v sich verabreden; **out of ~** veraltet

date[2] [deit] n Dattel f

daughter ['dɔːtə] n Tochter f

daughter-in-law ['dɔːtərinlɔː] n (pl daughters-) Schwiegertochter f

dawn [dɔːn] n Morgendämmerung f; Tagesanbruch m

day [dei] n Tag m; **by ~** bei Tage; **~ trip** Tagesausflug m; **per ~** pro Tag; **the ~ before yesterday** vorgestern

daybreak ['deibreik] n Tagesanbruch m

daylight ['deilait] n Tageslicht nt

dead [ded] adj tot; verstorben

deaf [def] adj taub

deal [diːl] n Transaktion f, Geschäft nt

***deal** [diːl] v austeilen; **~ with** v sich befassen mit; Geschäfte machen mit

dealer ['diːlə] n Kaufmann m, Kauffrau f, Händler m, -in f

dear [diə] adj lieb; teuer; wert

death [deθ] n Tod m; **~ penalty** Todesstrafe f

debate [di'beit] n Debatte f

debit ['debit] n Soll nt

debt [det] n Schuld f

decaf(feinated) [diː'kæfineitid] adj koffeinfrei(er Kaffee)

deceit [di'siːt] n Betrug m

deceive [di'siːv] v *betrügen

December [di'sembə] Dezember

decent ['diːsənt] adj anständig

decide [di'said] v *beschließen, sich *entschließen, *entscheiden

decision [di'siʒən] n Beschluss m, Entscheidung f

deck [dek] n Deck nt; **~ chair** Liegestuhl m

declaration [ˌdeklə'reiʃən] n Erklärung f

declare [di'kleə] v erklären; *angeben; verzollen

decorate ['dekəreit] v verzieren, schmücken

decoration [ˌdekə'reiʃən] n Dekoration f

decrease [diː'kriːs] v vermindern; *abnehmen; n Abnahme f

dedicate ['dedikeit] v widmen

deduce [di'djuːs] v ableiten

deduct [di'dʌkt] v *abziehen

deed [diːd] n Handlung f, Tat f

deep [diːp] adj tief

deep-freeze [ˌdiːp'friːz] n Tiefkühltruhe f

deer [diə] n (pl ~) Rotwild nt

defeat [di'fiːt] v besiegen; n Niederlage f

defective [di'fektiv] adj schadhaft, mangelhaft

defence [di'fens] n Verteidigung f; Abwehr f

defend [di'fend] v verteidigen

defense [di'fens] nAm Verteidigung f; Abwehr f

deficiency [di'fiʃənsi] n Mangel m

deficit ['defisit] n Defizit nt

define [di'fain] v definieren,

bestimmen

definite ['definit] *adj* bestimmt

definition [,defi'niʃən] *n*
Bestimmung *f*, Definition *f*

deformed [di'fɔːmd] *adj*
missgestaltet, entstellt

degree [di'griː] *n* Grad *m*; Titel *m*

delay [di'lei] *v* verzögern;
*aufschieben; *n* Verspätung *f*,
Verzögerung *f*; Aufschub *m*

delegate ['deligət] *n* Abgesandte *m/f*

delegation [,deli'geiʃən] *n*
Delegation *f*

deliberate¹ [di'libəreit] *v*
beratschlagen, überlegen

deliberate² [di'libərət] *adj* absichtlich

deliberation [di,libə'reiʃən] *n*
Erörterung *f*, Beratung *f*

delicacy ['delikəsi] *n* Leckerbissen *m*

delicate ['delikət] *adj* fein; zart;
misslich

deli(catessen) [,delikə'tesən] *n*
Feinkost *f*; Feinkostgeschäft *nt*

delicious [di'liʃəs] *adj* lecker, köstlich

delight [di'lait] *n* Genuss *m*; *v*
entzücken

delighted [di'laitəd] *adj* erfreut

delightful [di'laitfəl] *adj* köstlich,
entzückend

deliver [di'livə] *v* abliefern, ausliefern;
erlösen

delivery [di'livəri] *n* Zustellung *f*,
Lieferung *f*; Entbindung *f*; Erlösung
f; ~ **van** Lieferwagen *m*

demand [di'mɑːnd] *v* verlangen,
fordern; *n* Forderung *f*; Nachfrage *f*

democracy [di'mɔkrəsi] *n*
Demokratie *f*

democratic [,demə'krætik] *adj*
demokratisch

demolish [di'mɔliʃ] *v* *niederreißen

demolition [,demə'liʃən] *n* Abbruch
m

demonstrate ['demənstreit] *v*

*beweisen; demonstrieren

demonstration [,demən'streiʃən] *n*
Demonstration *f*; Kundgebung *f*

den [den] *n* Höhle *f*

Denmark ['denmɑːk] Dänemark

denomination [di,nɔmi'neiʃən] *n*
Bezeichnung *f*; Konfession *f*

dense [dens] *adj* dicht

dent [dent] *n* Beule *f*

dentist ['dentist] *n* Zahnarzt *m*,
Zahnärztin *f*

denture ['dentʃə] *n* Gebiss *nt*

deny [di'nai] *v* leugnen; versagen,
verweigern, nicht *anerkennen

deodorant [diː'oudərənt] *n*
Deodorant *nt*

depart [di'pɑːt] *v* *weggehen,
abreisen; *sterben

department [di'pɑːtmənt] *n*
Abteilung *f*; ~ **store** Kaufhaus *nt*

departure [di'pɑːtʃə] *n* Abreise *f*,
Abfahrt *f*

dependant [di'pendənt] *adj* abhängig

depend on [di'pend] *v* *abhängen von;
that depends das kommt darauf an

deposit [di'pɔzit] *n* Pfand *nt*;
Sediment *nt*, Ablagerung *f*; *v*
hinterlegen

depository [di'pɔzitəri] *n* Lagerraum
m

depot ['depou] *n* Lager *nt*; *nAm*
Bahnhof *m*

depress [di'pres] *v* deprimieren

depressed [di'prest] *adj*
niedergeschlagen

depression [di'preʃən] *n*
Niedergeschlagenheit *f*; Tief *nt*;
Rückgang *m*

deprive of [di'praiv] *v* berauben;
*entziehen; *vorenthalten

depth [depθ] *n* Tiefe *f*

deputy ['depjuti] *n* Abgeordnete *m/f*;
Stellvertreter *m*, -in *f*

descend [di'send] *v* *herabsteigen

descendant [di'sendənt] n
Nachkomme m

descent [di'sent] n Abstieg m

describe [di'skraib] v *beschreiben

description [di'skripʃən] n
Beschreibung f

desert¹ ['dezət] n Wüste f; adj wüst,
verlassen

desert² [di'zə:t] v desertieren;
*verlassen

deserve [di'zə:v] v verdienen

design [di'zain] v *entwerfen; n
Entwurf m; Zweck m

designate ['dezigneit] v bezeichnen;
bestimmen; *ernennen

desirable [di'zaiərəbəl] adj
begehrenswert, wünschenswert

desire [di'zaiə] n Wunsch m; Lust f,
Verlangen nt; v begehren, verlangen,
wünschen

desk [desk] n Schreibtisch m; Pult nt;
Schulbank f

despair [di'spɛə] n Verzweiflung f; v
verzweifeln

despatch [di'spætʃ] v *versenden

desperate ['despərət] adj verzweifelt

despise [di'spaiz] v verachten

despite [di'spait] prep trotz

dessert [di'zə:t] n Nachtisch m

destination [,desti'neiʃən] n
Bestimmungsort m

destine ['destin] v bestimmen

destiny ['destini] n Verhängnis nt,
Schicksal nt

destroy [di'strɔi] v zerstören,
vernichten

destruction [di'strʌkʃən] n
Zerstörung f; Untergang m

detach [di'tætʃ] v trennen, loslösen;
detached separat; distanziert

detail ['di:teil] n Einzelheit f

detailed ['di:teild] adj ausführlich,
eingehend

detect [di'tekt] v entdecken

detective [di'tektiv] n Detektiv m, -in
f; ~ **story** Kriminalroman m

detergent [di'tə:dʒənt] n
Reinigungsmittel nt

determine [di'tə:min] v festsetzen,
bestimmen

determined [di'tə:mind] adj
entschlossen

detest [di'test] v verabscheuen,
hassen

detour ['di:tuə] n Umweg m;
Umleitung f

devaluation [,di:vælju'eiʃən] n
Abwertung f

devalue [,di:'vælju:] v entwerten

develop [di'veləp] v entwickeln

development [di'veləpmənt] n
Entwicklung f

deviate ['di:vieit] v *abweichen

devil ['devəl] n Teufel m

devise [di'vaiz] v *ausdenken

devote [di'vout] v widmen

dew [dju:] n Tau m

diabetes [,daiə'bi:ti:z] n Diabetes m,
Zuckerkrankheit f

diabetic [,daiə'betik] n Diabetiker m,
-in f

diagnose [,daiəg'nouz] v
diagnostizieren; feststellen

diagnosis [,daiəg'nousis] n (pl -ses)
Diagnose f

diagonal [dai'ægənəl] n Diagonale f;
adj diagonal

diagram ['daiəgræm] n Schema nt;
grafische Darstellung

dial ['daiəl] n Zifferblatt nt; v wählen

dialect ['daiəlekt] n Mundart f

diamond ['daiəmənd] n Diamant m

diaper ['daiəpə] nAm Windel f

diarrh(o)ea [,daiə'riə] n Durchfall m

diary ['daiəri] n Notizbuch nt;
Tagebuch nt nt

dictate [dik'teit] v diktieren

dictation [dik'teiʃən] n Diktat nt

dictator [dik'teitə] n Diktator m

dictionary ['dikʃənəri] n Wörterbuch nt

did [did] v (p do)

die [dai] v *sterben

diesel ['diːzəl] n Diesel m

diet ['daiət] n Diät f

differ ['difə] v sich *unterscheiden

difference ['difərəns] n Unterschied m

different ['difərənt] adj verschieden; ander

difficult ['difikəlt] adj schwierig; schwer

difficulty ['difikəlti] n Schwierigkeit f; Mühe f

***dig** [dig] v *graben

digest [di'dʒest] v verdauen

digestible [di'dʒestəbəl] adj verdaulich

digestion [di'dʒestʃən] n Verdauung f

digit ['didʒit] n Ziffer f

digital ['didʒitəl] adj digital

dignified ['dignifaid] adj würdevoll

dignity ['digniti] n Würde f

dike [daik] n Deich m; Damm m

dilapidated [di'læpideitid] adj baufällig

diligence ['dilidʒəns] n Fleiß m, Eifer m

diligent ['dilidʒənt] adj fleißig, eifrig

dilute [dai'ljuːt] v verdünnen

dim [dim] adj trübe, matt; dunkel

dine [dain] v zu Abend *essen

dinghy ['diŋgi] n Jolle f

dining car ['dainiŋkɑː] n Speisewagen m

dining room ['dainiŋruːm] n Esszimmer nt; Speisesaal m

dinner ['dinə] n Hauptmahlzeit f; Abendessen nt, Mittagessen nt

dinner jacket ['dinə,dʒækit] n Smoking m

diphtheria [dif'θiəriə] n Diphtherie f

diploma [di'ploumə] n Diplom nt

diplomat ['dipləmæt] n Diplomat m, -in f

direct[1] ['direkt] adj unmittelbar, direkt

direct[2] [di'rekt] v richten; *weisen; führen

direction [di'rekʃən] n Richtung f; Anweisung f; Regie f; Verwaltung f, Vorstand m; **directions for use** Gebrauchsanweisung f

directive [di'rektiv] n Richtlinie f

director [di'rektə] n Direktor m, -in f; Regisseur m, -in f

directory [di'rektəri] n Adress-, Telefonbuch nt

dirt [dəːt] n Schmutz m

dirty ['dəːti] adj schmierig, dreckig, schmutzig

disabled [di'seibəld] adj körperbehindert, invalide

disadvantage [,disəd'vɑːntidʒ] n Nachteil m

disagree [,disə'griː] v uneins *sein, nicht übereinstimmen

disagreeable [,disə'griːəbəl] adj unangenehm

disappear [,disə'piə] v *verschwinden

disappoint [,disə'pɔint] v enttäuschen

disappointment [,disə'pɔintmənt] n Enttäuschung f

disapprove [,disə'pruːv] v missbilligen

disaster [di'zɑːstə] n Katastrophe f; Missgeschick nt, Unheil nt

disastrous [di'zɑːstrəs] adj verheerend

disc [disk] n Scheibe f; Schallplatte f; **slipped ~** Bandscheibenvorfall m

discard [di'skɑːd] v ausrangieren

discharge [dis'tʃɑːdʒ] v *entladen,

*ausladen; ~ of *entbinden von

discipline ['disiplin] *n* Disziplin *f*

discolo(u)r [dis'kʌlə] *v* sich verfärben

disconnect [,diskə'nekt] *v* trennen; ausschalten

discontented [,diskən'tentid] *adj* unzufrieden

discontinue [,diskən'tinju:] *v* einstellen, aufhören mit

discount ['diskaunt] *n* Rabatt *m*

discourage [dis'kʌrədʒ] *v* entmutigen, abschrecken

discover [dis'kʌvə] *v* entdecken

discovery [dis'kʌvəri] *n* Entdeckung *f*

discuss [di'skʌs] *v* erörtern; diskutieren

discussion [di'skʌʃən] *n* Diskussion *f*; Gespräch *nt*, Besprechung *f*, Auseinandersetzung *f*

disease [di'zi:z] *n* Krankheit *f*

disembark [,disim'bɑ:k] *v* an Land *gehen, landen

disgrace [dis'greis] *n* Schande *f*

disguise [dis'gaiz] *v* sich verkleiden; *n* Verkleidung *f*

disgust [dis'gʌst] *n* Ekel *m*, Abscheu *m*; *v* ekeln, anwidern

disgusting [dis'gʌstiŋ] *adj* widerlich, ekelhaft

dish [diʃ] *n* Teller *m*; Platte *f*, Schüssel *f*; Gericht *nt*

dishonest [dis'sonist] *adj* unehrlich

dishwasher ['diʃwoʃə] *n* Geschirrspülmaschine *f*; Tellerwäscher *m*, -in *f*

disinfect [,disin'fekt] *v* desinfizieren

disinfectant [,disin'fektənt] *n* Desinfektionsmittel *nt*

disk [disk] *n* Scheibe *f*; Diskette *f*; **hard ~** Festplatte *f*

dislike [dis'laik] *v* nicht ausstehen *können, nicht *mögen; *n* Abneigung *f*, Widerwille *m*,

Antipathie *f*

dislocated ['disləkeitid] *adj* verrenkt

dismiss [dis'mis] *v* fortschicken; *entlassen

disorder [di'sɔ:də] *n* Unordnung *f*

dispatch [di'spætʃ] *v* verschicken, abfertigen

display [di'splei] *v* auslegen; zeigen; *n* Ausstellung *f*, Auslage *f*

displease [di'spli:z] *v* verstimmen, *missfallen

disposable [di'spouzəbəl] *adj* wegwerfbar

disposal [di'spouzəl] *n* Verfügung *f*; Beseitigung *f*

dispose of [di'spouz] *v* verfügen über; beseitigen

dispute [di'spju:t] *n* Auseinandersetzung *f*; Zank *m*, Streitigkeit *f*; *v* *streiten, *bestreiten

dissatisfied [di'sætisfaid] *adj* unzufrieden

dissolve [di'zolv] *v* auflösen

dissuade from [di'sweid] *v* *abraten

distance ['distəns] *n* Entfernung *f*; ~ **in kilometres** (*Am* **kilometers**) Kilometerzahl *f*

distant ['distənt] *adj* entfernt

distinct [di'stiŋkt] *adj* deutlich; verschieden

distinction [di'stiŋkʃən] *n* Unterscheidung *f*, Unterschied *m*

distinguish [di'stiŋgwiʃ] *v* *unterscheiden

distinguished [di'stiŋgwiʃt] *adj* vornehm

distress [di'stres] *n* Not *f*; ~ **signal** Notsignal *nt*

distribute [di'stribju:t] *v* verteilen

distributor [di'stribjutə] *n* Stromverteiler *m*

district ['distrikt] *n* Bezirk *m*; Gegend *f*

disturb [di'stə:b] *v* stören

disturbance [di'stə:bəns] n Störung f; Verwirrung f

ditch [ditʃ] n Graben m

dive [daiv] v tauchen

diversion [dai'və:ʃən] n Umleitung f; Ablenkung f

divide [di'vaid] v teilen; verteilen; trennen

divine [di'vain] adj göttlich

division [di'viʒən] n Teilung f; Trennung f; Abteilung f

divorce [di'vɔ:s] n Scheidung f; v *scheiden

dizziness ['dizinəs] n Schwindel m

dizzy ['dizi] adj schwindlig

*do [du:] v *tun; genügen

dock [dɔk] n Dock nt; Kai m; v anlegen

docker ['dɔkə] n Hafenarbeiter m

doctor ['dɔktə] n Doktor m, -in f, Arzt m, Ärztin f

document ['dɔkjumənt] n Urkunde f

dog [dɔg] n Hund m

dogged ['dɔgid] adj hartnäckig

doll [dɔl] n Puppe f

dollar ['dɔlə] n Dollar m

dome [doum] n Kuppel f

domestic [də'mestik] adj häuslich; inländisch; ~ **animal** Haustier nt

domicile ['dɔmisail] n Wohnsitz m

domination [,dɔmi'neiʃən] n Herrschaft f

dominion [də'minjən] n Herrschaft f

donate [dou'neit] v spenden

donation [dou'neiʃən] n Spende f, Schenkung f

done [dʌn] v (pp do)

donkey ['dɔŋki] n Esel m

donor ['dounə] n Spender m

door [dɔ:] n Tür f; **revolving ~** Drehtür f; **sliding ~** Schiebetür f

doorbell ['dɔ:bel] n Türklingel f

doorkeeper ['dɔ:,ki:pə] n Portier m

doorman ['dɔ:mən] n (pl -men)

Portier m

dormitory ['dɔ:mitri] n Schlafsaal m

dose [dous] n Dosis f

dot [dɔt] n Punkt m

double ['dʌbəl] adj doppelt

doubt [daut] v bezweifeln, zweifeln; Zweifel m; **without ~** ohne Zweifel

doubtful ['dautfəl] adj zweifelhaft; ungewiss

dough [dou] n Teig m

down[1] [daun] adv herab; hinab, herunter, nieder; adj niedergeschlagen; prep entlang, hinab; **~ payment** Anzahlung f

down[2] [daun] n Daune f

downpour ['daunpɔ:] n Regenguss m

downstairs [,daun'stɛəz] adv hinunter, unten

downstream [,daun'stri:m] adv stromabwärts

down-to-earth [,dauntu'ə:θ] adj sachlich

downwards ['daunwədz] adv nach unten, abwärts

dozen ['dʌzən] n (pl ~, ~s) Dutzend nt

draft [drɑ:ft] n Entwurf m; Am (Luft)Zug m

drag [dræg] v schleppen

dragon ['drægən] n Drache m

drain [drein] v trockenlegen; entwässern; n Abfluss m

drama ['drɑ:mə] n Drama nt; Trauerspiel nt; Theater nt

dramatic [drə'mætik] adj dramatisch

drank [dræŋk] v (p drink)

draught [drɑ:ft] n Luftzug m; **draughts** Damespiel nt; **~ beer** Fassbier nt

draw [drɔ:] n Ziehung f

*draw [drɔ:] v zeichnen; *ziehen; *abheben; **~ up** abfassen

drawbridge ['drɔ:bridʒ] n Zugbrücke f

drawer ['drɔ:ə] n Schublade f;

drawers Unterhose f

drawing ['drɔːiŋ] n Zeichnung f; ~ **pin** Reißzwecke f

dread [dred] v befürchten; n Angst f

dreadful ['dredfəl] adj schrecklich, furchtbar

dream [driːm] n Traum m

*****dream** [driːm] v träumen

dress [dres] v ankleiden; sich kleiden, sich ankleiden; *verbinden; n Kleid nt

dressing gown ['dresiŋgaun] n Morgenrock m

dressing room ['dresiŋruːm] n Umkleidekabine ft

dressmaker ['dres,meikə] n Schneiderin f

drill [dril] v bohren; trainieren; n Bohrer m

drink [driŋk] n Aperitif m, Drink m

*****drink** [driŋk] v *trinken

drinking water ['driŋkiŋ,wɔːtə] n Trinkwasser nt

drip-dry [,drip'drai] adj bügelfrei

drive [draiv] n Weg m; Fahrt f

*****drive** [draiv] v *fahren

driver ['draivə] n Fahrer m, -in f; **driver's licence**, Brit **driving licence** Führerschein m

drizzle ['drizəl] n Sprühregen m

drop [drɔp] v fallen *lassen; n Tropfen m

drought [draut] n Dürre f

drown [draun] v *ertrinken; *ertränken; *be drowned *ertrinken

drug [drʌg] n Droge f; Arznei f

drugstore ['drʌgstɔː] nAm Drogerie f, Apotheke f; Warenhaus nt

drum [drʌm] n Trommel f

drunk [drʌŋk] adj (pp drink) betrunken

dry [drai] adj trocken; v trocknen; abtrocknen

dry-clean [,drai'kliːn] v chemisch reinigen

dry cleaner's [,drai'kliːnəz] n chemische Reinigung

dryer ['draiə] n Trockner m

duchess [dʌtʃis] n Herzogin f

duck [dʌk] n Ente f

due [djuː] adj schuldig; fällig; angemessen

dues [djuːz] pl Gebühren

dug [dʌg] v (p, pp dig)

duke [djuːk] n Herzog m

dull [dʌl] adj langweilig; matt; stumpf

dumb [dʌm] adj stumm; blöde, dumm

dune [djuːn] n Düne f

dung [dʌŋ] n Mist m, Dung m

dunghill ['dʌŋhil] n Misthaufen m

duration [dju'reifən] n Dauer f

during ['djuəriŋ] prep während

dusk [dʌsk] n Abenddämmerung f

dust [dʌst] n Staub m

dustbin ['dʌstbin] n Abfalleimer m

dusty ['dʌsti] adj staubig

Dutch [dʌtʃ] adj niederländisch, holländisch

duty ['djuːti] n Pflicht f; Aufgabe f; Einfuhrzoll m; **customs ~** Zoll m

duty-free [,djuːti'friː] adj zollfrei

dwarf [dwɔːf] n Zwerg m

dye [dai] v färben; n Farbe f

dynamo ['dainəmou] n (pl ~s) Dynamo m

E

each [i:tʃ] *adj* jeder; ~ **other** einander

eager ['i:gə] *adj* begierig

eagle ['i:gəl] *n* Adler *m*

ear [iə] *n* Ohr *nt*

earache ['iəreik] *n* Ohrenschmerzen *mpl*

eardrum ['iədrʌm] *n* Trommelfell *nt*

earl [ə:l] *n* Graf *m*

early ['ə:li] *adj* früh

earn [ə:n] *v* verdienen

earnest ['ə:nist] *adj* ernst; *n* Ernst *m*

earnings ['ə:niŋz] *pl* Einnahmen, Verdienst *m*

earring ['iəriŋ] *n* Ohrring *m*

earth [ə:θ] *n* Erde *f*; Boden *m*

earthenware ['ə:θənwɛə] *n* Steingut(geschirr) *nt*

earthquake ['ə:θkweik] *n* Erdbeben *nt*

ease [i:z] *n* Ungezwungenheit *f*, Leichtigkeit *f*; Wohlbefinden *nt*

east [i:st] *n* Osten *m*

Easter ['i:stə] Ostern

easterly ['i:stəli] *adj* östlich

eastern ['i:stən] *adj* östlich

easy ['i:zi] *adj* bequem; behaglich; ~ **chair** Lehnstuhl *m*

easy-going ['i:zi,gouiŋ] *adj* lässig

*eat [i:t] *v* *essen; speisen

ebony ['ebəni] *n* Ebenholz *nt*

eccentric [ik'sentrik] *adj* überspannt

echo ['ekou] *n* (pl ~es) Widerhall *m*, Echo *nt*

eclipse [i'klips] *n* Finsternis *f*

economic [,i:kə'nɔmik] *adj* wirtschaftlich

economical [,i:kə'nɔmikəl] *adj* sparsam

economist [i'kɔnəmist] *n* Volkswirt *m*, -in *f*

economize [i'kɔnəmaiz] *v* sparen

economy [i'kɔnəmi] *n* Wirtschaft *f*

ecstasy ['ekstəzi] *n* Verzückung *f*

Ecuador ['ekwədɔ:] Ekuador

Ecuadorian [,ekwə'dɔ:riən] *adj* ekuadorianisch; *n* Ekuadorianer *m*, -in *f*

eczema ['eksimə] *n* Ekzem *nt*

edge [edʒ] *n* Kante *f*, Rand *m*

edible ['edibəl] *adj* essbar

edit ['edit] *v* herausgeben, redigieren

edition [i'diʃən] *n* Ausgabe *f*

editor ['editə] *n* Redakteur *m*, -in *f*

educate ['edʒukeit] *v* ausbilden

education [,edʒu'keiʃən] *n* Erziehung *f*

eel [i:l] *n* Aal *m*

effect [i'fekt] *n* Ergebnis *nt*, Wirkung *f*; *v* zustande *bringen; **in ~** tatsächlich

effective [i'fektiv] *adj* wirksam, wirkungsvoll

efficient [i'fiʃənt] *adj* leistungsfähig, zweckmäßig

effort ['efət] *n* Anstrengung *f*

egg [eg] *n* Ei *nt*

eggcup ['egkʌp] *n* Eierbecher *m*

eggplant ['egplɑ:nt] *n* Aubergine *f*

egg yolk ['egjouk] *n* Eidotter *nt*

ego(t)istic [,egou'istik] *adj* egoistisch

Egypt ['i:dʒipt] Ägypten

Egyptian [i'dʒipʃən] *adj* ägyptisch; *n* Ägypter *m*, -in *f*

eiderdown ['aidədaun] *n* Daunendecke *f*

eight [eit] *num* acht

eighteen [,ei'ti:n] *num* achtzehn

eighteenth [,ei'ti:nθ] *num* achtzehnte

eighth [eitθ] *num* achte

eighty ['eiti] *num* achtzig

either ['aiðə] *pron* einer von beiden; **either ... or** entweder ... oder

elaborate [i'læbəreit] *v* ausarbeiten

elastic [i'læstik] *adj* elastisch;

dehnbar; n Gummiband nt

elasticity [,elæ'stisəti] n Spannkraft f

elbow ['elbou] n Ellbogen m

elder ['eldə] adj älter

eldest ['eldist] adj ältest

elect [i'lekt] v wählen

election [i'lekʃən] n Wahl f

electric [i'lektrik] adj elektrisch; ~ **razor** Rasierapparat m; ~ **cord** Kabel nt

electrician [,ilek'triʃən] n Elektriker m, -in f

electricity [,ilek'trisəti] n Elektrizität f

electronic [ilek'trɔnik] adj elektronisch

elegance ['eligəns] n Eleganz f

elegant ['eligənt] adj elegant

element ['elimənt] n Bestandteil m, Element nt

elephant ['elifənt] n Elefant m

elevator ['eliveitə] nAm Aufzug m

eleven [i'levən] num elf

eleventh [i'levənθ] num elfte

elf [elf] n (pl elves) Elfe f

eliminate [i'limineit] v beseitigen

elm [elm] n Ulme f

else [els] adv sonst

elsewhere [,el'sweə] adv anderswo

elucidate [i'lu:sideit] v erläutern

e-mail ['i:meil] n E-Mail f; v mailen, per E-Mail verschicken

emancipation [i,mænsi'peiʃən] n Emanzipation f

embankment [im'bæŋkmənt] n Damm m

embargo [em'ba:gou] n (pl ~es) Embargo nt

embark [im'ba:k] v sich einschiffen; *einsteigen

embarkation [,emba:'keiʃən] n Einschiffung f

embarrass [im'bærəs] v verwirren; in Verlegenheit *bringen; hindern;

embarrassed verlegen;

embarrassing peinlich;

embarrassment Verlegenheit f

embassy ['embəsi] n Botschaft f

emblem ['embləm] n Emblem nt

embrace [im'breis] v umarmen; n Umarmung f

embroider [im'brɔidə] v sticken

embroidery [im'brɔidəri] n Stickerei f

emerald ['emərəld] n Smaragd m

emergency [i'mə:dʒənsi] n Notfall m; Notlage f; ~ **exit** Notausgang m

emigrant ['emigrənt] n Auswanderer m, -in f

emigrate ['emigreit] v auswandern

emigration [,emi'greiʃən] n Auswanderung f

emotion [i'mouʃən] n Rührung f, Erregung f

emotional [i'mouʃənəl] adj emotional, gefühlsmäßig, -betont

emperor ['empərə] n Kaiser m

emphasize ['emfəsaiz] v betonen

empire ['empaiə] n Kaiserreich nt, Reich nt

employ [im'plɔi] v beschäftigen; *verwenden

employee [,emplɔi'i:] n Arbeitnehmer m, -in f, Angestellte m/f

employer [im'plɔiə] n Arbeitgeber m, -in f

employment [im'plɔimənt] n Beschäftigung f, Tätigkeit f; ~ **exchange** Arbeitsamt nt

empress ['empris] n Kaiserin f

empty ['empti] adj leer; v leeren

enable [i'neibəl] v befähigen; ermöglichen

enamel [i'næməl] n Email f

enamelled [i'næməld] adj emailliert

enchanting [in'tʃɑ:ntiŋ] adj zauberhaft, bezaubernd

encircle [in'sə:kəl] v einkreisen,

*umschließen; *einschließen

enclose [in'klouz] v beilegen

enclosure [in'klouʒə] n Beilage f

encounter [in'kauntə] v begegnen; n Begegnung f

encourage [in'kʌridʒ] v ermutigen

encyclop(a)edia [en,saiklə'pi:diə] n Enzyklopädie f

end [end] n Schluss m, Ende nt; v beenden; enden

ending ['endiŋ] n Ende nt

endless ['endləs] adj unendlich

endorse [in'dɔ:s] v abzeichnen, indossieren

endure [in'djuə] v *ertragen

enemy ['enəmi] n Feind m, -in f

energetic [,enə'dʒetik] adj energisch

energy ['enədʒi] n Energie f; Kraft f

engage [in'geidʒ] v anstellen; mieten; sich verpflichten; **engaged** verlobt; beschäftigt, besetzt

engagement [in'geidʒmənt] n Verlobung f; Verpflichtung f; Verabredung f; ~ **ring** Verlobungsring m

engine ['endʒin] n Maschine f, Motor m; Lokomotive f

engineer [,endʒi'niə] n Ingenieur m, -in f

England ['iŋglənd] England

English ['iŋgliʃ] adj englisch; **the ~ Channel** der Ärmelkanal; **the ~** die Engländer

Englishman ['iŋgliʃmən] n (pl -men) Engländer m

Englishwoman ['iŋgliʃ,wumən] n (pl -women) Engländerin f

engrave [in'greiv] v gravieren

engraving [in'greiviŋ] n Gravierung f

enigma [i'nigmə] n Rätsel nt

enjoy [in'dʒɔi] v *genießen

enjoyable [in'dʒɔiəbəl] adj erfreulich, gefällig, angenehm; schmackhaft

enjoyment [in'dʒɔimənt] n Genuss m

enlarge [in'lɑ:dʒ] v vergrößern; erweitern

enlargement [in'lɑ:dʒmənt] n Vergrößerung f

enormous [i'nɔ:məs] adj riesig, ungeheuer

enough [i'nʌf] adv genug; adj genügend

enquire [in'kwaiə] v sich erkundigen; untersuchen

enquiry [in'kwaiəri] n Erkundigung f; Untersuchung f; Umfrage f

enter ['entə] v *betreten, *eintreten; *einschreiben

enterprise ['entəpraiz] n Unternehmen nt

entertain [,entə'tein] v *unterhalten, amüsieren; bewirten

entertaining [,entə'teiniŋ] adj unterhaltsam, amüsant

entertainment [,entə'teinmənt] n Unterhaltung f

enthusiasm [in'θju:ziæzəm] n Begeisterung f

enthusiastic [in,θju:zi'æstik] adj begeistert

entire [in'taiə] adj ganz

entirely [in'taiəli] adv völlig, gänzlich

entrance ['entrəns] n Eingang m; Zutritt m; Eintritt m; ~ **fee** Eintrittsgeld nt

entry ['entri] n Eingang m, Eintritt m; Zugang m; Eintragung f; **no ~** Eintritt verboten

envelop [in'veləp] v einwickeln, einhüllen

envelope ['envəloup] n Briefumschlag m

envious ['enviəs] adj neidisch, eifersüchtig

environment [in'vaiərənmənt] n Umwelt f; Umgebung f

envoy ['envɔi] n Abgesandte m/f

envy ['envi] n Neid m; v beneiden

epic ['epik] n Epos nt; adj episch

epidemic [,epi'demik] n Epidemie f

epilepsy ['epilepsi] n Epilepsie f

episode ['episoud] n Episode f

equal ['i:kwəl] adj gleich

equality [i'kwɔləti] n Gleichheit f

equalize ['i:kwəlaiz] v *ausgleichen

equally ['i:kwəli] adv ebenso

equator [i'kweitə] n Äquator m

equip [i'kwip] v ausrüsten, ausstatten

equipment [i'kwipmənt] n Ausrüstung f

equivalent [i'kwivələnt] adj entsprechend, gleichwertig

eraser [i'reizə] n Radiergummi m

erect [i'rekt] v aufbauen, errichten, aufrichten; adj aufrecht

err [ə:] v sich irren; irren

error ['erə] n Fehler m, Irrtum m

escalator ['eskəleitə] n Rolltreppe f

escape [i'skeip] v *entkommen; *fliehen, flüchten, *entgehen; n Flucht f

especially [i'speʃəli] adv hauptsächlich, besonders

esplanade [,esplə'neid] n Promenade f

essay ['esei] n Essay m; Abhandlung f, Aufsatz m

essence ['esəns] n Essenz f; Kern m, Wesen nt

essential [i'senʃəl] adj unentbehrlich; grundlegend, wesentlich

essentially [i'senʃəli] adv vor allem

establish [i'stæbliʃ] v gründen; feststellen

estate [i'steit] n Landsitz m

esteem [i'sti:m] n Respekt m, Achtung f; v schätzen

estimate¹ ['estimeit] v veranschlagen, schätzen

estimate² ['estimət] n Voranschlag m

estuary ['estʃuəri] n Flussmündung f, Meeresarm m

etcetera [et'setərə] und so weiter

etching ['etʃiŋ] n Radierung f

eternal [i'tə:nəl] adj ewig

eternity [i'tə:nəti] n Ewigkeit f

ether ['i:θə] n Äther m

Ethiopia [iθi'oupiə] Äthiopien

Ethiopian [iθi'oupiən] adj äthiopisch; n Äthiopier m, -in f

EU ['i:'ju] EU, Europäische Union f

Euro ['juːrou] n Euro m

Europe ['juərəp] Europa

European [,juərə'piːən] adj europäisch; n Europäer m, -in f

evacuate [i'vækjueit] v evakuieren

evade [i'veid] v ausweichen, entkommen

evaluate [i'væljueit] v veranschlagen

evaporate [i'væpəreit] v verdampfen

even ['i:vən] adj glatt, eben, gleich; stetig; gerade; adv sogar

evening ['i:vniŋ] n Abend m; ~ dress Abendkleid m ; Frack m

event [i'vent] n Ereignis nt; Vorfall m

eventually [i'ventʃuəli] adv schließlich, endlich

ever ['evə] adv jemals; immer

every ['evri] adj jeder, jede, jedes

everybody ['evri,bɔdi] pron jedermann

everyday ['evridei] adj alltäglich

everyone ['evriwʌn] pron jeder, jedermann

everything ['evriθiŋ] pron alles

everywhere ['evriwɛə] adv überall

evidence ['evidəns] n Beweis m

evident ['evidənt] adj offensichtlich

evil ['i:vəl] n Übel nt; adj böse, schlecht

evolution [,i:və'lu:ʃən] n Evolution f

exact [ig'zækt] adj präzis, genau

exactly [ig'zæktli] adv genau

exaggerate [ig'zædʒəreit] v *übertreiben

exam [ig'zæmi] colloquial,

examination [ig,zæmi'neiʃən] n
Examen nt; Untersuchung f; Verhör
nt

examine [ig'zæmin] v prüfen

example [ig'zɑːmpəl] n Beispiel nt;
for ~ zum Beispiel

excavation [,ekskə'veiʃən] n
Ausgrabung f

exceed [ik'siːd] v *überschreiten;
*übertreffen

excel [ik'sel] v sich auszeichnen

excellent ['eksələnt] adj
ausgezeichnet, hervorragend

except [ik'sept] prep ausgenommen,
außer

exception [ik'sepʃən] n Ausnahme f

exceptional [ik'sepʃənəl] adj
ungewöhnlich, außergewöhnlich

excerpt ['eksəpt] n Auszug m

excess [ik'ses] n Ausschreitung f

excessive [ik'sesiv] adj übertrieben

exchange [iks'tʃeindʒ] v
auswechseln, wechseln, austauschen;
n Tausch m; Börse f; **~ office**
Wechselstube f; **~ rate** Wechselkurs
m

excite [ik'sait] v aufregen, erregen

excited [ik'saitəd] adj aufgeregt,
erregt

excitement [ik'saitmənt] n Erregung
f, Aufregung f

exciting [ik'saitiŋ] adj aufregend

exclaim [ik'skleim] v *ausrufen

exclamation [,eksklə'meiʃən] n
Ausruf m

exclude [ik'skluːd] v *ausschließen

exclusive [ik'skluːsiv] adj exklusiv

exclusively [ik'skluːsivli] adv
ausschließlich, nur

excursion [ik'skəːʃən] n Ausflug m

excuse [ik'skjuːs] n Entschuldigung
f; v *verzeihen, entschuldigen

execute ['eksikjuːt] v ausführen,
*vollziehen

execution [,eksi'kjuːʃən] n
Hinrichtung f

executive [ig'zekjutiv] adj
vollziehend; n Exekutive f; leitende
Angestellte m/f

exempt [ig'ʒempt] v befreien,
*ausnehmen; adj befreit

exemption [ig'ʒempʃən] n Befreiung
f

exercise ['eksəsaiz] n Übung f;
Aufgabe f; v üben; ausüben

exhale [eks'heil] v ausatmen

exhaust [ig'zɔːst] n Auspuff m; v
erschöpfen; **~ gases** Auspuffgase
ntpl

exhibit [ig'zibit] v ausstellen;
vorführen

exhibition [,eksi'biʃən] n Ausstellung
f

exile ['eksail] n Verbannung f

exist [ig'zist] v *bestehen, existieren,
*vorkommen

existence [ig'zistəns] n Dasein nt

exit ['eksit] n Ausgang m; Ausfahrt f

exotic [ig'zɔtik] adj exotisch

expand [ik'spænd] v ausbreiten;
ausdehnen; entfalten

expansion [ik'spænʃən] n
Ausbreitung f, Ausweitung f,
Expansion f

expect [ik'spekt] v erwarten

expectation [,ekspek'teiʃən] n
Erwartung f

expedition [,ekspə'diʃən] n Versand
m; Expedition f

expel [ik'spel] v *ausweisen;
*vertreiben

expenditure [ik'spenditʃə] n
Aufwand m

expense [ik'spens] n Ausgabe f;
expenses pl Unkosten pl

expensive [ik'spensiv] adj
kostspielig, teuer; kostbar

experience [ik'spiəriəns] n

Erfahrung f; v *erfahren, erleben;
experienced erfahren

experiment [ik'sperimənt] n Versuch
m, Experiment nt; v experimentieren

expert ['ekspə:t] n Fachmann m,
Fachfrau f, Sachverständige m/f; adj
fachkundig

expire [ik'spaiə] v *verfallen,
aufhören, *ablaufen; ausatmen;
expired verfallen

explain [ik'splein] v erläutern,
erklären

explanation [,eksplə'neiʃən] n
Erläuterung f, Erklärung f

explicit [ik'splisit] adj ausdrücklich

explode [ik'sploud] v explodieren

exploit [ik'sploit] v ausbeuten,
ausnutzen

explore [ik'splo:] v erforschen

explosion [ik'splouʒən] n Explosion f

explosive [ik'splousiv] adj explosiv; n
Sprengstoff m

export[1] [ik'spo:t] v ausführen,
exportieren

export[2] ['ekspo:t] n Export m

exportation [,ekspo:'teiʃən] n
Ausfuhr f

exports ['ekspo:ts] pl Ausfuhr f

exposition [,ekspə'ziʃən] n
Ausstellung f

exposure [ik'spouʒə] n Belichtung f

expose [ik'spous] v aussetzen;
aufdecken; belichten

express [ik'spres] v ausdrücken;
Ausdruck *geben, äußern; adj Eil-;
ausdrücklich; ~ train Schnellzug m

expression [ik'spreʃən] n Ausdruck
m; Äußerung f

exquisite [ik'skwizit] adj auserlesen

extend [ik'stend] v verlängern;
erweitern; gewähren

extension [ik'stenʃən] n
Verlängerung f; Ausdehnung f;
Nebenanschluss m; ~ cord
Verlängerungsschnur f

extensive [ik'stensiv] adj
umfangreich; umfassend, ausgedehnt

extent [ik'stent] n Ausmaß nt

exterior [ek'stiəriə] adj äußerlich; n
Außenseite f

external [ek'stə:nəl] adj äußerlich

extinguish [ik'stiŋgwiʃ] v löschen,
auslöschen

extort [ik'sto:t] v erpressen

extortion [ik'sto:ʃən] n Erpressung f

extract[1] [ik'strækt] v *ausziehen,
*ausreißen

extract[2] ['ekstrækt] n Auszug m;
Extrakt m

extradite ['ekstrədait] v ausliefern

extraordinary [ik'stro:dənri] adj
außerordentlich

extravagant [ik'strævəgənt] adj
übertrieben, extravagant

extreme [ik'stri:m] adj extrem;
höchst, äußerst; n Extrem nt

exuberant [ig'zju:bərənt] adj
überschwänglich

eye [ai] n Auge nt

eyebrow ['aibrau] n Augenbraue f; ~
pencil Augenbrauenstift m

eyelash ['ailæʃ] n Augenwimper f

eyelid ['ailid] n Augenlid nt

eyewitness ['ai,witnəs] n
Augenzeuge m, Augenzeugin f

F

fable ['feibəl] *n* Fabel *f*

fabric ['fæbrik] *n* Stoff *m*; Struktur *f*

façade [fə'sɑːd] *n* Fassade *f*

face [feis] *n* Gesicht *nt*; *v* *gegenüberstehen; ~ **cream** Gesichtscreme *f*; ~ **massage** Gesichtsmassage *f*; ~ **pack** Gesichtspackung *f*; **facing** gegenüber

facilities [fə'silətis] *pl* Anlage(n) *f(pl)*, Einrichtung(en) *f(pl)*; **cooking ~** Kochgelegenheit *f*

fact [fækt] *n* Tatsache *f*; **in ~** tatsächlich

factor ['fæktə] *n* Faktor *m*

factory ['fæktəri] *n* Fabrik *f*

factual ['fæktʃuəl] *adj* tatsächlich

faculty ['fækəlti] *n* Gabe *f*; Begabung *f*, Talent *nt*, Fähigkeit *f*; Fakultät *f*

fade [feid] *v* verblassen, *verschießen

fail [feil] *v* versagen; fehlen; mangeln; versäumen; *durchfallen; **without ~** unbedingt

failure ['feiljə] *n* Misserfolg *m*; Fehlschlag *m*

faint [feint] *v* ohnmächtig *werden; *adj* schwach, vage

fair [feə] *n* Kirmes *f*; Messe *f*; *adj* redlich, gerecht; blond; hübsch

fairly ['feəli] *adv* recht, leidlich, ziemlich

fairy ['feəri] *n* Fee *f*

fairytale ['feəriteil] *n* Märchen *nt*

faith [feiθ] *n* Glaube *m*; Vertrauen *nt*

faithful ['feiθful] *adj* treu

fake [feik] *n* Fälschung *f*; *v* fälschen; vortäuschen

fall [fɔːl] *n* Sturz *m*; *nAm* Herbst *m*

*fall [fɔːl] *v* *fallen

false [fɔːls] *adj* falsch; verkehrt, unwahr, unecht; ~ **teeth** künstliches Gebiss

falter ['fɔːltə] *v* wanken; stammeln

fame [feim] *n* Name *m*, Ruhm *m*; Ruf *m*

familiar [fə'miljə] *adj* vertraut; vertraulich

family ['fæməli] *n* Familie *f*; Verwandtschaft *f*; ~ **name** Nachname *m*

famous ['feiməs] *adj* berühmt

fan [fæn] *n* Ventilator *m*; Fächer *m*; Fan *m*

fanatical [fə'nætikəl] *adj* fanatisch

fancy ['fænsi] *v* *mögen, Lust *haben zu; sich einbilden, sich vorstellen; *n* Laune *f*, Fantasie *f*

fantastic [fæn'tæstik] *adj* fantastisch

fantasy ['fæntəzi] *n* Einbildungskraft *f*, (Tag)Traum *m*

far [fɑː] *adj* fern; *adv* viel; **by ~** bei weitem; **so ~** bis jetzt; ~ **away** weit entfernt

fare [feə] *n* Fahrgeld *nt*; Kost *f*, Speise *f*

farm [fɑːm] *n* Bauernhof *m*

farmer ['fɑːmə] *n* Bauer *m*; **farmer's wife** Bäuerin *f*

farmhouse ['fɑːmhaus] *n* Bauernhaus *nt*

far-off ['fɑːrɔf] *adj* abgelegen

farther ['fɑːðə] *adj* weiter, ferner

fascinate ['fæsineit] *v* fesseln; faszinieren

fascism ['fæʃizəm] *n* Faschismus *m*

fascist ['fæʃist] *adj* faschistisch; *n* Faschist *m*, -in *f*

fashion ['fæʃən] *n* Mode *f*; Weise *f*

fashionable ['fæʃənəbəl] *adj* modern

fast [fɑːst] *adj* rasch, schnell; fest

fasten ['fɑːsən] *v* festmachen, befestigen; *schließen

fastener ['fɑːsənə] *n* Verschluss *m*

fat [fæt] *adj* fett, dick; *n* Fett *nt*

fatal ['feitəl] *adj* unheilvoll, tödlich, verhängnisvoll

fate [feit] *n* Schicksal *nt*

father ['fɑːðə] *n* Vater *m*; Pater *m*

father-in-law ['fɑːðərinlɔː] *n* (pl fathers-) Schwiegervater *m*

fatty ['fæti] *adj* fettig

faucet ['fɔːsit] *nAm* Wasserhahn *m*

fault [fɔːlt] *n* Fehler *m*; Mangel *m*, Defekt *m*

faultless ['fɔːltləs] *adj* tadellos; einwandfrei

faulty ['fɔːlti] *adj* mangelhaft, fehlerhaft

favo(u)r ['feivə] *n* Gefälligkeit *f*; *v* begünstigen

favo(u)rable ['feivərəbəl] *adj* günstig

favo(u)rite ['feivərit] *n* Liebling *m*, Favorit *m*, -in *f*; *adj* Lieblings-

fax [fæks] *n* Fax *nt*; *v* faxen

fear [fiə] *n* Furcht *f*, Angst *f*; *v* fürchten

feasible ['fiːzəbəl] *adj* durchführbar

feast [fiːst] *n* Fest *nt*

feat [fiːt] *n* Glanzleistung *f*

feather ['feðə] *n* Feder *f*

feature ['fiːtʃə] *n* Kennzeichen *nt*; Gesichtszug *m*

February ['februəri] Februar

federal ['fedərəl] *adj* Bundes-

federation [,fedə'reiʃən] *n* Föderation *f*; Verband *m*

fee [fiː] *n* Honorar *nt*

feeble ['fiːbəl] *adj* schwach

*feed [fiːd] *v* ernähren; **fed up with** überdrüssig

*feel [fiːl] *v* fühlen; betasten; **~ like** Lust *haben zu

feeling ['fiːliŋ] *n* Gefühl *nt*

feet (pl foot)

fell [fel] *v* (p fall)

felt¹ [felt] *n* Filz *m*

felt² [felt] *v* (p, pp feel)

female ['fiːmeil] *adj* weiblich

feminine ['feminin] *adj* weiblich

fence [fens] *n* Zaun *m*; Gatter *nt*; *v* *fechten

ferment [fəːment] *v* *gären

ferry ['feri] *n* Fährboot *nt*

fertile ['fəːtail] *adj* fruchtbar

festival ['festivəl] *n* Festival *nt*

festive ['festiv] *adj* festlich

fetch [fetʃ] *v* holen; abholen

feudal ['fjuːdəl] *adj* feudal

fever ['fiːvə] *n* Fieber *nt*

feverish ['fiːvəriʃ] *adj* fiebrig

few [fjuː] *adj* wenig

fiancé [fi'ãːsei] *n* Verlobte *m*

fiancée [fi'ãːsei] *n* Verlobte *f*

fibre ['faibə] *n* Faser *f*

fiction ['fikʃən] *n* Fiktion *f*

field [fiːld] *n* Acker *m*, Feld *nt*; Gebiet *nt*; **~ glasses** Feldstecher *m*

fierce [fiəs] *adj* wild; wüst, heftig

fifteen [,fif'tiːn] *num* fünfzehn

fifteenth [,fif'tiːnθ] *num* fünfzehnte

fifth [fifθ] *num* fünfte

fifty ['fifti] *num* fünfzig

fig [fig] *n* Feige *f*

fight [fait] *n* Streit *m*, Kampf *m*

*fight [fait] *v* sich *schlagen, kämpfen

figure ['figə] *n* Figur *f*, Gestalt *f*; Zahl *f*

file [fail] *n* Feile *f*; Akten; Reihe *f*

fill [fil] *v* füllen; **~ in**, *Am* **~ out** ausfüllen

filling ['filiŋ] *n* Plombe *f*; Füllung *f*

filling station ['filiŋ,steiʃən] *n* Tankstelle *f*

film [film] *n* Film *m*; *v* filmen

filter ['filtə] *n* Filter *m*

filthy ['filθi] *adj* dreckig, schmutzig

final ['fainəl] *adj* letzt

finally ['fainəli] *adv* schließlich, zuletzt

finance [fai'næns] *v* finanzieren

finances [fai'nænsiz] *pl* Finanzen *pl*

financial [fai'nænʃəl] *adj* finanziell

finch [fintʃ] *n* Fink *m*

*find [faind] *v* *finden

fine [fain] *n* Geldstrafe *f; adj* fein;
schön; ausgezeichnet, prächtig; **~ arts**
die schönen Künste

finger ['fiŋgə] *n* Finger *m*

fingerprint ['fiŋgəprint] *n*
Fingerabdruck *m*

finish ['finiʃ] *v* fertig machen,
beenden; enden; *n* Schluss *m*;
Ziellinie *f*; **finished** fertig; alle

Finland ['finlənd] Finnland

Finnish ['finiʃ] *adj* finnisch

fire [faiə] *n* Feuer *nt*; Brand *m; v*
*schießen; *entlassen; **~ alarm**
Feueralarm *m*; **~ brigade**, *Am* **~**
department Feuerwehr *f*; **~ escape**
Nottreppe *f*; **~ extinguisher**
Feuerlöscher *m*

firefighter ['faiə,faitə] *n*
Feuerwehrmann *m*, -frau *f*

fireplace ['faiəpleis] *n* Kamin *m*

fireproof ['faiəpru:f] *adj* feuersicher;
feuerfest

firm [fə:m] *adj* fest; solide; *n* Firma *f*

first [fə:st] *num* erste; **at ~** zuerst;
anfangs; **~ name** Vorname *m*

first aid [,fə:st'eid] *n* erste Hilfe; **~ kit**
Verbandskasten *m*; **~ post**
Unfallstation *f*

first-class [,fə:st'kla:s] *adj*
erstklassig

first-rate [,fə:st'reit] *adj* vorzüglich,
erstrangig

fir tree ['fə:tri:] *n* Tanne *f*

fish¹ [fiʃ] *n* (pl ~, ~es) Fisch *m*; **~ shop**
Fischhandlung *f; v* fischen; angeln;
fishing gear Angelgeräte *ntpl*;
fishing hook Angelhaken *m*;
fishing industry Fischerei *f*; **fishing**
licence Angelschein *m*; **fishing line**
Angelschnur *f*; **fishing net** Fischnetz
nt; **fishing rod** Angelrute *f*; **fishing**
tackle Angelgeräte *ntpl*

fishbone ['fiʃboun] *n* Gräte *f*,
Fischgräte *f*

fisherman ['fiʃəmən] *n* (pl -men)
Fischer *m*

fisherwoman ['fiʃəwumən] *n* (pl
-women) Fischerin *f*

fist [fist] *n* Faust *f*

fit [fit] *adj* tauglich; *n* Anfall *m; v*
passen;

five [faiv] *num* fünf

fix [fiks] *v* richten

fixed [fikst] *adj* fest

fizz [fiz] *n* Brause *f*

flag [flæg] *n* Fahne *f*

flame [fleim] *n* Flamme *f*

flamingo [flə'miŋgou] *n* (pl ~s, ~es)
Flamingo *m*

flannel ['flænəl] *n* Flanell *m*

flash [flæʃ] *n* Blitz *m*; **~ bulb** Blitzlicht
nt

flashlight ['flæʃlait] *n* Taschenlampe
f

flask [fla:sk] *n* Flakon *nt*; **thermos ~**
Thermosflasche *f*

flat [flæt] *adj* eben, flach; *n* Wohnung
f; **~ tyre**, *Am* **~ tire** Reifenpanne *f*

flavour ['fleivə] *n* Geschmack *m; v*
würzen

flee [fli:] *v* fliehen, flüchten

fleet [fli:t] *n* Flotte *f*

flesh [fleʃ] *n* Fleisch *nt*

flew [flu:] *v* (p fly)

flex [fleks] *n* Kabel *nt*

flexible ['fleksibəl] *adj* geschmeidig;
biegsam

flight [flait] *n* Flug *m*; **charter ~**
Charterflug *m*

float [flout] *v* *schwimmen, *treiben;
n Schwimmer *m*

flock [flɔk] *n* Herde *f*

flood [flʌd] *n* Überschwemmung *f*;
Flut *f*

floor [flɔ:] *n* Fußboden *m*; Geschoss
nt, Stockwerk *nt*; **~ show** Kabarett *nt*

florist ['flɔrist] n Blumenhändler m, -in f

flour [flauə] n Mehl nt

flow [flou] v strömen, *fließen

flower [flauə] n Blume f

flowerbed ['flauəbed] n Blumenbeet nt

flower shop ['flauəʃɔp] n Blumenhandlung f

flown [floun] v (pp fly)

flu [fluː] n Grippe f

fluent ['fluːənt] adj fließend

fluid ['fluːid] adj flüssig; n Flüssigkeit f

flute [fluːt] n Flöte f

fly [flai] n Fliege f; Schlitz m

*fly [flai] v *fliegen

foam [foum] n Schaum m; v schäumen; ~ **rubber** Schaumgummi m

focus ['foukəs] n Brennpunkt m

fog [fɔg] n Nebel m

foggy ['fɔgi] adj nebelig

foglamp ['fɔglæmp] n Nebellampe f

fold [fould] v falten; zusammenfalten; n Falte f

folk [fouk] n Volk nt; ~ **dance** Volkstanz m; ~ **song** Volkslied nt

folklore ['fouklɔː] n Folklore f

follow ['fɔlou] v folgen; **following** adj nächst, folgend

fond: **be ~ of* [bi: fɔnd ɔv] gern *mögen

food [fuːd] n Nahrung f; Kost f; Essen nt; ~ **poisoning** Nahrungsmittelvergiftung f

foodstuffs ['fuːdstʌfs] pl Nahrungsmittel ntpl

fool [fuːl] n Dummkopf m, Narr m, Närrin f; v zum Narren *halten

foolish ['fuːliʃ] adj albern, töricht

foot [fut] n (pl feet) Fuß m; **on ~** zu Fuß

football ['futbɔːl] n Fußball m; ~ **match** Fußballspiel nt

foot brake ['futbreik] n Fußbremse f

footpath ['futpɑːθ] n Fußweg m

footwear ['futwɛə] n Schuhwerk nt

for [fɔː, fə] prep für; während; nach; wegen, aus; conj denn

*forbid [fə'bid] v *verbieten

force [fɔːs] v *zwingen; forcieren; n Macht f, Kraft f; Gewalt f; **by ~** zwangsweise; **driving ~** Treibkraft f

forecast ['fɔːkɑːst] n Vorhersage f; v voraussagen

foreground ['fɔːgraund] n Vordergrund m

forehead ['fɔred] n Stirn f

foreign ['fɔrin] adj ausländisch; fremd

foreigner ['fɔrinə] n Fremde m/f; Ausländer m, -in f

foreman ['fɔːmən] n (pl -men) Werkmeister m

foremost ['fɔːmoust] adj erste

forest ['fɔrist] n Forst m, Wald m

forester ['fɔristə] n Förster m, -in f

forever, for ever [fə'revə] adv für immer; ständig

forge [fɔːdʒ] v fälschen

*forget [fə'get] v *vergessen

forgetful [fə'getfəl] adj vergesslich

forgive [fə'giv] v entschuldigen, *verzeihen

fork [fɔːk] n Gabel f; Gabelung f; v sich gabeln

form [fɔːm] n Form f; Formular nt; Klasse f; v formen

formal ['fɔːməl] adj förmlich

formality [fɔː'mæləti] n Formalität f

former ['fɔːmə] adj ehemalig; früher; **formerly** früher

formula ['fɔːmjulə] n (pl ~e, ~s) Formel f; Rezept nt

fortnight ['fɔːtnait] n vierzehn Tage

fortress ['fɔːtris] n Festung f

fortunate ['fɔːtʃənət] adj glücklich; **fortunately** adv glücklicherweise

fortune ['fɔːtʃuːn] n Vermögen nt; Geschick nt, Glück nt

forty ['fɔːti] num vierzig

forward ['fɔːwəd] adv voraus, vorwärts; v *nachsenden

foster parents ['fɒstə,peərənts] pl Pflegeeltern pl

fought [fɔːt] v (p, pp fight)

foul [faul] adj schmutzig; niederträchtig

found¹ [faund] v (p, pp find)

found² [faund] v gründen, errichten, stiften

foundation [faun'deiʃən] n Stiftung f; ~ **cream** Make-up-Unterlage

fountain ['fauntin] n Springbrunnen m; Quelle f; ~ **pen** Füller m

four [fɔː] num vier

fourteen [,fɔː'tiːn] num vierzehn

fourteenth [,fɔː'tiːnθ] num vierzehnte

fourth [fɔːθ] num vierte

fowl [faul] n (pl ~s, ~) Geflügel nt

fox [fɒks] n Fuchs m

foyer ['fɔiei] n Foyer nt

fraction ['frækʃən] n Bruchstück nt

fracture ['fræktʃə] v *brechen; n Bruch m

fragile ['frædʒail] adj zerbrechlich

fragment ['frægmənt] n Fragment nt; Bruchstück nt

frame [freim] n Rahmen m; Gestell nt

France [frɑːns] Frankreich

franchise ['fræntʃaiz] n Wahlrecht nt

fraud [frɔːd] n Schwindel m, Betrug m

fray [frei] v zerfasern

free [friː] adj frei; gratis; ~ **of charge** kostenlos; ~ **ticket** Freikarte f

freedom ['friːdəm] n Freiheit f

***freeze** [friːz] v *frieren; *gefrieren

freezer ['friːzə] n Tiefkühltruhe f, Gefrierfach n

freezing ['friːziŋ] adj eisig

freezing point ['friːziŋpɔint] n Gefrierpunkt m

freight [freit] n Ladung f, Fracht f; ~ **train** Güterzug m

French [frentʃ] adj französisch; **the** ~ pl die Franzosen; ~ **fries** pl Pommes frites

frequency ['friːkwənsi] n Frequenz f; Häufigkeit f

frequent ['friːkwənt] adj üblich, häufig; **frequently** oft

fresh [freʃ] adj frisch; erfrischend; ~ **water** Süßwasser nt

friction ['frikʃən] n Reibung f

Friday ['fraidi] Freitag m

fridge [fridʒ] n Kühlschrank m

friend [frend] n Freund m, -in f

friendly ['frendli] adj freundlich; freundschaftlich

friendship ['frendʃip] n Freundschaft f

fright [frait] n Angst f, Schreck m

frighten ['fraitən] v *erschrecken

frightened ['fraitənd] adj verängstigt; ***be** ~ *erschrecken

frightful ['fraitfəl] adj fürchterlich, schrecklich

fringe [frindʒ] n Franse f

frock [frɒk] n Kutte f, Kittel m, Kleid nt

frog [frɒg] n Frosch m

from [frɒm] prep von; aus; von … an

front [frʌnt] n Vorderseite f; **in** ~ **of** vor

frontier ['frʌntiə] n Grenze f

frost [frɒst] n Frost m

froth [frɒθ] n Schaum m

frozen ['frouzən] adj gefroren

fruit [fruːt] n Obst nt; Frucht f

fry [frai] v *braten

frying pan ['fraiiŋpæn] n Bratpfanne f

fuck [fʌk] v vulgar ficken, vögeln

fuel ['fjuːəl] n Brennstoff m; Benzin nt; ~ **pump** Am Benzinpumpe f

full [ful] *adj* voll; ~ **board** Vollpension *f*; ~ **stop** Punkt *m*; ~ **up** vollbesetzt

fun [fʌn] *n* Vergnügen *nt*, Spaß *m*

function ['fʌŋkʃən] *n* Funktion *f*

fund [fʌnd] *n* Fonds *m*

fundamental [‚fʌndə'mentəl] *adj* grundlegend

funeral ['fju:nərəl] *n* Begräbnis *nt*

funnel ['fʌnəl] *n* Trichter *m*

funny ['fʌni] *adj* spaßig, komisch; sonderbar

fur [fə:] *n* Pelz *m*; ~ **coat** Pelzmantel *m*

furious ['fjuəriəs] *adj* rasend, wütend

furnace ['fə:nis] *n* Ofen *m*

furnish ['fə:niʃ] *v* liefern, verschaffen; möblieren, einrichten; ~ **with** *versehen mit

furniture ['fə:nitʃə] *n* Möbel *ntpl*

further ['fə:ðə] *adj* ferner; weiter

furthermore ['fə:ðəmɔ:] *adv* überdies

furthest ['fə:ðist] *adj* entferntest

fuss [fʌs] *n* Getue *nt*; Wichtigtuerei *f*

future ['fju:tʃə] *n* Zukunft *f*; *adj* zukünftig

G

gable ['geibəl] *n* Giebel *m*

gain [gein] *v* *gewinnen; *n* Gewinn *m*

gale [geil] *n* Sturm *m*

gall [gɔ:l] *n* Galle *f*; ~ **bladder** Gallenblase *f*

gallery ['gæləri] *n* Galerie *f*

gallon ['gælən] *n* Gallone *f* (Brit 4,55 l; Am 3,79 l)

gallop ['gæləp] *n* Galopp *m*

gallstone ['gɔ:lstoun] *n* Gallenstein *m*

game [geim] *n* Spiel *nt*; Wild *nt*; ~ **reserve** Wildpark *m*

gang [gæŋ] *n* Bande *f*; Schicht *f*

gap [gæp] *n* Lücke *f*

garage ['gærɑ:ʒ] *n* Garage *f*; *v* einstellen

garbage ['gɑ:bidʒ] *n* Müll *m*, Abfall *m*

garden ['gɑ:dən] *n* Garten *m*; **public ~** Anlage *f*; **zoological gardens** zoologischer Garten

gardener ['gɑ:dənə] *n* Gärtner *m*, -in *f*

gargle ['gɑ:gəl] *v* gurgeln

garlic ['gɑ:lik] *n* Knoblauch *m*

gas [gæs] *n* Gas *nt*; *nAm* Benzin *nt*; ~ **cooker** Gasherd *m*; ~ **pump** *Am* Benzinpumpe *f*; ~ **station** *Am* Tankstelle *f*; ~ **stove** Gasofen *m*; ~ **tank** *Am* Benzintank *m*

gasoline ['gæsəli:n] *nAm* Benzin *nt*

gastric ['gæstrik] *adj* Magen-; ~ **ulcer** Magengeschwür *nt*

gate [geit] *n* Tor *nt*

gather ['gæðə] *v* sammeln; sich versammeln; einholen

gauge [geidʒ] *n* Messer *m*

gave [geiv] *v* (p give)

gay [gei] *adj* lustig; bunt; *colloquial* schwul

gaze [geiz] *v* starren

gear [giə] *n* Gang *m*; Ausrüstung *f*; **change ~** schalten; ~ **lever**, ~ **shift** *Am* Schalthebel *m*, Gangschaltung *f*

gearbox ['giəbɔks] *n* Getriebe *nt*

geese (pl goose)

gem [dʒem] *n* Juwel *nt*, Edelstein *m*; Kleinod *nt*

gender ['dʒendə] *n* Geschlecht *nt*

general ['dʒenərəl] *adj* allgemein; *n* General *m*; ~ **practitioner**

praktischer Arzt; **in** ~ im Allgemeinen

generate ['dʒenəreit] *v* erzeugen

generation [,dʒenə'reiʃən] *n* Generation *f*

generator ['dʒenəreitər] *n* Generator *m*

generous ['dʒenərəs] *adj* freigebig, großzügig

genius ['dʒi:niəs] *n* Genie *nt*

gentle ['dʒentəl] *adj* sanft; zart, leicht; behutsam

gentleman ['dʒentəlmən] *n* (pl -men) Herr *m*

genuine ['dʒenjuin] *adj* echt

geography [dʒi'ɔgrəfi] *n* Erdkunde *f*

geology [dʒi'ɔlədʒi] *n* Geologie *f*

geometry [dʒi'ɔmətri] *n* Geometrie *f*

germ [dʒə:m] *n* Bazille *f*; Keim *m*

German ['dʒə:mən] *adj* deutsch; *n* Deutsche *m/f*

Germany ['dʒə:məni] Deutschland

gesticulate [dʒi'stikjuleit] *v* gestikulieren

*get [get] *v* *bekommen; holen; *werden; ~ **back** *zurückbekommen; *zurückgehen; ~ **off** *aussteigen; ~ **on** *einsteigen; *vorwärts kommen; ~ **up** *aufstehen

ghost [goust] *n* Geist *m*

giant ['dʒaiənt] *n* Riese *m*

giddiness ['gidinəs] *n* Schwindelgefühl *nt*

giddy ['gidi] *adj* schwindlig

gift [gift] *n* Geschenk *nt*; Gabe *f*

gifted ['giftid] *adj* begabt

gigantic [dʒai'gæntik] *adj* riesenhaft

giggle ['gigəl] *v* kichern

gill [gil] *n* Kieme *f*

gilt [gilt] *adj* vergoldet

ginger ['dʒindʒə] *n* Ingwer *m*

girl [gə:l] *n* Mädchen *nt*; ~ **guide** Pfadfinderin *f*

girlfriend ['gə:lfrend] *n* Freundin *f*

(eines Jungen)

*give [giv] *v* *geben; überreichen; ~ **away** *verraten; ~ **in** *nachgeben; ~ **up** *aufgeben

glacier ['glæsiə] *n* Gletscher *m*

glad [glæd] *adj* erfreut, froh; **gladly** mit Vergnügen, gerne

gladness ['glædnəs] *n* Freude *f*

glamorous ['glæmərəs] *adj* bezaubernd

glamour ['glæmə] *n* Reiz *m*

glance [glɑ:ns] *n* Blick *m*; *v* erblicken

gland [glænd] *n* Drüse *f*

glare [glɛə] *n* grelles Licht; Glanz *m*

glaring ['glɛəriŋ] *adj* blendend

glass [glɑ:s] *n* Glas *nt*; gläsern; **glasses** Brille *f*

glaze [gleiz] *v* glasieren

glide [glaid] *v* *gleiten

glider ['glaidə] *n* Segelflugzeug *nt*

glimpse [glimps] *n* Blick *m*; *v* erblicken

global ['gloubəl] *adj* weltumfassend

globe [gloub] *n* Erdball *m*

gloom [glu:m] *n* Düsterkeit *f*

gloomy ['glu:mi] *adj* düster

glorious ['glɔ:riəs] *adj* prächtig

glory ['glɔ:ri] *n* Ehre *f*, Ruhm *m*; Lob *nt*

gloss [glɔs] *n* Glanz *m*

glossy ['glɔsi] *adj* glänzend

glove [glʌv] *n* Handschuh *m*

glow [glou] *v* glühen; *n* Glut *f*

glue [glu:] *n* Leim *m*

*go [gou] *v* *gehen; *werden; ~ **ahead** *fortfahren; ~ **away** *weggehen; ~ **back** *zurückgehen; ~ **home** *heimgehen; ~ **in** *hineingehen; ~ **on** *weitergehen; *fortfahren; ~ **out** *ausgehen; ~ **through** durchmachen

goal [goul] *n* Ziel *nt*, Tor *nt*

goalkeeper ['goul,ki:pə] *n* Torwart *m*, -in *f*

goat [gout] *n* Ziegenbock *m*, Ziege *f*

god [gɔd] n Gott m

goddess ['gɔdis] n Göttin f

godfather ['gɔd,fɑːðə] n Pate m

godmother ['gɔd,mʌðə] n Patin f

goggles ['gɔgəlz] pl Schutzbrille f

gold [gould] n Gold nt; ~ **leaf** Blattgold nt

golden ['gouldən] adj golden

goldsmith ['gouldsmiθ] n Goldschmied m, -in f

golf [gɔlf] n Golf nt; **~club** Golfklub m; Golfschläger m; **~ course, ~ links** Golfplatz m

gondola ['gɔndələ] n Gondel f

gone [gɔn] adv (pp go) fort

good [gud] adj gut; lecker; brav, artig

goodbye! [,gud'bai] auf Wiedersehen!

good-humo(u)red [,gud'hjuːməd] adj gut gelaunt

good-looking [,gud'lukiŋ] adj hübsch

good-natured [,gud'neitʃəd] adj gutmütig

goods [gudz] pl Waren, Güter ntpl; **~ train** Güterzug m

good-tempered [,gud'tempəd] adj gut gelaunt

goodwill [,gud'wil] n Wohlwollen nt

goose [guːs] n (pl geese) Gans f; **~ bumps** Am, **~ flesh** Gänsehaut f

gooseberry ['guzbəri] n Stachelbeere f

gorge [gɔːdʒ] n Schlucht f

gorgeous ['gɔːdʒəs] adj prächtig

gossip ['gɔsip] n Tratsch m; v tratschen

got [gɔt] v (p, pp get)

gourmet ['guəmei] n Feinschmecker m, -in f

gout [gaut] n Gicht f

govern ['gʌvən] v regieren

government ['gʌvənmənt] n Verwaltung f, Regierung f

gown [gaun] n Kleid nt

grace [greis] n Gunst f, Gnade f

graceful ['greisfəl] adj reizend

grade [greid] n Rang m; Klasse f; Note f; v einstufen

gradient ['greidiənt] n Gefälle nt

gradual ['grædʒuəl] adj allmählich

graduate ['grædʒueit] v ein Diplom erlangen

grain [grein] n Korn nt, Getreide nt

gram [græm] n Gramm nt

grammar ['græmə] n Grammatik f

grand [grænd] adj großartig

grandchild ['græn,tʃaild] n Enkel m, -in f

granddad ['grændæd] n Opa m

granddaughter ['græn,dɔːtə] n Enkelin f

grandfather ['græn,fɑːðə] n Großvater m; Opa m

grandmother ['græn,mʌðə] n Großmutter f; Oma f

grandparents ['græn,peərənts] pl Großeltern pl

grandson ['grænsʌn] n Enkel m

granite ['grænit] n Granit m

grant [grɑːnt] v bewilligen, *verleihen; gewähren; n Zuschuss m, Stipendium nt

grapefruit ['greipfruːt] n Pampelmuse f

grapes [greips] pl Trauben fpl

graph [græf] n Grafik f

graphic ['græfik] adj grafisch

grasp [grɑːsp] v *ergreifen; n Griff m

grass [grɑːs] n Gras nt

grasshopper ['grɑːs,hɔpə] n Heuschrecke f

grate [greit] n Rost m; v raspeln

grateful ['greitfəl] adj erkenntlich, dankbar

grater ['greitə] n Reibe f

gratis ['greitis] adj umsonst

gratitude ['grætitjuːd] n Dankbarkeit f

gratuity [grə'tjuːəti] n Trinkgeld nt

grave [greiv] n Grab nt; adj ernst

gravel ['grævəl] n Kies m

gravestone ['greivstoun] n Grabstein m

graveyard ['greivjɑːd] n Friedhof m

gravity ['grævəti] n Schwerkraft f; Ernst m

gravy ['greivi] n Bratensoße f

graze [greiz] v weiden; n Schramme f

grease [griːs] n Fett nt; v schmieren

greasy ['griːsi] adj fett, fettig

great [greit] adj groß; **Great Britain** Großbritannien

Greece [griːs] n Griechenland

greed [griːd] n Gier f

greedy ['griːdi] adj gierig; gefräßig

Greek [griːk] adj griechisch; n Grieche m, Griechin f

green [griːn] adj grün; ~ card grüne Versicherungskarte; nAm Aufenthaltsgenehmigung f

greengrocer ['griːnˌgrousə] n Gemüsehändler m, -in f

greenhouse ['griːnhaus] n Treibhaus nt, Gewächshaus nt

greens [griːnz] pl Gemüse nt

greet [griːt] v grüßen

greeting ['griːtiŋ] n Gruß m

grey [grei] adj grau

greyhound ['greihaund] n Windhund m

grief [griːf] n Leid nt; Kummer m

grieve [griːv] v sich grämen

grill [gril] n Bratrost m; v grillen

grim [grim] adj grimmig, grausam; schrecklich

grin [grin] v grinsen; n Grinsen nt

*****grind** [graind] v mahlen; *zerreiben

grip [grip] v fassen; n Halt m, Griff m; nAm Handköfferchen nt

groan [groun] v stöhnen

grocer ['grousə] n Lebensmittelhändler m, -in f;

grocer's, grocery Lebensmittelgeschäft nt

groceries ['grousəriz] pl Lebensmittel pl

groin [groin] n Leiste f

groom [gruːm] n Pferdepfleger m, -in f, Stallbursche m; Bräutigam m; v pflegen

groove [gruːv] n Rille f

gross¹ [grous] n (pl ~) Gros nt

gross² [grous] adj grob; brutto

grotto ['grotou] n (pl ~es, ~s) Grotte f

ground¹ [graund] n Boden m, Grund m; ~ floor Erdgeschoss nt; **grounds** Grundstück nt

ground² [graund] v (p, pp grind)

group [gruːp] n Gruppe f

grouse [graus] n (pl ~) Moorhuhn nt

*****grow** [grou] v *wachsen; züchten; *werden

growl [graul] v brummen

grown-up ['grounʌp] adj erwachsen; n Erwachsene m/f

growth [grouθ] n Wuchs m; Geschwulst f

grudge [grʌdʒ] v missgönnen

guarantee [ˌgærən'tiː] n Garantie f; Bürgschaft f; v garantieren

guard [gɑːd] n Wache f; v bewachen

guess [ges] v *raten; *denken, vermuten; n Vermutung f

guest [gest] n Gast m; ~ **house** Pension f; ~ **room** Gästezimmer nt

guide [gaid] n Führer m, -in f; v führen; ~ **dog** Blindenhund m

guidebook ['gaidbuk] n Führer m

guideline ['gaidlain] n Richtlinie f

guilt [gilt] n Schuld f

guilty ['gilti] adj schuldig

guinea pig ['ginipig] n Meerschweinchen nt; Versuchskaninchen nt

guitar [gi'tɑː] n Gitarre f

gulf [gʌlf] n Golf m

gull [gʌl] n Möwe f
gum [gʌm] n Zahnfleisch nt; Gummi m; Klebstoff m
gun [gʌn] n Gewehr nt, Revolver m; Kanone f
gunpowder ['gʌn,paudə] n Schießpulver nt
gust [gʌst] n Windstoß m
gusty ['gʌsti] adj windig
gut [gʌt] n Darm m; **guts** Mumm m
guy [gai] n Bursche m

gym [dʒim] n colloquial Fitnessclub m; Turnhalle f
gymnasium [dʒim'neiziəm] n (pl ~s, -sia) Turnhalle f
gymnast ['dʒimnæst] n Turner m, -in f
gymnastics [dʒim'næstiks] pl Turnen nt
gynaecologist [,gainə'kɔlədʒist] n Gynäkologe m, Gynäkologin f, Frauenarzt m, Frauenärztin f

H

habit ['hæbit] n Gewohnheit f
habitable ['hæbitəbəl] adj bewohnbar
habitual [hə'bitʃuəl] adj gewohnt
had [hæd] v (p, pp have)
haddock ['hædək] n (pl ~) Schellfisch m
haemorrhage ['heməridʒ] n Blutsturz m
haemorrhoids ['hemərɔidz] pl Hämorrhoiden fpl
hail [heil] n Hagel m
hair [hɛə] n Haar nt; ~ piece Toupet nt
hairbrush ['hɛəbrʌʃ] n Haarbürste f
haircut ['hɛəkʌt] n Haarschnitt m
hairdo ['hɛədu:] n Frisur f
hairdresser ['hɛə,dresə] n Friseur m, -in f
hairdryer ['hɛədraiə] n Föhn m
hairgrip ['hɛəgrip] n Haarklemme f
hairpin ['hɛəpin] n Haarnadel f
hairy ['hɛəri] adj haarig
half [hɑ:f] adj halb; n (pl halves) Hälfte f
half time [,hɑ:f'taim] n Halbzeit f
halfway [,hɑ:f'wei] adv auf halbem Wege; halbwegs
halibut ['hælibət] n (pl ~) Heilbutt m

hall [hɔːl] n Halle f; Saal m
halt [hɔːlt] v *anhalten
halve [hɑːv] v halbieren
ham [hæm] n Schinken m
hammer ['hæmə] n Hammer m
hammock ['hæmək] n Hängematte f
hand [hænd] n Hand f; v *übergeben; ~ cream Handkrem f
handbag ['hændbæg] n Handtasche f
handbook ['hændbuk] n Handbuch nt
handbrake ['hændbreik] n Handbremse f
handcuffs ['hændkʌfs] pl Handschellen fpl
handful ['hændful] n Hand voll f
handicap ['hændikæp] n Handikap nt; Behinderung f; v benachteiligen; behindern
handicraft ['hændikrɑːft] n Handarbeit f; Handwerk nt
handkerchief ['hæŋkətʃif] n Taschentuch nt
handle ['hændəl] n Stiel m, Handgriff m; v handhaben; behandeln
hand-made [,hænd'meid] adj handgearbeitet
handshake ['hændʃeik] n

Händedruck *m*

handsome ['hænsəm] *adj* stattlich, gutaussehend (Mann)

handwork ['hændwə:k] *n* Handarbeit *f*

handwriting ['hænd,raitiŋ] *n* Handschrift *f*

handy ['hændi] *adj* handlich

*hang [hæŋ] *v* aufhängen; *hängen

hanger ['hæŋə] *n* Kleiderbügel *m*; Aufhänger *m*

hangover ['hæŋ,ouvə] *n* Kater *m*

happen ['hæpən] *v* *geschehen, passieren, sich ereignen

happening ['hæpəniŋ] *n* Ereignis *nt*

happiness ['hæpinəs] *n* Glück *nt*

happy ['hæpi] *adj* zufrieden, glücklich

harbour ['ha:bə] *n* Hafen *m*

hard [ha:d] *adj* hart; schwierig; ~ **disk** Festplatte *f*; **hardly** kaum

hardware ['ha:dwεə] *n* Eisenwaren *fpl*; ~ **store** Eisenwarenhandlung *f*

hare [hεə] *n* Hase *m*

harm [ha:m] *n* Schaden *m*; Übel *nt*, Böse *nt*; *v* schaden

harmful ['ha:mfəl] *adj* nachteilig, schädlich

harmless ['ha:mləs] *adj* harmlos

harmony ['ha:məni] *n* Harmonie *f*

harp [ha:p] *n* Harfe *f*

harpsichord ['ha:psikɔ:d] *n* Cembalo *nt*

harsh [ha:ʃ] *adj* rau; streng; grausam

harvest ['ha:vist] *n* Ernte *f*

has [hæz] *v* (pr have)

haste [heist] *n* Hast *f*, Eile *f*

hasten ['heisən] *v* eilen

hasty ['heisti] *adj* hastig

hat [hæt] *n* Hut *m*; ~ **rack** Garderobenständer *m*

hatch [hætʃ] *n* Luke *f*

hate [heit] *v* hassen; *n* Hass *m*

hatred ['heitrid] *n* Hass *m*

haughty ['hɔ:ti] *adj* hochmütig

haul [hɔ:l] *v* schleppen

*have [hæv] *v* *haben; machen; ~ **to** *müssen

hawk [hɔ:k] *n* Habicht *m*; Falke *m*

hay [hei] *n* Heu *nt*; ~ **fever** Heuschnupfen *m*

hazard ['hæzəd] *n* Risiko *nt*

haze [heiz] *n* Dunst *m*; Nebel *m*

hazelnut ['heizəlnʌt] *n* Haselnuss *f*

hazy ['heizi] *adj* diesig

he [hi:] *pron* er

head [hed] *n* Kopf *m*; Haupt *nt*; *v* leiten; ~ **of state** Staatsoberhaupt *nt*; ~ **teacher** Schulleiter *m*, -in *f*, Schuldirektor *m*, -in *f*

headache ['hedeik] *n* Kopfschmerzen *mpl*

heading ['hediŋ] *n* Überschrift *f*

headlamp ['hedlæmp] *n* Scheinwerfer *m*

headland ['hedlənd] *n* Landzunge *f*

headlight ['hedlait] *n* Scheinwerfer *m*

headline ['hedlain] *n* Schlagzeile *f*

headmaster [,hed'ma:stə] *n* Schulleiter *m*; Direktor *m*, Schuldirektor *m*

headquarters [,hed'kwɔ:təz] *pl* Hauptquartier *nt*

head-strong ['hedstrɔŋ] *adj* starrköpfig

head waiter [,hed'weitə] *n* Oberkellner *m*

heal [hi:l] *v* heilen

health [helθ] *n* Gesundheit *f*; ~ **centre** (*Am* **center**) Beratungsstelle *f*

healthy ['helθi] *adj* gesund

heap [hi:p] *n* Stapel *m*, Haufen *m*

*hear [hiə] *v* hören

hearing ['hiəriŋ] *n* Gehör *nt*

heart [ha:t] *n* Herz *nt*; Kern *m*; **by** ~ auswendig; ~ **attack** Herzschlag *m*

heartburn ['ha:tbə:n] *n* Sodbrennen *nt*

hearth [ha:θ] *n* Herd *m*

heartless ['hɑːtləs] adj herzlos
hearty ['hɑːti] adj herzlich
heat [hiːt] n Wärme f, Hitze f; v heizen; **heating pad** Heizkissen nt
heater ['hiːtə] n Heizofen m; **immersion ~** Tauchsieder m
heath [hiːθ] n Heide f
heathen ['hiːðən] n Heide m; heidnisch
heather ['heðə] n Heidekraut nt
heating ['hiːtiŋ] n Heizung f
heaven ['hevən] n Himmel m
heavy ['hevi] adj schwer
Hebrew ['hiːbruː] n Hebräisch nt
hedge [hedʒ] n Hecke f
hedgehog ['hedʒhɔg] n Igel m
heel [hiːl] n Ferse f; Absatz m
height [hait] n Höhe f; Gipfel m, Höhepunkt m
heir [eə] n Erbe m
heiress ['eəres] n Erbin f
helicopter ['helikʌptə] n Hubschrauber m
hell [hel] n Hölle f
hello! [he'lou] hallo!; guten Tag!; **say hello to** (be)grüßen
helm [helm] n Ruder nt
helmet ['helmit] n Helm m
helmsman ['helmzmən] n Steuermann m
help [help] v *helfen; n Hilfe f
helper ['helpə] n Helfer m, -in f
helpful ['helpfəl] adj hilfreich
helping ['helpiŋ] n Portion f
hem [hem] n Saum m
hemp [hemp] n Hanf m
hen [hen] n Henne f; Huhn nt
her [həː] pron sie, ihr
herb [həːb] n Kraut nt
herd [həːd] n Herde f
here [hiə] adv hier; **~ you are** bitte
hereditary [hi'reditəri] adj erblich
hernia ['həːniə] n Bruch m
hero ['hiərou] n (pl ~es) Held m

heron ['herən] n Reiher m
herring ['heriŋ] n (pl ~, ~s) Hering m
herself [həː'self] pron sich; selbst
hesitate ['heziteit] v zögern
heterosexual [,hetərə'sekʃuəl] adj heterosexuell
hiccup ['hikʌp] n Schluckauf m
hide [haid] n Haut f
*hide [haid] v verstecken; *verbergen
hideous ['hidiəs] adj abscheulich
hierarchy ['haiərɑːki] n Hierarchie f
high [hai] adj hoch
highway ['haiwei] n Landstraße f; nAm Autobahn f
hijack ['haidʒæk] v (Flugzeug) entführen
hijacker ['haidʒækə] n (Flugzeug)Entführer m, -in f
hike [haik] v wandern
hill [hil] n Hügel m
hillock ['hilək] n Erhebung f
hillside ['hilsaid] n Hang m
hilly ['hili] adj hügelig
him [him] pron ihn, ihm
himself [him'self] pron sich; selbst
hinder ['hində] v hindern
hinge [hindʒ] n Scharnier nt
hint [hint] n Andeutung f, Wink m; v andeuten
hip [hip] n Hüfte f
hire [haiə] v mieten; **for ~** zu vermieten
his [hiz] adj sein
historian [hi'stɔːriən] n Historiker m, -in f
historic [hi'stɔrik] adj historisch
historical [hi'stɔrikəl] adj geschichtlich
history ['histəri] n Geschichte f
hit [hit] n Schlager m
*hit [hit] v *schlagen; *treffen
hitchhike ['hitʃhaik] v per Anhalter *fahren
hitchhiker ['hitʃ,haikə] n Anhalter m,

-in f

hoarse [hɔːs] *adj* rau, heiser

hobby ['hɔbi] *n* Hobby *nt*, Steckenpferd *nt*

hobbyhorse ['hɔbihɔːs] *n* Steckenpferd *nt*

hockey ['hɔki] *n* Hockey *nt*

hoist [hɔist] *v* *hochziehen

hold [hould] *n* Griff *m*; Halt *m*; Stütze *f*

***hold** [hould] *v* *festhalten; *halten; *freihalten; ~ **on** sich *festhalten; ~ **up** stützen

hold-up ['houldʌp] *n* Überfall *m*

hole [houl] *n* Grube *f*, Loch *nt*

holiday ['hɔlədi] *n* Urlaub *m*; Feiertag *m*; ~ **camp** Ferienlager *nt*; ~ **resort** Erholungsort *m*; **on** ~ auf Urlaub

Holland ['hɔlənd] Holland

hollow ['hɔlou] *adj* hohl

holy ['houli] *adj* heilig

homage ['hɔmidʒ] *n* Huldigung *f*

home [houm] *n* Heim *nt*; Haus *nt*; *adv* zu Hause, nach Hause; **at** ~ zu Hause

home-made [,houm'meid] *adj* selbstgemacht

homesickness ['houm,siknəs] *n* Heimweh *nt*

homework ['houm,wəːk] *n* Hausaufgaben *pl*

homosexual [,houmə'sekʃuəl] *adj* homosexuell

honest ['ɔnist] *adj* ehrlich; aufrichtig

honesty ['ɔnisti] *n* Ehrlichkeit *f*

honey ['hʌni] *n* Honig *m*

honeymoon ['hʌnimuːn] *n* Hochzeitsreise *f*, Flitterwochen *fpl*

honk [hʌŋk] *vAm* hupen

honour ['ɔnə] *n* Ehre *f*; *v* ehren, huldigen

honourable ['ɔnərəbəl] *adj* ehrenwert; rechtschaffen

hood [hud] *n* Kapuze *f*; *nAm* Motorhaube *f*

hoof [huːf] *n* Huf *m*

hook [huk] *n* Haken *m*

hoot [huːt] *v* hupen; johlen

hooter ['huːtə] *n* Hupe *f*

hoover ['huːvə] *v* staubsaugen

hop[1] [hɔp] *v* hüpfen; *n* Hüpfer *m*

hop[2] [hɔp] *n* Hopfen *m*

hope [houp] *n* Hoffnung *f*; *v* hoffen

hopeful ['houpfəl] *adj* hoffnungsvoll

hopeless ['houpləs] *adj* hoffnungslos

horizon [hə'raizən] *n* Horizont *m*

horizontal [,hɔri'zɔntəl] *adj* waagerecht

horn [hɔːn] *n* Horn *nt*; Horn *f*; Hupe *f*

horrible ['hɔribəl] *adj* entsetzlich; schrecklich, grauenhaft, scheußlich

horror ['hɔrə] *n* Schauder *m*, Entsetzen *nt*

hors d'œuvre [ɔː'dəːvr] *n* Horsd'œuvre *nt*, Vorspeise *f*

horse [hɔːs] *n* Pferd *nt*

horseman ['hɔːsmən] *n* (pl -men) Reiter *m*, -in *f*

horsepower ['hɔːs,pauə] *n* Pferdestärke *f*

horserace ['hɔːsreis] *n* Pferderennen *nt*

horseradish ['hɔːs,rædiʃ] *n* Meerrettich *m*

horseshoe ['hɔːsʃuː] *n* Hufeisen *nt*horticulture** ['hɔːtikʌltʃə] *n* Gartenbau *m*

hospitable ['hɔspitəbəl] *adj* gastfreundlich

hospital ['hɔspitəl] *n* Klinik *f*, Krankenhaus *nt*

hospitality [,hɔspi'tæləti] *n* Gastfreundschaft *f*

host [houst] *n* Gastgeber *m*

hostage ['hɔstidʒ] *n* Geisel *f*

hostel ['hɔstəl] *n* Herberge *f*

hostess ['houstis] *n* Gastgeberin *f*

hostile ['hɔstail] *adj* feindlich

hot [hɔt] *adj* warm, heiß

hotel [hou'tel] n Hotel nt
hot-tempered [,hɔt'tempəd] adj jähzornig
hour [auə] n Stunde f
hourly ['auəli] adj stündlich
house [haus] n Haus nt; Wohnung f; Gebäude nt; ~ **block** Am Häuserblock m; **public** ~ Wirtshaus nt
houseboat ['hausbout] n Wohnboot nt
household ['haushould] n Haushalt m
housekeeper ['haus,ki:pə] n Haushälter m, -in f
housekeeping ['haus,ki:piŋ] n Hausarbeit f, Haushalt m
housemaid ['hausmeid] n Hausangestellte f
housewife ['hauswaif] n Hausfrau f
housework ['hauswə:k] n Hausarbeiten fpl
how [hau] adv wie; ~ **many** wie viel; ~ **much** wie viel
however [hau'evə] conj dennoch, jedoch
hug [hʌg] v umarmen; liebkosen; n Umarmung f
huge [hju:dʒ] adj gewaltig, ungeheuer, riesig
hum [hʌm] v summen
human ['hju:mən] adj menschlich; ~ **being** Mensch m
humanity [hju'mænəti] n Menschheit f
humble ['hʌmbəl] adj bescheiden
humid ['hju:mid] adj feucht

humidity [hju'midəti] n Feuchtigkeit f
humorous ['hju:mərəs] adj spaßig, witzig, humorvoll
humo(u)r ['hju:mə] n Humor m
hundred ['hʌndrəd] n hundert
Hungarian [hʌŋ'gɛəriən] adj ungarisch; n Ungar m, -in f
Hungary ['hʌŋgəri] Ungarn
hunger ['hʌŋgə] n Hunger m
hungry ['hʌŋgri] adj hungrig
hunt [hʌnt] v jagen; n Jagd f; ~ **for** suchen
hunter ['hʌntə] n Jäger m, -in f
hurricane ['hʌrikən] n Wirbelsturm m
hurry ['hʌri] v sich beeilen, eilen; n Eile f; **in a** ~ eilig
***hurt** [hə:t] v weh*tun, verletzen; kränken
hurtful ['hə:tfəl] adj schädlich
husband ['hʌzbənd] n Gatte m, Mann m
hut [hʌt] n Hütte f
hydrogen ['haidrədʒən] n Wasserstoff m
hygiene ['haidʒi:n] n Hygiene f
hygienic [hai'dʒi:nik] adj hygienisch
hymn [him] n Hymne f
hyphen ['haifən] n Bindestrich m
hypocrisy [hi'pɔkrəsi] n Heuchelei f
hypocrite ['hipəkrit] n Heuchler m, -in f
hypocritical [,hipə'kritikəl] adj heuchlerisch, scheinheilig
hysterical [hi'sterikəl] adj hysterisch

I

I [ai] pron ich
ice [ais] n Eis nt; ~ **bag** Eisbeutel m; ~ **cream** Eis nt
ice-cube ['aiskju:b] n Eiswürfel m

Iceland ['aislənd] Island
Icelandic [ais'lændik] *adj* isländisch
icon ['aikən] *n* Ikone *f*
idea [ai'diə] *n* Idee *f*; Einfall *m*, Gedanke *m*; Vorstellung *f*, Anschauung *f*
ideal [ai'diəl] *adj* ideal; *n* Ideal *nt*
identical [ai'dentikəl] *adj* identisch
identification [ai,dentifi'keiʃən] *n* Identifizierung *f*
identify [ai'dentifai] *v* identifizieren
identity [ai'dentəti] *n* Identität *f*; ~ **card** Ausweis *m*
idiomatic [,idiə'mætik] *adj* idiomatisch
idiot ['idiət] *n* Idiot *m*, -in *f*
idiotic [,idi'ɔtik] *adj* verrückt
idle ['aidəl] *adj* müßig; faul; nutzlos
idol ['aidəl] *n* Idol *nt*
if [if] *conj* wenn; falls
ignition [ig'niʃən] *n* Zündung *f*; ~ **coil** Zündung *f*
ignorant ['ignərənt] *adj* unwissend
ignore [ig'nɔː] *v* ignorieren
ill [il] *adj* krank; schlecht; böse
illegal [i'liːgəl] *adj* illegal, ungesetzlich
illegible [i'ledʒəbəl] *adj* unleserlich
illiterate [i'litərət] *n* Analphabet *m*, -in *f*
illness ['ilnəs] *n* Krankheit *f*
illuminate [i'luːmineit] *v* erleuchten
illumination [i,luːmi'neiʃən] *n* Beleuchtung *f*
illusion [i'luːʒən] *n* Illusion *f*; Täuschung *f*
illustrate ['iləstreit] *v* illustrieren
illustration [,ilə'streiʃən] *n* Illustration *f*
image ['imidʒ] *n* Bild *nt*
imaginary [i'mædʒinəri] *adj* imaginär
imagination [i,mædʒi'neiʃən] *n* Einbildung *f*
imagine [i'mædʒin] *v* sich vorstellen;

sich einbilden; sich *denken
imitate ['imiteit] *v* nachmachen, nachahmen
imitation [,imi'teiʃən] *n* Nachahmung *f*, Imitation *f*
immediate [i'miːdjət] *adj* unmittelbar
immediately [i'miːdjətli] *adv* unverzüglich, sogleich, sofort
immense [i'mens] *adj* unendlich, ungeheuer, unermesslich
immigrant ['imigrənt] *n* Einwanderer *m*, -in *f*
immigrate ['imigreit] *v* einwandern
immigration [,imi'greiʃən] *n* Einwanderung *f*
immodest [i'mɔdist] *adj* unbescheiden
immunity [i'mjuːnəti] *n* Immunität *f*
immunize ['imjunaiz] *v* immunisieren
impartial [im'paːʃəl] *adj* unparteiisch
impatient [im'peiʃənt] *adj* ungeduldig
impede [im'piːd] *v* hindern
impediment [im'pedimənt] *n* Hindernis *nt*
imperfect [im'pəːfikt] *adj* unvollkommen
imperial [im'piəriəl] *adj* kaiserlich; Reichs-
impersonal [im'pəːsənəl] *adj* unpersönlich
impertinence [im'pəːtinəns] *n* Unverschämtheit *f*
impertinent [im'pəːtinənt] *adj* frech, unverschämt
implement[1] ['implimənt] *n* Werkzeug *nt*, Gerät *nt*
implement[2] ['impliment] *v* ausführen
imply [im'plai] *v* *beinhalten; zur Folge *haben; andeuten
impolite [,impə'lait] *adj* unhöflich
import[1] [im'pɔːt] *v* einführen, importieren

import² ['impɔːt] n Importware f, Einfuhr f, Import m; **~ duty** Einfuhrzoll m

importance [im'pɔːtəns] n Bedeutung f, Wichtigkeit f

important [im'pɔːtənt] adj bedeutend, wichtig

importer [im'pɔːtə] n Importeur m, -in f

imposing [im'pouziŋ] adj imposant

impossible [im'pɔsəbəl] adj unmöglich

impotence ['impətəns] n Impotenz f

impotent ['impətənt] adj impotent

impress [im'pres] v imponieren, beeindrucken

impression [im'preʃən] n Eindruck m

impressive [im'presiv] adj eindrucksvoll

imprison [im'prizən] v inhaftieren

imprisonment [im'prizənmənt] n Haft f

improbable [im'prɔbəbəl] adj unwahrscheinlich

improper [im'prɔpə] adj unpassend

improve [im'pruːv] v verbessern

improvement [im'pruːvmənt] n Verbesserung f

improvise ['imprəvaiz] v improvisieren

impudent ['impjudənt] adj unverschämt

impulse ['impʌls] n Impuls m; Anregung f

impulsive [im'pʌlsiv] adj impulsiv

in [in] prep in; adv hinein

inaccessible [i,næk'sesəbəl] adj unzugänglich

inaccurate [i'nækjurət] adj ungenau

inadequate [i'nædikwət] adj unzulänglich

incapable [iŋ'keipəbəl] adj unfähig

incense ['insens] n Weihrauch m

inch ['intʃ] n Zoll m (2,54 cm)

incident ['insidənt] n Zwischenfall m

incidental [,insi'dentəl] adj zufällig

incite [in'sait] v anregen

inclination [,iŋkli'neiʃən] n Neigung f

incline [iŋ'klain] n Neigung f

inclined [iŋ'klaind] adj gewillt, geneigt; ***be ~ to** v neigen

include [iŋ'kluːd] v *enthalten, *einschließen

inclusive [iŋ'kluːsiv] adj einschließlich

income ['iŋkəm] n Einkommen nt; **~ tax** Einkommenssteuer f

incompetent [iŋ'kɔmpətənt] adj unfähig

incomplete [,inkəm'pliːt] adj unvollständig

inconceivable [,iŋkən'siːvəbəl] adj unfassbar

inconspicuous [,iŋkən'spikjuəs] adj unauffällig

inconvenience [,iŋkən'viːnjəns] n Unbequemlichkeit f, Unannehmlichkeit f

inconvenient [,iŋkən'viːnjənt] adj ungelegen; lästig

incorrect [,iŋkə'rekt] adj ungenau, unrichtig

increase¹ [iŋ'kriːs] v vergrößern; *anwachsen, *zunehmen

increase² ['iŋkriːs] n Zunahme f; Erhöhung f

incredible [iŋ'kredəbəl] adj unglaublich

incurable [iŋ'kjuərəbəl] adj unheilbar

indecent [in'diːsənt] adj unanständig

indeed [in'diːd] adv wirklich

indefinite [in'definit] adj unbestimmt

indemnity [in'demnəti] n Entschädigung f, Schadenersatz m

independence [,indi'pendəns] n Unabhängigkeit f

independent [ˌindiˈpendənt] adj
unabhängig; selbständig

index [ˈindeks] n Verzeichnis nt, Index
m; ~ **finger** Zeigefinger m

India [ˈindiə] Indien

Indian [ˈindiən] adj indisch;
indianisch; n Inder m, -in f; Indianer
m, -in f

indicate [ˈindikeit] v *angeben,
zeigen

indication [ˌindiˈkeiʃən] n Merkmal
nt, Anzeichen nt

indicator [ˈindikeitə] n Blinker m

indifferent [inˈdifərənt] adj
gleichgültig

indigestion [ˌindiˈdʒestʃən] n
Magenverstimmung f

indignation [ˌindigˈneiʃən] n
Entrüstung f

indirect [ˌindiˈrekt] adj indirekt

individual [ˌindiˈvidʒuəl] adj einzeln,
individuell; n Einzelne m/f,
Individuum nt

Indonesia [ˌindəˈniːziə] Indonesien

Indonesian [ˌindəˈniːziən] adj
indonesisch; n Indonesier m, -in f

indoor [ˈindɔː] adj im Haus

indoors [ˌinˈdɔːz] adv im Haus

indulge [inˈdʌldʒ] v *nachgeben

industrial [inˈdʌstriəl] adj industriell;
~ **area** Industriegebiet nt

industrious [inˈdʌstriəs] adj fleißig

industry [ˈindəstri] n Industrie f

inedible [iˈnedibəl] adj ungenießbar

inefficient [ˌiniˈfiʃənt] adj
unzweckmäßig

inevitable [iˈnevitəbəl] adj
unvermeidlich

inexpensive [ˌinikˈspensiv] adj billig

inexperienced [ˌinikˈspiəriənst] adj
unerfahren

infant [ˈinfənt] n Säugling m

infantry [ˈinfəntri] n Infanterie f

infect [inˈfekt] v anstecken

infection [inˈfekʃən] n Infektion f

infectious [inˈfekʃəs] adj ansteckend

infer [inˈfəː] v ableiten

inferior [inˈfiəriə] adj geringer,
minderwertig; unter

infinite [ˈinfinət] adj unendlich

infinitive [inˈfinitiv] n Infinitiv m

inflammable [inˈflæməbəl] adj
entzündbar

inflammation [ˌinfləˈmeiʃən] n
Entzündung f

inflatable [inˈfleitəbəl] adj aufblasbar

inflate [inˈfleit] v aufblähen

inflation [inˈfleiʃən] n Inflation f

inflict [inˈflikt] v zufügen; aufbürden

influence [ˈinfluəns] n Einfluss m;
beeinflussen

influential [ˌinfluˈenʃəl] adj
einflussreich

influenza [ˌinfluˈenzə] n Grippe f

inform [inˈfɔːm] v informieren;
berichten, mitteilen

informal [inˈfɔːməl] adj informell

information [ˌinfəˈmeiʃən] n
Auskunft f; Nachricht f, Mitteilung f

infra-red [ˌinfrəˈred] adj infrarot

ingredient [inˈgriːdiənt] n Zutat f,
Bestandteil m

inhabit [inˈhæbit] v bewohnen

inhabitable [inˈhæbitəbəl] adj
bewohnbar

inhabitant [inˈhæbitənt] n Einwohner
m, -in f; Bewohner m, -in f

inhale [inˈheil] v einatmen

inherit [inˈherit] v erben

inheritance [inˈheritəns] n Erbschaft
f

inhibit [inˈhibit] v hemmen,
verhindern

initial [iˈniʃəl] adj Anfangs-, erste; n
Anfangsbuchstabe m; v abzeichnen

initiate [iˈniʃieit] v in die Wege leiten;
einführen

initiative [iˈniʃətiv] n Initiative f

inject [in'dʒekt] v einspritzen

injection [in'dʒekʃən] n Injektion f

injure ['indʒə] v verletzen; kränken

injury ['indʒəri] n Verletzung f;
Verwundung f

injustice [in'dʒʌstis] n Unrecht nt

ink [iŋk] n Tinte f

inlet ['inlet] n Bucht f

inn [in] n Gasthof m

inner ['inə] adj inwendig; **~ tube**
Schlauch m

innocence ['inəsəns] n Unschuld f

innocent ['inəsənt] adj unschuldig

inoculate [i'nɔkjuleit] v impfen

inoculation [i,nɔkju'leiʃən] n
Impfung f

inquire [iŋ'kwaiə] v nachfragen, sich
erkundigen

inquiry [iŋ'kwaiəri] n Frage f,
Nachfrage f; Untersuchung f; **~ office**
Auskunftsbüro nt

inquisitive [iŋ'kwizətiv] adj
neugierig

insane [in'sein] adj wahnsinnig

inscription [in'skripʃən] n Inschrift f

insect ['insekt] n Insekt nt; **~
repellent** Insektenschutzmittel nt

insecticide [in'sektisaid] n
Insektengift nt

insensitive [in'sensətiv] adj
unempfindlich

insert [in'sə:t] v einfügen

inside [,in'said] n Innenseite f; adj
inner; adv drinnen; im Innern; prep
in, innerhalb; **~ out** verkehrt; **insides**
Eingeweide pl

insight ['insait] n Einsicht f

insignificant [,insig'nifikənt] adj
unbedeutend; unerheblich, nichts
sagend; belanglos

insist [in'sist] v *bestehen

insolence ['insələns] n
Unverschämtheit f

insolent ['insələnt] adj frech,

unverschämt

insomnia [in'sɔmniə] n
Schlaflosigkeit f

inspect [in'spekt] v inspizieren

inspection [in'spekʃən] n Inspektion
f; Kontrolle f

inspector [in'spektə] n Inspektor m,
-in f

inspire [in'spaiə] v begeistern;
anregen

instal(l) [in'stɔ:l] v installieren

installation [,instə'leiʃən] n
Einrichtung f

instal(l)ment [in'stɔ:lmənt] n
Ratenzahlung f

instance ['instəns] n Beispiel nt; Fall
m; **for ~** zum Beispiel

instant ['instənt] n Augenblick m

instantly ['instəntli] adv
unverzüglich, augenblicklich, sofort

instead of [in'sted ɔv] anstatt

instinct ['instiŋkt] n Instinkt m

institute ['institju:t] n Institut nt;
Anstalt f; v einrichten

institution [,insti'tju:ʃən] n
Einrichtung f, Institution f

instruct [in'strʌkt] v *unterweisen

instruction [in'strʌkʃən] n
Unterweisung f; Unterricht m;
Schulung f; Anweisung f

instructive [in'strʌktiv] adj lehrreich

instructor [in'strʌktə] n Lehrer m, -in
f

instrument ['instrumənt] n
Instrument nt; **musical ~**
Musikinstrument nt

insufficient ['insə'fiʃənt] adj
ungenügend

insulate ['insjuleit] v isolieren

insulation [,insju'leiʃən] n Isolierung
f

insult¹ [in'sʌlt] v beleidigen

insult² ['insʌlt] n Beleidigung f

insurance [in'ʃuərəns] n

Versicherung *f*; **~ policy**
Versicherungspolice *f*

insure [in'ʃuə] *v* versichern

intact [in'tækt] *adj* unversehrt

integrate ['intəgreit] *v* integrieren, eingliedern

intellect ['intəlekt] *n* Intellekt *m*, Verstand *m*

intellectual [,intə'lektʃuəl] *adj* intellektuell

intelligence [in'telidʒəns] *n* Intelligenz *f*

intelligent [in'telidʒənt] *adj* intelligent

intend [in'tend] *v* beabsichtigen

intense [in'tens] *adj* intensiv; heftig

intensify [in'tensifai] *v* (sich) verstärken, steigern, intensivieren

intention [in'tenʃən] *n* Absicht *f*

intentional [in'tenʃənəl] *adj* absichtlich

intercourse ['intəkɔːs] *n* Umgang *m*; Geschlechtsverkehr *m*

interest ['intrəst] *n* Interesse *nt*; Nutzen *m*; Zins *m*; *v* interessieren

interested ['intristid] *adj* interessiert

interesting ['intrəstiŋ] *adj* interessant

interfere [,intə'fiə] *v* *einschreiten; **~ with** sich einmischen

interference [,intə'fiərəns] *n* Eingreifen *nt*

interim ['intərim] *n* Zwischenzeit *f*

interior [in'tiəriə] *n* Innere *nt*

interlude ['intəluːd] *n* Zwischenspiel *nt*

intermediary [,intə'miːdjəri] *n* Vermittler *m*, -in *f*

intermission [,intə'miʃən] *n* Pause *f*

internal [in'təːnəl] *adj* inner, intern

international [,intə'næʃənəl] *adj* international

Internet ['intənet] *n* Internet *nt*

interpret [in'təːprit] *v* dolmetschen; darstellen

interpreter [in'təːpritə] *n* Dolmetscher *m*, -in *f*

interrogate [in'terəgeit] *v* verhören

interrogation [in,terə'geiʃən] *n* Verhör *nt*

interrogative [,intə'rɔgətiv] *adj* fragend

interrupt [,intə'rʌpt] *v* *unterbrechen

interruption [,intə'rʌpʃən] *n* Unterbrechung *f*

intersection [,intə'sekʃən] *n* Kreuzung *f*

interval ['intəvəl] *n* Pause *f*

intervene [,intə'viːn] *v* eingreifen, einschreiten

interview ['intəvjuː] *n* Unterredung *f*, Interview *nt*

intestine [in'testin] *n* Darm *m*; **intestines** Eingeweide *pl*

intimate ['intimət] *adj* intim

into ['intu] *prep* in

intolerable [in'tɔlərəbəl] *adj* unerträglich

intoxicated [in'tɔksikeitid] *adj* berauscht, betrunken

intrigue [in'triːg] *n* Komplott *nt*; *v* faszinieren, neugierig machen

introduce [,intrə'djuːs] *v* vorstellen; einführen

introduction [,intrə'dʌkʃən] *n* Vorstellung *f*; Einführung *f*

invade [in'veid] *v* *eindringen

invalid¹ ['invəlid] *n* Invalide *m/f*; *adj* invalide

invalid² [in'vælid] *adj* ungültig

invasion [in'veiʒən] *n* Einfall *m*, Invasion *f*

invent [in'vent] *v* *erfinden; *ersinnen

invention [in'venʃən] *n* Erfindung *f*

inventive [in'ventiv] *adj* erfinderisch

inventor [in'ventə] *n* Erfinder *m*, -in *f*

inventory ['invəntri] *n* Inventar *nt*

invert [in'vəːt] *v* umdrehen

invest [in'vest] v investieren; anlegen

investigate [in'vestigeit] v untersuchen

investigation [in,vesti'geiʃən] n Untersuchung f

investment [in'vestmənt] n Investition f, Anlage f, Geldanlage f

invisible [in'vizəbəl] adj unsichtbar

invitation [,invi'teiʃən] n Einladung f

invite [in'vait] v auffordern, *einladen

invoice ['invɔis] n Rechnung f

involve [in'vɔlv] v *verwickeln, *hineinziehen; *angehen; erfordern; **involved** beteiligt

inwards ['inwədz] adv nach innen

iodine ['aiədi:n] n Jod nt

Iran [i'rɑ:n] Iran

Iranian [i'reiniən] adj iranisch; n Iraner m, -in f

Iraq [i'rɑ:k] Irak

Iraqi [i'rɑ:ki] adj irakisch

Ireland ['aiələnd] Irland

Irish ['aiəriʃ] adj irisch

iron ['aiən] n Eisen nt; Bügeleisen nt; eisern; v bügeln

ironical [ai'rɔnikəl] adj ironisch

irony ['aiərəni] n Ironie f

irregular [i'regjulə] adj unregelmäßig

irreparable [i'repərəbəl] adj

irreparabel

irrevocable [i'revəkəbəl] adj unwiderruflich

irritable ['iritəbəl] adj reizbar

irritate ['iriteit] v reizen, irritieren

is [iz] v (pr be)

island ['ailənd] n Insel f

isolate ['aisəleit] v isolieren

isolation [,aisə'leiʃən] n Isolation f; Isolierung f

Israel ['izreil] Israel

Israeli [iz'reili] adj israelisch; n Israeli m/f

issue ['iʃu:] v *ausgeben; n Ausgabe f, Auflage f, Frage f, Punkt m; Ergebnis nt, Resultat nt, Folge f, Abschluss m, Ende nt; Ausweg m

it [it] pron es

Italian [i'tæljən] adj italienisch; n Italiener m, -in f

Italy ['itəli] Italien

itch [itʃ] n Jucken nt; v jucken

item ['aitəm] n Posten m; Punkt m

itinerary [ai'tinərəri] n Reiseplan m

its [its] sein(e), ihr(e), dessen, deren

itself [it'self] sich, sich selbst, selbst; **by ~** von allein, von selbst

ivory ['aivəri] n Elfenbein nt

ivy ['aivi] n Efeu m

J

jack [dʒæk] n Wagenheber m

jacket ['dʒækit] n Jacke f, Jackett nt; Umschlag m

jade [dʒeid] n Jade m

jail [dʒeil] n Gefängnis nt

jam [dʒæm] n Marmelade f; Verkehrsstauung f

janitor ['dʒænitə] n Hausmeister m, -in f

January ['dʒænjuəri] Januar

Japan [dʒə'pæn] Japan

Japanese [,dʒæpə'ni:z] adj japanisch; n Japaner m, -in f

jar [dʒɑ:] n Krug m

jaundice ['dʒɔ:ndis] n Gelbsucht f

jaw [dʒɔ:] n Kiefer m

jealous ['dʒeləs] adj eifersüchtig

jealousy ['dʒeləsi] n Eifersucht f

jeans [dʒiːnz] *pl* Bluejeans *pl*
jelly ['dʒeli] *n* Gelee *nt*
jellyfish ['dʒelifɪʃ] *n* Qualle *f*
jersey ['dʒɜːzi] *n* Jersey *m*;
  Wollpullover *m*; Trikot *nt*
jet [dʒet] *n* Strahl *m*; Düsenflugzeug
  nt
jetty ['dʒeti] *n* Pier *m*
Jew [dʒuː] *n* Jude *m*, Jüdin *f*
jewel ['dʒuːəl] *n* Juwel *nt*
jeweller ['dʒuːələ] *n* Juwelier *m*
jewellery, *Am* **jewelry** ['dʒuːəlri] *n*
  Schmuck *m*
Jewish ['dʒuːiʃ] *adj* jüdisch
job [dʒɔb] *n* Arbeit *f*; Stellung *f*,
  Beschäftigung *f*
jobless ['dʒɔbles] *adj* arbeitslos
jockey ['dʒɔki] *n* Jockei *m*
join [dʒɔin] *v* *verbinden; sich
  beteiligen an, sich *anschließen;
  zusammenfügen, vereinigen
joint [dʒɔint] *n* Gelenk *nt*; Lötstelle *f*;
  adj verbunden, gemeinschaftlich
jointly ['dʒɔintli] *adv* gemeinsam
joke [dʒouk] *n* Witz *m*
jolly ['dʒɔli] *adj* fröhlich
Jordan ['dʒɔːdən] Jordanien
Jordanian [dʒɔːˈdeiniən] *adj*
  jordanisch; *n* Jordanier *m*, -in *f*
journal ['dʒɜːnəl] *n* Zeitschrift *f*
journalism ['dʒɜːnəlizəm] *n*
  Journalismus *m*
journalist ['dʒɜːnəlist] *n* Journalist

m, -in *f*
journey ['dʒɜːni] *n* Reise *f*
joy [dʒɔi] *n* Wonne *f*, Freude *f*
joyful ['dʒɔifəl] *adj* froh, freudig
jubilee ['dʒuːbiliː] *n* Jubiläum *nt*
judge [dʒʌdʒ] *n* Richter *m*, -in *f*; *v*
  urteilen; beurteilen
judgment ['dʒʌdʒmənt] *n* Urteil *nt*
jug [dʒʌg] *n* Krug *m*
juggle ['dʒʌgəl] *v* jonglieren
juggler ['dʒʌglə] *n* Jongleur *m*, -in *f*
juice [dʒuːs] *n* Saft *m*
juicy ['dʒuːsi] *adj* saftig
July [dʒuˈlai] Juli
jump [dʒʌmp] *v* *springen; *n* Sprung
  m
jumper [dʒʌmpə] *n* Pullover *m*; *Am*
  Trägerkleid *nt*
junction ['dʒʌŋkʃən] *n*
  Straßenkreuzung *f*; Knotenpunkt *m*
June [dʒuːn] Juni
jungle ['dʒʌŋgəl] *n* Urwald *m*,
  Dschungel *m*
junior ['dʒuːnjə] *adj* jünger
junk [dʒʌŋk] *n* Plunder *m*; Müll *m*
jury ['dʒuəri] *n* Preisgericht *nt*
just [dʒʌst] *adj* berechtigt, gerecht;
  richtig; *adv* gerade; genau
justice ['dʒʌstis] *n* Recht *nt*;
  Gerechtigkeit *f*
justify ['dʒʌstifai] *v* rechtfertigen
juvenile ['dʒuːvənail] *adj* jugendlich

K

kangaroo [ˌkæŋgəˈruː] *n* Känguru *nt*
keel [kiːl] *n* Kiel *m*
keen [kiːn] *adj* begeistert; scharf
***keep** [kiːp] *v* *halten; bewahren;
  *bleiben; **~ away from** sich

*fernhalten von; **~ off** nicht anrühren;
  ~ on *fortfahren mit; **~ quiet**
  *schweigen; **~ up** ausharren; **~ up**
  with Schritt *halten mit
kennel ['kenəl] *n* Hundehütte *f*

Kenya ['kenjə] Kenia
kerosene ['kerəsi:n] n Kerosin nt
kettle ['ketəl] n Kessel m
key [ki:] n Schlüssel m
keyhole ['ki:houl] n Schlüsselloch nt
keyboard ['ki:bɔ:d] n Tastatur f
khaki ['kɑ:ki] n Khaki nt
kick [kik] v *stoßen, *treten; n Tritt m, Fußtritt m
kickoff [,ki'kɔf] n Anstoß m
kid [kid] n Kind nt; Ziegenleder nt; v foppen
kidney ['kidni] n Niere f
kill [kil] v *umbringen, töten
kilogram ['kiləgræm] n Kilo nt
kilometre ['kilə,mi:tə] n, Am kilometer Kilometer m
kind [kaind] adj nett, freundlich; gütig; n Sorte f
kindergarten ['kində,gɑ:tən] n Kindergarten m
king [kiŋ] n König m
kingdom ['kiŋdəm] n Königreich nt; Reich nt
kiosk ['ki:ɔsk] n Kiosk m
kiss [kis] n Kuss m; v küssen
kit [kit] n Ausrüstung f
kitchen ['kitʃin] n Küche f; ~ towel Geschirrtuch nt
knapsack ['næpsæk] n Rucksack m
knave [neiv] n Bube m
knee [ni:] n Knie nt
kneecap ['ni:kæp] n Kniescheibe f
*kneel [ni:l] v knien
knew [nju:] v (p know)
knife [naif] n (pl knives) Messer nt
knight [nait] n Ritter m
*knit [nit] v stricken
knob [nɔb] n Knauf m
knock [nɔk] v klopfen; n Klopfen nt; ~ against *zusammenstoßen mit; ~ down *niederschlagen
knot [nɔt] n Knoten m; v knoten
*know [nou] v *wissen, *kennen
knowledge ['nɔlidʒ] n Kenntnis f
knuckle ['nʌkəl] n Fingergelenk nt

L

label ['leibəl] n Etikett nt; v beschriften
laboratory [lə'bɔrətəri] n Laboratorium nt
labo(u)r ['leibə] n Arbeit f; Wehen fpl; v sich abmühen; labor permit Am Arbeitsbewilligung f
labourer ['leibərə] n Arbeiter m, -in f
labour-saving ['leibə,seiviŋ] adj arbeitssparend
labyrinth ['læbərinθ] n Labyrinth nt
lace [leis] n Spitze f; Schnürsenkel m
lack [læk] n Mangel m; v mangeln
lacquer ['lækə] n Lack m
lad [læd] n Junge m, Bursche m
ladder ['lædə] n Leiter f
lady ['leidi] n Dame f; ladies' room Damentoilette f
lagoon [lə'gu:n] n Lagune f
lake [leik] n See m
lamb [læm] n Lamm nt; Lammfleisch nt
lame [leim] adj gelähmt, lahm
lamentable ['læməntəbəl] adj jämmerlich
lamp [læmp] n Lampe f
lampshade ['læmpʃeid] n Lampenschirm m
land [lænd] n Land nt; v landen; an Land *gehen

landlady ['lænd,leidi] n Wirtin f

landlord ['lændlɔ:d] n Hausbesitzer m; Wirt m

landmark ['lændmɑ:k] n Meilenstein m; Wahrzeichen n

landscape ['lændskeip] n Landschaft f

lane [lein] n Gasse f, Pfad m; Fahrbahn f

language ['læŋgwidʒ] n Sprache f; ~ **laboratory** Sprachlabor nt

lantern ['læntən] n Laterne f

lap ['læp] n Schoß m; Runde f; v lecken, schlecken

larder ['lɑ:də] n Speisekammer f

large [lɑ:dʒ] adj groß; geräumig; **largely** größtenteils, weitgehend

lark [lɑ:k] n Lerche f

laryngitis [,lærin'dʒaitis] n Halsentzündung f

last [lɑ:st] adj letzt; vorhergehend; v dauern; **at ~** endlich; schließlich; zuletzt

lasting ['lɑ:stiŋ] adj bleibend, dauerhaft

latchkey ['lætʃki:] n Hausschlüssel m

late [leit] adj spät; verspätet

lately ['leitli] adv in letzter Zeit, kürzlich

lather ['lɑ:ðə] n Schaum m

Latin America ['lætin ə'merikə] Lateinamerika

Latin-American [,lætinə'merikən] adj lateinamerikanisch; n Lateinamerikaner m, -in f

latitude ['lætitju:d] n Breitengrad m

laugh [lɑ:f] v lachen; n Lachen nt

laughter ['lɑ:ftə] n Gelächter nt

launch [lɔ:ntʃ] v in Gang *bringen; *abschießen; n Barkasse f

launching ['lɔ:ntʃiŋ] n Stapellauf m

launderette [,lɔ:ndə'ret] n Münzwäscherei f

laundry ['lɔ:ndri] n Wäscherei f;

Wäsche f

lavatory ['lævətəri] n Toilette f

lavish ['læviʃ] adj verschwenderisch

law [lɔ:] n Gesetz nt; Recht nt; ~ **court** Gerichtshof m

lawful ['lɔ:fəl] adj gesetzlich

lawn [lɔ:n] n Rasen m

lawsuit ['lɔ:su:t] n Prozess m, Gerichtsverfahren nt

lawyer ['lɔ:jə] n Rechtsanwalt m, Rechtsanwältin f; Jurist m, -in f

laxative ['læksətiv] n Abführmittel n

*****lay** [lei] v stellen, setzen, legen; ~ **bricks** mauern

layer [leiə] n Schicht f

layman ['leimən] n Laie m

lazy ['leizi] adj faul

lead¹ [li:d] n Vorsprung m; Leitung f; Leine f

lead² [led] n Blei nt

*****lead** [li:d] v führen

leader ['li:də] n Anführer m, -in f, Leiter m, -in f

leadership ['li:dəʃip] n Führung f

leading ['li:diŋ] adj Haupt-, führend

leaf [li:f] n (pl leaves) Blatt nt

league [li:g] n Bund m

leak [li:k] v lecken; n Leck nt

leaky ['li:ki] adj leck

lean [li:n] adj mager

*****lean** [li:n] v lehnen

leap [li:p] n Sprung m

*****leap** [li:p] v *springen

leap year ['li:pjiə] n Schaltjahr nt

*****learn** [lə:n] v lernen

learner ['lə:nə] n Anfänger m, -in f

lease [li:s] n Mietvertrag m; Pacht f; v verpachten, vermieten; mieten

leash [li:ʃ] n Leine f

least [li:st] adj geringst, mindest; kleinst; **at ~** wenigstens; zumindest

leather ['leðə] n Leder nt; Leder-, ledern

leave [li:v] n Urlaub m

*leave [li:v] v *weggehen, *verlassen; *lassen; **~ behind** *zurücklassen; **~ out** *auslassen

Lebanese [,lebə'ni:z] adj libanesisch; n Libanese m, Libanesin f

Lebanon ['lebənən] Libanon

lecture ['lektʃə] n Vorlesung f, Vortrag m

left¹ [left] adj linke

left² [left] v (p, pp leave)

left-hand ['lefthænd] adj linke

left-handed [,left'hændid] adj linkshändig

leg [leg] n Bein nt

legacy ['legəsi] n Erbschaft f

legal ['li:gəl] adj gesetzmäßig, gesetzlich; rechtlich

legible ['ledʒibəl] adj leserlich

legitimate [li'dʒitimət] adj rechtmäßig

leisure ['leʒə] n Muße f; adj Freizeit-

lemon ['lemən] n Zitrone f

lemonade [,lemə'neid] n Limonade f

*lend [lend] v *leihen

length [leŋθ] n Länge f

lengthen ['leŋθən] v verlängern

lengthways ['leŋθweiz] adv der Länge nach

lens [lenz] n Linse f; Objektiv nt

leprosy ['leprəsi] n Lepra f

less [les] adv weniger

lessen ['lesən] v vermindern

lesson ['lesən] n Lektion f; Schulstunde f

level ['levəl] adj gleich; platt, flach, eben; n Stand m, Niveau nt; Wasserwaage f; **~ crossing** Bahnübergang m

letter ['letə] n Brief m; Buchstabe m; **~ opener** Am Brieföffner m

letterbox ['letəbɔks] n Briefkasten m

lettuce ['letis] n Salat m

lever ['li:və] n Hebel m

Levis ['li:vaiz] pl Bluejeans pl

liability [,laiə'biləti] n Verantwortlichkeit f

liable ['laiəbəl] adj verantwortlich; **~ to** unterworfen

liar ['laiə] n Lügner m, -in f

liberal ['libərəl] adj liberal; großzügig, freigebig

liberation [,libə'reiʃən] n Befreiung f

Liberia [lai'biəriə] Liberia

Liberian [lai'biəriən] adj liberisch; n Liberier m, -in f

liberty ['libəti] n Freiheit f

library ['laibrəri] n Bibliothek f

licence ['laisəns] n Lizenz f; Konzession f; **driving ~** Führerschein m; **~ number** (Auto)Kennzeichen nt

license ['laisəns] v konzessionieren; nAm Lizenz f, Konzession f; **~ plate** Am Nummernschild nt

lick [lik] v lecken

lid [lid] n Deckel m; (Augen)Lid nt

lie [lai] v *lügen; n Lüge f

*lie [lai] v *liegen; **~ down** sich niederlegen

life [laif] n (pl lives) Leben nt; **~ insurance** Lebensversicherung f; **~ jacket** Schwimmweste f

lifebelt ['laifbelt] n Rettungsgürtel m

lifetime ['laiftaim] n Leben nt

lift [lift] v *aufheben, *heben; n Aufzug m

light [lait] n Licht nt; adj leicht; hell; **~ bulb** Birne f

*light [lait] v anzünden

lighter ['laitə] n Anzünder m; Feuerzeug nt

lighthouse ['laithaus] n Leuchtturm m

lighting ['laitiŋ] n Beleuchtung f

lightning ['laitniŋ] n Blitz m

like [laik] v gern *mögen; gern *haben, *mögen; adj gleich; conj wie

likely ['laikli] adj wahrscheinlich

like-minded [,laik'maindid] adj gleichgesinnt

likewise ['laikwaiz] adv ebenso, ebenfalls

lily ['lili] n Lilie f

limb [lim] n Glied nt

lime [laim] n Kalk m; Linde f; Limone f

limetree ['laimtri:] n Linde m

limit ['limit] n Grenze f; v beschränken

limp [limp] v hinken; adj schlaff

line [lain] n Zeile f; Strich m; Schnur f; Linie f; Reihe f; **stand in ~** Am Schlange *stehen

linen ['linin] n Leinen nt; Wäsche f

lingerie ['lɔ-ʒəri:] n Damenunterwäsche f

lining ['lainiŋ] n Futter nt

link [liŋk] v *verbinden; n Verbindung f; Glied nt

lion ['laiən] n Löwe m

lip [lip] n Lippe f

lipstick ['lipstik] n Lippenstift m

liqueur [li'kjuə] n Likör m

liquid ['likwid] adj flüssig; n Flüssigkeit f

liquor ['likə] n Spirituosen pl; **~ store** Am Spirituosenladen

liquorice ['likəris] n Lakritze f

list [list] n Liste f; v *eintragen

listen ['lisən] v anhören, zuhören

listener ['lisnə] n Zuhörer m, -in f

literary ['litrəri] adj literarisch

literature ['litrətʃə] n Literatur f

litre ['li:tə] n Liter m

litter ['litə] n Abfall m; Schutt m; Wurf m

little ['litəl] adj klein; wenig

live[1] [liv] v leben; wohnen

live[2] [laiv] adj lebend; live

livelihood ['laivlihud] n Unterhalt m

lively ['laivli] adj lebhaft

liver ['livə] n Leber f

living ['liviŋ] n Leben nt; Lebensunterhalt m; adj lebend(ig); **~ room** Wohnzimmer nt

lizard ['lizəd] n Eidechse f

load [loud] n Last f; v *laden

loaf [louf] n (pl loaves) Laib m

loan [loun] n Anleihe f

lobby ['lɔbi] n Foyer nt

lobster ['lɔbstə] n Hummer m

local ['loukəl] adj lokal, örtlich; **~ call** Ortsgespräch nt; **~ train** Nahverkehrszug m

locate [lou'keit] v ausfindig machen

location [lou'keiʃən] n Lage f

lock [lɔk] v *verschließen; n Schloss nt; Schleuse f; **~ up** einsperren

locker ['lɔkə] n Spind m, Schließfach n

locomotive [,loukə'moutiv] n Lokomotive f

lodge [lɔdʒ] v beherbergen

lodger ['lɔdʒə] n Untermieter m, -in f

lodgings ['lɔdʒiŋz] pl Unterkunft f

log [lɔg] n Klotz m; **~ in** v einloggen; **~ off** v ausloggen

logic ['lɔdʒik] n Logik f

logical ['lɔdʒikəl] adj logisch

lonely ['lounli] adj einsam

long [lɔŋ] adj lang; langwierig; **~ for** v sich sehnen nach; **no longer** nicht mehr

longing ['lɔŋiŋ] n Sehnsucht f

longitude ['lɔndʒitju:d] n Längengrad m

look [luk] v gucken, schauen; *scheinen, *aussehen; n Blick m; Aussehen nt, Anblick m; **~ after** versorgen, aufpassen auf, sich kümmern um; **~ at** anschauen, *ansehen; **~ for** suchen; **~ out** *Acht geben, sich *vorsehen

looking-glass ['lukiŋglɑ:s] n Spiegel m

loop [lu:p] *n* Schlinge *f*

loose [lu:s] *adj* lose

loosen ['lu:sən] *v* lockern

loser ['lu:sə] *n* Verlierer *m*, -in *f*; Versager *m*, -in *f*

lord [lɔ:d] *n* Lord *m*

lorry ['lɔri] *n* Lastwagen *m*

*****lose** [lu:z] *v* einbüßen, *verlieren

loss [lɔs] *n* Verlust *m*

lost [lɔst] *adj* verirrt; weg; **~ and found** Fundsachen *fpl*; **~ property office** Fundbüro *nt*

lot [lɔt] *n* Los *nt*; Haufen *m*, Menge *f*

aftershave lotion Rasierwasser *nt*

lottery ['lɔtəri] *n* Lotterie *f*

loud [laud] *adj* laut

loudspeaker [,laud'spi:kə] *n* Lautsprecher *m*

louse [laus] *n* (pl lice) Laus *f*

love [lʌv] *v* gern *haben, lieben; *n* Liebe *f*; **in ~** verliebt

lovely ['lʌvli] *adj* herrlich, wunderbar, hübsch

lover ['lʌvə] *n* Liebhaber *m*, -in *f*

love story ['lʌv,stɔ:ri] *n* Liebesgeschichte *f*

low [lou] *adj* niedrig, tief; niedergeschlagen; **~ tide** Ebbe *f*

lower ['louə] *v* *herunterlassen; herabsetzen; *streichen; *adj* unter, niedrig

lowlands ['loulədz] *pl* Tiefland *nt*

loyal ['lɔiəl] *adj* loyal

lubricate ['lu:brikeit] *v* ölen, schmieren

lubrication [,lu:bri'keiʃən] *n* Schmierung *f*; **~ oil** Schmieröl *nt*; **~ system** Schmiersystem *nt*

luck [lʌk] *n* Glück *nt*; Zufall *m*; **bad ~** Pech *nt*; **good ~!** viel Glück!

lucky ['lʌki] *adj* glücklich; **~ charm** Amulett *nt*

ludicrous ['lu:dikrəs] *adj* lächerlich, lachhaft

luggage ['lʌgidʒ] *n* Gepäck *nt*; **hand ~** Handgepäck *nt*; **left ~ office** Gepäckaufbewahrung *f*; **~ rack** Gepäcknetz *nt*; **~ van** Gepäckwagen *m*

lukewarm ['lu:kwɔ:m] *adj* lauwarm

lumbago [lʌm'beigou] *n* Hexenschuss *m*

luminous ['lu:minəs] *adj* leuchtend

lump [lʌmp] *n* Brocken *m*, Klumpen *m*, Stück *nt*; Beule *f*; **~ of sugar** Stück Zucker; **~ sum** Pauschalsumme *f*

lumpy ['lʌmpi] *adj* klumpig

lunacy ['lu:nəsi] *n* Irrsinn *m*

lunatic ['lu:nətik] *adj* irrsinnig; *n* Irre *m/f*

lunch [lʌntʃ] *n* Imbiss *m*, Mittagessen *nt*

luncheon ['lʌntʃən] *n* Mittagessen *nt*

lung [lʌŋ] *n* Lunge *f*

luxurious [lʌg'ʒuəriəs] *adj* luxuriös

luxury ['lʌkʃəri] *n* Luxus *m*

M

machine [mə'ʃi:n] *n* Apparat *m*, Maschine *f*

machinery [mə'ʃi:nəri] *n* Mechanismus *m*

mackerel ['mækrəl] *n* (pl ~) Makrele *f*

mackintosh ['mækintɔʃ] *n* Regenmantel *m*

mad [mæd] *adj* irre, toll, verrückt; wütend

madam ['mædəm] *n* gnädige Frau

madness ['mædnəs] n Wahnsinn m

magazine [,mægə'zi:n] n Zeitschrift f

magic ['mædʒik] n Zauberei f, Magie f; adj Zauber-

magician [mə'dʒiʃən] n Zauberer m

magistrate ['mædʒistreit] n Richter m, -in f

magnetic [mæg'netik] adj magnetisch

magneto [mæg'ni:tou] n (pl ~s) Magnet m

magnificent [mæg'nifisənt] adj prächtig; großartig, glänzend

magnify ['mægnifai] v vergrößern; übertreiben

magpie ['mægpai] n Elster f

maiden name ['meidən neim] Mädchenname m

mail [meil] n Post f; v *aufgeben; ~ order Am Postanweisung f

mailbox ['meilbɔks] nAm Briefkasten m

main [mein] adj Haupt-, wichtigste; größt; ~ deck Oberdeck nt; ~ line Hauptstrecke f; ~ road Hauptstraße f; ~ street Hauptstraße f

mainland ['meinlənd] n Festland nt

mainly ['meinli] adv hauptsächlich

mains [meinz] pl Hauptleitung f

maintain [mein'tein] v *aufrechterhalten

maintenance ['meintənəns] n Instandhaltung f

maize [meiz] n Mais m

major ['meidʒə] adj groß; Haupt-; größer; n Major m

majority [mə'dʒɔrəti] n Mehrheit f

*make [meik] v machen; verdienen; *schaffen; ~ do with sich *behelfen mit; ~ good vergüten; ~ up zusammenstellen

make-up ['meikʌp] n Schminke f

malaria [mə'lɛəriə] n Malaria f

Malaysia [mə'leiziə] Malaysia

Malaysian [mə'leiziən] adj malaiisch

male [meil] adj männlich

malicious [mə'liʃəs] adj boshaft

malignant [mə'lignənt] adj bösartig

mall [mɔːl] nAm Einkaufszentrum

malnutrition [,mælnju'triʃən] n Unterernährung f

mammal ['mæməl] n Säugetier nt

mammoth ['mæməθ] n Mammut nt

man [mæn] n (pl men) Mann m; Mensch m; **men's room** Herrentoilette f

manage ['mænidʒ] v verwalten; bewerkstelligen, zustande bringen

manageable ['mænidʒəbəl] adj handlich

management ['mænidʒmənt] n Verwaltung f; Führung f

manager ['mænidʒə] n Chef m, -in f, Direktor m, -in f

mandarin ['mændərin] n Mandarine f

mandate ['mændeit] n Mandat f

manger ['meindʒə] n Krippe f

manicure ['mænikjuə] n Maniküre f; v maniküren

manipulate [mə'nipjulait] v manipulieren, beeinflussen; handhaben

mankind [mæn'kaind] n Menschheit f

mannequin ['mænəkin] n Mannequin nt

manner ['mænə] n Art f, Weise f; **manners** pl Manieren fpl

manor ['mænə] n (Land)Gut nt

mansion ['mænʃən] n Herrschaftshaus nt

manual ['mænjuəl] adj Hand-

manufacturer [,mænju'fæktʃərə] n Hersteller m, -in f; Fabrikant m, -in f

manure [mə'njuə] n Dünger m

manuscript ['mænjuskript] n Manuskript nt

many ['meni] adj viel(e)

map [mæp] n Karte f; Landkarte f;

Plan m

maple ['meipəl] n Ahorn m

marble ['ma:bəl] n Marmor m; Murmel f

March [ma:tʃ] März

march [ma:tʃ] v marschieren; n Marsch m

mare [mɛə] n Stute f

margarine [,ma:dʒə'ri:n] n Margarine f

margin ['ma:dʒin] n Rand m

maritime ['mæritaim] adj maritim

mark [ma:k] v ankreuzen; bezeichnen, zeichnen; kennzeichnen; n Zeichen nt; Zensur f; Zielscheibe f

market ['ma:kit] n Markt m

marketplace ['ma:kitpleis] n Marktplatz m

marmalade ['ma:məleid] n Marmelade f

marriage ['mæridʒ] n Ehe f

marrow ['mærou] n Mark nt

marry ['mæri] v heiraten; **married** verheiratet; **married couple** Ehepaar nt

marsh [ma:ʃ] n Sumpf m

martyr ['ma:tə] n Märtyrer m, -in f

marvel ['ma:vəl] n Wunder nt; v sichwundern, staunen

marvellous ['ma:vələs] adj wunderbar

mascara [mæ'ska:rə] n Wimperntusche f

masculine ['mæskjulin] adj männlich

mash [mæʃ] v zerstampfen; **mashed potatoes** npl Kartoffelbrei

mask [ma:sk] n Maske f

Mass [mæs] n Messe f

mass [mæs] n Menge f; ~ **production** Massenproduktion f

massage ['mæsa:ʒ] n Massage f; v massieren

masseur [mæ'sə:] n Masseur m

massive ['mæsiv] adj massiv

mast [ma:st] n Mast m

master ['ma:stə] n Meister m; Studienrat m, Lehrer m; v beherrschen

masterpiece ['ma:stəpi:s] n Meisterstück nt

mat [mæt] n Matte f; adj matt, glanzlos

match [mætʃ] n Streichholz nt; Spiel nt; v passen zu, übereinstimmen

matchbox ['mætʃbɔks] n Streichholzschachtel f

material [mə'tiəriəl] n Material nt; adj stofflich, materiell

mathematical [,mæθə'mætikəl] adj mathematisch

mathematics [,mæθə'mætiks] n Mathematik f

matrimony ['mætriməni] n Ehe f

matter ['mætə] n Stoff m, Materie f; Sache f, Frage f; v von Bedeutung *sein; **as a ~ of fact** tatsächlich

matter-of-fact [,mætərəv'fækt] adj nüchtern

mattress ['mætrəs] n Matratze f

mature [mə'tjuə] adj reif

maturity [mə'tjuərəti] n Reife f

mausoleum [,mɔ:sə'li:əm] n Mausoleum nt

May [mei] Mai

*may [mei] v *mögen; *dürfen

maybe ['meibi:] adv vielleicht

mayor [mɛə] n Bürgermeister m, -in f

me [mi:] pron mich; mir

meadow ['medou] n Wiese f

meal [mi:l] n Mahl nt, Mahlzeit f

mean [mi:n] adj niederträchtig; n Durchschnitt m

*mean [mi:n] v bedeuten; meinen

meaning ['mi:niŋ] n Bedeutung f

meaningless ['mi:niŋləs] adj sinnlos

means [mi:nz] n Mittel nt; **by no ~** keineswegs, keinesfalls

meantime: in the ~ [in ðə 'mi:ntaim]

mittlerweile, inzwischen

meanwhile ['mi:nwail] *adv* inzwischen, mittlerweile

measles ['mi:zəlz] *n* Masern *pl*

measure ['meʒə] *v* *messen; *n* Maß *nt*; Maßnahme *f*

meat [mi:t] *n* Fleisch *nt*

mechanic [mi'kænik] *n* Monteur *m*, -in *f*, Mechaniker *m*, -in *f*

mechanical [mi'kænikəl] *adj* mechanisch

mechanism ['mekənizəm] *n* Mechanismus *m*

medal ['medəl] *n* Medaille *f*

media ['mi:diə] *pl* Medien *npl*

mediaeval [,medi'i:vəl] *adj* mittelalterlich

mediate ['mi:dieit] *v* vermitteln

mediator ['mi:dieitə] *n* Vermittler *m*, -in *f*

medical ['medikəl] *adj* ärztlich, medizinisch

medicine ['medsin] *n* Medizin *f*

meditate ['mediteit] *v* meditieren

Mediterranean [,meditə'reiniən] Mittelmeer *nt*

medium ['mi:diəm] *adj* mittelmäßig, durchschnittlich, mittler...; *n* Medium *nt*; Mitte *f*

***meet** [mi:t] *v* *treffen; begegnen

meeting ['mi:tiŋ] *n* Versammlung *f*, Treffen *nt*; **~ place** Treffpunkt *m*

melancholy ['melənkəli] *n* Schwermut *f*

mellow ['melou] *adj* mild

melody ['melədi] *n* Melodie *f*

melon ['melən] *n* Melone *f*

melt [melt] *v* *schmelzen

member ['membə] *n* Mitglied *nt*; **Member of Parliament** Abgeordnete *m/f*

membership ['membəʃip] *n* Mitgliedschaft *f*

memorable ['memərəbəl] *adj* denkwürdig

memorial [mə'mɔ:riəl] *n* Denkmal *nt*

memorize ['meməraiz] *v* auswendig lernen

memory ['meməri] *n* Gedächtnis *nt*; Erinnerung *f*; Andenken *nt*

mend [mend] *v* flicken, ausbessern

menstruation [,menstru'eiʃən] *n* Menstruation *f*

mental ['mentəl] *adj* geistig

mention ['menʃən] *v* *nennen, erwähnen; *n* Meldung *f*, Erwähnung *f*

menu ['menju:] *n* Speisekarte *f*

merchandise ['mə:tʃəndaiz] *n* Handelsware *f*, Ware *f*

merchant ['mə:tʃənt] *n* Händler *m*, -in *f*, Kaufmann *m*, Kauffrau *f*

mercury ['mə:kjuri] *n* Quecksilber *nt*

mere [miə] *adj* bloß

merely ['miəli] *adv* nur

merge [mə:dʒ] *v* verschmelzen; fusionieren

merger ['mə:dʒə] *n* Fusion *f*

merit ['merit] *v* verdienen; *n* Verdienst *nt*

merry ['meri] *adj* fröhlich

merry-go-round ['merigou,raund] *n* Karussell *nt*

mesh [meʃ] *n* Masche *f*

mess [mes] *n* Durcheinander *nt*, Unordnung *f*; **~ up** in Unordnung *bringen

message ['mesidʒ] *n* Nachricht *f*, Bescheid *m*

messenger ['mesindʒə] *n* Bote *m*, Botin *f*

metal ['metəl] *n* Metall *nt*; metallisch

meter ['mi:tə] *n* Zähler *m*

method ['meθəd] *n* Methode *f*; Ordnung *f*

methodical [mə'θɔdikəl] *adj* methodisch

metre ['mi:tə] *n* Meter *nt*

metric ['metrik] *adj* metrisch

Mexican ['meksikən] *adj* mexikanisch; *n* Mexikaner *m*, -in *f*

Mexico ['meksikou] Mexiko

mice (pl mouse)

microphone ['maikrəfoun] *n* Mikrofon *nt*

microwave oven ['maikrouweiv 'ʌvən] *n* Mikrowellenherd *m*

midday ['middei] *n* Mittag *m*

middle ['midəl] *n* Mitte *f*; *adj* mittler; **Middle Ages** Mittelalter *nt*; ~ **class** Mittelstand *m*; **middle-class** *adj* bürgerlich

midnight ['midnait] *n* Mitternacht *f*

midsummer ['mid,sʌmə] *n* Hochsommer *m*

midwife ['midwaif] *n* (pl -wives) Hebamme *f*

might [mait] *n* Macht *f*

***might** [mait] *v* *können

mighty ['maiti] *adj* mächtig

migraine ['migrein] *n* Migräne *f*

mild [maild] *adj* mild

mildew ['mildju] *n* Schimmel *m*

mile [mail] *n* Meile *f*

mileage ['maildʒ] *n* Meilenstand *m*

milestone ['mailstoun] *n* Meilenstein *m*

milieu ['mi:ljə:] *n* Milieu *nt*

military ['militəri] *adj* militärisch

milk [milk] *n* Milch *f*

milkshake ['milkʃeik] *n* Milkshake *m*

milky ['milki] *adj* milchig

mill [mil] *n* Mühle *f*; Fabrik *f*

miller ['milə] *n* Müller *m*, -in *f*

million ['miljən] *n* Million *f*

millionaire [,miljə'nεə] *n* Millionär *m*, -in *f*

mince [mins] *v* zerhacken

mind [maind] *n* Geist *m*; *v* etwas einzuwenden *haben gegen; *Acht geben auf, kümmern, achten auf

mine [main] *n* Bergwerk *nt*

miner ['mainə] *n* Bergmann *m*

mineral ['minərəl] *n* Mineral *nt*; ~ **water** Mineralwasser *nt*

mingle ['mingl] *v* (sich) vermischen; *v* sich einmischen

miniature ['minjətʃə] *n* Miniatur *f*

minimum ['miniməm] *n* Minimum *nt*

mining ['mainiŋ] *n* Bergbau *m*

minister ['ministə] *n* Minister *m*, -in *f*; Geistliche *m/f*; **Prime Minister** Ministerpräsident *m*, -in *f*

ministry ['ministri] *n* Ministerium *nt*

mink [miŋk] *n* Nerz *m*

minor ['mainə] *adj* klein, gering, kleiner; untergeordnet; *n* Minderjährige *m/f*

minority [mai'nɔrəti] *n* Minderheit *f*

mint [mint] *n* Minze *f*

minus ['mainəs] *prep* weniger

minute¹ ['minit] *n* Minute *f*; **minutes** Protokoll *nt*

minute² [mai'nju:t] *adj* winzig

miracle ['mirəkəl] *n* Wunder *nt*

miraculous [mi'rækjuləs] *adj* wunderbar

mirror ['mirə] *n* Spiegel *m*

misbehave [,misbi'heiv] *v* sich schlecht *benehmen

miscarriage [mis'kæridʒ] *n* Fehlgeburt *f*

miscellaneous [,misə'leiniəs] *adj* vermischt

mischief ['mistʃif] *n* Unfug *m*; Unheil *nt*, Schaden *m*

mischievous ['mistʃivəs] *adj* boshaft; schelmisch

miserable ['mizərəbəl] *adj* erbärmlich, elend

misery ['mizəri] *n* Jammer *m*, Elend *nt*; Not *f*

misfortune [mis'fɔ:tʃen] *n* Unglück *nt*, Missgeschick *nt*

mishap ['mishæp] *n* Panne *f*, Unglück *n*

***mislay** [mis'lei] *v* verlegen

misplaced [mis'pleist] *adj* unangebracht

mispronounce [,misprə'nauns] *v* falsch *aussprechen

miss¹ [mis] Fräulein *nt*

miss² [mis] *v* verpassen

missing ['misiŋ] *adj* fehlend; ~ **person** Vermisste *m/f*

mist [mist] *n* Nebel *m*

mistake [mi'steik] *n* Versehen *nt*, Irrtum *m*, Fehler *m*

*****mistake** [mi'steik] *v* verwechseln

mistaken [mi'steikən] *adj* falsch; *be ~ sich täuschen, sich irren

mister ['mistə] Herr *m*

mistress ['mistrəs] *n* Herrin *f*; Lehrerin *f*

mistrust [mis'trʌst] *v* misstrauen

misty ['misti] *adj* nebelig

*****misunderstand** [,misʌndə'stænd] *v* *missverstehen

misunderstanding [,misʌndə'stændiŋ] *n* Missverständnis *nt*

misuse [mis'ju:s] *n* Missbrauch *m*

mittens ['mitənz] *pl* Fausthandschuhe *mpl*

mix [miks] *v* mischen; ~ **with** verkehren mit

mixed [mikst] *adj* meliert, gemischt

mixer ['miksə] *n* Mixer *m*

mixture ['mikstʃə] *n* Mischung *f*

moan [moun] *v* stöhnen

mobile ['moubail] *adj* mobil, beweglich; ~ **phone** Handy *nt*

mock [mɔk] *v* verspotten

mockery ['mɔkəri] *n* Spott *m*

model ['mɔdəl] *n* Modell *nt*; Mannequin *nt*; *v* formen, modellieren

modem ['moudem] *n* Modem *nt*

moderate ['mɔdərət] *adj* gemäßigt, mäßig; mittelmäßig

modern ['mɔdən] *adj* modern

modest ['mɔdist] *adj* bescheiden

modesty ['mɔdisti] *n* Bescheidenheit *f*

modify ['mɔdifai] *v* modifizieren

mohair ['mouheə] *n* Mohair *m*

moist [mɔist] *adj* nass, feucht

moisten ['mɔisən] *v* anfeuchten

moisture ['mɔistʃə] *n* Feuchtigkeit *f*; **moisturizing cream** Feuchtigkeitskrem *f*

molar ['moulə] *n* Backenzahn *m*

moment ['moumənt] *n* Moment *m*, Augenblick *m*

monarch ['mɔnək] *n* Monarch *m*, -in *f*

monarchy ['mɔnəki] *n* Monarchie *f*

monastery ['mɔnəstri] *n* Kloster *nt*

Monday ['mʌndi] Montag *m*

monetary unit ['mʌnitəri ,junit] Währungseinheit *f*

money ['mʌni] *n* Geld *nt*; ~ **exchange** Wechselstube *f*; ~ **order** Anweisung *f*

monk [mʌŋk] *n* Mönch *m*

monkey ['mʌŋki] *n* Affe *m*

monologue ['mɔnɔlɔg] *n* Monolog *m*

monopoly [mə'nɔpəli] *n* Monopol *m*

monotonous [mə'nɔtənəs] *adj* monoton

month [mʌnθ] *n* Monat *m*

monthly ['mʌnθli] *adj* monatlich

monument ['mɔnjumənt] *n* Monument *nt*, Denkmal *nt*

mood [mu:d] *n* Laune *f*, Stimmung *f*

moon [mu:n] *n* Mond *m*

moonlight ['mu:nlait] *n* Mondlicht *nt*

moor [muə] *n* Heide *f*, Moor *nt*

moose [mu:s] *n* (pl ~, ~s) Elch *m*

moped ['mouped] *n* Moped *nt*

moral ['mɔrəl] *n* Moral *f*; *adj* sittlich, moralisch; **morals** Sitten

morality [mə'ræləti] *n* Moral *f*

more [mɔ:] *adj* mehr; **once ~** noch einmal

moreover [mɔ:'rouvə] *adv* ferner, außerdem

morning ['mɔːniŋ] n Morgen m; ~ **paper** Morgenzeitung f; **this ~** heute Morgen

Moroccan [məˈrɔkən] adj marokkanisch; n Marokkaner m, -in f

Morocco [məˈrɔkou] Marokko

morphia ['mɔːfiə] n Morphium nt

morphine ['mɔːfiːn] n Morphium nt

morsel ['mɔːsəl] n Stück nt

mortal ['mɔːtəl] adj tödlich, sterblich

mortgage ['mɔːgidʒ] n Hypothek f

mosaic [məˈzeiik] n Mosaik nt

mosque [mɔsk] n Moschee f

mosquito [məˈskiːtou] n (pl ~es) Mücke f; Moskito m; ~ **net** Moskitonetz nt

moss [mɔs] n Moos nt

most [moust] adj meist; **at ~** allenfalls, höchstens; ~ **of all** besonders

mostly ['moustli] adv meistens

motel [mou'tel] n Motel nt

moth [mɔθ] n Motte f

mother ['mʌðə] n Mutter f; ~ **tongue** Muttersprache f

mother-in-law ['mʌðərinlɔː] n (pl mothers-) Schwiegermutter f

mother of pearl [,mʌðərəv'pəːl] n Perlmutt nt

motion ['mouʃən] n Bewegung f; Antrag m

motivate ['moutiveit] v motivieren, anspornen

motive ['moutiv] n Motiv nt

motor ['moutə] n Motor m; v im Auto *fahren; ~ **body** Am Karosserie f; **starter** ~ Anlasser m

motorbike ['moutəbaik] nAm Moped nt

motorboat ['moutəbout] n Motorboot nt

motorcycle ['moutə,saikəl] n Motorrad nt

motorist ['moutərist] n Autofahrer m, -in f

motorway ['moutəwei] n Autobahn f

motto ['mɔtou] n (pl ~es, ~s) Devise f

mouldy ['mouldi] adj schimmelig

mound [maund] n Erhebung f

mount [maunt] v *besteigen; n Berg m

mountain ['mauntin] n Berg m; ~ **pass** Gebirgspass m; ~ **range** Bergkette f

mountaineering [,maunti'niəriŋ] n Bergsteigen nt

mountainous ['mauntinəs] adj gebirgig

mourning ['mɔːniŋ] n Trauer f

mouse [maus] n (pl mice) Maus f

moustache [məˈstɑːʃ] n Schnurrbart m

mouth [mauθ] n Mund m; Maul nt; Mündung f

mouthwash ['mauθwɔʃ] n Mundwasser nt

movable ['muːvəbəl] adj beweglich

move [muːv] v bewegen; versetzen; *umziehen; rühren; n Zug m, Schritt m; Umzug m

movement ['muːvmənt] n Bewegung f

movie ['muːvi] n Film m; **movies** Am Kino nt; ~ **theater** Am Kino nt

much [mʌtʃ] adj viel; **as ~** ebenso viel; ebenso sehr

muck [mʌk] n Dreck m

mud [mʌd] n Schlamm m

muddle ['mʌdəl] n Wirrwarr m, Durcheinander m, Durcheinander nt; v *durcheinander bringen

muddy ['mʌdi] adj schlammig

muffler ['mʌflə] nAm Auspufftopf m

mug [mʌg] n Becher m

mule [mjuːl] n Maultier nt, Maulesel m

multiplication [,mʌltipli'keiʃən] n Multiplikation f

multiply ['mʌltiplai] v multiplizieren

mumps [mʌmps] *n* Mumps *m*

municipal [mju:'nisipəl] *adj* städtisch

municipality [mju:,nisi'pæləti] *n* Stadtverwaltung *f*

murder ['mə:də] *n* Mord *m*; *v* morden

murderer ['mə:dərə] *n* Mörder *m*, -in *f*

muscle ['mʌsəl] *n* Muskel *m*

muscular ['mʌskjulə] *adj* muskulös

museum [mju:'zi:əm] *n* Museum *nt*

mushroom ['mʌʃru:m] *n* Champignon *m*; Pilz *m*

music ['mju:zik] *n* Musik *f*; ~ **academy** Konservatorium *f*

musical ['mju:zikəl] *adj* musikalisch; *n* Musical *nt*

music hall ['mju:zikhɔ:l] *n* Varietétheater *nt*

musician [mju:'ziʃən] *n* Musiker *m*, -in *f*

mussel ['mʌsəl] *n* Muschel *f*

*must [mʌst] *v* *müssen

mustard ['mʌstəd] *n* Senf *m*

mute [mju:t] *adj* stumm

mutiny ['mju:tini] *n* Meuterei *f*

mutton ['mʌtən] *n* Hammelfleisch *nt*

mutual ['mju:tʃuəl] *adj* wechselseitig, gegenseitig

my [mai] *adj* mein

myself [mai'self] *pron* mich; selbst

mysterious [mi'stiəriəs] *adj* rätselhaft, geheimnisvoll

mystery ['mistəri] *n* Rätsel *nt*, Geheimnis *nt*

myth [miθ] *n* Mythos *m*

N

nail [neil] *n* Nagel *m*; ~ **file** Nagelfeile *f*; **polish** Nagellack *m*; ~ **scissors** Nagelschere *f*

nailbrush ['neilbrʌʃ] *n* Nagelbürste *f*

naïve [nɑ:'i:v] *adj* naiv

naked ['neikid] *adj* bloß, nackt; kahl

name [neim] *n* Name *m*; *v* *nennen; **in the ~ of** im Namen von

namely ['neimli] *adv* nämlich

napkin ['næpkin] *n* Serviette *f*

nappy ['næpi] *n* Windel *f*

narcosis [nɑ:'kousis] *n* (pl -ses) Narkose *f*

narcotic [nɑ:'kɔtik] *n* Rauschgift *nt*

narrow ['nærou] *adj* eng, schmal

narrow-minded [,nærou'maindid] *adj* engstirnig

nasty ['nɑ:sti] *adj* unangenehm, widrig; garstig

nation ['neiʃən] *n* Nation *f*; Volk *nt*

national ['næʃənəl] *adj* national; Volks-; Staats-; ~ **anthem** Nationalhymne *f*; ~ **dress** Tracht *f*; ~ **park** Naturschutzpark *m*

nationality [,næʃə'næləti] *n* Staatsangehörigkeit *f*

native ['neitiv] *n* Eingeborene *m/f*; *adj* einheimisch; ~ **country** Vaterland *nt*, Heimatland *nt*; ~ **language** Muttersprache *f*

natural ['nætʃərəl] *adj* natürlich; angeboren

naturally ['nætʃərəli] *adv* natürlich, selbstverständlich

nature ['neitʃə] *n* Natur *f*; Wesensart *f*

naughty ['nɔ:ti] *adj* ungezogen, unartig

nausea ['nɔ:siə] *n* Übelkeit *f*

naval ['neivəl] *adj* Marine-

navel ['neivəl] *n* Nabel *m*

navigable ['nævigəbəl] *adj* befahrbar

navigate ['nævigeit] *v* steuern

navigation [,nævi'geiʃən] *n* Navigation *f*; Schifffahrt *f*

navy ['neivi] *n* Marine *f*

near [niə] *prep* bei; *adj* nahe

nearby ['niəbai] *adj* nahe

nearly ['niəli] *adv* fast, beinahe

neat [ni:t] *adj* nett, sorgfältig

necessary ['nesəsəri] *adj* nötig, notwendig

necessity [nə'sesəti] *n* Notwendigkeit *f*

neck [nek] *n* Hals *m*; **nape of the ~** Nacken *m*

necklace [,nækli'g. ['nekləs] *n* Halskette *f*

necktie ['nektai] *n* Krawatte *f*

need [ni:d] *v* brauchen, nötig *haben; n* Not *f*, Bedürfnis *nt*; Notwendigkeit *f*; **~ to** *müssen

needle ['ni:dəl] *n* Nadel *f*

needlework ['ni:dəlwə:k] *n* Handarbeit *f*

negative ['negətiv] *adj* verneinend, negativ; *n* Negativ *nt*

neglect [ni'glekt] *v* vernachlässigen; *n* Vernachlässigung *f*

neglectful [ni'glektfəl] *adj* nachlässig

negotiate [ni'gouʃieit] *v* verhandeln

negotiation [ni,gouʃi'eiʃən] *n* Verhandlung *f*

neighbo(u)r ['neibə] *n* Nachbar *m*, -in *f*

neighbo(u)rhood ['neibəhud] *n* Nachbarschaft *f*

neighbo(u)ring ['neibəriŋ] *adj* benachbart

neither ['naiðə] *pron* keiner von beiden; **neither ... nor** weder ... noch

nephew ['nefju:] *n* Neffe *m*

nerve [nə:v] *n* Nerv *m*; Kühnheit *f*

nervous ['nə:vəs] *adj* nervös

nest [nest] *n* Nest *nt*

net [net] *n* Netz *nt*; *adj* netto

Netherlands ['neðələndz]: **the ~** Niederlande *fpl*

network ['netwə:k] *n* Netz *nt*

neuralgia [njuə'rældʒə] *n* Neuralgie *f*

neurosis [njuə'rousis] *n* Neurose *f*

neuter ['nju:tə] *adj* sächlich

neutral ['nju:trəl] *adj* neutral

never ['nevə] *adv* nie, niemals

nevertheless [,nevəðə'les] *adv* nichtsdestoweniger

new [nju:] *adj* neu; **New Year** Neujahr

news [nju:z] *n* Nachrichten, Neuigkeit *f*

newsagent ['nju:,zeidʒənt] *n* Zeitungshändler *m*

newspaper ['nju:z,peipə] *n* Zeitung *f*

newsreel ['nju:zri:l] *n* Wochenschau *f*

newsstand ['nju:zstænd] *n* Zeitungsstand *m*

New Zealand [nju: 'zi:lənd] Neuseeland

next [nekst] *adj* nächst; **~ to** neben

next-door [,nekst'dɔ:] *adv* nebenan

nice [nais] *adj* nett, hübsch; wohl schmeckend; sympathisch

nickel ['nikəl] *n* Nickel *m*

nickname ['nikneim] *n* Spitzname *m*

nicotine ['nikəti:n] *n* Nikotin *f*

niece [ni:s] *n* Nichte *f*

Nigeria [nai'dʒiəriə] Nigeria

Nigerian [nai'dʒiəriən] *adj* nigerianisch; *n* Nigerianer *m*, -in *f*

night [nait] *n* Nacht *f*; Abend *m*; **by ~** bei Nacht; **~ cream** Nachtcreme *f*; **~ flight** Nachtflug *m*; **~ rate** Nachttarif *m*; **~ train** Nachtzug *m*

nightclub ['naitklʌb] *n* Nachtlokal *nt*

nightdress ['naitdres] *n* Nachthemd *nt*

nightingale ['naitiŋgeil] *n* Nachtigall *f*

nightly ['naitli] *adj* nächtlich

nightmare ['naitmeə] n Alptraum m

nil [nil] nichts

nine [nain] num neun

nineteen [,nain'ti:n] num neunzehn

nineteenth [,nain'ti:nθ] num
neunzehnte

ninety ['nainti] num neunzig

ninth [nainθ] num neunte

nitrogen ['naitrədʒən] n Stickstoff m

no [nou] nein; adj kein; ~ one
niemand

nobility [nou'biləti] n Adel m

noble ['noubəl] adj adlig; edel

nobody ['noubɔdi] pron niemand

nod [nɔd] n Nicken nt; v nicken

noise [nɔiz] n Geräusch nt; Krach m,
Lärm m

noisy ['nɔizi] adj laut

nominal ['nɔminəl] adj nominell

nominate ['nɔmineit] v *ernennen

nomination [,nɔmi'neiʃən] n
Ernennung f

none [nʌn] pron keiner

nonsense ['nɔnsəns] n Unsinn m

non-smoker [,nɔn'smoukə] n
Nichtraucher m, -in f

noon [nu:n] n Mittag m

nor ['nɔ:] auch nicht; **neither ... nor**
weder ... noch

normal ['nɔ:məl] adj gewohnt, normal

north [nɔ:θ] n Norden m; adj nördlich;
North Pole Nordpol m

north-east [,nɔ:θ'i:st] n Nordosten m

northerly ['nɔ:ðəli] adj nördlich

northern ['nɔ:ðən] adj nördlich

north-west [,nɔ:θ'west] n
Nordwesten m

Norway ['nɔ:wei] Norwegen

Norwegian [nɔ:'wi:dʒən] adj
norwegisch; n Norweger m, -in f

nose [nouz] n Nase f

nosebleed ['nouzbli:d] n
Nasenbluten nt

nostril ['nɔstril] n Nasenloch nt

nosy ['nouzi] adj colloquial neugierig

not [nɔt] adv nicht

notary ['noutəri] n Notar m, -in f

note [nout] n Aufzeichnung f, Notiz f;
Vermerk m; Ton m; v anmerken;
*wahrnehmen, bemerken

notebook ['noutbuk] n Notizbuch nt;
Notebook nt

noted ['noutid] adj berühmt

notepaper ['nout,peipə] n
Schreibpapier nt, Briefpapier nt

nothing ['nʌθiŋ] n nichts

notice ['noutis] v feststellen, merken,
bemerken; *sehen; n Anzeige f,
Bericht m; Aufmerksamkeit f, Acht f

noticeable ['noutisəbəl] adj
wahrnehmbar; bemerkenswert

notify ['noutifai] v mitteilen;
benachrichtigen

notion ['nouʃən] n Begriff m, Ahnung
f

notorious [nou'tɔ:riəs] adj berüchtigt

nougat ['nu:gɑ:] n Nougat m

nought [nɔ:t] n Null f

noun [naun] n Hauptwort nt,
Substantiv nt

nourishing ['nʌriʃiŋ] adj nahrhaft

novel ['nɔvəl] n Roman m

novelist ['nɔvəlist] n
Romanschriftsteller m, -in f

November [nou'vembə] November

now [nau] adv jetzt; ~ **and then** hin
und wieder

nowadays ['nauədeiz] adv
heutzutage

nowhere ['nouweə] adv nirgends

nozzle ['nɔzəl] n Schnabel m

nuance [nju:'ɑ:s] n Nuance f

nuclear ['nju:kliə] adj Kern-, nuklear;
~ **energy** Kernenergie f

nucleus ['nju:kliəs] n Kern m

nude [nju:d] adj nackt; n Akt m

nuisance ['nju:səns] n Unfug m

numb [nʌm] adj starr; erstarrt

number ['nʌmbə] *n* Nummer *f*; Ziffer *f*, Zahl *f*; Anzahl *f*

numeral ['nju:mərəl] *n* Zahlwort *nt*

numerous ['nju:mərəs] *adj* zahlreich

nun [nʌn] *n* Nonne *f*

nurse [nə:s] *n* Schwester *f*, Krankenschwester *f*, Krankenpfleger *m*; Kindermädchen *nt*; *v* pflegen; stillen

nursery ['nə:səri] *n* Kinderzimmer *nt*; Kinderkrippe *f*; Baumschule *f*

nut [nʌt] *n* Nuss *f*; Schraubenmutter *f*

nutcrackers ['nʌt,krækəz] *pl* Nussknacker *m*

nutmeg ['nʌtmeg] *n* Muskatnuss *f*

nutritious [nju:'trifəs] *adj* nahrhaft

nutshell ['nʌtfel] *n* Nussschale *f*

nylon ['nailɔn] *n* Nylon *nt*

O

oak [ouk] *n* Eiche *f*

oar [ɔ:] *n* Ruder *nt*

oasis [ou'eisis] *n* (pl oases) Oase *f*

oath [ouθ] *n* Eid *m*

oats [outs] *pl* Hafer *m*

obedience [ə'bi:diəns] *n* Gehorsam *m*

obedient [ə'bi:diənt] *adj* gehorsam

obesity [ə'bi:siti] *n* Fettleibigkeit *f*

obey [ə'bei] *v* gehorchen

object[1] ['ɔbdʒikt] *n* Objekt *nt*; Gegenstand *m*; Ziel *nt*

object[2] [əb'dʒekt] *v* *einwenden; ~ to Einwand *erheben gegen

objection [əb'dʒekfən] *n* Widerspruch *m*, Einwand *m*

objective [əb'dʒektiv] *adj* objektiv; *n* Zweck *m*

obligatory [ə'bligətəri] *adj* obligatorisch

oblige [ə'blaidʒ] *v* verpflichten; *be obliged to* verpflichtet *sein zu; *müssen

obliging [ə'blaidʒiŋ] *adj* gefällig

oblong ['ɔblɔŋ] *adj* länglich; *n* Rechteck *nt*

obscene [əb'si:n] *adj* obszön

obscure [əb'skjuə] *adj* unklar, dunkel

observation [,ɔbzə'veifən] *n* Beobachtung *f*

observatory [əb'zə:vətri] *n* Observatorium *nt*

observe [əb'zə:v] *v* beobachten; beachten

obsession [əb'sefən] *n* Besessenheit *f*

obstacle ['ɔbstəkəl] *n* Hindernis *nt*

obstinate ['ɔbstinət] *adj* starrköpfig; hartnäckig

obtain [əb'tein] *v* erlangen, *erhalten

obtainable [əb'teinəbəl] *adj* erhältlich

obvious ['ɔbviəs] *adj* offensichtlich

occasion [ə'keiʒən] *n* Gelegenheit *f*; Anlass *m*

occasionally [ə'keiʒənəli] *adv* ab und zu, gelegentlich

occupant ['ɔkjupənt] *n* Bewohner *m*, -in *f*; Insasse *m*, -in *f*

occupation [,ɔkju'peifən] *n* Beschäftigung *f*; Besetzung *f*

occupy ['ɔkjupai] *v* *einnehmen, besetzen; **occupied** *adj* besetzt

occur [ə'kə:] *v* *geschehen, *vorkommen, sich ereignen

occurrence [ə'kʌrəns] *n* Vorkommen *nt*; Ereignis *nt*

ocean ['oufən] *n* Ozean *m*

October [ɔk'toubə] Oktober

octopus ['ɔktəpəs] n Polyp m

oculist ['ɔkjulist] n Augenarzt m, Augenärztin f

odd [ɔd] adj seltsam, sonderbar; ungerade

odour ['oudə] n Geruch m

of [ɔv, əv] prep von

off [ɔf] adv ab; weg; prep von

offence [ə'fens] n Vergehen nt; Beleidigung f, Verstoß m

offend [ə'fend] v kränken, beleidigen; sich *vergehen

offensive [ə'fensiv] adj beleidigend, anstößig; offensiv; n Offensive f

offer ['ɔfə] v *anbieten; leisten; n Angebot nt

office ['ɔfis] n Büro nt; Amt nt; ~ hours Bürostunden fpl

officer ['ɔfisə] n Offizier m, -in f

official [ə'fiʃəl] adj offiziell

often ['ɔfən] adv häufig, oft

oil [ɔil] n Öl nt; Petroleum nt; fuel ~ Heizöl nt; ~ filter Ölfilter nt; ~ painting Ölgemälde nt; ~ refinery Ölraffinerie f; ~ well Ölquelle f

oily ['ɔili] adj ölig

ointment ['ɔintmənt] n Salbe f

okay! [,ou'kei] in Ordnung!

old [ould] adj alt; ~ age Alter nt

old-fashioned [,ould'fæʃənd] adj altmodisch

olive ['ɔliv] n Olive f; ~ oil Olivenöl nt

omelette ['ɔmlət] n Eierkuchen m

ominous ['ɔminəs] adj unheilvoll

omit [ə'mit] v *auslassen

omnipotent [ɔm'nipətənt] adj allmächtig

on [ɔn] prep auf; an

once [wʌns] adv einst, einmal; at ~ sofort; for ~ ausnahmsweise; ~ more noch einmal

oncoming ['ɔn,kʌmiŋ] adj entgegenkommend, herannahend

one [wʌn] num eins; pron man

oneself [wʌn'self] pron selbst

onion ['ʌnjən] n Zwiebel f

only ['ounli] adj einzig; adv nur, bloß; conj jedoch

onwards ['ɔnwədz] adv vorwärts

onyx ['ɔniks] n Onyx m

opal ['oupəl] n Opal m

open ['oupən] v öffnen; adj offen; offenherzig; **opener** Öffner m

opening ['oupəniŋ] n Öffnung f

opera ['ɔpərə] n Oper f; ~ house Opernhaus n

operate ['ɔpəreit] v wirken, arbeiten; operieren

operation [,ɔpə'reiʃən] n Funktion f; Operation f

operator ['ɔpəreitə] n Bediener m, -in f; (Telefon)Vermittlung f

operetta [,ɔpə'retə] n Operette f

opinion [ə'pinjən] n Ansicht f, Meinung f

opponent [ə'pounənt] n Gegner m, -in f

opportunity [,ɔpə'tju:nəti] n Gelegenheit f

oppose [ə'pouz] v sich widersetzen

opposite ['ɔpəzit] prep gegenüber; adj gegensätzlich, entgegengesetzt

opposition [,ɔpə'ziʃən] n Opposition f

oppress [ə'pres] v bedrücken, unterdrücken

optician [ɔp'tiʃən] n Optiker m, -in f

optimism ['ɔptimizəm] n Optimismus m

optimist ['ɔptimist] n Optimist m, -in f

optimistic [,ɔpti'mistik] adj optimistisch

optional ['ɔpʃənəl] adj beliebig; wahlweise; Sonder-

or [ɔː] conj oder

oral ['ɔːrəl] adj mündlich

orange ['ɔrindʒ] n Apfelsine f; adj orange

orbit ['ɔːbit] n Umlaufbahn f

orchard ['ɔːtʃəd] n Obstgarten m

orchestra ['ɔːkistrə] n Orchester nt

order ['ɔːdə] v *befehlen; bestellen; n Reihenfolge f, Ordnung f; Auftrag m, Befehl m; Bestellung f; ~ **form** Bestellzettel m; **in** ~ in Ordnung; **in** ~ **to** um zu; **made to** ~ auf Bestellung gemacht; **out of** ~ funktionsunfähig; **postal** ~ Postanweisung f

ordinary ['ɔːdənri] adj alltäglich, gewöhnlich

ore [ɔː] n Erz nt

organ ['ɔːgən] n Organ nt; Orgel f

organic [ɔː'gænik] adj organisch

organization [,ɔːgənai'zeiʃən] n Organisation f

organize ['ɔːgənaiz] v organisieren

Orient ['ɔːriənt] n Orient m

oriental [,ɔːri'entəl] adj orientalisch

orientate ['ɔːriənteit] v sich orientieren

origin ['ɔridʒin] n Abstammung f, Ursprung m; Herkunft f

original [ə'ridʒinəl] adj ursprünglich, originell

originally [ə'ridʒinəli] adv ursprünglich

ornament ['ɔːnəmənt] n Verzierung f

ornamental [,ɔːnə'mentəl] adj dekorativ

orphan ['ɔːfən] n Waise f

orthodox ['ɔːθədɔks] adj orthodox

ostrich ['ɔstritʃ] n Strauß m

other ['ʌðə] adj ander

otherwise ['ʌðəwaiz] conj sonst; adv anders

ought [ɔːt] v sollte (-st, -t, -n)

ounce [auns] n Unze f

our [auə] pron unser(e)

ours ['auəz] pron unsere(s)

ourselves [auə'selvz] pron uns; selbst

out [aut] adv heraus, hinaus; ~ **of** außer, aus

outbreak ['autbreik] n Ausbruch m

outburst ['autbəːst] n Gefühls- etc. Ausbruch m

outcome ['autkʌm] n Ergebnis nt

***outdo** [,aut'duː] v *übertreffen

outdoors [,aut'dɔːz] adv draußen

outer [autə] adj äußer

outfit ['autfit] n Ausrüstung f

outing ['autiŋ] n Ausflug m

outline ['autlain] n Umriss m; v *umreißen

outlook ['autluk] n Aussicht f; Anschauung f

output ['autput] n Ausstoß m; Ertrag m

outrage ['autreidʒ] n Gewaltakt m

outside [,aut'said] adv draußen; prep außerhalb; n Äußere nt, Außenseite f

outsize ['autsaiz] n Übergröße f

outskirts ['autskəːts] pl Außenbezirke mpl

outstanding [,aut'stændiŋ] adj außergewöhnlich, hervorragend

outward ['autwəd] adj äußere(r, -s)

outwards ['autwədz] adv nach draußen

oval ['ouvəl] adj oval

oven ['ʌvən] n Backofen m

over ['ouvə] prep oberhalb, über; adv über; nieder; adj vorbei; ~ **there** drüben

overall ['ouvərɔːl] adj gesamt

overalls ['ouvərɔːlz] pl Arbeitsanzug m

overcast ['ouvəkaːst] adj bewölkt

overcoat ['ouvəkout] n Mantel m

***overcome** [,ouvə'kʌm] v *überwinden

overdo [,ouvə'duː] v übertreiben; zu weit gehen; zu lange garen

overdraft ['ouvədraːft] n Kontoüberziehung f

overdraw [‚ouvə'drɔ:] *v* Konto *nt*
überziehen

overdue [‚ouvə'dju:] *adj* überfällig;
rückständig

overgrown [‚ouvə'groun] *adj*
überwachsen, überwuchert

overhaul [‚ouvə'hɔ:l] *v* überholen

overhead [‚ouvə'hed] *adv* oben

overlook [‚ouvə'luk] *v* *übersehen

overnight [‚ouvə'nait] *adv* über
Nacht

overseas [‚ouvə'si:z] *adj* überseeisch

oversight ['ouvəsait] *n* Versehen *nt*

*oversleep [‚ouvə'sli:p] *v*
*verschlafen

overstrung [‚ouvə'strʌŋ] *adj*
überspannt

*overtake [‚ouvə'teik] *v* überholen;
no overtaking Überholen verboten

over-tired [‚ouvə'taiəd] *adj*

übermüdet

overture ['ouvətʃə] *n* Ouvertüre *f*

overweight ['ouvəweit] *n*
Übergewicht *nt*

overwhelm [‚ouvə'welm] *v*
überwältigen

overwork [‚ouvə'wə:k] *v* sich
überarbeiten

owe [ou] *v* schuldig *sein, schulden;
verdanken; **owing to** aufgrund,
infolge

owl [aul] *n* Eule *f*

own [oun] *v* *besitzen; *adj* eigen

owner ['ounə] *n* Besitzer *m*, -in *f*,
Eigentümer *m*, -in *f*

ox [ɔks] *n* (pl oxen) Ochse *m*

oxygen ['ɔksidʒən] *n* Sauerstoff *m*

oyster ['ɔistə] *n* Auster *f*

ozone ['ouzoun] *n* Ozon *nt*

P

pace [peis] *n* Gang *m*; Schritt *m*;
Tempo *nt*

Pacific Ocean [pə'sifik 'ouʃən] Stille
Ozean, Pazifik

pacifism ['pæsifizəm] *n* Pazifismus *m*

pacifist ['pæsifist] *n* Pazifist *m*, -in *f*,
pazifistisch

pack [pæk] *v* packen; **~ up** einpacken

package ['pækidʒ] *n* Paket *nt*

packet ['pækit] *n* Päckchen *nt*

packing ['pækiŋ] *n* Verpackung *f*

pact ['pækt] *n* Pakt *m*, Vertrag *m*

pad [pæd] *n* Polster *nt*; Schreibblock
m

paddle ['pædəl] *n* Paddel *nt*

padlock ['pædlɔk] *n* Vorhängeschloss
nt

pagan ['peigən] *adj* heidnisch; *n*

Heide *m*, Heidin *f*

page [peidʒ] *n* Blatt *nt*, Seite *f*

pail [peil] *n* Eimer *m*

pain [pein] *n* Schmerz *m*; **pains** Mühe
f

painful ['peinfəl] *adj* schmerzhaft

painkiller ['peinkilə] *n* Schmerzmittel
nt

painless ['peinləs] *adj* schmerzlos

paint [peint] *n* Farbe *f*; *v* malen;
*anstreichen

paintbox ['peintbɔks] *n* Malkasten *m*

paintbrush ['peintbrʌʃ] *n* Pinsel *m*

painter ['peintə] *n* Maler *m*, -in *f*

painting ['peintiŋ] *n* Gemälde *nt*

pair [pɛə] *n* Paar *nt*

Pakistan [‚pɑ:ki'stɑ:n] Pakistan

Pakistani [‚pɑ:ki'stɑ:ni] *adj*

pakistanisch; *n* Pakistaner *m*, -in *f*

pal ['pæl] *n colloquial* Kumpel *m*, Freund *m*, -in *f*

palace ['pæləs] *n* Palast *m*

pale [peil] *adj* bleich; hell

palm [pɑːm] *n* Palme *f*; Handfläche *f*

palpable ['pælpəbəl] *adj* fühlbar

palpitation [,pælpi'teiʃən] *n* Herzklopfen *nt*

pan [pæn] *n* Pfanne *f*

pane [pein] *n* Scheibe *f*

panel ['pænəl] *n* Paneel *nt*

panelling ['pænəliŋ] *n* Täfelung *f*

panic ['pænik] *n* Panik *f*

pancake ['pæŋkeik] *n* Pfannkuchen *m*

pant [pænt] *v* keuchen

panties ['pæntiz] *pl* Schlüpfer *m*

pants [pænts] *pl* Unterhose *f*; *plAm* Hose *f*

pant suit ['pæntsuːt] *n* Hosenanzug *m*

panty hose ['pæntihouz] *n* Strumpfhose *f*

paper ['peipə] *n* Papier *nt*; Zeitung *f*; ~ **bag** Tüte *f*; ~ **napkin** Papierserviette *f*; **wrapping** ~ Packpapier *nt*

paperback ['peipəbæk] *n* Taschenbuch *nt*

parade [pə'reid] *n* Parade *f*, Umzug *m*

paradise ['pærədais] *n* Paradies *nt*

paraffin ['pærəfin] *n* Petroleum *nt*

paragraph ['pærəgrɑːf] *n* Absatz *m*

parallel ['pærəlel] *adj* parallel; *n* Parallele *f*

paralyse, *Am* **paralyze** ['pærəlaiz] *v* lähmen

parcel ['pɑːsəl] *n* Paket *nt*

pardon ['pɑːdən] *n* Verzeihung *f*

parent ['pɛərənt] *n* Elternteil *m*

parents ['pɛərənts] *pl* Eltern *pl*

parents-in-law ['pɛərəntsinlɔː] *pl* Schwiegereltern *pl*

park [pɑːk] *n* Park *m*; *v* parken; **no**

parking Parken verboten; **parking** Parkplatz *m*; **parking fee** Parkgebühr *f*; **parking light** Parkleuchte *f*; **parking lot** *Am* Parkplatz *m*; **parking meter** Parkuhr *f*; **parking zone** Parkzone *f*

parliament ['pɑːləmənt] *n* Parlament *nt*

parliamentary [,pɑːlə'mentəri] *adj* parlamentarisch

parrot ['pærət] *n* Papagei *m*

parsley ['pɑːsli] *n* Petersilie *f*

parson ['pɑːsən] *n* Pfarrer *m*, -in *f*

parsonage ['pɑːsənidʒ] *n* Pfarrhaus *nt*

part [pɑːt] *n* Teil *m*; Stück *nt*; *v* trennen; **spare** ~ Ersatzteil *nt*

partial ['pɑːʃəl] *adj* teilweise; parteiisch

participant [pɑː'tisipənt] *n* Teilnehmer *m*, -in *f*

participate [pɑː'tisipeit] *v* *teilnehmen

particular [pə'tikjulə] *adj* besonder; wählerisch; **in** ~ speziell

parting ['pɑːtiŋ] *n* Abschied *m*; Scheitel *m*

partition [pɑː'tiʃən] *n* Teilung *f*

partly ['pɑːtli] *adv* teils, teilweise

partner ['pɑːtnə] *n* Partner *m*, -in *f*; Teilhaber *m*, -in *f*

partridge ['pɑːtridʒ] *n* Rebhuhn *nt*

party ['pɑːti] *n* Partei *f*; Party *f*; Gruppe *f*

pass [pɑːs] *v* *vergehen, passieren; überholen; reichen; *bestehen; *vAm* *vorbeifahren; **no passing** *Am* Überholen verboten; ~ **by** *vorbeigehen; ~ **through** durchqueren

passage ['pæsidʒ] *n* Durchgang *m*; Überfahrt *f*; Stelle *f*; Durchfahrt *f*

passenger ['pæsəndʒə] *n* Passagier *m*, -in *f*; ~ **car** *Am* Wagen *m*; ~ **train**

Personenzug *m*

passer-by [‚pɑːsə'bai] *n* Passant *m*,
-in *f*

passion ['pæʃən] *n* Leidenschaft *f*,
Passion *f*; Wut *f*

passionate ['pæʃənət] *adj*
leidenschaftlich

passive ['pæsiv] *adj* passiv

passport ['pɑːspɔːt] *n* Pass *m*; ~
control Passkontrolle *f*, ~
photograph Passfoto *nt*

password ['pɑːswɜːd] *n* Passwort *nt*

past [pɑːst] *n* Vergangenheit *f*; *adj*
vorig, letzt, vergangen; *prep* entlang,
an … vorbei

paste [peist] *n* Paste *f*; *v* kleben

pastime ['pɑːstaim] *n* Zeitvertreib *m*

pastry ['peistri] *n* Gebäck *nt*; ~ **shop**
Konditorei *f*

pasture ['pɑːstʃə] *n* Weide *f*

pasty ['pɑːsti] *n* (Fleisch- oder
Gemüse-)Pastete *f*

patch [pætʃ] *v* flicken

patent ['peitənt] *n* Patent *nt*

path [pɑːθ] *n* Pfad *m*

patience ['peiʃəns] *n* Geduld *f*

patient ['peiʃənt] *adj* geduldig; *n*
Patient *m*, -in *f*

patriot ['peitriət] *n* Patriot *m*, -in *f*

patrol [pə'troul] *n* Streife *f*; *v*
patrouillieren; überwachen

pattern ['pætən] *n* Motiv *nt*, Muster *nt*

pause [pɔːz] *n* Pause *f*; *v* pausieren

pave [peiv] *v* pflastern

pavement ['peivmənt] *n* Bürgersteig
m; Pflaster *nt*

pavilion [pə'viljən] *n* Pavillon *m*

paw [pɔː] *n* Pfote *f*

pawn [pɔːn] *v* verpfänden; *n* Bauer *m*

pay [pei] *n* Gehalt *nt*, Lohn *m*; ~ **desk**
Kasse *f*; ~ **phone** Münzfernsprecher
m

***pay** [pei] *v* bezahlen, zahlen; sich
lohnen; ~ **attention to** achten auf;

paying rentabel; ~ **off** tilgen; ~ **on**
account abzahlen

payee [pei'iː] *n* Zahlungsempfänger
m, -in *f*

payment ['peimənt] *n* Bezahlung *f*

pea [piː] *n* Erbse *f*

peace [piːs] *n* Frieden *m*

peaceful ['piːsfəl] *adj* friedlich

peach [piːtʃ] *n* Pfirsich *m*

peacock ['piːkɔk] *n* Pfau *m*

peak [piːk] *n* Gipfel *m*; Spitze *f*; ~
hour Hauptverkehrszeit *f*; ~ **season**
Hochsaison *f*

peanut ['piːnʌt] *n* Erdnuss *f*

pear [pɛə] *n* Birne *f*

pearl [pɜːl] *n* Perle *f*

peasant ['pezənt] *n* Bauer *m*

pebble ['pebəl] *n* Kieselstein *m*

peculiar [pi'kjuːljə] *adj* eigentümlich;
speziell, sonderbar

peculiarity [pi‚kjuːli'ærəti] *n*
Eigentümlichkeit *f*

pedal ['pedəl] *n* Pedal *nt*

pedestrian [pi'destriən] *n* Fußgänger
m, -in *f*; **no pedestrians** Fußgänger
verboten; ~ **crossing**
Fußgängerübergang *m*

peel [piːl] *v* schälen; *n* Schale *f*

peep [piːp] *v* spähen

peg [peg] *n* Kleiderhaken *m*

pelican ['pelikən] *n* Pelikan *m*

pelvis ['pelvis] *n* Becken *nt*

pen [pen] *n* Feder *f*

penalty ['penəlti] *n* Buße *f*; Strafe *f*; ~
kick Strafstoß *m*

pencil ['pensəl] *n* Bleistift *m*; ~
sharpener Bleistiftspitzer *m*

pendant ['pendənt] *n* Anhänger *m*

penetrate ['penitreit] *v*
*durchdringen

penguin ['peŋgwin] *n* Pinguin *m*

penicillin [‚peni'silin] *n* Penicillin *m*

peninsula [pə'ninsjulə] *n* Halbinsel *f*

penknife ['pennaif] *n* (pl -knives)

Taschenmesser *nt*
penny ['peni] *n*; (*pl* pennies, pence) Penny *m*
pension¹ ['pɑ̃ːsiɔ̃ː] *n* Pension *f*
pension² ['penʃən] *n* Rente *f*
Pentecost ['pentikast] *n* Pfingsten *nt*
people ['piːpəl] *pl* Leute *pl*; *n* Volk *nt*
pepper ['pepə] *n* Pfeffer *m*
peppermint ['pepəmint] *n* Pfefferminze *f*
per [pəː] *prep* per, pro, für; ~ **cent** Prozent
perceive [pə'siːv] *v* *wahrnehmen
percent [pə'sent] *n* Prozent *nt*
percentage [pə'sentidʒ] *n* Prozentsatz *m*
perceptible [pə'septibəl] *adj* wahrnehmbar
perception [pə'sepʃən] *n* Empfindung *f*
perch [pəːtʃ] (*pl* ~) Barsch *m*
percolator ['pəːkəleitə] *n* Kaffeemaschine *f*
perfect ['pəːfikt] *adj* vollkommen
perfection [pə'fekʃən] *n* Perfektion *f*, Vollkommenheit *f*
perform [pə'fɔːm] *v* ausführen, verrichten
performance [pə'fɔːməns] *n* Aufführung *f*
perfume ['pəːfjuːm] *n* Parfüm *nt*
perhaps [pə'hæps] *adv* vielleicht
peril ['peril] *n* Gefahr *f*
perilous ['periləs] *adj* gefährlich
period ['piəriəd] *n* Zeitraum *m*, Zeitabschnitt *m*; Punkt *m*
periodical [,piəri'ɔdikəl] *n* Zeitschrift *f*; *adj* periodisch
perish ['periʃ] *v* *umkommen
perishable ['periʃəbəl] *adj* leicht verderblich
perjury ['pəːdʒəri] *n* Meineid *m*
perm [pəːm] *n* Dauerwelle *f*
permanent ['pəːmənənt] *adj* dauerhaft, dauernd; beständig, fest; ~ **press** mit Dauerbügelfalte; ~ **wave** Dauerwelle *f*
permission [pə'miʃən] *n* Erlaubnis *f*, Genehmigung *f*; Bewilligung *f*, Konzession *f*
permit¹ [pə'mit] *v* gestatten, erlauben
permit² ['pəːmit] *n* Genehmigung *f*
peroxide [pə'rɔksaid] *n* Wasserstoffperoxid *nt*
perpendicular [,pəːpən'dikjulə] *adj* senkrecht
Persia ['pəːʃə] Persien
Persian ['pəːʃən] *adj* persisch; *n* Perser *m*, -in *f*
person ['pəːsən] *n* Person *f*; **per** ~ pro Person
personal ['pəːsənəl] *adj* persönlich
personality [,pəːsə'næləti] *n* Persönlichkeit *f*
personnel [,pəːsə'nel] *n* Personal *nt*
perspective [pə'spektiv] *n* Perspektive *f*
perspiration [,pəːspə'reiʃən] *n* Schweiß *m*
perspire [pə'spaiə] *v* transpirieren, schwitzen
persuade [pə'sweid] *v* bereden, überreden; überzeugen
persuasion [pə'sweiʒən] *n* Überzeugung *f*
pessimism ['pesimizəm] *n* Pessimismus *m*
pessimist ['pesimist] *n* Pessimist *m*, -in *f*
pessimistic [,pesi'mistik] *adj* pessimistisch
pet [pet] *n* Haustier *nt*; Liebling *m*
petal ['petəl] *n* Blütenblatt *nt*
petrol ['petrəl] *n* Benzin *nt*; ~ **pump** Benzinpumpe *f*; ~ **station** Tankstelle *f*; ~ **tank** Benzintank *m*
petroleum [pi'trouliəm] *n* Petroleum *nt*

petty ['peti] *adj* klein, unbedeutend, geringfügig; **~ cash** Kleingeld *nt*

pewit ['pi:wit] *n* Kiebitz *m*

pewter ['pju:tə] *n* Zinn *nt*

phantom ['fæntəm] *n* Gespenst *nt*

pharmacy ['fɑ:məsi] *n* Apotheke *f*; Drogerie *f*

pharmacist ['fɑ:məsist] *n* Apotheker *m*

phase [feiz] *n* Phase *f*

pheasant ['fezənt] *n* Fasan *m*

Philippine ['filipain] *adj* philippinisch

Philippines ['filipi:nz] *pl* Philippinen *pl*

philosopher [fi'lɔsəfə] *n* Philosoph *m*, -in *f*

philosophy [fi'lɔsəfi] *n* Philosophie *f*

phone [foun] *n* Fernsprecher *m*; *v* *anrufen, telefonieren

phone card ['founkɑ:d] *n* Telefonkarte *f*

phonetic [fə'netik] *adj* phonetisch

photo ['foutou] *n* (pl ~s) Foto *nt*

photocopy ['foutəkɔpi] *n* Fotokopie *f*; *v* fotokopieren

photograph ['foutəgrɑ:f] *n* Lichtbild *nt*; *v* fotografieren

photographer [fə'tɔgrəfə] *n* Fotograf *m*, -in *f*

photography [fə'tɔgrəfi] *n* Fotografie *f*

phrase [freiz] *n* Redewendung *f*; **~ book** Sprachführer *m*

physical ['fizikəl] *adj* physisch

physician [fi'ziʃən] *n* Arzt *m*, Ärztin *f*

physicist ['fizisist] *n* Physiker *m*, -in *f*

physics ['fiziks] *n* Physik *f*, Naturwissenschaft *f*

physiology [,fizi'ɔlədʒi] *n* Physiologie *f*

pianist ['pi:ənist] *n* Pianist *m*, -in *f*

piano [pi'ænou] *n* Klavier *nt*; **grand ~** Flügel *m*

pick [pik] *v* pflücken; wählen; *n* Wahl

f; **~ up** *aufnehmen; abholen; **pick-up van** Lieferwagen *m*

picnic ['piknik] *n* Picknick *nt*; *v* picknicken

picture ['piktʃə] *n* Gemälde *nt*; Abbildung *f*, Stich *m*; Bild *nt*; **~ postcard** Ansichtskarte *f*; **pictures** Kino *nt*

picturesque [,piktʃə'resk] *adj* pittoresk, malerisch

pie [pai] *n* Pastete *f*

piece [pi:s] *n* Stück *nt*

pier [piə] *n* Pier *m*

pierce [piəs] *v* durchbohren

pig [pig] *n* Schwein *nt*

pigeon ['pidʒən] *n* Taube *f*

piggy bank ['pigibæŋk] *n* Sparschwein *nt*

pig-headed [,pig'hedid] *adj* starrköpfig

piglet ['piglət] *n* Ferkel *nt*

pigskin ['pigskin] *n* Schweinsleder *nt*

pike [paik] (pl ~) Hecht *m*

pile [pail] *n* Haufen *m*; *v* anhäufen; **piles** *pl* Hämorrhoiden *fpl*

pilgrim ['pilgrim] *n* Pilger *m*, -in *f*

pilgrimage ['pilgrimidʒ] *n* Pilgerfahrt *f*

pill [pil] *n* Pille *f*

pillar ['pilə] *n* Pfeiler *m*, Säule *f*

pillarbox ['piləbɔks] *n* Briefkasten *m*

pillow ['pilou] *n* Kissen *nt*, Kopfkissen *nt*

pillowcase ['piloukeis] *n* Kissenbezug *m*

pilot ['pailət] *n* Pilot *m*, -in *f*; Lotse *m*

pimple ['pimpəl] *n* Pickel *m*

pin [pin] *n* Stecknadel *f*; *v* feststecken; **bobby ~** *Am* Haarklemme *f*

pincers ['pinsəz] *pl* Kneifzange *f*

pinch [pintʃ] *v* *kneifen

pineapple ['pai,næpəl] *n* Ananas *f*

ping-pong ['piŋpɔŋ] *n* Tischtennis *nt*

pink [piŋk] *adj* rosa

pint [paint] *n* Maßeinheit: 0,57 l, Am 0,47 l *colloquial* Halbe *f* (Bier)

pioneer [ˌpaiə'niə] *n* Pionier *m*, -in *f*

pious ['paiəs] *adj* fromm

pip [pip] *n* Kern *m*

pipe [paip] *n* Pfeife *f*; Rohr *nt*; ~ **cleaner** Pfeifenreiniger *m*; ~ **tobacco** Tabak *m*

pipeline ['paiplain] *n* Rohrleitung *f*, Pipeline *f*

pirate ['paiərət] *n* Seeräuber *m*

pistol ['pistəl] *n* Pistole *f*

piston ['pistən] *n* Kolben *m*; ~ **ring** Kolbenring

pit [pit] *n* Grube *f*

pitcher ['pitʃə] *n* Krug *m*

pity ['piti] *n* Mitleid *nt*; *v* Mitleid *haben mit, bemitleiden; **what a pity!** schade!

placard ['plækɑːd] *n* Plakat *nt*

place [pleis] *n* Ort *m*; *v* setzen, stellen; ~ **of birth** Geburtsort *m*; *take ~ *stattfinden

plague [pleig] *n* Plage *f*; Pest *f*

plaice [pleis] (pl ~) Scholle *f*

plain [plein] *adj* deutlich; gewöhnlich, schlicht; *n* Ebene *f*

plan [plæn] *n* Plan *m*; Grundriss *m*; *v* planen

plane [plein] *adj* flach; *n* Flugzeug *nt*; ~ **crash** Flugzeugabsturz *m*

planet ['plænit] *n* Planet *m*

planetarium [ˌplæni'teəriəm] *n* Planetarium *nt*

plank [plæŋk] *n* Brett *nt*

plant [plɑːnt] *n* Pflanze *f*; Werk *nt*; *v* pflanzen

plantation [plæn'teiʃən] *n* Plantage *f*

plaster ['plɑːstə] *n* Putz *m*, Gips *m*; Pflaster *nt*, Heftpflaster *nt*

plastic ['plæstik] *adj* Kunststoff-; *n* Kunststoff *m*; ~ **bag** Plastikbeutel *m*, Plastiktüte *f*

plate [pleit] *n* Teller *m*; Platte *f*

plateau ['plætou] *n* (pl ~x, ~s) Hochebene *f*

platform ['plætfɔːm] *n* Bahnsteig *m*

platinum ['plætinəm] *n* Platin *nt*

play [plei] *v* spielen; *n* Spiel *nt*; Schauspiel *nt*; ~ **truant** schwänzen

player [pleiə] *n* Spieler *m*, -in *f*

playground ['pleigraund] *n* Spielplatz *m*

playing card ['pleiiŋkɑːd] *n* Spielkarte *f*

plea [pliː] *n* Verteidigungsrede *f*

plead [pliːd] *v* (inständig) bitten; plädieren

pleasant ['plezənt] *adj* angenehm, nett

please [pliːz] bitte; *v* *gefallen; **pleased** erfreut; **pleasing** angenehm

pleasure ['pleʒə] *n* Vergnügen *nt*, Spaß *m*, Freude *f*

plentiful ['plentifəl] *adj* reichlich

plenty ['plenti] *n* Fülle *f*; Menge *f*

pliers [plaiəz] *pl* Zange *f*

plimsolls ['plimsəlz] *pl* Turnschuhe *mpl*

plot [plɔt] *n* Verschwörung *f*, Komplott *nt*; Handlung *f*; Parzelle *f*

plough [plau] *n* Pflug *m*; *v* pflügen

plucky ['plʌki] *adj* mutig

plug [plʌg] *n* Stecker *m*; ~ **in** einstöpseln

plum [plʌm] *n* Pflaume *f*

plumber ['plʌmə] *n* Installateur *m*, -in *f*

plump [plʌmp] *adj* mollig

plural ['pluərəl] *n* Mehrzahl *f*

plus [plʌs] *prep* plus

pneumatic [njuː'mætik] *adj* pneumatisch

pneumonia [njuː'mouniə] *n* Lungenentzündung *f*

poach [poutʃ] *v* wildern

pocket ['pɔkit] *n* Tasche *f*

pocketknife ['pɔkitnaif] n (pl -knives) Taschenmesser nt

poem ['pouim] n Gedicht nt

poet ['pouit] n Dichter m, -in f

poetry ['pouitri] n Dichtung f

point [pɔint] n Punkt m; Spitze f; v zeigen; ~ **of view** Standpunkt m

pointed ['pɔintid] adj spitz

poison ['pɔizən] n Gift nt; v vergiften

poisonous ['pɔizənəs] adj giftig

Poland ['poulənd] Polen

pole [poul] n Pfosten m

police [pə'li:s] pl Polizei f

policeman [pə'li:smən] n (pl -men) Schutzmann m, Polizist m

policewoman [pə'li:swumən] n (pl -women) Polizistin f

police station [pə'li:s,steiʃən] n Polizeiwache f

policy ['pɔlisi] n Vorgehen nt, Politik f; Police f

polio ['pouliou] n Polio f, Kinderlähmung f

Polish ['pouliʃ] adj polnisch

polish ['pɔliʃ] v polieren

polite [pə'lait] adj höflich

political [pə'litikəl] adj politisch

politician [,pɔli'tiʃən] n Politiker m, -in f

politics ['pɔlitiks] n Politik f

poll [poul] n Umfrage f, Wahl f; **go to the polls** zur Wahl gehen

pollute [pə'lu:t] v verschmutzen; verderben

pollution [pə'lu:ʃən] n Verschmutzung f, Verunreinigung f

pond [pɔnd] n Teich m

pony ['pouni] n Pony nt

pool [pu:l] n Teich m; Schwimmbecken nt; Poolbillard nt; ~ **attendant** Bademeister m, -in f

poor [puə] adj arm; ärmlich; schwach

pope [poup] n Papst m

pop music [pɔp 'mju:zik] Popmusik f

poppy ['pɔpi] n Klatschmohn m; Mohn m

popular ['pɔpjulə] adj beliebt; Volks-

population [,pɔpju'leiʃən] n Bevölkerung f

populous ['pɔpjuləs] adj dicht bevölkert

porcelain ['pɔ:səlin] n Porzellan nt

porcupine ['pɔ:kjupain] n Stachelschwein m

pork [pɔ:k] n Schweinefleisch nt

port [pɔ:t] n Hafen m; Backbord nt

portable ['pɔ:təbəl] adj tragbar

porter ['pɔ:tə] n Träger m; Pförtner m, -in f

porthole ['pɔ:thoul] n Luke f

portion ['pɔ:ʃən] n Portion f

portrait ['pɔ:trit] n Porträt nt

Portugal ['pɔ:tjugəl] Portugal

Portuguese [,pɔ:tju'gi:z] adj portugiesisch; n Portugiese m, Portugiesin f

posh [pɔʃ] adj colloquial piekfein,

position [pə'ziʃən] n Position f; Lage f; Haltung f; Stellung f

positive ['pɔzətiv] adj positiv; n Positiv m

possess [pə'zes] v *besitzen; **possessed** adj besessen

possession [pə'zeʃən] n Besitz m

possessions Habe f

possibility [,pɔsə'biləti] n Möglichkeit f

possible ['pɔsəbəl] adj möglich; eventuell

post [poust] n Pfosten m; Posten m; Post f; v *aufgeben; ~ **office** ['poustɔfis] n Post(amt nt) f

postage ['poustidʒ] n Porto nt; ~ **paid** portofrei; ~ **stamp** Briefmarke f

postcard ['poustkɑ:d] n Postkarte f; Ansichtskarte f

poster ['poustə] n Plakat nt

poste restante [poust re'stɑ̃:t]

postlagernd

postman ['poustmən] *n* (pl -men) Postbote *m*

post-paid [,poust'peid] *adj* franko

postpone [pə'spoun] *v* *aufschieben

pot [pɔt] *n* Topf *m*

potato [pə'teitou] *n* (pl ~es) Kartoffel *f*

pottery ['pɔtəri] *n* Töpferware *f*

pouch [pautʃ] *n* Beutel *m*

poulterer ['poultərə] *n* Geflügelhändler *m*, -in *f*

poultry ['poultri] *n* Geflügel *nt*

pound [paund] *n* Pfund *nt*

pour [pɔ:] *v* einschenken, schenken, *gießen

poverty ['pɔvəti] *n* Armut *f*

powder ['paudə] *n* Puder *m*; ~ **compact** Puderdose *f*; ~ **room** Damentoilette *f*

power [pauə] *n* Kraft *f*; Energie *f*; Macht *f*

powerful ['pauəfəl] *adj* mächtig; stark

powerless ['pauələs] *adj* machtlos

power station ['pauə,steiʃən] *n* Kraftwerk *nt*

practical ['præktikəl] *adj* praktisch

practically ['præktikli] *adv* nahezu, so gut wie

practice ['præktis] *n* Praxis *f*

practise ['præktis] *v* ausüben; sich üben

praise [preiz] *v* loben; *n* Lob *nt*

pram [præm] *n* Kinderwagen *m*

prawn [prɔ:n] *n* Krabbe *f*

pray [prei] *v* beten

prayer [preə] *n* Gebet *nt*

preach [pri:tʃ] *v* predigen

precarious [pri'kɛəriəs] *adj* heikel

precaution [pri'kɔ:ʃən] *n* Vorsicht *f*; Vorsichtsmaßnahme *f*

precede [pri'si:d] *v* *vorangehen

preceding [pri'si:diŋ] *adj* vorhergehend

precious ['preʃəs] *adj* teuer

precipice ['presipis] *n* Abgrund *m*

precipitation [pri,sipi'teiʃən] *n* Niederschläge *mpl*

precise [pri'sais] *adj* präzis, exakt, genau

predecessor ['pri:disesə] *n* Vorgänger *m*, -in *f*

predict [pri'dikt] *v* vorhersagen

prefer [pri'fə:] *v* *vorziehen

preferable ['prefərəbəl] *adj* vorzuziehend

preference ['prefərəns] *n* Vorzug *m*

prefix ['pri:fiks] *n* Präfix *nt*

pregnant ['pregnənt] *adj* schwanger

prejudice ['predʒədis] *n* Vorurteil *nt*

preliminary [pri'liminəri] *adj* einleitend; vorläufig

premature ['premətʃuə] *adj* vorzeitig

premier ['premiə] *n* Premierminister *m*, -in *f*

premises ['premisiz] *pl* Örtlichkeit *n*; Gebäude *nt*

premium ['pri:miəm] *n* Prämie *f*

prepaid [,pri:'peid] *adj* vorausbezahlt

preparation [,prepə'reiʃən] *n* Vorbereitung *f*

prepare [pri'pɛə] *v* vorbereiten; fertig machen

prepared [pri'pɛəd] *adj* bereit

preposition [,prepə'ziʃən] *n* Präposition *f*

prescribe [pri'skraib] *v* *verschreiben

prescription [pri'skripʃən] *n* Rezept *nt*

presence ['prezəns] *n* Anwesenheit *f*; Gegenwart *f*

present¹ ['prezənt] *n* Präsent *nt*, Geschenk *nt*; Gegenwart *f*; *adj* gegenwärtig; anwesend

present² [pri'zent] *v* vorstellen; *anbieten

presently ['prezəntli] *adv* sofort,

sogleich

preserve [pri'zə:v] *v* bewahren; einmachen

president ['prezidənt] *n* Präsident *m*, -in *f*; Vorsitzende *m/f*

press [pres] *n* Presse *f*; *v* drücken; bügeln; **~ conference** Pressekonferenz *f*

pressing ['presiŋ] *adj* dringend

pressure ['preʃə] *n* Druck *m*; Spannung *f*; **atmospheric ~** Luftdruck *m*; **~ cooker** Schnellkochtopf *m*

prestige [pre'sti:ʒ] *n* Prestige *nt*

presumable [pri'zju:məbəl] *adj* vermutlich

presume [pri'zju:m] *v* vermuten, annehmen

presumptuous [pri'zʌmpʃəs] *adj* übermütig; überheblich

pretence [pri'tens] *n* Heuchelei *f*; Verstellung *f*

pretend [pri'tend] *v* sich verstellen, *vorgeben

pretext ['pri:tekst] *n* Vorwand *m*

pretty ['priti] *adj* schön, hübsch; *adv* ziemlich, beträchtlich

prevent [pri'vent] *v* *anhalten, verhindern; verhüten

preventive [pri'ventiv] *adj* vorbeugend

preview ['privju:] *n* Vorschau *f*

previous ['pri:viəs] *adj* vorig, früher, vorhergehend

pre-war [,pri:'wɔ:] *adj* Vorkriegs-

price [prais] *v* den Preis festsetzen; **~ list** Preisliste *f*

priceless ['praisləs] *adj* unschätzbar

price list ['prais,list] *n* Preisliste *f*

prick [prik] *v* *stechen

pride [praid] *n* Stolz *m*

priest [pri:st] *n* Priester *m*, -in *f*

primary ['praiməri] *adj* Grund-; Anfangs-, hauptsächlich; elementar

prince [prins] *n* Prinz *m*

princess [prin'ses] *n* Prinzessin *f*

principal ['prinsəpəl] *adj* wichtigste; *n* Schulleiter *m*, -in *f*, Direktor *m*, -in *f*

principle ['prinsəpəl] *n* Grundsatz *m*, Prinzip *nt*

print [print] *v* drucken; *n* Abzug *m*; Stich *m*; **printed matter** Drucksache *f*

printer ['printə] *n* Drucker *m*

printout ['print,aut] *n* (Computer)Ausdruck *m*

prior [praiə] *adj* früher

priority [prai'ɔrəti] *n* Priorität *f*, Vorrang *m*; Vorfahrt *f*

prison ['prizən] *n* Gefängnis *nt*

prisoner ['prizənə] *n* Häftling *m*, Gefangene *m/f*; **~ of war** Kriegsgefangene *m/f*

privacy ['praivəsi] *n* Privatleben *nt*

private ['praivit] *adj* privat; persönlich

privilege ['privilidʒ] *n* Vorrecht *nt*

prize [praiz] *n* Preis *m*; Belohnung *f*

probable ['prɔbəbəl] *adj* vermutlich, wahrscheinlich

probably ['prɔbəbli] *adv* wahrscheinlich

problem ['prɔbləm] *n* Problem *nt*; Frage *f*

procedure [prə'si:dʒə] *n* Verfahren *nt*

proceed [prə'si:d] *v* *fortfahren; *verfahren

process ['prouses] *n* Verfahren *nt*, Vorgang *m*; Prozess *m*

procession [prə'seʃən] *n* Prozession *f*, Zug *m*

proclaim [prə'kleim] *v* proklamieren

produce¹ [prə'dju:s] *v* herstellen

produce² ['prɔdju:s] *n* Erlös *m*, Ertrag *m*

producer [prə'dju:sə] *n* Produzent *m*, -in *f*

product ['prɔdʌkt] *n* Produkt *nt*

production [prə'dʌkʃən] n
Produktion f

profession [prə'feʃən] n Fach nt,
Beruf m

professional [prə'feʃənəl] adj
beruflich

professor [prə'fesə] n Professor m,
-in f

profit ['prɔfit] n Vorteil m, Gewinn m;
Nutzen m; v profitieren

profitable ['prɔfitəbəl] adj einträglich

programme ['prougræm] n
Programm nt

progress[1] ['prougres] n Fortschritt m

progress[2] [prə'gres] v
*weiterkommen

progressive [prə'gresiv] adj
fortschrittlich, progressiv;
zunehmend

prohibit [prə'hibit] v *verbieten

prohibition [,proui'biʃən] n Verbot nt

prohibitive [prə'hibitiv] adj
unerschwinglich

project ['prɔdʒekt] n Plan m, Projekt
nt

promenade [,prɔmə'nɑ:d] n
Promenade f

promise ['prɔmis] n Versprechen nt; v
*versprechen

promote [prə'mout] v fördern,
befördern

promotion [prə'mouʃən] n
Beförderung f; Werbung f

prompt [prɔmpt] adj sofortig,
unverzüglich

pronoun ['prounaun] n Fürwort nt

pronounce [prə'nauns] v
*aussprechen

pronunciation [,prənʌnsi'eiʃən] n
Aussprache f

proof [pru:f] n Beweis m

propaganda [,prɔpə'gændə] n
Propaganda f

propel [prə'pel] v *antreiben

propeller [prə'pelə] n Schraube f,
Propeller m

proper ['prɔpə] adj richtig,
gebührend, passend, angebracht,
geeignet

property ['prɔpəti] n Besitz m,
Eigentum nt; Eigenschaft f

prophet ['prɔfit] n Prophet m, -in f

proportion [prə'pɔːʃən] n Verhältnis
nt

proportional [prə'pɔːʃənəl] adj
proportional

proposal [prə'pouzəl] n Vorschlag m

propose [prə'pouz] v *vorschlagen

proposition [,prɔpə'ziʃən] n
Vorschlag m

proprietor [prə'praiətə] n
Eigentümer m, -in f

prospect ['prɔspekt] n Aussicht f

prospectus [prə'spektəs] n Prospekt
m

prosperity [prɔ'sperəti] n Wohlstand
m

prosperous ['prɔspərəs] adj
wohlhabend

prostitute ['prɔstitjuːt] n
Prostituierte f

protect [prə'tekt] v schützen

protection [prə'tekʃən] n Schutz m

protein ['proutiːn] n Protein nt;
Eiweiß nt

protest[1] ['proutest] n Protest m

protest[2] [prə'test] v protestieren

Protestant ['prɔtistənt] n Protestant
m, -in f, adj protestantisch

proud [praud] adj stolz; hochmütig

prove [pruːv] v zeigen, *beweisen;
sich herausstellen

proverb ['prɔvəːb] n Sprichwort nt

provide [prə'vaid] v liefern,
beschaffen; versorgen mit

provided that vorausgesetzt dass

province ['prɔvins] n Provinz f

provincial [prə'vinʃəl] adj provinziell

provisional [prə'viʒənəl] adj
vorläufig

provisions [prə'viʒənz] pl Vorrat m

prune [pru:n] n Backpflaume f

psychiatrist [sai'kaiətrist] n
Psychiater m, -in f

psychic ['saikik] adj psychisch

psychoanalyst [,saikou'ænəlist] n
Psychoanalytiker m, -in f

psychological [,saikə'lɔdʒikəl] adj
psychologisch

psychologist [sai'kɔlədʒist] n
Psychologe m, Psychologin f

psychology [sai'kɔlədʒi] n
Psychologie f

pub [pʌb] n Wirtshaus nt; Kneipe f

public ['pʌblik] adj öffentlich;
allgemein; n Publikum nt; ~ **garden**
Anlage f; ~ **house** Wirtshaus nt

publication [,pʌbli'keiʃən] n
Veröffentlichung f

publicity [pʌ'blisəti] n Reklame f;
Bekanntheit f

publish ['pʌbliʃ] v veröffentlichen,
*herausgeben

publisher ['pʌbliʃə] n Verleger m, -in
f

puddle ['pʌdəl] n Pfütze f

pull [pul] v *ziehen; ~ **out** *abfahren; ~
up *anhalten

pulley ['puli] n (pl ~s) Rolle f;
Flaschenzug m

pullover ['pu,louvə] n Pullover m

pulpit ['pulpit] n Kanzel f

pulse [pʌls] n Pulsschlag m, Puls m

pump [pʌmp] n Pumpe f; v pumpen

pun [pʌn] n Wortspiel nt

punctual ['pʌŋktʃuəl] adj genau,
pünktlich

puncture ['pʌŋktʃə] n Reifenpanne f

punctured ['pʌŋktʃəd] adj
durchstochen

punish ['pʌniʃ] v strafen

punishment ['pʌniʃmənt] n Strafe f

pupil ['pju:pəl] n Schüler m, -in f

puppet-show ['pʌpitʃou] n
Marionettentheater nt;
Puppentheater nt

purchase ['pə:tʃəs] v kaufen; n
Erwerb m, Kauf m; ~ **price** Kaufpreis
m

purchaser ['pə:tʃəsə] n Käufer m, -in
f

pure [pjuə] adj klar, rein

purple ['pə:pəl] adj violett

purpose ['pə:pəs] n Absicht f, Zweck
m; **on** ~ absichtlich

purse [pə:s] n Börse f, Geldbeutel m

pursue [pə'sju:] v verfolgen;
nachstreben

pus [pʌs] n Eiter m

push [puʃ] n Schub m, Stoß m; v
*stoßen; *schieben; drängen; ~
button Druckknopf m

***put** [put] v setzen, legen, stellen;
stecken; ~ **away** weglegen; ~ **off**
*verschieben; ~ **on** *anziehen; ~ **out**
auslöschen

puzzle ['pʌzəl] n Rätsel nt; v
verwirren; **jigsaw** ~ Puzzlespiel nt

puzzling ['pʌzliŋ] adj rätselhaft

pyjamas [pə'dʒɑ:məz] pl Pyjama m

Q

quail [kweil] n (pl ~, ~s) Wachtel f

quaint [kweint] adj seltsam;
altmodisch

qualification [,kwɔlifi'keiʃən] n

Vorbehalt *m*, Eignung *f*; Einschränkung *f*

qualified ['kwɔlifaid] *adj* qualifiziert; befugt

qualify ['kwɔlifai] *v* sich eignen

quality ['kwɔləti] *n* Qualität *f*; Eigenschaft *f*

quantity ['kwɔntəti] *n* Quantität *f*; Anzahl *f*

quarantine ['kwɔrənti:n] *n* Quarantäne *f*

quarrel ['kwɔrəl] *v* zanken, *streiten; *n* Streit *m*, Zank *m*

quarry ['kwɔri] *n* Steinbruch *m*

quarter ['kwɔ:tə] *n* Viertel *nt*; Quartal *nt*; Stadtviertel *nt*; ~ **of an hour** Viertelstunde *f*

quarterly ['kwɔ:təli] *adj* vierteljährlich

quay [ki:] *n* Kai *m*

queen [kwi:n] *n* Königin *f*

queer [kwiə] *adj* sonderbar; komisch

query ['kwiəri] *n* Frage *f*; *v* befragen;

bezweifeln

question ['kwestʃən] *n* Frage *f*; Problem *nt*; *v* befragen; in Zweifel *ziehen; ~ **mark** Fragezeichen *nt*

queue [kju:] *n* Schlange *f*; *v* Schlange *stehen

quick [kwik] *adj* schnell

quick-tempered [,kwik'tempəd] *adj* reizbar

quiet ['kwaiət] *adj* still, ruhig, gelassen; *n* Stille *f*, Ruhe *f*

quilt [kwilt] *n* Steppdecke *f*

quit [kwit] *v* aufhören mit, *aufgeben; *verlassen

quite [kwait] *adv* völlig, durchaus; leidlich, ziemlich, beträchtlich; sehr, ganz

quiz [kwiz] *n* (pl ~zes) Quiz *nt*

quota ['kwoutə] *n* Quote *f*

quotation [kwou'teiʃən] *n* Zitat *nt*; ~ **marks** Anführungszeichen *ntpl*

quote [kwout] *v* zitieren

R

rabbit ['ræbit] *n* Kaninchen *nt*

rabies ['reibiz] *n* Tollwut *f*

race [reis] *n* Wettlauf *m*, Rennen *nt*; Rasse *f*

racecourse ['reiskɔ:s] *n* Rennbahn *f*

racehorse ['reishɔ:s] *n* Rennpferd *nt*

racetrack ['reistræk] *n* Rennbahn *f*, Rennstrecke *f*

racial ['reiʃəl] *adj* Rassen-

racket ['rækit] *n* Tumult *m*, (Tennis)Schläger *m*

radiator ['reidieitə] *n* Heizkörper *m*

radical ['rædikəl] *adj* radikal

radio ['reidiou] *n* Radio *nt*

radish ['rædiʃ] *n* Rettich *m*

radius ['reidiəs] *n* (pl radii) Umkreis *m*

raft [rɑ:ft] *n* Floß *nt*

rag [ræg] *n* Lumpen *m*

rage [reidʒ] *n* Wut *f*; *v* rasen, wüten

raid [reid] *n* Überfall *m*

rail [reil] *n* Brüstung *f*, Geländer *nt*

railing ['reiliŋ] *n* Gitter *nt*

railroad ['reilroud] *nAm* Eisenbahn *f*

railway ['reilwei] *n* Bahn *f*, Eisenbahn *f*

rain [rein] *n* Regen *m*; *v* regnen

rainbow ['reinbou] *n* Regenbogen *m*

raincoat ['reinkout] *n* Regenmantel *m*

rainproof ['reinpru:f] *adj* wasserdicht

rainy ['reini] *adj* regnerisch

raise [reiz] *v* *heben; erhöhen; *aufziehen, anbauen, züchten; *erheben; *nAm* Lohnerhöhung *f*, Erhöhung *f*

raisin ['reizən] *n* Rosine *f*

rake [reik] *n* Harke *f*

rally ['ræli] *n* Versammlung *f*

ramp [ræmp] *n* Rampe *f*

ramshackle ['ræm‚fækəl] *adj* wacklig

rancid ['rænsid] *adj* ranzig

rang [ræŋ] *v* (p ring)

range [reindʒ] *n* Bereich *m*; ~ **finder** Entfernungsmesser *m*

rank [ræŋk] *n* Rang *m*; Reihe *f*

ransom ['rænsəm] *n* Lösegeld *nt*

rape [reip] *v* vergewaltigen

rapid ['ræpid] *adj* schnell

rapids ['ræpidz] *pl* Stromschnelle *f*

rare [rɛə] *adj* selten

rarely ['rɛəli] *adv* selten, kaum

rascal ['rɑːskəl] *n* Schalk *m*, Schelm *m*

rash [ræʃ] *n* Hautausschlag *m*, Ausschlag *m*; *adj* übereilt, unbesonnen

raspberry ['rɑːzbəri] *n* Himbeere *f*

rat [ræt] *n* Ratte *f*

rate [reit] *n* Satz *m*, Tarif *m*; Geschwindigkeit *f*, **at any ~** jedenfalls, auf jeden Fall; **~ of exchange** Kurs *m*

rather ['rɑːðə] *adv* recht, ziemlich, vielmehr; lieber, eher

ration ['ræʃən] *n* Ration *f*

raven ['reivən] *n* Rabe *m*

raw [rɔː] *adj* roh; ~ **material** Rohmaterial *nt*

ray [rei] *n* Strahl *m*

rayon ['reiən] *n* Kunstseide *f*

razor ['reizə] *n* Rasierapparat *m*; ~ **blade** Rasierklinge *f*

reach [riːtʃ] *v* erreichen; *n* Bereich *m*

react [ri'ækt] *v* reagieren

reaction [ri'ækʃən] *n* Reaktion *f*

*read [riːd] *v* *lesen

reader ['riːdə] *n* Leser *m*, -in *f*; Lektor *m*, -in *f*

reading lamp ['riːdiŋlæmp] *n* Leselampe *f*

reading room ['riːdiŋruːm] *n* Lesesaal *m*

ready ['redi] *adj* fertig, bereit

ready-made [‚redi'meid] *adj* Konfektions-

real [riəl] *adj* wirklich

reality [ri'æləti] *n* Wirklichkeit *f*

realize ['riəlaiz] *v* sich vergegenwärtigen; realisieren, verwirklichen

really ['riəli] *adv* tatsächlich, wirklich; eigentlich

rear [riə] *n* Hinterseite *f*; *v* *großziehen; ~ **light** Schlusslicht *nt*

reason ['riːzən] *n* Ursache *f*, Grund *m*; Verstand *m*, Vernunft *f*; *v* logisch *durchdenken

reasonable ['riːzənəbəl] *adj* vernünftig; billig

reassure [‚riːə'ʃuə] *v* beruhigen

rebate ['riːbeit] *n* Ermäßigung *f*, Rabatt *m*

rebellion [ri'beljən] *n* Aufstand *m*, Aufruhr *m*

recall [ri'kɔːl] *v* sich erinnern; *zurückrufen; *widerrufen

receipt [ri'siːt] *n* Quittung *f*; Empfang *m*

receive [ri'siːv] *v* *bekommen, *empfangen

receiver [ri'siːvə] *n* Hörer *m*.

recent ['riːsənt] *adj* jüngst

recently ['riːsəntli] *adv* kürzlich, neulich

reception [ri'sepʃən] *n* Empfang *m*; Aufnahme *f*; ~ **office** Rezeption *f*

receptionist [ri'sepʃənist] *n*

Empfangsdame f

recession [ri'seʃən] n Rückgang m

recipe ['resipi] n (Koch)Rezept nt

reckon ['rekən] v rechnen; *halten für; *denken

recognition [,rekəg'niʃən] n Anerkennung f

recognize ['rekəgnaiz] v *erkennen; *anerkennen

recollect [,rekə'lekt] v sich *entsinnen

recommence [,ri:kə'mens] v wieder *beginnen

recommend [,rekə'mend] v *empfehlen; *anraten

recommendation [,rekəmen'deiʃən] n Empfehlung f

reconciliation [,rekənsili'eiʃən] n Versöhnung f

record¹ ['rekɔ:d] n Schallplatte f; Rekord m; Akte f

record² [ri'kɔ:d] v aufzeichnen

recording [ri'kɔ:diŋ] n Aufnahme f

record player ['rekɔ:d,pleiə] n Plattenspieler m

recover [ri'kʌvə] v wiedererlangen; sich erholen, *genesen

recovery [ri'kʌvəri] n Genesung f

recreation [,rekri'eiʃən] n Erholung f; ~ **ground** Spielplatz m

recruit [ri'kru:t] n Rekrut m, -in f

rectangle ['rektæŋgəl] n Rechteck nt

rectangular [rek'tæŋgjulə] adj rechteckig

rector ['rektə] n Pfarrer m, -in f, Pastor m, -in f

rectum ['rektəm] n Mastdarm m

recycle [,ri:'saikəl] v wieder verwerten

red [red] adj rot

redeem [ri'di:m] v erlösen

reduce [ri'dju:s] v reduzieren, vermindern, herabsetzen

reduction [ri'dʌkʃən] n Rabatt m, Preisnachlass m; Verkleinerung f

redundant [ri'dʌndənt] adj überflüssig

reed [ri:d] n Schilfrohr nt

reef [ri:f] n Riff nt

reference ['refrəns] n Referenz f, Verweis m; Beziehung f; **with ~ to** hinsichtlich

refer to [ri'fə:] *verweisen auf

referee [,refə'ri:] n Schiedsrichter m, -in f

refill ['ri:fil] n Ersatzfüllung f

refinery [ri'fainəri] n Raffinerie f

reflect [ri'flekt] v widerspiegeln

reflection [ri'flekʃən] n Spiegelung f; Spiegelbild nt

reflector [ri'flektə] n Reflektor m

reformation [,refə'meiʃən] n Reformation f

refresh [ri'freʃ] v erfrischen

refreshment [ri'freʃmənt] n Erfrischung f

refrigerator [ri'fridʒəreitə] n Eisschrank m, Kühlschrank m

refugee [,refju'dʒi:] n Flüchtling m

refund¹ [ri'fʌnd] v rückvergüten

refund² ['ri:fʌnd] n Rückvergütung f

refusal [ri'fju:zəl] n Verweigerung f

refuse¹ [ri'fju:z] v verweigern

refuse² ['refju:s] n Abfall m

regard [ri'ga:d] v *ansehen; betrachten; n Respekt m; **as regards** hinsichtlich, in Bezug auf, was … betrifft

regarding [ri'ga:diŋ] prep betreffs, hinsichtlich; in Anbetracht

regatta [ri'gætə] n Regatta f

régime [rei'ʒi:m] n Regime nt

region ['ri:dʒən] n Gegend f; Gebiet nt

regional ['ri:dʒənəl] adj örtlich

register ['redʒistə] v sich *einschreiben; *einschreiben; **registered letter** Einschreiben n

registration [,redʒi'streiʃən] n

Eintragung f; **~ number**
Kennzeichen nt; **~ plate**
Nummernschild nt

regret [ri'gret] v bedauern; n
Bedauern nt

regular ['regjulə] adj regelmäßig;
gewohnt, normal

regulate ['regjuleit] v regeln

regulation [,regju'leifən] n Vorschrift
f; Regelung f

rehabilitation [,ri:hə,bili'teifən] n
Rehabilitation f

rehearsal [ri'hə:səl] n Probe f

rehearse [ri'hə:s] v proben

reign [rein] n Herrschaft f; v regieren

reimburse [,ri:im'bə:s] v
zurückzahlen, erstatten

reject [ri'dʒekt] v ablehnen,
*zurückweisen; *verwerfen

relate [ri'leit] v erzählen

related [ri'leitid] adj verwandt

relation [ri'leifən] n Beziehung f,
Verbindung f; Verwandte m/f

relationship [ri'leifənfip] n
(Liebes)Beziehung f, Verhältnis nt

relative ['relətiv] n Verwandte m/f;
adj verhältnismäßig, relativ

relax [ri'læks] v sich entspannen

relaxation [,rilæk'seifən] n
Entspannung f

reliable [ri'laiəbəl] adj zuverlässig

relic ['relik] n Reliquie f

relief [ri'li:f] n Erleichterung f;
Unterstützung f; Relief nt

relieve [ri'li:v] v erleichtern; ablösen

religion [ri'lidʒən] n Religion f

religious [ri'lidʒəs] adj religiös

rely on [ri'lai] sich *verlassen auf

remain [ri'mein] v *bleiben; *übrig
bleiben

remainder [ri'meində] n Restbestand
m, Überbleibsel nt, Rest m

remaining [ri'meiniŋ] adj übrig

remark [ri'ma:k] n Bemerkung f; v

bemerken

remarkable [ri'ma:kəbəl] adj
merkwürdig

remedy ['remədi] n Heilmittel nt;
Mittel nt

remember [ri'membə] v sich
erinnern; *behalten

remembrance [ri'membrəns] n
Andenken nt, Erinnerung f

remind [ri'maind] v erinnern

remit [ri'mit] v *überweisen

remittance [ri'mitəns] n
Überweisung f

remnant ['remnənt] n Überbleibsel
nt, Rest m, Überrest m

remote [ri'mout] adj abgelegen,
entfernt

removal [ri'mu:vəl] n Beseitigung f

remove [ri'mu:v] v beseitigen

remunerate [ri'mju:nəreit] v
entschädigen

remuneration [ri,mju:nə'reifən] n
Entlohnung f; Entschädigung f

renew [ri'nju:] v erneuern; verlängern

rent [rent] v mieten; n Miete f

repair [ri'peə] v reparieren; n
Instandsetzung f

reparation [,repə'reifən] n
Wiederherstellung f, Reparatur f

***repay** [ri'pei] v zurückzahlen

repayment [ri'peimənt] n
Rückzahlung f

repeat [ri'pi:t] v wiederholen

repellent [ri'pelənt] adj widerwärtig,
abstoßend

repentance [ri'pentəns] n Reue f

repertory ['repətəri] n Repertoire nt

repetition [,repə'tifən] n
Wiederholung f

replace [ri'pleis] v ersetzen

reply [ri'plai] v antworten; n Antwort
f; **in ~** als Antwort

report [ri'po:t] v berichten; melden;
sich melden; n Meldung f, Bericht m

reporter [ri'pɔːtə] *n* Berichterstatter *m*, -in *f*

represent [ˌrepri'zent] *v* *vertreten; vorstellen

representation [ˌreprizen'teiʃən] *n* Vertretung *f*

representative [ˌrepri'zentətiv] *adj* repräsentativ; *n* Vertreter *m*, -in *f*; Abgeordnete *m/f*

reprimand ['reprimɑːnd] *v* tadeln

reproach [ri'proutʃ] *n* Vorwurf *m*; *v* *vorwerfen

reproduce [ˌriːprə'djuːs] *v* reproduzieren

reproduction [ˌriːprə'dʌkʃən] *n* Reproduktion *f*

reptile ['reptail] *n* Reptil *nt*

republic [ri'pʌblik] *n* Republik *f*

republican [ri'pʌblikən] *adj* republikanisch

repulsive [ri'pʌlsiv] *adj* widerwärtig

reputation [ˌrepju'teiʃən] *n* Ruf *m*; Ansehen *nt*

request [ri'kwest] *n* Bitte *f*; *v* *bitten

require [ri'kwaiə] *v* erfordern

requirement [ri'kwaiəmənt] *n* Erfordernis *nt*

requisite ['rekwizit] *adj* erforderlich

rescue ['reskjuː] *v* retten; *n* Rettung *f*

research [ri'səːtʃ] *n* Forschung *f*

resemblance [ri'zembləns] *n* Ähnlichkeit *f*

resemble [ri'zembəl] *v* *gleichen

resent [ri'zent] *v* *übel nehmen

reservation [ˌrezə'veiʃən] *n* Reservierung *f*

reserve [ri'zəːv] *v* reservieren; vorbestellen; *n* Reserve *f*

reserved [ri'zəːvd] *adj* reserviert

reservoir ['rezəvwɑː] *n* Reservoir *nt*

reside [ri'zaid] *v* wohnen

residence ['rezidəns] *n* Wohnsitz *m*; ~ **permit** Aufenthaltsgenehmigung *f*

resident ['rezidənt] *n* Ortsansässige *m/f*; *adj* wohnhaft; intern

resign [ri'zain] *v* *zurücktreten

resignation [ˌrezig'neiʃən] *n* Rücktritt *m*

resin ['rezin] *n* Harz *m*

resist [ri'zist] *v* sich widersetzen

resistance [ri'zistəns] *n* Widerstand *m*

resolute ['rezəluːt] *adj* resolut, entschlossen

respect [ri'spekt] *n* Respekt *m*; Ehrfurcht *f*, Achtung *f*, Ehrerbietung *f*; *v* achten

respectable [ri'spektəbəl] *adj* achtbar, ehrbar

respectful [ri'spektfəl] *adj* ehrerbietig

respective [ri'spektiv] *adj* jeweilig

respiration [ˌrespə'reiʃən] *n* Atmung *f*

respite ['respait] *n* Aufschub *m*

responsibility [riˌsponsə'biləti] *n* Verantwortlichkeit *f*

responsible [ri'sponsəbəl] *adj* verantwortlich; haftbar

rest [rest] *n* Rast *f*; Rest *m*; *v* ausruhen, ruhen

restaurant ['restərɔ-ː] *n* Restaurant *nt*

restful ['restfəl] *adj* ruhig; erholsam

rest home ['resthoum] *n* Erholungsheim *nt*

restless ['restləs] *adj* unruhig; ruhelos

restrain [ri'strein] *v* in Schranken *halten, *zurückhalten

restriction [ri'strikʃən] *n* Einschränkung *f*

rest room ['restruːm] *nAm* Toilette *f*

result [ri'zʌlt] *n* Ergebnis *nt*; Folge *f*; *v* sich *ergeben

resume [ri'zjuːm] *v* *wieder aufnehmen

résumé ['rezjumei] *n*

Zusammenfassung *f*; *Am*
Lebenslauf *m*
retail ['ri:teil] *v* im Einzelhandel
verkaufen; **~ trade** Einzelhandel *m*,
Kleinhandel *m*,
retailer ['ri:teilə] *n* Einzelhändler *m*,
-in *f*, Kleinhändler *m*, -in *f*;
Wiederverkäufer *m*, -in *f*
retina ['retinə] *n* Netzhaut *f*
retire [ri'taiə] *v* sich zurückziehen; in
Rente gehen
retired [ri'taiəd] *adj* pensioniert
retirement [ri'taiəmənt] *n* Ruhestand
m
return [ri'tɔ:n] *v* *zurückkommen,
zurückkehren; *n* Rückkehr *f*; **~ flight**
Rückflug *m*; **~ journey** Rückreise *f*,
Rückfahrt *f*; **~ ticket** *n* Rückfahrkarte
f **reunite** [,ri:ju:'nait] *v*
wiedervereinigen
reveal [ri'vi:l] *v* offenbaren, enthüllen
revelation [,revə'leiʃən] *n*
Enthüllung *f*
revenge [ri'vendʒ] *n* Rache *f*
revenue ['revənju:] *n* Einkünfte *fpl*,
Einkommen *nt*
reverse [ri'vɔ:s] *n* Gegenteil *nt*;
Kehrseite *f*; Rückwärtsgang *m*;
Umschwung *m*, Rückschlag *m*; *adj*
umgekehrt; *v* rückwärts *fahren
review [ri'vju:] *n* Besprechung *f*;
Zeitschrift *f*
revise [ri'vaiz] *v* überarbeiten
revision [ri'viʒən] *n* Überarbeitung *f*
revival [ri'vaivəl] *n*
Wiederherstellung *f*
revolt [ri'voult] *v* rebellieren; *n*
Aufstand *m*, Aufruhr *m*
revolting [ri'voultiŋ] *adj* widerwärtig,
empörend, abstoßend
revolution [,revə'lu:ʃən] *n*
Revolution *f*; Umdrehung *f*
revolutionary [,revə'lu:ʃənəri] *adj*
revolutionär

revolver [ri'vɔlvə] *n* Revolver *m*
revue [ri'vju:] *n* Kabarett *nt*
reward [ri'wɔ:d] *n* Belohnung *f*; *v*
belohnen
rheumatism ['ru:mətizəm] *n*
Rheumatismus *m*
rhinoceros [rai'nɔsərəs] *n* (pl ~, ~es)
Nashorn *nt*
rhubarb ['ru:ba:b] *n* Rhabarber *m*
rhyme [raim] *n* Reim *m*
rhythm ['riðəm] *n* Rhythmus *m*
rib [rib] *n* Rippe *f*
ribbon ['ribən] *n* Band *nt*
rice [rais] *n* Reis *m*
rich [ritʃ] *adj* reich
riches ['ritʃiz] *pl* Reichtum *m*
rid [rid] *v* befreien (of von); **get ~ of**
loswerden
riddle ['ridəl] *n* Rätsel *nt*
ride [raid] *n* Fahrt *f*
*ride [raid] *v* *fahren; *reiten
rider ['raidə] *n* Reiter *m*, -in *f*
ridge [ridʒ] *n* Grat *m*
ridiculous [ri'dikjuləs] *adj* lächerlich
riding ['raidiŋ] *n* Reitsport *m*; **~
school** Reitschule *f*
rifle ['raifəl] *v* Gewehr *nt*
right [rait] *n* Recht *nt*; *adj* gut, richtig;
recht; redlich, gerecht; **all right!**
einverstanden!; ***be ~** Recht *haben;
~ of way Vorfahrtsrecht *nt*
righteous ['raitʃəs] *adj* gerecht
right-hand ['raithænd] *adj* recht
rightly ['raitli] *adv* mit Recht
rim [rim] *n* Felge *f*; Rand *m*
ring [riŋ] *n* Ring *m*; Kreis *m*;
Zirkusarena *f*
*ring [riŋ] *v* läuten; **~ up** *anrufen
rinse [rins] *v* spülen; *n* Spülung *f*
riot ['raiət] *n* Aufruhr *m*
rip [rip] *v* *zerreißen
ripe [raip] *adj* reif
rise [raiz] *n* Gehaltserhöhung *f*,
Erhöhung *f*; Anhöhe *f*; Steigung *f*;

Aufstieg *m*

*rise [raiz] *v* *aufstehen; *aufgehen; *steigen

rising ['raiziŋ] *n* Aufstand *m*

risk [risk] *n* Risiko *nt*; Gefahr *f*; *v* wagen

risky ['riski] *adj* gewagt, riskant

rival ['raivəl] *n* Rivale *m*, Rivalin *f*; Konkurrent *m*, -in *f*; *v* rivalisieren

rivalry ['raivəlri] *n* Rivalität *f*; Konkurrenz *f*

river ['rivə] *n* Fluss *m*; ~ **bank** Flussufer *nt*

riverside ['rivəsaid] *n* Flussufer *nt*

road [roud] *n* Straße *f*; ~ **fork** *n* Weggabelung *f*; ~ **map** Autokarte *f*; ~ **system** Straßennetz *nt*; ~ **up** Straßenarbeiten *fpl*

roadhouse ['roudhaus] *n* Gaststätte *f*

roadside ['roudsaid] *n* Straßenseite *f*; ~ **restaurant** Gaststätte *f*

roadway ['roudwei] *nAm* Fahrbahn *f*

roam [roum] *v* umherschweifen

roar [rɔ:] *v* heulen, brüllen; *n* Brüllen *nt*, Dröhnen *nt*

roast [roust] *v* *braten, rösten

rob [rɔb] *v* rauben

robber ['rɔbə] *n* Räuber *m*, -in *f*

robbery ['rɔbəri] *n* Raub *m*, Diebstahl *m*

robe [roub] *n* Kleid *nt*; Gewand *nt*

robin ['rɔbin] *n* Rotkehlchen *nt*

robust [rou'bʌst] *adj* robust

rock [rɔk] *n* Felsen *m*; *v* schaukeln

rocket ['rɔkit] *n* Rakete *f*

rocky ['rɔki] *adj* felsig

rod [rɔd] *n* Stange *f*

roe [rou] *n* Rogen *m*

role [roul] *n* Rolle *f*

roll [roul] *v* rollen; *n* Rolle *f*; Brötchen *nt*

Roman Catholic ['roumən 'kæθəlik] römisch-katholisch

romance [rə'mæns] *n* Romanze *f*

romantic [rə'mæntik] *adj* romantisch

roof [ru:f] *n* Dach *nt*; **thatched** ~ Strohdach *nt*

room [ru:m] *n* Raum *m*, Zimmer *nt*; Platz *m*; ~ **and board** Zimmer mit Vollpension; ~ **service** Zimmerservice *m*; ~ **temperature** Zimmertemperatur *f*

roomy ['ru:mi] *adj* geräumig

root [ru:t] *n* Wurzel *f*

rope [roup] *n* Seil *nt*

rosary ['rouzəri] *n* Rosenkranz *m*

rose [rouz] *n* Rose *f*; *adj* rosa

rotten ['rɔtən] *adj* verdorben

rouge [ru:ʒ] *n* Rouge *nt*

rough [rʌf] *adj* uneben, rau, holperig; stürmisch

roulette [ru:'let] *n* Roulett *nt*

round [raund] *adj* rund; *prep* um … herum, um; *n* Runde *f*; ~ **trip** *Am* Hin- und Rückfahrt

rounded ['raundid] *adj* auf- oder abgerundet

route [ru:t] *n* Route *f*

routine [ru:'ti:n] *n* Routine *f*

row¹ [rou] *n* Reihe *f*; *v* rudern

row² [rau] *n* Krach *m*

rowdy ['raudi] *adj* streitsüchtig

rowing boat ['rouiŋbout] *n* Ruderboot *nt*

royal ['rɔiəl] *adj* königlich

rub [rʌb] *v* *reiben

rubber ['rʌbə] *n* Gummi *m*; Radiergummi *m*; ~ **band** Gummiband *nt*

rubbish ['rʌbiʃ] *n* Abfall *m*; Quatsch *m*, Unsinn *m*; ~ **bin** Abfalleimer *m*; **talk** ~ quatschen

ruby ['ru:bi] *n* Rubin *m*

rucksack ['rʌksæk] *n* Rucksack *m*

rudder ['rʌdə] *n* Steuerruder *nt*

rude [ru:d] *adj* grob

rug [rʌg] *n* Vorleger *m*

ruin ['ru:in] *v* ruinieren; *n* Untergang

m; **ruins** Ruine *f*
rule [ru:l] *n* Regel *f*; Verwaltung *f*, Regierung *f*, Herrschaft *f*; *v* regieren, herrschen; **as a ~** gewöhnlich, in der Regel
ruler ['ru:lə] *n* Monarch *m*, -in *f*, Herrscher *m*, -in *f*; Lineal *nt*
Rumania [ru:'meiniə] Rumänien
Rumanian [ru:'meiniən] *adj* rumänisch; *n* Rumäne *m*, Rumänin *f*
rumour ['ru:mə] *n* Gerücht *nt*
***run** [rʌn] *v* *laufen; **~ into** zufällig begegnen
runaway ['rʌnəwei] *n* Ausreißer *m*,

-in *f*
rung [rʌŋ] *v* (pp ring)
runner ['rʌnə] *n* Läufer *m*, -in *f*
runway ['rʌnwei] *n* Startbahn *f*
rural ['ruərəl] *adj* ländlich
ruse [ru:z] *n* List *f*
rush [rʌʃ] *v* eilen; *n* Binse *f*; **~ hour** Hauptverkehrszeit *f*
Russia ['rʌʃə] Russland
Russian ['rʌʃən] *adj* russisch; *n* Russe *m*, Russin *f*
rust [rʌst] *n* Rost *m*
rustic ['rʌstik] *adj* ländlich
rusty ['rʌsti] *adj* rostig

S

sack [sæk] *n* Sack *m*
sacred ['seikrid] *adj* heilig
sacrifice ['sækrifais] *n* Opfer *nt*; *v* aufopfern
sad [sæd] *adj* traurig; niedergeschlagen, betrübt, trübsinnig
saddle ['sædəl] *n* Sattel *m*
sadness ['sædnəs] *n* Traurigkeit *f*
safe [seif] *adj* sicher; *n* Safe *m*
safety ['seifti] *n* Sicherheit *f*; **~ belt** Sicherheitsgurt *m*; **~ pin** Sicherheitsnadel *f*; **~ razor** Rasierapparat *m*
sail [seil] *v* *befahren, *fahren; *n* Segel *nt*
sailing boat ['seiliŋbout] *n* Segelboot *nt*
sailor ['seilə] *n* Matrose *m*
saint [seint] *n* Heilige *m/f*
salad ['sæləd] *n* Salat *m*; **~ dressing** Salatsoße *f*; **~ oil** Salatöl *nt*
salary ['sæləri] *n* Lohn *m*, Gehalt *nt*
sale [seil] *n* Verkauf *m*; **clearance ~**

Ausverkauf *m*; **for ~** zu verkaufen; **sales** Schlussverkauf *m*; **sales tax** Verbrauchssteuer *f*
saleable ['seiləbəl] *adj* verkäuflich
salesgirl ['seilzgə:l] *n* Verkäuferin *f*
salesman ['seilzmən] *n* (pl -men) Verkäufer *m*
salmon ['sæmən] *n* (pl ~) Lachs *m*
salon ['sælɔ̃:] *n* Salon *m*
saloon [sə'lu:n] *n* Bar *f*
salt [sɔ:lt] *n* Salz *nt*; **~ cellar** *n*, *Am* **~ shaker** Salzstreuer *m*
salty ['sɔ:lti] *adj* salzig
salute [sə'lu:t] *v* grüßen
salve [sɑ:v] *n* Salbe *f*
same [seim] *adj* selb
sample ['sɑ:mpəl] *n* Muster *nt*
sanatorium [ˌsænə'tɔ:riəm] *n* (pl ~s, -ria) Sanatorium *n*
sand [sænd] *n* Sand *m*
sandal ['sændəl] *n* Sandale *f*
sandpaper ['sænd,peipə] *n* Schmirgelpapier *nt*
sandwich ['sænwidʒ] *n* Sandwich *nt*;

Butterbrot nt

sandy ['sændi] adj sandig

sanitary ['sænitəri] adj sanitär; ~ **napkin**, ~ **towel** Damenbinde f

sapphire ['sæfaiə] n Saphir m

sardine [sɑːˈdiːn] n Sardine f

satellite ['sætəlait] n Satellit m; ~ **television** Satellitenfernsehen nt

satin ['sætin] n Satin m

satisfaction [ˌsætisˈfækʃən] n Befriedigung f, Genugtuung f

satisfactory [ˌsætisˈfæktəri] adj befriedigend, zufrieden stellend

satisfy ['sætisfai] v zufriedenstellen, befriedigen; **satisfied** satt, zufrieden

Saturday ['sætədi] Sonnabend m; Samstag m

sauce [sɔːs] n Soße f

saucepan ['sɔːspən] n Pfanne f

saucer ['sɔːsə] n Untertasse f

Saudi Arabia [ˌsaudiəˈreibiə] Saudi-Arabien

Saudi Arabian [ˌsaudiəˈreibiən] adj saudiarabisch

sauna ['sɔːnə] n Sauna f

sausage ['sɔsidʒ] n Wurst f

savage ['sævidʒ] adj wild

save [seiv] v retten; sparen

savings ['seiviŋz] pl Ersparnisse fpl; ~ **bank** Sparkasse f

saviour ['seivjə] n Retter m, -in f

savoury ['seivəri] adj schmackhaft; pikant

saw¹ [sɔː] v (p see)

saw² [sɔː] n Säge f

sawdust ['sɔːdʌst] n Sägemehl nt

***say** [sei] v sagen

scaffolding ['skæfəldiŋ] n Gerüst nt

scale [skeil] n Maßstab m; Tonleiter f; Schuppe f; **scales** pl Waage f

scandal ['skændəl] n Skandal m

Scandinavia [ˌskændiˈneiviə] Skandinavien

Scandinavian [ˌskændiˈneiviən] adj skandinavisch; n Skandinavier m, -in f

scapegoat ['skeipgout] n Sündenbock m

scar [skɑː] n Narbe f

scarce [skɛəs] adj knapp

scarcely ['skɛəsli] adv kaum

scarcity ['skɛəsəti] n Mangel m

scare [skɛə] v *erschrecken; n Schreck m

scarf [skɑːf] n (pl ~s, scarves) Schal m

scarlet ['skɑːlət] adj scharlachrot

scary ['skɛəri] adj unheimlich

scatter ['skætə] v verstreuen

scene [siːn] n Szene f

scenery ['siːnəri] n Landschaft f

scenic ['siːnik] adj malerisch

scent [sent] n Parfüm nt

schedule ['ʃedjuːl] n Fahrplan m, Plan m

scheme [skiːm] n Schema nt; Plan m

scholar ['skɔlə] n Gelehrte m/f; Schüler m, -in f

scholarship ['skɔləʃip] n Stipendium nt

school [skuːl] n Schule f

schoolboy ['skuːlbɔi] n Schüler m

schoolgirl ['skuːlgəːl] n Schülerin f

schoolmaster ['skuːlˌmɑːstə] n Lehrer m, Volksschullehrer m

schoolteacher ['skuːlˌtiːtʃə] n Lehrer m, -in f

science ['saiəns] n Wissenschaft f

scientific [ˌsaiənˈtifik] adj wissenschaftlich

scientist ['saiəntist] n Wissenschaftler m, -in f

scissors ['sizəz] pl Schere f

scold [skould] v schimpfen

scooter ['skuːtə] n Motorroller m; Roller m

score [skɔː] n Spielstand m; v *anschreiben

scorn [skɔːn] n Hohn m, Verachtung

f, v verachten

Scot [skɔt] *n* Schotte *m*, Schottin *f*

Scotch [skɔtʃ] *adj* schottisch;

scotch tape Selbstklebeband *nt*

Scotland ['skɔtlənd] Schottland *nt*

Scottish ['skɔtiʃ] *adj* schottisch

scout [skaut] *n* Pfadfinder *m*

scrap [skræp] *n* Stückchen *nt*; Fetzen *m*; Rest *m*

scrapbook ['skræpbuk] *n* Sammelalbum *nt*

scrape [skreip] *v* schaben

scratch [skrætʃ] *v* kratzen; *n* Kratzer *m*, Schramme *f*

scream [skri:m] *v* kreischen, *schreien; *n* Ruf *m*, Schrei *m*

screen [skri:n] *n* Schirm *m*; Bildschirm *m*, Filmleinwand *f*

screw [skru:] *n* Schraube *f; v* schrauben

screwdriver ['skru:,draivə] *n* Schraubenzieher *m*

scrub [skrʌb] *v* scheuern; *n* Gestrüpp *nt*

sculptor ['skʌlptə] *n* Bildhauer *m*, -in *f*

sculpture ['skʌlptʃə] *n* Skulptur *f*

sea [si:] *n* Meer *nt*

seabird ['si:bə:d] *n* Seevogel *m*

seafood ['si:,fu:d] *n* Meeresfrüchte *pl*

seagull ['si:gʌl] *n* Seemöwe *f*

seal [si:l] *n* Siegel *nt*; Robbe *f*, Seehund *m*

seam [si:m] *n* Naht *f*

seaman ['si:mən] *n* (pl -men) Matrose *m*

seamless ['si:mləs] *adj* nahtlos

seaport ['si:pɔ:t] *n* Seehafen *m*

search [sə:tʃ] *v* suchen; durchsuchen; *n* Suche *f*

searchlight ['sə:tʃlait] *n* Scheinwerfer *m*

seashell ['si:ʃel] *n* Muschel *f*

seashore ['si:ʃɔ:] *n* Meeresküste *f*

seasick ['si:sik] *adj* seekrank

seasickness ['si:,siknəs] *n* Seekrankheit *f*

seaside ['si:said] *n* Küste *f*; **~ resort** Seebad *nt*

season ['si:zən] *n* Jahreszeit *f*, Saison *f*; **high ~** Hochsaison *f*; **low ~** Nachsaison *f*; **off ~** außer Saison; **~ ticket** Dauerkarte *f*

seat [si:t] *n* Sitz *m*; Platz *m*; **~ belt** Sicherheitsgurt *m*

sea urchin ['si:,ə:tʃin] *n* Seeigel *m*

sea water ['si:,wɔ:tə] *n* Meerwasser *nt*

second ['sekənd] *num* zweite; *n* Sekunde *f*; Augenblick *m*

secondary ['sekəndəri] *adj* untergeordnet; **~ school** höhere Schule

second-hand [,sekənd'hænd] *adj* gebraucht

secret ['si:krət] *n* Geheimnis *nt*; *adj* geheim

secretary ['sekrətri] *n* Sekretär *m*, -in *f*

section ['sekʃən] *n* Abschnitt *m*; Fach *nt*, Abteilung *f*

secure [si'kjuə] *adj* sicher; *v* sich sichern

security [si'kjuərəti] *n* Sicherheit *f*; Pfand *nt*

sedative ['sedətiv] *n* Beruhigungsmittel *nt*

seduce [si'dju:s] *v* verführen

***see** [si:] *v* *sehen; *begreifen, *einsehen; **~ to** sorgen für

seed [si:d] *n* Samen *m*

***seek** [si:k] *v* suchen

seem [si:m] *v* *erscheinen, *scheinen

seen [si:n] *v* (pp see)

seesaw ['si:sɔ:] *n* Wippe *f*

seize [si:z] *v* *ergreifen

seldom ['seldəm] *adv* selten

select [si'lekt] *v* *auslesen,

auswählen; *adj* erlesen

selection [si'lekʃən] *n* Wahl *f*, Auswahl *f*

self [self] selves; *n* Selbst *n*, Ich *n*; selbst..., Selbst...

self-employed [,selfim'plɔid] *adj* selbständig

self-evident [,sel'fevidənt] *adj* selbstverständlich

self-government [,self'gʌvəmənt] *n* Selbstverwaltung *f*

selfish ['selfiʃ] *adj* selbstsüchtig

selfishness ['selfiʃnəs] *n* Selbstsucht *f*

self-service [,self'səːvis] *n* Selbstbedienung *f*; ~ **restaurant** Selbstbedienungsrestaurant *nt*

***sell** [sel] *v* verkaufen

semblance ['sembləns] *n* Anschein *m*

semi- ['semi] Halb-

semicircle ['semi,səːkəl] *n* Halbkreis *m*

semicolon [,semi'koulən] *n* Strichpunkt *m*

senate ['senət] *n* Senat *m*

senator ['senətə] *n* Senator *m*, -in *f*

***send** [send] *v* schicken, *senden; ~ **back** zurückschicken, *zurücksenden; ~ **for** kommen *lassen; ~ **off** *absenden

sender ['sendə] *n* Absender *m*, -in *f*

senile ['siːnail] *adj* senil

senior ['siːnjə] *n* Ältere *m/f*; Vorgesetzte *m/f*; *adj* senior; älter, ranghöher; ~ **citizen** Rentner *m*, -in *f*

sensation [sen'seiʃən] *n* Sensation *f*; Eindruck *m*, Empfindung *f*

sensational [sen'seiʃənəl] *adj* aufsehenerregend, sensationell

sense [sens] *n* Sinn *m*; Verstand *m*, Vernunft *f*; Bedeutung *f*; *v* spüren; ~ **of honour** Ehrgefühl *nt*

senseless ['sensləs] *adj* unsinnig

sensible ['sensəbəl] *adj* verständig

sensitive ['sensitiv] *adj* empfindlich

sentence ['sentəns] *n* Satz *m*; Urteil *nt*; *v* verurteilen

sentimental [,senti'mentəl] *adj* sentimental

separate¹ ['sepəreit] *v* trennen

separate² ['sepərət] *adj* besonder, getrennt

separately ['sepərətli] *adv* getrennt, separat

September [sep'tembə] September

septic ['septik] *adj* septisch; ***become** ~ entzünden

sequel ['siːkwəl] *n* Folge *f*

sequence ['siːkwəns] *n* Reihenfolge *f*; Folge *f*

serene [sə'riːn] *adj* ruhig; klar

serial ['siəriəl] *n* Serie *f*; *adj* Fortsetzungs-...

series ['siəriːz] *n* (pl ~) Folge *f*, Serie *f*

serious ['siəriəs] *adj* seriös, ernst

seriousness ['siəriəsnəs] *n* Ernst *m*

sermon ['səːmən] *n* Predigt *f*

serum ['siərəm] *n* Serum *nt*

servant ['səːvənt] *n* Diener *m*, -in *f*

serve [səːv] *v* bedienen

service ['səːvis] *n* Dienst *m*; Bedienung *f*; ~ **charge** Bedienung *f*; ~ **station** Tankstelle *f*

serviette [,səːvi'et] *n* Serviette *f*

session ['seʃən] *n* Sitzung *f*

set [set] *n* Satz *m*, Gruppe *f*

***set** [set] *v* stellen; ~ **menu** festes Menü; ~ **out** abreisen

setting ['setiŋ] *n* Umgebung *f*

settle ['setəl] *v* erledigen, regeln; ~ **down** sich *niederlassen

settlement ['setəlmənt] *n* Regelung *f*, Vergleich *m*, Übereinkunft *f*

seven ['sevən] *num* sieben

seventeen [,sevən'tiːn] *num* siebzehn

seventeenth [,sevən'tiːnθ] *num*

siebzehnte

seventh ['sevənθ] *num* siebente

seventy ['sevənti] *num* siebzig

several ['sevərəl] *adj* etliche, mehrere

severe [si'viə] *adj* heftig, streng, ernst

sew [sou] *v* nähen; ~ **up** nähen

sewing machine ['souiŋmə,ʃi:n] *n* Nähmaschine *f*

sex [seks] *n* Geschlecht *nt*; Sex *m*

sexual ['seksuəl] *adj* sexuell

sexuality [,seksu'æləti] *n* Sexualität *f*

shade [ʃeid] *n* Schatten *m*; Farbton *m*

shadow ['ʃædou] *n* Schatten *m*

shady ['ʃeidi] *adj* schattig

*****shake** [ʃeik] *v* schütteln

shaky ['ʃeiki] *adj* wacklig

*****shall** [ʃæl] *v* *werden; sollen

shallow ['ʃælou] *adj* seicht

shame [ʃeim] *n* Schande *f*; **shame!** pfui!

shampoo [ʃæm'pu:] *n* Shampoo *nt*

shamrock ['ʃæmrɔk] *n* Kleeblatt *nt*

shape [ʃeip] *n* Form *f*; *v* bilden

share [ʃɛə] *v* teilen; *n* Teil *m*; Aktie *f*

shark [ʃɑ:k] *n* Hai *m*

sharp [ʃɑ:p] *adj* scharf

sharpen ['ʃɑ:pən] *v* *schleifen, schärfen

shave [ʃeiv] *v* sich rasieren

shaver ['ʃeivə] *n* Rasierapparat *m*

shaving brush ['ʃeiviŋbrʌʃ] *n* Rasierpinsel *m*

shaving cream ['ʃeiviŋkri:m] *n* Rasierkrem *f*

shaving soap ['ʃeiviŋsoup] *n* Rasierseife *f*

shawl [ʃɔ:l] *n* Umschlagtuch *nt*, Schal *m*

she [ʃi:] *pron* sie

shed [ʃed] *n* Schuppen *m*

*****shed** [ʃed] *v* *vergießen; verbreiten

sheep [ʃi:p] *n* (pl ~) Schaf *nt*

sheer [ʃiə] *adj* absolut, rein; dünn, durchscheinend

sheet [ʃi:t] *n* Laken *nt*; Blatt *nt*; Platte *f*

shelf [ʃelf] *n* (pl shelves) Regal *nt*

shell [ʃel] *n* Muschel *f*; Schale *f*

shellfish ['ʃelfiʃ] *n* Schalentier *nt*

shelter ['ʃeltə] *n* Schutz *m*; *v* schützen

shepherd ['ʃepəd] *n* Hirt *m*, -in *f*

shift [ʃift] *n* Schicht *f*

*****shine** [ʃain] *v* strahlen; leuchten, glänzen

ship [ʃip] *n* Schiff *nt*; *v* *versenden; **shipping line** Schifffahrtslinie *f*

shipowner ['ʃi,pounə] *n* Reeder *m*, -in *f*

shipyard ['ʃipjɑ:d] *n* Schiffswerft *f*

shirt [ʃə:t] *n* Hemd *nt*

shiver ['ʃivə] *v* zittern, frösteln; *n* Frösteln *nt*

shock [ʃɔk] *n* Schock *m*; *v* schockieren; ~ **absorber** Stoßdämpfer *m*

shocking ['ʃɔkiŋ] *adj* empörend

shoe [ʃu:] *n* Schuh *m*; **gym shoes** Turnschuhe *mpl*; ~ **polish** Schuhkrem *f*; ~ **shop** Schuhgeschäft *nt*

shoelace ['ʃu:leis] *n* Schnürsenkel *m*

shoemaker ['ʃu:,meikə] *n* Schuhmacher *m*, -in *f*

shook [ʃuk] *v* (p shake)

*****shoot** [ʃu:t] *v* *schießen

shop [ʃɔp] *n* Geschäft *nt*; *v* einkaufen; ~ **assistant** *n* Verkäufer *m*, -in *f*

shopkeeper ['ʃɔp,ki:pə] *n* Ladeninhaber *m*, -in *f*

shopping ['ʃɔpiŋ] *n* Einkauf *m*; **go ~** einkaufen gehen; ~ **bag** Einkaufstasche *f*; ~ **centre**, ~ **mall** Einkaufszentrum *nt*

shopwindow [,ʃɔp'windou] *n* Schaufenster *nt*

shore [ʃɔ:] *n* Ufer *nt*, Küste *f*

short [ʃɔ:t] *adj* kurz; klein; ~ **circuit** Kurzschluss *m*

shortage ['ʃɔːtidʒ] n Mangel m, Knappheit f

shorten ['ʃɔːtən] v verkürzen

shorthand ['ʃɔːthænd] n Stenografie f

shortly ['ʃɔːtli] adv in Kürze, bald

shorts [ʃɔːts] pl kurze Hose; plAm Unterhose f

short-sighted [,ʃɔːt'saitid] adj kurzsichtig

shot [ʃɔt] n Schuss m; Spritze f; Aufnahme f

***should** [ʃud] v *müssen

shoulder ['ʃouldə] n Schulter f

shout [ʃaut] v *schreien, *rufen; n Schrei m

shovel ['ʃʌvəl] n Schaufel f

show [ʃou] n Aufführung f, Vorstellung f; Ausstellung f

***show** [ʃou] v zeigen; sehen *lassen, ausstellen; *beweisen

showcase ['ʃoukeis] n Vitrine f

shower ['ʃauə] n Dusche f; Schauer m, Regenschauer m

showroom ['ʃouruːm] n Ausstellungsraum m

shriek [ʃriːk] v kreischen; n Gekreisch nt

shrimp [ʃrimp] n Garnele f

shrine [ʃrain] n Heiligtum nt, Schrein m

***shrink** [ʃriŋk] v schrumpfen

shrinkproof ['ʃriŋkpruːf] adj nicht einlaufend

shrub [ʃrʌb] n Strauch m

shudder ['ʃʌdə] n Schauder m

shuffle ['ʃʌfəl] v mischen

***shut** [ʃʌt] v *abschließen, *schließen; **shut** zu, geschlossen; **~ in** *einschließen

shutter ['ʃʌtə] n Fensterladen; Verschluss m

shy [ʃai] adj scheu, schüchtern

shyness ['ʃainəs] n Schüchternheit f

sick [sik] adj krank; übel

sickness ['siknəs] n Krankheit f; Übelkeit f

side [said] n Seite f; Partei f; **one-sided** adj einseitig

sideburns ['saidbəːnz] pl Koteletten

sidelight ['saidlait] n Seitenlicht nt

side street ['saidstriːt] n Seitenstraße f

sidewalk ['saidwɔːk] nAm Gehweg m, Bürgersteig m

sideways ['saidweiz] adv seitwärts

siege [siːdʒ] n Belagerung f

sieve [siv] n Sieb nt; v sieben

sift [sift] v sieben

sight [sait] n Aussicht f; Sicht f, Anblick m; Sehenswürdigkeit f

sightseeing ['sait,siːiŋ] n Besichtigung f; **~ tour** Rundreise f, Stadtrundfahrt f

sign [sain] n Zeichen nt; Gebärde f, Wink m; v unterzeichnen, *unterschreiben

signal ['signəl] n Signal nt; Zeichen nt; v signalisieren

signature ['signətʃə] n Unterschrift f

significant [sig'nifikənt] adj bedeutungsvoll

signpost ['sainpoust] n Wegweiser m

silence ['sailəns] n Stille f; v zum Schweigen *bringen

silencer ['sailənsə] n Auspufftopf m

silent ['sailənt] adj schweigend, still; ***be ~** *schweigen

silk [silk] n Seide f

silly ['sili] adj albern; dumm

silver ['silvə] n Silber nt; silbern

silverware ['silvəwɛə] n Silber nt

similar ['similə] adj derartig, ähnlich

similarity [,simi'lærəti] n Ähnlichkeit f

simple ['simpəl] adj schlicht, einfach; üblich

simply ['simpli] adv einfach

simulate ['simjuleit] v heucheln; vortäuschen

simultaneous [,siməl'teiniəs] adj gleichzeitig

sin [sin] n Sünde f

since [sins] prep seit; adv seither; conj seitdem; da

sincere [sin'siə] adj aufrichtig; **yours sincerely** mit freundlichen Grüßen

sinew ['sinju:] n Sehne f

*sing [siŋ] v *singen

singer ['siŋə] n Sänger m, -in f

single ['siŋgəl] adj einzig; ledig

singular ['siŋgjulə] n Einzahl f; adj merkwürdig

sinister ['sinistə] adj unheilvoll

sink [siŋk] n Ausguss m

*sink [siŋk] v *sinken

sip [sip] n Schlückchen nt

sir [sə:] mein Herr

siren ['saiərən] n Sirene f

sister ['sistə] n Schwester f

sister-in-law ['sistərinlɔ:] n (pl sisters-) Schwägerin f

*sit [sit] v *sitzen; **~ down** sich setzen

site [sait] n Gelände nt; Lage f

sitting room ['sitiŋru:m] n Wohnzimmer nt

situated ['sitʃueitid] adj gelegen

situation [,sitʃu'eiʃən] n Lage f

six [siks] num sechs

sixteen [,siks'ti:n] num sechzehn

sixteenth [,siks'ti:nθ] num sechzehnte

sixth [siksθ] num sechste

sixty ['siksti] num sechzig

size [saiz] n Größe f, Nummer f; Ausmaß nt; Format nt

skate [skeit] v *eislaufen; n Schlittschuh m

skating rink ['skeitiŋriŋk] n Eisbahn f

skeleton ['skelitən] n Gerippe nt, Skelett nt

sketch [sketʃ] n Zeichnung f, Skizze f;

v zeichnen, skizzieren

ski¹ [ski:] v Ski *laufen

ski² [ski:] n (pl ~, ~s) Ski m; **~ boots** Skischuhe mpl; **~ jump** Skisprung m; **~ lift** Skilift m; **~ pants** Skihose f; **~ poles** Am Skistöcke mpl; **~ sticks** Skistöcke mpl

skid [skid] v schleudern

skier ['ski:ə] n Skiläufer m, -in f

skiing ['ski:iŋ] n Skilauf m

skil(l)ful ['skilfəl] adj geschickt, gewandt

skill [skil] n Fertigkeit f

skilled [skild] adj geübt, geschickt; erfahren

skin [skin] n Fell nt, Haut f, Schale f; **~ cream** Hautkrem f

skip [skip] v hüpfen; *übergehen; ausfallen *lassen

skirt [skə:t] n Rock m

skull [skʌl] n Schädel m

sky [skai] n Himmel m; Luft f

skyscraper ['skai,skreipə] n Wolkenkratzer m

slack [slæk] adj träge

slacks [slæks] pl Hose f

slam [slæm] v *zuschlagen

slander ['slɑ:ndə] n Verleumdung f

slang [slæŋ] n Slang m, Jargon m

slant [slɑ:nt] v sich neigen

slanting ['slɑ:ntiŋ] adj schief, abschüssig, schräg

slap [slæp] v *schlagen; n Schlag m

slate [sleit] n Schiefer m

slave [sleiv] n Sklave m, Sklavin f

sled [sled] nAm Schlitten m

sledge [sledʒ] n Schlitten m

sleep [sli:p] n Schlaf m

*sleep [sli:p] v *schlafen

sleeping bag ['sli:piŋbæg] n Schlafsack m

sleeping car ['sli:piŋkɑ:] n Schlafwagen m

sleeping pill ['sli:piŋpil] n

Schlafmittel *nt*
sleepless ['sli:pləs] *adj* schlaflos
sleepy ['sli:pi] *adj* schläfrig
sleeve [sli:v] *n* Ärmel *m*; Hülle *f*
sleigh [slei] *n* Schlitten *m*
slender ['slendə] *adj* schlank
slice [slais] *n* Schnitte *f*
slide [slaid] *n* Rutschbahn *f*; Dia *nt*
*slide [slaid] *v* *gleiten
slight [slait] *adj* leicht; geringfügig
slim [slim] *adj* schlank; *v* *abnehmen
slip [slip] *v* *ausgleiten *f*, ausrutschen;
    entwischen; *n* Fehltritt *m*; Unterrock
    m
slipper ['slipə] *n* Hausschuh *m*,
    Pantoffel *m*
slippery ['slipəri] *adj* glitschig,
    schlüpfrig
slogan ['slougən] *n* Wahlspruch *m*,
    Schlagwort *nt*
slope [sloup] *n* Abhang *m*; *v* *abfallen
sloping ['sloupiŋ] *adj* abschüssig
sloppy ['slɔpi] *adj* schlampig
slot [slɔt] *n* Schlitz *m*; ~ **machine**
    Automat *m*
slovenly ['slʌvənli] *adj* unordentlich
slow [slou] *adj* schwerfällig, langsam;
    ~ **down** verzögern, verlangsamen;
    abbremsen
sluice [slu:s] *n* Schleuse *f*
slum [slʌm] *n* Elendsviertel *nt*
slump [slʌmp] *n* Preissturz *m*
slush [slʌʃ] *n* Matsch *m*
sly [slai] *adj* listig
smack [smæk] *v* *schlagen; *n* Klaps *m*
small [smɔ:l] *adj* klein; gering
smallpox ['smɔ:lpɔks] *n* Pocken *fpl*
smart [smɑ:t] *adj* elegant; gewandt,
    gescheit
smash [smæʃ] *n* heftiger Schlag;
    Schmetterschlag *m*; *v* zertrümmern;
    schmettern
smell [smel] *n* Geruch *m*
*smell [smel] *v* *riechen; *stinken

smelly ['smeli] *adj* übel riechend
smile [smail] *v* lächeln; *n* Lächeln *nt*
smith [smiθ] *n* Schmied *m*, -in *f*
smog [smɔg] *n* Smog *m*, Dunstglocke
    f
smoke [smouk] *v* rauchen; *n* Rauch
    m; **no smoking** Rauchen verboten
smoker ['smoukə] *n* Raucher *m*, -in *f*;
    Raucherabteil *nt*
smoking compartment
    ['smoukiŋkəm,pa:tmənt] *n*
    Raucherabteil *nt*
smooth [smu:ð] *adj* eben, flach, glatt;
    geschmeidig
smuggle ['smʌgəl] *v* schmuggeln
snack [snæk] *n* Imbiss *m*; ~ **bar**
    Snackbar *f*
snail [sneil] *n* Schnecke *f*
snake [sneik] *n* Schlange *f*
snapshot ['snæpʃɔt] *n*
    Schnappschuss *m*
sneakers ['sni:kəz] *plAm*
    Turnschuhe *mpl*
sneeze [sni:z] *v* niesen
sniper ['snaipə] *n* Heckenschütze *m*
snooty ['snu:ti] *adj* hochnäsig
snore [snɔ:] *v* schnarchen
snorkel ['snɔ:kəl] *n* Schnorchel *m*
snout [snaut] *n* Schnauze *f*
snow [snou] *n* Schnee *m*; *v* schneien
snowstorm ['snoustɔ:m] *n*
    Schneesturm *m*
snowy ['snoui] *adj* schneebedeckt,
    verschneit
so [sou] *conj* also; *adv* so; dermaßen;
    and ~ on und so weiter; ~ **far** bisher; ~
    that sodass, damit
soak [souk] *v* einweichen, weichen,
    durchnässen
soap [soup] *n* Seife *f*; ~ **powder**
    Seifenpulver *nt*
sober ['soubə] *adj* nüchtern;
    besonnen
so-called [,sou'kɔ:ld] *adj* so genannt

soccer ['sɔkə] n Fußball m; ~ **team**
Elf f

social ['souʃəl] adj Gesellschafts-,
sozial

socialism ['souʃəlizəm] n
Sozialismus m

socialist ['souʃəlist] adj sozialistisch;
n Sozialist m, -in f

society [sə'saiəti] n Gesellschaft f;
Verein m

sock [sɔk] n Socke f

socket ['sɔkit] n Fassung f

soda ['soudə] nAm Limo(nade) f; ~
water Selterswasser nt, Sodawasser
nt

sofa ['soufə] n Sofa nt

soft [sɔft] adj weich; ~ **drink**
alkoholfreies Getränk

soften ['sɔfən] v mildern

software ['sɔftweə] n Software f

soil [sɔil] n Erde f; Erdboden m,
Boden m

soiled [sɔild] adj beschmutzt

solar ['soulə] adj Sonnen...; ~ **system**
Sonnensystem nt

sold [sould] v (p, pp sell); ~ **out**
ausverkauft

soldier ['sould3ə] n Soldat m, -in f

sole¹ [soul] adj einzig

sole² [soul] n Sohle f; Seezunge f

solely ['soulli] adv ausschließlich

solemn ['sɔləm] adj feierlich

solicitor [sə'lisitə] n Anwalt m,
Anwältin f

solid ['sɔlid] adj stark, fest; massiv; n
Festkörper m

soluble ['sɔljubəl] adj löslich

solution [sə'lu:ʃən] n Lösung f

solve [sɔlv] v lösen

sombre ['sɔmbə] adj düster

some [sʌm] adj einige; pron manche;
was; ~ **day** eines Tages; ~ **more** etwas
mehr; ~ **time** einmal

somebody ['sʌmbədi] pron jemand

somehow ['sʌmhau] adv irgendwie

someone ['sʌmwʌn] pron jemand

something ['sʌmθiŋ] pron etwas

sometimes ['sʌmtaimz] adv
manchmal

somewhat ['sʌmwɔt] adv ziemlich

somewhere ['sʌmweə] adv irgendwo

son [sʌn] n Sohn m

song [sɔŋ] n Lied nt

son-in-law ['sʌninlɔ:] n (pl sons-)
Schwiegersohn m

soon [su:n] adv in Kürze, bald; **as ~
as** so bald wie

sooner ['su:nə] adv lieber

sore [sɔ:] adj schmerzhaft, wund; n
wunde Stelle; Geschwür nt; ~ **throat**
Halsschmerzen mpl

sorrow ['sɔrou] n Leid nt, Kummer m

sorry ['sɔri] adj bekümmert; **sorry!**
Verzeihung!, Entschuldigung!

sort [sɔ:t] v sortieren, ordnen; n Art f,
Sorte f; **all sorts of** allerlei

soul [soul] n Seele f; Geist m

sound [saund] n Klang m, Schall m; v
*klingen, erschallen; adj zuverlässig

soundproof ['saundpru:f] adj
schalldicht

soup [su:p] n Suppe f

sour [sauə] adj sauer

source [sɔ:s] n Quelle f

south [sauθ] n Süden m; **South Pole**
Südpol m

South Africa [sauθ 'æfrikə] Südafrika

southeast [,sauθ'i:st] n Südosten m

southerly ['sʌðəli] adj südlich

southern ['sʌðən] adj südlich

southwest [,sauθ'west] n Südwesten
m

souvenir ['su:vəniə] n Andenken nt

sovereign ['sɔvrin] n Herrscher m,
-in f

***sow** [sou] v säen

spa [spa:] n Heilbad nt

space [speis] n Raum m; Abstand m,

Zwischenraum *m*; Weltraum *m*; *v* in Abständen anordnen; **~shuttle** Raumfähre *f*

spacious ['speiʃəs] *adj* geräumig

spade [speid] *n* Schaufel *f*, Spaten *m*

Spain [spein] Spanien

Spaniard ['spænjəd] *n* Spanier *m*, -in *f* **Spanish** ['spæniʃ] *adj* spanisch

spanking ['spæŋkiŋ] *n* Prügel *pl*

spanner ['spænə] *n* Schraubenschlüssel *m*

spare [spɛə] *adj* Reserve-, überschüssig; *v* entbehren; **~ part** Ersatzteil *nt*; **~ room** Gästezimmer *nt*; **~ time** Freizeit *f*; **~ tyre** Ersatzreifen *m*; **~ wheel** Reserverad *nt*

spark [spɑːk] *n* Funken *m*

sparking plug ['spɑːkiŋplʌg] *n* Zündkerze *f*

sparkling ['spɑːkliŋ] *adj* funkelnd; perlend

sparrow ['spærou] *n* Sperling *m*

spasm ['spæzəm] *n* Krampf *m*, Spasmus *m*

speak [spiːk] *v* *sprechen

speaker ['spiːkə] *n* Sprecher *m*, -in *f*

spear [spiə] *n* Speer *m*

special ['speʃəl] *adj* besonder, speziell

specialist ['speʃəlist] *n* Spezialist *m*, -in *f*

speciality [,speʃi'æləti] *n* Spezialität *f*

specialize ['speʃəlaiz] *v* sich spezialisieren

specially ['speʃəli] *adv* im einzelnen

species ['spiːʃiːz] *n* (pl ~) Art *f*

specific [spə'sifik] *adj* spezifisch

specimen ['spesimən] *n* Exemplar *nt*

speck [spek] *n* Fleck *m*

spectacle ['spektəkəl] *n* Schauspiel *nt*; **spectacles** Brille *f*

spectator [spek'teitə] *n* Zuschauer *m*, -in *f*

speculate ['spekjuleit] *v* spekulieren

speech [spiːtʃ] *n* Sprache *f*; Ansprache *f*, Rede *f*

speechless ['spiːtʃləs] *adj* sprachlos

speed [spiːd] *n* Geschwindigkeit *f*; Schnelligkeit *f*, Eile *f*; **cruising ~** Reisegeschwindigkeit *f*; **~ limit** Höchstgeschwindigkeit *f*, Geschwindigkeitsbegrenzung *f*

*speed [spiːd] *v* rasen; zu schnell *fahren

speeding ['spiːdiŋ] *n* Geschwindigkeitsübertretung *f*

speedometer [spiː'dɔmitə] *n* Geschwindigkeitsmesser *m*

spell [spel] *n* Zauber *m*

*spell [spel] *v* buchstabieren

spelling ['speliŋ] *n* Rechtschreibung *f*

*spend [spend] *v* verausgaben, *ausgeben; *verbringen

sphere [sfiə] *n* Kugel *f*; Kreis *m*

spice [spais] *n* Gewürz *nt*

spiced [spaist] *adj* gewürzt

spicy ['spaisi] *adj* pikant

spider ['spaidə] *n* Spinne *f*; **spider's web** Spinnwebe *f*

*spill [spil] *v* verschütten

*spin [spin] *v* *spinnen; wirbeln

spinach ['spinidʒ] *n* Spinat *m*

spine [spain] *n* Rückgrat *nt*

spinster ['spinstə] *n* alte Jungfer

spire [spaiə] *n* (Kirchturm)Spitze *f*

spirit ['spirit] *n* Geist *m*; Laune *f*; **spirits** alkoholische Getränke, Spirituosen *pl*; Stimmung *f*; **~ stove** Spirituskocher *m*

spiritual ['spiritʃuəl] *adj* geistig

spit [spit] *n* Speichel *m*, Spucke *f*; Bratspieß *m*

*spit [spit] *v* spucken

spite [spait] *n* Gehässigkeit *f*; *v* j-m eins auswischen; **in ~ of** ungeachtet, trotz

spiteful ['spaitfəl] *adj* gehässig

splash [splæʃ] v bespritzen

splendid ['splendid] adj prächtig, herrlich

splendour ['splendə] n Pracht f

splint [splint] n Schiene f

splinter ['splintə] n Splitter m

*__split__ [split] v spalten

*__spoil__ [spɔil] v *verderben; verwöhnen

spoke[1] [spouk] v (p speak)

spoke[2] [spouk] n Speiche f

sponge [spʌndʒ] n Schwamm m

spook [spu:k] n Gespenst nt, Geist m

spool [spu:l] n Spule f

spoon [spu:n] n Löffel m

spoonful ['spu:nful] n Löffel voll

sport [spɔ:t] n Sport m

sports car ['spɔ:tska:] n Sportwagen m

sports jacket ['spɔ:ts,dʒækit] n Sportjacke f

sportsman ['spɔ:tsmən] n (pl -men) Sportler m

sportswear ['spɔ:tsweə] n Sportkleidung f

sportswoman ['spɔ:tswumən] n (pl -women) Sportlerin f

spot [spɔt] n Klecks m, Fleck m; Stelle f, Platz m

spotless ['spɔtləs] adj fleckenlos

spotlight ['spɔtlait] n Scheinwerfer m

spotted ['spɔtid] adj gesprenkelt

spout [spaut] n Strahl m

sprain [sprein] v verstauchen; n Verstauchung f

spray [sprei] n Gischt f; Spray(dose f) nt; v (ver)sprühen; Pflanzen spritzen

*__spread__ [spred] v ausbreiten

spring [spriŋ] n Frühling m; Feder f; Quelle f

springtime ['spriŋtaim] n Frühling m

sprouts [sprauts] pl Rosenkohl m

spy [spai] n Spion m, -in f

square [skweə] adj quadratisch; n Quadrat nt; Platz m

squash [skwɔʃ] n Fruchtsaft m; Am Zucchini f; Squash nt

squeeze [skwi:z] v quetschen, drücken; Obst auspressen

squirrel ['skwirəl] n Eichhörnchen nt

squirt [skwə:t] n Strahl m

stable ['steibəl] adj stabil; n Stall m

stack [stæk] n Stapel m

stadium ['steidiəm] n Stadion nt

staff [sta:f] n Personal nt

stage [steidʒ] n Bühne f; Phase f, Stadium nt; Etappe f

stain [stein] v beflecken; n Klecks m, Fleck m; **stained glass** buntes Glas; ~ **remover** Fleckenreinigungsmittel nt

stainless ['steinləs] adj fleckenlos; ~ **steel** rostfreier Stahl, Edelstahl m

staircase ['steəkeis] n Treppe f

stairs [steəz] pl Treppe f

stale [steil] adj altbacken

stamp [stæmp] n Briefmarke f; Stempel m; v frankieren; stampfen

stand [stænd] n Stand m; Tribüne f

*__stand__ [stænd] v *stehen

standard ['stændəd] n Norm f, Maßstab m; Standard-; ~ **of living** Lebensstandard m

stanza ['stænzə] n Strophe f

staple ['steipəl] n Heftklammer f

star [sta:] n Stern m

starboard ['sta:bəd] n Steuerbord nt

stare [steə] v starren

starling ['sta:liŋ] n Star m

start [sta:t] v *anfangen; n Anfang m

starting point ['sta:tiŋpɔint] n Ausgangspunkt m

state [steit] n Staat m; Zustand m; v nennen, erklären; darlegen

the States Vereinigte Staaten von Amerika

statement ['steitmənt] n Erklärung f

statesman ['steitsmən] n (pl -men)

Staatsmann *m*

station ['steiʃən] *n* Bahnhof *m*; Stelle *f*

stationary ['steiʃənəri] *adj* stillstehend

stationer's ['steiʃənəz] *n* Schreibwarenhandlung *f*

stationery ['steiʃənəri] *n* Schreibwaren *fpl*

statistics [stə'tistiks] *pl* Statistik *f*

statue ['stætʃuː] *n* Standbild *nt*

stay [stei] *v* *bleiben; verweilen, sich *aufhalten; *n* Aufenthalt *m*

steadfast ['stedfaːst] *adj* standhaft

steady ['stedi] *adj* beständig

steak [steik] *n* Steak *nt*

***steal** [stiːl] *v* *stehlen

steam [stiːm] *n* Dampf *m*

steamer ['stiːmə] *n* Dampfer *m*

steel [stiːl] *n* Stahl *m*

steep [stiːp] *adj* schroff, steil

steeple ['stiːpəl] *n* Kirchturm *m*

steer [stiə] *v* steuern, lenken

steering wheel ['stiəriŋwiːl] *n* Steuerrad *nt*

steersman ['stiəzmən] *n* (pl -men) Steuermann *m*

stem [stem] *n* Stiel *m*

step [step] *n* Schritt *m*, Tritt *m*; Stufe *f*; *v* *treten

stepchild ['steptʃaild] *n* (pl -children) Stiefkind *nt*

stepfather ['step,faːðə] *n* Stiefvater *m*

stepmother ['step,mʌðə] *n* Stiefmutter *f*

stereo [steriou] *n* Stereo *nt*; *colloquial* Stereogerät *nt*

sterile ['sterail] *adj* steril

sterilize ['sterilaiz] *v* sterilisieren

steward ['stjuːəd] *n* Steward *m*

stewardess ['stjuːədes] *n* Stewardess *f*

stick [stik] *n* Stock *m*

***stick** [stik] *v* kleben, ankleben

sticker ['stikə] *n* Aufkleber *m*

sticky ['stiki] *adj* klebrig

stiff [stif] *adj* steif

still [stil] *adv* noch; dennoch; *adj* still

stimulant ['stimjulənt] *n* Reizmittel *nt*

stimulate ['stimjuleit] *v* anspornen

sting [stiŋ] *n* Stich *m*

***sting** [stiŋ] *v* *stechen

stingy ['stindʒi] *adj* kleinlich

***stink** [stiŋk] *v* *stinken

stipulate ['stipjuleit] *v* vereinbaren, festsetzen

stipulation [,stipju'leiʃən] *n* Klausel *f*

stir [stəː] *v* bewegen; rühren

stitch [stitʃ] *n* Stich *m*, Stechen *nt*

stock [stɔk] *n* Vorrat *m*; *v* vorrätig *haben; ~ **exchange** Börse *f*; ~ **market** Börse *f*; **stocks and shares** Aktien

stocking ['stɔkiŋ] *n* Strumpf *m*

stole[1] [stoul] *v* (p steal)

stole[2] [stoul] *n* Stola *f*

stomach ['stʌmək] *n* Magen *m*; ~ **ache** Bauchschmerzen *mpl*, Magenschmerzen *mpl*

stone [stoun] *n* Stein *m*; Edelstein *m*; Kern *m*; steinern

stood [stud] *v* (p, pp stand)

stop [stɔp] *v* aufhören; aufhören mit, einstellen; *n* Haltestelle *f*; **stop!** halt!

stopper ['stɔpə] *n* Stöpsel *m*

storage ['stɔːridʒ] *n* Lagerung *f*

store [stɔː] *n* Vorrat *m*; Laden *m*; *v* lagern; ~ **house** Lagerhaus *nt*

storey ['stɔːri] *n* Etage *f*, Stockwerk *nt*

stork [stɔːk] *n* Storch *m*

storm [stɔːm] *n* Sturm *m*

stormy ['stɔːmi] *adj* stürmisch

story ['stɔːri] *n* Geschichte *f*

stout [staut] *adj* dick, stämmig, korpulent

stove [stouv] *n* Ofen *m*; Herd *m*

straight [streit] *adj* gerade; ehrlich; *adv* geradewegs; **~ ahead** geradeaus; **~ away** sofort; **~ on** geradeaus

strain [strein] *n* Anstrengung *f*; Anspannung *f*; *v* forcieren; sich anstrengen; abgießen

strainer ['streinə] *n* Sieb *m*

strange [streindʒ] *adj* fremd; komisch

stranger ['streindʒə] *n* Fremde *m/f*; Unbekannte *m/f*

strangle ['stræŋgəl] *v* erwürgen

strap [stræp] *n* Riemen *m*

straw [strɔ:] *n* Stroh *nt*

strawberry ['strɔ:bəri] *n* Erdbeere *f*

stream [stri:m] *n* Bach *m*; *v* strömen

street [stri:t] *n* Straße *f*

streetcar ['stri:tkɑ:] *nAm* Straßenbahn *f*

strength [streŋθ] *n* Stärke *f*, Kraft *f*

stress [stres] *n* Spannung *f*; Betonung *f*; *v* betonen

stretch [stretʃ] *v* dehnen; *n* Strecke *f*

strict [strikt] *adj* streng

strike [straik] *n* Streik *m*

***strike** [straik] *v* *schlagen; *zuschlagen; *auffallen; streiken; *streichen

striking ['straikiŋ] *adj* treffend, erstaunlich, auffallend

string [striŋ] *n* Schnur *f*; Saite *f*

strip [strip] *n* Streifen *m*

stripe [straip] *n* Streifen *m*

striped [straipt] *adj* gestreift

stroke [strouk] *n* Schlaganfall *m*

stroll [stroul] *v* bummeln; *n* Bummel *m*

strong [strɔŋ] *adj* stark; kräftig

stronghold ['strɔŋhould] *n* Burg *f*

structure ['strʌktʃə] *n* Struktur *f*

struggle ['strʌgəl] *n* Kampf *m*, Ringen *nt*; *v* *ringen, kämpfen

stub [stʌb] *n* Kontrollabschnitt *m*

stubborn ['stʌbən] *adj* hartnäckig

student ['stju:dənt] *n* Student *m*, -in *f*

studies ['stʌdiz] *n pl* Studium *nt*

study ['stʌdi] *v* studieren; *n* Studium *nt*

stuff [stʌf] *n* Stoff *m*; Zeug *nt*

stuffed [stʌft] *adj* gefüllt

stuffing ['stʌfiŋ] *n* Füllung *f*

stuffy ['stʌfi] *adj* stickig

stumble ['stʌmbəl] *v* stolpern

stung [stʌŋ] *v* (p, pp sting)

stupid ['stju:pid] *adj* dumm

style [stail] *n* Stil *m*

subject[1] ['sʌbdʒikt] *n* Subjekt *nt*; Staatsangehörige *m/f*; **~ to** ausgesetzt

subject[2] [səb'dʒekt] *v* *unterwerfen

submarine ['sʌbməri:n] *n* U-Boot *nt*

submit [səb'mit] *v* sich *unterwerfen

subordinate [sə'bɔ:dinət] *adj* Unter-; untergeordnet

subscriber [səb'skraibə] *n* Abonnent *m*, -in *f*

subscription [səb'skripʃən] *n* Abonnement *nt*

subsequent ['sʌbsikwənt] *adj* folgend

subsidy ['sʌbsidi] *n* Subvention *f*

substance ['sʌbstəns] *n* Substanz *f*

substantial [səb'stænʃəl] *adj* sachlich; wirklich; bedeutend

substitute ['sʌbstitju:t] *v* ersetzen; *n* Ersatz *m*; Stellvertreter *m*, -in *f*

subtitle ['sʌb,taitəl] *n* Untertitel *m*

subtle ['sʌtəl] *adj* subtil

subtract [səb'trækt] *v* subtrahieren

suburb ['sʌbə:b] *n* Vorort *m*, Vorstadt *f*

suburban [sə'bə:bən] *adj* vorstädtisch

subway ['sʌbwei] *nAm* Untergrundbahn *f*

succeed [sək'si:d] *v* *gelingen; nachfolgen

success [sək'ses] *n* Erfolg *m*

successful [sək'sesfəl] *adj* erfolgreich

succumb [sə'kʌm] v *erliegen

such [sʌtʃ] adj solch; adv so; ~ **as** wie

suck [sʌk] v saugen; lutschen

sudden ['sʌdən] adj plötzlich

suddenly ['sʌdənli] adv plötzlich

suede [sweid] n Wildleder nt

suffer ['sʌfə] v *leiden; *erleiden

suffering ['sʌfəriŋ] n Leiden nt

suffice [sə'fais] v reichen

sufficient [sə'fiʃənt] adj hinreichend, genügend

suffrage ['sʌfridʒ] n Wahlrecht nt

sugar ['ʃugə] n Zucker m

suggest [sə'dʒest] v *vorschlagen

suggestion [sə'dʒestʃən] n Vorschlag m

suicide ['su:isaid] n Selbstmord m

suit [su:t] v passen; anpassen an; kleiden; n Anzug m

suitable ['su:təbəl] adj angemessen, geeignet

suitcase ['su:tkeis] n Handkoffer m

sum [sʌm] n Summe f

summary ['sʌməri] n Zusammenfassung f

summer ['sʌmə] n Sommer m; ~ **time** Sommerzeit f

summit ['sʌmit] n Gipfel m

sun [sʌn] n Sonne f

sunbathe ['sʌnbeið] v sich sonnen

sunburn ['sʌnbə:n] n Sonnenbrand m

Sunday ['sʌndi] n Sonntag m

sunglasses ['sʌn,glɑːsiz] pl Sonnenbrille f

sunlight ['sʌnlait] n Sonnenlicht nt

sunny ['sʌni] adj sonnig

sunrise ['sʌnraiz] n Sonnenaufgang m

sunset ['sʌnset] n Sonnenuntergang m

sunshade ['sʌnʃeid] n Sonnenschirm m

sunshine ['sʌnʃain] n Sonnenschein m

sunstroke ['sʌnstrouk] n Sonnenstich m

suntan oil ['sʌntænɔil] Sonnenöl nt

super ['sju:pə] adj colloquial super, toll, geil; Super ...

superb [su'pə:b] adj großartig, prächtig

superficial [,su:pə'fiʃəl] adj oberflächlich

superfluous [su'pə:fluəs] adj überflüssig

superior [su'piəriə] adj überlegen, besser, überragend, ober

superlative [su'pə:lətiv] adj überragend; n Superlativ m

supermarket ['su:pə,mɑːkit] n Supermarkt m

superstition [,su:pə'stiʃən] n Aberglaube m

supervise ['su:pəvaiz] v beaufsichtigen

supervision [,su:pə'viʒən] n Kontrolle f, Aufsicht f

supper ['sʌpə] n Abendessen nt

supple ['sʌpəl] adj biegsam, geschmeidig, gelenkig

supplement ['sʌplimənt] n Beilage f

supply [sə'plai] n Zufuhr f, Lieferung f; Vorrat m; Angebot nt; v liefern

support [sə'pɔ:t] v unterstützen, stützen; n Unterstützung f

supporter [sə'pɔ:tə] n Anhänger m, -in f

suppose [sə'pouz] v vermuten, *annehmen; **supposing that** angenommen dass

suppository [sə'pozitəri] n Zäpfchen nt

suppress [sə'pres] v unterdrücken

surcharge ['sə:tʃɑːdʒ] n Zuschlag m

sure [ʃuə] adj sicher

surely ['ʃuəli] adv sicherlich

surface ['sə:fis] n Oberfläche f

surfboard ['sə:fbɔːd] n Surfbrett nt

surgeon ['sə:dʒən] *n* Chirurg *m*, -in *f*;
 veterinary ~ Tierarzt *m*, Tierärztin *f*
surgery ['sə:dʒəri] *n* Operation *f*;
 Sprechzimmer *nt*
surname ['sə:neim] *n* Familienname
 m
surplus ['sə:pləs] *n* Überschuss *m*
surprise [sə'praiz] *n* Überraschung *f*;
 v überraschen; erstaunen
surrender [sə'rendə] *v* sich *ergeben;
 n Übergabe *f*
surround [sə'raund] *v* umringen,
 *umgeben
surrounding [sə'raundiŋ] *adj*
 umliegend
surroundings [sə'raundiŋz] *pl*
 Umgebung *f*
survey ['sə:vei] *n* Übersicht *f*
survival [sə'vaivəl] *n* Überleben *nt*
survive [sə'vaiv] *v* überleben
suspect[1] [sə'spekt] *v* verdächtigen;
 vermuten
suspect[2] ['sʌspekt] *n* Verdächtige *m/f*
suspend [sə'spend] *v* suspendieren
suspenders [sə'spendəz] *plAm*
 Hosenträger *mpl*
suspension [sə'spenʃən] *n* Federung
 f, Aufhängung *f*; **~ bridge**
 Hängebrücke *f*
suspicion [sə'spiʃən] *n* Verdacht *m*
 Misstrauen *nt*
suspicious [sə'spiʃəs] *adj* verdächtig;
 misstrauisch
sustain [sə'stein] *v* *aushalten
Swahili [swə'hi:li] *n* Suaheli *nt*
swallow ['swɔlou] *v* *verschlingen,
 schlucken; *n* Schwalbe *f*
swam [swæm] *v* (p swim)
swamp [swɔmp] *n* Morast *m*
swan [swɔn] *n* Schwan *m*
swap [swɔp] *v* tauschen
***swear** [sweə] *v* *schwören; fluchen
sweat [swet] *n* Schweiß *m*; *v*
 schwitzen

sweater ['swetə] *n* Pullover *m*
Swede [swi:d] *n* Schwede *m*,
 Schwedin *f*
Sweden ['swi:dən] Schweden
Swedish ['swi:diʃ] *adj* schwedisch
***sweep** [swi:p] *v* fegen
sweet [swi:t] *adj* süß; lieb; *n* Bonbon
 m; Nachtisch *m*; **sweets** Süßigkeiten
 fpl
sweeten ['swi:tən] *v* süßen
sweetheart ['swi:tha:t] *n* Schatz *m*,
 Liebling *m*
sweetshop ['swi:tʃɔp] *n*
 Süßwarengeschäft *nt*
swell [swel] *adj* wunderbar
***swell** [swel] *v* *schwellen
swelling ['sweliŋ] *n* Geschwulst *f*
swift [swift] *adj* geschwind
***swim** [swim] *v* *schwimmen
swimmer ['swimə] *n* Schwimmer *m*,
 -in *f*
swimming ['swimiŋ] *n*
 Schwimmsport *m*; **~ pool**
 Schwimmbad *nt*
swimmingtrunks ['swimiŋtrʌŋks] *n*
 Badehose *f*
swimsuit ['swimsu:t] *n* Badeanzug *m*
swindle ['swindəl] *v* *betrügen; *n*
 Betrug *m*
swindler ['swindlə] *n* Betrüger *m*, -in
 f
swing [swiŋ] *n* Schaukel *f*
***swing** [swiŋ] *v* schaukeln
Swiss [swis] *adj* schweizerisch; *n*
 Schweizer *m*, -in *f*
switch [switʃ] *n* Schalter *m*; *v*
 wechseln; **~ off** ausschalten; **~ on**
 einschalten
Switzerland ['switsələnd] Schweiz *f*
sword [sɔ:d] *n* Schwert *nt*
swum [swʌm] *v* (pp swim)
syllable ['siləbəl] *n* Silbe *f*
symbol ['simbəl] *n* Symbol *nt*
sympathetic [,simpə'θetik] *adj*

sympathisch, mitfühlend
sympathy ['simpəθi] n Sympathie f; Mitgefühl nt
symphony ['simfəni] n Symphonie f
symptom ['simtəm] n Symptom nt
synagogue ['sinəgɔg] n Synagoge f
synonym ['sinənim] n Synonym nt
synthetic [sin'θetik] adj synthetisch
Syria ['siriə] Syrien

Syrian ['siriən] adj syrisch; n Syrer m, -in f
syringe [si'rindʒ] n Spritze f
syrup ['sirəp] n Sirup m
system ['sistəm] n System nt; Ordnung f; **decimal ~** Dezimalsystem nt
systematic [,sistə'mætik] adj systematisch

T

table ['teibəl] n Tisch m; Tabelle f; **~ of contents** Inhaltsverzeichnis nt; **~ tennis** Tischtennis nt
tablecloth ['teibəlklɔθ] n Tischtuch nt
tablespoon ['teibəlspu:n] n Esslöffel m
tablet ['tæblit] n Tablette f
taboo [tə'bu:] n Tabu nt
tactics ['tæktiks] pl Taktik f
tag [tæg] n Etikett nt
tail [teil] n Schwanz m
taillight ['teillait] n Rücklicht nt
tailor ['teilə] n Schneider m
tailor-made ['teiləmeid] adj nach Maß
***take** [teik] v *nehmen; *greifen; *bringen; *verstehen, kapieren; **~ away** entfernen; *wegnehmen; **~ off** starten; **~ out** *herausnehmen; **~ over** *übernehmen; **~ place** *stattfinden; **~ up** *einnehmen
take-off ['teikɔf] n Start m
tale [teil] n Geschichte f, Erzählung f
talent ['tælənt] n Begabung f, Talent nt
talented ['tæləntid] adj begabt
talk [tɔ:k] v reden, *sprechen; n Gespräch nt

talkative ['tɔ:kətiv] adj gesprächig
tall [tɔ:l] adj hoch; lang, groß
tame [teim] adj zahm; v zähmen
tampon ['tæmpən] n Tampon m
tangerine [,tændʒə'ri:n] n Mandarine f
tangible ['tændʒibəl] adj greifbar, handfest
tank [tæŋk] n Tank m
tanker ['tæŋkə] n Tankschiff nt
tanned [tænd] adj braun
tap [tæp] n Hahn m; Klopfen nt; v pochen
tape [teip] n Band nt; Kordel f; **adhesive ~** Klebestreifen m; Heftpflaster nt
tar [ta:] n Teer m
target ['ta:git] n Ziel nt, Zielscheibe f
tariff ['tærif] n Tarif m
task [ta:sk] n Aufgabe f
taste [teist] n Geschmack m; v schmecken; kosten
tasteless ['teistləs] adj geschmacklos
tasty ['teisti] adj lecker, schmackhaft
taught [tɔ:t] v (p, pp teach)
tavern ['tævən] n Schenke f
tax [tæks] n Steuer f; v besteuern
taxation [tæk'seiʃən] n Besteuerung f
tax-free ['tæksfri:] adj steuerfrei

taxi ['tæksi] *n* Taxi *nt*; ~ **driver** Taxichauffeur *m*, -in *f*; ~ **rank** Taxistand *m*; ~ **stand** *Am* Taxistand *m*

taximeter ['tæksi,mi:tə] *n* Taxameter *m*

tea [ti:] *n* Tee *m*; Teestunde *f*; ~ **cloth** Geschirrtuch *nt*; ~ **set** Teeservice *nt*

*teach [ti:tʃ] *v* lehren, unterrichten

teacher ['ti:tʃə] *n* Lehrer *m*, -in *f*; Volksschullehrer *m*, -in *f*, Schullehrer *m*, -in *f*

teachings ['ti:tʃiŋz] *pl* Lehre *f*

teacup ['ti:kʌp] *n* Teetasse *f*

team [ti:m] *n* Team *nt*, Mannschaft *f*

teapot ['ti:pɔt] *n* Teekanne *f*

tear[1] [tiə] *n* Träne *f*

tear[2] [tɛə] *n* Riss *m*; ***tear** *v* *reißen

tearjerker ['tiə,dʒə:kə] *n* Schnulze *f*

tease [ti:z] *v* necken

tea-shop ['ti:ʃɔp] *n* Teestube *f*

teaspoon ['ti:spu:n] *n* Teelöffel *m*

teaspoonful ['ti:spu:n,ful] *n* Teelöffel voll *m*

technical ['teknikəl] *adj* technisch

technician [tek'niʃən] *n* Techniker *m*, -in *f*

technique [tek'ni:k] *n* Technik *f*

technology [tek'nɔlədʒi] *n* Technologie *f*

technological [,teknə'lɔdʒikəl] *adj* technologisch

teenager ['ti:,neidʒə] *n* Teenager *m*

telegram ['teligræm] *n* Telegramm *nt*

telephone ['telifoun] *n* Telefon *nt*; ~ **book** *Am* Telefonbuch *nt*; ~ **call** Anruf *m*, Telefonanruf *m*; ~ **directory** Telefonbuch *nt*; ~ **exchange** Telefonzentrale *f*

television ['teliviʒən] *n* Fernsehen *nt*; ~ **set** Fernsehgerät *nt*

*tell [tel] *v* sagen; erzählen

telly ['teli] *n colloquial* Fernseher *m*; Fernsehen *nt*

temper ['tempə] *n* Laune *f*, Stimmung *f*; Temperament *nt*

temperature ['temprətʃə] *n* Temperatur *f*

tempest ['tempist] *n* Unwetter *nt*

temple ['tempəl] *n* Tempel *m*; Schläfe *f*

temporary ['tempərəri] *adj* vorläufig, zeitweilig

tempt [tempt] *v* versuchen

temptation [temp'teiʃən] *n* Versuchung *f*

ten [ten] *num* zehn

tenant ['tenənt] *n* Mieter *m*, -in *f*

tend [tend] *v* neigen; pflegen; ~ **to** neigen zu

tendency ['tendənsi] *n* Neigung *f*, Tendenz *f*

tender ['tendə] *adj* zärtlich, zart

tendon ['tendən] *n* Sehne *f*

tennis ['tenis] *n* Tennis *nt*; ~ **court** Tennisplatz *m*; ~ **shoes** Tennisschuhe *mpl*

tense [tens] *adj* gespannt

tension ['tenʃən] *n* Spannung *f*

tent [tent] *n* Zelt *nt*

tenth [tenθ] *num* zehnte

tepid ['tepid] *adj* lauwarm

term [tə:m] *n* Ausdruck *m*; Laufzeit *f*, Dauer *f*; Bedingung *f*

terminal ['tə:minəl] *n* Endstation *f*

terrace ['terəs] *n* Terrasse *f*

terrain [te'rein] *n* Gelände *nt*

terrible ['teribəl] *adj* abscheulich, furchtbar, schrecklich

terrific [tə'rifik] *adj* großartig

terrify ['terifai] *v* *erschrecken; **terrifying** furchterregend

territory ['teritəri] *n* Gebiet *nt*

terror ['terə] *n* Furcht *f*

terrorism ['terərizəm] *n* Terrorismus *m*, Terror *m*

terrorist ['terərist] *n* Terrorist *m*, -in *f*

test [test] *n* Probe *f*, Test *m*; *v* testen,

prüfen

testify ['testifai] v bezeugen

text [tekst] n Text m

textbook ['teksbuk] n Lehrbuch nt

textile ['tekstail] n Textilien pl

texture ['tekstʃə] n Struktur f

Thai [tai] adj thailändisch; n Thailänder m, -in f

Thailand ['tailænd] Thailand

than [ðæn] conj als

thank [θæŋk] v danken; ~ you danke schön

thankful ['θæŋkfəl] adj dankbar

that [ðæt] adj jener; pron das; der; conj dass

thaw [θɔː] v tauen, auftauen; n Tauwetter nt

the [ðə, ði] art der art; **the ... the** je ... je

theatre, theater ['θiətə] n Schauspielhaus nt, Theater nt

theft [θeft] n Diebstahl m

their [ðeə] adj ihr

them [ðem] pron sie; ihnen

theme [θiːm] n Thema nt, Stoff m

themselves [ðəm'selvz] pron sich; selbst

then [ðen] adv damals; darauf, dann

theology [θi'ɔlədʒi] n Theologie f

theoretical [θiə'retikəl] adj theoretisch

theory ['θiəri] n Theorie f

therapy ['θerəpi] n Therapie f

there [ðeə] adv dort; dorthin

therefore ['ðeəfɔː] conj darum

thermometer [θə'mɔmitə] n Thermometer nt

thermostat ['θɔːməstæt] n Thermostat m

these [ðiːz] adj diese

thesis ['θiːsis] n (pl theses) These f

they [ðei] pron sie

thick [θik] adj dick; dicht

thicken ['θikən] v verdicken

thickness ['θiknəs] n Dicke f

thief [θiːf] n (pl thieves) Dieb m

thigh [θai] n Oberschenkel m

thimble ['θimbəl] n Fingerhut m

thin [θin] adj dünn; mager

thing [θiŋ] n Ding nt

*think [θiŋk] v *denken; *nachdenken; ~ of *denken an; ~ over überlegen

thinker ['θiŋkə] n Denker m, -in f

third [θəːd] num dritte

thirst [θəːst] n Durst m

thirsty ['θəːsti] adj durstig

thirteen [,θəː'tiːn] num dreizehn

thirteenth [,θəː'tiːnθ] num dreizehnte

thirtieth ['θəːtiəθ] num dreißigste

thirty ['θəːti] num dreißig

this [ðis] adj dieser; pron dies

thistle ['θisəl] n Distel f

thorn [θɔːn] n Dorn m

thorough ['θʌrə] adj gründlich, sorgfältig

thoroughfare ['θʌrəfɛə] n Durchgangsstraße f, Hauptverkehrsstraße f

those [ðouz] adj jene

though [ðou] conj obwohl, wenn auch, obgleich; adv jedoch

thought¹ [θɔːt] v (p, pp think)

thought² [θɔːt] n Gedanke m

thoughtful ['θɔːtfəl] adj nachdenklich; zuvorkommend

thousand ['θauzənd] num tausend

thread [θred] n Faden m; Zwirn m; v aufreihen

threadbare ['θredbɛə] adj verschlissen

threat [θret] n Drohung f, Bedrohung f

threaten ['θretən] v drohen, bedrohen; **threatening** bedrohlich

three [θriː] num drei

three-quarter [,θri'kwɔːtə] adj Dreiviertel-

threshold ['θreʃould] n Schwelle f

threw [θru:] v (p throw)

thrifty ['θrifti] adj sparsam

throat [θrout] n Kehle f; Hals m

throne [θroun] n Thron m

through [θru:] prep durch

throughout [θru:'aut] adv überall

throw [θrou] n Wurf m

***throw** [θrou] v schleudern, *werfen

thrush [θrʌʃ] n Drossel f

thumb [θʌm] n Daumen m

thumbtack ['θʌmtæk] nAm Reißnagel m

thump [θʌmp] v *schlagen

thunder ['θʌndə] n Donner m; v donnern

thunderstorm ['θʌndəstɔ:m] n Gewitter nt

Thursday ['θə:zdi] Donnerstag m

thus [ðʌs] adv so

thyme [taim] n Thymian m

tick off [tik'ɔf] v abhaken

ticket ['tikit] n Karte f; Anzeige f; ~ collector Schaffner m, -in f; ~ machine Fahrkartenautomat m

tickle ['tikəl] v kitzeln

tide [taid] n Tide f; **high** ~ Flut f; **low** ~ Ebbe f

tidy ['taidi] adj ordentlich; ~ up aufräumen

tie [tai] v knoten, *binden; n Krawatte f

tiger ['taigə] n Tiger m

tight [tait] adj stramm; eng, knapp; adv fest

tighten ['taitən] v *zusammenziehen, straffen, spannen; enger machen; enger *werden

tights [taits] pl Trikot nt

tile [tail] n Kachel f; Dachziegel m

till [til] prep bis zu, bis; conj bis

timber ['timbə] n Bauholz nt

time [taim] n Zeit f; Mal nt; **all the** ~ immerzu; **in** ~ rechtzeitig; ~ **of arrival** Ankunftszeit f; ~ **of departure** Abfahrtszeit f

time-saving ['taim,seiviŋ] adj zeitsparend

timetable ['taim,teibəl] n Fahrplan m

timid ['timid] adj schüchtern

timidity [ti'midəti] n Schüchternheit f

tin [tin] n Zinn nt; Büchse f; **tinned food** Konserven fpl; ~ **opener** Dosenöffner m

tiny ['taini] adj winzig

tip [tip] n Spitze f; Trinkgeld nt

tire[1] [taiə] n Reifen m

tire[2] [taiə] v ermüden

tired [taiəd] adj erschöpft, müde; ~ **of** überdrüssig

tiring ['taiəriŋ] adj ermüdend

tissue ['tiʃu:] n Gewebe nt; Papiertaschentuch nt

title ['taitəl] n Titel m

to [tu:] prep bis; zu, vor, nach; um zu

toad [toud] n Kröte f

toadstool ['toudstu:l] n ungenießbarer Pilz m

toast [toust] n Toast m; Trinkspruch m

tobacco [tə'bækou] n (pl ~s) Tabak m; ~ **pouch** Tabaksbeutel m

tobacconist [tə'bækənist] n Tabakhändler m; **tobacconist's** Tabakladen m

today [tə'dei] adv heute

toddler ['tɔdlə] n Kleinkind nt

toe [tou] n Zehe f

toffee ['tɔfi] n Sahnebonbon m

together [tə'geðə] adv zusammen

toilet ['tɔilət] n Toilette f; ~ **paper** Toilettenpapier nt

toiletry ['tɔilətri] n Toilettenartikel mpl

token ['toukən] n Zeichen nt; Beweis m; Münze f

told [tould] v (p, pp tell)

tolerable ['tɔlərəbəl] adj erträglich

toll [toul] n Maut f

tomato [tə'mɑːtou] n (pl ~es) Tomate f

tomb [tuːm] n Grab nt

tombstone ['tuːmstoun] n Grabstein m

tomorrow [tə'mɔrou] adv morgen

ton [tʌn] n Tonne f

tone [toun] n Ton m; Klang m

tongs [tɔŋz] pl Zange f

tongue [tʌŋ] n Zunge f

tonight [tə'nait] adv heute Nacht, heute Abend

tonsilitis [,tɔnsə'laitis] n Mandelentzündung f

tonsils ['tɔnsəlz] pl Mandeln

too [tuː] adv zu; auch

took [tuk] v (p take)

tool [tuːl] n Gerät nt, Werkzeug nt; ~ kit Werkzeugtasche f

toot [tuːt] vAm hupen

tooth [tuːθ] n (pl teeth) Zahn m

toothache ['tuːθeik] n Zahnschmerzen ntpl

toothbrush ['tuːθbrʌʃ] n Zahnbürste f

toothpaste ['tuːθpeist] n Zahnpasta f

toothpick ['tuːθpik] n Zahnstocher m

top [tɔp] n Gipfel m; Spitze f; Deckel m; oberst; **on ~ of** oben auf; ~ **side** Oberseite f; v bedecken; übertreffen

topic ['tɔpik] n Thema nt

topical ['tɔpikəl] adj aktuell

torch [tɔːtʃ] n Fackel f; Taschenlampe f

torment¹ [tɔː'ment] v quälen

torment² ['tɔːment] n Qual f

torture ['tɔːtʃə] n Folter f; v foltern

toss [tɔs] v *werfen

tot [tɔt] n kleines Kind

total ['toutəl] adj total; ganz, gänzlich; n Gesamtsumme f

totalitarian [,toutæli'tɛəriən] adj totalitär

touch [tʌtʃ] v berühren, anrühren; *betreffen; n Kontakt m, Berührung f; Tastsinn m

touching ['tʌtʃiŋ] adj rührend

tough [tʌf] adj zäh

tour [tuə] n Rundreise f

tourism ['tuərizəm] n Fremdenverkehr m

tourist ['tuərist] n Tourist m, -in f; ~ **class** Touristenklasse f

tournament ['tuənəmənt] n Turnier nt

tow [tou] v schleppen

towards [tə'wɔːdz] prep nach; zu

towel [tauəl] n Handtuch nt

towelling ['tauəliŋ] n Frottierstoff m

tower [tauə] n Turm m

town [taun] n Stadt f; ~ **centre** (Am **center**) Stadtzentrum nt; ~ **hall** Rathaus nt

townspeople ['taunz,piːpəl] pl Städter mpl

toxic ['tɔksik] adj toxisch

toy [tɔi] n Spielzeug nt

toyshop ['tɔiʃɔp] n Spielwarenladen m

trace [treis] n Spur f

track [træk] n Gleis nt; Bahn f

tractor ['træktə] n Traktor m

trade [treid] n Gewerbe nt, Handel m; Fach nt, Beruf m; v handeln

trader ['treidə] n Händler m, -in f

tradesman ['treidzmən] n (pl -men) Geschäftsmann m

tradeswoman ['treidzwumən] n (pl -women) Geschäftsfrau f

trade union [,treid'juːnjən] n Gewerkschaft f

tradition [trə'diʃən] n Tradition f

traditional [trə'diʃənəl] adj traditionell

traffic ['træfik] n Verkehr m; ~ **jam** Verkehrsstauung f; ~ **light** Verkehrsampel f

tragedy ['trædʒədi] n Tragödie f

tragic ['trædʒik] adj tragisch

trail [treil] n Fährte f, Pfad m

trailer ['treilə] n Anhänger m; nAm Wohnwagen m

train [trein] n Zug m; v dressieren, ausbilden; **through ~** durchgehender Zug; **~ ferry** Eisenbahnfähre f

trainee [trei'ni:] n Auszubildende m/f; Trainee m/f

trainer ['treinə] n Ausbilder m, -in f; Trainer m, -in f

training ['treiniŋ] n Ausbildung f

trait [treit] n Zug m

traitor ['treitə] n Verräter m, -in f

tram [træm] n Straßenbahn f

tramp [træmp] v wandern

tranquil ['træŋkwil] adj ruhig

tranquillizer ['træŋkwilaizə] n Beruhigungsmittel nt

transaction [træn'zækʃən] n Transaktion f

transatlantic [,trænzət'læntik] adj transatlantisch

transfer [træns'fə:] v *übertragen

transform [træns'fɔ:m] v verwandeln

transformer [træns'fɔ:mə] n Transformator m

transition [træn'siʃən] n Übergang m

translate [træns'leit] v übersetzen

translation [træns'leiʃən] n Übersetzung f

translator [træns'leitə] n Übersetzer m, -in f

transmission [trænz'miʃən] n Sendung f

transmit [trænz'mit] v *senden

transmitter [trænz'mitə] n Sender m

transparent [træn'spɛərənt] adj durchsichtig

transport¹ ['trænspɔ:t] n Beförderung f

transport² [træn'spɔ:t] v transportieren

transportation [,trænspɔ:'teiʃən] n Transport m

trap [træp] n Falle f

trash [træʃ] n Müll m; **~ can** Am Abfalleimer m

travel ['trævəl] v reisen; **~ agency** Reisebüro nt; **~ insurance** Reiseversicherung f; **travel(l)ing expenses** Reisespesen pl

travel(l)er ['trævələ] n Reisende m/f; **traveller's cheque,** Am **traveler's check** Reisescheck m

tray [trei] n Tablett nt

treason ['tri:zən] n Verrat m

treasure ['treʒə] n Schatz m

treat [tri:t] v behandeln

treatment ['tri:tmənt] n Behandlung f

treaty ['tri:ti] n Vertrag m

tree [tri:] n Baum m

tremble ['trembəl] v zittern; beben

tremendous [tri'mendəs] adj ungeheuer

trendy ['trendi] adj colloquial modisch, modern, in

trespass ['trespəs] v *eindringen

trespasser ['trespəsə] n Eindringling m

trial [traiəl] n Gerichtsverfahren nt; Versuch m

triangle ['traiæŋgəl] n Dreieck nt

triangular [trai'æŋgjulə] adj dreieckig

tribe [traib] n Stamm m

tributary ['tribjutəri] n Nebenfluss m

tribute ['tribju:t] n Huldigung f

trick [trik] n Trick m

trigger ['trigə] n Abzug m

trim [trim] v stutzen

trip [trip] n Ausflug m, Reise f

triumph ['traiəmf] n Triumph m; v triumphieren

triumphant [trai'ʌmfənt] adj triumphierend

troops [tru:ps] pl Truppen fpl

tropical ['trɔpikəl] adj tropisch

tropics ['trɔpiks] pl Tropen pl

trouble ['trʌbəl] n Sorge f, Mühe f, Last f; v bemühen

troublesome ['trʌbəlsəm] adj lästig

trousers ['trauzəz] pl Hose f

trouser ['trauzə] adj Hosen...

trout [traut] n (pl ~) Forelle f

truck [trʌk] nAm Lastwagen m

true [tru:] adj wahr; wirklich, echt; treu, aufrichtig

trumpet ['trʌmpit] n Trompete f

trunk [trʌŋk] n Koffer m; Stamm m; nAm Kofferraum m; **trunks** pl Turnhose f

trust [trʌst] v vertrauen; n Vertrauen nt

trustworthy ['trʌst,wə:ði] adj zuverlässig

truth [tru:θ] n Wahrheit f

truthful ['tru:θfəl] adj wahrhaft

try [trai] v versuchen; probieren, sich bemühen; n Versuch m; ~ **on** anprobieren

tube [tju:b] n Röhre f, Rohr nt; Tube f

tuberculosis [tju:,bə:kju'lousis] n Tuberkulose f

Tuesday ['tju:zdi] Dienstag m

tug [tʌg] v schleppen; n Schlepper m; Ruck m

tuition [tju:'iʃən] n Unterricht m; (Studien)Gebühren fpl

tulip ['tju:lip] n Tulpe f

tumbler ['tʌmblə] n Becher m

tumour ['tju:mə] n Geschwulst f, Tumor m

tuna ['tju:nə] n (pl ~, ~s) Thunfisch m

tune [tju:n] n Lied nt, Melodie f; ~ **in** einstellen

tuneful ['tju:nfəl] adj melodisch

tunic ['tju:nik] n Tunika f

Tunisia [tju:'niziə] Tunesien

Tunisian [tju:'niziən] adj tunesisch; n

Tunesier m, -in f

tunnel ['tʌnəl] n Tunnel m

turbine ['tə:bain] n Turbine f

Turkey ['tə:ki] Türkei

turkey ['tə:ki] n Truthahn m

Turkish ['tə:kiʃ] adj türkisch; ~ **bath** Schwitzbad nt

turn [tə:n] v *wenden; kehren, umdrehen; n Wendung f, Drehung f; Biegung f; Reihe f; ~ **back** umkehren; ~ **down** *verwerfen; ~ **into** sich verwandeln in; ~ **off** abdrehen; ~ **on** einschalten; andrehen; ~ **over** *umwenden; ~ **round** umkehren; sich umdrehen

turning ['tə:niŋ] n Kurve f; ~ **point** Wendepunkt m

turnover ['tə:,nouvə] n Umsatz m; ~ **tax** Umsatzsteuer f

turnpike ['tə:npaik] nAm gebührenpflichtige Verkehrsstraße

turpentine ['tə:pəntain] n Terpentin nt

turtle ['tə:təl] n Schildkröte f

tutor ['tju:tə] n Privatlehrer m; Vormund m; Tutor m, -in f

tuxedo [tʌk'si:dou] nAm (pl ~s, ~es) Smoking m

TV [,ti:'vi:] n colloquial Fernseher m; Fernsehen nt; **on** ~ im Fernsehen

tweed [twi:d] n Tweed m

tweezers ['twi:zəz] pl Pinzette f

twelfth [twelfθ] num zwölfte

twelve [twelv] num zwölf

twentieth ['twentiəθ] num zwanzigste

twenty ['twenti] num zwanzig

twice [twais] adv zweimal

twig [twig] n Zweig m

twilight ['twailait] n Zwielicht nt

twine [twain] n Schnur f

twins [twinz] pl Zwillinge mpl; **twin beds** Doppelbett nt

twist [twist] v *winden; drehen; n Drehung f

two [tu:] *num* zwei
two-piece [,tu:'pi:s] *adj* zweiteilig
type [taip] *v* tippen, Maschine *schreiben; *n* Typ *m*
typewriter ['taipraitə] *n* Schreibmaschine *f*

typhoid ['taifɔid] *n* Typhus *m*
typical ['tipikəl] *adj* bezeichnend, typisch
tyrant ['taiərənt] *n* Tyrann *m*, -in *f*
tyre [taiə] *n* Reifen *m*; ~ **pressure** Reifendruck *m*

U

ugly ['ʌgli] *adj* hässlich
ulcer ['ʌlsə] *n* Geschwür *nt*
ultimate ['ʌltimət] *adj* letzt
ultraviolet [,ʌltrə'vaiələt] *adj* ultraviolett
umbrella [ʌm'brelə] *n* Regenschirm *m*
umpire ['ʌmpaiə] *n* Schiedsrichter *m*, -in *f*
unable [ʌ'neibəl] *adj* unfähig
unacceptable [,ʌnək'septəbəl] *adj* unannehmbar
unaccountable [,ʌnə'kauntəbəl] *adj* unerklärlich
unaccustomed [,ʌnə'kʌstəmd] *adj* ungewohnt
unanimous [ju:'næniməs] *adj* einstimmig
unanswered [,ʌ'nɑːnsəd] *adj* unbeantwortet
unauthorized [,ʌ'nɔ:θəraizd] *adj* unbefugt
unavoidable [,ʌnə'vɔidəbəl] *adj* unvermeidlich
unaware [,ʌnə'wɛə] *adj* unbewusst
unbearable [ʌn'bɛərəbəl] *adj* unerträglich
unbreakable [ʌn'breikəbəl] *adj* unzerbrechlich
unbroken [,ʌn'broukən] *adj* unversehrt
unbutton [,ʌn'bʌtən] *v* aufknöpfen

uncertain [ʌn'sə:tən] *adj* unsicher
uncle ['ʌŋkəl] *n* Onkel *m*
uncomfortable [ʌn'kʌmfətəbəl] *adj* ungemütlich
uncommon [ʌn'kɔmən] *adj* ungewöhnlich, selten
unconditional [,ʌnkən'diʃənəl] *adj* bedingungslos
unconscious [ʌn'kɔnʃəs] *adj* bewusstlos
uncork [,ʌn'kɔ:k] *v* entkorken
uncover [ʌn'kʌvə] *v* aufdecken
uncultivated [,ʌn'kʌltiveitid] *adj* unkultiviert
under ['ʌndə] *prep* unterhalb, unter
undercurrent ['ʌndə,kʌrənt] *n* Unterströmung *f*
underestimate [,ʌndə'restimeit] *v* unterschätzen
underground ['ʌndəgraund] *adj* unterirdisch; *n* U-Bahn *f*
underline [,ʌndə'lain] *v* *unterstreichen
underneath [,ʌndə'ni:θ] *adv* unten
underpants ['ʌndəpænts] *plAm* Unterhose *f*
undershirt ['ʌndəʃə:t] *n* Unterhemd *nt*
*understand [,ʌndə'stænd] *v* *begreifen, *verstehen
understanding [,ʌndə'stændiŋ] *n* Verständigung *f*

understate [ˌʌndə'steit] v
untertreiben

understatement [ˌʌndə'steitmənt] n
Untertreibung f

*undertake [ˌʌndə'teik] v
*unternehmen

undertaking [ˌʌndə'teikiŋ] n
Unternehmung f

underwater ['ʌndə,wɔːtə] adj
Unterwasser-

underwear ['ʌndəwɛə] n
Unterwäsche fpl

undesirable [ˌʌndi'zaiərəbəl] adj
unerwünscht

*undo [ˌʌn'duː] v aufmachen

undoubtedly [ʌn'dautidli] adv
zweifellos

undress [ˌʌn'dres] v sich entkleiden

unearned [ˌʌ'nɔːnd] adj unverdient

uneasy [ʌ'niːzi] adj unruhig

uneducated [ˌʌ'nedjukeitid] adj
ungebildet

unemployed [ˌʌnim'plɔid] adj
arbeitslos

unemployment [ˌʌnim'plɔimənt] n
Arbeitslosigkeit f

unequal [ˌʌ'niːkwəl] adj ungleich

uneven [ˌʌ'niːvən] adj ungleich,
uneben

unexpected [ˌʌnik'spektid] adj
unvorhergesehen, unerwartet

unfair [ˌʌn'fɛə] adj ungerecht, unfair

unfaithful [ˌʌn'feiθfəl] adj untreu

unfamiliar [ˌʌnfə'miljə] adj
unbekannt

unfasten [ˌʌn'fɑːsən] v aufmachen

unfavo(u)rable [ˌʌn'feivərəbəl] adj
ungünstig

unfit [ˌʌn'fit] adj untauglich

unfold [ʌn'fould] v entfalten

unfortunate [ʌn'fɔːtʃənət] adj
unglücklich

unfortunately [ʌn'fɔːtʃənətli] adv
unglücklicherweise, leider

unfriendly [ˌʌn'frendli] adj
unfreundlich

unfurnished [ˌʌn'fɔːniʃt] adj
unmöbliert

ungrateful [ʌn'greitfəl] adj
undankbar

unhappy [ʌn'hæpi] adj unglücklich

unhealthy [ʌn'helθi] adj ungesund

unhurt [ʌn'hɔːt] adj unverletzt

uniform ['juːnifɔːm] n Uniform f; adj
gleichförmig

unimportant [ˌʌnim'pɔːtənt] adj
unwichtig

uninhabitable [ˌʌnin'hæbitəbəl] adj
unbewohnbar

uninhabited [ˌʌnin'hæbitid] adj
unbewohnt

unintentional [ˌʌnin'tenʃənəl] adj
unabsichtlich

union ['juːnjən] n Vereinigung f;
Union f

unique [juː'niːk] adj einzigartig

unit ['juːnit] n Einheit f

unite [juː'nait] v vereinigen

united [juː'naitid] adj vereinigt;
United States [juː'naitid steits]
Vereinigte Staaten

unity ['juːnəti] n Einheit f

universal [ˌjuːni'vɔːsəl] adj
allgemein, universal

universe ['juːnivɔːs] n Weltall nt

university [ˌjuːni'vɔːsəti] n
Universität f

unjust [ˌʌn'dʒʌst] adj ungerecht

unkind [ʌn'kaind] adj unfreundlich

unknown [ˌʌn'noun] adj unbekannt

unlawful [ˌʌn'lɔːfəl] adj rechtswidrig

unleaded [ˌʌn'ledid] adj bleifrei

unlearn [ˌʌn'lɔːn] v verlernen

unless [ən'les] conj außer wenn

unlike [ˌʌn'laik] adj unähnlich

unlikely [ʌn'laikli] adj
unwahrscheinlich

unlimited [ʌn'limitid] adj unbegrenzt,

unbeschränkt

unload [ˌʌn'loud] v *ausladen, *abladen

unlock [ˌʌn'lɔk] v *aufschließen

unlucky [ʌn'lʌki] adj unglücklich

unnecessary [ʌn'nesəsəri] adj unnötig

unoccupied [ˌʌ'nɔkjupaid] adj unbesetzt

unpack [ˌʌn'pæk] v auspacken

unpleasant [ʌn'plezənt] adj langweilig, unangenehm; unerfreulich

unpopular [ˌʌn'pɔpjulə] adj unpopulär, unbeliebt

unprotected [ˌʌnprə'tektid] adj ungeschützt

unqualified [ˌʌn'kwɔlifaid] adj unqualifiziert

unreal [ˌʌn'riəl] adj unwirklich

unreasonable [ʌn'ri:zənəbəl] adj unvernünftig

unreliable [ˌʌnri'laiəbəl] adj unzuverlässig

unrest [ˌʌn'rest] n Unruhe f; Ruhelosigkeit f

unsafe [ˌʌn'seif] adj unsicher

unsatisfactory [ˌʌnsætis'fæktəri] adj unbefriedigend

unscrew [ˌʌn'skru:] v abschrauben

unselfish [ˌʌn'selfiʃ] adj selbstlos

unskilled [ˌʌn'skild] adj ungelernt

unsound [ˌʌn'saund] adj ungesund

unstable [ˌʌn'steibəl] adj labil

unsteady [ˌʌn'stedi] adj wacklig

unsuccessful [ˌʌnsək'sesfəl] adj erfolglos

unsuitable [ˌʌn'su:təbəl] adj ungeeignet

unsurpassed [ˌʌnsə'pɑ:st] adj unübertroffen

untidy [ʌn'taidi] adj unordentlich

untie [ˌʌn'tai] v aufknoten

until [ən'til] prep bis

untrue [ˌʌn'tru:] adj unwahr

untrustworthy [ˌʌn'trʌst,wə:ði] adj unzuverlässig

unusual [ʌn'ju:ʒuəl] adj ungebräuchlich, ungewöhnlich

unwell [ˌʌn'wel] adj unwohl

unwilling [ˌʌn'wiliŋ] adj unwillig

unwise [ˌʌn'waiz] adj unüberlegt

unwrap [ˌʌn'ræp] v auspacken

up [ʌp] adv nach oben, hinauf

upholster [ʌp'houlstə] v polstern, *überziehen

upkeep ['ʌpki:p] n Unterhalt m

uplands ['ʌpləndz] pl Hochland nt

upon [ə'pɔn] prep auf

upper ['ʌpə] adj höher, ober

upright ['ʌprait] adj aufrecht; adv aufrecht

upset [ʌp'set] v stören; adj bestürzt

upside down [ˌʌpsaid'daun] adv verkehrt herum

upstairs [ˌʌp'stɛəz] adv oben; nach oben

upstream [ˌʌp'stri:m] adv stromaufwärts

upwards ['ʌpwədz] adv aufwärts

urban ['ə:bən] adj städtisch

urge [ə:dʒ] v drängen; n Impuls m

urgency ['ə:dʒənsi] n Dringlichkeit f

urgent ['ə:dʒənt] adj dringend

urine ['juərin] n Urin m

Uruguay ['juərəgwai] Uruguay

Uruguayan [ˌjuərə'gwaiən] adj uruguayisch

us [ʌs] pron uns

usable ['ju:zəbəl] adj brauchbar

usage ['ju:zidʒ] n Brauch m

use¹ [ju:z] v benutzen, gebrauchen; *be used to gewohnt *sein; ~ up verbrauchen

use² [ju:s] n Gebrauch m; Nutzen m; *be of ~ nützen

useful ['ju:sfəl] adj brauchbar, nützlich

useless ['ju:sləs] *adj* nutzlos

user ['ju:zə] *n* Benutzer *m*, -in *f*

usher ['ʌʃə] *n* Platzanweiser *m*

usherette [ˌʌʃə'ret] *n* Platzanweiserin *f*

usual ['ju:ʒuəl] *adj* gewöhnlich

usually ['ju:ʒuəli] *adv* gewöhnlich, normalerweise

utensil [ju:'tensəl] *n* Werkzeug *nt*, Gerät *nt*; Gebrauchsgegenstand *m*

utility [ju:'tiləti] *n* Nutzen *m*

utilize ['ju:tilaiz] *v* benutzen

utmost ['ʌtmoust] *adj* äußerst

utter ['ʌtə] *adj* völlig, gänzlich; *v* äußern

V

vacant ['veikənt] *adj* frei

vacate [və'keit] *v* räumen

vacation [və'keiʃən] *n* Ferien *pl*

vaccinate ['væksineit] *v* impfen

vaccination [ˌvæksi'neiʃən] *n* Impfung *f*

vacuum ['vækjuəm] *n* Vakuum *nt*; *vAm* staubsaugen; ~ **cleaner** Staubsauger *m*; ~ **flask** Thermosflasche *f*

vague [veig] *adj* undeutlich

vain [vein] *adj* eitel; unnütz; **in** ~ vergebens, umsonst

valet ['vælit] *n* Diener *m*

valid ['vælid] *adj* gültig

valley ['væli] *n* Tal *nt*

valuable ['væljubəl] *adj* wertvoll, kostbar; **valuables** *pl* Wertsachen *fpl*

value ['vælju:] *n* Wert *m*; *v* schätzen

valve [vælv] *n* Ventil *nt*

van [væn] *n* Lieferwagen *m*, Transporter *m*

vanilla [və'nilə] *n* Vanille *f*

vanish ['væniʃ] *v* *verschwinden

vapour ['veipə] *n* Dunst *m*

variable ['veəriəbəl] *adj* veränderlich

variation [ˌveəri'eiʃən] *n* Abwechslung *f*; Veränderung *f*

varied ['veərid] *adj* verschieden

variety [və'raiəti] *n* Auswahl *f*; ~ **theatre** Varietétheater *nt*

various ['veəriəs] *adj* allerlei, verschiedene

varnish ['vɑ:niʃ] *n* Lack *m*, Firnis *m*; *v* lackieren

vary ['veəri] *v* variieren, wechseln; verändern; verschieden *sein

vase [vɑ:z] *n* Vase *f*

vaseline ['væsəli:n] *n* Vaseline *f*

vast [vɑ:st] *adj* unermesslich, weit

vault [vɔ:lt] *n* Gewölbe *nt*

veal [vi:l] *n* Kalbfleisch *nt*

vegetable ['vedʒətəbəl] *n* Gemüse *nt*; ~ **merchant** Gemüsehändler *m*, -in *f*

vegetarian [ˌvedʒi'teəriən] *n* Vegetarier *m*, -in *f*

vegetation [ˌvedʒi'teiʃən] *n* Vegetation *f*

vehicle ['vi:əkəl] *n* Fahrzeug *nt*

veil [veil] *n* Schleier *m*

vein [vein] *n* Ader *f*; **varicose** ~ Krampfader *f*

velvet ['velvit] *n* Samt *m*

venerable ['venərəbəl] *adj* ehrwürdig

venereal disease [vi'niəriəl di'zi:z] Geschlechtskrankheit *f*

Venezuela [ˌveni'zweilə] Venezuela

Venezuelan [ˌveni'zweilən] *adj* venezolanisch; *n* Venezolaner *m*, -in *f*

ventilate ['ventileit] *v* ventilieren;

lüften

ventilation [ˌventiˈleiʃn] n
Ventilation f; Lüftung f

ventilator [ˈventileitə] n Ventilator m

venture [ˈventʃə] v wagen

veranda [vəˈrændə] n Veranda f

verb [vəːb] n Zeitwort nt

verbal [ˈvəːbəl] adj mündlich

verdict [ˈvəːdikt] n Urteil nt,
Urteilsspruch m

verge [vəːdʒ] n Rand m

verify [ˈverifai] v nachprüfen

verse [vəːs] n Vers m

version [ˈvəːʃən] n Darstellung f;
Übersetzung f

versus [ˈvəːsəs] prep gegen

vertical [ˈvəːtikəl] adj senkrecht

very [ˈveri] adv sehr; adj wahr,
wirklich, exakt; äußerst

vessel [ˈvesəl] n Schiff nt; Gefäß nt

vest [vest] n Hemd nt; nAm Weste f

veterinary surgeon [ˈvetrinəri
ˈsəːdʒən] Tierarzt m, Tierärztin f

via [vaiə] prep über

viaduct [ˈvaiədʌkt] n Viadukt m

vibrate [vaiˈbreit] v vibrieren

vibration [vaiˈbreiʃən] n Schwingung
f

vicar [ˈvikə] n Vikar m, Vikarin f

vice president [ˌvaisˈprezidənt] n
Vizepräsident m, -in f

vicinity [viˈsinəti] n Nähe f,
Nachbarschaft f

vicious [ˈviʃəs] adj bösartig

victim [ˈviktim] n Opfer nt

victory [ˈviktəri] n Sieg m

video [ˈvidiou] n Video nt, Videofilm
m; Videoband nt, -kassette f; ~
cassette Videokassette f; ~ **game**
Videospiel nt; ~ **recorder**
Videorekorder m; ~ **recording**
Videoaufzeichnung f

view [vjuː] n Aussicht f; Meinung f,
Ansicht f; v besichtigen

viewfinder [ˈvjuːˌfaində] n Sucher m

vigilant [ˈvidʒilənt] adj wachsam

villa [ˈvilə] n Villa f

village [ˈvilidʒ] n Dorf nt

vine [vain] n Weinrebe f

vinegar [ˈvinigə] n Essig m

vineyard [ˈvinjəd] n Weinberg m

vintage [ˈvintidʒ] n Weinlese f

violation [vaiəˈleiʃən] n Verletzung f

violence [ˈvaiələns] n Gewalt f

violent [ˈvaiələnt] adj gewaltsam;
heftig

violet [ˈvaiələt] n Veilchen nt; adj
violett

violin [vaiəˈlin] n Geige f

VIP [ˌviː ai ˈpiː] n Prominente m/f

virgin [ˈvəːdʒin] n Jungfrau f

virtue [ˈvəːtʃuː] n Tugend f

visa [ˈviːzə] n Visum nt

visibility [ˌvizəˈbiləti] n Sichtweite f

visible [ˈvizəbəl] adj sichtbar

vision [ˈviʒən] n Einsicht f

visit [ˈvizit] v besuchen; n Besuch m

visitor [ˈvizitə] n Gast m

vital [ˈvaitəl] adj wesentlich

vitamin [ˈvitəmin] n Vitamin nt

vivid [ˈvivid] adj lebhaft

vocabulary [vəˈkæbjuləri] n
Vokabular nt, Wortschatz m

vocal [ˈvoukəl] adj vokal

vocalist [ˈvoukəlist] n Sänger m, -in f

voice [vɔis] n Stimme f

void [vɔid] adj nichtig

volcano [vɔlˈkeinou] n (pl ~es, ~s)
Vulkan m

volt [voult] n Volt nt

voltage [ˈvoultidʒ] n Spannung f

volume [ˈvɔljum] n Volumen nt; Teil
m, Band m

voluntary [ˈvɔləntəri] adj freiwillig

volunteer [ˌvɔlənˈtiə] n Freiwillige
m/f

vomit [ˈvɔmit] v sich *übergeben,
*erbrechen

vote [vout] v stimmen; n Stimme f; Abstimmung f

voter ['voutə] n Wähler m, -in f

voucher ['vautʃə] n Beleg m, Gutschein m

vow [vau] n Eid m; v *schwören

vowel [vauəl] n Selbstlaut m

voyage ['vɔiidʒ] n Reise f

vulgar ['vʌlgə] adj gemein; Volks-, ordinär

vulnerable ['vʌlnərəbəl] adj verletzbar

vulture ['vʌltʃə] n Geier m

W

wade [weid] v waten

waffle ['wɔfəl] n Waffel f

wages ['weidʒiz] pl Lohn m

waggon ['wægən] n Waggon m

waist [weist] n Taille f

waistcoat ['weiskout] n Weste f

wait [weit] v warten; ~ **on** bedienen

waiter ['weitə] n Ober m, Kellner m

waiting n das Warten; ~ **list** Warteliste f; ~ **room** Wartezimmer nt

waitress ['weitris] n Kellnerin f

***wake** [weik] v wecken; ~ **up** aufwachen, wach *werden

walk [wɔ:k] v *gehen; spazieren; n Spaziergang m; Gang m; **walking** zu Fuß

walker ['wɔ:kə] n Spaziergänger m, -in f

walking stick ['wɔ:kiŋstik] n Spazierstock m

wall [wɔ:l] n Mauer f; Wand f

wallet ['wɔlit] n Brieftasche f

wallpaper ['wɔ:l,peipə] n Tapete f

walnut ['wɔ:lnʌt] n Walnuss f

waltz [wɔ:ls] n Walzer m

wander ['wɔndə] v umherschweifen, umherwandern

want [wɔnt] v *wollen; wünschen; n Bedarf m; Mangel m, Fehlen nt

war [wɔ:] n Krieg m

warden ['wɔ:dən] n Wächter m, -in f

wardrobe ['wɔ:droub] n Kleiderschrank m, Garderobe f

warehouse ['wɛəhaus] n Lager nt, Depot nt

wares [wɛəz] pl Waren

warm [wɔ:m] adj heiß, warm; v wärmen

warmth [wɔ:mθ] n Wärme f

warn [wɔ:n] v warnen

warning ['wɔ:niŋ] n Warnung f

wary ['wɛəri] adj bedächtig

was [wɔz] v (p be)

wash [wɔʃ] v *waschen; ~ **and wear** bügelfrei; ~ **up** *abwaschen

washable ['wɔʃəbəl] adj waschbar

washbasin ['wɔʃ,beisən] n Waschbecken nt

washing ['wɔʃiŋ] n Waschen nt; Wäsche f; ~ **machine** Waschmaschine f; ~ **powder** Waschpulver nt

washroom ['wɔʃruːm] nAm Toilette f

wasp [wɔsp] n Wespe f

waste [weist] v vergeuden; n Verschwendung f; adj brach

wasteful ['weistfəl] adj verschwenderisch

wastepaper basket [weist'peipə,ba:skit] n Papierkorb m

watch [wɔtʃ] v *Acht geben auf,

beobachten; überwachen; n Uhr f; ~ out aufpassen

watchmaker ['wɔtʃ,meikə] n Uhrmacher m, -in f

water ['wɔːtə] n Wasser nt; **iced ~** Eiswasser nt; **running ~** fließendes Wasser; **~ pump** Wasserpumpe f; **~ ski** Wasserschi m

watercolo(u)r ['wɔːtə,kʌlə] n Wasserfarbe f; Aquarell nt

watercress ['wɔːtəkres] n Brunnenkresse f

waterfall ['wɔːtəfɔːl] n Wasserfall m

watermelon ['wɔːtə,melən] n Wassermelone f

waterproof ['wɔːtəpruːf] adj wasserdicht

waterway ['wɔːtəwei] n Wasserstraße f

watt [wɔt] n Watt nt

wave [weiv] n Welle f; v winken

wavelength ['weivleŋθ] n Wellenlänge f

wavy ['weivi] adj wellig

wax [wæks] n Wachs nt

waxworks ['wækswəːks] pl Wachsfigurenkabinett nt

way [wei] n Art f, Weise f; Weg m; Seite f, Richtung f; Entfernung f; **any ~** wie auch immer; **by the ~** übrigens; **out of the ~** entlegen; **the other ~ round** andersherum; **~ back** Rückweg m; **~ in** Eingang m; **~ out** Ausgang m

wayside ['weisaid] n Wegrand m

we [wiː] pron wir

weak [wiːk] adj schwach; dünn

weakness ['wiːknəs] n Schwäche f

wealth [welθ] n Reichtum m

wealthy ['welθi] adj reich

weapon ['wepən] n Waffe f

*wear [weə] v *anhaben, *tragen; **~ out** *abtragen

weary ['wiəri] adj überdrüssig, müde

weather ['weðə] n Wetter nt; **~ forecast** Wetterbericht m

*weave [wiːv] v weben

weaver ['wiːvə] n Weber m, -in f

wedding ['wediŋ] n Heirat f, Hochzeit f; **~ ring** Ehering m

wedge [wedʒ] n Keil m

Wednesday ['wenzdi] Mittwoch m

weed [wiːd] n Unkraut nt

week [wiːk] n Woche f

weekday ['wiːkdei] n Wochentag m

weekend ['wiːkend] n Wochenende nt

weekly ['wiːkli] adj wöchentlich

*weep [wiːp] v weinen

weigh [wei] v *wiegen

weighing machine ['weiiŋmə,ʃiːn] n Waage f

weight [weit] n Gewicht nt

welcome ['welkəm] adj willkommen; n Willkommen nt v begrüßen

weld [weld] v schweißen

welfare ['welfeə] n Wohlbefinden nt

well¹ [wel] adv gut; adj gesund; **as ~** auch, ebenfalls; **as ~ as** ebenso wie; **well!** gut!

well² [wel] n Quelle f, Brunnen m

well-founded [,wel'faundid] adj wohl begründet

well-known ['welnoun] adj bekannt

well-to-do [,weltə'duː] adj wohlhabend

went [went] v (p go)

were [wəː] v (p be)

west [west] n Westen m

westerly ['westəli] adj westlich

western ['westən] adj westlich

wet [wet] adj nass; feucht

whale [weil] n Wal m

wharf [wɔːf] n (pl ~s, wharves) Kai m

what [wɔt] pron was; **~ for** wozu

whatever [wɔ'tevə] pron was auch immer

wheat [wiːt] n Weizen m

wheel [wi:l] n Rad nt

wheelbarrow ['wi:l,bærou] n Schubkarren m

wheelchair ['wi:ltʃɛə] n Rollstuhl m

when [wen] adv wann; conj als, wenn

whenever [we'nevə] conj wann immer

where [wɛə] adv wo; conj wo

wherever [wɛə'revə] conj wo immer

whether ['weðə] conj ob; **whether ... or** ob ... oder

which [witʃ] pron welcher; der

whichever [wi'tʃevə] adj welcher auch immer

while [wail] conj während; n Weile f

whilst [wailst] conj während, obwohl

whim [wim] n Grille f, Laune f

whip [wip] n Peitsche f; v *schlagen

whisper ['wispə] v flüstern; n Geflüster nt

whistle ['wisəl] v *pfeifen; n Pfeife f

white [wait] adj weiß

whiting ['waitiŋ] n (pl ~) Weißfisch m

Whitsun ['witsən] Pfingsten

who [hu:] pron welcher

whoever [hu:'evə] pron wer auch immer

whole [houl] adj vollständig, ganz; unbeschädigt; n Ganze nt

wholesale ['houlseil] n Großhandel m; ~ **dealer** Großhändler m, -in f

wholesome ['houlsəm] adj bekömmlich

wholly ['houlli] adv gänzlich

whom [hu:m] pron wem

whore [hɔ:] n Hure f

whose [hu:z] pron dessen; wessen

why [wai] adv warum

wicked ['wikid] adj böse

wide [waid] adj weit, breit

widen ['waidən] v erweitern

widow ['widou] n Witwe f

widower ['widouə] n Witwer m

width [widθ] n Breite f

wife [waif] n (pl wives) Gattin f, Frau f

wig [wig] n Perücke f

wild [waild] adj wild; wüst

will [wil] n Wille m; Testament nt

***will** [wil] v *wollen; *werden

willing ['wiliŋ] adj willig

willingly ['wiliŋli] adv gern

willpower ['wilpauə] n Willenskraft f

***win** [win] v *gewinnen

wind [wind] n Wind m

***wind** [waind] v sich *winden; *aufziehen, *winden

winding ['waindiŋ] adj gewunden

windmill ['windmil] n Windmühle f

window ['windou] n Fenster nt

windowsill ['windousil] n Fensterbrett nt

windscreen ['windskri:n] n Windschutzscheibe f; ~ **wiper** Scheibenwischer m

windshield ['windʃi:ld] nAm Windschutzscheibe f; ~ **wiper** Am Scheibenwischer m

windy ['windi] adj windig

wine [wain] n Wein m; ~ **cellar** Weinkeller m; ~ **list** Weinkarte f; ~ **merchant** Weinhändler m, -in f

wing [wiŋ] n Flügel m

winner ['winə] n Sieger m, -in f

winning ['winiŋ] adj gewinnend; **winnings** pl Gewinn m

winter ['wintə] n Winter m; ~ **sports** Wintersport m

wipe [waip] v abwischen; auswischen

wire [waiə] n Draht m

wireless ['waiələs] adj drahtlos

wisdom ['wizdəm] n Weisheit f

wise [waiz] adj weise

wish [wiʃ] v begehren, wünschen; n Begehren nt, Wunsch m

wit ['wit] n Witz m, Geist m

witch [witʃ] n Hexe f

with [wið] prep mit; bei; von

***withdraw** [wið'drɔ:] v *zurückziehen

within [wi'ðin] *prep* innerhalb; *adv* im Innern

without [wi'ðaut] *prep* ohne

witness ['witnəs] *n* Zeuge *m*, Zeugin *f*

wits [wits] *pl* Verstand *m*

witty ['witi] *adj* geistreich

wolf [wulf] *n* (pl wolves) Wolf *m*

woman ['wumən] *n* (pl women) Frau *f*

womb [wu:m] *n* Gebärmutter *f*

won [wʌn] *v* (p, pp win)

wonder ['wʌndə] *n* Wunder *nt*; Verwunderung *f*; *v* sich fragen

wonderful ['wʌndəfəl] *adj* prächtig, wunderbar; herrlich

wood [wud] *n* Holz *nt*; Wald *m*

wooded ['wudid] *adj* bewaldet

wooden ['wudən] *adj* hölzern; **~ shoe** Holzschuh *m*

wool [wul] *n* Wolle *f*; **darning ~** Stopfgarn *nt*

woollen ['wulən] *adj* wollen

word [wə:d] *n* Wort *nt*

wore [wɔ:] *v* (p wear)

work [wə:k] *n* Arbeit *f*; Tätigkeit *f*; *v* arbeiten; funktionieren; **~ of art** Kunstwerk *nt*; **~ permit** Arbeitsbewilligung *f*

worker ['wə:kə] *n* Arbeiter *m*, -in *f*

working ['wə:kiŋ] *n* Betrieb *m*

working day ['wə:kiŋ] *n* Werktag *m*

workman ['wə:kmən] *n* (pl -men) Arbeiter *m*

works [wə:ks] *pl* Fabrik *f*

workshop ['wə:kʃɔp] *n* Werkstatt *f*

world [wə:ld] *n* Welt *f*; **~ war** Weltkrieg *m*

world-famous [,wə:ld'feiməs] *adj* weltberühmt

world-wide ['wə:ldwaid] *adj* weltweit

worm [wə:m] *n* Wurm *m*

worn [wɔ:n] *adj* (pp wear) abgetragen

worn-out [,wɔ:n'aut] *adj* abgenutzt

worried ['wʌrid] *adj* beunruhigt

worry ['wʌri] *v* sich beunruhigen; *n* Sorge *f*, Besorgtheit *f*

worse [wə:s] *adj* schlechter; *adv* schlechter

worship ['wə:ʃip] *v* verehren; *n* Gottesdienst *m*

worst [wə:st] *adj* schlechtest; *adv* am schlechtesten

worth [wə:θ] *n* Wert *m*; ***be ~** wert *sein; ***be worth-while** sich lohnen

worthless ['wə:θləs] *adj* wertlos

worthy of ['wə:ði əv] würdig

would [wud] *v* (p will) würde; pflegt(e) zu

wound¹ [wu:nd] *n* Wunde *f*; *v* verletzen, verwunden

wound² [waund] *v* (p, pp wind)

wrap [ræp] *v* einwickeln

wreck [rek] *n* Wrack *nt*; *v* vernichten

wrench [rentʃ] *n* Schraubenschlüssel *m*; Ruck *m*; *v* verdrehen

wrinkle ['riŋkəl] *n* Falte *f*

wrist [rist] *n* Handgelenk *nt*

wristwatch ['ristwɔtʃ] *n* Armbanduhr *f*

*write [rait] *v* *schreiben; **in writing** schriftlich; **~ down** *aufschreiben

writer ['raitə] *n* Schriftsteller *m*, -in *f*

writing pad ['raitiŋpæd] *n* Notizblock *m*, Schreibblock *m*

writing paper ['raitiŋ,peipə] *n* Schreibpapier *nt*

written ['ritən] *adj* (pp write) schriftlich

wrong [rɔŋ] *adj* unrecht, falsch; *n* Unrecht *nt*; *v* unrecht *tun; ***be ~** Unrecht *haben

wrote [rout] *v* (p write)

X

Xmas ['krisməs] Weihnachten

X-ray ['eksrei] n Röntgenbild nt; v röntgen

Y

yacht [jɔt] n Jacht f; ~ **club** Segelklub m

yachting ['jɔtiŋ] n Segelsport m

yard [jɑːd] n Hof m

yarn [jɑːn] n Garn nt

yawn [jɔːn] v gähnen

year [jiə] n Jahr nt

yearly ['jiəli] adj jährlich

yeast [jiːst] n Hefe f

yell [jel] v *schreien; n Schrei m

yellow ['jelou] adj gelb

yes [jes] ja

yesterday ['jestədi] adv gestern

yet [jet] adv noch; conj dennoch, jedoch, doch

yield [jiːld] v *einbringen; *nachgeben

yoke [jouk] n Joch nt

yolk [jouk] n Dotter nt

you [juː] pron du; dir; ; dich; Sie; Ihnen; ihr; euch

young [jʌŋ] adj jung

your [jɔː] adj Ihr; dein; euer

yours [jɔːz] pron dein, Ihr

yourself [jɔːˈself] pron dich; selbst

yourselves [jɔːˈselvz] pron euch; selbst

youth [juːθ] n Jugend f; ~ **hostel** Jugendherberge f

Z

zap [zæp] v zappen

zeal [ziːl] n Eifer m

zealous ['zeləs] adj eifrig

zebra ['ziːbrə] n Zebra nt

zebra crossing ['ziːbrə krɔsiŋ] n Zebrastreifen m

zenith ['zeniθ] n Zenit m; Höhepunkt m

zero ['ziərou] n (pl ~s) Null f

zest [zest] n Begeisterung f

zinc [ziŋk] n Zink nt

zip [zip] n Reißverschluss m; ~ **code** Am Postleitzahl f

zipper ['zipə] n Reißverschluss m

zone [zoun] n Zone f; Gebiet nt

zoo [zuː] n (pl ~s) Zoo m

zoology [zouˈɔlədʒi] n Zoologie f

Menu Reader

Food

almond Mandel

anchovy Sardelle

angel food cake Kuchen aus Eiweißschnee

angels on horseback auf Toast servierte, in Speck eingerollte und gegrillte Austern

appetizer Appetithäppchen

apple Apfel

~ dumpling Apfel im Schlafrock

~ sauce Apfelmus

apricot Aprikose

Arbroath smoky geräucherter Schellfisch

artichoke Artischocke

asparagus Spargel

~ tip Spargelspitze

aspic Aspik, Gelee, Sülze

assorted gemischt

avocado (pear) Avocado

bacon Speck

~ and eggs Spiegeleier und Speck

bagel Brötchen in Kranzform

baked im Ofen gebacken

~ Alaska norwegisches Omelett

~ beans gebackene weiße Bohnen mit Tomatensoße

~ potato gebackene Pellkartoffel

Bakewell tart Kuchen aus gemahlenen Mandeln und Marmelade

baloney eine Art Mortadella

banana Banane

~ split halbierte Banane, verschiedene Eiskremsorten, Nüsse und Sirup oder Schokolade

barbecue 1) Rindfleischgehacktes, mit pikanter Tomatensoße in einem Brötchen serviert 2) Grillparty

~ sauce pikante Tomatensoße

barbecued über offenem Holzfeuer gegrillt

basil Basilikum

bass Barsch

bean Bohne

beef Rindfleisch

~ olive Rinderroulade

beefburger gehacktes Beefsteak, gegrillt und in einem Brötchen serviert

beet, beetroot rote Rübe

bilberry Heidel-, Blaubeere

bill Rechnung

~ of fare Speisekarte

biscuit 1) Kleingebäck, Keks (GB) 2) kleines Brötchen (US)

blackberry Brombeere

blackcurrant schwarze Johannisbeere

black pudding Blutwurst

bloater Bückling

blood sausage Blutwurst

blueberry Heidel-, Blaubeere

boiled gekocht, gesotten

Bologna (sausage) eine Art Mortadella

bone Knochen

boned ausgebeint

Boston baked beans weiße Bohnen, Speckwürfel und Melasse im Ofen gebacken

Boston cream pie mehrschichtige Torte mit Kremfüllung und Schokoladenglasur

brains Hirn

braised gedämpft, geschmort

bramble pudding Brombeerpudding, oft mit Apfelscheiben

braunschweiger Leberwurst

bread Brot

breaded paniert

breakfast Frühstück

bream Brasse

breast Brust, Brüstchen

brisket Bruststück

broad bean Saubohne

broth Fleischbrühe, Bouillon

brown Betty eine Art Charlotte aus Äpfeln und Gewürzen, mit Paniermehl bestreut

brunch spätes, reichhaltiges Frühstück, das zugleich das Mittagessen ersetzt; Gabelfrühstück

brussels sprout Rosenkohl

bubble and squeak eine Art Pfannkuchen aus Kartoffeln und Weißkohl

bun 1) süßes Milchbrötchen mit Rosinen oder anderen getrockneten Früchten (GB) 2) Hefebrötchen (US)

buttered gebuttert

cabbage Weißkohl

Caesar salad Salat mit Brotwürfeln, Sardellen, Knoblauch und geriebenem Käse

cake Kuchen

cakes Kekse

calf Kalb

Canadian bacon geräucherter Lendenspeck

canapé Appetitschnittchen, belegtes Brötchen

cantaloupe Melone

caper Kaper

capercaillie, capercailzie Auerhahn

carp Karpfen

carrot Mohrrübe, Karotte

cashew Cashewnuss, Elefantenlaus

casserole in der Kasserolle serviertes Gericht

catfish 1) Steinbeißer, Seewolf 2) Katzenwels

catsup Ketchup

cauliflower Blumenkohl

celery Sellerie

cereal Getreideflocken

   hot ~ Haferbrei

check Rechnung

Cheddar (cheese) fetter, orangegelber Hartkäse

cheese Käse

   ~ board Käseplatte

   ~ cake Käsekuchen

cheeseburger eine Art deutsches Beefsteak, mit geschmolzenem Käse in einem Brötchen serviert

chef's salad Salat mit Schinken, Rindfleisch, Hühnerfleisch, Eiern, Tomaten und Käse

cherry Kirsche

chestnut Esskastanie, Marone

chicken Huhn, Hühnchen

chicory 1) Brüsseler Endivie, Chicorée (GB) 2) Endivie (US)

chili con carne dicker Eintopf aus Rindfleisch mit roten Bohnen, Zwiebeln und Chilipfeffer

chili pepper Chilipfeffer

chips 1) Pommes frites (GB) 2) Kartoffelchips (US)

chitt(er)lings Schweinskaldaunen, -kutteln

chive Schnittlauch

chocolate Schokolade

choice Auswahl

chop Kotelett

   ~ suey Gericht aus fein geschnittenem Hühner- oder Schweinefleisch, Gemüse und Reis

chopped gehackt, feingeschnitten

chowder dicke Suppe mit Meeresfrüchten

Christmas pudding englischer Weihnachtspudding aus getrockneten Früchten, Paniermehl, Gewürzen; manchmal flambiert

chutney scharfgewürzte indische Tafelsoße

cinnamon Zimt

clam Sandmuschel

club sandwich doppeltes Sandwich mit gebratenem Frühstücksspeck, Hühnerfleisch, Tomaten, Salat und Mayonnaise

cobbler eine Art gedeckter Obstkuchen

cock-a-leekie soup Hühnerbrühe mit Porree

coconut Kokosnuss

cod Kabeljau, Dorsch

Colchester oyster die beste englische Auster

cold cuts/meat Aufschnitt

coleslaw Weißkohlsalat

compote Kompott

condiment Gewürz

consommé Fleischbrühe, Bouillon

cooked gekocht

cookie Keks

corn 1) Korn, Weizen (GB) 2) Mais (US)

~ **on the cob** Maiskolben

cornflakes geröstete Maisflocken

corned beef gepökeltes Rindfleisch

cottage cheese Bauernkäse aus Quark

cottage pie Auflauf aus Hackfleisch, Zwiebeln und Kartoffelpüree

course Gericht, Gang

cover charge Gedeck extra

crab Krabbe

cracker kleines knuspriges Salzgebäck

cranberry nordamerikanische Preiselbeere

~ **sauce** Preiselbeersoße

crawfish, crayfish 1) Krebs 2) Languste (GB) 3) Kaisergranat (US)

cream 1) Sahne 2) Krem 3) Kremsuppe

~ **cheese** Rahmkäse

~ **puff** Windbeutel

creamed potatoes Sahnekartoffeln

creole Kreolenart; meistens mit Tomaten, Paprikaschoten und Zwiebeln gewürzt, mit Reis serviert

cress Kresse

crisps Kartoffelchips

crumpet rundes, mit Butter bestrichenes Hefebrötchen, wird warm gegessen

cucumber Gurke

Cumberland ham bekannter englischer Räucherschinken

Cumberland sauce pikante Tafelsoße aus rotem Johannisbeergelee, Orangensaft und Wein

cupcake kleiner, runder Kuchen

cured geräuchert, gebeizt, gepökelt

currant 1) Korinthe 2) Johannisbeere

curried mit Curry

custard 1) englische Krem 2) Puddingtörtchen

cutlet Schnitzel, Kotelett

dab Kliesche, rauhe Scholle

Danish pastry Plundergebäck

date Dattel

Derby cheese blassgelber Schnittkäse von mildem bis würzigem Geschmack

devilled sehr stark gewürzt

devil's food cake Schokoladentorte

devils on horseback in Rotwein gekochte Backpflaumen, mit Mandeln und Sardellen gefüllt, in Speck eingerollt und gegrillt

Devonshire cream dicke Sahne

diced gewürfelt

diet food Diätkost

dinner (großes) Abendessen

dish Gericht, Gang

donut, doughnut süßer Krapfen, Berliner Pfannkuchen in Ringform

double cream Doppelrahm

Dover sole Dover-Seezunge, gilt als die beste Englands

dressing 1) Salatsoße 2) Füllung für Geflügel (US)

Dublin Bay prawn Kaisergranat

duck Ente

duckling junge Ente

dumpling Teigkloß, Knödel

Dutch apple pie Apfeltorte mit Streusel aus Rohzucker, Zimt und Butter

éclair Blitzkuchen, gefüllte Brandteigstange

eel Aal

egg Ei
   boiled ~ gekocht
   fried ~ Spiegelei
   hard-boiled ~ hartgekocht
   poached ~ pochiert, verloren
   scrambled ~ Rührei
   soft-boiled ~ weichgekocht

eggplant Aubergine

endive 1) Endivie (GB) 2) Brüsseler Endivie, Chicorée (US)

entrée 1) Vorspeise (GB) 2) Hauptgericht (US)

escalope Schnitzel

fennel Fenchel

fig Feige

fillet Fleisch- oder Fischfilet

finnan haddock geräucherter Schellfisch

fish Fisch
   ~ **and chips** fritierter Fisch und Pommes frites
   ~ **cake** Frikadelle aus Fisch und Kartoffelpüree

flan Obst-, Käsekuchen

flapjack kleiner, dicker Pfannkuchen

flounder Flunder

forcemeat gehacktes Füllfleisch

fowl Geflügel

French bean grüne Bohne

French bread Pariser Brot

French dressing 1) würzige kalte Kräutersoße (GB) 2) sahnige

Salatsoße mit Ketchup (US)

french fries Pommes frites

French toast armer Ritter, Goldschnitte

fresh frisch

fried gebraten oder in Öl gebacken

fritter Krapfen

frogs' legs Froschschenkel

frosting Zuckerguss, Glasur

fruit Obst

fry Fritüre

galantine Rollpastete

game Wild

gammon Räucherschinken

garfish Hornhecht

garlic Knoblauch

garnish Garnierung, Beilage

gherkin Essig-, Gewürzgurke

giblets Geflügelklein

ginger Ingwer

goose Gans
   ~**berry** Stachelbeere

grape Weintraube
   ~**fruit** Pampelmuse

grated gerieben

gravy Bratensaft, -soße

grayling Äsche

green bean grüne Bohne

green pepper grüne Paprikaschote

green salad grüner Salat, Gartensalat

greens grünes Gemüse

grilled gegrillt

grilse junger Lachs

grouse schottisches Moorhuhn

gumbo 1) Gombo (unreife Frucht einer mittelelamerikanischen Eibischart) 2) kreolisches Fleisch- oder Fischgericht mit *okra*

haddock Schellfisch

haggis Hammelmagen mit einer Füllung aus gehackten Innereien und Haferflocken

hake Seehecht

half Hälfte, halb

halibut Heilbutt
ham Schinken
~ **and eggs** Spiegeleier mit Schinken
hare Hase
haricot bean weiße Bohne
hash 1) gehacktes oder
feingeschnittenes Fleisch 2) Gericht
aus feingeschnittenem Fleisch,
Kartoffeln und Gemüse
hazelnut Haselnuss
heart Herz
herb Gewürzkraut
herring Hering
home-made hausgemacht
hominy grits Maisbrei
honey Honig
~ **dew melon** Honigmelone, sehr süß,
mit gelbgrünem Fruchtfleisch
hors-d'œuvre Vorspeise
horse-radish Meerrettich
hot 1) warm, heiß 2) scharf
~ **cross bun** Rosinenbrötchen mit
kreuzförmiger Verzierung (zur
Fastenzeit)
~ **dog** heißes Würstchen in einem
aufgeschnittenen Brötchen
huckleberry Heidel-, Blaubeere
hush puppy Krapfen aus Maismehl
ice-cream Speiseeis
iced eisgekühlt
icing Zuckerguss, Glasur
Idaho baked potato im Ofen
gebackene Pellkartoffel
Irish stew Eintopfgericht mit
Hammelfleisch, Kartoffeln und
Zwiebeln
Italian dressing würzige kalte
Kräutersoße
jam Marmelade
jellied in Gelee
Jell-O Geleenachspeise, Götterspeise
jelly Gelee, Sülze
Jerusalem artichoke Erdartischocke,
Topinambur

John Dory Heringskönig, Petersfisch
jugged hare Hasenpfeffer
juice Saft
juniper berry Wacholderbeere
junket gezuckerte Dickmilch
kale Kraus-, Grünkohl
kedgeree stark gewürztes
Frühstücksgericht aus
feingeschnittenem Fisch mit Reis,
Eiern und Butter
kidney Niere
kipper geräucherter Hering
lamb Lamm
Lancashire hot pot Eintopf aus
Lammkoteletts und -nieren,
Kartoffeln und Zwiebeln
larded gespickt
lean mager
leek Porree, Lauch
leg Keule, Schlegel
lemon Zitrone
~ **sole** Rotzunge
lentil Linse
lettuce Kopfsalat, Lattich
lima bean Limabohne
lime Limette, Zitrusfrucht mit grüner
Schale
liver Leber
loaf Brotlaib
lobster Hummer
loin Filet, Lendenstück
Long Island duck Long-Island-Ente,
besonders wohlschmeckend
low-calorie kalorienarm
lox Räucherlachs
lunch Mittagessen
macaroon Makrone
mackerel Makrele
maize Mais
mandarin Mandarine
maple syrup Ahornsirup
marinated mariniert, eingelegt
marjoram Majoran
marmalade Marmelade aus

Zitrusfrüchten (besonders
Apfelsinen)
marrow Mark
  ~ bone Markknochen
marshmallow eine Art türkischer
Honig
mashed potatoes Kartoffelpüree
meal Mahlzeit
meat Fleisch
  ~ ball Fleischkloß
  ~ loaf Hackbraten
medium (done) halb durchgebraten,
halbgar
melon Melone
melted geschmolzen
Melton Mowbray pie eine englische
Fleischpastete, wird kalt gegessen
menu Speisekarte
meringue Baiser, Meringe
milk Milch
mince Gehacktes, Hackfleisch
  ~ meat Hackfleisch
  ~ pie Kuchen oder Pastete mit
Füllung aus Äpfeln, Rosinen,
feingehacktes Orangeat und
Zitronat, Gewürze; mit oder ohne
Fleisch
minced gehackt
mint Minze
mixed gemischt
  ~ grill verschiedene Fleischstücke
mit Bratwürstchen,
Speckscheibchen, Tomaten, Pilzen
und Zwiebeln; gegrillt
molasses Melasse
morel Morchel
mousse eine Art Kremeis
mulberry Maulbeere
mullet Meerbarbe
mulligatawny soup stark gewürzte
indische Hühnersuppe
mushroom Pilz
muskmelon Melone
mussel Miesmuschel

mustard Senf
mutton Hammelfleisch
noodle Nudel
nut Nuss
oatmeal (porridge) Haferbrei
oil Öl
okra schlanke Gomboschote, Okra
omelet Omelett
onion Zwiebel
orange Apfelsine
ox tongue Ochsenzunge
oxtail Ochsenschwanz
oyster Auster
pancake Eierkuchen
parsley Petersilie
parsnip Pastinake, Hirschmöhre
partridge Rebhuhn
pastry feines Backwerk
pasty Pastetchen, Fleischpastete
pea Erbse
peach Pfirsich
peanut Erdnuss
pear Birne
pearl barley Perlgraupen
pepper Pfeffer
  ~mint Pfefferminze
perch Barsch
persimmon Dattel-, Kakipflaume
pheasant Fasan
pickerel junger Hecht
pickle 1) mit Kräutern und Gewürzen
in Essig eingelegte Gemüse und
Frucht 2) kleine Gewürzgurke (US)
pickled in Essig eingelegt, gepökelt
pie englische Pastete (mit würziger
oder süßer Füllung und meistens mit
Teigdeckel)
pig Schwein
pigeon Taube
pineapple Ananas
plaice Scholle
plain einfach, naturell
plate Teller, Platte, Gang
plum Pflaume

~ pudding englischer
Weihnachtspudding aus
getrockneten Früchten, Paniermehl,
Gewürzen; manchmal flambiert
poached pochiert
popcorn Puffmais
popover kleines, stark aufgegangenes
Brötchen
pork Schweinefleisch
porridge Haferbrei
porterhouse steak doppeltes
Lendensteak (vom Rind)
pot roast Schmorbraten mit
Gemüsebeilage
potato Kartoffel
~ chips 1) Pommes frites (GB) 2)
Kartoffelchips (US)
~ in its jacket Ofenkartoffel
potted shrimps in Butter
eingemachte Garnelen
poultry Geflügel
prawn Steingarnele
prune Backpflaume
ptarmigan Schneehuhn
pudding meist eine weiche oder feste
Mehlspeise, entweder mit Fleisch,
Fisch, Gemüse oder Früchten,
gebacken oder gedämpft
pumpkin Kürbis
quail Wachtel
quince Quitte
rabbit Kaninchen
radish Rettich, Radieschen
rainbow trout Regenbogenforelle
raisins Rosinen
rare halbgar
raspberry Himbeere
raw roh
red mullet Rotbarbe
red (sweet) pepper rote
Paprikaschote
redcurrant rote Johannisbeere
relish Würzsoße
rhubarb Rhabarber

rib (of beef) Rippenstück (vom Rind)
rice Reis
rissole Fleisch- oder Fischfrikadelle
river trout Bachforelle
roast Braten
roasted gebraten
Rock Cornish hen Masthühnchen
roe Rogen, Fischeier
roll Brötchen, Semmel
rollmop herring Rollmops
round steak Steak aus der
Rinderkeule
Rubens sandwich gepökeltes
Rindfleisch auf Toast mit
Sauerkraut, Käse und Salatsoße;
heiß serviert
rump steak Steak aus der
Rinderhüfte
rusk Zwieback
rye bread Roggenbrot
saddle Rücken
saffron Safran
sage Salbei
salad Salat
~ bar Auswahl an Salaten
~ cream leicht gezuckerte sahnige
Salatsoße
~ dressing Salatsoße
salmon Lachs
~ trout Lachsforelle
salt Salz
salted gesalzen
sauce Soße
sausage Wurst
sauté(ed) schnell gebraten,
geschwenkt
scallop 1) Jakobsmuschel 2)
Kalbsschnitzel
scone weicher Gersten- oder
Weizenmehlkuchen
Scotch broth Lammfleischbrühe mit
Gemüse
Scotch woodcock Toast mit fein
gehackten Eiern, Gewürzen und

Sardellenpaste

sea bass Wolfs-, Seebarsch

sea kale Meer-, Strandkohl

seafood Fisch und Meeresfrüchte

(in) season (je nach) Jahreszeit

seasoning Gewürz, Würze

service charge Bedienungszuschlag

service (not) included Bedienung (nicht) inbegriffen

set menu Gedeck, Menü

shad Alse, Maifisch

shallot Schalotte

shellfish Krusten- und Schalentiere

sherbet Sorbet, Schnee-Eis, Scherbett

shoulder Schulter

shredded wheat Weizenschrot (zum Frühstück)

shrimp Garnele, Krevette

silverside (of beef) bester Teil der Rinderkeule

sirloin steak Lendensteak (vom Rind)

skewer Bratspießchen

slice Scheibe

sliced aufgeschnitten

sloppy Joe gehacktes Rindfleisch mit Chilisoße, in einem Brötchen serviert

smelt Stint, Spierling (ein Lachsfisch)

smoked geräuchert

snack Imbiss

sole Seezunge

soup Suppe

sour sauer

soused herring in Essig und Gewürzen eingelegter Hering

spare rib Schweinerippchen

spice Gewürz

spinach Spinat

spiny lobster Languste

(on a) spit (am) Spieß

sponge cake leichter Hefekuchen

sprat Sprotte

squash Kürbis

starter Vorspeise

steak and kidney pie englische Rindfleisch- und Nierenpastete

steamed gedämpft

stew Ragout, Eintopf

Stilton (cheese) englischer Edelpilzkäse, weiß und mild oder blaugeädert und scharf

strawberry Erdbeere

string bean grüne Bohne

stuffed gefüllt

stuffing Füllung

suck(l)ing pig Spanferkel

sugar Zucker

sugarless ungezuckert

sundae Eisbecher mit Früchten, Nüssen, Schlagsahne und manchmal Sirup

supper Abendbrot

swede gelbe Kohlrübe

sweet 1) süß 2) Nachspeise

~ **corn** Zuckermais

~ **potato** Süßkartoffel

sweetbread Kalbsbries, -milch

Swiss cheese Schweizer Käse, Emmentaler

Swiss roll Biskuitrolle

Swiss steak mit Gemüse und Gewürzen geschmorte Rindfleischscheibe

T-bone steak Lendensteak (vom Rind)

table d'hôte Gedeck, Menü

tangerine Mandarinenart

tarragon Estragon

tart Törtchen, Torte, Obstkuchen

tenderloin Lendenstück (vom Rind oder Schwein)

Thousand Island dressing würzige Salatsoße aus Mayonnaise und feingehackten Paprikaschoten

thyme Thymian

toad-in-the-hole Fleischstücke oder Würste, in Teig eingehüllt und gebacken

toasted geröstet
~ **cheese** Toast mit geschmolzenem Käse
tomato Tomate
tongue Zunge
treacle Melasse
trifle mit Sherry oder Branntwein getränkte leichte Biskuitmasse, mit Mandeln, Marmelade, Schlagsahne und englischer Krem
tripe Kaldaunen, Kutteln
trout Forelle
truffle Trüffel
tuna, tunny Thunfisch
turbot Steinbutt
turkey Truthahn
turnip Kohlrübe
turnover gefülltes Törtchen, Tasche
turtle Schildkröte
underdone halbgar
vanilla Vanille
veal Kalbfleisch
~ **bird** Kalbsroulade
vegetable Gemüse
~ **marrow** Kürbischen, Zucchini
venison Wildbret
vichyssoise kalte Suppe mit Porree, Kartoffeln und Sahne
vinegar Essig

Virginia baked ham im Ofen gebackener Schinken, mit Gewürznelken gespickt, mit Ananasscheiben und Kirschen dekoriert und mit dem Saft dieser Früchte glasiert
wafer Oblate, Waffel
waffle heiße Waffel, mit Melasse oder Ahornsirup serviert
walnut Walnuss
water ice Fruchteis
watercress Brunnenkresse
watermelon Wassermelone
well-done durchgebraten, gar
Welsh rabbit/rarebit eine Art warme Käseschnitte
whelk Wellhorn(schnecke)
whipped cream Schlagsahne
whitebait Weißfischchen
wine list Weinkarte
woodcock Waldschnepfe
Worcestershire sauce aromatische Würzsoße
York ham bekannter englischer Räucherschinken
Yorkshire pudding eine Art Eierkuchen, im Ofen gebacken und als Beilage zu Roastbeef serviert

Drinks

ale obergäriges, kohlensäurearmes Bier, nicht zu kühl ausgeschenkt
bitter ~ goldgelbes, stark gehopftes Fassbier
brown ~ dunkles, süßliches Flaschenbier
light ~ helles Flaschenbier
mild ~ dunkles, süßliches Fassbier
pale ~ helles Flaschenbier

applejack amerikanischer Apfelbranntwein
Athol Brose schottisches Getränk aus Whisky, Honig und manchmal Hafermehl
Bacardi cocktail Mischgetränk aus Rum, Zucker, Granatapfelsirup und Limettensaft
barley water ein Getränk aus Gerste

mit Zitronengeschmack

barley wine starkes Bier

beer Bier

bottled ~ Flaschenbier

draft, draught ~ Fassbier

bitters aus Bitterextrakten hergestellte Aperitifs, Magenliköre usw.

black velvet Mischgetränk aus Champagner und *stout* (wird oft zu Austern serviert)

bloody Mary Wodka, Tomatensaft und Gewürze

bourbon amerikanischer Whisky, hauptsächlich aus Mais gebrannt

brandy 1) Branntwein 2) Weinbrand, Kognak

~ **Alexander** Weinbrand, Kakaolikör und Sahne

British wines Weine, die aus importierten Trauben oder Traubensäften in Großbritannien hergestellt werden

cherry brandy Kirschlikör

chocolate Schokolade

cider Apfelwein

~ **cup** Mischgetränk aus Apfelwein, Gewürzen, Zucker und Eis

claret roter Bordeauxwein

cobbler ein *long drink* aus Fruchtsaft mit Wein oder Likör und Eis

cocktail alkoholisches Mischgetränk, vor den Mahlzeiten serviert

coffee Kaffee

~ **with cream** Kaffee mit Sahne

black ~ schwarzer Kaffee

cafeine-free ~ koffeinfreier Kaffee

white ~ Milchkaffee

cordial magen- oder herzstärkender Likör

cream 1) Krem 2) Sahne

cup Erfrischungsgetränk aus eisgekühltem Wein, Sodawasser und einem Likör oder Alkohol, mit einer

Apfelsinen- oder Zitronenscheibe garniert

daiquiri Mischgetränk aus Rum, Limetten- und Ananassaft

double doppeltes Maß

Drambuie Likör aus Whisky und Honig

dry martini 1) trockener Wermut (GB) 2) Gin mit trockenem Wermut (US)

egg-nog warmes Mischgetränk aus Rum oder Branntwein, geschlagenem Eigelb und Zucker

gin and it Gin mit italienischem Wermut

gin-fizz Gin mit Zitronensaft, Zucker und Sodawasser

ginger ale alkoholfreies Getränk mit Ingwergeschmack

ginger beer leicht alkoholisches Getränk aus Ingwer und Zukker

grasshopper Mischgetränk aus Pfefferminz- und Kakaolikör mit Sahne

Guinness (stout) sehr dunkles, stark gehopftes Malzbier

half pint ungefähr 3 Deziliter

highball Whisky oder Branntwein mit Sodawasser oder *ginger ale* verdünnt

iced eisgekühlt

Irish coffee Kaffee mit Zucker, irischem Whisky und Schlagsahne

Irish Mist irischer Likör aus Whisky und Honig

Irish whiskey irischer Whisky; er enthält außer Gerste auch Roggen, Hafer und Weizen und ist etwas milder im Geschmack als der schottische Whisky

juice Saft

lager helles Lagerbier, kühl ausgeschenkt

lemon squash Zitronensaft mit Sodawasser

lemonade Limonade
lime juice Limettensaft
liqueur Likör
liquor Spirituosen
long drink alle alkoholischen Bargetränke, mit Wasser oder Sprudel verdünnt; mit Eiswürfeln
Manhattan amerikanischer Whisky, Wermut und Angosturabitter
milk Milch
mineral water Mineralwasser
mulled wine Glühwein
neat unverdünnt, pur
old-fashioned Cocktail aus Whisky, Zucker, Angosturabitter und Maraschinokirschen
on the rocks mit Eiswürfeln
Ovaltine Ovomaltine
Pimm's cup(s) eine Art Likör, wird mit Fruchtsaft oder Sodawasser gemischt
~ **No. 1** mit Gin
~ **No. 2** mit Whisky
~ **No. 3** mit Rum
~ **No. 4** mit Weinbrand
pink champagne Rosé-Sekt
pink lady Cocktail aus Eiweiß, Apfelbranntwein, Zitronensaft, Granatapfelsirup und Gin
pint ungefähr 6 Deziliter
port (wine) Portwein
porter starkes, dunkles Bier mit süßlichem Geschmack
quart 1,14 Liter (US 0,95 Liter)
root beer aus verschiedenen Wurzeln und Kräutern bereitete Brauselimonade
rye (whiskey) Roggenwhisky, eher

schwerer und kräftiger als *bourbon*
scotch (whisky) schottischer Whisky, meist aus Gerstenmalz- und Getreidewhisky »geblendet« (gemischt)
screwdriver Wodka und Orangensaft
shandy *bitter ale* mit Limonade oder *ginger beer*
short drink unverdünntes alkoholisches Getränk
shot ein Schuss Whisky, Kognak oder Branntwein
sloe gin-fizz Schlehenlikör mit Zitronensaft und Sodawasser
soda water Soda-, Sprudelwasser
soft drink alkoholfreies Erfrischungsgetränk
spirits Branntweine
stinger Kognak mit Pfefferminzlikör
stout sehr dunkles, stark gehopftes Malzbier
straight unverdünnt, pur
tea Tee
toddy eine Art Grog
Tom Collins Gin, Zitronensaft, Zucker und Sodawasser
tonic (water) Tonic(wasser); Sprudel, meist mit Chiningeschmack
vodka Wodka
water Wasser
whisky sour Whisky, Zitronensaft, Zucker und Maraschinokirschen
wine Wein
dry ~ trockener Wein
red ~ Rotwein
sparkling ~ Schaumwein, Sekt
sweet ~ Süßwein, Dessertwein
white ~ Weißwein

Englische Kurzgrammatik

Artikel

Der bestimmte Artikel (der, die, das) hat für alle drei Geschlechter, Singular und Plural, nur eine Form: *the.*

the room, the rooms   das Zimmer, die Zimmer

Der unbestimmte Artikel (ein, eine) hat zwei Formen: *a* vor Konsonanten und *an* vor Vokal oder stummem *h.*

a coat   ein Mantel
an umbrella   ein Schirm
an hour   eine Stunde

Some drückt eine unbestimmte Menge oder Anzahl aus.

I'd like some coffee, please.   Ich möchte etwas Kaffee, bitte.

Any wird in negativen Aussagen und in Fragen gebraucht.

There isn't any soap.   Es gibt keine Seife.
Do you have any stamps?   Haben Sie Briefmarken?

Substantiv

Der **Plural** der meisten Substantive wird durch Anhängen von *-(e)s* an den Singular gebildet.

cup — cups (Tasse — Tassen)   **dress — dresses** (Kleid — Kleider)

N.B.: Wenn ein Substantiv mit *-y* aufhört und ein Konsonant vorangeht, so ist die Pluralendung *-ies;* wenn dem *-y* ein Vokal vorangeht, wird der Plural normal gebildet.

lady — ladies (Dame — Damen)   **key — keys** (Schlüssel — Schlüssel)

Folgende Substantive bilden einen unregelmäßigen Plural:

man — men (Mann — Männer)   **woman — women** (Frau — Frauen)
child — children (Kind — Kinder)   **foot — feet** (Fuß — Füße)

Genitiv

1. Bei Personen: wenn das Substantiv nicht mit *-s* endet, wird *'s* angefügt.

the boy's room   das Zimmer des Jungen
the children's clothes   die Kleider der Kinder

Endet es mit *-s*, wird nur ein Apostroph (') angehängt.

the boys' rooms   die Zimmer der Jungen

2. Bei Gegenständen sowie für Mengen- und Maßangaben wird die Präposition *of* gebraucht.

the key of the door	der Schlüssel der Tür
a cup of tea	eine Tasse Tee

Adjektiv

Adjektive stehen normalerweise vor dem Substantiv.

a large brown suitcase	ein großer brauner Koffer

Die Steigerungsformen werden auf zwei Arten gebildet:

1. Alle einsilbigen und viele zweisilbige Adjektive erhalten *-(e)r* und *-(e)st* angefügt.

small (klein) — **smaller** — **smallest**
pretty (hübsch) — **prettier** — **prettiest***

2. Adjektive mit drei oder mehr Silben und einige zweisilbige bilden die Steigerungsformen mit *more* und *most*.

expensive (teuer) — **more expensive** — **most expensive**

Die folgenden Adjektive sind unregelmäßig:

good (gut)	**better**	best
bad (schlecht)	**worse**	worst
little (wenig)	**less**	least
much/many (viel)	**more**	most

Adverbien

Zahlreiche Adverbien werden gebildet, indem man dem Adjektiv *-ly* anhängt.

quick — **quickly**	schnell
slow — **slowly**	langsam

Einige wichtige Ausnahmen:

good — **well**	gut
fast — **fast**	rasch

Pronomen

	Subjekt	Objekt (Akk./Dat.)	Possessiv 1	2
ich	**I**	**me**	**my**	**mine**
du	**you**	**you**	**your**	**yours**

* *y* wird zu *i*, wenn ein Konsonant vorangeht.

er	he	him	his	his
sie	she	her	her	hers
es	it	it	its	—

wir	we	us	our	ours
ihr	you	you	your	yours
sie	they	them	their	theirs

Possessiv-Form 1 wird vor Substantiven gebraucht; Form 2 steht allein.

Where's my key? Wo ist mein Schlüssel?
That's not mine. Das ist nicht meiner.

N.B. Im Englischen wird zwischen »du« und »Sie« kein Unterschied gemacht, es gibt nur die Form *you*.

Give it to me. Geben Sie es mir.
He came with you. Er kam mit dir/Ihnen.

Hilfsverben (Präsens)

a) **to be** (sein)

	Kurzform	Negativ-Kurzformen	
I am	I'm		I'm not
you are	you're	you're not	you aren't
he is	he's	he's not	he isn't
she is	she's	she's not	she isn't
it is	it's	it's not	it isn't
we are	we're	we're not	we aren't
you are	you're	you're not	you aren't
they are	they're	they're not	they aren't

Fragend: **Am I? Are you? Is he?** usw.

N.B.: In der Umgangssprache werden fast ausschließlich die Kurzformen gebraucht.

Das Englische besitzt zwei Formen für das deutsche »es gibt«: *there is* (*there's*) vor einem Substantiv im Singular, *there are* vor einem Substantiv im Plural.

Negativ: **There isn't — There aren't**
Fragend: **Is there? — Are there?**

b) **to have** (haben)

	Kurzform		Kurzform
I have	I've	we have	we've
you have	you've	you have	you've
he/she/it has	he's/she's/it's	they have	they've

Negativ: **I have not (haven't)**
Fragend: **Have you? — Has he?**

c) **to do** (tun, machen)

I do, you do, he/she/it does, we do, you do, they do

Negativ: **I do not (I don't) — He does not (he doesn't)**
Fragend: **Do you? — Does he?**

Andere Verben

Die Infinitivform wird für alle Personen außer der 3. Person Singular, die auf -(e)s endet, verwendet:

	to love (lieben)	to come (kommen)	to go (gehen)
I	love	come	go
you	love	come	go
he/she/it	loves	comes	goes
we	love	come	go
you	love	come	go
they	love	come	go

Die negative Form wird durch das Hilfsverb *do* (3. Pers. *does*) + *not* + Infinitiv gebildet.

We do not (don't) like this hotel.   Wir mögen dieses Hotel nicht.

Fragen werden mit dem Hilfsverb *do* (3. Pers. *does*) + Subjekt + Infinitiv gebildet.

Do you drink wine?   Trinken Sie Wein?
Does he live here?   Wohnt er hier?

Präsens Verlaufsform

Diese Form gibt es im Deutschen nicht. Sie wird gebildet durch die entsprechende Form des Verbes *to be* + Partizip Präsens. Das Partizip Präsens wird durch Anhängen von -*ing* an den Infinitiv gebildet (ein -*e* am Ende des Verbs wird weggelassen). Die Verlaufsform kann nur mit bestimmten Verben verwendet werden, da sie ausdrückt, dass man gerade bei einer Beschäftigung ist oder dass ein Geschehen nocht andauert, während man spricht.

What are you doing?	Was machen Sie?
	(jetzt, in diesem Augenblick)
I'm writing a letter.	Ich schreibe gerade einen Brief.

Imperativ

Der Imperativ (Singular und Plural) hat dieselbe Form wie der Infinitiv (ohne *to*). Der negative Imperativ wird mit *don't* gebildet.

Please bring me some water.	Bringen Sie mir bitte etwas Wasser.
Don't be late.	Kommen Sie nicht zu spät.

Unregelmäßige Verben

Wir führen nachstehend die englischen unregelmäßigen Verben auf. Die Zusammensetzung und die Präfixverben werden ebenso konjugiert wie das zugrundeliegende Verb. Beispiel: *withdraw* konjugiert man wie *draw* und *mistake* wie *take*.

Infinitiv	Präteritum	Partizip Perfekt	
arise	arose	arisen	*sich erheben*
awake	awoke	awoken	*erwecken*
be	was	been	*sein*
bear	bore	borne	*(er)tragen*
beat	beat	beaten	*schlagen*
become	became	become	*werden*
begin	began	begun	*beginnen*
bend	bent	bent	*biegen*
bet	bet	bet	*wetten*
bid	bade/bid	bidden/bid	*gebieten*
bind	bound	bound	*binden*
bite	bit	bitten	*beißen*
bleed	bled	bled	*bluten*
blow	blew	blown	*blasen*
break	broke	broken	*brechen*
breed	bred	bred	*züchten*
bring	brought	brought	*bringen*
build	built	built	*bauen*
burn	burnt/burned	burnt/burned	*(ver)brennen*
burst	burst	burst	*platzen*
buy	bought	bought	*kaufen*
can*	could	—	*können*
cast	cast	cast	*werfen*
catch	caught	caught	*fangen*
choose	chose	chosen	*wählen*
cling	clung	clung	*sich klammern*
clothe	clothed/clad	clothed/clad	*kleiden*
come	came	come	*kommen*
cost	cost	cost	*kosten*
creep	crept	crept	*kriechen*
cut	cut	cut	*schneiden*
deal	dealt	dealt	*Handel treiben*
dig	dug	dug	*graben*

---

* Indikativ Präsens

do (**he does**)	did	done	*tun*
draw	drew	drawn	*ziehen, zeichnen*
dream	dreamt/dreamed	dreamt/dreamed	*träumen*
drink	drank	drunk	*trinken*
drive	drove	driven	*fahren*
dwell	dwelt	dwelt	*wohnen*
eat	ate	eaten	*essen*
fall	fell	fallen	*fallen*
feed	fed	fed	*füttern*
feel	felt	felt	*fühlen*
fight	fought	fought	*kämpfen*
find	found	found	*finden*
flee	fled	fled	*fliehen*
fling	flung	flung	*schleudern*
fly	flew	flown	*fliegen*
forsake	forsook	forsaken	*verlassen*
freeze	froze	frozen	*gefrieren*
get	got	got	*bekommen*
give	gave	given	*geben*
go	went	gone	*gehen*
grind	ground	ground	*mahlen*
grow	grew	grown	*wachsen*
hang	hung	hung	*hängen*
have	had	had	*haben*
hear	heard	heard	*hören*
hew	hewed	hewed/hewn	*hacken*
hide	hid	hidden	*verbergen*
hit	hit	hit	*schlagen*
hold	held	held	*halten*
hurt	hurt	hurt	*verletzen*
keep	kept	kept	*behalten*
kneel	knelt	knelt	*knien*
knit	knitted/knit	knitted/knit	*stricken*
know	knew	known	*kennen*
lay	laid	laid	*legen*
lead	led	led	*führen*
lean	leant/leaned	leant/leaned	*lehnen*
leap	leapt/leaped	leapt/leaped	*springen*
learn	learnt/learned	learnt/learned	*lernen*
leave	left	left	*verlassen*
lend	lent	lent	*leihen*
let	let	let	*lassen*
lie	lay	lain	*liegen*
light	lit/lighted	lit/lighted	*anzünden*

lose	lost	lost	*verlieren*
make	made	made	*machen*
may*	might	—	*dürfen*
mean	meant	meant	*bedeuten*
meet	met	met	*begegnen*
mow	mowed	mowed/mown	*mähen*
must*	—	—	*müssen*
ought (to)*	—	—	*sollen*
pay	paid	paid	*zahlen*
put	put	put	*legen*
read	read	read	*lesen*
rid	rid	rid	*sich entledigen*
ride	rode	ridden	*reiten*
ring	rang	rung	*läuten*
rise	rose	risen	*aufstehen*
run	ran	run	*rennen*
saw	sawed	sawn	*sägen*
say	said	said	*sagen*
see	saw	seen	*sehen*
seek	sought	sought	*suchen*
sell	sold	sold	*verkaufen*
send	sent	sent	*senden*
set	set	set	*setzen*
sew	sewed	sewed/sewn	*nähen*
shake	shook	shaken	*schütteln*
shall*	should	—	*sollen*
shed	shed	shed	*vergießen*
shine	shone	shone	*leuchten*
shoot	shot	shot	*schießen*
show	showed	shown	*zeigen*
shrink	shrank	shrunk	*schrumpfen*
shut	shut	shut	*schließen*
sing	sang	sung	*singen*
sink	sank	sunk	*sinken, versenken*
sit	sat	sat	*sitzen*
sleep	slept	slept	*schlafen*
slide	slid	slid	*gleiten*
sling	slung	slung	*schleudern*
slink	slunk	slunk	*schleichen*
slit	slit	slit	*schlitzen*
smell	smelled/smelt	smelled/smelt	*riechen*
sow	sowed	sown/sowed	*säen*

---

* Indikativ Präsens

speak	spoke	spoken	*sprechen*
speed	sped/speeded	sped/speeded	*eilen*
spell	spelt/spelled	spelt/spelled	*buchstabieren*
spend	spent	spent	*ausgeben, ver-bringen*
spill	spilt/spilled	spilt/spilled	*verschütten*
spin	spun	spun	*spinnen*
spit	spat	spat	*spucken*
split	split	split	*spalten*
spoil	spoilt/spoiled	spoilt/spoiled	*verderben*
spread	spread	spread	*ausbreiten*
spring	sprang	sprung	*springen*
stand	stood	stood	*stehen*
steal	stole	stolen	*stehlen*
stick	stuck	stuck	*kleben*
sting	stung	stung	*stechen*
stink	stank/stunk	stunk	*stinken*
strew	strewed	strewed/strewn	*streuen*
stride	strode	stridden	*schreiten*
strike	struck	struck/stricken	*schlagen*
string	strung	strung	*aufreihen*
strive	strove	striven	*streben*
swear	swore	sworn	*schwören*
sweep	swept	swept	*fegen*
swell	swelled	swollen	*schwellen*
swim	swam	swum	*schwimmen*
swing	swung	swung	*schwingen*
take	took	taken	*nehmen*
teach	taught	taught	*lehren*
tear	tore	torn	*zerreißen*
tell	told	told	*erzählen*
think	thought	thought	*denken*
throw	threw	thrown	*werfen*
thrust	thrust	thrust	*stoßen*
tread	trod	trodden	*treten*
wake	woke/waked	woken/waked	*(auf)wachen*
wear	wore	worn	*tragen (Kleider)*
weave	wove	woven	*weben*
weep	wept	wept	*weinen*
will*	would	—	*wollen*
win	won	won	*gewinnen*
wind	wound	wound	*winden*

* Indikativ Präsens

| wring | wrung | wrung | *(w)ringen* |
| write | wrote | written | *schreiben* |

Englische Abkürzungen

AA	*Automobile Association*	britischer Automobilklub
AAA	*American Automobile Association*	Amerikanischer Automobilklub
ABC	*American Broadcasting Company*	amerikanische Rundfunkgesellschaft
A.D.	*anno Domini*	nach Christus
Am.	*America; American*	Amerika; amerikanisch
a.m.	*ante meridiem (before noon)*	vormittags (genauer: von 00.01 bis 11.59 Uhr)
Amtrak	*American railroad corporation*	amerikanisches Eisenbahnkonsortium
att(n)	*attention*	zu Händen
AT & T	*American Telephone and Telegraph Company*	Amerikanische Telefon- und Telegrafengesellschaft
Ave.	*avenue*	Allee (Prachtstraße)
BBC	*British Broadcasting Corporation*	Britische Rundfunkgesellschaft
B.C.	*before Christ*	vor Christus
bldg.	*building*	Gebäude
Blvd.	*boulevard*	Boulevard (Ringstraße)
B.R.	*British Rail*	Britische Staatsbahnen
Brit.	*Britain; British*	Großbritannien; britisch
Bros.	*brothers*	Gebrüder
¢	*cent*	Cent, 1/100 vom Dollar
Can.	*Canada; Canadian*	Kanada; kanadisch
CBS	*Columbia Broadcasting System*	amerikanische Rundfunkgesellschaft
CID	*Criminal Investigation Department*	britische Kriminalpolizei
CNR	*Canadian National Railway*	Kanadische Bundesbahnen
c/o	*(in) care of*	bei, per Adresse
Co.	*company*	Handelsgesellschaft
Corp.	*corporation*	Handelsgesellschaft
CPR	*Canadian Pacific Railways*	kanadische Eisenbahngesellschaft
D.C.	*District of Columbia*	Bundesdistrikt der USA
DDS	*Doctor of Dental Science*	Doktor der Zahnheilkunde
dept.	*department*	Abteilung
EU	*European Union*	Europäische Union
e.g.	*for instance*	zum Beispiel
Eng.	*England; English*	England; englisch

excl.	*excluding; exclusive*	ausschließlich, nicht inbegriffen
ft.	*foot/feet*	Fuß (30,5 cm)
GB	*Great Britain*	Großbritannien
H.E.	*His/Her Excellency; His Eminence*	Seine/Ihre Exzellenz; Seine Eminenz
H.H.	*His Holiness*	Seine Heiligkeit
H.M.	*His/Her Majesty*	Seine/Ihre Majestät
H.M.S.	*Her Majesty's ship*	wörtlich: Schiff Ihrer Majestät (Kriegsmarine)
hp	*horsepower*	Pferdestärke
Hwy	*highway*	Schnellstraße
i.e.	*that is to say*	das heißt
in.	*inch*	Zoll (2,54 cm)
Inc.	*incorporated*	amerikanische Aktiengesellschaft
incl.	*including, inclusive*	einschließlich, inbegriffen
£	*pound sterling*	Pfund Sterling
L.A.	*Los Angeles*	Los Angeles
Ltd.	*limited*	Aktiengesellschaft
M.D.	*Doctor of Medicine*	Arzt
M.P.	*Member of Parliament*	Mitglied des Parlaments
mph	*miles per hour*	Meilen pro Stunde
Mr.	*Mister*	Herr
Mrs.	*Missis*	Frau
Ms.	*Missis/Miss*	Frau/Fräulein
nat.	*national*	staatlich
NBC	*National Broadcasting Company*	amerikanische Rundfunkgesellschaft
No.	*number*	Nummer
N.Y.C.	*New York City*	Stadt New York
O.B.E.	*Officer (of the Order) of the British Empire*	Offizier (des Ordens) des Britischen Weltreiches
p.	*page; penny/pence*	Seite; Penny, 1/100 vom Pfund Sterling
p.a.	*per annum*	pro Jahr
Ph.D.	*Doctor of Philosophy*	Doktor der Philosophie
p.m.	*post meridiem (after noon)*	nachmittags (genauer: von 12.01 bis 23.59 Uhr)
PO	*Post Office*	Postamt
POO	*post office order*	Postanweisung
pop.	*population*	Einwohner(zahl)
P.T.O.	*please turn over*	bitte wenden
RAC	*Royal Automobile Club*	Königlicher Automobilklub (von England)

RCMP	*Royal Canadian Mounted Police*	Königliche berittene Polizei von Kanada
Rd.	*road*	Straße, Weg
ref.	*reference*	vergleiche, siehe
Rev.	*reverend*	Pfarrer
RFD	*rural free delivery*	Briefzustellung per Postfach in ländlichen Gegenden
RR	*railroad*	Eisenbahn
RSVP	*please reply*	Antwort erbeten
$	*dollar*	Dollar
Soc.	*society*	Gesellschaft
St.	*saint; street*	Sankt; Straße
UK	*United Kingdom*	Vereinigtes Königreich
UN	*United Nations*	Vereinte Nationen
UPS	*United Parcel Service*	privater Paketbeförderungsdienst
US	*United States*	Vereinigte Staaten von Amerika
USS	*United States Ship*	wörtlich: Schiff der Vereinigten Staaten (Kriegsmarine)
VAT	*value added tax*	Mehrwertsteuer
VIP	*very important person*	bevorzugt behandelte Persönlichkeit (im Reiseverkehr usw.)
Xmas	*Christmas*	Weihnachten
yd.	*yard*	Yard
YMCA	*Young Men's Christian Association*	Christlicher Verein Junger Männer
YWCA	*Young Women's Christian Association*	Christlicher Verein Junger Mädchen
ZIP	*ZIP code*	Postleitzahl

Zahlwörter

Grundzahlen

0	zero
1	one
2	two
3	three
4	four
5	five
6	six
7	seven
8	eight
9	nine
10	ten
11	eleven
12	twelve
13	thirteen
14	fourteen
15	fifteen
16	sixteen
17	seventeen
18	eighteen
19	nineteen
20	twenty
21	twenty-one
22	twenty-two
23	twenty-three
24	twenty-four
25	twenty-five
30	thirty
40	forty
50	fifty
60	sixty
70	seventy
80	eighty
90	ninety
100	a/one hundred
230	two hundred and thirty
500	five hundred
1,000	a/one thousand
10,000	ten thousand
100,000	a/one hundred thousand
1,000,000	a/one million

Ordnungszahlen

1st	first
2nd	second
3rd	third
4th	fourth
5th	fifth
6th	sixth
7th	seventh
8th	eighth
9th	ninth
10th	tenth
11th	eleventh
12th	twelfth
13th	thirteenth
14th	fourteenth
15th	fifteenth
16th	sixteenth
17th	seventeenth
18th	eighteenth
19th	nineteenth
20th	twentieth
21st	twenty-first
22nd	twenty-second
23rd	twenty-third
24th	twenty-fourth
25th	twenty-fifth
26th	twenty-sixth
27th	twenty-seventh
28th	twenty-eighth
29th	twenty-ninth
30th	thirtieth
40th	fortieth
50th	fiftieth
60th	sixtieth
70th	seventieth
80th	eightieth
90th	ninetieth
100th	hundredth
230th	two hundred and thirtieth
500th	five hundredth
1,000th	thousandth

Uhrzeit

Engländer und Amerikaner verwenden allgemein das Zwölfstundensystem. Dabei bezeichnet die Abküzung *a.m.* (*ante meridiem*) die Stunden der ersten Tageshälfte, *p.m.* (*post meridiem*) die der zweiten. In Großbritannien allerdings geht man mehr und mehr zum Vierundzwanzigstundensystem über.

I'll come at seven a.m.	Ich werde um 7 Uhr morgens kommen.
I'll come at two p.m.	Ich werde um 2 Uhr nachmittags kommen.
I'll come at eight p.m.	Ich werde um 8 Uhr abends kommen.

Wochentage

Sunday	Sonntag	*Thursday*	Donnerstag
Monday	Montag	*Friday*	Freitag
Tuesday	Dienstag	*Saturday*	Samstag, Sonnabend
Wednesday	Mittwoch		

Conversion tables/ Umrechnungstabellen

Metres and Feet

The figure in the middle stands for both metres and feet, e.g. 1 metre = 3.281 ft. and 1 foot = 0.30 m.

Meter und Fuß

Die Zahlen in der Mitte gelten zugleich für Meter und Fuß, z. B. 1 Meter = 3,281 Fuß; 1 Fuß = 0,30 Meter.

Metres/Meter		Feet/Fuß
0.30	**1**	3.281
0.61	**2**	6.563
0.91	**3**	9.843
1.22	**4**	13.124
1.52	**5**	16.403
1.83	**6**	19.686
2.13	**7**	22.967
2.44	**8**	26.248
2.74	**9**	29.529
3.05	**10**	32.810
3.66	**12**	39.372
4.27	**14**	45.934
6.10	**20**	65.620
7.62	**25**	82.023
15.24	**50**	164.046
22.86	**75**	246.069
30.48	**100**	328.092

Temperature

To convert Centigrade to Fahrenheit, multiply by 1.8 and add 32.
To convert Fahrenheit to Centigrade, subtract 32 from Fahrenheit and divide by 1.8.

Temperatur

Um Celsius in Fahrenheit umzurechnen, multiplizieren Sie den Celsiuswert mit 1,8 und zählen zum Ergebnis 32 hinzu.
Um Fahrenheit in Celsius umzurechnen, ziehen Sie vom Fahrenheitwert 32 ab und dividieren die Summe durch 1,8.